HONDA

ODYSSEY
2001-10 REPAIR MANUAL

CHILTON'S

Covers U.S. and Canadian models of Honda Odyssey
2001 through 2010

by John Wegmann

CHILTON *Automotive Books*

PUBLISHED BY **HAYNES NORTH AMERICA, Inc.**

Haynes ®

APA AUTOMOTIVE PARTS & ACCESSORIES ASSOCIATION MEMBER

Manufactured in USA
©2012 Haynes North America, Inc.
ISBN-13: 978-1-56392-981-6
ISBN-10: 1-56392-981-3
Library of Congress Control Number 2012935834

Haynes Publishing Group
Sparkford Nr Yeovil
Somerset BA22 7JJ England

Haynes North America, Inc
861 Lawrence Drive
Newbury Park
California 91320 USA

ABCDE
FGHIJ
KLMNO
PQRST

Contents

Author, mechanic and photographer with a 2000 Honda Odyssey

ACKNOWLEDGEMENTS

Wiring diagrams originated by Valley Forge Technical Information Services. Technical writers who contributed to this project include Mike Stubblefield and Robert Maddox.

About this manual

ITS PURPOSE

The purpose of this manual is to help you get the best value from your vehicle. It can do so in several ways. It can help you decide what work must be done, even if you choose to have it done by a dealer service department or a repair shop; it provides information and procedures for routine maintenance and servicing; and it offers diagnostic and repair procedures to follow when trouble occurs.

We hope you use the manual to tackle the work yourself. For many simpler jobs, doing it yourself may be quicker than arranging an appointment to get the vehicle into a shop and making the trips to leave it and pick it up. More importantly, a lot of money can be saved by avoiding the expense the shop must pass on to you to cover its labor and overhead costs. An added benefit is the sense of satisfaction and accomplishment that you feel after doing the job yourself.

USING THE MANUAL

The manual is divided into Chapters. Each Chapter is divided into numbered Sections. Each Section consists of consecutively numbered paragraphs.

At the beginning of each numbered Section you will be referred to any illustrations which apply to the procedures in that Section. The reference numbers used in illustration captions pinpoint the pertinent Section and the Step within that Section. That is, illustration 3.2 means the illustration refers to Section 3 and Step (or paragraph) 2 within that Section.

Procedures, once described in the text, are not normally repeated. When it's necessary to refer to another Chapter, the reference will be given as Chapter and Section number. Cross references given without use of the word "Chapter" apply to Sections and/or paragraphs in the same Chapter. For example, "see Section 8" means in the same Chapter.

References to the left or right side of the vehicle assume you are sitting in the driver's seat, facing forward.

Even though we have prepared this manual with extreme care, neither the publisher nor the author can accept responsibility for any errors in, or omissions from, the information given.

➡ **NOTE**

A *Note* provides information necessary to properly complete a procedure or information which will make the procedure easier to understand.

❋❋ **CAUTION**

A *Caution* provides a special procedure or special steps which must be taken while completing the procedure where the Caution is found. Not heeding a Caution can result in damage to the assembly being worked on.

❋❋ **WARNING**

A *Warning* provides a special procedure or special steps which must be taken while completing the procedure where the Warning is found. Not heeding a Warning can result in personal injury.

Introduction

This manual covers the Honda Odyssey van. All models are equipped with a standard rear liftgate door and sliding side doors on the curb side (passenger side) and driver's side of the vehicle.

The transversely mounted V6 engines used in these models are equipped with Programmed Fuel Injection (PGM-FI), a "sequential multiport" system. The engine drives the front wheels through a four-speed or five-speed automatic transaxle via independent driveaxles.

Independent suspension, featuring coil spring/strut damper units, is used on the front, while the rear suspension utilizes trailing arms, shock absorber/coil spring units, one upper and two lower control arms.

The power-assisted rack-and-pinion steering unit is mounted behind the engine.

The brakes are disc-type at the front and the rear brakes are either drum or disc-type. An Anti-lock Braking System (ABS) is available on all models.

Vehicle identification numbers

Modifications are a continuing and unpublicized process in vehicle manufacturing. Since spare parts manuals and lists are compiled on a numerical basis, the individual vehicle numbers are essential to correctly identify the component required.

VEHICLE IDENTIFICATION NUMBER (VIN)

This very important identification number is stamped on a plate attached to the dashboard inside the windshield on the driver's side of

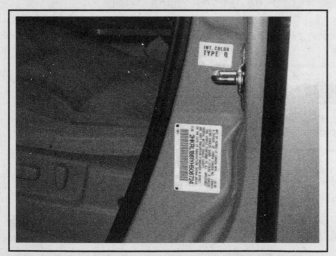

The Vehicle Identification Number (VIN) is located on a plate on top of the dash (visible through the windshield)

the vehicle (see illustration). It can also be found on the certification label located on the driver's side door post. The VIN also appears on the Vehicle Certificate of Title and Registration. It contains information such as where and when the vehicle was manufactured, the model year and the body style.

On the models covered by this manual the model year codes are:

1	2001
2	2002
3	2003
4	2004
5	2005
6	2006
7	2007
8	2008
9	2009
A	2010

CERTIFICATION LABEL

The certification label is attached to the driver's door post (see illustration). The plate contains the name of the manufacturer, the month and year of production, the Gross Vehicle Weight Rating (GVWR), the Gross Axle Weight Rating (GAWR) and the certification statement.

ENGINE IDENTIFICATION NUMBERS

The engine serial number can be found on the front side of the engine (see illustration).

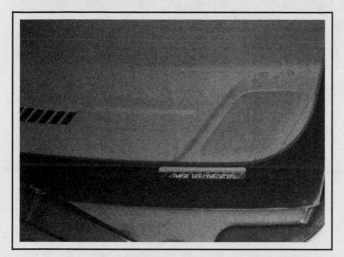

The vehicle certification label is located on the driver's door post

The engine serial number is located on the front side of the block

Buying parts

Replacement parts are available from many sources, which generally fall into one of two categories - authorized dealer parts departments and independent retail auto parts stores. Our advice concerning these parts is as follows:

Retail auto parts stores: Good auto parts stores will stock frequently needed components which wear out relatively fast, such as clutch components, exhaust systems, brake parts, tune-up parts, etc. These stores often supply new or reconditioned parts on an exchange basis, which can save a considerable amount of money. Discount auto parts stores are often very good places to buy materials and parts needed for general vehicle maintenance such as oil, grease, filters, spark plugs, belts, touch-up paint, bulbs, etc. They also usually sell

tools and general accessories, have convenient hours, charge lower prices and can often be found not far from home.

Authorized dealer parts department: This is the best source for parts which are unique to the vehicle and not generally available elsewhere (such as major engine parts, transmission parts, trim pieces, etc.).

Warranty information: If the vehicle is still covered under warranty, be sure that any replacement parts purchased - regardless of the source - do not invalidate the warranty!

To be sure of obtaining the correct parts, have engine and chassis numbers available and, if possible, take the old parts along for positive identification.

MAINTENANCE TECHNIQUES

There are a number of techniques involved in maintenance and repair that will be referred to throughout this manual. Application of these techniques will enable the home mechanic to be more efficient, better organized and capable of performing the various tasks properly, which will ensure that the repair job is thorough and complete.

Fasteners

Fasteners are nuts, bolts, studs and screws used to hold two or more parts together. There are a few things to keep in mind when working with fasteners. Almost all of them use a locking device of some type, either a lockwasher, locknut, locking tab or thread adhesive. All threaded fasteners should be clean and straight, with undamaged threads and undamaged corners on the hex head where the wrench fits. Develop the habit of replacing all damaged nuts and bolts with new ones. Special locknuts with nylon or fiber inserts can only be used once. If they are removed, they lose their locking ability and must be replaced with new ones.

Rusted nuts and bolts should be treated with a penetrating fluid to ease removal and prevent breakage. Some mechanics use turpentine in a spout-type oil can, which works quite well. After applying the rust penetrant, let it work for a few minutes before trying to loosen the nut or bolt. Badly rusted fasteners may have to be chiseled or sawed off or removed with a special nut breaker, available at tool stores.

If a bolt or stud breaks off in an assembly, it can be drilled and removed with a special tool commonly available for this purpose. Most automotive machine shops can perform this task, as well as other repair procedures, such as the repair of threaded holes that have been stripped out.

Flat washers and lockwashers, when removed from an assembly, should always be replaced exactly as removed. Replace any damaged washers with new ones. Never use a lockwasher on any soft metal surface (such as aluminum), thin sheet metal or plastic.

Fastener sizes

For a number of reasons, automobile manufacturers are making wider and wider use of metric fasteners. Therefore, it is important to be able to tell the difference between standard (sometimes called U.S. or SAE) and metric hardware, since they cannot be interchanged.

All bolts, whether standard or metric, are sized according to diameter, thread pitch and length. For example, a standard 1/2 - 13 x 1 bolt is 1/2 inch in diameter, has 13 threads per inch and is 1 inch long. An M12 - 1.75 x 25 metric bolt is 12 mm in diameter, has a thread pitch of 1.75 mm (the distance between threads) and is 25 mm long. The two bolts are nearly identical, and easily confused, but they are not interchangeable.

In addition to the differences in diameter, thread pitch and length, metric and standard bolts can also be distinguished by examining the bolt heads. To begin with, the distance across the flats on a standard bolt head is measured in inches, while the same dimension on a metric bolt is sized in millimeters (the same is true for nuts). As a result, a standard wrench should not be used on a metric bolt and a metric wrench should not be used on a standard bolt. Also, most standard bolts have slashes radiating out from the center of the head to denote the grade or strength of the bolt, which is an indication of the amount of torque that can be applied to it. The greater the number of slashes, the greater the strength of the bolt. Grades 0 through 5 are commonly used on automobiles. Metric bolts have a property class (grade) number, rather than a slash, molded into their heads to indicate bolt strength. In this case, the higher the number, the stronger the bolt. Property class numbers 8.8, 9.8 and 10.9 are commonly used on automobiles.

Strength markings can also be used to distinguish standard hex nuts from metric hex nuts. Many standard nuts have dots stamped into one side, while metric nuts are marked with a number. The greater the number of dots, or the higher the number, the greater the strength of the nut.

Metric studs are also marked on their ends according to property class (grade). Larger studs are numbered (the same as metric bolts), while smaller studs carry a geometric code to denote grade.

It should be noted that many fasteners, especially Grades 0 through 2, have no distinguishing marks on them. When such is the case, the only way to determine whether it is standard or metric is to measure the thread pitch or compare it to a known fastener of the same size.

Standard fasteners are often referred to as SAE, as opposed to metric. However, it should be noted that SAE technically refers to a non-metric fine thread fastener only. Coarse thread non-metric fasteners are referred to as USS sizes.

Since fasteners of the same size (both standard and metric) may have different strength ratings, be sure to reinstall any bolts, studs or nuts removed from your vehicle in their original locations. Also, when replacing a fastener with a new one, make sure that the new one has a strength rating equal to or greater than the original.

Tightening sequences and procedures

Most threaded fasteners should be tightened to a specific torque value (torque is the twisting force applied to a threaded component such as a nut or bolt). Overtightening the fastener can weaken it and cause it to break, while undertightening can cause it to eventually come loose. Bolts, screws and studs, depending on the material they are made of and their thread diameters, have specific torque values, many of which are noted in the Specifications at the end of each Chapter. Be sure to follow the torque recommendations closely. For fasteners not assigned a specific torque, a general torque value chart is presented here as a guide. These torque values are for dry (unlubricated) fasteners threaded into steel or cast iron (not aluminum). As was previously mentioned, the size and grade of a fastener determine the amount of torque that can safely be applied to it. The figures listed here are approximate for Grade 2 and Grade 3 fasteners. Higher grades can tolerate higher torque values.

Fasteners laid out in a pattern, such as cylinder head bolts, oil pan bolts, differential cover bolts, etc., must be loosened or tightened in sequence to avoid warping the component. This sequence will normally be shown in the appropriate Chapter. If a specific pattern is not given, the following procedures can be used to prevent warping.

Initially, the bolts or nuts should be assembled finger-tight only. Next, they should be tightened one full turn each, in a criss-cross or diagonal pattern. After each one has been tightened one full turn, return to the first one and tighten them all one-half turn, following the same

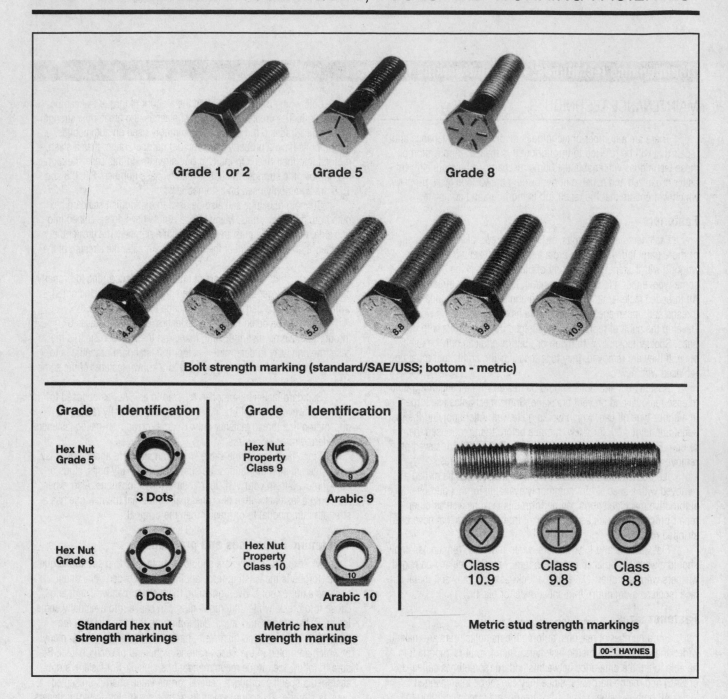

Grade 1 or 2   Grade 5   Grade 8

Bolt strength marking (standard/SAE/USS; bottom - metric)

Grade	Identification	Grade	Identification
Hex Nut Grade 5	3 Dots	Hex Nut Property Class 9	Arabic 9
Hex Nut Grade 8	6 Dots	Hex Nut Property Class 10	Arabic 10

Standard hex nut strength markings

Metric hex nut strength markings

Class 10.9   Class 9.8   Class 8.8

Metric stud strength markings

00-1 HAYNES

pattern. Finally, tighten each of them one-quarter turn at a time until each fastener has been tightened to the proper torque. To loosen and remove the fasteners, the procedure would be reversed.

Component disassembly

Component disassembly should be done with care and purpose to help ensure that the parts go back together properly. Always keep track of the sequence in which parts are removed. Make note of special characteristics or marks on parts that can be installed more than one way, such as a grooved thrust washer on a shaft. It is a good idea to lay the disassembled parts out on a clean surface in the order that they were removed. It may also be helpful to make sketches or take instant photos of components before removal.

When removing fasteners from a component, keep track of their locations. Sometimes threading a bolt back in a part, or putting the washers and nut back on a stud, can prevent mix-ups later. If nuts and bolts cannot be returned to their original locations, they should be kept in a compartmented box or a series of small boxes. A cupcake or muffin tin is ideal for this purpose, since each cavity can hold the bolts and nuts from a particular area (i.e. oil pan bolts, valve cover bolts, engine

Metric thread sizes	Ft-lbs	Nm
M-6	6 to 9	9 to 12
M-8	14 to 21	19 to 28
M-10	28 to 40	38 to 54
M-12	50 to 71	68 to 96
M-14	80 to 140	109 to 154

Pipe thread sizes		
1/8	5 to 8	7 to 10
1/4	12 to 18	17 to 24
3/8	22 to 33	30 to 44
1/2	25 to 35	34 to 47

U.S. thread sizes		
1/4 - 20	6 to 9	9 to 12
5/16 - 18	12 to 18	17 to 24
5/16 - 24	14 to 20	19 to 27
3/8 - 16	22 to 32	30 to 43
3/8 - 24	27 to 38	37 to 51
7/16 - 14	40 to 55	55 to 74
7/16 - 20	40 to 60	55 to 81
1/2 - 13	55 to 80	75 to 108

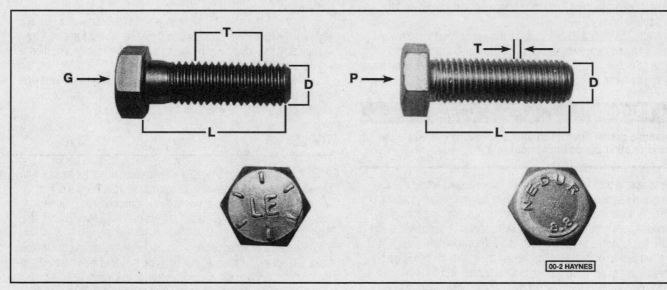

Standard (SAE and USS) bolt dimensions/grade marks

G   Grade marks (bolt strength)
L   Length (in inches)
T   Thread pitch (number of threads per inch)
D   Nominal diameter (in inches)

Metric bolt dimensions/grade marks

P   Property class (bolt strength)
L   Length (in millimeters)
T   Thread pitch (distance between threads in millimeters)
D   Diameter

mount bolts, etc.). A pan of this type is especially helpful when working on assemblies with very small parts, such as the carburetor, alternator, valve train or interior dash and trim pieces. The cavities can be marked with paint or tape to identify the contents.

Whenever wiring looms, harnesses or connectors are separated, it is a good idea to identify the two halves with numbered pieces of masking tape so they can be easily reconnected.

Gasket sealing surfaces

Throughout any vehicle, gaskets are used to seal the mating surfaces between two parts and keep lubricants, fluids, vacuum or pressure contained in an assembly.

Many times these gaskets are coated with a liquid or paste-type gasket sealing compound before assembly. Age, heat and pressure can sometimes cause the two parts to stick together so tightly that they are very difficult to separate. Often, the assembly can be loosened by striking it with a soft-face hammer near the mating surfaces. A regular hammer can be used if a block of wood is placed between the hammer and the part. Do not hammer on cast parts or parts that could be easily damaged. With any particularly stubborn part, always recheck to make sure that every fastener has been removed.

Avoid using a screwdriver or bar to pry apart an assembly, as

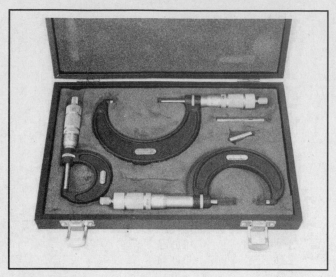

Micrometer set

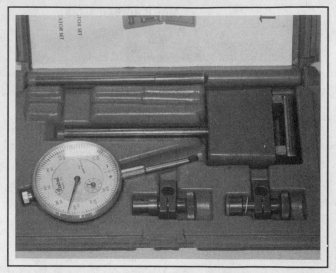

Dial indicator set

they can easily mar the gasket sealing surfaces of the parts, which must remain smooth. If prying is absolutely necessary, use an old broom handle, but keep in mind that extra clean up will be necessary if the wood splinters.

After the parts are separated, the old gasket must be carefully scraped off and the gasket surfaces cleaned. Stubborn gasket material can be soaked with rust penetrant or treated with a special chemical to soften it so it can be easily scraped off.

✳✳ CAUTION:

Never use gasket removal solutions or caustic chemicals on plastic or other composite components.

A scraper can be fashioned from a piece of copper tubing by flattening and sharpening one end. Copper is recommended because it is usually softer than the surfaces to be scraped, which reduces the chance of gouging the part. Some gaskets can be removed with a wire brush, but regardless of the method used, the mating surfaces must be left clean and smooth. If for some reason the gasket surface is gouged, then a gasket sealer thick enough to fill scratches will have to be used during reassembly of the components. For most applications, a non-drying (or semi-drying) gasket sealer should be used.

Hose removal tips

✳✳ WARNING:

If the vehicle is equipped with air conditioning, do not disconnect any of the A/C hoses without first having the system depressurized by a dealer service department or a service station.

Hose removal precautions closely parallel gasket removal precautions. Avoid scratching or gouging the surface that the hose mates against or the connection may leak. This is especially true for radiator hoses. Because of various chemical reactions, the rubber in hoses can bond itself to the metal spigot that the hose fits over. To remove a hose, first loosen the hose clamps that secure it to the spigot. Then, with slip-joint pliers, grab the hose at the clamp and rotate it around the spigot. Work it back and forth until it is completely free, then pull it off. Silicone or other lubricants will ease removal if they can be applied between the hose and the outside of the spigot. Apply the same lubricant to the inside of the hose and the outside of the spigot to simplify installation.

As a last resort (and if the hose is to be replaced with a new one anyway), the rubber can be slit with a knife and the hose peeled from the spigot. If this must be done, be careful that the metal connection is not damaged.

If a hose clamp is broken or damaged, do not reuse it. Wire-type clamps usually weaken with age, so it is a good idea to replace them with screw-type clamps whenever a hose is removed.

TOOLS

A selection of good tools is a basic requirement for anyone who plans to maintain and repair his or her own vehicle. For the owner who has few tools, the initial investment might seem high, but when compared to the spiraling costs of professional auto maintenance and repair, it is a wise one.

To help the owner decide which tools are needed to perform the tasks detailed in this manual, the following tool lists are offered: *Maintenance and minor repair, Repair/overhaul and Special.*

The newcomer to practical mechanics should start off with the *maintenance and minor repair* tool kit, which is adequate for the simpler jobs performed on a vehicle. Then, as confidence and experience grow, the owner can tackle more difficult tasks, buying additional tools as they are needed. Eventually the basic kit will be expanded into the *repair and overhaul* tool set. Over a period of time, the experienced do-it-yourselfer will assemble a tool set complete enough for most repair and overhaul procedures and will add tools from the special category when it is felt that the expense is justified by the frequency of use.

Maintenance and minor repair tool kit

The tools in this list should be considered the minimum required for performance of routine maintenance, servicing and minor repair work. We recommend the purchase of combination wrenches (box-end and open-end combined in one wrench). While more expensive than open end wrenches, they offer the advantages of both types of wrench.

Combination wrench set (1/4-inch to 1 inch or 6 mm to 19 mm)
Adjustable wrench, 8 inch
Spark plug wrench with rubber insert

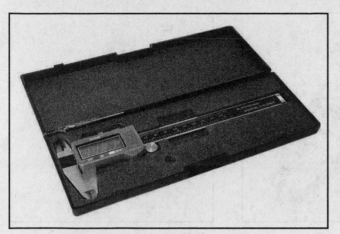

Dial caliper

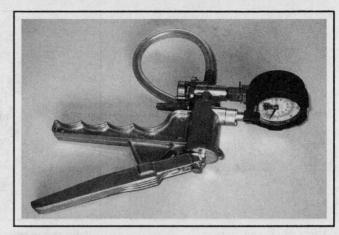

Hand-operated vacuum pump

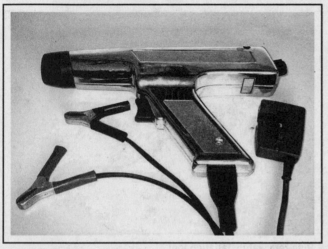

Timing light

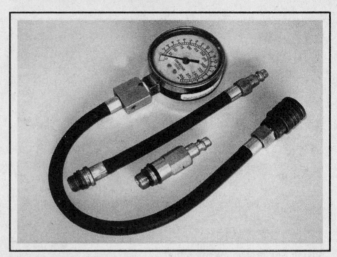

Compression gauge with spark plug hole adapter

Damper/steering wheel puller

General purpose puller

Hydraulic lifter removal tool

Spark plug gap adjusting tool
Feeler gauge set
Brake bleeder wrench
Standard screwdriver (5/16-inch x 6 inch)
Phillips screwdriver (No. 2 x 6 inch)
Combination pliers - 6 inch
Hacksaw and assortment of blades
Tire pressure gauge
Grease gun

Oil can
Fine emery cloth
Wire brush
Battery post and cable cleaning tool
Oil filter wrench
Funnel (medium size)
Safety goggles
Jackstands (2)
Drain pan

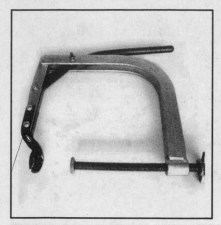

Valve spring compressor

Valve spring compressor

Ridge reamer

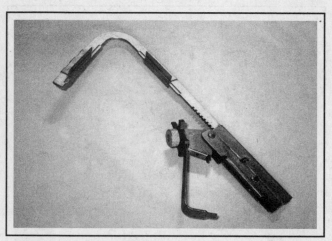

Piston ring groove cleaning tool

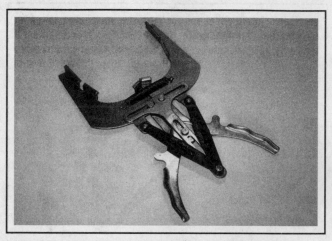

Ring removal/installation tool

Ring compressor

Cylinder hone

Brake hold-down spring tool

➡ **Note:** If basic tune-ups are going to be part of routine maintenance, it will be necessary to purchase a good quality stroboscopic timing light and combination tachometer/dwell meter. Although they are included in the list of special tools, it is mentioned here because they are absolutely necessary for tuning most vehicles properly.

Repair and overhaul tool set

These tools are essential for anyone who plans to perform major repairs and are in addition to those in the maintenance and minor repair tool kit. Included is a comprehensive set of sockets which, though expensive, are invaluable because of their versatility, especially when various extensions and drives are available. We recommend the 1/2-inch drive over the 3/8-inch drive. Although the larger drive is bulky and more expensive, it has the capacity of accepting a very wide range of large sockets. Ideally, however, the mechanic should have a 3/8-inch drive set and a 1/2-inch drive set.

Torque angle gauge

Clutch plate alignment tool

Socket set(s)
Reversible ratchet
Extension - 10 inch
Universal joint
Torque wrench (same size drive as sockets)
Ball peen hammer - 8 ounce
Soft-face hammer (plastic/rubber)
Standard screwdriver (1/4-inch x 6 inch)
Standard screwdriver (stubby - 5/16-inch)
Phillips screwdriver (No. 3 x 8 inch)
Phillips screwdriver (stubby - No. 2)
Pliers - vise grip
Pliers - lineman's
Pliers - needle nose
Pliers - snap-ring (internal and external)
Cold chisel - 1/2-inch
Scribe
Scraper (made from flattened copper tubing)
Centerpunch
Pin punches (1/16, 1/8, 3/16-inch)
Steel rule/straightedge - 12 inch
Allen wrench set (1/8 to 3/8-inch or 4 mm to 10 mm)
A selection of files
Wire brush (large)
Jackstands (second set)
Jack (scissor or hydraulic type)

➡ **Note: Another tool which is often useful is an electric drill with a chuck capacity of 3/8-inch and a set of good quality drill bits.**

Special tools

The tools in this list include those which are not used regularly, are expensive to buy, or which need to be used in accordance with their manufacturer's instructions. Unless these tools will be used frequently, it is not very economical to purchase many of them. A consideration would be to split the cost and use between yourself and a friend or friends. In addition, most of these tools can be obtained from a tool rental shop on a temporary basis.

This list primarily contains only those tools and instruments widely available to the public, and not those special tools produced by the vehicle manufacturer for distribution to dealer service departments. Occasionally, references to the manufacturer's special tools are included in the text of this manual. Generally, an alternative method of doing the job without the special tool is offered. However, sometimes

there is no alternative to their use. Where this is the case, and the tool cannot be purchased or borrowed, the work should be turned over to the dealer service department or an automotive repair shop.

Valve spring compressor
Piston ring groove cleaning tool
Piston ring compressor
Piston ring installation tool
Cylinder compression gauge
Cylinder ridge reamer
Cylinder surfacing hone
Cylinder bore gauge
Micrometers and/or dial calipers
Hydraulic lifter removal tool
Balljoint separator
Universal-type puller
Impact screwdriver
Dial indicator set
Stroboscopic timing light (inductive pick-up)
Hand operated vacuum/pressure pump
Tachometer/dwell meter
Universal electrical multimeter
Cable hoist
Brake spring removal and installation tools
Floor jack

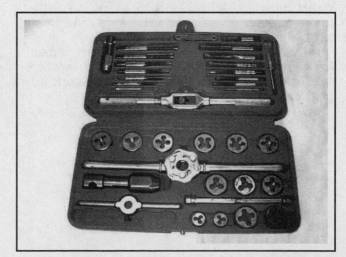

Tap and die set

Buying tools

For the do-it-yourselfer who is just starting to get involved in vehicle maintenance and repair, there are a number of options available when purchasing tools. If maintenance and minor repair is the extent of the work to be done, the purchase of individual tools is satisfactory. If, on the other hand, extensive work is planned, it would be a good idea to purchase a modest tool set from one of the large retail chain stores. A set can usually be bought at a substantial savings over the individual tool prices, and they often come with a tool box. As additional tools are needed, add-on sets, individual tools and a larger tool box can be purchased to expand the tool selection. Building a tool set gradually allows the cost of the tools to be spread over a longer period of time and gives the mechanic the freedom to choose only those tools that will actually be used.

Tool stores will often be the only source of some of the special tools that are needed, but regardless of where tools are bought, try to avoid cheap ones, especially when buying screwdrivers and sockets, because they won't last very long. The expense involved in replacing cheap tools will eventually be greater than the initial cost of quality tools.

Care and maintenance of tools

Good tools are expensive, so it makes sense to treat them with respect. Keep them clean and in usable condition and store them properly when not in use. Always wipe off any dirt, grease or metal chips before putting them away. Never leave tools lying around in the work area. Upon completion of a job, always check closely under the hood for tools that may have been left there so they won't get lost during a test drive.

Some tools, such as screwdrivers, pliers, wrenches and sockets, can be hung on a panel mounted on the garage or workshop wall, while others should be kept in a tool box or tray. Measuring instruments, gauges, meters, etc. must be carefully stored where they cannot be damaged by weather or impact from other tools.

When tools are used with care and stored properly, they will last a very long time. Even with the best of care, though, tools will wear out if used frequently. When a tool is damaged or worn out, replace it. Subsequent jobs will be safer and more enjoyable if you do.

HOW TO REPAIR DAMAGED THREADS

Sometimes, the internal threads of a nut or bolt hole can become stripped, usually from overtightening. Stripping threads is an all-too-common occurrence, especially when working with aluminum parts, because aluminum is so soft that it easily strips out.

Usually, external or internal threads are only partially stripped. After they've been cleaned up with a tap or die, they'll still work. Sometimes, however, threads are badly damaged. When this happens, you've got three choices:

1) *Drill and tap the hole to the next suitable oversize and install a larger diameter bolt, screw or stud.*
2) *Drill and tap the hole to accept a threaded plug, then drill and tap the plug to the original screw size. You can also buy a plug already threaded to the original size. Then you simply drill a hole to the specified size, then run the threaded plug into the hole with a bolt and jam nut. Once the plug is fully seated, remove the jam nut and bolt.*
3) *The third method uses a patented thread repair kit like Heli-Coil or Slimsert. These easy-to-use kits are designed to repair damaged threads in straight-through holes and blind holes. Both are available as kits which can handle a variety of sizes and thread patterns. Drill the hole, then tap it with the special included tap. Install the Heli-Coil and the hole is back to its original diameter and thread pitch.*

Regardless of which method you use, be sure to proceed calmly and carefully. A little impatience or carelessness during one of these relatively simple procedures can ruin your whole day's work and cost you a bundle if you wreck an expensive part.

WORKING FACILITIES

Not to be overlooked when discussing tools is the workshop. If anything more than routine maintenance is to be carried out, some sort of suitable work area is essential.

It is understood, and appreciated, that many home mechanics do not have a good workshop or garage available, and end up removing an engine or doing major repairs outside. It is recommended, however, that the overhaul or repair be completed under the cover of a roof.

A clean, flat workbench or table of comfortable working height is an absolute necessity. The workbench should be equipped with a vise that has a jaw opening of at least four inches.

As mentioned previously, some clean, dry storage space is also required for tools, as well as the lubricants, fluids, cleaning solvents, etc. which soon become necessary.

Sometimes waste oil and fluids, drained from the engine or cooling system during normal maintenance or repairs, present a disposal problem. To avoid pouring them on the ground or into a sewage system, pour the used fluids into large containers, seal them with caps and take them to an authorized disposal site or recycling center. Plastic jugs, such as old antifreeze containers, are ideal for this purpose.

Always keep a supply of old newspapers and clean rags available. Old towels are excellent for mopping up spills. Many mechanics use rolls of paper towels for most work because they are readily available and disposable. To help keep the area under the vehicle clean, a large cardboard box can be cut open and flattened to protect the garage or shop floor.

Whenever working over a painted surface, such as when leaning over a fender to service something under the hood, always cover it with an old blanket or bedspread to protect the finish. Vinyl covered pads, made especially for this purpose, are available at auto parts stores.

Jacking and towing

JACKING

The jack supplied with the vehicle should only be used for raising the vehicle for changing a tire or placing jackstands under the frame.

✳✳ WARNING:

Never crawl under the vehicle or start the engine when the jack is being used as the only means of support.

All vehicles are supplied with a scissors-type jack. When jacking the vehicle, it should be engaged with the rocker panel flange, between the two cutouts (see illustration).

The vehicle should be on level ground with the wheels blocked and the transmission in Park. Pry off the hub cap (if equipped) using the tapered end of the lug wrench. Loosen the lug nuts one-half turn and leave them in place until the wheel is raised off the ground.

Place the jack under the side of the vehicle in the indicated position. Use the supplied wrench to turn the jackscrew clockwise until the wheel is raised off the ground. Remove the lug nuts, pull off the wheel and install the spare.

The jack fits over the rocker panel flange (there are two jacking points on each side of the vehicle)

With the beveled side in, install the lug nuts and tighten them until snug. Lower the vehicle by turning the jackscrew counterclockwise. Remove the jack and tighten the nuts in a diagonal pattern to the torque listed in the Chapter 1 Specifications. If a torque wrench is not available, have the torque checked by a service station as soon as possible. Install the hubcap by placing it in position and using the heel of your hand or a rubber mallet to seat it.

TOWING

As a general rule, the vehicle should be towed with the front (drive) wheels off the ground or, preferably, on a flat bed car carrier. If the front wheels can't be raised or a carrier isn't available, place them on a dolly. The ignition key must be in the ACC position, since the steering lock mechanism isn't strong enough to hold the front wheels straight while towing.

In emergency situations the vehicle can be towed from the front with all four wheels on the ground, provided that speeds don't exceed 35 mph and the distance is not over 50 miles. Before towing, check the transaxle fluid level (see Chapter 1). If the level is below the HOT mark on the dipstick, add fluid.

Towing equipment specifically designed for this purpose should be used and should be attached to the main structural members of the vehicle, not the bumper or brackets.

Safety is a major consideration when towing and all applicable state and local laws must be obeyed. A safety chain system must be used for all towing.

While towing, the parking brake must be released and the transmission must be in Neutral. The steering must be unlocked (ignition switch in the Off position). Remember that power steering and power brakes will not work with the engine off.

TRACTION CONTROL

On models equipped with Traction-Control system, push in the TRAC switch (on the dashboard or floor console, depending on model) anytime the vehicle is on a "rolling road" tester such as a speedometer test machine or chassis dynamometer. The TRAC OFF indicator light should illuminate when the system is turned off.

Booster battery (jump) starting

Observe the following precautions when using a booster battery to start a vehicle:

a) *Before connecting the booster battery, make sure the ignition switch is in the Off position.*

b) *Turn off the lights, heater and other electrical loads.*

c) *Your eyes should be shielded. Safety goggles are a good idea.*

d) *Make sure the booster battery is the same voltage as the dead one in the vehicle.*

e) *The two vehicles MUST NOT TOUCH each other.*

f) *Make sure the transmission is in Park.*

g) *If the booster battery is not a maintenance-free type, remove the vent caps and lay a cloth over the vent holes.*

Connect the red jumper cable to the positive (+) terminals of each battery.

Connect one end of the black cable to the negative (-) terminal of the booster battery. The other end of this cable should be connected to a good ground on the engine block (see illustration). Make sure the cable will not come into contact with the fan, drivebelts or other moving parts of the engine.

Start the engine using the booster battery, then, with the engine running at idle speed, disconnect the jumper cables in the reverse order of connection

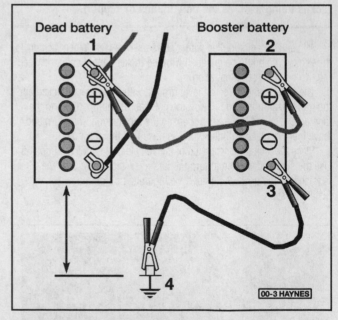

Make the booster battery cable connections in the numerical order shown (note that the negative cable of the booster battery is NOT attached to the negative terminal of the dead battery)

Automotive chemicals and lubricants

A number of automotive chemicals and lubricants are available for use during vehicle maintenance and repair. They include a wide variety of products ranging from cleaning solvents and degreasers to lubricants and protective sprays for rubber, plastic and vinyl.

CLEANERS

Carburetor cleaner and choke cleaner is a strong solvent for gum, varnish and carbon. Most carburetor cleaners leave a dry-type lubricant film which will not harden or gum up. Because of this film it is not recommended for use on electrical components.

Brake system cleaner is used to remove brake dust, grease and brake fluid from the brake system, where clean surfaces are absolutely necessary. It leaves no residue and often eliminates brake squeal caused by contaminants.

Electrical cleaner removes oxidation, corrosion and carbon deposits from electrical contacts, restoring full current flow. It can also be used to clean spark plugs, carburetor jets, voltage regulators and other parts where an oil-free surface is desired.

Demoisturants remove water and moisture from electrical components such as alternators, voltage regulators, electrical connectors and fuse blocks. They are non-conductive and non-corrosive.

Degreasers are heavy-duty solvents used to remove grease from the outside of the engine and from chassis components. They can be sprayed or brushed on and, depending on the type, are rinsed off either with water or solvent.

LUBRICANTS

Motor oil is the lubricant formulated for use in engines. It normally contains a wide variety of additives to prevent corrosion and reduce foaming and wear. Motor oil comes in various weights (viscosity ratings) from 0 to 50. The recommended weight of the oil depends on the season, temperature and the demands on the engine. Light oil is used in cold climates and under light load conditions. Heavy oil is used in hot climates and where high loads are encountered. Multi-viscosity oils are designed to have characteristics of both light and heavy oils and are available in a number of weights from 0W-20 to 20W 50.

Gear oil is designed to be used in differentials, manual transmissions and other areas where high-temperature lubrication is required.

Chassis and wheel bearing grease is a heavy grease used where increased loads and friction are encountered, such as for wheel bearings, ball-joints, tie-rod ends and universal joints.

High-temperature wheel bearing grease is designed to withstand the extreme temperatures encountered by wheel bearings in disc brake equipped vehicles. It usually contains molybdenum disulfide (moly), which is a dry-type lubricant.

White grease is a heavy grease for metal-to-metal applications where water is a problem. White grease stays soft under both low and high temperatures (usually from -100 to +190-degrees F), and will not wash off or dilute in the presence of water.

Assembly lube is a special extreme pressure lubricant, usually containing moly, used to lubricate high-load parts (such as main and rod bearings and cam lobes) for initial start-up of a new engine. The assembly lube lubricates the parts without being squeezed out or washed away until the engine oiling system begins to function.

Silicone lubricants are used to protect rubber, plastic, vinyl and nylon parts.

Graphite lubricants are used where oils cannot be used due to contamination problems, such as in locks. The dry graphite will lubricate metal parts while remaining uncontaminated by dirt, water, oil or acids. It is electrically conductive and will not foul electrical contacts in locks such as the ignition switch.

Moly penetrants loosen and lubricate frozen, rusted and corroded fasteners and prevent future rusting or freezing.

Heat-sink grease is a special electrically non-conductive grease that is used for mounting electronic ignition modules where it is essential that heat is transferred away from the module.

SEALANTS

RTV sealant is one of the most widely used gasket compounds. Made from silicone, RTV is air curing, it seals, bonds, waterproofs, fills surface irregularities, remains flexible, doesn't shrink, is relatively easy to remove, and is used as a supplementary sealer with almost all low and medium temperature gaskets.

Anaerobic sealant is much like RTV in that it can be used either to seal gaskets or to form gaskets by itself. It remains flexible, is solvent resistant and fills surface imperfections. The difference between an anaerobic sealant and an RTV-type sealant is in the curing. RTV cures when exposed to air, while an anaerobic sealant cures only in the absence of air. This means that an anaerobic sealant cures only after the assembly of parts, sealing them together.

Thread and pipe sealant is used for sealing hydraulic and pneumatic fittings and vacuum lines. It is usually made from a Teflon compound, and comes in a spray, a paint-on liquid and as a wrap-around tape.

CHEMICALS

Anti-seize compound prevents seizing, galling, cold welding, rust and corrosion in fasteners. High-temperature anti-seize, usually made with copper and graphite lubricants, is used for exhaust system and exhaust manifold bolts.

Anaerobic locking compounds are used to keep fasteners from vibrating or working loose and cure only after installation, in the absence of air. Medium strength locking compound is used for small nuts, bolts and screws that may be removed later. High-strength locking compound is for large nuts, bolts and studs which aren't removed on a regular basis.

Oil additives range from viscosity index improvers to chemical treatments that claim to reduce internal engine friction. It should be noted that most oil manufacturers caution against using additives with their oils.

Gas additives perform several functions, depending on their chemical makeup. They usually contain solvents that help dissolve gum and varnish that build up on carburetor, fuel injection and intake parts. They also serve to break down carbon deposits that form on the inside surfaces of the combustion chambers. Some additives contain upper cylinder lubricants for valves and piston rings, and others contain chemicals to remove condensation from the gas tank.

MISCELLANEOUS

Brake fluid is specially formulated hydraulic fluid that can withstand the heat and pressure encountered in brake systems. Care must be taken so this fluid does not come in contact with painted surfaces or plastics. An opened container should always be resealed to prevent contamination by water or dirt.

Weatherstrip adhesive is used to bond weatherstripping around doors, windows and trunk lids. It is sometimes used to attach trim pieces.

Undercoating is a petroleum-based, tar-like substance that is designed to protect metal surfaces on the underside of the vehicle from corrosion. It also acts as a sound-deadening agent by insulating the bottom of the vehicle.

Waxes and polishes are used to help protect painted and plated surfaces from the weather. Different types of paint may require the use of different types of wax and polish. Some polishes utilize a chemical or abrasive cleaner to help remove the top layer of oxidized (dull) paint on older vehicles. In recent years many non-wax polishes that contain a wide variety of chemicals such as polymers and silicones have been introduced. These non-wax polishes are usually easier to apply and last longer than conventional waxes and polishes.

CONVERSION FACTORS

LENGTH (distance)
Inches (in)	X 25.4	= Millimeters (mm)	X 0.0394	= Inches (in)
Feet (ft)	X 0.305	= Meters (m)	X 3.281	= Feet (ft)
Miles	X 1.609	= Kilometers (km)	X 0.621	= Miles

VOLUME (capacity)
Cubic inches (cu in; in³)	X 16.387	= Cubic centimeters (cc; cm³)	X 0.061	= Cubic inches (cu in; in³)
Imperial pints (Imp pt)	X 0.568	= Liters (l)	X 1.76	= Imperial pints (Imp pt)
Imperial quarts (Imp qt)	X 1.137	= Liters (l)	X 0.88	= Imperial quarts (Imp qt)
Imperial quarts (Imp qt)	X 1.201	= US quarts (US qt)	X 0.833	= Imperial quarts (Imp qt)
US quarts (US qt)	X 0.946	= Liters (l)	X 1.057	= US quarts (US qt)
Imperial gallons (Imp gal)	X 4.546	= Liters (l)	X 0.22	= Imperial gallons (Imp gal)
Imperial gallons (Imp gal)	X 1.201	= US gallons (US gal)	X 0.833	= Imperial gallons (Imp gal)
US gallons (US gal)	X 3.785	= Liters (l)	X 0.264	= US gallons (US gal)

MASS (weight)
Ounces (oz)	X 28.35	= Grams (g)	X 0.035	= Ounces (oz)
Pounds (lb)	X 0.454	= Kilograms (kg)	X 2.205	= Pounds (lb)

FORCE
Ounces-force (ozf; oz)	X 0.278	= Newtons (N)	X 3.6	= Ounces-force (ozf; oz)
Pounds-force (lbf; lb)	X 4.448	= Newtons (N)	X 0.225	= Pounds-force (lbf; lb)
Newtons (N)	X 0.1	= Kilograms-force (kgf; kg)	X 9.81	= Newtons (N)

PRESSURE
Pounds-force per square inch (psi; lbf/in²; lb/in²)	X 0.070	= Kilograms-force per square centimeter (kgf/cm²; kg/cm²)	X 14.223	= Pounds-force per square inch (psi; lbf/in²; lb/in²)
Pounds-force per square inch (psi; lbf/in²; lb/in²)	X 0.068	= Atmospheres (atm)	X 14.696	= Pounds-force per square inch (psi; lbf/in²; lb/in²)
Pounds-force per square inch (psi; lbf/in²; lb/in²)	X 0.069	= Bars	X 14.5	= Pounds-force per square inch (psi; lbf/in²; lb/in²)
Pounds-force per square inch (psi; lbf/in²; lb/in²)	X 6.895	= Kilopascals (kPa)	X 0.145	= Pounds-force per square inch (psi; lbf/in²; lb/in²)
Kilopascals (kPa)	X 0.01	= Kilograms-force per square centimeter (kgf/cm²; kg/cm²)	X 98.1	= Kilopascals (kPa)

TORQUE (moment of force)
Pounds-force inches (lbf in; lb in)	X 1.152	= Kilograms-force centimeter (kgf cm; kg cm)	X 0.868	= Pounds-force inches (lbf in; lb in)
Pounds-force inches (lbf in; lb in)	X 0.113	= Newton meters (Nm)	X 8.85	= Pounds-force inches (lbf in; lb in)
Pounds-force inches (lbf in; lb in)	X 0.083	= Pounds-force feet (lbf ft; lb ft)	X 12	= Pounds-force inches (lbf in; lb in)
Pounds-force feet (lbf ft; lb ft)	X 0.138	= Kilograms-force meters (kgf m; kg m)	X 7.233	= Pounds-force feet (lbf ft; lb ft)
Pounds-force feet (lbf ft; lb ft)	X 1.356	= Newton meters (Nm)	X 0.738	= Pounds-force feet (lbf ft; lb ft)
Newton meters (Nm)	X 0.102	= Kilograms-force meters (kgf m; kg m)	X 9.804	= Newton meters (Nm)

VACUUM
Inches mercury (in. Hg)	X 3.377	= Kilopascals (kPa)	X 0.2961	= Inches mercury
Inches mercury (in. Hg)	X 25.4	= Millimeters mercury (mm Hg)	X 0.0394	= Inches mercury

POWER
Horsepower (hp)	X 745.7	= Watts (W)	X 0.0013	= Horsepower (hp)

VELOCITY (speed)
Miles per hour (miles/hr; mph)	X 1.609	= Kilometers per hour (km/hr; kph)	X 0.621	= Miles per hour (miles/hr; mph)

FUEL CONSUMPTION *
Miles per gallon, Imperial (mpg)	X 0.354	= Kilometers per liter (km/l)	X 2.825	= Miles per gallon, Imperial (mpg)
Miles per gallon, US (mpg)	X 0.425	= Kilometers per liter (km/l)	X 2.352	= Miles per gallon, US (mpg)

TEMPERATURE
Degrees Fahrenheit $= (°C \times 1.8) + 32$ Degrees Celsius (Degrees Centigrade; °C) $= (°F - 32) \times 0.56$

*It is common practice to convert from miles per gallon (mpg) to liters/100 kilometers (l/100km), where mpg (Imperial) x l/100 km = 282 and mpg (US) x l/100 km = 235

FRACTION/DECIMAL/MILLIMETER EQUIVALENTS

DECIMALS TO MILLIMETERS

Decimal	mm	Decimal	mm
0.001	0.0254	0.500	12.7000
0.002	0.0508	0.510	12.9540
0.003	0.0762	0.520	13.2080
0.004	0.1016	0.530	13.4620
0.005	0.1270	0.540	13.7160
0.006	0.1524	0.550	13.9700
0.007	0.1778	0.560	14.2240
0.008	0.2032	0.570	14.4780
0.009	0.2286	0.580	14.7320
		0.590	14.9860
0.010	0.2540		
0.020	0.5080		
0.030	0.7620		
0.040	1.0160	0.600	15.2400
0.050	1.2700	0.610	15.4940
0.060	1.5240	0.620	15.7480
0.070	1.7780	0.630	16.0020
0.080	2.0320	0.640	16.2560
0.090	2.2860	0.650	16.5100
		0.660	16.7640
0.100	2.5400	0.670	17.0180
0.110	2.7940	0.680	17.2720
0.120	3.0480	0.690	17.5260
0.130	3.3020		
0.140	3.5560		
0.150	3.8100		
0.160	4.0640	0.700	17.7800
0.170	4.3180	0.710	18.0340
0.180	4.5720	0.720	18.2880
0.190	4.8260	0.730	18.5420
		0.740	18.7960
0.200	5.0800	0.750	19.0500
0.210	5.3340	0.760	19.3040
0.220	5.5880	0.770	19.5580
0.230	5.8420	0.780	19.8120
0.240	6.0960	0.790	20.0660
0.250	6.3500		
0.260	6.6040		
0.270	6.8580	0.800	20.3200
0.280	7.1120	0.810	20.5740
0.290	7.3660	0.820	21.8280
		0.830	21.0820
0.300	7.6200	0.840	21.3360
0.310	7.8740	0.850	21.5900
0.320	8.1280	0.860	21.8440
0.330	8.3820	0.870	22.0980
0.340	8.6360	0.880	22.3520
0.350	8.8900	0.890	22.6060
0.360	9.1440		
0.370	9.3980		
0.380	9.6520		
0.390	9.9060		
		0.900	22.8600
0.400	10.1600	0.910	23.1140
0.410	10.4140	0.920	23.3680
0.420	10.6680	0.930	23.6220
0.430	10.9220	0.940	23.8760
0.440	11.1760	0.950	24.1300
0.450	11.4300	0.960	24.3840
0.460	11.6840	0.970	24.6380
0.470	11.9380	0.980	24.8920
0.480	12.1920	0.990	25.1460
0.490	12.4460	1.000	25.4000

FRACTIONS TO DECIMALS TO MILLIMETERS

Fraction	Decimal	mm	Fraction	Decimal	mm
1/64	0.0156	0.3969	33/64	0.5156	13.0969
1/32	0.0312	0.7938	17/32	0.5312	13.4938
3/64	0.0469	1.1906	35/64	0.5469	13.8906
1/16	0.0625	1.5875	9/16	0.5625	14.2875
5/64	0.0781	1.9844	37/64	0.5781	14.6844
3/32	0.0938	2.3812	19/32	0.5938	15.0812
7/64	0.1094	2.7781	39/64	0.6094	15.4781
1/8	0.1250	3.1750	5/8	0.6250	15.8750
9/64	0.1406	3.5719	41/64	0.6406	16.2719
5/32	0.1562	3.9688	21/32	0.6562	16.6688
11/64	0.1719	4.3656	43/64	0.6719	17.0656
3/16	0.1875	4.7625	11/16	0.6875	17.4625
13/64	0.2031	5.1594	45/64	0.7031	17.8594
7/32	0.2188	5.5562	23/32	0.7188	18.2562
15/64	0.2344	5.9531	47/64	0.7344	18.6531
1/4	0.2500	6.3500	3/4	0.7500	19.0500
17/64	0.2656	6.7469	49/64	0.7656	19.4469
9/32	0.2812	7.1438	25/32	0.7812	19.8438
19/64	0.2969	7.5406	51/64	0.7969	20.2406
5/16	0.3125	7.9375	13/16	0.8125	20.6375
21/64	0.3281	8.3344	53/64	0.8281	21.0344
11/32	0.3438	8.7312	27/32	0.8438	21.4312
23/64	0.3594	9.1281	55/64	0.8594	21.8281
3/8	0.3750	9.5250	7/8	0.8750	22.2250
25/64	0.3906	9.9219	57/64	0.8906	22.6219
13/32	0.4062	10.3188	29/32	0.9062	23.0188
27/64	0.4219	10.7156	59/64	0.9219	23.4156
7/16	0.4375	11.1125	15/16	0.9375	23.8125
29/64	0.4531	11.5094	61/64	0.9531	24.2094
15/32	0.4688	11.9062	31/32	0.9688	24.6062
31/64	0.4844	12.3031	63/64	0.9844	25.0031
1/2	0.5000	12.7000	1	1.0000	25.4000

Regardless of how enthusiastic you may be about getting on with the job at hand, take the time to ensure that your safety is not jeopardized. A moment's lack of attention can result in an accident, as can failure to observe certain simple safety precautions. The possibility of an accident will always exist, and the following points should not be considered a comprehensive list of all dangers. Rather, they are intended to make you aware of the risks and to encourage a safety conscious approach to all work you carry out on your vehicle.

ESSENTIAL DOS AND DON'TS

DON'T rely on a jack when working under the vehicle. Always use approved jackstands to support the weight of the vehicle and place them under the recommended lift or support points.

DON'T attempt to loosen extremely tight fasteners (i.e. wheel lug nuts) while the vehicle is on a jack - it may fall.

DON'T start the engine without first making sure that the transmission is in Neutral (or Park where applicable) and the parking brake is set.

DON'T remove the radiator cap from a hot cooling system - let it cool or cover it with a cloth and release the pressure gradually.

DON'T attempt to drain the engine oil until you are sure it has cooled to the point that it will not burn you.

DON'T touch any part of the engine or exhaust system until it has cooled sufficiently to avoid burns.

DON'T siphon toxic liquids such as gasoline, antifreeze and brake fluid by mouth, or allow them to remain on your skin.

DON'T inhale brake lining dust - it is potentially hazardous (see Asbestos below).

DON'T allow spilled oil or grease to remain on the floor - wipe it up before someone slips on it.

DON'T use loose fitting wrenches or other tools which may slip and cause injury.

DON'T push on wrenches when loosening or tightening nuts or bolts. Always try to pull the wrench toward you. If the situation calls for pushing the wrench away, push with an open hand to avoid scraped knuckles if the wrench should slip.

DON'T attempt to lift a heavy component alone - get someone to help you.

DON'T rush or take unsafe shortcuts to finish a job.

DON'T allow children or animals in or around the vehicle while you are working on it.

DO wear eye protection when using power tools such as a drill, sander, bench grinder, etc. and when working under a vehicle.

DO keep loose clothing and long hair well out of the way of moving parts.

DO make sure that any hoist used has a safe working load rating adequate for the job.

DO get someone to check on you periodically when working alone on a vehicle.

DO carry out work in a logical sequence and make sure that everything is correctly assembled and tightened.

DO keep chemicals and fluids tightly capped and out of the reach of children and pets.

DO remember that your vehicle's safety affects that of yourself and others. If in doubt on any point, get professional advice.

STEERING, SUSPENSION AND BRAKES

These systems are essential to driving safety, so make sure you have a qualified shop or individual check your work. Also, compressed suspension springs can cause injury if released suddenly - be sure to use a spring compressor.

AIRBAGS

Airbags are explosive devices that can CAUSE injury if they deploy while you're working on the vehicle. Follow the manufacturer's instructions to disable the airbag whenever you're working in the vicinity of airbag components.

ASBESTOS

Certain friction, insulating, sealing, and other products - such as brake linings, brake bands, clutch linings, torque converters, gaskets, etc. - may contain asbestos or other hazardous friction material. Extreme care must be taken to avoid inhalation of dust from such products, since it is hazardous to health. If in doubt, assume that they do contain asbestos.

FIRE

Remember at all times that gasoline is highly flammable. Never smoke or have any kind of open flame around when working on a vehicle. But the risk does not end there. A spark caused by an electrical short circuit, by two metal surfaces contacting each other, or even by static electricity built up in your body under certain conditions, can ignite gasoline vapors, which in a confined space are highly explosive. Do not, under any circumstances, use gasoline for cleaning parts. Use an approved safety solvent.

Always disconnect the battery ground (-) cable at the battery before working on any part of the fuel system or electrical system. Never risk spilling fuel on a hot engine or exhaust component. It is strongly recommended that a fire extinguisher suitable for use on fuel and electrical fires be kept handy in the garage or workshop at all times. Never try to extinguish a fuel or electrical fire with water.

FUMES

Certain fumes are highly toxic and can quickly cause unconsciousness and even death if inhaled to any extent. Gasoline vapor falls into this category, as do the vapors from some cleaning solvents. Any draining or pouring of such volatile fluids should be done in a well ventilated area.

When using cleaning fluids and solvents, read the instructions on the container carefully. Never use materials from unmarked containers.

Never run the engine in an enclosed space, such as a garage. Exhaust fumes contain carbon monoxide, which is extremely poisonous. If you need to run the engine, always do so in the open air, or at least have the rear of the vehicle outside the work area.

THE BATTERY

Never create a spark or allow a bare light bulb near a battery. They normally give off a certain amount of hydrogen gas, which is highly explosive.

Always disconnect the battery ground (-) cable at the battery before working on the fuel or electrical systems.

If possible, loosen the filler caps or cover when charging the battery from an external source (this does not apply to sealed or maintenance-free batteries). Do not charge at an excessive rate or the battery may burst.

Take care when adding water to a non maintenance-free battery and when carrying a battery. The electrolyte, even when diluted, is very corrosive and should not be allowed to contact clothing or skin.

Always wear eye protection when cleaning the battery to prevent the caustic deposits from entering your eyes.

HOUSEHOLD CURRENT

When using an electric power tool, inspection light, etc., which operates on household current, always make sure that the tool is correctly connected to its plug and that, where necessary, it is properly grounded. Do not use such items in damp conditions and, again, do not create a spark or apply excessive heat in the vicinity of fuel or fuel vapor.

SECONDARY IGNITION SYSTEM VOLTAGE

A severe electric shock can result from touching certain parts of the ignition system (such as the spark plug wires) when the engine is running or being cranked, particularly if components are damp or the insulation is defective. In the case of an electronic ignition system, the secondary system voltage is much higher and could prove fatal.

HYDROFLUORIC ACID

This extremely corrosive acid is formed when certain types of synthetic rubber, found in some O-rings, oil seals, fuel hoses, etc. are exposed to temperatures above 750-degrees F (400-degrees C). The rubber changes into a charred or sticky substance containing the acid. *Once formed, the acid remains dangerous for years. If it gets onto the skin, it may be necessary to amputate the limb concerned.*

When dealing with a vehicle which has suffered a fire, or with components salvaged from such a vehicle, wear protective gloves and discard them after use.

Troubleshooting

CONTENTS

This section provides an easy reference guide to the more common problems which may occur during the operation of your vehicle. These problems and their possible causes are grouped under headings denoting various components or systems, such as Engine, Cooling system, etc. They also refer you to the chapter and/or section which deals with the problem.

Remember that successful troubleshooting is not a mysterious black art practiced only by professional mechanics. It is simply the result of the right knowledge combined with an intelligent, systematic approach to the problem. Always work by a process of elimination, starting with the simplest solution and working through to the most complex - and never overlook the obvious. Anyone can run the gas tank dry or leave the lights on overnight, so don't assume that you are exempt from such oversights.

Finally, always establish a clear idea of why a problem has occurred and take steps to ensure that it doesn't happen again. If the electrical system fails because of a poor connection, check the other connections in the system to make sure that they don't fail as well. If a particular fuse continues to blow, find out why - don't just replace one fuse after another. Remember, failure of a small component can often be indicative of potential failure or incorrect functioning of a more important component or system.

ENGINE AND PERFORMANCE

1   Engine will not rotate when attempting to start

1   Battery terminal connections loose or corroded (Chapter 1).
2   Battery discharged or faulty (Chapter 1).
3   Automatic transaxle not completely engaged in Park (Chapter 7).
4   Broken, loose or disconnected wiring in the starting circuit (Chapters 5 and 12).
5   Starter motor pinion jammed in flywheel ring gear (Chapter 5).
6   Starter solenoid faulty (Chapter 5).
7   Starter motor faulty (Chapter 5).
8   Ignition switch faulty (Chapter 12).
9   Neutral start switch faulty (Chapter 7).
10   Starter pinion or driveplate teeth worn or broken (Chapter 5).

2   Engine rotates but will not start

1   Fuel tank empty.
2   Battery discharged (engine rotates slowly) (Chapter 5).
3   Battery terminal connections loose or corroded (Chapter 1).
4   Leaking fuel injector(s), fuel pump, pressure regulator, etc. (Chapter 4).
5   Fuel not reaching fuel injection system (Chapter 4).
6   Ignition components damp or damaged (Chapter 5).
7   Worn, faulty or incorrectly gapped spark plugs (Chapter 1).
8   Broken, loose or disconnected wiring in the starting circuit (Chapter 5).
9   Broken, loose or disconnected wires at the ignition coil(s) or faulty coil(s) (Chapter 5).

3   Engine hard to start when cold

1   Battery discharged or low (Chapter 1).
2   Fuel system malfunctioning (Chapter 4).
3   Emissions or engine control system malfunctioning (Chapter 6).

4   Engine hard to start when hot

1   Air filter clogged (Chapter 1).
2   Fuel not reaching the fuel injection system (Chapter 4).
3   Corroded battery connections, especially ground (Chapter 1).
4   Emissions or engine control system malfunctioning (Chapter 6).

5   Starter motor noisy or excessively rough in engagement

1   Pinion or driveplate gear teeth worn or broken (Chapter 5).
2   Starter motor mounting bolts loose or missing (Chapter 5).

6   Engine starts but stops immediately

1   Loose or faulty electrical connections at coil pack or alternator (Chapter 5).
2   Insufficient fuel reaching the fuel injectors (Chapter 4).
3   Vacuum leak at the gasket between the intake manifold/plenum and throttle body (Chapters 1 and 4).
4   Restricted exhaust system (most likely the catalytic converter) (Chapters 4 and 6).

7   Oil puddle under engine

1   Oil pan gasket and/or oil pan drain bolt seal leaking (Chapters 1 and 2).
2   Oil pressure sending unit leaking (Chapter 2).
3   Rocker arm cover gaskets leaking (Chapter 2).
4   Engine oil seals leaking (Chapter 2).

8   Engine lopes while idling or idles erratically

1   Vacuum leakage (Chapter 4).
2   Leaking EGR valve or plugged PCV valve (Chapter 6).
3   Air filter clogged (Chapter 1).
4   Fuel pump not delivering sufficient fuel to the fuel injection system (Chapter 4).
5   Leaking head gasket (Chapter 2).
6   Camshaft lobes worn (Chapter 2).

9   Engine misses at idle speed

1   Spark plugs worn or not gapped properly (Chapter 1).
2   Faulty spark plug wires (Chapter 1).
3   Vacuum leaks (Chapters 1 and 4).
4   Uneven or low compression (Chapter 2C).

10   Engine misses throughout driving speed range

1   Fuel filter clogged and/or impurities in the fuel system (Chapters 1 and 4).
2   Low fuel output at the injector (Chapter 4).
3   Faulty or incorrectly gapped spark plugs (Chapter 1).
4   Leaking spark plug wires (Chapter 1).
5   Faulty emission system components (Chapter 6).
6   Low or uneven cylinder compression pressures (Chapter 2).
7   Weak or faulty ignition system (Chapter 5).
8   Vacuum leak in fuel injection system, intake manifold or vacuum hoses (Chapter 4).

11   Engine stumbles on acceleration

1   Spark plugs fouled (Chapter 1).
2   Fuel injection system needs adjustment or repair (Chapter 4).
3   Fuel filter clogged (Chapter 1).
4   Intake manifold air leak (Chapter 4).

12   Engine surges while holding accelerator steady

1   Intake air leak (Chapter 4).
2   Fuel pump faulty (Chapter 4).
3   Loose fuel injector harness connections (Chapter 4).
4   Defective ECM (Chapter 6).

13   Engine stalls

1   Idle speed incorrect (Chapters 1 and 4).
2   Fuel filter clogged and/or water and impurities in the fuel system (Chapters 1 and 4).
3   Ignition components damp or damaged (Chapter 5).
4   Faulty emissions system components (Chapter 6).
5   Faulty or incorrectly gapped spark plugs (Chapter 1).
6   Faulty spark plug wires (Chapter 1).
7   Vacuum leak in the intake manifold or vacuum hoses (Chapter 4).

14   Engine lacks power

1   Faulty or incorrectly gapped spark plugs (Chapter 1).
2   Restricted exhaust system (most likely the catalytic converter (Chapters 4 and 6).
3   Fuel injection system malfunctioning (Chapter 4).
4   Faulty coil(s) (Chapter 5).
5   Brakes binding (Chapter 1).
6   Automatic transaxle fluid level incorrect (Chapter 1).
7   Fuel filter clogged and/or impurities in the fuel system (Chapter 1).
8   Emission control system not functioning properly (Chapter 6).
9   Low or uneven cylinder compression pressures (Chapter 2).

15   Engine backfires

1   Emissions system not functioning properly (Chapter 6).
2   Fuel injection system malfunctioning (Chapter 4).
3   Vacuum leak at fuel injectors, intake manifold or vacuum hoses (Chapter 4).
4   Valves sticking (Chapter 2).

16   Pinging or knocking engine sounds during acceleration or uphill

1   Incorrect grade of fuel.
2   Fuel injection system malfunctioning Chapter 4).
3   Improper or damaged spark plugs or wires (Chapter 1).
4   Worn or damaged ignition components (Chapter 5).
5   Faulty emissions system (Chapter 6).
6   Vacuum leak (Chapter 4).

17   Engine runs with oil pressure light on

1   Low oil level (Chapter 1).
2   Short in wiring circuit (Chapter 12).
3   Faulty oil pressure sender (Chapter 2).
4   Oil viscosity too low or oil diluted.
5   Worn engine bearings and/or oil pump (Chapter 2).

18   Engine diesels (continues to run) after switching off

1   Excessive engine operating temperature (Chapter 3).
2   Excessive carbon deposits on valves and pistons.

ENGINE ELECTRICAL SYSTEM

19   Battery will not hold a charge

1   Alternator drivebelt defective or not adjusted properly (Chapter 1).
2   Battery terminals loose or corroded (Chapter 1).
3   Alternator not charging properly (Chapter 5).
4   Loose, broken or faulty wiring in the charging circuit (Chapter 5).
5   Short in vehicle wiring (Chapters 5 and 12).
6   Internally defective battery (Chapters 1 and 5).

20   Voltage warning light fails to go out

1   Faulty alternator or charging circuit (Chapter 5).
2   Alternator drivebelt defective or out of adjustment (Chapter 1).
3   Alternator voltage regulator inoperative (Chapter 5).

21   Voltage warning light fails to come on when key is turned on

1   Warning light bulb defective (Chapter 12).
2   Fault in the printed circuit, dash wiring or bulb holder (Chapter 12).

FUEL SYSTEM

22   Excessive fuel consumption

1   Dirty or clogged air filter element (Chapter 1).
2   Emissions system not functioning properly (Chapter 6).
3   Fuel injection system malfunctioning (Chapter 4).
4   Low tire pressure or incorrect tire size (Chapter 1).

23 Fuel leakage and/or fuel odor

1 Leak in a fuel feed or vent line (Chapter 4).
2 Tank overfilled.
3 Evaporative emissions control canister defective (Chapters 1 and 6).
4 Fuel injector seals faulty (Chapter 4).

COOLING SYSTEM

24 Overheating

1 Insufficient coolant in system (Chapter 1).
2 Water pump drivebelt defective or out of adjustment (Chapter 1).
3 Radiator core blocked or grille restricted (Chapter 3).
4 Thermostat faulty (Chapter 3).
5 Electric cooling fan blades broken or cracked (Chapter 3).
6 Radiator cap not maintaining proper pressure (Chapter 3).

25 Overcooling

Incorrect (opening temperature too low) or faulty thermostat (Chapter 3).

26 External coolant leakage

1 Deteriorated/damaged hoses or loose clamps (Chapters 1 and 3).
2 Water pump seal defective (Chapters 1 and 3).
3 Leakage from radiator core (Chapter 3).
4 Engine drain or water jacket core plugs leaking (Chapter 2).

27 Internal coolant leakage

1 Leaking cylinder head gasket (Chapter 2).
2 Cracked cylinder bore or cylinder head (Chapter 2).

28 Coolant loss

1 Too much coolant in system (Chapter 1).
2 Coolant boiling away because of overheating (Chapter 3).
3 Internal or external leakage (Chapter 3).
4 Faulty radiator cap (Chapter 3).

29 Poor coolant circulation

1 Inoperative water pump (Chapter 3).
2 Restriction in cooling system (Chapters 1 and 3).
3 Water pump drivebelt defective or out of adjustment (Chapter 1).
4 Thermostat sticking (Chapter 3).

AUTOMATIC TRANSAXLE

➡ **Note: Due to the complexity of the automatic transaxle, it's difficult for the home mechanic to properly diagnose and service this component. For problems other than the following, the vehicle should be taken to a dealer service department or a transmission shop.**

30 Fluid leakage

1 Automatic transmission fluid is a deep red color. Fluid leaks should not be confused with engine oil, which can easily be blown by airflow to the transaxle.
2 To pinpoint a leak, first remove all built-up dirt and grime from the transaxle housing with degreasing agents and/or steam cleaning. Drive the vehicle at low speeds so air flow will not blow the leak far from its source. Raise the vehicle and determine where the leak is coming from. Common areas of leakage are:

   a) *Fluid pan*
   b) *Fill plug (Chapter 1)*
   c) *Fluid cooler lines (Chapter 7)*
   d) *Vehicle Speed Sensor (Chapter 6)*

31 Transaxle fluid brown or has a burned smell

Transaxle overheated. Change fluid (Chapter 1).

32 General shift mechanism problems

1 Chapter 7 deals with checking and adjusting the shift linkage on automatic transaxles. Common problems which may be attributed to a poorly adjusted linkage are:

   a) *Engine starting in gears other than Park or Neutral.*
   b) *Indicator on shifter pointing to a gear other than the one actually being used.*
   c) *Vehicle moves when in Park.*

2 Refer to Chapter 7 for the shift linkage adjustment procedure.

33 Engine will start in gears other than Park or Neutral

Transmission range switch malfunctioning (Chapter 6).

34 Transaxle slips, shifts roughly, is noisy or has no drive in forward or reverse gears

There are many probable causes for the above problems, but the home mechanic should be concerned with only one possibility - fluid level. Before taking the vehicle to a repair shop, check the level and condition of the fluid as described in Chapter 1.

Correct the fluid level as necessary or change the fluid and filter if needed. If the problem persists, have a professional diagnose the probable cause.

DRIVEAXLES

35 Clicking noise in turns

Worn or damaged outer CV joint. Check for cut or damaged boots (Chapter 1). Repair as necessary (Chapter 8).

36 Knock or clunk when accelerating after coasting

Worn or damaged CV joint. Check for cut or damaged boots (Chapter 1). Repair as necessary (Chapter 8).

37   Shudder or vibration during acceleration

1   Worn or damaged CV joints. Repair or replace as necessary (Chapter 8).
2   Sticking inner joint assembly. Correct or replace as necessary (Chapter 8).

BRAKES

➡ **Note: Before assuming that a brake problem exists, make sure . . .**

a)   The tires are in good condition and properly inflated (Chapter 1).
b)   The front end alignment is correct (Chapter 10).
c)   The vehicle isn't loaded with weight in an unequal manner.

38   Vehicle pulls to one side during braking

1   Incorrect tire pressures (Chapter 1).
2   Front end out of alignment (have the front end aligned).
3   Unmatched tires on same axle.
4   Restricted brake lines or hoses (Chapter 9).
5   Sticking caliper or wheel cylinder piston (Chapter 9).
6   Loose suspension parts (Chapter 10).
7   Contaminated brake pad or shoe material (Chapter 9).

39   Noise (grinding or high-pitched squeal) when the brakes are applied

1   Disc brake pads worn out. Replace pads with new ones immediately (Chapter 9).
2   Drum brake shoes worn out. Replace the shoes immediately (Chapter 9).

40   Brake roughness or chatter (pedal pulsates)

1   Excessive brake disc lateral runout or brake drum out-of-round (Chapter 9).
2   Parallelism of disc not within specifications (Chapter 9).
3   Uneven pad wear caused by caliper not sliding due to improper clearance or dirt (Chapter 9).
4   Defective brake disc (Chapter 9).

41   Excessive pedal effort required to stop vehicle

1   Malfunctioning power brake booster (Chapter 9).
2   Partial system failure (Chapter 9).
3   Excessively worn pads (Chapter 9).
4   One or more caliper or wheel cylinder pistons seized or sticking (Chapter 9).
5   Brake pads contaminated with oil or grease (Chapter 9).
6   New pads or shoes installed and not yet seated. It will take a while for the new material to seat.

42   Excessive brake pedal travel

1   Partial brake system failure (Chapter 9).
2   Insufficient fluid in master cylinder (Chapters 1 and 9).
3   Air trapped in system (Chapter 9).
4   Faulty master cylinder (Chapter 9).

43   Dragging brakes

1   Master cylinder pistons not returning correctly (Chapter 9).
2   Restricted brake lines or hoses (Chapters 1 and 9).
3   Incorrect parking brake adjustment (Chapter 9).
4   Defective brake calipers (Chapter 9).

44   Grabbing or uneven braking action

1   Malfunction of proportioning valve (Chapter 9).
2   Malfunction of power brake booster unit (Chapter 9).
3   Binding brake pedal mechanism (Chapter 9).
4   Contaminated brake linings (Chapter 9).

45   Brake pedal feels spongy when depressed

1   Air in hydraulic lines (Chapter 9).
2   Master cylinder mounting bolts loose (Chapter 9).
3   Master cylinder defective (Chapter 9).

46   Brake pedal travels to the floor with little resistance

Little or no fluid in the master cylinder reservoir caused by leaking caliper, or loose, damaged or disconnected brake lines (Chapter 9).

47   Parking brake does not hold

Parking brake cables improperly adjusted (Chapter 9).

SUSPENSION AND STEERING SYSTEMS

➡ **Note: Before attempting to diagnose the suspension and steering systems, perform the following preliminary checks:**

a)   Check the tire pressures and look for uneven wear.
b)   Check the steering universal joints or coupling from the column to the steering gear for loose fasteners and wear.
c)   Check the front and rear suspension and the steering gear assembly for loose and damaged parts.
d)   Look for out-of-round or out-of-balance tires, bent rims and loose and/or rough wheel bearings.

48   Vehicle pulls to one side

1   Mismatched or uneven tires (Chapter 10).
2   Broken or sagging springs (Chapter 10).
3   Wheel alignment incorrect (Chapter 10).
4   Front brakes dragging (Chapter 9).

49   Abnormal or excessive tire wear

1   Front wheel alignment incorrect (Chapter 10).
2   Sagging or broken springs (Chapter 10).
3   Tire out-of-balance (Chapter 10).
4   Worn strut or shock absorber (Chapter 10).
5   Overloaded vehicle.
6   Tires not rotated regularly.

50 Wheel makes a "thumping" noise

1 Blister or bump on tire (Chapter 1).
2 Improper strut or shock absorber action (Chapter 10).

51 Shimmy, shake or vibration

1 Tire or wheel out-of-balance or out-of-round (Chapter 10).
2 Loose or worn wheel bearings (Chapter 10).
3 Worn tie-rod ends (Chapter 10).
4 Worn balljoints (Chapter 10).
5 Excessive wheel runout (Chapter 10).
6 Blister or bump on tire (Chapter 1).

52 Hard steering

1 Lack of lubrication at balljoints, tie-rod ends and steering gear assembly (Chapter 10).
2 Front wheel alignment incorrect (Chapter 10).
3 Low tire pressure (Chapter 1).

53 Steering wheel does not return to center position correctly

1 Lack of lubrication at balljoints and tie-rod ends (Chapters 1 and 10).
2 Binding in steering column (Chapter 10).
3 Defective rack-and-pinion assembly (Chapter 10).
4 Front wheel alignment problem (Chapter 10).

54 Abnormal noise at the front end

1 Lack of lubrication at balljoints and tie-rod ends (Chapter 1).
2 Loose upper strut mount (Chapter 10).
3 Worn tie-rod ends (Chapter 10).
4 Loose stabilizer bar (Chapter 10).
5 Loose wheel lug nuts (Chapter 1).
6 Loose suspension bolts (Chapter 10).

55 Wander or poor steering stability

1 Mismatched or uneven tires (Chapter 10).
2 Lack of lubrication at balljoints or tie-rod ends (Chapters 1 and 10).
3 Worn struts or shock absorbers (Chapter 10).
4 Loose stabilizer bar (Chapter 10).
5 Broken or sagging springs (Chapter 10).
6 Front wheel alignment incorrect.
7 Worn steering gear clamp bushing (Chapter 10).

56 Erratic steering when braking

1 Wheel bearings worn (Chapter 10).
2 Broken or sagging springs (Chapter 10).
3 Leaking caliper (Chapter 9).
4 Warped brake discs (Chapter 9).
5 Worn steering gear clamp bushing (Chapter 10).
6 Wheel alignment incorrect.

57 Excessive pitching and/or rolling around corners or during braking

1 Loose stabilizer bar (Chapter 10).
2 Worn struts/shock absorbers or mounts (Chapter 10).
3 Broken or sagging springs (Chapter 10).
4 Overloaded vehicle.

58 Suspension bottoms

1 Overloaded vehicle.
2 Worn struts or shock absorbers (Chapter 10).
3 Incorrect, broken or sagging springs (Chapter 10).

59 Cupped tires

1 Front wheel alignment incorrect (Chapter 10).
2 Worn struts or shock absorbers (Chapter 10).
3 Wheel bearings worn (Chapter 10).
4 Excessive tire or wheel runout (Chapter 10).
5 Worn balljoints (Chapter 10).

60 Excessive tire wear on outside edge

1 Inflation pressures incorrect (Chapter 1).
2 Excessive speed in turns.
3 Wheel alignment incorrect (excessive toe-in or positive camber). Have professionally aligned.
4 Suspension arm bent or twisted (Chapter 10).

61 Excessive tire wear on inside edge

1 Inflation pressures incorrect (Chapter 1).
2 Wheel alignment incorrect (toe-out or excessive negative camber). Have professionally aligned.
3 Loose or damaged steering components (Chapter 10).

62 Tire tread worn in one place

1 Tires out-of-balance.
2 Damaged or buckled wheel. Inspect and replace if necessary.
3 Defective tire (Chapter 1).

63 Excessive play or looseness in steering system

1 Wheel bearings worn (Chapter 10).
2 Tie-rod end loose or worn (Chapter 10).
3 Steering gear loose (Chapter 10).

64 Rattling or clicking noise in steering gear

1 Steering gear mounting bolts loose (Chapter 10).
2 Steering gear defective (Chapter 10).

1

TUNE-UP AND ROUTINE MAINTENANCE

1 Maintenance schedule

The maintenance intervals in this manual are provided with the assumption that you, not the dealer, will be doing the work. These are the minimum maintenance intervals recommended by the factory for vehicles that are driven daily. If you wish to keep your vehicle in peak condition at all times, you may wish to perform some of these procedures even more often. Because frequent maintenance enhances the efficiency, performance and resale value of your car, we encourage you to do so. If you drive in dusty areas, tow a trailer, idle or drive at low speeds for extended periods or drive for short distances (less than four miles) in below freezing temperatures, shorter intervals are also recommended.

When your vehicle is new, follow the maintenance schedule to the letter, record the maintenance performed in your owners manual and keep all receipts to protect the new vehicle warranty. In many cases, the initial maintenance check is done at no cost to the owner.

EVERY 250 MILES (400 KM) OR WEEKLY, WHICHEVER COMES FIRST

Check the engine oil level (Section 4)
Check the engine coolant level (Section 4)
Check the windshield washer fluid level (Section 4)
Check the brake fluid level (Section 4)
Check the power steering fluid level (Section 4)
Check the automatic transaxle fluid level (Section 4)
Check the tires and tire pressures (Section 5)
Check the operation of all lights
Check the horn operation

EVERY 3000 MILES (4800 KM) OR 3 MONTHS, WHICHEVER COMES FIRST

All items listed above plus:
Change the engine oil and oil filter (Section 6)

EVERY 7500 MILES (12,000 KM) OR 6 MONTHS, WHICHEVER COMES FIRST

All items listed above plus:
Inspect (and replace, if necessary) the windshield wiper blades (Section 7)
Check and service the battery (Section 8)
Check the cooling system (Section 9)
Rotate the tires (Section 10)
Check the seat belts (Section 11)
Inspect the brake system (Section 12)

EVERY 15,000 MILES (24,000 KM) OR 12 MONTHS, WHICHEVER COMES FIRST

All items listed above plus:
Inspect the suspension and steering components driveaxle boots (Section 13)*
Inspect and replace, if necessary, all underhood hoses (Section 14)
Replace the air filter (Section 15)*
Replace the interior ventilation filter (Section 16)
Inspect the fuel system (Section 17)
Check the exhaust system (Section 18)
Check the driveaxle boots (Section 19)
Valve clearance check and adjustment (only if noisy) (see Chapter 2A)

EVERY 30,000 (48,000 KM) MILES OR 24 MONTHS, WHICHEVER COMES FIRST

All items listed above plus:
Check and adjust, if necessary, the engine drivebelts (Section 20)
Replace the brake fluid (Section 21)
Service the cooling system (drain, flush and refill) (Section 22)

EVERY 45,000 MILES (72,400 KM) OR 36 MONTHS, WHICHEVER COMES FIRST

Change the automatic transaxle fluid (Section 23)**

EVERY 105,000 MILES (169,000 KM) OR 84 MONTHS, WHICHEVER COMES FIRST

Replace the spark plugs (see Section 24)
Check and adjust, if necessary, the engine idle speed (Section 25)
Check and adjust, if necessary, the valve clearance (see Chapter 2A)
Replace the timing belt, and inspect the water pump (see Chapter 2A and Chapter 3)

*This item is affected by "severe" operating conditions as described below. If your vehicle is operated under "severe" conditions, perform all maintenance indicated with a * at 7500 mile/6 month intervals. Severe conditions are indicated if you mainly operate your vehicle under one or more of the following conditions:*

Operating in dusty areas
Towing a trailer
Idling for extended periods and/or low speed operation
Operating when outside temperatures remain below freezing and when most trips are less than five miles

**If operated under one or more of the following conditions, change the automatic transaxle fluid every 15,000 miles:*

In heavy city traffic where the outside temperature regularly reaches 90-degrees F (32-degrees C) or higher
In hilly or mountainous terrain

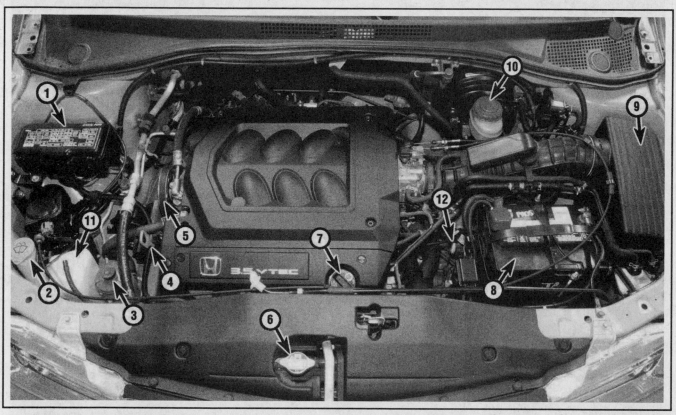

Typical engine compartment layout

1	Fuse/relay block	5	Power steering drivebelt	9	Air filter housing
2	Windshield washer fluid reservoir	6	Radiator cap	10	Brake fluid reservoir
3	Power steering fluid reservoir	7	Engine oil filler cap	11	Engine coolant reservoir
4	Engine oil dipstick	8	Battery	12	Automatic transaxle fluid dipstick

Typical front underside components

1	Engine oil filter	4	Front disc brake caliper	7	Air conditioning compressor
2	Engine oil drain plug	5	Exhaust pipe	8	Radiator drain fitting
3	Automatic transaxle drain plug	6	Catalytic converter		

Typical rear underside components

1 Exhaust system hanger	4 Rear drum brake assembly	7 Shock absorber
2 Muffler	5 Brake hose	8 Fuel filler hose
3 Fuel tank	6 Parking brake cable	

2 Introduction

This Chapter is designed to help the home mechanic maintain the Odyssey with the goals of maximum performance, economy, safety and reliability in mind.

Included is a master maintenance schedule, followed by procedures dealing specifically with each item on the schedule. Visual checks, adjustments, component replacement and other helpful items are included. Refer to the accompanying illustrations of the engine compartment and the underside of the vehicle for the locations of various components.

Servicing the vehicle, in accordance with the mileage/time maintenance schedule and the step-by-step procedures will result in a planned maintenance program that should produce a long and reliable service life. Keep in mind that it is a comprehensive plan, so maintaining some items but not others at the specified intervals will not produce the same results.

As you service the vehicle, you will discover that many of the procedures can - and should - be grouped together because of the nature of the particular procedure you're performing or because of the close proximity of two otherwise unrelated components to one another.

For example, if the vehicle is raised for chassis lubrication, you should inspect the exhaust, suspension, steering and fuel systems while you're under the vehicle. When you're rotating the tires, it makes good sense to check the brakes since the wheels are already removed. Finally, let's suppose you have to borrow or rent a torque wrench. Even if you only need it to tighten the spark plugs, you might as well check the torque of as many critical fasteners as time allows.

The first step in this maintenance program is to prepare yourself before the actual work begins. Read through all the procedures you're planning to do, then gather up all the parts and tools needed. If it looks like you might run into problems during a particular job, seek advice from a mechanic or an experienced do-it-yourselfer.

OWNER'S MANUAL AND VECI LABEL INFORMATION

Your vehicle owner's manual was written for your year and model and contains very specific information on component locations, specifications, fuse ratings, part numbers, etc. The Owner's Manual is an important resource for the do-it-yourselfer to have; if one was not supplied with your vehicle, it can generally be ordered from a dealer parts department.

Among other important information, the Vehicle Emissions Control Information (VECI) label contains specifications and procedures for applicable tune-up adjustments and, in some instances, spark plugs (see Chapter 6 for more information on the VECI label). The information on this label is the exact maintenance data recommended by the manufacturer. This data often varies by intended operating altitude, local emissions regulations, month of manufacture, etc.

This Chapter contains procedural details, safety information and more ambitious maintenance intervals than you might find in manufacturer's literature. However, you may also find procedures or specifications in your Owner's Manual or VECI label that differ with what's printed here. In these cases, the Owner's Manual or VECI label can be considered correct, since it is specific to your particular vehicle.

3 Tune-up general information

The term tune-up is used in this manual to represent a combination of individual operations rather than one specific procedure.

If, from the time the vehicle is new, the routine maintenance schedule is followed closely and frequent checks are made of fluid levels and high wear items, as suggested throughout this manual, the engine will be kept in relatively good running condition and the need for additional work will be minimized.

More likely than not, however, there will be times when the engine is running poorly due to lack of regular maintenance. This is even more likely if a used vehicle, which has not received regular and frequent maintenance checks, is purchased. In such cases, an engine tune-up will be needed outside of the regular routine maintenance intervals.

The first step in any tune-up or diagnostic procedure to help correct a poor running engine is a cylinder compression check. A compression check (see Chapter 2B) will help determine the condition of internal engine components and should be used as a guide for tune-up and repair procedures. If, for instance, a compression check indicates serious internal engine wear, a conventional tune-up will not improve the performance of the engine and would be a waste of time and money. Because of its importance, the compression check should be done by someone with the right equipment and the knowledge to use it properly.

The following procedures are those most often needed to bring a generally poor running engine back into a proper state of tune.

MINOR TUNE-UP

Check all engine related fluids (Section 4)
Clean, inspect and test the battery (Section 8)
Check and adjust the drivebelts (Section 20)
Check all underhood hoses (Section 14)
Check the cooling system (Section 9)
Check the air filter (Section 15)

MAJOR TUNE-UP

All items listed under minor tune-up, plus . . .
Replace the spark plugs (Section 24)
Replace the air filter (Section 15)
Check the idle speed (Section 25)
Check the fuel system (Section 17)

4 Fluid level checks (every 250 miles [400km] or weekly)

1 Fluids are an essential part of the lubrication, cooling, brake, clutch and other systems. Because these fluids gradually become depleted and/or contaminated during normal operation of the vehicle, they must be periodically replenished. See *Recommended lubricants, fluids* and *Capacities* in this Chapter's Specifications before adding fluid to any of the following components.

➡ **Note: The vehicle must be on level ground before fluid levels can be checked.**

ENGINE OIL

▶ **Refer to illustrations 4.4 and 4.6**

2 The engine oil level is checked with a dipstick located at the front side of the engine (see engine compartment layout illustration at the beginning of this Chapter). The dipstick extends through a metal tube from which it protrudes down into the engine oil pan.

3 The oil level should be checked before the vehicle has been driven, or about 5 minutes after the engine has been shut off. If the oil is checked immediately after driving the vehicle, some of the oil will remain in the upper engine components, producing an inaccurate reading on the dipstick.

4 Pull the dipstick from the tube and wipe all the oil from the end with a clean rag or paper towel. Insert the clean dipstick all the way back into its metal tube and pull it out again. Observe the oil at the end of the dipstick. At its highest point, the level should be between the upper and lower holes (see illustration).

5 It takes one quart of oil to raise the level from the lower hole to the upper hole on the dipstick. Do not allow the level to drop below the lower hole or oil starvation may cause engine damage. Conversely, overfilling the engine (adding oil above the upper hole) may cause oil fouled spark plugs, oil leaks or oil seal failures.

6 Remove the threaded cap from the valve cover to add oil (see illustration). Use an oil can spout or funnel to prevent spills. After adding the oil, install the filler cap hand tight. Start the engine and look carefully for any small leaks around the oil filter or drain plug. Stop the

engine and check the oil level again after it has had sufficient time to drain from the upper block and cylinder head galleys.

7 Checking the oil level is an important preventive maintenance step. A continually dropping oil level indicates oil leakage through damaged seals, from loose connections, or past worn rings or valve guides. If the oil looks milky in color or has water droplets in it, a cylinder head gasket may be blown or the oil cooler could be leaking. The engine should be checked immediately. The condition of the oil should also be checked. Each time you check the oil level, slide your thumb and index finger up the dipstick before wiping off the oil. If you see small dirt or metal particles clinging to the dipstick, the oil should be changed (see Section 8).

ENGINE COOLANT

▶ **Refer to illustration 4.9**

❄ WARNING:

Do not allow antifreeze to come in contact with your skin or painted surfaces of the vehicle. Flush contaminated areas immediately with plenty of water. Don't store new coolant or leave old coolant lying around where it's accessible to children or pets - they're attracted by its sweet smell. Ingestion of even a small amount of coolant can be fatal! Wipe up garage floor and drip pan spills immediately. Keep antifreeze containers covered and repair cooling system leaks as soon as they're noticed.

8 All vehicles covered by this manual are equipped with a pressurized coolant recovery system. A coolant reservoir, located on the right side of the engine compartment, is connected by a hose to the base of the radiator filler neck. If the coolant heats up during engine operation, coolant can escape through the pressurized filler cap, then through the connecting hose into the reservoir. As the engine cools, the coolant is automatically drawn back into the cooling system to maintain the correct level.

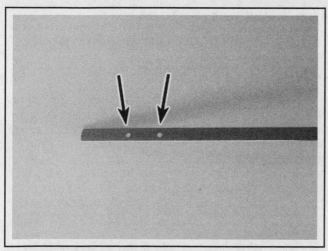

4.4 The oil level should be in the safe range - if it's below the MIN or ADD mark, add enough oil to bring it up to or near the MAX or FULL mark

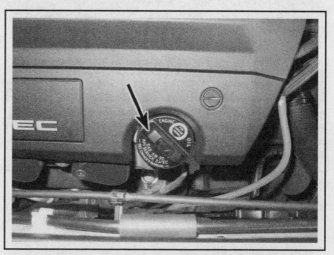

4.6 The oil filler cap is located on the valve cover - always make sure the area around the opening is clean before unscrewing the cap to prevent dirt from contaminating the engine

4.9 When the engine is cold, the engine coolant level should be at the MIN mark

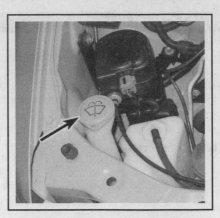

4.14 The windshield/rear window washer fluid reservoir is located in the right front corner of the engine compartment

4.16 The brake fluid level should be kept between the MIN and MAX marks on the translucent plastic reservoir

9   The coolant level in the reservoir should be checked regularly. It must be between the MAX and MIN lines on the tank. The level will vary with the temperature of the engine. When the engine is cold, the coolant level should be at or slightly above the MIN mark on the tank. Once the engine has warmed up, the level should be at or near the MAX mark. If it isn't, allow the fluid in the tank to cool, then remove the cap from the reservoir (see illustration) and add coolant to bring the level up to the MAX line.

※※ WARNING:

Do not remove the radiator cap to check the coolant level when the engine is warm!

Use only the recommended coolant and water in the mixture ratio listed in this Chapter's Specifications. Do not use supplemental inhibitors or additives. If only a small amount of coolant is required to bring the system up to the proper level, water can be used. However, repeated additions of water will dilute the recommended antifreeze and water solution. In order to maintain the proper ratio of antifreeze and water, it is advisable to top up the coolant level with the correct mixture.

10   If the coolant level drops within a short time after replenishment, there may be a leak in the system. Inspect the radiator, hoses, engine coolant filler cap, drain plugs and water pump. If no leak is evident, have the radiator cap pressure tested.

※※ WARNING:

Never remove the radiator cap or the coolant reservoir cap when the engine is running or has just been shut down, because the cooling system is hot. Escaping steam and scalding liquid could cause serious injury.

11   If it is necessary to open the radiator cap, wait until the system has cooled completely, then wrap a thick cloth around the cap and turn it to the first stop. If any steam escapes, wait until the system has cooled further, then remove the cap.

12   When checking the coolant level, always note its condition. It should be relatively clear. If it is brown or rust colored, the system should be drained, flushed and refilled. Even if the coolant appears to be normal, the corrosion inhibitors wear out with use, so it must be replaced at the specified intervals.

13   Do not allow antifreeze to come in contact with your skin or painted surfaces of the vehicle. Flush contacted areas immediately with plenty of water.

WINDSHIELD WASHER FLUID

▶ **Refer to illustration 4.14**

14   Fluid for the windshield washer system is stored in a plastic reservoir which is located at the right front corner of the engine compartment (see illustration). Check the fluid level by detaching the cap and pulling up the dipstick. In milder climates, plain water can be used to top up the reservoir, but the reservoir should be kept no more than 2/3 full to allow for expansion should the water freeze. In colder climates, the use of a specially designed windshield washer fluid, available at your dealer and any auto parts store, will help lower the freezing point of the fluid. Mix the solution with water in accordance with the manufacturer's directions on the container. Do not use regular antifreeze. It will damage the vehicle's paint.

BRAKE FLUID

▶ **Refer to illustration 4.16**

15   The brake master cylinder is located on the driver's side of the engine compartment firewall.

16   The level should be maintained at the MAX mark on the reservoir (see illustration).

17   If additional fluid is necessary to bring the level up, use a rag to clean all dirt off the top of the reservoir. If any foreign matter enters the master cylinder when the cap is removed, blockage in the brake system lines can occur. Also, make sure all painted surfaces around the master cylinder are covered, since brake fluid will ruin paint. Carefully pour new, clean brake fluid into the master cylinder. Be careful not to spill the fluid on painted surfaces. Be sure the specified fluid is used; mixing different types of brake fluid can cause damage to the system. See *Recommended lubricants and fluids* in this Chapter's Specifications or your owner's manual.

18   At this time the fluid and the master cylinder can be inspected for contamination. If deposits, dirt particles or water droplets are seen in the fluid, the system should be drained and refilled with fresh fluid (see Section 21).

19   Reinstall the master cylinder cap.

4.23 The power steering fluid reservoir is located at the right front side of the engine compartment

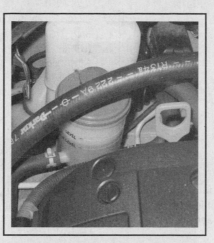

4.26 At normal operating temperature, the power steering fluid level should be between the MAX and MIN marks

4.32 The transaxle dipstick is located on the left side of the engine compartment

20 The brake fluid in the master cylinder will drop slightly as the brake shoes or pads at each wheel wear down during normal operation. If the master cylinder requires repeated replenishing to keep the level up, it's an indication of leaks in the brake system, which should be corrected immediately. Check all brake lines and connections, along with the wheel cylinders and booster (see Chapter 9 for more information).

21 If you discover that the reservoir is empty or nearly empty, the brake system should be filled, bled (see Chapter 9) and checked for leaks.

POWER STEERING FLUID

▶ **Refer to illustrations 4.23 and 4.26**

22 Check the power steering fluid level periodically to avoid steering system problems, such as damage to the pump.

✳ CAUTION:

DO NOT hold the steering wheel against either stop (extreme left or right turn) for more than five seconds. If you do, the power steering pump could be damaged.

23 The power steering reservoir, located at the right side of the engine compartment (see illustration), has MIN and MAX fluid level marks on the side. The fluid level can be seen without removing the reservoir cap.

24 Park the vehicle on level ground and apply the parking brake.

25 Run the engine until it has reached normal operating temperature. With the engine at idle, turn the steering wheel back and forth about 10 times to get any air out of the steering system. Shut the engine off with the wheels in the straight-ahead position.

26 Note the fluid level on the side of the reservoir. It should be between the two marks (see illustration).

27 Add small amounts of fluid until the level is correct.

✳ CAUTION:

Do not overfill the reservoir. If too much fluid is added, remove the excess with a clean syringe or suction pump.

28 Check the power steering hoses and connections for leaks and wear.

AUTOMATIC TRANSAXLE FLUID

▶ **Refer to illustrations 4.32 and 4.34**

29 The level of the automatic transaxle fluid should be carefully maintained. Low fluid level can lead to slipping or loss of drive, while overfilling can cause foaming, loss of fluid and transaxle damage.

30 The transaxle fluid level should only be checked when the transaxle is hot (at its normal operating temperature). If the vehicle has just been driven over 10 miles (15 miles in a frigid climate), and the fluid temperature is 160 to 175-degrees F, the transaxle is hot.

✳ CAUTION:

If the vehicle has just been driven for a long time at high speed or in city traffic in hot weather, or if it has been pulling a trailer, an accurate fluid level reading cannot be obtained. Allow the fluid to cool down for about 30 minutes.

31 If the vehicle has not just been driven, park the vehicle on level ground, set the parking brake and start the engine. While the engine is idling, depress the brake pedal and move the selector lever through all the gear ranges, beginning and ending in Park.

32 Turn off the engine and remove the dipstick from its tube (see illustration).

33 Wipe the fluid from the dipstick with a clean rag and reinsert it back into the filler tube until the cap seats.

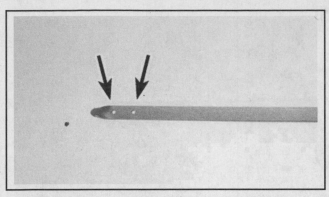

4.34 The automatic transaxle fluid level should be between the two holes in the dipstick - if it isn't, add enough oil to bring the level to or near the upper hole

34 Pull the dipstick out again and note the fluid level (see illustration). The fluid level should be in the operating temperature range (between the upper and lower mark). If the level is at the low side of either range, add the specified automatic transmission fluid through the dipstick tube with a funnel.

35 Add just enough of the recommended fluid to fill the transaxle to the proper level. It takes about one pint to raise the level from the low mark to the high mark when the fluid is hot, so add the fluid a little at a time and keep checking the level until it is correct.

36 The condition of the fluid should also be checked along with the level. If the fluid at the end of the dipstick is black or a dark reddish brown color, or if it emits a burned smell, the fluid should be changed (see Section 23). If you are in doubt about the condition of the fluid, purchase some new fluid and compare the two for color and smell.

5 Tire and tire pressure checks (every 250 miles [400 km] or weekly)

▶ **Refer to illustrations 5.2, 5.3, 5.4a, 5.4b and 5.8**

1 Periodic inspection of the tires may spare you from the inconvenience of being stranded with a flat tire. It can also provide you with vital information regarding possible problems in the steering and suspension systems before major damage occurs.

2 Normal tread wear can be monitored with a simple, inexpensive device known as a tread depth indicator (see illustration). When the tread depth reaches the specified minimum, replace the tire(s).

3 Note any abnormal tread wear (see illustration). Tread pattern irregularities such as cupping, flat spots and more wear on one side than the other are indications of front end alignment and/or balance problems. If any of these conditions are noted, take the vehicle to a tire shop or service station to correct the problem.

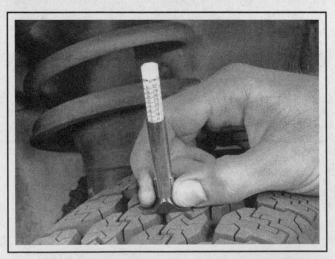

5.2 A tire tread depth indicator should be used to monitor tire wear - they are available at auto parts stores and service stations and cost very little

4 Look closely for cuts, punctures and embedded nails or tacks. Sometimes a tire will hold its air pressure for a short time or leak down very slowly even after a nail has embedded itself into the tread. If a slow leak persists, check the valve core to make sure it is tight (see illustration). Examine the tread for an object that may have embedded itself into the tire or for a "plug" that may have begun to leak (radial tire punctures are repaired with a plug that is installed in a puncture). If a puncture is suspected, it can be easily verified by spraying a solution of soapy water onto the puncture area (see illustration). The soapy solution will bubble if there is a leak. Unless the puncture is inordinately large, a tire shop or gas station can usually repair the punctured tire.

5 Carefully inspect the inner side of each tire for evidence of brake fluid leakage. If you see any, inspect the brakes immediately.

6 Correct tire air pressure adds miles to the lifespan of the tires, improves mileage and enhances overall ride quality. Tire pressure cannot be accurately estimated by looking at a tire, particularly if it is a radial. A tire pressure gauge is therefore essential. Keep an accurate gauge in the glovebox. The pressure gauges fitted to the nozzles of air hoses at gas stations are often inaccurate.

7 Always check tire pressure when the tires are cold. "Cold," in this case, means the vehicle has not been driven over a mile in the three hours preceding a tire pressure check. A pressure rise of four to eight pounds is not uncommon once the tires are warm.

8 Unscrew the valve cap protruding from the wheel or hubcap and push the gauge firmly onto the valve (see illustration). Note the reading on the gauge and compare this figure to the recommended tire pressure shown on the tire placard on the left door jamb. Be sure to reinstall the valve cap to keep dirt and moisture out of the valve stem mechanism. Check all four tires and, if necessary, add enough air to bring them up to the recommended pressure levels.

9 Don't forget to keep the spare tire inflated to the specified pressure (consult your owner's manual). Note that the air pressure specified for the compact spare is significantly higher than the pressure of the regular tires.

UNDERINFLATION

CUPPING

OVERINFLATION

INCORRECT TOE-IN OR EXTREME CAMBER

Cupping may be caused by:

- Underinflation and/or mechanical irregularities such as out-of-balance condition of wheel and/or tire, and bent or damaged wheel.
- Loose or worn steering tie-rod or steering idler arm.
- Loose, damaged or worn front suspension parts.

FEATHERING DUE TO MISALIGNMENT

5.3 This chart will help you determine the condition of your tires, the probable cause(s) of abnormal wear and the corrective action necessary

5.4a If a tire loses air on a steady basis, check the valve core first to make sure it's snug (special inexpensive wrenches are commonly available at auto parts stores)

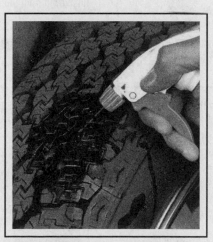

5.4b If the valve core is tight, raise the corner of the vehicle with the low tire and spray a soapy water solution onto the tread as the tire is turned slowly - slow leaks will cause small bubbles to appear

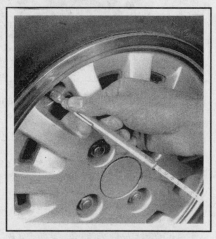

5.8 To extend the life of your tires, check the air pressure at least once a week with an accurate gauge (don't forget the spare!)

6 Engine oil and oil filter change (every 3000 miles [4800 km] or 3 months)

▶ **Refer to illustrations 6.2, 6.7, 6.12 and 6.14**

1   Frequent oil changes are the best preventive maintenance the home mechanic can give the engine, because aging oil becomes diluted and contaminated, which leads to premature engine wear.

2   Make sure you have all the necessary tools before you begin this procedure (see illustration). You should also have plenty of rags or newspapers handy for mopping up any spills.

3   Access to the underside of the vehicle is greatly improved if the vehicle can be lifted on a hoist, driven onto ramps or supported by jackstands.

⁂ WARNING:

Do not work under a vehicle which is supported only by a bumper, hydraulic or scissors-type jack.

4   If this is your first oil change, get under the vehicle and familiarize yourself with the locations of the oil drain plug and the oil filter. The engine and exhaust components will be warm during the actual work, so try to anticipate any potential problems before the engine and accessories are hot.

5   Park the vehicle on a level spot. Start the engine and allow it to reach its normal operating temperature. Warm oil and sludge will flow out more easily. Turn off the engine when it's warmed up. Remove the filler cap from the valve cover.

6   Raise the vehicle and support it securely on jackstands.

⁂ WARNING:

Never get beneath the vehicle when it is supported only by a jack. The jack provided with your vehicle is designed solely for raising the vehicle to remove and replace the wheels. Always use jackstands to support the vehicle when it becomes necessary to place your body underneath the vehicle.

7   Being careful not to touch the hot exhaust components, place the drain pan under the drain plug in the bottom of the pan and remove the plug (see illustration). You may want to wear gloves while unscrewing the plug the final few turns if the engine is hot.

8   Allow the old oil to drain into the pan. It may be necessary to move the pan farther under the engine as the oil flow slows to a trickle. Inspect the old oil for the presence of metal shavings and chips.

9   After all the oil has drained, wipe off the drain plug with a clean rag. Even minute metal particles clinging to the plug would immediately contaminate the new oil.

10 Clean the area around the drain plug opening, reinstall the plug and tighten it securely, but do not strip the threads.

11 Move the drain pan into position under the oil filter.

12 Loosen the oil filter (see illustration) by turning it counterclockwise with an oil filter wrench. Once the filter is loose, use your hands to unscrew it from the block. Keep the open end pointing up to prevent the

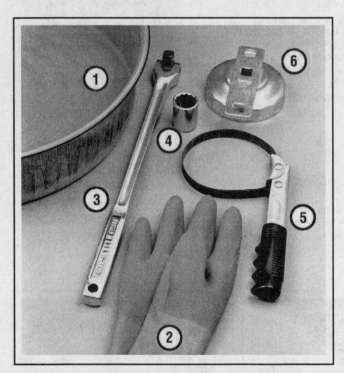

6.2 These tools are required when changing the engine oil and filter

1   *Drain pan* - *It should be fairly shallow in depth, but wide in order to prevent spills*

2   *Rubber gloves* - *When removing the drain plug and filter, it is inevitable that you will get oil on your hands (the gloves will prevent burns)*

3   *Breaker bar* - *Sometimes the oil drain plug is pretty tight and a long breaker bar is needed to loosen it*

4   *Socket* - *To be used with the breaker bar or a ratchet (must be the correct size to fit the drain plug)*

5   *Filter wrench* - *This is a metal band-type wrench, which requires clearance around the filter to be effective*

6   *Filter wrench* - *This type fits on the bottom of the filter and can be turned with a ratchet or beaker bar (different size wrenches are available for different types of filters)*

6.7 Use a proper size box-end wrench or socket to remove the oil drain plug and avoid rounding it off

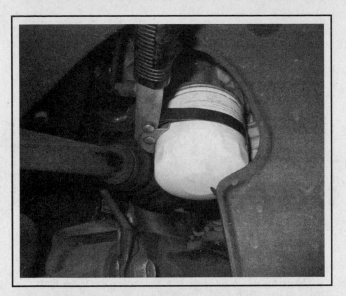

6.12 Use an oil filter wrench to remove the filter

6.14 Lubricate the oil filter gasket with clean engine oil before installing the filter on the engine

oil inside the filter from spilling out.

> ❊❊ **WARNING:**
>
> **The exhaust system may still be hot, so be careful.**

13 With a clean rag, wipe off the mounting surface on the block. If a residue of old oil is allowed to remain, it will smoke when the block is heated up. Also make sure that none of the old gasket remains stuck to the mounting surface. It can be removed with a scraper if necessary.

14 Compare the old filter with the new one to make sure they are the same type. Smear some clean engine oil on the rubber gasket of the new filter (see illustration).

15 Attach the new filter to the engine, following the tightening directions printed on the filter canister or packing box. Most filter manufacturers recommend against using a filter wrench due to the possibility of overtightening and damaging the seal.

16 Remove all tools, rags, etc. from under the vehicle, being careful not to spill the oil in the drain pan, then lower the vehicle.

17 Add new oil to the engine through the oil filler cap in the valve cover. Use a funnel, if necessary, to prevent oil from spilling onto the top of the engine. Pour three quarts of fresh oil into the engine. Wait a few minutes to allow the oil to drain into the pan, then check the level on the oil dipstick (see Section 4). If the oil level is at or near the upper hole on the dipstick, install the filler cap hand tight, start the engine and allow the new oil to circulate.

18 Allow the engine to run for about a minute. While the engine is running, look under the vehicle and check for leaks at the oil pan drain plug and around the oil filter. If either is leaking, stop the engine and tighten the plug or filter.

19 Wait a few minutes to allow the oil to trickle down into the pan, then recheck the level on the dipstick and, if necessary, add enough oil to bring the level to the upper hole.

20 During the first few trips after an oil change, make it a point to check frequently for leaks and proper oil level.

21 The old oil drained from the engine cannot be reused in its present state and should be disposed of. Check with your local auto parts store, disposal facility or environmental agency to see if they will accept the oil for recycling. After the oil has cooled it can be drained into a container (capped plastic jugs, topped bottles, milk cartons, etc.) for transport to one of these disposal sites. Don't dispose of the oil by pouring it on the ground or down a drain!

---

7   Windshield wiper blade inspection and replacement (every 7500 miles [12,000 km] or 6 months)

▶ **Refer to illustrations 7.5a and 7.5b**

1   The windshield wiper and blade assembly should be inspected periodically for damage, loose components and cracked or worn blade elements.

2   Road film can build up on the wiper blades and affect their effi- ciency, so they should be washed regularly with a mild detergent solu- tion.

3   The action of the wiping mechanism can loosen bolts, nuts and fasteners, so they should be checked and tightened, as necessary, at the same time the wiper blades are checked.

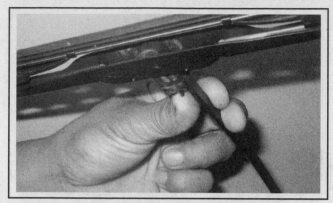

7.5a To release the blade holder, push the release lever . . .

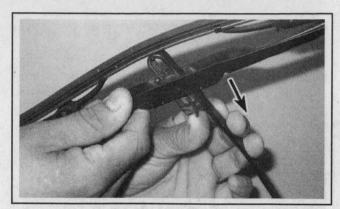

7.5b . . . and pull the wiper blade in the direction of the arrow to separate it from the arm

4   If the wiper blade elements are cracked, worn or warped, or no longer clean adequately, they should be replaced with new ones.

5   Lift the arm assembly away from the glass for clearance, press on the release lever, then slide the wiper blade assembly out of the hook at the end of the arm (see illustrations).

6   Attach the new wiper to the arm. Connection can be confirmed by an audible click.

8   Battery check, maintenance and charging (every 7500 miles [12,000 km] or 6 months)

▶ **Refer to illustrations 8.1, 8.6a, 8.6b, 8.7a, 8.7b and 8.8**

✳✳ WARNING:

Certain precautions must be followed when checking and servicing the battery. Hydrogen gas, which is highly flammable, is always present in the battery cells, so keep lighted tobacco and all other open flames and sparks away from the battery. The electrolyte inside the battery is actually diluted sulfuric acid, which will cause injury if splashed on your skin or in your eyes. It will also ruin clothes and painted surfaces. When removing the battery cables, always detach the negative cable first and hook it up last!

1   A routine preventive maintenance program for the battery in your vehicle is the only way to ensure quick and reliable starts. But before performing any battery maintenance, make sure that you have the proper equipment necessary to work safely around the battery (see illustration).

2   There are also several precautions that should be taken whenever battery maintenance is performed. Before servicing the battery, always turn the engine and all accessories off and disconnect the cable from the negative terminal of the battery (see Chapter 5, Section 1).

3   The battery produces hydrogen gas, which is both flammable and explosive. Never create a spark, smoke or light a match around the battery. Always charge the battery in a ventilated area.

4   Electrolyte contains poisonous and corrosive sulfuric acid. Do not

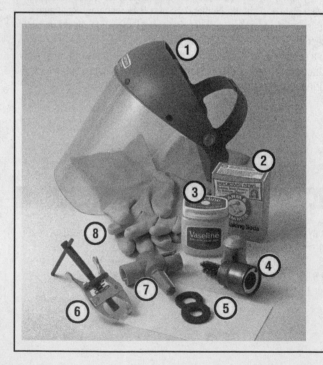

8.1 Tools and materials required for battery maintenance

1   ***Face shield/safety goggles*** - *When removing corrosion with a brush, the acidic particles can easily fly up into your eyes*

2   ***Baking soda*** - *A solution of baking soda and water can be used to neutralize corrosion*

3   ***Petroleum jelly*** - *A layer of this on the battery posts will help prevent corrosion*

4   ***Battery post/cable cleaner*** - *This wire brush cleaning tool will remove all traces of corrosion from the battery posts and cable clamps*

5   ***Treated felt washers*** - *Placing one of these on each post, directly under the cable clamps, will help prevent corrosion*

6   ***Puller*** - *Sometimes the cable clamps are very difficult to pull off the posts, even after the nut/bolt has been completely loosened. This tool pulls the clamp straight up and off the post without damage*

7   ***Battery post/cable cleaner*** - *Here is another cleaning tool which is a slightly different version of number 4 above, but it does the same thing*

8   ***Rubber gloves*** - *Another safety item to consider when servicing the battery; remember that's acid inside the battery*

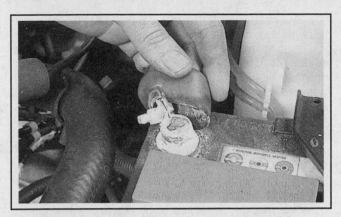

8.6a Battery terminal corrosion usually appears as light, fluffy powder

8.6b Removing a cable from the battery post with a wrench - sometimes a pair of special battery pliers are required for this procedure if corrosion has caused deterioration of the nut hex (always remove the ground (-) cable first and hook it up last!)

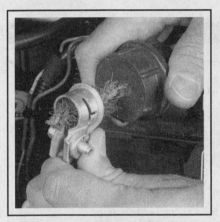

8.7a When cleaning the cable clamps, all corrosion must be removed (the inside of the clamp is tapered to match the taper on the post, so don't remove too much material)

8.7b Regardless of the type of tool used to clean the battery posts, a clean, shiny surface should be the result

8.8 Make sure the battery hold-down fasteners are tight

allow it to get in your eyes, on your skin on your clothes. Never ingest it. Wear protective safety glasses when working near the battery. Keep children away from the battery.

5   Note the external condition of the battery. If the positive terminal and cable clamp on your vehicle's battery is equipped with a rubber protector, make sure that it's not torn or damaged. It should completely cover the terminal. Look for any corroded or loose connections, cracks in the case or cover or loose hold-down clamps. Also check the entire length of each cable for cracks and frayed conductors.

6   If corrosion, which looks like white, fluffy deposits (see illustration) is evident, particularly around the terminals, the battery should be removed for cleaning. Loosen the cable clamp bolts with a wrench, being careful to remove the ground cable first, and slide them off the terminals (see illustration). Then disconnect the hold-down clamp bolt and nut, remove the clamp and lift the battery from the engine compartment.

7   Clean the cable clamps thoroughly with a battery brush or a terminal cleaner and a solution of warm water and baking soda (see

illustration). Wash the terminals and the top of the battery case with the same solution but make sure that the solution doesn't get into the battery. When cleaning the cables, terminals and battery top, wear safety goggles and rubber gloves to prevent any solution from coming in contact with your eyes or hands. Wear old clothes too - even diluted, sulfuric acid splashed onto clothes will burn holes in them. If the terminals have been extensively corroded, clean them up with a terminal cleaner (see illustration). Thoroughly wash all cleaned areas with plain water.

8   Make sure that the battery tray is in good condition and the hold-down clamp fasteners are tight (see illustration). If the battery is removed from the tray, make sure no parts remain in the bottom of the tray when the battery is reinstalled. When reinstalling the hold-down clamp bolts, do not overtighten them.

9   Information on removing and installing the battery can be found in Chapter 5. If you disconnected the cable(s) from the negative and/or positive battery terminals, see Chapter 5, Section 1. Information on jump starting can be found at the front of this manual.

CLEANING

10 Corrosion on the hold-down components, battery case and surrounding areas can be removed with a solution of water and baking soda. Thoroughly rinse all cleaned areas with plain water.

11 Any metal parts of the vehicle damaged by corrosion should be covered with a zinc-based primer, then painted.

CHARGING

⁂ WARNING:

When batteries are being charged, hydrogen gas, which is very explosive and flammable, is produced. Do not smoke or allow open flames near a charging or a recently charged battery. Wear eye protection when near the battery during charging. Also, make sure the charger is unplugged before connecting or disconnecting the battery from the charger.

12 Slow-rate charging is the best way to restore a battery that's discharged to the point where it will not start the engine. It's also a good way to maintain the battery charge in a vehicle that's only driven a few miles between starts. Maintaining the battery charge is particularly important in the winter when the battery must work harder to start the engine and electrical accessories that drain the battery are in greater use.

13 It's best to use a one or two-amp battery charger (sometimes called a "trickle" charger). They are the safest and put the least strain on the battery. They are also the least expensive. For a faster charge, you can use a higher amperage charger, but don't use one rated more than 1/10th the amp/hour rating of the battery. Rapid boost charges that claim to restore the power of the battery in one to two hours are hardest on the battery and can damage batteries not in good condition. This type of charging should only be used in emergency situations.

14 The average time necessary to charge a battery should be listed in the instructions that come with the charger. As a general rule, a trickle charger will charge a battery in 12 to 16 hours.

9   Cooling system check (every 7500 miles [12,000 km] or 6 months)

▶ **Refer to illustration 9.4**

1   Many major engine failures can be attributed to a faulty cooling system. The cooling system also cools the transaxle fluid and thus plays an important role in prolonging transaxle life.

2   The cooling system should be checked with the engine cold. Do this before the vehicle is driven for the day or after the engine has been shut off for at least three hours.

3   Remove the radiator cap by turning it to the left until it reaches a stop. If you hear a hissing sound (indicating there is still pressure in the system), wait until it stops. Now press down on the cap with the palm of your hand and continue turning to the left until the cap can be removed. Thoroughly clean the cap, inside and out, with clean water. Also clean the filler neck on the radiator. All traces of corrosion should be removed. The coolant inside the radiator should be relatively transparent. If it's rust colored, the system should be drained and refilled (see Section 22). If the coolant level isn't up to the top, add additional antifreeze/coolant mixture (see Section 4).

4   Carefully check the large upper and lower radiator hoses along with the smaller diameter heater hoses which run from the engine to the firewall. Inspect each hose along its entire length, replacing any hose which is cracked, swollen or shows signs of deterioration. Cracks may become more apparent if the hose is squeezed (see illustration). Regardless of condition, it's a good idea to replace hoses with new ones every two years.

5   Make sure that all hose connections are tight. A leak in the cooling system will usually show up as white or rust colored deposits on the areas adjoining the leak. If wire-type clamps are used at the ends of the hoses, it may be a good idea to replace them with more secure screw-type clamps.

6   Use compressed air or a soft brush to remove bugs, leaves, etc. from the front of the radiator or air conditioning condenser. Be careful not to damage the delicate cooling fins or cut yourself on them.

7   Every other inspection, or at the first indication of cooling system problems, have the cap and system pressure tested. If you don't have a pressure tester, most gas stations and repair shops will do this for a minimal charge.

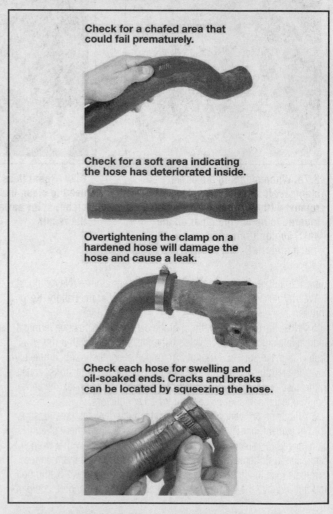

Check for a chafed area that could fail prematurely.

Check for a soft area indicating the hose has deteriorated inside.

Overtightening the clamp on a hardened hose will damage the hose and cause a leak.

Check each hose for swelling and oil-soaked ends. Cracks and breaks can be located by squeezing the hose.

9.4 Hoses, like drivebelts, have a habit of failing at the worst possible time - to prevent the inconvenience of a blown radiator or heater hose, inspect them carefully as shown here

10 Tire rotation (every 7500 miles [12,000 km] or 6 months)

▶ **Refer to illustrations 10.2a and 10.2b**

1   The tires should be rotated at the specified intervals and whenever uneven wear is noticed. Since the vehicle will be raised and the tires removed anyway, check the brakes (see Section 12) at this time.

2   Radial tires must be rotated in a specific pattern (see illustrations). Most models are equipped with non-directional tires, but some models may have directional tires, which have a different rotation pattern. When rotating tires, examine the sidewalls. Directional tires have arrows on the sidewall that indicate the direction they must turn, and a set of these tires includes two left-side tires and two right-side tires. The left and right side tires must not be rotated to the other side.

3   Refer to the information in *Jacking and towing* at the front of this manual for the proper procedures to follow when raising the vehicle and changing a tire. If the brakes are to be checked, do not apply the parking brake as stated. Make sure the tires are blocked to prevent the vehicle from rolling.

4   Preferably, the entire vehicle should be raised at the same time. This can be done on a hoist or by jacking up each corner and then lowering the vehicle onto jackstands placed under the frame rails. Always use four jackstands and make sure the vehicle is firmly supported.

5   After rotation, check and adjust the tire pressures as necessary and be sure to check the lug nut tightness. Ideally, lug nuts should be tightened to the torque listed in this Chapter's Specifications with a torque wrench, and rechecked after 25 miles of driving.

6   For further information on the wheels and tires, refer to Chapter 10.

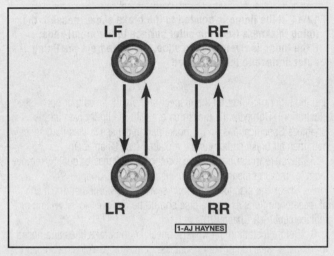

10.2a The recommended rotation pattern for *directional* radial tires

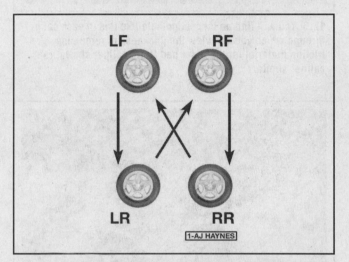

10.2b The recommended rotation pattern for *non-directional* radial tires

11 Seat belt check (every 7500 miles [12,000 km] or 6 months)

1   Check seat belts, buckles, latch plates and guide loops for obvious damage and signs of wear.

2   See if the seat belt reminder light comes on when the key is turned to the Run or Start position. A chime should also sound. On passive restraint systems, the shoulder belt should move into position in the A-pillar.

3   The seat belts are designed to lock up during a sudden stop or impact, yet allow free movement during normal driving. Make sure the retractors return the belt against your chest while driving and rewind the belt fully when the buckle is unlatched.

4   If any of the above checks reveal problems with the seat belt system, replace parts as necessary.

12 Brake system check (every 7500 miles [12,000 km] or 6 months)

❉❉ **WARNING:**

The dust created by the brake system is harmful to your health. Never blow it out with compressed air and don't inhale any of it. An approved filtering mask should be worn when working on the brakes. Do not, under any circumstances, use petroleum-based solvents to clean brake parts. Use brake system cleaner only!

➡ **Note: For detailed photographs of the brake system, refer to Chapter 9.**

1   In addition to the specified intervals, the brakes should be inspected every time the wheels are removed or whenever a defect is suspected.

2   Any of the following symptoms could indicate a potential brake system defect: The vehicle pulls to one side when the brake pedal is depressed; the brakes make squealing or dragging noises when applied; brake pedal travel is excessive; the pedal pulsates; or brake fluid leaks, usually onto the inside of the tire or wheel.

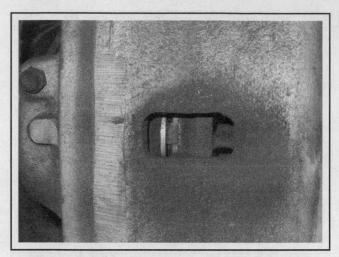

12.6 You will find an inspection hole like this in each caliper through which you can view the thickness of remaining friction material for the inner pad (front caliper shown, rear caliper similar)

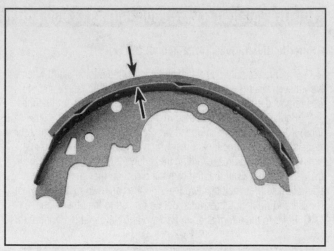

12.14 If the lining is bonded to the brake shoe, measure the lining thickness from the outer surface to the metal shoe; if the lining is riveted to the shoe, measure from the lining outer surface to the rivet head

12.16 Pull the boot away from the cylinder and check for fluid leakage

DISC BRAKES

▶ **Refer to illustration 12.6**

3 Disc brakes can be visually checked without removing any parts except the wheels. Remove the hub caps (if applicable) and loosen the wheel lug nuts a quarter turn each.

4 Raise the vehicle and place it securely on jackstands.

❈❈ **WARNING:**

Never work under a vehicle that is supported only by a jack!

5 Remove the wheels. Now visible is the disc brake caliper which contains the pads. There is an outer brake pad and an inner pad. Both must be checked for wear.

6 Measure the thickness of the outer pad at each end of the caliper

and the inner pad through the inspection hole in the caliper body (see illustration). Compare the measurement with the limit given in this Chapter's Specifications; if any brake pad thickness is less than specified, then all brake pads must be replaced (see Chapter 9).

7 If you're in doubt as to the exact pad thickness or quality, remove them for measurement and further inspection (see Chapter 9).

8 Check the disc for score marks, wear and burned spots. If any of these conditions exist, the disc should be removed for servicing or replacement (see Chapter 9).

9 Before installing the wheels, check all the brake lines and hoses for damage, wear, deformation, cracks, corrosion, leakage, bends and twists, particularly in the vicinity of the rubber hoses and calipers.

10 Install the wheels, lower the vehicle and tighten the wheel lug nuts to the torque given in this Chapter's Specifications.

DRUM BRAKES

▶ **Refer to illustrations 12.14 and 12.16**

11 On models with rear drum brakes, make sure the parking brake is off then tap on the outside of the drum with a rubber mallet to loosen it.

12 Remove the brake drums. If the drum still won't come off, refer to Chapter 9

13 With the drums removed, carefully clean the brake assembly with brake system cleaner.

❈❈ **WARNING:**

Don't blow the dust out with compressed air and don't inhale any of it (it is harmful to your health).

14 Note the thickness of the lining material on both front and rear brake shoes (see illustration). Compare the measurement with the limit given in this Chapter's Specifications; if any lining thickness is less than specified, then all of the brake shoes must be replaced (see Chapter 9). The shoes should also be replaced if they're cracked, glazed (shiny areas), or covered with brake fluid.

15 Make sure all the brake assembly springs are connected and in

good condition.

16 Check the brake components for signs of fluid leakage. With your finger or a small screwdriver, carefully pry back the rubber cups on the wheel cylinder located at the top of the brake shoes (see illustration). Any leakage here is an indication that the wheel cylinders should be replaced immediately (see Chapter 9). Also, check all hoses and connections for signs of leakage.

17 Wipe the inside of the drum with a clean rag and denatured alcohol or brake cleaner. Again, be careful not to breathe the dangerous asbestos dust.

18 Check the inside of the drum for cracks, score marks, deep scratches and "hard spots" which will appear as small discolored areas. If imperfections cannot be removed with fine emery cloth, the drum must be taken to an automotive machine shop for resurfacing.

19 Repeat the procedure for the remaining wheel. If the inspection reveals that all parts are in good condition, reinstall the brake drums, install the wheels and lower the vehicle to the ground.

BRAKE BOOSTER CHECK

20 Sit in the driver's seat and perform the following sequence of tests.

21 With the brake fully depressed, start the engine - the pedal should move down a little when the engine starts.

22 With the engine running, depress the brake pedal several times - the travel distance should not change.

23 Depress the brake, stop the engine and hold the pedal in for about 30 seconds - the pedal should neither sink nor rise.

24 Restart the engine, run it for about a minute and turn it off. Then firmly depress the brake several times - the pedal travel should decrease with each application.

25 If your brakes do not operate as described, the brake booster has failed. Refer to Chapter 9 for the replacement procedure.

---

13 Steering and suspension check (every 15,000 miles [24,000 km] or 12 months)

➡ **Note: For detailed illustrations of the steering and suspension components, refer to Chapter 10.**

WITH THE WHEELS ON THE GROUND

1 With the vehicle stopped and the front wheels pointed straight ahead, rock the steering wheel gently back and forth. If freeplay is excessive, a front wheel bearing, steering shaft universal joint or lower arm balljoint is worn or the steering gear is out of adjustment or broken. Refer to Chapter 10 for the appropriate repair procedure.

2 Other symptoms, such as excessive vehicle body movement over rough roads, swaying (leaning) around corners and binding as the steering wheel is turned, may indicate faulty steering and/or suspension components.

3 Check the shock absorbers by pushing down and releasing the vehicle several times at each corner. If the vehicle does not come back to a level position within one or two bounces, the shocks/struts are worn and must be replaced. When bouncing the vehicle up and down, listen for squeaks and noises from the suspension components.

4 Check the shock absorbers for evidence of fluid leakage. A light film of fluid is no cause for concern. Make sure that any fluid noted is from the shocks and not from some other source. If leakage is noted, replace the shocks as a set.

5 Check the shocks to be sure they are securely mounted and undamaged. Check the upper mounts for damage and wear. If damage or wear is noted, replace the shocks as a set (front and rear).

6 If the shocks must be replaced, refer to Chapter 10 for the procedure.

UNDER THE VEHICLE

♦ **Refer to illustrations 13.10 and 13.11**

7 Raise the vehicle with a floor jack and support it securely on jackstands. See *Jacking and towing* at the front of this book for the proper jacking points.

8 Check the tires for irregular wear patterns and proper inflation.

See Section 5 in this Chapter for information regarding tire wear and Chapter 10 for information on wheel bearing replacement.

9 Inspect the universal joint between the steering shaft and the steering gear housing. Check the steering gear housing for lubricant leakage. Make sure that the dust seals and boots are not damaged and that the boot clamps are not loose. Check the steering linkage for looseness or damage. Check the tie-rod ends for excessive play. Look for loose bolts, broken or disconnected parts and deteriorated rubber bushings on all suspension and steering components. While an assistant turns the steering wheel from side to side, check the steering components for free movement, chafing and binding. If the steering components do not seem to be reacting with the movement of the steering wheel, try to determine where the slack is located.

10 Check the balljoints for wear by trying to move each control arm up and down with a pry bar (see illustration) to ensure that its balljoint has no play. If any balljoint does have play, replace it. See Chapter 10 for the balljoint replacement procedure.

13.10 To check a balljoint for wear, try to pry the control arm up and down to make sure there is no play in the balljoint (if there is, replace it)

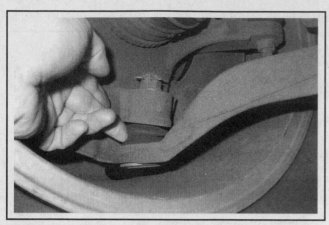

13.11 Push on the balljoint boot to check for tears, cracks and leaking grease

11 Inspect the balljoint boots for damage and leaking grease (see illustration). Replace the balljoints with new ones if they are damaged (see Chapter 10).

12 At the rear of the vehicle, inspect the suspension arm bushings for deterioration. Additional information on suspension components can be found in Chapter 10.

14 Underhood hose check and replacement (every 15,000 miles [24,000 km] or 12 months)

✳ WARNING:

Replacement of air conditioning hoses must be left to a dealer service department or air conditioning shop that has the equipment to depressurize the system safely. Never remove air conditioning components or hoses until the system has been depressurized.

GENERAL

1 High temperatures under the hood can cause deterioration of the rubber and plastic hoses used for engine, accessory and emission systems operation. Periodic inspection should be made for cracks, loose clamps, material hardening and leaks.

2 Information specific to the cooling system hoses can be found in Section 9.

3 Most (but not all) hoses are secured to the fittings with clamps. Where clamps are used, check to be sure they haven't lost their tension, allowing the hose to leak. If clamps aren't used, make sure the hose has not expanded and/or hardened where it slips over the fitting, allowing it to leak.

PCV SYSTEM HOSE

4 To reduce hydrocarbon emissions, crankcase blow-by gas is vented through the PCV valve in the rocker arm cover to the intake manifold via a rubber hose on most models. The blow-by gases mix with incoming air in the intake manifold before being burned in the combustion chambers.

5 Check the PCV hose for cracks, leaks and other damage. Disconnect it from the valve cover and the intake manifold and check the inside for obstructions. If it's clogged, clean it out with solvent.

VACUUM HOSES

6 It's quite common for vacuum hoses, especially those in the emissions system, to be color coded or identified by colored stripes molded into them. Various systems require hoses with different wall thickness, collapse resistance and temperature resistance. When replacing hoses, be sure the new ones are made of the same material.

7 Often the only effective way to check a hose is to remove it completely from the vehicle. If more than one hose is removed, be sure to label the hoses and fittings to ensure correct installation.

8 When checking vacuum hoses, be sure to include any plastic T-fittings in the check. Inspect the fittings for cracks and the hose where it fits over each fitting for distortion, which could cause leakage.

9 A small piece of vacuum hose (1/4-inch inside diameter) can be used as a stethoscope to detect vacuum leaks. Hold one end of the hose to your ear and probe around vacuum hoses and fittings, listening for the "hissing" sound characteristic of a vacuum leak.

✳ WARNING:

When probing with the vacuum hose stethoscope, be careful not to come into contact with moving engine components such as drivebelts, the cooling fan, etc.

FUEL HOSE

✳ WARNING:

Gasoline is flammable, so take extra precautions when you work on any part of the fuel system. Don't smoke or allow open flames or bare light bulbs near the work area, and don't work in a garage where a gas-type appliance (such as a water heater or clothes dryer) is present. Since fuel is carcinogenic, wear latex gloves when there's a possibility of being exposed to fuel, and, if you spill any fuel on your skin, rinse it off immediately with soap and water. Mop up any spills immediately and do not store fuel-soaked rags where they could ignite. The fuel system is under constant pressure, so, if any fuel lines are to be disconnected, the fuel pressure in the system must be relieved first (see Chapter 4 for more information). When you perform any kind of work on the fuel system, wear safety glasses and have a Class B type fire extinguisher on hand.

10 The fuel lines are usually under pressure, so if any fuel lines are to be disconnected be prepared to catch spilled fuel.

> ## ✳✳ WARNING:
>
> **Your vehicle is equipped with fuel injection and you must relieve the fuel system pressure before servicing the fuel lines. Refer to Chapter 4 for the fuel system pressure relief procedure.**

11 Check all flexible fuel lines for deterioration and chafing. Check especially for cracks in areas where the hose bends and just before fittings, such as where a hose attaches to the fuel pump, fuel filter and fuel injection unit.

12 When replacing a hose, use only hose that is specifically designed for your fuel injection system.

13 Spring-type clamps are sometimes used on fuel return or vapor lines. These clamps often lose their tension over a period of time, and can be "sprung" during removal. Replace all spring-type clamps with screw clamps whenever a hose is replaced. Some fuel lines use spring-lock type couplings, which require a special tool to disconnect. See Chapter 4 for more information on this type of coupling.

METAL LINES

14 Sections of metal line are often used for fuel line between the fuel pump and the fuel injection unit. Check carefully to make sure the line isn't bent, crimped or cracked.

15 If a section of metal fuel line must be replaced, use seamless steel tubing only, since copper and aluminum tubing do not have the strength necessary to withstand vibration caused by the engine.

16 Check the metal brake lines where they enter the master cylinder and brake proportioning unit (if used) for cracks in the lines and loose fittings. Any sign of brake fluid leakage calls for an immediate thorough inspection of the brake system.

15 Air filter replacement (every 15,000 miles [24,000 km] or 12 months)

▶ **Refer to illustrations 15.1a and 15.1b**

1 The air filter is located inside a housing at the left (driver's) side of the engine compartment. To remove the air filter, loosen the screw securing the two small coolant pipes to the cover and detach the pipes, remove the screws securing the two halves of the air filter housing together, then separate the cover halves and remove the air filter element (see illustrations).

2 Inspect the outer surface of the filter element. If it is dirty, replace it. If it is only moderately dusty, It can be reused by blowing it clean from the back to the front surface with compressed air. Because it is a pleated paper type filter, it cannot be washed or oiled. If it cannot be cleaned satisfactorily with compressed air, discard and replace it. While the cover is off, be careful not to drop anything down into the housing.

> ## ✳✳ CAUTION:
>
> **Never drive the vehicle with the air cleaner removed. Excessive engine wear could result and backfiring could even cause a fire under the hood.**

3 Wipe out the inside of the air cleaner housing.

4 Place the new filter into the air cleaner housing, making sure it seats properly.

5 Installation of the housing is the reverse of removal.

15.1a Loosen the screw securing the coolant pipes to the cover (A), detach the pipes, then remove the screws securing the two halves of the air cleaner housing (B)

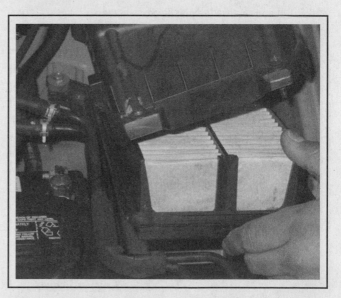

15.1b Pull the cover out of the way and lift the element out

16 Interior ventilation filter replacement (every 15,000 miles [24,000 km] or 12 months)

▶ Refer to illustrations 16.3, 16.4, 16.5 and 16.6

✳✳ WARNING:

The models covered by this manual are equipped with a Supplemental Restraint System (SRS), more commonly known as airbags. Always disable the airbag system before working in the vicinity of any airbag system component to avoid the possibility of accidental deployment of the airbag, which could cause personal injury (see Chapter 12).

1   These models are equipped with an air filtering element in the air conditioning system, located in a housing next to the evaporator, under the right side of the instrument panel.

2   Remove the glove box (see Chapter 11).

2004 AND EARLIER MODELS

3   If you're changing the filter for the first time, you'll need to cut out the plastic cross brace (see illustration).

4   Remove the glove box frame (see illustration).

5   Release the tab at the top and remove the filter door (see illustration).

6   Remove the filter from the air evaporator housing (see illustration).

7   Installation is the reverse of the removal procedure.

2005 AND LATER MODELS

8   Pull out the filter housing, then lift the filter from the housing.

9   Installation is the reverse of removal.

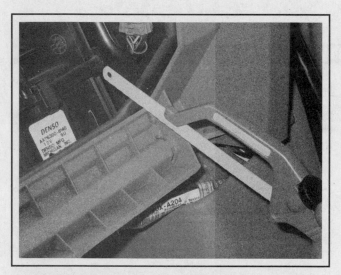

16.3 Cut and remove the plastic cross brace

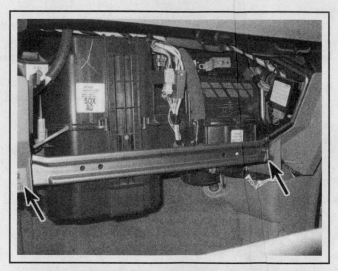

16.4 Remove the fasteners securing the glovebox frame

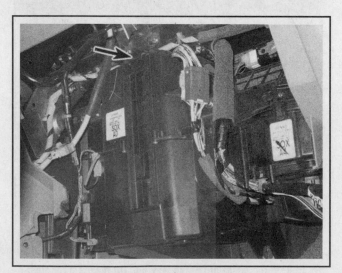

16.5 Release the tab securing the filter door

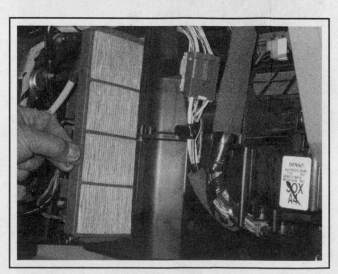

16.6 Slide the filter from the housing

17 Fuel system check (every 15,000 miles [24,000 km] or 12 months)

▶ Refer to illustration 17.6

17.6 Check the fuel tank filler hose connection for leaks and damage

> ❋❋ **WARNING:**
>
> Gasoline is flammable, so take extra precautions when you work on any part of the fuel system. Don't smoke or allow open flames or bare light bulbs near the work area, and don't work in a garage where a gas-type appliance (such as a water heater or clothes dryer) is present. Since fuel is carcinogenic, wear latex gloves when there's a possibility of being exposed to fuel, and, if you spill any fuel on your skin, rinse it off immediately with soap and water. Mop up any spills immediately and do not store fuel-soaked rags where they could ignite. When you perform any kind of work on the fuel system, wear safety glasses and have a Class B type fire extinguisher on hand. The fuel system is under constant pressure, so, before any lines are disconnected, the fuel system pressure must be relieved (see Chapter 4).

1 If you smell gasoline while driving or after the vehicle has been sitting in the sun, inspect the fuel system immediately.

2 Remove the fuel filler cap and inspect if for damage and corrosion. The gasket should have an unbroken sealing imprint. If the gasket is damaged or corroded, install a new cap.

3 Inspect the fuel feed line for cracks. Make sure that the connections between the fuel lines and the fuel injection system.

> ❋❋ **WARNING:**
>
> Your vehicle is fuel injected, so you must relieve the fuel system pressure before servicing fuel system components. The fuel system pressure relief procedure is outlined in Chapter 4.

4 Since some components of the fuel system - the fuel tank and the fuel lines, for example - are underneath the vehicle, they can be inspected more easily with the vehicle raised on a hoist. If that's not possible, raise the vehicle and support it on jackstands.

5 With the vehicle raised and safely supported, inspect the gas tank and filler neck for punctures, cracks and other damage. The connection between the filler neck and the tank is particularly critical. Sometimes a rubber filler neck will leak because of loose clamps or deteriorated rubber. Inspect all fuel tank mounting brackets and straps to be sure that the tank is securely attached to the vehicle.

> ❋❋ **WARNING:**
>
> Do not, under any circumstances, try to repair a fuel tank (except rubber components). A welding torch or any open flame can easily cause fuel vapors inside the tank to explode.

6 Carefully check all hoses and lines leading away from the fuel tank. Check for loose connections, deteriorated hoses, crimped lines and other damage (see illustration). Repair or replace damaged sections as necessary (see Chapter 4).

18 Exhaust system check (every 15,000 miles [24,000 km] or 12 months)

▶ Refer to illustration 18.2

1 With the engine cold (at least three hours after the vehicle has been driven), check the complete exhaust system from the engine to the end of the tailpipe. Ideally, the inspection should be done with the vehicle on a hoist to permit unrestricted access. If a hoist isn't available, raise the vehicle and support it securely on jackstands.

2 Check the exhaust pipes and connections for evidence of leaks, severe corrosion and damage. Make sure that all brackets and hangers are in good condition and tight (see illustration).

3 At the same time, inspect the underside of the body for holes, corrosion, open seams, etc. which may allow exhaust gases to enter the passenger compartment. Seal all body openings with silicone or body putty.

4 Rattles and other noises can often be traced to the exhaust system, especially the mounts and hangers. Try to move the pipes, muffler and catalytic converter. If the components can come in contact with the body or suspension parts, secure the exhaust system with new mounts.

5 Check the running condition of the engine by inspecting inside the end of the tailpipe. The exhaust deposits here are an indication of

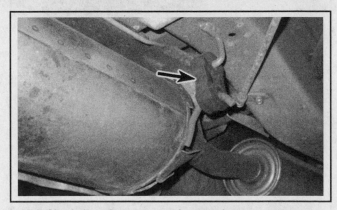

18.2 Check the exhaust system for rust, damage, or worn rubber hangers

engine state-of-tune. If the pipe is black and sooty or coated with white deposits, the engine may need a tune-up, including a thorough fuel system inspection and adjustment.

19 Driveaxle boot check (every 15,000 miles [24,000 km] or 12 months)

▶ **Refer to illustration 19.2**

1   The driveaxle boots are very important because they prevent dirt, water and foreign material from entering and damaging the constant velocity (CV) joints. Oil and grease can cause the boot material to deteriorate prematurely, so it's a good idea to wash the boots with soap and water. Because it constantly pivots back and forth following the steering action of the front hub, the outer CV boot wears out sooner and should be inspected regularly.

2   Inspect the boots for tears and cracks as well as loose clamps (see illustration). If there is any evidence of cracks or leaking lubricant, they must be replaced as described in Chapter 8.

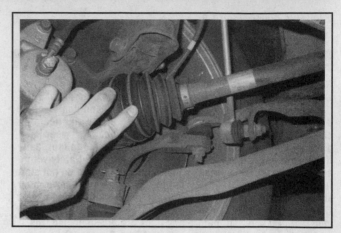

19.2 Flex the driveaxle boots by hand to check for tears, cracks and leaking grease

20 Drivebelt check, adjustment and replacement (every 30,000 miles [48,000 km] or 24 months)

✳ WARNING:

The electric cooling fan(s) on these models can activate at any time the ignition switch is in the ON position. Make sure the ignition is OFF when working in the vicinity of the fan(s).

1   The drivebelts are located at the front of the engine and play an important role in the operation of the vehicle and its components. Due to their function and material makeup, the belts are prone to failure after a period of time and should be inspected and adjusted periodically to prevent major damage.

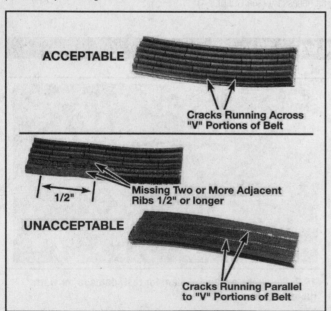

20.3 Here are some of the more common problems associated with drivebelts (check the belts very carefully to prevent an untimely breakdown)

2   These vehicles are equipped with two belts. One belt transmits power from the crankshaft to the alternator and air conditioning compressor. The power steering pump is driven by its own belt.

CHECK

▶ **Refer to illustrations 20.3, 20.4 and 20.5**

3   With the engine off, open the hood and use your fingers (and a flashlight, if necessary), to move along the belt checking for cracks and separation of the belt plies. Also check for fraying and glazing, which gives the belt a shiny appearance. Also check the ribs on the underside of the belt. They should all be the same depth, with none of the surface uneven (see illustration).

4   The power steering belt tension is checked by pushing on it at a distance halfway between the pulleys. Apply about 20 pounds of force with your thumb and see how much the belt moves down (deflects). Measure the deflection with a ruler (see illustration). The belt should deflect about 1/4-inch if the distance between pulleys is between 7 and 11 inches and around 1/2-inch if the distance is between 12 and 16 inches.

5   The alternator/air conditioning compressor belt tension is adjusted by an automatic tensioner. Look at the wear indicator on the tensioner (see illustration). The marks should be within the specified range; if not, the belt will have to be replaced.

ADJUSTMENT (POWER STEERING BELT)

▶ **Refer to illustration 20.6**

6   Loosen the power steering pump mounting bolt and nut, then turn the adjuster bolt to set the belt tension (see illustration). When you have obtained the desired tension, tighten the pump fasteners securely.

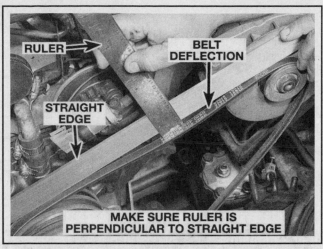

20.4 Measure drivebelt deflection with a straightedge and ruler - make sure the ruler is perpendicular to the straightedge

20.5 Details of the alternator/air conditioning compressor drivebelt tensioner (2001 model tensioner shown, later models similar)

1   Maximum length (belt worn out)
2   Belt length indicator

20.6 Power steering pump belt adjustment details

1   Power steering pump mounting bolt and nut
2   Adjustment nut

20.8 With a wrench, rotate the tensioner counterclockwise to release the tension (2001 model shown)

REPLACEMENT

➡ **Note: Since belts tend to wear out more or less at the same time, it's a good idea to replace both of them at the same time.**

7   Apply the parking brake, loosen the right (passenger's side) front wheel lug nuts, raise the front of the vehicle and support it securely on jackstands. Remove the wheel, then remove the drivebelt splash shield.

Alternator/air conditioning compressor belt

▶ **Refer to illustration 20.8**

8   The automatic tensioner must be released to allow drivebelt replacement. Place a wrench or a socket on the tensioner pulley bolt and rotate it counterclockwise until the belt can be removed (see illustration).

➡ **Note: On 2001 models, place the wrench on the tensioner pulley bolt. On 2002 and later models, place the wrench on the cast-in hex on the tensioner arm.**

Remove the belt and slowly release the tensioner. Install the new belt then rotate the tensioner counterclockwise to allow the belt to slip over it, then release the tensioner slowly until it contacts the drivebelt.

9   When installing the belt, make sure the belt is centered on the pulleys.

10   Install the drivebelt splash shield, wheel and lug nuts. Lower the vehicle and tighten the lug nuts to the torque listed in this Chapter's Specifications.

Power steering belt

11   Remove the alternator/air conditioning compressor drivebelt (see Steps 8 through 10).

12   Follow Step 6 for drivebelt adjustment, but loosen the belt and slip the belt off the pulleys and remove it.

13 When installing the belt, make sure the belt is centered on the pulleys.

14 Adjust the belt as described in Step 6.

15 Install the drivebelt splash shield, wheel and lug nuts. Lower the vehicle and tighten the lug nuts to the torque listed in this Chapter's Specifications.

AUTOMATIC TENSIONER REPLACEMENT

16 Remove the alternator/air conditioning compressor drivebelt (see

Steps 8 through 10).

17 Unscrew the tensioner mounting bolt and remove the tensioner.

19 Install the new tensioner assembly by reversing the removal procedure. Tighten the mounting bolt to the torque listed in this Chapter's Specifications.

20 Install the drivebelt as described previously in this Section.

21 Install the drivebelt splash shield, wheel and lug nuts. Lower the vehicle and tighten the lug nuts to the torque listed in this Chapter's Specifications.

21 Brake fluid change (every 30,000 miles [48,000 km] or 24 months)

❋❋ WARNING:

Brake fluid can harm your eyes and damage painted surfaces, so use extreme caution when handling or pouring it. Do not use brake fluid that has been standing open or is more than one year old. Brake fluid absorbs moisture from the air. Excess moisture can cause a dangerous loss of braking effectiveness.

1 At the specified intervals, the brake fluid should be drained and replaced. Since the brake fluid may drip or splash when pouring it, place plenty of rags around the master cylinder to protect any surrounding painted surfaces.

2 Before beginning work, purchase the specified brake fluid (see *Recommended lubricants and fluids* in this Chapter is Specifications).

3 Remove the cap from the master cylinder reservoir.

4 Using a hand suction pump or similar device, withdraw the fluid from the master cylinder reservoir.

5 Add new fluid to the master cylinder until it rises to the base of the filler neck.

6 Bleed the brake system as described in Chapter 9 at all four brakes until new and uncontaminated fluid is expelled from the bleeder screw. Be sure to maintain the fluid level in the master cylinder as you perform the bleeding process. If you allow the master cylinder to run dry, air will enter the system.

7 Refill the master cylinder with fluid and check the operation of the brakes. The pedal should feel solid when depressed, with no sponginess.

❋❋ WARNING:

Do not operate the vehicle if you are in doubt about the effectiveness of the brake system.

22 Cooling system servicing (draining, flushing and refilling) (every 30,000 miles [48,000 km] or 24 months)

❋❋ WARNING:

Do not allow antifreeze to come in contact with your skin or painted surfaces of the vehicle. Rinse off spills immediately with plenty of water. Antifreeze is highly toxic if ingested. Never leave antifreeze lying around in an open container or in puddles on the floor; children and pets are attracted by its sweet smell and may drink it. Check with local authorities about disposing of used antifreeze. Many communities have collection centers which will see that antifreeze is disposed of safely. Never dump used antifreeze on the ground or pour it into drains.

1 Periodically, the cooling system should be drained, flushed and refilled to replenish the antifreeze mixture and prevent formation of rust and corrosion, which can impair the performance of the cooling system and cause engine damage. When the cooling system is serviced, all hoses and the radiator cap should be checked and replaced if necessary.

DRAINING

▶ **Refer to illustrations 22.3 and 22.4**

2 Apply the parking brake and block the wheels.

❋❋ WARNING:

If the vehicle has just been driven, wait several hours to allow the engine to cool down before beginning this procedure.

Turn the heater control to maximum heat.

3 Move a large container under the radiator drain to catch the coolant. The radiator drain plug is located on the right side lower corner of the radiator (see illustration). Unscrew the drain plug until coolant starts flowing from the drain hole (a pair of pliers may be required to turn it).

4 Remove the radiator cap and allow the radiator to drain, then,

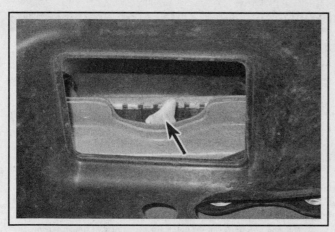

22.3 The drain fitting is located at the bottom of the radiator

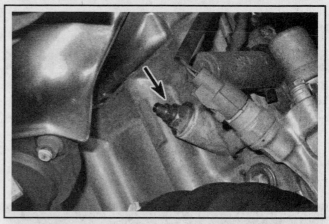

22.4 The engine has a coolant drain plug located on the side of the engine

move the container under the engine. Loosen the engine block drain plug and allow the coolant in the block to drain (see illustration).

5   While the coolant is draining, check the condition of the radiator hoses, heater hoses and clamps (refer to Section 9 if necessary).

6   Replace any damaged clamps or hoses. Close the drain plugs.

FLUSHING

▶ **Refer to illustration 22.9**

7   Once the system is completely drained, remove the thermostat from the engine (see Chapter 3), then reinstall the thermostat housing without the thermostat. This will allow the system to be thoroughly flushed.

8   Turn the heating system controls to Hot, so that the heater core will be flushed at the same time as the rest of the cooling system.

9   Disconnect the upper radiator hose from the radiator, then place a garden hose in the upper radiator inlet and flush the system until the water runs clear at the upper radiator hose (see illustration).

10 In severe cases of contamination or clogging of the radiator, remove the radiator (see Chapter 3) and have a radiator repair facility clean and repair it if necessary.

11 Many deposits can be removed by the chemical action of a cleaner available at auto parts stores. Follow the procedure outlined in the manufacturer's instructions.

➡ **Note: When the coolant is regularly drained and the system refilled with the correct antifreeze/water mixture, there should be no need to use chemical cleaners or descalers.**

12 Remove the overflow hose from the coolant recovery reservoir. Drain the reservoir and flush it with clean water, then reconnect the hose.

REFILLING

13 Reconnect the upper radiator hose and reinstall the thermostat.

14 Fill the cooling system with the proper type and mixture of anti-freeze (see this Chapter's Specifications), up to the base of the radiator cap filler neck.

15 Start the engine and run it at approximately 1500 rpm until the radiator fan comes on two times. Feel the upper radiator hose - it should be warm, indicating the thermostat has opened.

16 Turn off the engine and let it cool down. Slowly remove the radiator cap and check the coolant level, adding as necessary.

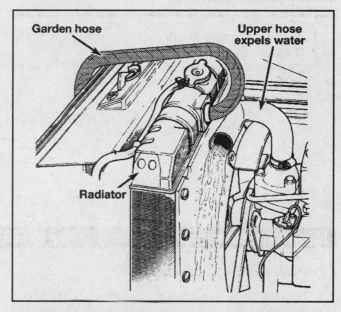

Garden hose

Upper hose expels water

Radiator

22.9 With the thermostat removed, disconnect the upper radiator hose and flush the radiator and engine block with a garden hose

❋❋ **WARNING:**

If you hear a hissing sound as you unscrew the cap, STOP. Let the engine cool down longer.

17 Place the heater control to minimum heat. Start the engine and run it at approximately 1500 rpm for five minutes.

18 Turn off the engine and let it cool down. Slowly remove the radiator cap and check the coolant level, adding as necessary.

❋❋ **WARNING:**

If you hear a hissing sound as you unscrew the cap, STOP. Let the engine cool down longer.

19 Place the heater control to maximum heat. Start the engine and run it at approximately 1500 rpm for five minutes.

20 Turn off the engine and let it cool down. Slowly remove the radiator cap and check the coolant level, adding as necessary.

⚹⚹ WARNING:

If you hear a hissing sound as you unscrew the cap, STOP. Let the engine cool down longer.

21 Place the heater control to minimum heat. Start the engine and run it at approximately 1500 rpm for three minutes.

22 Turn off the engine and let it cool down. Slowly remove the radiator cap and check the coolant level, adding as necessary.

WARNING:

If you hear a hissing sound as you unscrew the cap, STOP. Let the engine cool down longer.

23 Place the heater control to maximum heat. Start the engine and run it at approximately 1500 rpm for three minutes.

24 Turn off the engine and let it cool down. Slowly remove the radiator cap and check the coolant level, adding as necessary.

⚹⚹ WARNING:

If you hear a hissing sound as you unscrew the cap, STOP. Let the engine cool down longer.

25 Repeat Steps 21 through 24 until the cooling system no longer requires any more coolant, then install the radiator cap, but don't tighten it.

26 Place the heater control to minimum heat. Start the engine and run it at approximately 2500 rpm for one minute.

27 Place the front and rear heater controls to maximum heat and check the temperature of the air coming out of the rear floor vents; it should be quite warm, if not actually hot. If it isn't, repeat Steps 21 through 24 a few more times, then repeat this Step.

28 With the engine running, listen for the sound of flowing water at the rear heater unit, which would indicate that air is still in the system. If you do hear flowing water, repeat Steps 21 through 24 a few more times until you don't.

29 Let the engine cool down completely, then check the coolant level in the radiator again, adding as necessary. Fill the coolant reservoir up to the MIN mark, if necessary.

30 Start the engine, allow it to reach normal operating temperature and check for leaks.

23 Automatic transaxle fluid change (every 45,000 miles [72,400 km] or 36 months)

▶ **Refer to illustrations 23.6 and 23.8**

1 The automatic transaxle fluid should be changed at the recommended intervals.

2 Before beginning work, purchase the specified transmission fluid (see *Recommended lubricants and fluids* in this Chapter's Specifications).

3 Other tools necessary for this job include jackstands to support the vehicle in a raised position, wrenches, drain pan capable of holding at least four quarts, newspapers and clean rags.

4 The fluid should be drained immediately after the vehicle has been driven. Hot fluid is more effective than cold fluid at removing built up sediment.

⚹⚹ WARNING:

Fluid temperature can exceed 350-degrees F in a hot transaxle. Wear protective gloves.

5 After the vehicle has been driven to warm up the fluid, raise the front of the vehicle and support it securely on jackstands.

⚹⚹ WARNING:

Never work under a vehicle that is supported only by a jack!

6 Place the drain pan under the drain plug in the transaxle pan and remove the drain plug (see illustration). Be sure the drain pan is in position, as fluid will come out with some force. Once the fluid is drained, reinstall the drain plug securely. Measure the amount of fluid drained and write down this figure for reference when refilling.

23.6 Remove the transaxle drain plug

7   Lower the vehicle.

8   With the engine off, remove the fill plug (see illustration), then add new fluid to the transaxle *(see Recommended lubricants and fluids* for the recommended fluid type). Begin the refill procedure by initially adding 1/3 of the amount drained. Then, with the engine running, add 1/2-pint at a time (cycling the shifter through each gear position between additions) until the level is correct on the dipstick.

9   If desired, repeat Steps 5 through 8 once to flush any contaminated fluid from the torque converter.

23.8 The transaxle fill plug is located at the top of the transaxle

---

24   Spark plug check and replacement (every 105,000 miles [169,000 km] or 84 months, whichever comes first)

▶ **Refer to illustrations 24.2, 24.5, 24.8a, 24.8b, 24.8c, 24.10, 24.11, 24.12a and 24.12b**

1   The spark plugs are located in the center of each cylinder head.

2   In most cases the tools necessary for spark plug replacement include a spark plug socket which fits onto a ratchet (this special socket is padded inside to protect the porcelain insulators on the new plugs and hold them in place), various extensions and a feeler gauge to check and adjust the spark plug gap (see illustration). Since these engines are equipped with an aluminum cylinder head, a torque wrench should be used when tightening the spark plugs.

3   The best approach when replacing the spark plugs is to purchase the new spark plugs beforehand, adjust them to the proper gap and then replace each plug one at a time. When buying the new spark plugs, be

sure to obtain the correct plug for your specific engine. This information can be found in this Chapter's Specifications, in your owner's manual or on the Vehicle Emissions Control Information (VECI) label located under the hood. If differences exist between the sources, purchase the spark plug type specified on the VECI label as it was printed for your specific engine.

4   Allow the engine to cool completely before attempting to remove any of the plugs. During this cooling off time, each of the new spark plugs can be inspected for defects and the gaps can be checked.

5   The gap is checked by inserting the proper thickness gauge between the electrodes at the tip of the plug (see illustration). The gap between the electrodes should be as listed in this Chapter's Specifications or in your owner's manual.

❊❊ CAUTION:

The manufacturer recommends against adjusting the gap on platinum-tipped spark plugs; if the gap is out of specification, replace the plug.

Also, at this time check for cracks in the spark plug body (if any are found, the plug must not be used).

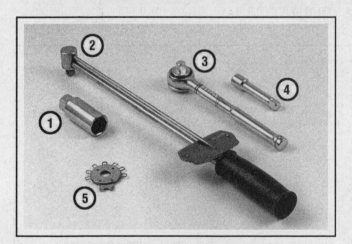

24.2 Tools required for changing spark plugs

1   *Spark plug socket* - This will have special padding inside to protect the spark plug porcelain insulator

2   *Torque wrench* - Although not mandatory, use of this tool is the best way to ensure that the plugs are tightened properly

3   *Ratchet* - Standard hand tool to fit the plug socket

4   *Extension* - Depending on model and accessories, you may need special extensions and universal joints to reach one or more of the plugs

5   *Spark plug gap gauge* - This gauge for checking the gap comes in a variety of styles. Make sure the gap for your engine is included

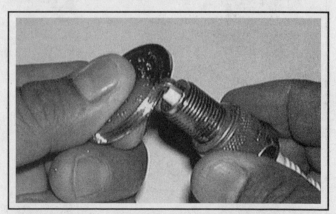

24.5 Spark plug manufacturers recommend using a tapered thickness gauge when checking the gap - slide the thin side into the gap and turn it until the gauge just fills the gap, then read the thickness on the gauge - do not force the tool into the gap

24.8a Disconnect the coil electrical connector . . .

24.8b . . . remove the retaining screw . . .

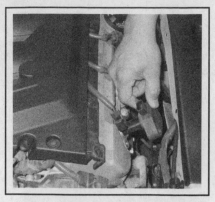

24.8c . . . then pull straight up and out to remove the coil

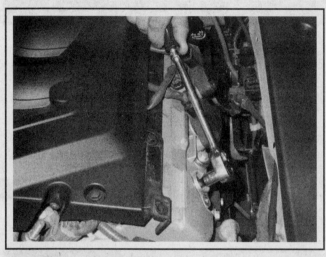

24.10 Use a ratchet and extension to remove the spark plug

6 Cover the fender to prevent damage to the paint. Fender covers are available from auto parts stores but an old blanket will work just fine.

7 Remove the intake manifold cover and the ignition coil cover (see Chapter 2A).

8 Remove the ignition coils (see illustrations).

9 If compressed air is available, use it to blow any dirt or foreign material away from the spark plug area.

❊ **CAUTION:**

Wear eye protection! The idea here is to eliminate the possibility of material falling into the cylinder through the spark plug hole as the spark plug is removed.

10 Place the spark plug socket over the plug and remove it from the engine by turning it in a counterclockwise direction (see illustration).

11 Compare the spark plug with the chart (see illustration) to get an

A normally worn spark plug should have light tan or gray deposits on the firing tip.

A carbon fouled plug, identified by soft, sooty, black deposits, may indicate an improperly tuned vehicle. Check the air cleaner, ignition components and engine control system.

An oil fouled spark plug indicates an engine with worn piston rings and/or bad valve seals allowing excessive oil to enter the chamber.

This spark plug has been left in the engine too long, as evidenced by the extreme gap- Plugs with such an extreme gap can cause misfiring and stumbling accompanied by a noticeable lack of power.

A physically damaged spark plug may be evidence of severe detonation in that cylinder. Watch that cylinder carefully between services, as a continued detonation will not only damage the plug, but could also damage the engine.

A bridged or almost bridged spark plug, identified by a build-up between the electrodes caused by excessive carbon or oil build-up on the plug.

24.11 Spark plug chart

24.12a Apply a thin coat of anti-seize compound to the spark plug threads - DO NOT get any on the electrodes!

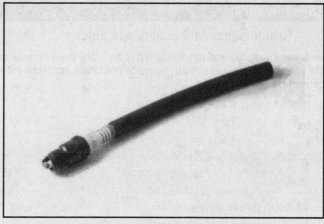

24.12b A length of snug-fitting rubber hose will save time and prevent damaged threads when installing the spark plugs

indication of the overall running condition of the engine.

12 Apply a small amount of anti-seize compound to the spark plug threads (see illustration). Install one of the new plugs into the hole until you can no longer turn it with your fingers, then tighten it with a torque wrench (if available) or the ratchet. It is a good idea to slip a short length of rubber hose over the end of the plug to use as a tool to thread it into place (see illustration). The hose will grip the plug well enough

to turn it, but will start to slip if the plug begins to cross-thread in the hole - this will prevent damaged threads and the accompanying repair costs.

13 Attach the coil to the new spark plug using a twisting motion until it is firmly seated on the end of the spark plug. Tighten the mounting bolts securely.

14 Repeat the procedure for the remaining spark plugs.

25 Idle speed check and adjustment (105,000 miles [169,000 km] or 84 months)

CHECK

1   Engine idle speed is the speed at which the engine operates when no accelerator pedal pressure is applied, as when stopped at a traffic light. The speed is critical to the performance of the engine itself, as well as many subsystems.

2   Set the parking brake firmly and block the wheels to prevent the vehicle from rolling. Place the transaxle in Park.

3   Connect a hand-held tachometer in accordance with the tool manufacturer's instructions.

4   Disconnect the two-pin electrical connector from the EVAP purge control solenoid (see Chapter 5).

5   Start the engine and run it at 3000 rpm until it warms up to normal operating temperature (the cooling fan comes on).

6   Slowly release the accelerator until the idle drops to normal speed. Make sure all accessories are turned off and the transaxle is in Neutral.

7   Note the idle speed on the tachometer and compare it to that listed on the VECI label or in this Chapter's Specifications.

➡ **Note: If the idle speed listed on the VECI label is different than that listed in this Chapter's Specifications, use the specification shown on the VECI label.**

ADJUSTMENT

♦ **Refer to illustration 25.9**

8   Before adjusting the idle speed, make sure the engine cooling fan is off.

25.9 Use a small screwdriver to turn the idle adjustment screw

9   If the idle speed is too low or too high, remove the plug and turn the idle speed adjusting screw to obtain the specified idle speed (see illustration). Make changes only in quarter-turn increments. Allow the idle to stabilize for one minute and recheck the idle speed.

10 Turn off the engine and disconnect the tachometer. Reconnect the EVAP solenoid.

Specifications

Recommended lubricants and fluids

➡ **Note: The fluids and lubricants listed here are those recommended by the manufacturer at the time this manual was written. Vehicle manufacturers occasionally upgrade their fluid and lubricant specifications, so check with your local auto parts store for the most current recommendations.**

Engine oil
   Type   API "Certified for gasoline engines"
   Viscosity
      2001 models   SAE 5W-30
      2002 and later models   SAE 5W-20
Automatic transaxle fluid   Honda ATF-Z1 or equivalent
Brake fluid type   DOT 3 brake fluid
Power steering system fluid   Honda power steering fluid or equivalent
Fuel type   Unleaded gasoline, 86 octane or higher
Engine coolant   50/50 mixture of Honda All Season Antifreeze/Coolant Type 2
                                    or equivalent

Capacities*

Engine oil (including oil filter)   4.6 quarts (4.2 liters)
Automatic transaxle fluid (drain and refill)**
   2001 models   3.1 quarts (2.9 liters)
   2002 and later models   3.5 quarts (3.3 liters)
Cooling system
   Without rear A/C   5.8 quarts (5.5 liters)
   With rear A/C   7.9 quarts (7.5 liters)

All capacities approximate. Add as necessary to bring to appropriate level.

** *If you want to flush the converter during a fluid change, purchase twice the amount of fluid listed here.*

Ignition system

Spark plug type and gap
   Type
      2004 and earlier models   NGK PZFR5F-11
      2005 through 2007 models   NGK IZFR5K11
      2008 and later models   NGK ILZKR7B11
   Gap   0.039 to 0.043 inch (1.0 to 1.1 mm)
Engine firing order   1-4-2-5-3-6

```
 ( 1 )  ( 2 )  ( 3 )      FRONT OF
                          VEHICLE
 ( 4 )  ( 5 )  ( 6 )         |
   1-4-2-5-3-6               ↓
                     42035-B-SPECS HAYNES
```
Cylinder locations

Engine idle speed (in Park or Neutral)

2001 models   730+/-50 rpm
2002 and later models   710+/-50 rpm

Cooling system

Thermostat rating
   Starts to open
      2001 models   163-degrees F (73-degrees C)
      2002 and later models   169-degrees F (76-degrees C)
   Fully open   194-degrees F (90-degrees C)

Accessory drivebelt deflection

Power steering pump	
New belt	0.33 to 0.43-inch (8.5 to 11.0 mm)
Old belt	0.51 to 0.65-inch (13.0 to 16.5 mm)
Alternator	See tension indicator on vehicle

Brakes

Disc brake pad lining thickness (minimum), front or rear	1/16-inch (1.6 mm)
Drum brake shoe lining thickness (minimum)	5/64-inch (2.0 mm)
Parking brake adjustment	
Drum rear brake	3 to 5 clicks
Disc rear brake	4 to 6 clicks

Torque specifications	Ft-lbs (unless otherwise indicated)	Nm

➡ **Note: One foot-pound (ft-lb) of torque is equivalent to 12 inch-pounds (in-lbs) of torque. Torque values below approximately 15 foot-pounds are expressed in inch-pounds, because most foot-pound torque wrenches are not accurate at these smaller values.**

Engine oil drain plug	29	39
Automatic transaxle		
Drain plug	36	49
Filler plug	33	44
Spark plugs	156 in-lbs	18
Wheel lug nuts		
2004 and earlier models	80	108
2005 and later models	94	127

Notes

2A

ENGINE

Section

Reference to other Chapters

1   General information

This Part of Chapter 2 is devoted to in-vehicle repair procedures for the 3.5L V6 VTEC engine. Since these procedures are based on the assumption that the engine is installed in the vehicle, many of the steps outlined in this Part of Chapter 2 will not apply if the engine has been removed.

The Specifications included in this Part of Chapter 2 apply only to the procedures contained in this Part. Information concerning engine/transaxle removal and engine overhaul or replacement can be found in Part B of this Chapter.

2   Repair operations possible with the engine in the vehicle

Many major repair operations can be accomplished without removing the engine from the vehicle.

Clean the engine compartment and the exterior of the engine with some type of degreaser before any work is done. It will make the job easier and help keep dirt out of the internal areas of the engine.

Depending on the components involved, it may be helpful to remove the hood to improve access to the engine as repairs are performed (refer to Chapter 11 if necessary). Cover the fenders to prevent damage to the paint. Special pads are available, but an old bedspread or blanket will also work.

If vacuum, exhaust, oil or coolant leaks develop, indicating a need for gasket or seal replacement, the repairs can generally be made with the engine in the vehicle. The intake and exhaust manifold gaskets, oil pan gasket, crankshaft front oil seal and cylinder head gaskets are all accessible with the engine in place.

Exterior engine components, such as the intake and exhaust manifolds, the oil pan, the oil pump, the water pump (see Chapter 3), the starter motor, the alternator, the ignition coils (see Chapter 5) and the fuel system components (see Chapter 4) can be removed for repair with the engine in place.

Since the cylinder heads can be removed without pulling the engine, valve component servicing can also be accomplished with the engine in the vehicle. Replacement of the camshafts, timing belt and sprockets is also possible with the engine in the vehicle.

In extreme cases caused by a lack of necessary equipment, repair or replacement of piston rings, pistons, connecting rods and rod bearings is possible with the engine in the vehicle. However, this practice is not recommended because of the cleaning and preparation work that must be done to the components involved.

3   Top Dead Center (TDC) for number one piston - locating

▶ **Refer to illustrations 3.5 and 3.6**

1   Top Dead Center (TDC) is the highest point in the cylinder that each piston reaches as it travels up-and-down during crankshaft rotation. Each piston reaches TDC on the compression stroke and again on the exhaust stroke, but TDC generally refers to piston position on the compression stroke.

2   Positioning the piston(s) at TDC is an essential part of many other repair procedures discussed in this manual.

3   Before beginning this procedure, be sure to place the transaxle in Neutral and apply the parking brake or block the rear wheels. Remove the spark plugs, as this will make the crankshaft much easier to turn (see Chapter 1).

4   In order to bring any piston to TDC, the crankshaft must be turned using one of the methods outlined below. When looking at the front of the engine, normal crankshaft rotation is clockwise.

   a) *The preferred method is to turn the crankshaft with a socket and ratchet attached to the bolt threaded into the front of the crankshaft.*

   b) *A remote starter switch, which may save some time, can also be used. Follow the instructions included with the switch. Once the piston is close to TDC, use a socket and ratchet as described in the previous paragraph.*

   c) *If an assistant is available to turn the ignition switch to the Start position in short bursts, you can get the piston close to TDC without a remote starter switch. Make sure your assistant is out of the vehicle, away from the ignition switch, then use a socket and ratchet as described in Paragraph a) to complete the procedure.*

5   Turn the crankshaft until the TDC notch on the crankshaft pulley is aligned with the pointer on the timing belt lower cover (see illustration).

6   Locate the camshaft sprocket timing mark on the front cylinder bank. Look through the hole in the timing belt cover to check that the camshaft sprocket timing mark is aligned with the mark on the rear cover (see illustration). If no mark is present, rotate the crankshaft clockwise one revolution and realign the marks.

7   When the crankshaft pulley timing marks are aligned, and the camshaft sprocket timing marks are aligned, the number one piston is at TDC on the compression stroke.

8   After the number one piston has been positioned at TDC on the compression stroke, TDC for any of the remaining pistons can be located by turning the crankshaft and following the firing order, aligning the cylinder number on the camshaft sprocket with the pointer on the timing belt cover (they're arranged in the firing order).

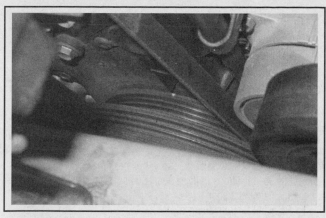

3.5 Align the TDC mark on the crankshaft pulley with the pointer

3.6 Position the inspection hole cover aside and check the alignment of the camshaft sprocket timing mark with the mark on the timing belt cover (there is an inspection hole on each cylinder bank) - the numeral 1 is visible when the number 1 piston is at TDC

4 Valve covers - removal and installation

REMOVAL

1 Disconnect the cable from the negative battery terminal (see Chapter 5, Section 1).

2 Remove the ignition coil assemblies (see Chapter 5).

3 Refer to Section 6 and remove the upper intake manifold.

2004 and earlier models

4 At the front valve cover, pull the PCV hose from the left side of the valve cover (see Chapter 6).

5 At the rear valve cover, remove the bolt retaining the power steering hose bracket and move the hose aside.

2005 and later models

Front valve cover

6 Unbolt the interfering wiring harnesses and set them aside.

Rear valve cover

7 Remove the drivebelt (see Chapter 1).

8 On 2007 and later models, remove the power steering pump (see Chapter 10). Set it aside but don't disconnect the hoses. On earlier models, simply disconnect the power steering hose support bracket.

9 Unbolt the interfering wiring harnesses and brackets, then set them aside.

All models

▶ **Refer to illustrations 4.10a and 4.10b**

10 Remove the retaining bolts (see illustrations), then detach the valve cover. If the cover is stuck to the head, bump the end with a block of wood and a hammer to jar it loose.

✳✳ CAUTION:

Don't pry at the cover-to-head joint or damage to the sealing surfaces may occur, leading to oil leaks after the cover is reinstalled.

11 Remove the original gasket and seal washers and clean the mat-

4.10a Remove the valve cover retaining bolts (rear valve cover)

4.10b Remove the valve cover retaining bolts (front valve cover)

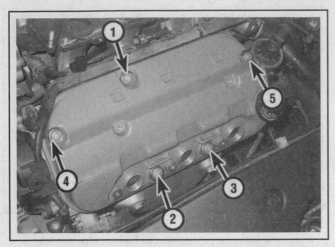

4.13 Valve cover tightening sequence - front shown, rear valve cover tightening sequence is identical

ing surfaces of the cylinder head and valve cover. If you removed the rear valve cover, inspect the PCV valve (see Chapter 6) before reattaching it to the valve cover.

INSTALLATION

▶ **Refer to illustration 4.13**

12 Position a new gasket in the groove and install new seal washers on the bolts.

13 Install the cover and tighten the bolts to the torque listed in this Chapter's Specifications in three equal steps. Follow the correct torque sequence (see illustration).

14 Reinstall the remaining components.

15 Reconnect the battery. Refer to Chapter 5, Section 1.

16 Run the engine and check for oil leaks.

5 Valve clearance - check and adjustment

CHECK

1 The valve clearance generally does not need adjustment unless valvetrain components have been replaced or a valve job has been performed, or if the valves are noisy.

2 The simplest check for proper valve adjustment is to listen carefully to the engine running with the hood open. If the valvetrain is noisy, adjustment is necessary.

3 The valve clearance must be checked and adjusted with the engine cold.

ADJUSTMENT

▶ **Refer to illustrations 5.6, 5.7 and 5.9**

4 Remove the valve covers (see Section 4).

5 Rotate the crankshaft clockwise and position the number one piston at TDC (see Section 3). When positioned correctly at TDC, the pointer on the front timing belt cover will align with the sprocket mark (see illustration 3.6).

6 In this position, adjust the valves for cylinder number one (see illustration). There are four valves for each cylinder. Check and adjust the valve clearance.

7 Starting with the intake valve. Insert a feeler gauge of the correct thickness (see this Chapter's Specifications) between the valve stem and the rocker arm (see illustration). Withdraw it; you should feel a slight drag. If there's no drag or a heavy drag, loosen the adjuster nut and back off the adjuster screw. Carefully tighten the adjuster screw until you can feel a slight drag on the feeler gauge as you withdraw it.

8 Hold the adjuster screw with a screwdriver to keep it from turning and tighten the locknut. Recheck the clearance to make sure it hasn't changed. Repeat the procedure in this Step and the previous Step on

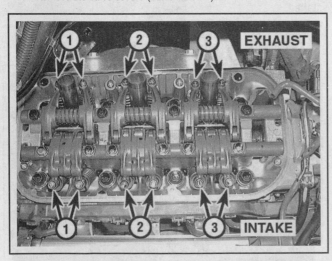

5.6 Valve layout for the rear cylinder bank - three intake rocker arm arrangement shown (2002 and later models), the adjustment on the two rocker arm VTEC (2001 models) arrangement is similar

5.7 Insert a feeler gauge between the valve stem and the rocker arm, loosen the locknut with a box end wrench and adjust the clearance with a screwdriver

the other intake valve, then on the two exhaust valves.

9 Rotate the crankshaft pulley clockwise until the number 4 on the camshaft sprocket is aligned with the pointer on the timing belt cover (see illustration 3.6). Check and adjust the number four cylinder valves (see illustration).

10 Rotate the crankshaft pulley 120-degrees clockwise until the number two cylinder is at TDC. Check and adjust the number two cylinder valves.

11 Rotate the crankshaft pulley clockwise, follow the firing order listed in this Chapter's Specifications and adjust the remaining valves.

12 Refer to Section 4 and install the valve covers.

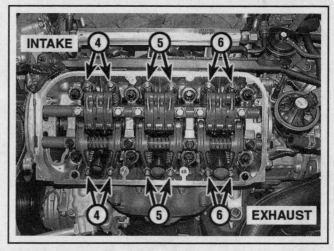

5.9 Valve layout for the front cylinder bank

---

6   Intake manifold - removal and installation

✳✳ WARNING:

Wait until the engine is completely cool before beginning this procedure.

UPPER INTAKE MANIFOLD

▶ **Refer to illustrations 6.5, 6.6a, 6.6b, 6.9a, 6.9b and 6.9c**

1 Relieve the fuel pressure (see Chapter 4).

2 Disconnect the cable from the negative battery terminal (see Chapter 5, Section 1).

3 Clamp-off the coolant hoses to the throttle body, then detach them. Be prepared for a little coolant spillage.

4 Refer to Chapter 4 and remove the air intake duct, then disconnect the throttle linkage, hoses and other connections from the throttle body.

5 Remove the intake manifold cover (see illustration).

➡ **Note: On 2002 and later models, follow the reverse order of the tightening sequence on the intake manifold cover (see illustration 6.9b or 6.9c).**

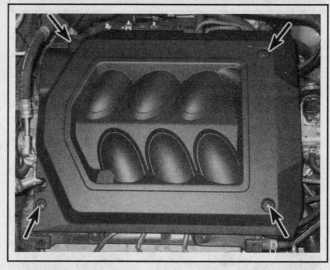

6.5 Intake manifold cover mounting screw locations on 2001 models

6.6a Vacuum line locations on the rear side of the upper intake manifold

6.6b Vacuum hose location for the PCV valve

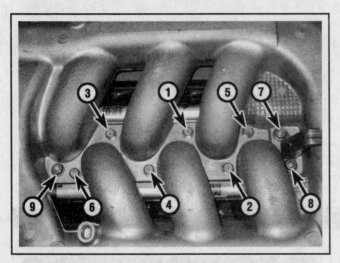

6.9a Upper intake manifold bolt tightening sequence (2001 models shown, later models similar)

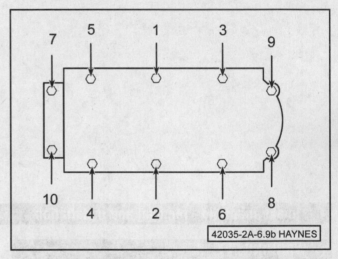

6.9b Intake manifold cover bolt tightening sequence on 2002 through 2004 models

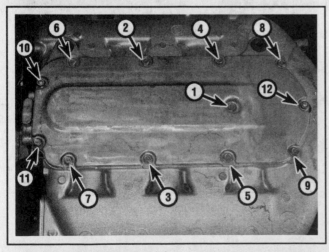

6.9c Upper intake manifold cover bolt tightening sequence on 2005 and later models

6 Disconnect the vacuum hoses from the rear side of the intake manifold (see illustrations). Be sure to mark each hose with tape to insure correct reassembly.

7 Remove the engine harness connectors (IAT, TPS, IAC, MAP, EVAP canister [2002 and later]) from their respective components. Label each connector with tape to insure correct reassembly.

8 Following the reverse of the tightening sequence (see illustration 6.9a), remove the bolts and nuts and remove the manifold with the throttle body attached.

9 To install the upper manifold, clean the mounting surfaces of the lower manifold with lacquer thinner and remove all traces of the old gasket material or sealant. Install the new gasket over the studs on the lower manifold, then install the upper intake manifold. Tighten the nuts and bolts in sequence (see illustrations) to the torque listed in this Chapter's Specifications. Check the coolant level and add some, if necessary (see Chapter 1).

10 Reconnect the battery. Refer to Chapter 5, Section 1.

6.13 Location of the lower intake manifold mounting nuts - the four corner nuts are hidden from view

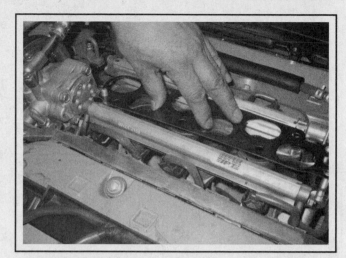

6.15 Position the gasket over the dowels in the cylinder head and install the lower intake manifold(s)

LOWER INTAKE MANIFOLD

▶ **Refer to illustrations 6.13 and 6.15**

11 Remove the power steering pump and position it aside, without disconnecting the hoses (see Chapter 10).

12 Disconnect the electrical connectors at the fuel injectors (label all connectors first) and remove the fuel rails from the lower intake manifold (see Chapter 4).

13 Remove the mounting nuts and bolts, then detach the two lower intake manifold sections from the cylinder heads (see illustration). If they are stuck, don't pry between the gasket mating surfaces or damage may result.

➡ **Note: The fuel injectors may be left installed in the lower intake manifolds during removal.**

14 Carefully use a scraper to remove all traces of old gasket material and sealant from the manifold and cylinder heads, then clean the mating surfaces with lacquer thinner or acetone.

15 Install new gaskets (see illustration), then position the lower manifolds on the cylinder heads. Make sure the gaskets and manifolds are aligned over the dowels in the cylinder heads and install the nuts/bolts.

16 Tighten the fasteners, in three equal steps, to the torque listed in this Chapter's Specifications. Work from the center out towards the ends to avoid warping the manifolds.

17 Install the upper intake manifold (see Step 9).

18 The remainder of the installation is the reverse of the removal procedure. Check the coolant level and add some, if necessary (see Chapter 1). Run the engine and check for fuel, vacuum and coolant leaks.

7 Exhaust manifolds - removal and installation

✺✺ WARNING:

The engine must be completely cool before beginning this procedure.

REMOVAL

▶ **Refer to illustrations 7.3a, 7.3b, 7.4, 7.5 and 7.6**

1 Disconnect the cable from the negative battery terminal (see Chapter 5, Section 1).

2 Spray penetrating oil on the exhaust manifold fasteners and allow it to soak in.

3 Block the rear wheels to prevent the vehicle from rolling. Set the parking brake and place the transaxle in Park. Raise the front of the vehicle and support it securely on jackstands. Remove the splash guard from below the engine compartment (see illustrations).

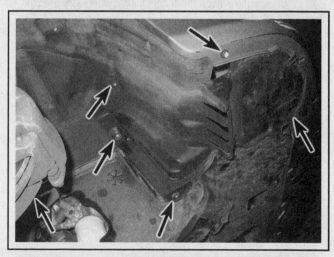

7.3a First, remove only the mounting screws and push-pins from the inner fender shield that connect to the splash shield

7.3b Remove the push-pin fasteners from the splash shield and remove it from the body

7.4 Remove the exhaust pipe-to-manifold nuts

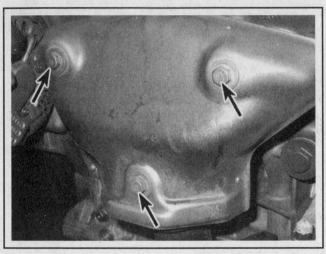

7.5 Remove the heat shield bolts and the heat shield

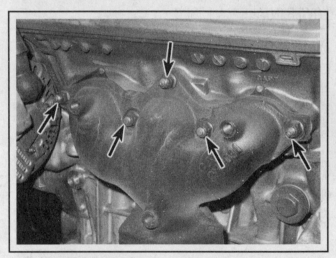

7.6 Exhaust manifold nuts

4   Disconnect the exhaust pipes from the manifolds and lower the pipes (see illustration).

5   Remove the bolts and the heat shields from each manifold (see illustration).

6   Remove the self-locking nuts retaining the manifold to the cylinder head and remove the manifold (see illustration). Discard the self-locking nuts and obtain new ones for reassembly.

7   Carefully inspect the manifold for cracks and warpage. If the manifold is cracked or warped, replace it with a new one.

INSTALLATION

8   Use a scraper to remove any traces of old gasket material and carbon deposits from the manifold and cylinder head mating surfaces.

9   Position a new gasket over the cylinder head studs.

10 Install the manifold and thread the mounting nuts into place. Working from the center out, tighten the nuts to the torque listed in this Chapter's Specifications in three equal steps.

11 Reinstall the remaining parts in the reverse order of removal. Apply engine oil to the studs and install new self-locking nuts.

12 Reconnect the battery. Refer to Chapter 5, Section 1.

13 Run the engine and check for exhaust leaks.

8 Timing belt and sprockets - removal, inspection and installation

REMOVAL

▶ **Refer to illustrations 8.10a, 8.10b, 8.11, 8.12a, 8.12b, 8.13, 8.14, 8.15, 8.16, 8.17, 8.18 and 8.19**

1   Disconnect the cable from the negative battery terminal (see Chapter 5, Section 1).

2   Place the transaxle in Park or neutral, apply the parking brake and block the rear wheels.

3   Remove the drivebelts (see Chapter 1).

4   Remove the alternator and power steering pump (see Chapters 5 and 10).

5   Remove the spark plugs to make it easier to turn the crankshaft (see Chapter 1), then position the number one piston at TDC (see Section 3).

6   Loosen the lug nuts on the right front wheel. Raise the front of the vehicle and support it securely on jackstands. Remove the right front wheel.

7   Remove the right front inner fender splash guard (see Chapter 11).

8   Support the engine by placing a floor jack under the oil pan with a block of wood on the jack to protect the pan. Remove the splash shield under the radiator (see Chapter 3).

9   Remove the two bolts and the wiring harness retainer holding the passenger-side engine mount to the block, remove the through-bolt, and remove the mount (see Section 18). Remove the engine mount bracket. Remove the engine oil dipstick tube.

10 Remove the upper timing belt covers (see illustrations).

11 If you intend to re-use the belt, mark the belt to indicate the direction of rotation (see illustration).

12 Make sure the timing marks are properly aligned (see illustrations).

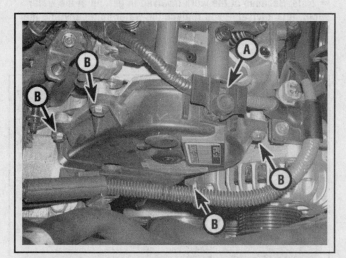

8.10a Detach the wiring harness from the retainer (A) and remove the bolts (B) from the upper timing belt cover (front cylinder bank)

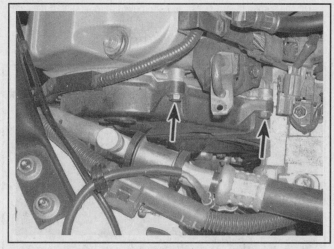

8.10b Remove the upper timing belt cover (arrows indicate two of the four bolts) from the rear cylinder bank

8.11 Mark the direction of rotation on the timing belt

8.12a Camshaft timing marks (front cylinder bank) - align the mark on the sprocket with the mark on the rear cover

8.12b Camshaft sprocket timing marks - rear cylinder bank

13 Using a strap wrench or equivalent tool to hold the crankshaft, loosen the crankshaft pulley bolt (see illustration). Remove the crankshaft pulley.

➡ **Note: When the crankshaft pulley bolt is loosened, the position of the timing marks on the crankshaft pulley and the camshafts may be disturbed. Check and align them again. Temporarily reinstall the crankshaft pulley bolt to turn the crankshaft.**

14 Remove the lower timing belt cover (see illustration).

15 Slip the timing belt guide off the crankshaft sprocket, noting how it's installed. Also note the alignment of the crankshaft sprocket timing marks (see illustration).

16 Remove one of the long hold-down bolts from the battery tray and bevel the threaded end somewhat with a file or grinder. Thread the bolt into the boss so that it pushes against the timing belt adjuster - the bolt is used to hold the adjuster in position (see illustration). Do not apply any more than hand pressure in tightening.

17 Remove the engine mount bracket and loosen the idler pulley bolt six turns, then remove the timing belt (see illustration).

18 The camshaft sprockets can be removed at this point, if they are damaged or to replace the oil seals (see illustration). Remove the keys from the shafts so they don't fall out and get lost.

CAUTION:

Don't allow the camshaft(s) to turn.

19 If it's worn or damaged, or if you're replacing the crankshaft front oil seal, the crankshaft sprocket can now be removed (see illustration). If it won't come off by hand, carefully pry it off. Also remove the timing belt guide, noting how it's installed.

INSPECTION

20 Inspect the sprocket teeth for wear and damage. Check the timing belt for any cracks or oil residue. Also check the camshaft for excessive endplay (see Section 12). Check the timing belt tensioner for smooth operation. Replace any worn parts with new ones.

21 Now that the timing belt is removed, inspect the water pump (see Chapter 3).

➡ **Note: Because of the work involved in getting at the water pump, it is advisable you replace the water pump anytime the timing belt is removed.**

8.13 Remove the crankshaft pulley bolt using a strap or chain wrench to hold the pulley (if you use a chain wrench, be sure to wrap the crankshaft pulley with an old piece of drivebelt to protect it)

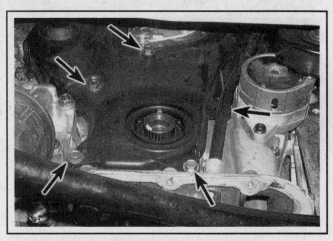

8.14 Remove the bolts and the lower timing belt cover

8.15 Crankshaft sprocket timing marks

8.16 Thread the long battery hold-down bolt (A) into the boss as shown to hold the timing belt adjuster (B) in position

8.17 Loosen the timing belt idler bolt about six turns

INSTALLATION

▶ **Refer to illustration 8.26**

22 Remove all dirt and oil from the timing belt area. Clean the teeth of the sprockets with lacquer thinner.

23 If any of the timing belt sprockets were removed, install them now with their keys and tighten the bolts to the torque listed in this Chapter's Specifications.

24 If removed, install the timing belt guide over the crankshaft sprocket with the chamfered edge facing away from the belt.

25 Recheck the position of the timing marks (see illustrations 8.12a, 8.12b and 8.15). Install the timing belt in a clockwise direction, starting at the crankshaft sprocket and tensioner pulley, then rear camshaft sprocket, water pump, front camshaft sprocket, and idler pulley. If you're re-using the original belt, the arrow you made in Step 11 should point in the normal direction of rotation.

➡ **Note: If the tensioner piston has extended and you're unable to install the timing belt, remove the tensioner and compress the piston as described below.**

26 Install the outer timing belt guide over the crankshaft sprocket with the chamfered edge facing away from the belt (see illustration).

27 Tighten the idler pulley bolt to the torque listed in this Chapter's Specifications. Remove the battery hold-down bolt that was holding the tensioner pulley in position (see illustration 8.16).

28 Turn the crankshaft slowly six revolutions clockwise using a socket and breaker bar on the crankshaft pulley bolt to seat the belt, then return to TDC. Recheck the alignment of cam and crank timing marks.

❊❊ CAUTION:

If you feel any resistance, back up and recheck the belt timing. Do not force the crankshaft to turn or engine damage will occur!

29 Install the lower timing belt cover.

30 Install the crankshaft pulley, aligning the pulley keyway with the crankshaft key. Install the bolt and tighten it to the torque listed in this Chapter's Specifications. Use the method described in Step 13 to keep the crankshaft from turning.

31 Recheck the timing marks (see illustrations 8.12a and 8.12b and 8.15).

❊❊ CAUTION:

If the timing marks are not aligned exactly as shown, repeat the timing belt installation procedure. DO NOT start the engine until you're absolutely certain that the timing belt is installed correctly. Serious and costly engine damage could occur if the belt is installed wrong.

32 Reinstall the remaining parts in the reverse order of removal.
33 Reconnect the battery. Refer to Chapter 5, Section 1.

TENSIONER ADJUSTMENT

34 The belt tensioner does not normally need to be removed or adjusted for a timing belt replacement procedure (unless the tensioner piston has extended), but there other engine procedures (water pump

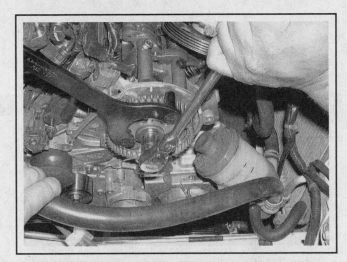

8.18 Prevent the camshaft from turning by inserting a two-pin spanner through the holes in the sprocket while you loosen the bolt

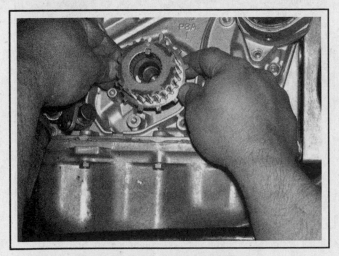

8.19 Carefully remove the crankshaft sprocket

8.26 Install the outer timing belt guide as shown

replacement, etc.) that require the tensioner be removed. Once removed, the tensioner piston will extend in length. The following Steps apply only if the tensioner has been removed from the engine.

35 To remove the tensioner, remove the long bolt used in Step 16, and unbolt the tensioner from the block.

36 To retract the tensioner, align the holes in the rod and the tensioner body by collapsing the assembly in a vise or a press. When the holes are aligned, insert a small pin or drill to lock the rod in the retracted position.

37 Reinstall the service bolt in the tensioner. Install the tensioner, being careful not to dislodge the pin, and tighten the mounting bolts to the torque listed in this Chapter's Specifications. After completing the remainder of the timing belt installation procedure, pull out the pin.

9 Crankshaft front oil seal - replacement

▶ **Refer to illustrations 9.2 and 9.4**

1 Remove the timing belt and crankshaft sprocket (see Section 8).

2 Carefully pry the seal out of the engine with a screwdriver or seal removal tool (see illustration). If you use a screwdriver, don't scratch the housing bore or damage the crankshaft (if the crankshaft is damaged, the new seal will end up leaking).

3 Clean the oil seal bore and coat the outer edge of the new seal with a small amount of engine oil to ease installation. Apply multi-purpose grease to the seal lip.

4 Using a seal-driver or a socket with an outside diameter slightly smaller than the outside diameter of the seal, carefully drive the new seal into place with a hammer (see illustration). Make sure it's installed squarely and driven in to the same depth as the original. If a socket isn't available, a short section of large-diameter pipe will also work. Check the seal after installation to make sure the garter spring didn't pop out of place.

5 Reinstall the crankshaft sprocket and timing belt (see Section 8).

6 Run the engine and check for oil leaks at the front seal.

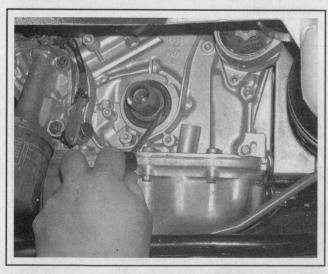

9.2 Carefully pry out the oil seal

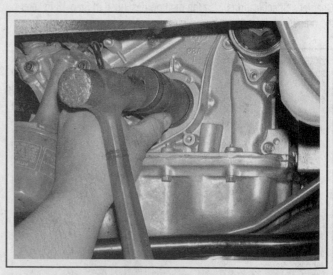

9.4 Lubricate the seal lip and tap the new crankshaft seal into place with a large socket or piece of pipe and a hammer

10 VTEC and i-VTEC VCM systems - general description and component checks

GENERAL DESCRIPTION

VTEC system

1   The VTEC system is Honda's design for Variable Valve Timing and Lift Electronic Control.

2   The differences between conventional engines and the VTEC system is strictly in the components and operation of the valve train.

3   The engine management computer has the ability to change which camshaft intake lobes are being used to operate the intake valves. The computer turns the system ON or OFF, depending on sensor input.

4   The following are used to determine VTEC operation:

    a) *Engine speed (rpm)*
    b) *Vehicle speed (mph)*
    c) *Throttle position*
    d) *Engine load measured by Manifold Absolute Pressure (MAP) sensor*
    e) *Coolant temperature*

5   The camshaft has two different intake valve lobe profiles (lift and duration specifications).

6   At low speeds, the secondary intake valve operates on its own camshaft lobe, which has lift and duration profiles designed specifically for the torque applications for that year and model. This limited valve operation is designed to provide good low end torque and responsiveness.

7   When performance is needed, the primary and secondary rocker arms are locked together through the use of an electrically controlled hydraulic system. Hydraulically operated synchronizing pistons lock the rocker arms together. When activated, the intake valves open to the higher lift and duration of the rocker arm, which has its own camshaft lobe designed with the higher lift profile.

➡ **Note: Refer to this Chapter's Specifications for the exact camshaft lobe lift profiles.**

i-VTEC VCM system

8   Variable Cylinder Management (VCM) is used on later models equipped with the J35A7 engine, VCM is a variation of the i-VTEC system that is used for improved economy.

9   Under certain driving conditions such as deceleration and cruise, the rocker arms for some of the rear cylinders are de-activated and their fuel injectors are shut off. This allows the engine to temporarily operate as either a 3 or 4-cylinder engine.

COMPONENT CHECKS

➡ **Note: The VTEC system will require specialized diagnostic equipment to access the on-board computer to test the associated electrical circuits, actuators and sensors. However, there are some mechanical tests of the VTEC system that the home mechanic can perform to check for obvious and simple problems within the system. If these simple checks don't reveal any problems, have the VTEC system diagnosed by a dealer service department or other qualified automotive repair facility. Also, some checks and inspections of the VTEC components requires removal of the rocker arm assembly (see Section 11).**

VTEC lock-up control solenoid valve

▶ **Refer to illustrations 10.10 and 10.11**

➡ **Note: Most common problems in the VTEC system are associated with the solenoid valve and its filter. Regular engine oil and filter changes are necessary for trouble-free operation of the valve.**

10   The lock-up VTEC solenoid valve and switch are located on the oil filter housing at the right-rear side of the engine, best viewed through the right fenderwell (see illustration).

11   Remove the oil filter adapter housing from the engine and check the filter/O-ring for clogging (see illustration). Clean and reinstall with a new O-ring. A clogged filter screen is often the cause of system problems.

Rocker arms

▶ **Refer to illustration 10.13**

12   Position the number one piston at Top Dead Center (see Section 3). Remove the valve cover (see Section 4).

10.10 The VTEC solenoid is located on top of the oil filter housing

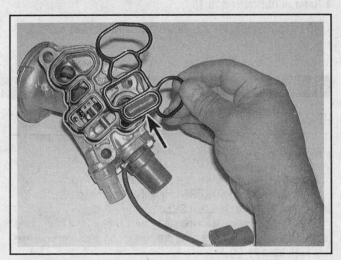

10.11 Whenever problems are suspected in the VTEC system, check the O-ring and filter behind the oil filter adapter housing

10.13 Push down on the mid-rocker of cylinder number 1 to check the action of the VTEC rocker assembly - it should move independently of the primary and secondary intake rockers (2002 through 2004 models shown)

10.15 Push down on the plunger of each lost motion assembly - they should move smoothly (2002 and later models shown)

10.18 Check for smooth movement of the piston in each VTEC rocker arm (2002 and later models shown)

13 Press on the secondary (2001 models) or the mid (2002 and later models) intake rocker arm for cylinder number 1 to see that it moves independently of the primary and secondary intake rockers (see illustration). Check the rockers for the other cylinders at their own TDC positions.

Lost motion assembly

▶ **Refer to illustration 10.15**

14 The lost motion assemblies sit in three pockets in each cylinder head. The rocker arms/shafts must be removed for access to the lost motion assemblies (see Section 11).

15 Test each lost motion assembly by pushing the plunger with your finger (see illustration). A light pressure should move the plunger slightly, and firmer pressure will move it further. If the assembly doesn't move smoothly, replace it.

Synchronizing assembly

▶ **Refer to illustration 10.18**

16 Once the rocker arm assemblies have been removed and disas-

sembled (see Section 11), separate the rocker arms and synchronizing components.

VTEC components:

  a) *Primary rocker arm*
  b) *Secondary rocker arm*
  c) *Mid rocker arm (2002 and later models)*
  d) *Synchronizing piston A*
  e) *Synchronizing piston B*
  f) *Timing piston*

17 Inspect the timing spring, making sure it's not broken or collapsed. Replace it if necessary.

18 Inspect all other parts (rocker arms and synchronizing pistons) for wear, galling, scoring or signs of overheating (bluish in color). Use your finger to push on the rocker arm pistons to check for smooth movement (see illustration). Replace any parts necessary.

19 Reassemble each cylinder's components and wrap a rubber band around the rocker arms before trying to assemble them on the rocker shaft (see Section 11).

11 Rocker arm assembly - removal, inspection and installation

REMOVAL

▶ **Refer to illustration 11.4**

1 Remove the valve cover (see Section 4).

2 Position the engine at TDC for number 1 piston (see Section 3) and remove the timing belt (see Section 8).

3 Loosen the rocker shaft mounting bolts 1/4-turn at a time, in the reverse of the tightening sequence, until the spring pressure is relieved (see illustration 11.11).

4 Lift the rocker arms and shaft assembly from the cylinder head (see illustration). Do not remove the shaft mounting bolts, they will keep the rocker arm assembly components together.

INSPECTION

▶ **Refer to illustrations 11.5 and 11.6**

5 If you wish to disassemble and inspect the rocker arm assembly, a good idea as long as you have them off, remove the mounting bolts and slip the rocker arms and springs off the shafts (see illustration). Mark the relationship of the shafts to the bearing caps and keep the parts in order so you can reassemble them in the same positions.

➡ **Note: On 2002 and later models, keep the three intake rockers for each cylinder together by wrapping them with a heavy rubber band. On 2001 models, wrap the secondary and primary rocker arms with a heavy rubber band.**

6   Thoroughly clean the parts and inspect them for wear and damage. Check the rocker arm faces that contact the camshaft and the rocker arm tips (see illustration). Check the surfaces of the shafts that the rocker arms ride on, as well as the bearing surfaces inside the rocker arms, for scoring and excessive wear. Replace any parts that are damaged or excessively worn. Also, make sure the oil holes in the shafts are not plugged. Check the roller tips for wear and smoothness of operation.

7   Remove the lost motion assemblies from the cylinder head (see illustration 10.13), and clean them. Check for smoothness of plunger operation by pushing down gently with your finger.

8   Check the smoothness of operation of the VTEC pistons in each intake rocker arm (see illustration 10.16).

INSTALLATION

▶ **Refer to illustration 11.11**

9   Lubricate all components with engine oil and reassemble the shafts. When installing the rocker arms, shafts and springs, note the markings and the difference between the left and right side parts.

10   Coat the wear surfaces of the rocker arms with camshaft installation lubricant and install the rocker arm assembly.

11   Tighten the rocker shaft mounting bolts a little at a time, following the recommended tightening sequence (see illustration) to the torque listed in this Chapter's Specifications.

12   The remainder of installation is the reverse of removal.

13   Check the valve clearance and adjust to Specifications (see Section 5).

14   Run the engine and check for oil leaks and proper operation.

11.4 Leave the rocker assembly mounting bolts in place as you remove the assembly (this will keep the components in order on the shafts)

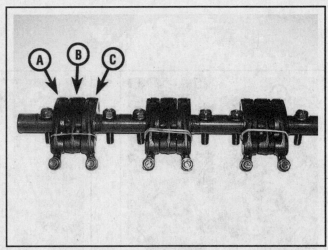

11.5 Intake rocker arm assembly components - rear cylinder bank; on the front cylinder bank, A and C are reversed (2002 and later models shown)

A   Primary intake rocker arm
B   Mid intake rocker arm
C   Secondary intake rocker arm

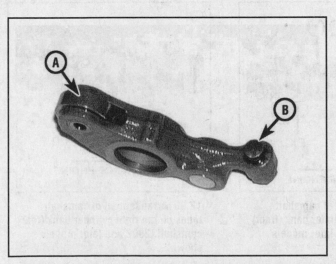

11.6 Inspect the rockers arms for wear and damage at the roller (A) and the valve stem end of the adjusters (B)

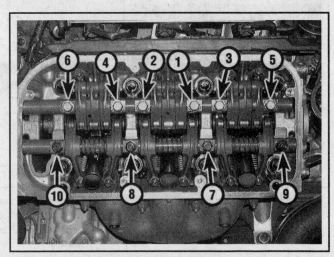

11.11 Rocker arm/shaft mounting bolts TIGHTENING sequence

12 Camshafts - removal, inspection and installation

REMOVAL

▶ **Refer to illustrations 12.4, 12.5 and 12.6**

1 Remove the valve covers (see Section 4).
2 Remove the timing belt and sprockets (see Section 8).
3 Remove the rocker arms/shafts as an assembly (see Section 11).

➡ **Note: Refer to the Inspection procedures below and check camshaft endplay before removing the camshafts.**

4 Remove the EGR valve (see Chapter 6) to access the rear plate for the camshaft (see illustration).
5 Remove the camshaft retainer plate (see illustration).
6 Carefully slide the camshaft out of the cylinder head, being careful not to nick the lobes or journals as you withdraw it (see illustration).

INSPECTION

▶ **Refer to illustrations 12.8, 12.9a and 12.9b**

7 Keeping careful track of the location of the components (see illustration 11.5), remove the rocker arms and springs from the rocker shafts and bolt the bare rocker shafts to the cylinder head, tightening them to the torque listed in this Chapter's Specifications.

8 Mount a dial indicator so that it contacts the nose of the camshaft (see illustration). Pry the camshaft forwards and back with a screwdriver, with the tip taped to prevent damage to the camshaft. Record the movement of the dial indicator and compare it to this Chapter's Specifications. If the endplay is excessive, the camshaft must be replaced.

9 After the endplay check, remove the rocker shafts and withdraw the camshaft. Measure the journal diameters and lobe heights on each camshaft. Be sure to use the Specifications in this Part of Chapter 2. Check also for visual signs of wear, scoring, pitting or overheating.

➡ **Note: The arrangement of lobes is different between the front and rear camshafts (see illustrations).**

12.4 To access the camshaft plate for the front camshaft, remove the EGR valve (A), then the two bolts on the plate (B) located behind the EGR valve

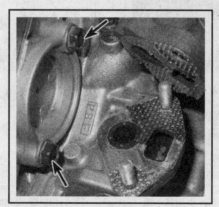

12.5 Remove the bolts and the camshaft retainer plate

12.6 Pull the camshaft straight out of the cylinder head, taking care not to nick the journals or bearings

12.8 Check the camshaft endplay with a dial indicator (2002 and later models shown)

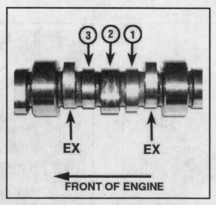

12.9a Arrangement of camshaft lobes on the left cylinder bank (front) camshaft (2002 and later models shown)

1 Primary intake lobe
2 Mid intake lobe
3 Secondary intake lobe

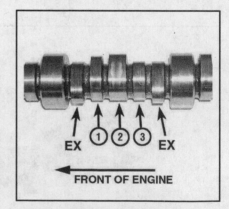

12.9b Arrangement of camshaft lobes on the right cylinder bank (rear) camshaft (2002 and later models shown)

1 Primary intake lobe
2 Mid intake lobe
3 Secondary intake lobe

INSTALLATION

▶ **Refer to illustrations 12.10, 12.11 and 12.12**

10 Remove the timing belt rear covers from each cylinder head to access the camshaft seals (see illustration).

11 The camshaft oil seal should be replaced whenever the camshaft is removed or replaced. Pry the old seal out with a screwdriver or seal removal tool (see illustration).

12 Lubricate the lips with engine oil, then install a new camshaft oil seal by driving it in squarely with a seal installation tool to the same depth as the original seal (see illustration). A socket of the appropriate size will also work.

13 Clean the camshaft thoroughly with solvent, then lubricate the

journals and lobes with camshaft installation lubricant and carefully install the camshaft into the cylinder head.

14 Lubricate and install a new O-ring at the end of the camshaft retainer plate and bolt the retainer plates in place.

15 Install the other camshaft in the same manner.

16 Reinstall the remaining components in the reverse order of removal. Refer to Section 5 for the valve adjustment procedure.

17 Run the engine and check for oil leaks at the camshaft seals. Run the engine at low speed for five minutes to allow the air to bleed from the lost motion assemblies, then check for leaks and proper operation.

➡ **Note: There will be some tappet noise during the first few minutes of operation. If the noise continues, it may indicate a problem with one of the lost motion assemblies.**

12.10 Remove the two bolts and the timing belt rear cover from each cylinder head

12.11 Pry out the old camshaft oil seal with a screwdriver

12.12 If a seal driver is not available, use a hammer and a section of pipe or a large socket to drive the new seal into place

13 Cylinder heads - removal and installation

❄❄ WARNING:

Allow the engine to cool completely before beginning this procedure.

REMOVAL

▶ **Refer to illustrations 13.12 and 13.15**

1   Relieve the fuel pressure, disconnect the electrical connectors from the fuel injectors, disconnect the fuel lines, and remove the fuel rails (see Chapter 4).

2   Disconnect the cable from the negative battery terminal (see Chapter 5, Section 1).

3   Drain the cooling system, including both block drains (see Chapter 1).

4   Remove the alternator (see Chapter 5).

5   Remove the ignition coils from the valve covers (see Chapter 5).

6   Remove the power steering pump and set it aside without disconnecting the hoses (see Chapter 10).

7   Remove the upper and lower intake manifolds (see Section 6).

8   Remove the exhaust manifolds (see Section 7).

9   Remove the timing belt covers (see Section 8).

10 Detach the timing belt and remove the camshaft sprockets (see Section 8).

11 Correctly label and remove all the electrical connectors at the lower intake manifold.

13.12 Remove the coolant passage mounting bolts from both cylinder heads - lightly tap the passage with a soft-faced hammer to break the gasket seal and remove the coolant passage

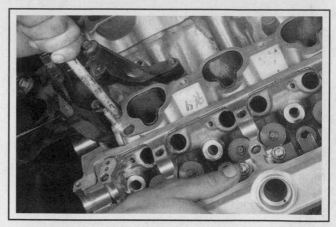

13.15 Pry up carefully on a casting protrusion

13.23 Cylinder head bolt TIGHTENING sequence

12 Remove the coolant passage assembly from the cylinder head (see illustration).

13 Refer to Section 11 and remove the rocker arms/shafts assembly.

14 Using a socket and breaker bar, loosen the cylinder head bolts in 1/4-turn increments until they can be removed by hand. Loosen them in a sequence opposite that of the tightening sequence (see illustration 13.23)

15 Lift the cylinder head off the engine block. If the head is stuck, pry against an external casting protrusion (see illustration).

❋❋ CAUTION:

Don't pry between the head and block. The gasket surfaces may be damaged and leaks could result.

16 Repeat Steps 13 through 15 for the other head.

INSTALLATION

▶ **Refer to illustration 13.23**

17 The mating surfaces of the cylinder heads and block must be perfectly clean when the heads are installed. Use a gasket scraper to remove all traces of carbon and old gasket material. Be careful not to gouge the delicate aluminum. Clean the mating surfaces with lacquer thinner or acetone. If there's oil on the mating surfaces when the head is installed, the gasket may not seal correctly and leaks could develop. When working on the block, stuff the cylinders with clean shop rags to keep out debris. Use a vacuum cleaner to remove material that falls into the cylinders.

18 Check the block and head mating surfaces for nicks, deep scratches and other damage. If damage is slight, it can be removed with a file; if it's excessive, machining may be the only alternative.

19 Use a tap of the correct size to chase the threads in the head bolt holes, then clean the holes with compressed air - make sure that nothing remains in the holes.

❋❋ WARNING:

Wear eye protection when using compressed air!

20 Mount each bolt in a vise and run a die down the threads to remove corrosion and restore the threads. Dirt, corrosion, sealant and damaged threads will affect torque readings.

21 Clean the oil-control jets thoroughly and reinstall them with new O-rings. Position the new gaskets over the oil-control jets and locating dowels in the block.

22 Carefully set the head on the block without disturbing the gasket. On 2007 and later engines, measure the thread diameter of each head bolt at 1.8 inches and 2 inches from the end of the bolt. If any measurement is less than the minimum shown in this Chapter's Specifications, that bolt must be replaced with a new one.

23 Before installing the head bolts, apply a small amount of clean engine oil to the threads and under the bolt heads. Install the bolts and special washers and tighten them finger tight. Following the recommended sequence (see illustration), tighten the bolts to the torque listed in this Chapter's Specifications in three steps.

➡ **Note: On 2006 and earlier models, perform each step twice; torque all bolts to the Specification for the first step, then again torque all to the same Specification before proceeding to the second step.**

Repeat the entire procedure to install the other cylinder head, if necessary. If you're working on a 2007 or later model and you've replaced one or more head bolts, be sure to tighten each new bolt an extra 90-degrees (see this Chapter's Specifications).

24 The remaining installation steps are the reverse of removal.

25 Reconnect the battery. Refer to Chapter 5, Section 1.

26 Refill the cooling system, change the oil and filter (see Chapter 1), run the engine and check for leaks. Run the engine at low speed for five minutes to allow the air to bleed from the lost motion assemblies, then check for leaks and proper operation.

➡ **Note: There will be some tappet noise during the first few minutes of operation. If the noise continues, it may indicate a problem with one of the lost motion assemblies.**

14 Oil pan - removal and installation

REMOVAL

▶ **Refer to illustrations 14.6a and 14.6b**

1 Disconnect the cable from the negative battery terminal (see Chapter 5, Section 1).

2 Block the rear wheels and set the parking brake. Raise the front of the vehicle and support it securely on jackstands.

3 Remove the lower splash shield (see illustrations 7.3a and 7.3b).

4 Drain the engine oil and remove the oil filter (see Chapter 1).

5 Unbolt the exhaust pipe from the manifolds (see Section 6) and unbolt the flange at the catalytic converter (see Chapter 4). Remove the pipe. On later models with the J35A7 engine, remove the cover from the CKP sensor and the bolt, then disconnect the sensor wire.

6 Remove the torque converter cover, then remove the bolts/nuts (see illustration) and lower the oil pan. The bolts at the timing belt end of the engine can be removed with a 1/4-inch drive flex-socket, extension and ratchet. If the pan is stuck, use a dull pry tool at the tabs on the casting corners (see illustration). Don't damage the mating surfaces of the pan and block or oil leaks could develop.

INSTALLATION

▶ **Refer to illustration 14.11**

7 Use a scraper to remove all traces of old sealant from the block and oil pan. Be careful not to gouge the delicate aluminum block. Clean the mating surfaces with lacquer thinner or acetone.

8 Make sure the threaded bolt holes in the block are clean.

9 Inspect the oil pump pick-up screen assembly for damage and a blocked strainer (see Section 15).

10 Position a new gasket on the oil pan.

11 Carefully position the oil pan on the engine block and install the bolts. Follow the correct torque sequence (see illustration) and tighten them to the torque listed in this Chapter's Specifications in three steps.

12 The remainder of installation is the reverse of removal. Be sure to add oil and install a new oil filter.

➡ **Note: If the oil pump has been replaced, wait 20 minutes (to allow the sealant to cure) before adding oil.**

13 Reconnect the battery. Refer to Chapter 5, Section 1.

14 Run the engine and check for oil pressure and leaks.

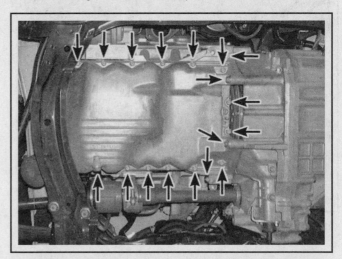

14.6a Remove the bolts from around the perimeter of the oil pan and the oil pan-to-transaxle case bolts (four bolts hidden from view behind the subframe)

14.6b Use a dull screwdriver to pry the pan loose at the cast tabs - DO NOT pry on the gasket surface

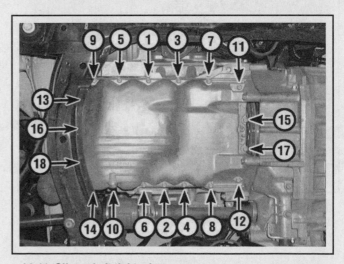

14.11 Oil pan bolt tightening sequence

15 Oil pump - removal, inspection and installation

REMOVAL

▶ **Refer to illustrations 15.3 and 15.5**

1   Remove the timing belt, crankshaft sprocket and idler pulley (see Section 8).

2   Refer to Chapter 6 and remove the crankshaft position sensor.

3   Remove the oil pan (see Section 14) and oil pick-up screen (see illustration). If equipped, remove the oil level sensor.

4   Remove the oil filter adapter housing/VTEC solenoid assembly from the front of the oil pump (see Section 10).

5   Remove the bolts and detach the oil pump housing from the engine (see illustration). You may have to pry carefully between the main bearing cap and the pump housing with a screwdriver.

INSPECTION

▶ **Refer to illustrations 15.6 and 15.7**

6   Use a large Phillips screwdriver to remove the screws holding the pump cover to the rear of the housing (see illustration).

7   Lift the cover off and inspect the pump rotors (see illustration). If any wear or damage is evident, replace the pump. Check the rotor clearance with a feeler gauge and compare it to this Chapter's Specifications.

8   Use a scraper to remove any traces of old sealant from the pump body and engine block, being careful not to damage the delicate aluminum.

15.3 Oil pick-up screen bolt locations

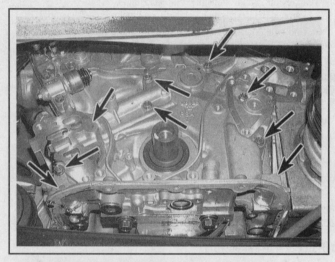

15.5 Oil pump housing bolt locations

15.6 Remove the screws from the pump cover and replace the O-ring seal (A)

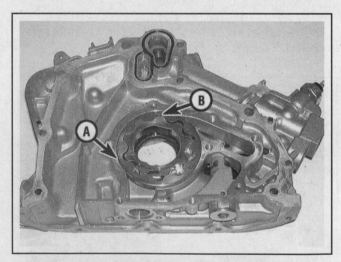

15.7 Inspect the condition of the rotors and the inside of the cover - with feeler gauges, measure the clearances at (A) (outer rotor-to-housing) and (B) (inner rotor-to-outer rotor), lay a straightedge across the face of the pump housing and measure the housing-to-rotor axial clearance and compare to Specifications

INSTALLATION

9 Replace the old crankshaft oil seal (see Section 9). Apply multi-purpose grease to the seal lip.

10 Pack the pump cavity with petroleum jelly and install the cover. Apply thread-locking compound to the threads and tighten the screws securely following a criss-cross pattern.

11 Use acetone or lacquer thinner and a clean rag to remove all traces of oil from the gasket surfaces.

12 Apply a bead of anaerobic sealant to the oil pump flange and the threads of the mounting bolts. Avoid using an excessive amount of sealant, especially around oil passages and bolt holes. Parts must be assembled within five minutes of sealant application, otherwise the material must be removed and reapplied. Wherever O-rings are employed, use new ones.

13 Engage the flat surfaces on the oil pump drive rotor with the matching flats on the crankshaft and slide the pump into place.

14 Install the pump mounting bolts in their original locations and tighten them to the torque listed in this Chapter's Specifications in a criss-cross pattern.

15 Using a new O-ring, install the oil pick-up screen and tighten the fasteners to the torque listed in this Chapter's Specifications.

16 Reinstall the remaining parts in the reverse order of removal.

17 Wait 20 minutes to allow the sealant to cure, then add oil, start the engine and check for oil leaks and pressure.

18 Recheck the engine oil level after operating the engine.

16 Driveplate - removal and installation

1 Remove the engine and transaxle (see Chapter 2B), then separate the transaxle from the engine (see Chapter 7).

2 Remove the bolts that secure the driveplate to the crankshaft.

3 Clean the driveplate and inspect the surface for cracks. Check for worn, cracked or broken ring-gear teeth. Lay the driveplate on a flat surface and use a straightedge to check for warpage.

4 Clean and inspect the mating surfaces of the driveplate and the crankshaft. If the crankshaft oil seal is leaking, replace it before rein- stalling the driveplate (see Section 17).

5 Position the driveplate against the crankshaft. Note that offset bolt holes ensure correct installation.

6 Follow a criss cross pattern and tighten the bolts in several stages to the torque listed in this Chapter's Specifications.

7 The remainder of installation is the reverse of the removal procedure.

17 Rear main oil seal - replacement

▶ **Refer to illustrations 17.2 and 17.3**

1 The transaxle must be removed from the vehicle for this procedure and the driveplate must be removed from the engine. Refer to Chapter 7 and Section 16 as necessary.

2 The seal can be replaced without removing the oil pan or removing the seal retainer. However, the lip of the seal is quite stiff and it's possible to cock the seal in the retainer bore or damage it during installation. Pry out the old seal with a screwdriver (see illustration).

3 Apply multi-purpose grease to the crankshaft seal journal and the lip of the new seal and carefully drive the new seal into place (see illustration). Install the seal with the spring side in. Use a socket, section of pipe or seal installation tool. The lip is stiff so carefully work it onto the seal journal of the crankshaft. Don't rush it or you may damage the seal.

➡ **Note: Drive the seal in squarely and only until it is flush with the back of the seal plate, no further.**

4 The remaining steps are the reverse of removal.

17.2 Carefully pry the rear main seal out - don't damage the surface of the crankshaft or the new seal will leak

17.3 Drive the new seal in squarely until flush with the housing

18 Engine mounts - check and replacement

CHECK

1 There are four engine mounts on these vehicles. The front mount on models not equipped with the Active Engine Mount (ACM) system is computer controlled and is operated by engine vacuum (see Section 19). The front and rear mounts are electrically operated on vehicles with ACM.

2 During the check, the engine must be raised slightly to remove the weight from the mounts.

3 Raise the vehicle and support it securely on jackstands, then position a jack under the engine oil pan. Place a large block of wood between the jack head and the oil pan, then carefully raise the engine just enough to take the weight off the mounts.

18.9 Remove the through-bolt from the passenger's side engine mount

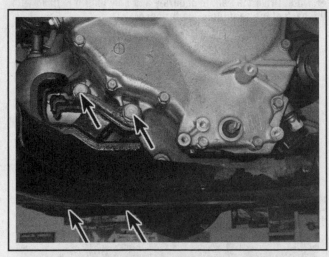

18.11 Remove the two upper mounting bolts and the two lower mounting bolts (accessible through holes in the subframe structure) and remove the driver's side transaxle mount

✳ WARNING:

DO NOT place any part of your body under the engine when it's supported only by a jack!

4 Check the mounts to see if the rubber is cracked, hardened or separated from the casing.

5 Check for relative movement between the mount plates and the engine or frame. Use a large screwdriver or prybar to attempt to move the mounts. If movement is noted, lower the engine and tighten the mount fasteners.

6 Rubber preservative should be applied to the mounts to slow deterioration.

7 Apply the parking brake, block the rear wheels, raise the front of the vehicle and support it securely on jackstands (if not already done).

REPLACEMENT

▶ Refer to illustrations 18.9, 18.11, 18.15 and 18.20

➡ Note: On 2007 and later models with Variable Cylinder Management (VCM), disconnect the wiring from each engine mount/actuator before removing the fasteners.

Right (passenger-side) mount

8 Use a floor jack under the engine to take the weight from the mount.

9 Remove the through-bolt from the mount (see illustration), then remove the bolts holding the engine bracket in place. Remove the three mount-to-chassis bolts and remove the mount.

10 Installation is the reverse of removal.

➡ Note: Tighten the bolts to Specifications only after the powertrain weight is back onto the mounts and the jack is removed. Proceed to Step 24.

Left (driver's-side) mount

11 The driver's-side mount is between the bottom of the transaxle and the subframe (see illustration).

12 With the engine/transaxle supported, remove the two nuts from below the subframe, the two bolts at the transaxle, and remove the mount.

13 Installation is the reverse of removal.

➡ Note: Tighten the bolts securely only after the powertrain weight is back onto the mounts and the jack is removed. Proceed to Step 24.

Front mount

14 The front mount is located between the engine and radiator.

15 Remove the large nut where the mount stud goes through the engine bracket (see illustration).

16 Remove the four bolts holding the mount to the chassis, then disconnect the vacuum hose from the bottom of the mount.

17 Raise the engine enough for the stud to clear the upper bracket and remove the mount.

18 Installation is the reverse of removal.

➡ Note: Tighten the bolts to Specifications only after the powertrain weight is back onto the mounts and the jack is removed. Proceed to Step 24.

Rear mount

19 The rear mount is positioned between the subframe and the engine above the catalytic converter.

20 Remove the large nut and through bolt from the rear mount assembly (see illustration).

21 Remove the four bolts holding the mount to the subframe.

22 Raise the engine enough for the stud to clear the upper bracket and remove the mount.

23 Installation is the reverse of removal.

➡ Note: Tighten the bolts securely only after the powertrain weight is back onto the mounts and the jack is removed. Proceed to Step 24.

Final tightening, all mounts

24 To ensure maximum bushing life and prevent excessive noise and vibration, the vehicle should be level and the engine weight should be on the mounts during the final tightening stage.

➡ Note: Use non-hardening thread locking compound on the nuts/bolts.

Ensure that the bushings are not twisted or offset. If you have replaced more than one mount, or when you are installing the engine, tighten the mounts in the following order: front, rear, passenger's-side and driver's-side.

18.15 Remove the upper nut from the mount stud on the front engine mount

18.20 Remove the through-bolt from the rear engine mount

19 Engine Mount Control System - description and check

MODELS WITHOUT VARIABLE CYLINDER MANAGEMENT (VCM)

Description

1 These models have a special front engine mount that is computer-controlled to reduce idle speed vibrations from the engine. The interior of the liquid-filled mount has two chambers. When the engine is idling, the Powertrain Control Module (PCM) signals a control solenoid valve, which allows manifold vacuum to the mount. There a diaphragm changes the flow of liquid between the two chambers, to cancel vibrations at idle speeds. At engine speeds over 1000 rpm, the vacuum is shut off and the motor mount changes to its normal mode.

Check

▸ **Refer to illustration 19.2**

2 If abnormal vibration is noticed at idle, check the vacuum hose (see illustration) to the engine mount control solenoid for signs of damage or leakage.

19.2 Location of the vacuum line to the front engine mount

3   With the vehicle idling warm (less than 800 rpm), have an assistant put the car in gear with their foot on the brake and the parking brake on, while you connect and disconnect the connector on the solenoid valve. There should be a noticeable change in smoothness.

4   Any further diagnostic procedures should be performed by a dealer service department or other qualified automotive repair facility.

MODELS WITH VARIABLE CYLINDER MANAGEMENT (VCM)

Description

5   Because these vehicles sometimes operate on three or four cylinders, engine vibration is a problem. The engine mounts are part of the Active Engine Mount Control (ACM) system. This system is made up of the special engine mount/actuators, the engine mount control unit and the Powertrain Control Module (PCM).

6   When the engine mount control unit receives data from the PCM indicating that the engine is not operating on all six cylinders, it signals the engine mount/actuators to electrically generate a separate vibration that will help to cancel out the engine vibration.

Check

7   Because the system is computer controlled, diagnosis is impossible without a Honda factory scan tool. See a dealer service department or other qualified repair facility if you notice excessive engine vibration.

Specifications

General

Cylinder numbers (timing belt end-to-transaxle end)

Rear (firewall) side	1-2-3
Front (radiator) side	4-5-6
Firing order	1-4-2-5-3-6
Bore	3.5 inches (89.0 mm)
Stroke	Not available
Displacement	214 cubic inches (3.5 liters)

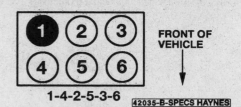

1-4-2-5-3-6

42035-B-SPECS HAYNES

Cylinder locations

Valve adjustment

Intake	0.008 to 0.009 inch (0.20 to 0.22 mm)
Exhaust	0.011 to 0.013 inch (0.28 to 0.32 mm)

Camshaft and rocker arms

Camshaft bearing oil clearance

Standard	0.0020 to 0.0035 inch (0.050 to 0.089 mm)
Service limit	0.006 inch (0.15 mm)

Camshaft lobe height

2001 models

Intake

Primary	1.4107 inches (35.832 mm)
Secondary	1.2231 inches (31.066 mm)
Exhaust	1.4080 inches (35.763 mm)

2002 through 2004 models

Intake

Primary	1.368 inches (34.74 mm)
Mid	1.435 inches (36.45 mm)
Secondary	1.375 inches (34.92 mm)
Exhaust	1.430 inches (36.33 mm)

Camshaft lobe height (continued)

2005 and later J35A6 engine

Intake

Primary	1.380 inches (35.04 mm)
Mid	1.435 inches (36.45 mm)
Secondary	1.390 inches (35.28 mm)
Exhaust	1.430 inches (36.37 mm)

2005 and 2006 J35A7 engine

Intake

Primary front	1.423 inches (36.15 mm)
Primary rear	1.394 inches (35.41 mm)
Secondary	1.134 inches (28.80 mm)

Exhaust

Primary front	1.412 inches (35.86 mm)
Primary rear	1.458 inches (37.04 mm)
Secondary	1.260 inches (32.00 mm)

Specifications (continued)

Camshaft lobe height (continued)

2007 J35A7 engine

Intake

Front	1.423 inches (36.15 mm)
Rear	1.394 inches (35.41 mm)

Exhaust

Front	1.412 inches (35.86 mm)
Rear	1.458 inches (37.04 mm)

2008 and later J35A7 engine

Intake

Front	1.384 inches (35.16 mm)
Rear	1.384 inches (35.16 mm)

Exhaust

Front	1.439 inches (36.54 mm)
Rear	1.438 inches (36.51 mm)

Camshaft endplay

Standard	0.002 to 0.008 inch (0.05 to 0.20 mm)
Service limit	0.008 inch (0.20 mm)
Camshaft runout limit (total indicator reading)	0.002 inch (0.05 mm)
Cylinder head bolt minimum diameter (2007 and later models)	0.445 inch (11.30 mm)

Rocker arm-to-shaft oil clearance

Intake

Standard	0.0010 to 0.0026 inch (0.026 to 0.067 mm)
Service limit	0.0026 inch (0.067 mm)

Exhaust

Standard	0.0010 to 0.0030 inch (0.026 to 0.077 mm)
Service limit	0.0030 inch (0.077 mm)

Oil pump

Outer rotor-to-body clearance	0.004 to 0.007 inch (0.10 to 0.19 mm)
Outer rotor-to-inner rotor clearance	0.002 to 0.006 inch (0.05 to 0.15 mm)
Housing-to-rotor clearance	0.001 to 0.003 inch (0.02 to 0.07 mm)

Torque specifications	Ft-lbs (unless otherwise indicated)	Nm

➡ Note: One foot-pound (ft-lb) of torque is equivalent to 12 inch-pounds (in-lbs) of torque. Torque values below approximately 15 foot-pounds are expressed in inch-pounds, because most foot-pound torque wrenches are not accurate at these smaller values.

Camshaft thrust plate bolts	16	22
Camshaft sprocket bolts	67	90
Crankshaft pulley bolt	181	245
Cylinder head bolts (in sequence - see illustration 13.23)		
2006 and earlier models		
Step 1*	29	39
Step 2*	51	69
Step 3*	72	98
2007 and later models		
Step 1	22	30
Step 2	Tighten an additional 90 degrees	
Step 3	Tighten an additional 90 degrees	
Step 4 (use on each NEW bolt only)	Tighten an additional 90 degrees	

Torque specifications (continued) Ft-lbs (unless otherwise indicated) Nm

➡ **Note:** One foot-pound (ft-lb) of torque is equivalent to 12 inch-pounds (in-lbs) of torque. Torque values below approximately 15 foot-pounds are expressed in inch-pounds, because most foot-pound torque wrenches are not accurate at these smaller values.

	Ft-lbs	Nm
Valve cover bolts	104 in-lbs	12
Driveplate bolts	54	74
Exhaust manifold nuts	23	31
Exhaust heat shield bolts	16	22
Engine mount bracket bolts	33	44
Engine mount nuts (use NEW nuts)	54	74
Engine mount bolts (use NEW bolts)	40	54
Intake manifold upper cover bolts	104 in-lbs	12
Intake manifold bolts		
Upper intake manifold	16	22
Lower intake manifold(s)	16	22
Oil pan bolts	104 in-lbs	12
Oil pan-to-transaxle bolts	28	38
Oil pick-up screen mounting bolts	104 in-lbs	12
Oil pump mounting bolts	104 in-lbs	12
Rocker arm shaft bolts	17	24
Timing belt tensioner bolts	104 in-lbs	12
Timing belt idler pulley bolt	33	44
Timing belt cover bolts	104 in-lbs	12
Rear main oil seal retainer bolts	104 in-lbs	12

Perform each Step twice

Notes

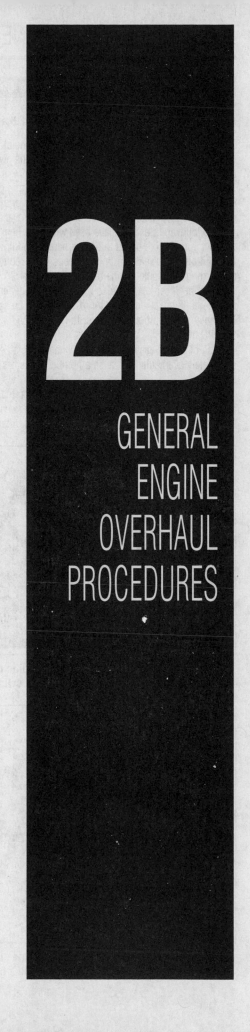

2B

GENERAL ENGINE OVERHAUL PROCEDURES

1 General information - engine overhaul

▶ **Refer to illustrations 1.1, 1.2, 1.3, 1.4, 1.5 and 1.6**

Included in this portion of Chapter 2 are general information and diagnostic testing procedures for determining the overall mechanical condition of your engine.

The information ranges from advice concerning preparation for an overhaul and the purchase of replacement parts and/or components to detailed, step-by-step procedures covering removal and installation.

The following Sections have been written to help you determine whether your engine needs to be overhauled and how to remove and install it once you've determined it needs to be rebuilt. For information concerning in-vehicle engine repair, see Chapter 2A or 2B.

The Specifications included in this part are general in nature and include only those necessary for testing the oil pressure and checking the engine compression. Refer to Chapter 2A for additional engine Specifications.

It's not always easy to determine when, or if, an engine should be completely overhauled, because a number of factors must be considered.

High mileage is not necessarily an indication that an overhaul is needed, while low mileage doesn't preclude the need for an overhaul. Frequency of servicing is probably the most important consideration.

An engine that's had regular and frequent oil and filter changes, as well as other required maintenance, will most likely give many thousands of miles of reliable service. Conversely, a neglected engine may require an overhaul very early in its service life.

Excessive oil consumption is an indication that piston rings, valve seals and/or valve guides are in need of attention. Make sure that oil leaks aren't responsible before deciding that the rings and/or guides are bad. Perform a cylinder compression check to determine the extent of the work required (see Section 3). Also check the vacuum readings under various conditions (see Section 4).

Check the oil pressure with a gauge installed in place of the oil pressure sending unit and compare it to this Chapter's Specifications (see Section 2). If it's extremely low, the bearings and/or oil pump are probably worn out.

Loss of power, rough running, knocking or metallic engine noises, excessive valve train noise and high fuel consumption rates may also point to the need for an overhaul, especially if they're all present at the same time. If a complete tune-up doesn't remedy the situation, major mechanical work is the only solution.

An engine overhaul involves restoring the internal parts to the specifications of a new engine. During an overhaul, the piston rings are replaced and the cylinder walls are reconditioned (rebored and/or honed) (see illustrations 1.1 and 1.2). If a rebore is done by an automotive machine shop, new oversize pistons will also be installed. The main bearings and connecting rod bearings are generally replaced with new ones and, if necessary, the crankshaft may be reground to restore the journals (see illustration 1.3). Generally, the valves are serviced as well, since they're usually in less-than-perfect condition at this point. While the engine is being overhauled, other components, such as the starter and alternator, can be rebuilt as well. The end result should be a like-new engine that will give many trouble-free miles.

➡ **Note: Critical cooling system components such as the hoses, drivebelts, thermostat and water pump should be replaced with new parts when an engine is overhauled. The radiator should be checked carefully to ensure that it isn't clogged or leaking (see Chapter 3). If you purchase a rebuilt engine or short block, some rebuilders will not warranty their engines unless the radiator has been professionally flushed. Also, we don't recommend overhauling the oil pump - always install a new one when an engine is rebuilt.**

1.1 An engine block being bored. An engine rebuilder will use special machinery to recondition the cylinder bores

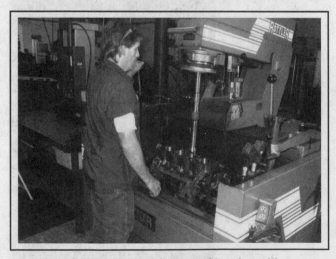

1.2 If the cylinders are bored, the machine shop will normally hone the engine on a machine like this

1.3 A crankshaft having a main bearing journal ground

1.4 A machinist checks for a bent connecting rod, using specialized equipment

1.5 A bore gauge being used to check the main bearing bore

1.6 Uneven piston wear like this indicates a bent connecting rod

Overhauling the internal components on today's engines is a difficult and time-consuming task that requires a significant amount of specialty tools and is best left to a professional engine rebuilder (see illustrations 1.4, 1.5 and 1.6). A competent engine rebuilder will handle the inspection of your old parts and offer advice concerning the reconditioning or replacement of the original engine. Never purchase parts or have machine work done on other components until the block has been thoroughly inspected by a professional machine shop. As a general rule, time is the primary cost of an overhaul, especially since the vehicle may be tied up for a minimum of two weeks or more. Be aware that some engine builders only have the capability to rebuild the engine you bring them while other rebuilders have a large inventory of rebuilt exchange engines in stock. Also be aware that many machine shops could take as much as two weeks time to completely rebuild your engine depending on shop workload. Sometimes it makes more sense to simply exchange your engine for another engine that's already rebuilt to save time.

2 Oil pressure check

▶ **Refer to illustration 2.2**

1 Low engine oil pressure can be a sign of an engine in need of rebuilding. A "low oil pressure" indicator (often called an "idiot light") is not a test of the oiling system. Such indicators only come on when the oil pressure is dangerously low. Even a factory oil pressure gauge in the instrument panel is only a relative indication, although much better for driver information than a warning light. A better test is with a mechanical (not electrical) oil pressure gauge.

2 Locate the oil pressure indicator sending unit on the engine block. The oil pressure sending unit is located on the oil pump housing next to the VTEC solenoid (see illustration).

3 Unscrew and remove the oil pressure sending unit and then screw in the hose for your oil pressure gauge (see illustration). If necessary, install an adapter fitting. Use Teflon tape or thread sealant on the threads of the adapter and/or the fitting on the end of your gauge's hose.

4 Connect an accurate tachometer to the engine, according to the tachometer manufacturer's instructions.

5 Check the oil pressure with the engine running (normal operating temperature) at the specified engine speed, and compare it to this Chapter's Specifications. If it's extremely low, the bearings and/or oil pump are probably worn out.

2.2 The oil pressure sending unit is located on top of the oil pump, near the VTEC solenoid

3 Cylinder compression check

▸ **Refer to illustration 3.6**

1   A compression check will tell you what mechanical condition the upper end of your engine (pistons, rings, valves, head gaskets) is in. Specifically, it can tell you if the compression is down due to leakage caused by worn piston rings, defective valves and seats or a blown head gasket.

➡ **Note: The engine must be at normal operating temperature and the battery must be fully charged for this check.**

2   Begin by cleaning the area around the spark plugs before you remove them (compressed air should be used, if available). The idea is to prevent dirt from getting into the cylinders as the compression check is being done.

3   Remove all of the spark plugs from the engine (see Chapter 1).

4   Block the throttle wide open.

5   Disable the ignition and fuel systems by unplugging the wiring harness connectors from the ignition coils (see Chapter 5) and by removing the fuel pump relay (see Chapter 4).

6   Install a compression gauge in the spark plug hole (see illustration).

7   Crank the engine over at least seven compression strokes and watch the gauge. The compression should build up quickly in a healthy engine. Low compression on the first stroke, followed by gradually increasing pressure on successive strokes, indicates worn piston rings. A low compression reading on the first stroke, which doesn't build up during successive strokes, indicates leaking valves or a blown head gasket (a cracked head could also be the cause). Deposits on the undersides of the valve heads can also cause low compression. Record the highest gauge reading obtained.

8   Repeat the procedure for the remaining cylinders and compare the results to this Chapter's Specifications.

9   Add some engine oil (about three squirts from a plunger-type oil can) to each cylinder, through the spark plug hole, and repeat the test.

10 If the compression increases after the oil is added, the piston

3.6 Use a compression gauge with a threaded fitting for the spark plug hole, not the type that requires hand pressure to

rings are definitely worn. If the compression doesn't increase significantly, the leakage is occurring at the valves or head gasket. Leakage past the valves may be caused by burned valve seats and/or faces or warped, cracked or bent valves.

11 If two adjacent cylinders have equally low compression, there's a strong possibility that the head gasket between them is blown. The appearance of coolant in the combustion chambers or the crankcase would verify this condition.

12 If one cylinder is slightly lower than the others, and the engine has a slightly rough idle, a worn lobe on the camshaft could be the cause.

13 If the compression is unusually high, the combustion chambers are probably coated with carbon deposits. If that's the case, the cylinder head(s) should be removed and decarbonized.

14 If compression is way down or varies greatly between cylinders, it would be a good idea to have a leak-down test performed by an automotive repair shop. This test will pinpoint exactly where the leakage is occurring and how severe it is.

4 Vacuum gauge diagnostic checks

▸ **Refer to illustrations 4.4 and 4.6**

1   A vacuum gauge provides inexpensive but valuable information about what is going on in the engine. You can check for worn rings or cylinder walls, leaking head or intake manifold gaskets, restricted exhaust, stuck or burned valves, weak valve springs, improper ignition or valve timing and ignition problems.

2   Unfortunately, vacuum gauge readings are easy to misinterpret, so they should be used in conjunction with other tests to confirm the diagnosis.

3   Both the absolute readings and the rate of needle movement are important for accurate interpretation. Most gauges measure vacuum in inches of mercury (in-Hg). The following references to vacuum assume the diagnosis is being performed at sea level. As elevation increases (or atmospheric pressure decreases), the reading will decrease. For every 1,000-foot increase in elevation above approximately 2000 feet, the gauge readings will decrease about one inch of mercury.

4   Connect the vacuum gauge directly to the intake manifold vacuum, not to ported (throttle body) vacuum (see illustration). Be sure no hoses are left disconnected during the test or false readings will result.

5   Before you begin the test, allow the engine to warm up completely. Block the wheels and set the parking brake. With the transmis-

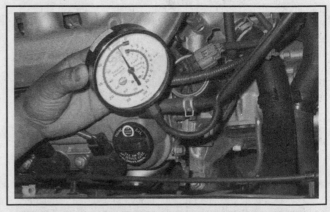

4.4 A simple vacuum gauge can be handy in diagnosing engine condition and performance. Connect it to an intake manifold vacuum source, not a ported (throttle body) source

sion in Park, start the engine and allow it to run at normal idle speed.

✳✳ WARNING:

Keep your hands and the vacuum gauge clear of the fans and drivebelts.

6   Read the vacuum gauge; an average, healthy engine should normally produce about 17 to 22 in-Hg with a fairly steady needle (see illustration). Refer to the following vacuum gauge readings and what they indicate about the engine's condition:

7   A low steady reading usually indicates a leaking gasket between the intake manifold and cylinder head(s) or throttle body, a leaky vacuum hose, late ignition timing or incorrect camshaft timing. Check ignition timing with a timing light and eliminate all other possible causes, utilizing the tests provided in this Chapter before you remove the timing belt cover to check the timing marks.

8   If the reading is three to eight inches below normal and it fluctuates at that low reading, suspect an intake manifold gasket leak at an intake port or a faulty fuel injector.

9   If the needle has regular drops of about two-to-four inches at a steady rate, the valves are probably leaking. Perform a compression check or leak-down test to confirm this.

10 An irregular drop or down-flick of the needle can be caused by a sticking valve or an ignition misfire. Perform a compression check or leak-down test and read the spark plugs.

11 A rapid vibration of about four in-Hg variation at idle combined with exhaust smoke indicates worn valve guides. Perform a leak-down test to confirm this. If the rapid vibration occurs with an increase in engine speed, check for a leaking intake manifold gasket or head gasket, weak valve springs, burned valves or ignition misfire.

12 A slight fluctuation, say one inch up and down, may mean ignition problems. Check all the usual tune-up items and, if necessary, run the engine on an ignition analyzer.

13 If there is a large fluctuation, perform a compression or leak-down test to look for a weak or dead cylinder or a blown head gasket.

14 If the needle moves slowly through a wide range, check for a clogged PCV system, incorrect idle fuel mixture, throttle body or intake manifold gasket leaks.

15 Check for a slow return after revving the engine by quickly snapping the throttle open until the engine reaches about 2,500 rpm and let it shut. Normally the reading should drop to near zero, rise above normal idle reading (about 5 in-Hg over) and then return to the previous idle reading. If the vacuum returns slowly and doesn't peak when the throttle is snapped shut, the rings may be worn. If there is a long delay, look for a restricted exhaust system (often the muffler or catalytic converter). An easy way to check this is to temporarily disconnect the exhaust ahead of the suspected part and redo the test.

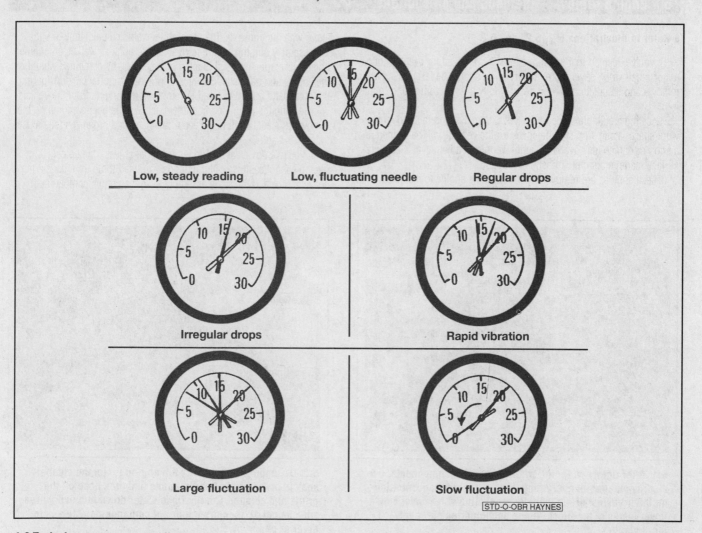

Low, steady reading

Low, fluctuating needle

Regular drops

Irregular drops

Rapid vibration

Large fluctuation

Slow fluctuation

STD-O-OBR HAYNES

4.6 Typical vacuum gauge readings

5 Engine rebuilding alternatives

The do-it-yourselfer is faced with a number of options when purchasing a rebuilt engine. The major considerations are cost, warranty, parts availability and the time required for the rebuilder to complete the project. The decision to replace the engine block, piston/connecting rod assemblies and crankshaft depends on the final inspection results of your engine. Only then can you make a cost effective decision whether to have your engine overhauled or simply purchase an exchange engine for your vehicle.

Some of the rebuilding alternatives include:

Individual parts - If the inspection procedures reveal that the engine block and most engine components are in reusable condition, purchasing individual parts and having a rebuilder rebuild your engine may be the most economical alternative. The block, crankshaft and piston/connecting rod assemblies should all be inspected carefully by a machine shop first.

Short block - A short block consists of an engine block with a crankshaft and piston/connecting rod assemblies already installed. All new bearings are incorporated and all clearances will be correct. The existing camshafts, valve train components, cylinder head and external parts can be bolted to the short block with little or no machine shop work necessary.

Long block - A long block consists of a short block plus an oil pump, oil pan, cylinder head, valve cover, camshaft and valve train components, timing sprockets and belt or gears and timing cover. All components are installed with new bearings, seals and gaskets incorporated throughout. The installation of manifolds and external parts is all that's necessary.

Low mileage used engines - Some companies now offer low mileage used engines that are a very cost effective way to get your vehicle up and running again. These engines often come from vehicles that have been in totaled in accidents or come from other countries that have a higher vehicle turn over rate. A low mileage used engine also usually has a similar warranty like the newly remanufactured engines.

Give careful thought to which alternative is best for you and discuss the situation with local automotive machine shops, auto parts dealers and experienced rebuilders before ordering or purchasing replacement parts.

6 Engine removal - methods and precautions

▶ **Refer to illustrations 6.1, 6.2, and 6.3**

If you've decided that an engine must be removed for overhaul or major repair work, several preliminary steps should be taken. Read all removal and installation procedures carefully prior to committing to this job.

Locating a suitable place to work is extremely important. Adequate work space, along with storage space for the vehicle, will be needed. If a shop or garage isn't available, at the very least a flat, level, clean work surface made of concrete or asphalt is required.

These engines are removed by lowering the engine to the floor, along with the transaxle, then raising the vehicle sufficiently to slide the assembly out; this will require a vehicle hoist as well as an engine hoist. Make sure the hoist is rated in excess of the combined weight of the engine and transaxle. Safety is of primary importance, considering the potential hazards involved in removing the engine from the vehicle.

Cleaning the engine compartment and engine before beginning the removal procedure will help keep tools clean and organized (see illustrations 6.1 and 6.2).

If you're a novice at engine removal, get at least one helper. One person cannot easily do all the things you need to do to remove a big heavy engine and transaxle assembly from the engine compartment.

6.1 After tightly wrapping water-vulnerable components, use a spray cleaner on everything, with particular concentration on the greasiest areas, usually around the valve cover and lower edges of the block. If one section dries out, apply more cleaner

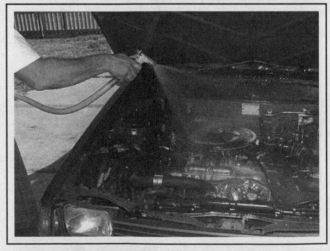

6.2 Depending on how dirty the engine is, let the cleaner soak in according to the directions and then hose off the grime and cleaner. Get the rinse water down into every area you can get at; then dry important components with a hair dryer or paper towels

Also helpful is to seek advice and assistance from someone who's experienced in engine removal.

Plan the operation ahead of time. Arrange for or obtain all of the tools and equipment you'll need prior to beginning the job (see illustration 6.3). Some of the equipment necessary to perform engine removal and installation safely and with relative ease are (in addition to a vehicle hoist and an engine hoist) a heavy duty floor jack (preferably fitted with a transmission jack head adapter), complete sets of wrenches and sockets as described in the front of this manual, wooden blocks, plenty of rags and cleaning solvent for mopping up spilled oil, coolant and gasoline.

Plan for the vehicle to be out of use for quite a while. A machine shop can do the work that is beyond the scope of the home mechanic. Machine shops often have a busy schedule, so before removing the engine, consult the shop for an estimate of how long it will take to rebuild or repair the components that may need work.

6.3 Get an engine stand sturdy enough to firmly support the engine while you're working on it. Stay away from three-wheeled models; they have a tendency to tip over more easily, so get a four-wheeled unit

7   Engine - removal and installation

✳ WARNING:

Gasoline is extremely flammable, so take extra precautions when you work on any part of the fuel system. Don't smoke or allow open flames or bare light bulbs near the work area, and don't work in a garage where a gas-type appliance (such as a water heater or clothes dryer) is present. Since gasoline is carcinogenic, wear fuel-resistant gloves when there's a possibility of being exposed to fuel, and, if you spill any fuel on your skin, rinse it off immediately with soap and water. Mop up any spills immediately and do not store fuel-soaked rags where they could ignite. The fuel system is under constant pressure, so, if any fuel lines are to be disconnected, the fuel pressure in the system must be relieved first (see Chapter 4 for more information). When you perform any kind of work on the fuel system, wear safety glasses and have a Class B type fire extinguisher on hand.

✳ WARNING:

The engine must be completely cool before beginning this procedure.

➡ **Note 1: Engine removal on these models is a difficult job, especially for the do-it-yourself mechanic working at home.**

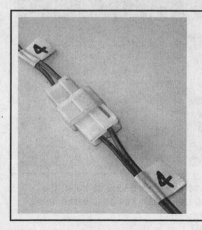

7.10 Label both ends of each wire or vacuum connection before disconnecting them

Because of the vehicle's design, the manufacturer states that the engine and transaxle have to be removed as a unit from the bottom of the vehicle, not the top. With a floor jack and jackstands, the vehicle can't be raised high enough and supported safely enough for the engine/transaxle assembly to slide out from underneath. The manufacturer recommends that removal of the engine transaxle assembly only be performed on a frame-contact type vehicle hoist.

➡ **Note 2: Read through the entire Section before beginning this procedure. The engine and transaxle are removed as a unit from below and then separated outside the vehicle.**

REMOVAL

▶ **Refer to illustrations 7.10 and 7.36**

1   Have the air conditioning system discharged by an automotive air conditioning technician.

2   Park the vehicle on a frame-contact type vehicle hoist, then engage the arms of the hoist with the jacking points of the vehicle. Raise the hoist arms until they contact the vehicle, but not so much that the wheels come off the ground.

3   Relieve the fuel system pressure (see Chapter 4).

4   Place protective covers on the fenders and cowl and remove the hood (see Chapter 11).

5   Remove the intake manifold cover (see Chapter 4) and the ignition coil assembly cover (see Chapter 5).

6   Remove the air filter housing (see Chapter 4).

7   Disconnect the accelerator cable (and cruise control cable, if equipped) and bracket from the engine and position them aside.

8   Remove the battery and the battery tray (see Chapter 5).

9   Disconnect the engine harness connectors near the battery tray and remove the ground cable, the relay bracket and the harness clamp. Position the components off to the side.

10 Clearly label and disconnect all vacuum lines, emissions hoses, wiring harness connectors, ground straps and fuel lines. Masking tape and/or a touch up paint applicator work well for marking items (see illustration). Take instant photos or sketch the locations of components and brackets.

11 Disconnect the electrical connectors from the PCM (see Chapter 6). Also detach any other electrical connectors between the engine and the vehicle.

➡ **Note: Remove the grommet mounting nuts and rotate the grommet counterclockwise. Pull the PCM connectors from the housing behind the grommet.**

12 Disconnect the inlet and return lines from the fuel rail (see Chapter 4).

13 Loosen the front wheel lug nuts, then raise the vehicle on the hoist.

➡ **Note: Keep in mind that during this procedure you'll have to adjust the height of the vehicle to perform certain operations.**

14 Drain the cooling system and engine oil and remove the drivebelts (see Chapter 1).

15 Remove the starter (see Chapter 5).

16 Remove the power steering pump and hose clamps at the subframe (see Chapter 10).

17 Detach the lower radiator hose from the engine (see Chapter 3).

18 Lower the vehicle and detach the heater hoses at the firewall.

19 Detach the upper radiator hose from the thermostat housing (see Chapter 3). Remove the heater hoses.

20 Remove the stabilizer bar links (see Chapter 10).

21 Disconnect the lower balljoints and remove the driveaxles (see Chapter 8).

22 Remove the cooling fan(s), shroud(s) and radiator (see Chapter 3).

23 Disconnect the shift cable from the transaxle (see Chapter 7). Also disconnect any wiring harness connectors from the transaxle.

24 Remove the air conditioning compressor (see Chapter 3).

25 Remove the transaxle mount nuts (see Chapter 7).

26 Remove the power steering gear mounts from the subframe (see Chapter 10).

➡ **Note: The power steering gear will have to be supported using rope, later, when the powertrain/subframe assembly is being lowered.**

27 Raise the vehicle on the hoist. Remove the front wheels.

28 Remove the rear engine mount bolts (see Chapter 2A).

29 Disconnect and plug the transaxle fluid hoses (see Chapter 7).

30 Unplug the downstream oxygen sensor electrical connector.

31 Detach the exhaust pipe from the exhaust manifold (see Chapter 4).

32 Remove the coolant bypass hoses (see Chapter 3).

33 Remove the torque converter bolts.

34 Lower the vehicle.

35 Support the engine with a floor jack and block of wood. Remove the left side and front engine mounts, including the portion that bolts to the engine. Attach one end of an engine lifting sling or chain to the lift mount near the intake manifold. Tighten the bolt securely. Attach the other end of the sling or chain to the lift mount located on the transaxle. Be sure the positioning of the chain or sling will support the engine and transaxle in a balanced attitude.

➡ **Note: The sling or chain must be long enough to allow the engine hoist to lower the engine/transaxle assembly to the ground, without letting the hoist arm contact the vehicle.**

36 Roll the hoist into position and attach the sling or chain to it (see illustration). Take up the slack until there is slight tension on the hoist, then remove the jack from under the engine. Remember that the transaxle end of the engine will be heavier, so position the chain on the hoist so it balances the engine and the transaxle level with the vehicle.

➡ **Note: Depending on the design of the engine hoist, it may be helpful to position the hoist from the side of the vehicle, so that when the engine/transaxle assembly is lowered, it will fit between the legs of the hoist.**

37 Recheck to be sure nothing except the remaining mounts are still connecting the engine to the vehicle or to the transaxle. Disconnect and label anything still remaining.

38 Carefully mark the position of the subframe in relation to the vehicle chassis.

39 Remove the upper engine mount (see Chapter 2A) and the subframe mounting bolts.

40 Slowly lower the engine/transaxle and subframe assembly onto the jackstands.

41 Disconnect the engine lifting hoist and raise the vehicle until it clears the powertrain.

42 Reconnect the chain or sling and raise the engine and transaxle. Support the engine with blocks of wood or another floor jack, while leaving the sling or chain attached to the right-side mounting boss. Support the transaxle with another floor jack, preferably one with a transmission jack head adapter. At this point the transaxle can be unbolted and removed from the engine. Be very careful to ensure that the components are supported securely so they won't topple off their supports during disconnection.

43 Reconnect the lifting chain to the engine, then raise the engine and attach it to an engine stand.

INSTALLATION

▶ **Refer to illustrations 7.44a, 7.44b and 7.44c**

44 Installation is the reverse of removal, noting the following points:
   a) *Check the engine/transaxle mounts. If they're worn or damaged, replace them.*
   b) *Attach the transaxle to the engine fol lowing the procedure described in Chapter 7.*
   c) *Add coolant, oil, power steering and transmission fluids as needed* (see Chapter 1).
   d) *Align the reference marks on the front subframe before tightening the bolts (see illustration).*
   e) *Tighten the subframe mounting bolts and bracket bolts to the torque listed in this Chapter's Specifications. Note the locations of the various size bolts (see illustration). Replace all the large subframe bolts (A) with new bolts.*
   f) *Run the engine and check for proper operation and leaks. Shut off the engine and recheck fluid levels.*

45 Reconnect the negative battery cable. Refer to Chapter 5, Section 1.

7.36 With the minivan positioned on a vehicle hoist, the engine/transaxle/subframe assembly can be lowered onto jackstands using an engine lift

7.44a Align the subframe marks with the edge of the body - right side shown

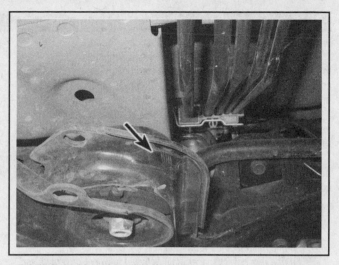

7.44b Left side subframe alignment marks

7.44c Location of the main subframe mounting bolts (A), the bracket bolts (B) and the special bolt (C)

8   Engine overhaul - disassembly sequence

1   It's much easier to remove the external components if it's mounted on a portable engine stand. A stand can often be rented quite cheaply from an equipment rental yard. Before the engine is mounted on a stand, the flywheel/driveplate should be removed from the engine.

2   If a stand isn't available, it's possible to remove the external engine components with it blocked up on the floor. Be extra careful not to tip or drop the engine when working without a stand.

3   If you're going to obtain a rebuilt engine, all external components must come off first, to be transferred to the replacement engine. These components include:

Driveplate
Ignition system components
Emissions-related components
Engine mounts and mount brackets
Engine rear cover (spacer plate between flywheel/driveplate and engine block)
Intake/exhaust manifolds

Fuel injection components
Oil filter
Spark plug wires and spark plugs
Thermostat and housing assembly
Water pump

➡ **Note: When removing the external components from the engine, pay close attention to details that may be helpful or important during installation. Note the installed position of gaskets, seals, spacers, pins, brackets, washers, bolts and other small items.**

4   If you're going to obtain a short block (assembled engine block, crankshaft, pistons and connecting rods), then remove the timing belt, cylinder heads, oil pan, oil pump pick-up tube, oil pump and water pump from your engine so that you can turn in your old short block to the rebuilder as a core. See *Engine rebuilding alternatives* for additional information regarding the different possibilities to be considered.

9   Pistons and connecting rods - removal and installation

REMOVAL

◆ **Refer to illustrations 9.1, 9.2 and 9.4**

➡ **Note: Prior to removing the piston/connecting rod assemblies, remove the cylinder heads and oil pan (see Chapter 2A).**

1   Use your fingernail to feel if a ridge has formed at the upper limit of ring travel (about 1/4-inch down from the top of each cylinder). If carbon deposits or cylinder wear have produced ridges, they must be completely removed with a special tool (see illustration). Follow the manufacturer's instructions provided with the tool. Failure to remove the ridges before attempting to remove the piston/connecting rod assemblies may result in piston breakage.

2   After the cylinder ridges have been removed, turn the engine so the crankshaft is facing up.

3   Before the connecting rods are removed, check the connecting rod endplay with feeler gauges. Slide them between the first connecting rod and the crankshaft throw until the play is removed (see illustration). Repeat this procedure for each connecting rod. The endplay is equal to the thickness of the feeler gauge(s). Check with an automotive machine shop for the endplay service limit (a typical end play limit should measure between 0.005 to 0.015 inch [0.127 to 0.369 mm]). If the play exceeds the service limit, new connecting rods will be required. If new rods (or a new crankshaft) are installed, the endplay may fall under the minimum allowable. If it does, the rods will have to be machined to restore it. If necessary, consult an automotive machine shop for advice.

4   Check the connecting rods and caps for identification marks. If they aren't plainly marked, use paint or marker (see illustration) to clearly identify each rod and cap (1, 2, 3, etc., depending on the cylinder they're associated with).

✳✳ **CAUTION:**

Do not use a punch and hammer to mark the connecting rods or they may be damaged.

9.1   Before you try to remove the pistons, use a ridge reamer to remove the raised material (ridge) from the top of the cylinders

9.3   Checking the connecting rod endplay (side clearance)

9.4   If the connecting rods or caps are not marked, use permanent ink or paint to mark the caps to the rods by cylinder number (for example, this would be number 4 cylinder connecting rod)

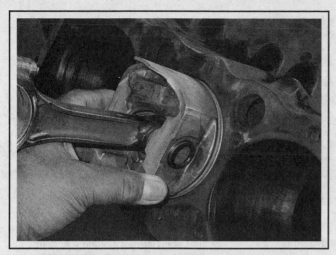

9.13 Install the piston ring into the cylinder then push it down into position using a piston so the ring will be square in the cylinder

9.14 With the ring square in the cylinder, measure the ring end gap with a feeler gauge

5   Loosen each of the connecting rod cap bolts 1/2-turn at a time until they can be removed by hand.

➡ **Note: New connecting rod cap bolts must be used when reassembling the engine, but save the old bolts for use when checking the connecting rod bearing oil clearance.**

6   Remove the number one connecting rod cap and bearing insert. Don't drop the bearing insert out of the cap.

7   Remove the bearing insert and push the connecting rod/piston assembly out through the top of the engine. Use a wooden or plastic hammer handle to push on the upper bearing surface in the connecting rod. If resistance is felt, double-check to make sure that all of the ridge was removed from the cylinder.

8   Repeat the procedure for the remaining cylinders.

9   After removal, reassemble the connecting rod caps and bearing inserts in their respective connecting rods and install the cap bolts finger tight. Leaving the old bearing inserts in place until reassembly will help prevent the connecting rod bearing surfaces from being accidentally nicked or gouged.

10   The pistons and connecting rods are now ready for inspection and overhaul at an automotive machine shop.

PISTON RING INSTALLATION

◗ **Refer to illustrations 9.13, 9.14, 9.15, 9.19a, 9.19b and 9.22**

11   Before installing the new piston rings, the ring end gaps must be checked. It's assumed that the piston ring side clearance has been checked and verified correct.

12   Lay out the piston/connecting rod assemblies and the new ring sets so the ring sets will be matched with the same piston and cylinder during the end gap measurement and engine assembly.

13   Insert the top (number one) ring into the first cylinder and square it up with the cylinder walls by pushing it in with the top of the piston (see illustration). The ring should be near the bottom of the cylinder, at the lower limit of ring travel.

14   To measure the end gap, slip feeler gauges between the ends of the ring until a gauge equal to the gap width is found (see illustration). The feeler gauge should slide between the ring ends with a slight amount of drag. A typical ring gap should fall between 0.010 and 0.020

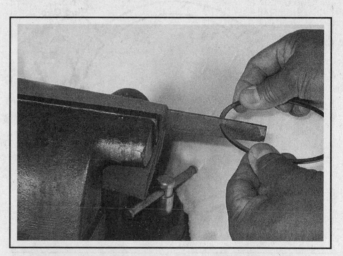

9.15 If the ring end gap is too small, clamp a file in a vise as shown and file the piston ring ends - be sure to remove all raised material

inch [0.25 to 0.50 mm] for compression rings and up to 0.030 inch [0.76 mm] for the oil ring steel rails. If the gap is larger or smaller than specified, double-check to make sure you have the correct rings before proceeding.

15   If the gap is too small, it must be enlarged or the ring ends may come in contact with each other during engine operation, which can cause serious damage to the engine. If necessary, increase the end gaps by filing the ring ends very carefully with a fine file. Mount the file in a vise equipped with soft jaws, slip the ring over the file with the ends contacting the file face and slowly move the ring to remove material from the ends. When performing this operation, file only by pushing the ring from the outside end of the file towards the vise (see illustration).

16   Excess end gap isn't critical unless it's greater than 0.040 inch (1.01 mm). Again, double-check to make sure you have the correct ring type.

17   Repeat the procedure for each ring that will be installed in the first cylinder and for each ring in the remaining cylinders. Remember to keep rings, pistons and cylinders matched up.

18   Once the ring end gaps have been checked/corrected, the rings can be installed on the pistons.

9.19a Installing the spacer/expander in the oil ring groove

9.19b DO NOT use a piston ring installation tool when installing the oil control side rails

9.22 Use a piston ring installation tool to install the number 2 and the number 1 (top) rings - be sure the directional mark on the piston ring(s) is facing toward the top of the piston

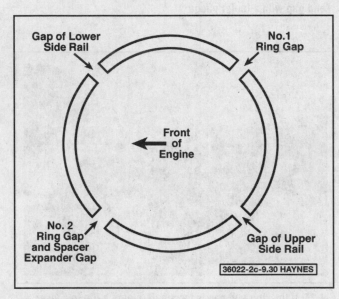

9.30 Position the piston ring end gaps as shown

19 The oil control ring (lowest one on the piston) is usually installed first. It's composed of three separate components. Slip the spacer/expander into the groove (see illustration). If an anti-rotation tang is used, make sure it's inserted into the drilled hole in the ring groove. Next, install the upper side rail in the same manner (see illustration). Don't use a piston ring installation tool on the oil ring side rails, as they may be damaged. Instead, place one end of the side rail into the groove between the spacer/expander and the ring land, hold it firmly in place and slide a finger around the piston while pushing the rail into the groove. Finally, install the lower side rail.

20 After the three oil ring components have been installed, check to make sure that both the upper and lower side rails can be rotated smoothly inside the ring grooves.

21 The number two (middle) ring is installed next. It's usually stamped with a mark which must face up, toward the top of the piston. Do not mix up the top and middle rings, as they have different cross-sections.

➡ **Note: Always follow the instructions printed on the ring package or box - different manufacturers may require different approaches.**

22 Use a piston ring installation tool and make sure the identification mark is facing the top of the piston, then slip the ring into the middle groove on the piston (see illustration). Don't expand the ring any more than necessary to slide it over the piston.

23 Install the number one (top) ring in the same manner. Make sure the mark is facing up. Be careful not to confuse the number one and number two rings.

24 Repeat the procedure for the remaining pistons and rings.

INSTALLATION

25 Before installing the piston/connecting rod assemblies, the cylinder walls must be perfectly clean, the top edge of each cylinder bore must be chamfered, and the crankshaft must be in place.

26 Remove the cap from the end of the number one connecting rod (refer to the marks made during removal). Remove the original bearing inserts and wipe the bearing surfaces of the connecting rod and cap with a clean, lint-free cloth. They must be kept spotlessly clean.

Connecting rod bearing oil clearance check

▶ **Refer to illustrations 9.30, 9.35, 9.37 and 9.41**

27 Clean the back side of the new upper bearing insert, then lay it in place in the connecting rod.

28 Make sure the tab on the bearing fits into the recess in the rod. Don't hammer the bearing insert into place and be very careful not to nick or gouge the bearing face. Don't lubricate the bearing at this time.

29 Clean the back side of the other bearing insert and install it in the rod cap. Again, make sure the tab on the bearing fits into the recess in the cap, and don't apply any lubricant. It's critically important that the mating surfaces of the bearing and connecting rod are perfectly clean and oil free when they're assembled.

30 Position the piston ring gaps at 90-degree intervals around the piston as shown (see illustration).

31 Lubricate the piston and rings with clean engine oil and attach a piston ring compressor to the piston. Leave the skirt protruding about 1/4-inch to guide the piston into the cylinder. The rings must be compressed until they're flush with the piston.

9.35 Use a plastic or wooden hammer handle to push the piston into the cylinder

9.37 Place Plastigage on each connecting rod bearing journal parallel to the crankshaft centerline

9.41 Use the scale on the Plastigage package to determine the bearing oil clearance - be sure to measure the widest part of the Plastigage and use the correct scale; it comes with both standard and metric scales

32 Rotate the crankshaft until the number one connecting rod journal is at BDC (bottom dead center) and apply a liberal coat of engine oil to the cylinder walls.

33 With the arrow on the top of the piston crown facing the front (timing belt end) of the engine, gently insert the piston/connecting rod assembly into the number one cylinder bore and rest the bottom edge of the ring compressor on the engine block. Install the pistons with the cavity mark(s) facing toward the timing belt.

34 Tap the top edge of the ring compressor to make sure it's contacting the block around its entire circumference.

35 Gently tap on the top of the piston with the end of a wooden or plastic hammer handle (see illustration) while guiding the end of the connecting rod into place on the crankshaft journal. The piston rings may try to pop out of the ring compressor just before entering the cylinder bore, so keep some downward pressure on the ring compressor. Work slowly, and if any resistance is felt as the piston enters the cylinder, stop immediately. Find out what's hanging up and fix it before proceeding. Do not, for any reason, force the piston into the cylinder - you might break a ring and/or the piston.

36 Once the piston/connecting rod assembly is installed, the connecting rod bearing oil clearance must be checked before the rod cap is permanently installed.

37 Cut a piece of the appropriate size Plastigage slightly shorter than the width of the connecting rod bearing and lay it in place on the number one connecting rod journal, parallel with the journal axis (see illustration).

38 Clean the connecting rod cap bearing face and install the rod cap. Make sure the mating mark on the cap is on the same side as the mark on the connecting rod (see illustration 9.4).

39 Install the old rod bolts, at this time, and tighten them to the torque listed in this Chapter's Specifications.

➡ **Note: Use a thin-wall socket to avoid erroneous torque readings that can result if the socket is wedged between the rod cap and the bolt or nut. If the socket tends to wedge itself between the fastener and the cap, lift up on it slightly until it no longer contacts the cap. DO NOT rotate the crankshaft at any time during this operation.**

40 Remove the fasteners and detach the rod cap, being very careful not to disturb the Plastigage. Discard the cap bolts at this time as they cannot be reused.

➡ **Note: You MUST use new connecting rod bolts.**

41 Compare the width of the crushed Plastigage to the scale printed on the Plastigage envelope to obtain the oil clearance (see illustration). The connecting rod oil clearance is usually about 0.001 to 0.002 inch. Consult an automotive machine shop for the clearance specified for the rod bearings on your engine.

42 If the clearance is not as specified, the bearing inserts may be the wrong size (which means different ones will be required). Before deciding that different inserts are needed, make sure that no dirt or oil was between the bearing inserts and the connecting rod or cap when the clearance was measured. Also, recheck the journal diameter. If the Plastigage was wider at one end than the other, the journal may be tapered. If the clearance still exceeds the limit specified, the bearing will have to be replaced with an undersize bearing.

❋❋ CAUTION:

When installing a new crankshaft always use a standard size bearing.

Final installation

43 Carefully scrape all traces of the Plastigage material off the rod journal and/or bearing face. Be very careful not to scratch the bearing - use your fingernail or the edge of a plastic card.

44 Make sure the bearing faces are perfectly clean, then apply a uniform layer of clean moly-base grease or engine assembly lube to both of them. You'll have to push the piston into the cylinder to expose the face of the bearing insert in the connecting rod.

45 Slide the connecting rod back into place on the journal, install the rod cap, install the nuts or new bolts and tighten them to the torque listed in this Chapter's Specifications. Again, work up to the torque in three steps.

❋❋ CAUTION:

If the connecting rod caps are secured to the rods with bolts (instead of nuts), install new connecting rod cap bolts. Do NOT reuse old bolts - they have stretched and cannot be reused.

ENGINE BEARING ANALYSIS

Debris

Babbitt bearing embedded with debris from machinings

Microscopic detail of debris

Microscopic detail of gouges

Overplated copper alloy bearing gouged by cast iron debris

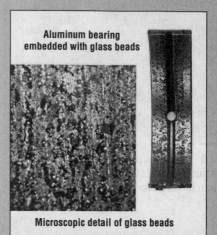

Aluminum bearing embedded with glass beads

Microscopic detail of glass beads

Damaged lining caused by dirt left on the bearing back

Misassembly

Result of a lower half assembled as an upper - blocking the oil flow

Excessive oil clearance is indicated by a short contact arc

Polished and oil-stained backs are a result of a poor fit in the housing bore

Result of a wrong, reversed, or shifted cap

Overloading

Damage from excessive idling which resulted in an oil film unable to support the load imposed

Damaged upper connecting rod bearings caused by engine lugging; the lower main bearings (not shown) were similarly affected

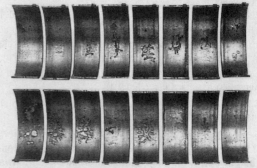

The damage shown in these upper and lower connecting rod bearings was caused by engine operation at a higher-than-rated speed under load

Misalignment

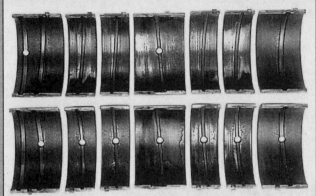

A warped crankshaft caused this pattern of severe wear in the center, diminishing toward the ends

A poorly finished crankshaft caused the equally spaced scoring shown

A tapered housing bore caused the damage along one edge of this pair

A bent connecting rod led to the damage in the "V" pattern

Lubrication

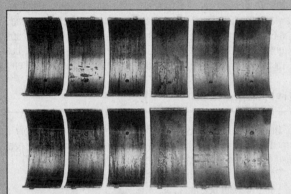

Result of dry start: The bearings on the left, farthest from the oil pump, show more damage

Result of a low oil supply or oil starvation

Severe wear as a result of inadequate oil clearance

Corrosion

Microscopic detail of corrosion

Corrosion is an acid attack on the bearing lining generally caused by inadequate maintenance, extremely hot or cold operation, or inferior oils or fuels

Microscopic detail of cavitation

Example of cavitation - a surface erosion caused by pressure changes in the oil film

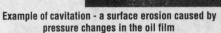

Damage from excessive thrust or insufficient axial clearance

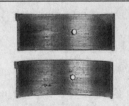

Bearing affected by oil dilution caused by excessive blow-by or a rich mixture

46 Repeat the entire procedure for the remaining pistons/connecting rods.

47 The important points to remember are:

a) *Keep the back sides of the bearing inserts and the insides of the connecting rods and caps perfectly clean when assembling them.*

b) *Make sure you have the correct piston/rod assembly for each cylinder.*

c) *The mark on the piston must face the front (timing belt end) of the engine.*

d) *Lubricate the cylinder walls liberally with clean oil.*

e) *Lubricate the bearing faces when installing the rod caps after the oil clearance has been checked.*

48 After all the piston/connecting rod assemblies have been correctly installed, rotate the crankshaft a number of times by hand to check for any obvious binding.

49 As a final step, check the connecting rod endplay again.

50 Compare the measured endplay to the tolerance listed in this Chapter's Specifications to make sure it's acceptable. If it was correct before disassembly and the original crankshaft and rods were reinstalled, it should still be correct. If new rods or a new crankshaft were installed, the endplay may be inadequate. If so, the rods will have to be removed and taken to an automotive machine shop for resizing.

10 Crankshaft - removal and installation

REMOVAL

▶ **Refer to illustrations 10.1 and 10.3**

➡ **Note: The crankshaft can be removed only after the engine has been removed from the vehicle. It's assumed that the driveplate, crankshaft pulley, timing belt, oil pan, oil pump body, oil filter and piston/connecting rod assemblies have already been removed. The rear main oil seal retainer must be unbolted and separated from the block before proceeding with crankshaft removal.**

1 Before the crankshaft is removed, measure the endplay. Mount a dial indicator with the indicator in line with the crankshaft and just touching the end of the crankshaft as shown (see illustration).

2 Pry the crankshaft all the way to the rear and zero the dial indicator. Next, pry the crankshaft to the front as far as possible and check the reading on the dial indicator. The distance traveled is the endplay. A typical crankshaft endplay will fall between 0.003 to 0.010 inch (0.076 to 0.254 mm). If it is greater than that, check the crankshaft thrust surfaces for wear after it's removed. If no wear is evident, new main bearings should correct the endplay.

3 If a dial indicator isn't available, feeler gauges can be used. Gently pry the crankshaft all the way to the front of the engine. Slip feeler gauges between the crankshaft and the front face of the thrust bearing or washer to determine the clearance (see illustration).

4 Loosen the main bearing cap bolts 1/4-turn at a time each, until they can be removed by hand.

5 Gently tap the main bearing caps with a soft-face hammer. Pull the main bearing caps straight up and off the cylinder block. Try not to drop the bearing inserts if they come out with the caps.

6 Carefully lift the crankshaft out of the engine. It may be a good idea to have an assistant available, since the crankshaft is quite heavy and awkward to handle. With the bearing inserts in place inside the engine block and main bearing caps, reinstall the main bearing caps and tighten the bolts finger tight. Make sure you install the main bearing caps with the arrows facing the front end (timing belt) of the engine.

INSTALLATION

7 Crankshaft installation is the first step in engine reassembly. It's assumed at this point that the engine block and crankshaft have been cleaned, inspected and repaired or reconditioned.

8 Position the engine block with the bottom facing up.

9 Remove main bearing caps.

10 If they're still in place, remove the original bearing inserts from the block and from the main bearing caps. Wipe the bearing surfaces of the block and main bearing cap assembly with a clean, lint-free cloth.

10.1 Checking crankshaft endplay with a dial indicator

10.3 Checking crankshaft endplay with feeler gauges at the thrust bearing journal

10.17 Place the Plastigage onto the crankshaft bearing journal as shown

They must be kept spotlessly clean. This is critical for determining the correct bearing oil clearance.

MAIN BEARING OIL CLEARANCE CHECK

▶ Refer to illustrations 10.17, 10.19 and 10.21

11 Without mixing them up, clean the back sides of the new upper main bearing inserts (with grooves and oil holes) and lay one in each main bearing saddle in the block. Each upper bearing has an oil groove and oil hole in it.

❋❋ CAUTION:

The oil holes in the block must line up with the oil holes in the upper bearing inserts.

The thrust washers must be installed in the number 3 crankshaft journal. Clean the back sides of the lower main bearing inserts and lay them in the corresponding location in the main bearing cap assembly. Make sure the tab on the bearing insert fits into the recess in the block or main bearing cap assembly. The upper bearings with the oil holes are installed into the engine block while the lower bearings without the oil holes are installed in the main bearing caps.

❋❋ CAUTION:

Do not hammer the bearing insert into place and don't nick or gouge the bearing faces. DO NOT apply any lubrication at this time.

12 Clean the faces of the bearing inserts in the block and the crankshaft main bearing journals with a clean, lint-free cloth.

13 Check or clean the oil holes in the crankshaft, as any dirt here can go only one way - straight through the new bearings.

14 Once you're certain the crankshaft is clean, carefully lay it in position in the cylinder block.

15 Before the crankshaft can be permanently installed, the main bearing oil clearance must be checked.

16 Cut several strips of the appropriate size of Plastigage. They must be slightly shorter than the width of the main bearing journal.

17 Place one piece on each crankshaft main bearing journal, parallel

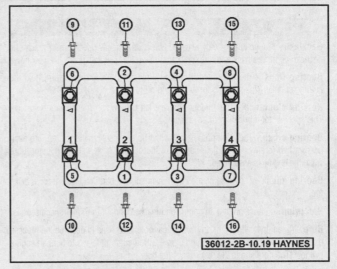

10.19 Main bearing cap bolt tightening sequence

10.21 Use the scale on the Plastigage package to determine the bearing oil clearance - be sure to measure the widest part of the Plastigage and use the correct scale; it comes

with the journal axis as shown (see illustration).

18 Clean the faces of the bearing inserts in the main bearing caps. Hold the bearing inserts in place and install the assembly onto the crankshaft and cylinder block. DO NOT disturb the Plastigage. Make sure you install the main bearing caps with the arrows facing the front (timing belt end) of the engine.

19 Apply clean engine oil to all bolt threads prior to installation, then install all bolts finger-tight. Tighten the main bearing cap bolts (the 8 main bolts followed by the 8 side bolts) in the sequence shown (see illustration) progressing in steps, to the torque listed in this Chapter's Specifications. DO NOT rotate the crankshaft at any time during this operation.

20 Remove the bolts in the reverse order of the tightening sequence and carefully lift the main bearing caps straight up and off the block. Do not disturb the Plastigage or rotate the crankshaft. If the main bearing caps are difficult to remove, tap them gently from side-to-side with a soft-face hammer to loosen it.

21 Compare the width of the crushed Plastigage on each journal to the scale printed on the Plastigage envelope to determine the main bearing oil clearance (see illustration). Check with an automotive machine shop for the oil clearance for your engine.

GLOSSARY

B

Backlash - The amount of play between two parts. Usually refers to how much one gear can be moved back and forth without moving the gear with which it's meshed.

Bearing Caps - The caps held in place by nuts or bolts which, in turn, hold the bearing surface. This space is for lubricating oil to enter.

Bearing clearance - The amount of space left between shaft and bearing surface. This space is for lubricating oil to enter.

Bearing crush - The additional height which is purposely manufactured into each bearing half to ensure complete contact of the bearing back with the housing bore when the engine is assembled.

Bearing knock - The noise created by movement of a part in a loose or worn bearing.

Blueprinting - Dismantling an engine and reassembling it to EXACT specifications.

Bore - An engine cylinder, or any cylindrical hole; also used to describe the process of enlarging or accurately refinishing a hole with a cutting tool, as to bore an engine cylinder. The bore size is the diameter of the hole.

Boring - Renewing the cylinders by cutting them out to a specified size. A boring bar is used to make the cut.

Bottom end - A term which refers collectively to the engine block, crankshaft, main bearings and the big ends of the connecting rods.

Break-in - The period of operation between installation of new or rebuilt parts and time in which parts are worn to the correct fit. Driving at reduced and varying speed for a specified mileage to permit parts to wear to the correct fit.

Bushing - A one-piece sleeve placed in a bore to serve as a bearing surface for shaft, piston pin, etc. Usually replaceable.

C

Camshaft - The shaft in the engine, on which a series of lobes are located for operating the valve mechanisms. The camshaft is driven by gears or sprockets and a timing chain. Usually referred to simply as the cam.

Carbon - Hard, or soft, black deposits found in combustion chamber, on plugs, under rings, on and under valve heads.

Cast iron - An alloy of iron and more than two percent carbon, used for engine blocks and heads because it's relatively inexpensive and easy to mold into complex shapes.

Chamfer - To bevel across (or a bevel on) the sharp edge of an object.

Chase - To repair damaged threads with a tap or die.

Combustion chamber - The space between the piston and the cylinder head, with the piston at top dead center, in which air-fuel mixture is burned.

Compression ratio - The relationship between cylinder volume (clearance volume) when the piston is at top dead center and cylinder volume when the piston is at bottom dead center.

Connecting rod - The rod that connects the crank on the crankshaft with the piston. Sometimes called a con rod.

Connecting rod cap - The part of the connecting rod assembly that attaches the rod to the crankpin.

Core plug - Soft metal plug used to plug the casting holes for the coolant passages in the block.

Crankcase - The lower part of the engine in which the crankshaft rotates; includes the lower section of the cylinder block and the oil pan.

Crank kit - A reground or reconditioned crankshaft and new main and connecting rod bearings.

Crankpin - The part of a crankshaft to which a connecting rod is attached.

Crankshaft - The main rotating member, or shaft, running the length of the crankcase, with offset throws to which the connecting rods are attached; changes the reciprocating motion of the pistons into rotating motion.

Cylinder sleeve - A replaceable sleeve, or liner, pressed into the cylinder block to form the cylinder bore.

D

Deburring - Removing the burrs (rough edges or areas) from a bearing.

Deglazer - A tool, rotated by an electric motor, used to remove glaze from cylinder walls so a new set of rings will seat.

E

Endplay - The amount of lengthwise movement between two parts. As applied to a crankshaft, the distance that the crankshaft can move forward and back in the cylinder block.

F

Face - A machinist's term that refers to removing metal from the end of a shaft or the face of a larger part, such as a flywheel.

Fatigue - A breakdown of material through a large number of loading and unloading cycles. The first signs are cracks followed shortly by breaks.

Feeler gauge - A thin strip of hardened steel, ground to an exact thickness, used to check clearances between parts.

Free height - The unloaded length or height of a spring.

Freeplay - The looseness in a linkage, or an assembly of parts, between the initial application of force and actual movement. Usually perceived as slop or slight delay.

Freeze plug - See Core plug.

G

Gallery - A large passage in the block that forms a reservoir for engine oil pressure.

Glaze - The very smooth, glassy finish that develops on cylinder walls while an engine is in service.

H

Heli-Coil - A rethreading device used when threads are worn or damaged. The device is installed in a retapped hole to reduce the thread size to the original size.

I

Installed height - The spring's measured length or height, as installed on the cylinder head. Installed height is measured from the spring seat to the underside of the spring retainer.

J

Journal - The surface of a rotating shaft which turns in a bearing.

K

Keeper - The split lock that holds the valve spring retainer in position on the valve stem.

Key - A small piece of metal inserted into matching grooves machined into two parts fitted together - such as a gear pressed onto a shaft - which prevents slippage between the two parts.

Knock - The heavy metallic engine sound, produced in the combustion chamber as a result of abnormal combustion - usually detonation. Knock is usually caused by a loose or worn bearing. Also referred to as detonation, pinging and spark knock. Connecting rod or main bearing knocks are created by too much oil clearance or insufficient lubrication.

L

Lands - The portions of metal between the piston ring grooves.

Lapping the valves - Grinding a valve face and its seat together with lapping compound.

Lash - The amount of free motion in a gear train, between gears, or in a mechanical assembly, that occurs before movement can begin. Usually refers to the lash in a valve train.

Lifter - The part that rides against the cam to transfer motion to the rest of the valve train.

M

Machining - The process of using a machine to remove metal from a metal part.

Main bearings - The plain, or babbitt, bearings that support the crankshaft.

Main bearing caps - The cast iron caps, bolted to the bottom of the block, that support the main bearings.

O

O.D. - Outside diameter.

Oil gallery - A pipe or drilled passageway in the engine used to carry engine oil from one area to another.

Oil ring - The lower ring, or rings, of a piston; designed to prevent excessive amounts of oil from working up the cylinder walls and into the combustion chamber. Also called an oil-control ring.

Oil seal - A seal which keeps oil from leaking out of a compartment. Usually refers to a dynamic seal around a rotating shaft or other moving part.

O-ring - A type of sealing ring made of a special rubberlike material; in use, the O-ring is compressed into a groove to provide the sealing action.

Overhaul - To completely disassemble a unit, clean and inspect all parts, reassemble it with the original or new parts and make all adjustments necessary for proper operation.

P

Pilot bearing - A small bearing installed in the center of the flywheel (or the rear end of the crankshaft) to support the front end of the input shaft of the transmission.

Pip mark - A little dot or indentation which indicates the top side of a compression ring.

Piston - The cylindrical part, attached to the connecting rod, that moves up and down in the cylinder as the crankshaft rotates. When the fuel charge is fired, the piston transfers the force of the explosion to the connecting rod, then to the crankshaft.

Piston pin (or wrist pin) - The cylindrical and usually hollow steel pin that passes through the piston. The piston pin fastens the piston to the upper end of the connecting rod.

Piston ring - The split ring fitted to the groove in a piston. The ring contacts the sides of the ring groove and also rubs against the cylinder wall, thus sealing space between piston and wall. There are two types of rings: Compression rings seal the compression pressure in the combustion chamber; oil rings scrape excessive oil off the cylinder wall.

Piston ring groove - The slots or grooves cut in piston heads to hold piston rings in position.

Piston skirt - The portion of the piston below the rings and the piston pin hole.

Plastigage - A thin strip of plastic thread, available in different sizes, used for measuring clearances. For example, a strip of plastigage is laid across a bearing journal and mashed as parts are assembled. Then parts are disassembled and the width of the strip is measured to determine clearance between journal and bearing. Commonly used to measure crankshaft main-bearing and connecting rod bearing clearances.

Press-fit - A tight fit between two parts that requires pressure to force the parts together. Also referred to as drive, or force, fit.

Prussian blue - A blue pigment; in solution, useful in determining the area of contact between two surfaces. Prussian blue is commonly used to determine the width and location of the contact area between the valve face and the valve seat.

R

Race (bearing) - The inner or outer ring that provides a contact surface for balls or rollers in bearing.

Ream - To size, enlarge or smooth a hole by using a round cutting tool with fluted edges.

Ring job - The process of reconditioning the cylinders and installing new rings.

Runout - Wobble. The amount a shaft rotates out-of-true.

S

Saddle - The upper main bearing seat.

Scored - Scratched or grooved, as a cylinder wall may be scored by abrasive particles moved up and down by the piston rings.

Scuffing - A type of wear in which there's a transfer of material between parts moving against each other; shows up as pits or grooves in the mating surfaces.

Seat - The surface upon which another part rests or seats. For example, the valve seat is the matched surface upon which the valve face rests. Also used to refer to wearing into a good fit; for example, piston rings seat after a few miles of driving.

Short block - An engine block complete with crankshaft and piston and, usually, camshaft assemblies.

Static balance - The balance of an object while it's stationary.

Step - The wear on the lower portion of a ring land caused by excessive side and back-clearance. The height of the step indicates the ring's extra side clearance and the length of the step projecting from the back wall of the groove represents the ring's back clearance.

Stroke - The distance the piston moves when traveling from top dead center to bottom dead center, or from bottom dead center to top dead center.

Stud - A metal rod with threads on both ends.

T

Tang - A lip on the end of a plain bearing used to align the bearing during assembly.

Tap - To cut threads in a hole. Also refers to the fluted tool used to cut threads.

Taper - A gradual reduction in the width of a shaft or hole; in an engine cylinder, taper usually takes the form of uneven wear, more pronounced at the top than at the bottom.

Throws - The offset portions of the crankshaft to which the connecting rods are affixed.

Thrust bearing - The main bearing that has thrust faces to prevent excessive endplay, or forward and backward movement of the crankshaft.

Thrust washer - A bronze or hardened steel washer placed between two moving parts. The washer prevents longitudinal movement and provides a bearing surface for thrust surfaces of parts.

Tolerance - The amount of variation permitted from an exact size of measurement. Actual amount from smallest acceptable dimension to largest acceptable dimension.

U

Umbrella - An oil deflector placed near the valve tip to throw oil from the valve stem area.

Undercut - A machined groove below the normal surface.

Undersize bearings - Smaller diameter bearings used with re-ground crankshaft journals.

V

Valve grinding - Refacing a valve in a valve-refacing machine.

Valve train - The valve-operating mechanism of an engine; includes all components from the camshaft to the valve.

Vibration damper - A cylindrical weight attached to the front of the crankshaft to minimize torsional vibration (the twist-untwist actions of the crankshaft caused by the cylinder firing impulses). Also called a harmonic balancer.

W

Water jacket - The spaces around the cylinders, between the inner and outer shells of the cylinder block or head, through which coolant circulates.

Web - A supporting structure across a cavity.

Woodruff key - A key with a radiused backside (viewed from the side).

22 If the clearance is not as specified, the bearing inserts may be the wrong size (which means different ones will be required). Before deciding if different inserts are needed, make sure that no dirt or oil was between the bearing inserts and the cap or block when the clearance was measured. If the Plastigage was wider at one end than the other, the crankshaft journal may be tapered. If the clearance still exceeds the limit specified, the bearing insert(s) will have to be replaced with an under-size bearing insert(s).

✳ CAUTION:

When installing a new crankshaft always install a standard bearing insert set.

23 Carefully scrape all traces of the Plastigage material off the main bearing journals and/or the bearing insert faces. Be sure to remove all residue from the oil holes. Use your fingernail or the edge of a plastic card - don't nick or scratch the bearing faces.

FINAL INSTALLATION

24 Carefully lift the crankshaft out of the cylinder block.

25 Clean the bearing insert faces in the cylinder block, then apply a thin, uniform layer of moly-base grease or engine assembly lube to each of the bearing surfaces. Be sure to coat the thrust faces as well as the journal face of the thrust bearing.

26 Make sure the crankshaft journals are clean, then lay the crankshaft back in place in the cylinder block.

27 Clean the bearing insert faces and then apply the same lubricant to them. Clean the engine block thoroughly. The surfaces must be free of oil residue.

28 Assemble the main bearing caps and bearings and install each main bearing cap onto the crankshaft and cylinder block. Make sure the arrows face the front (timing belt) of the engine.

29 Prior to installation, apply clean engine oil to all bolt threads wiping off any excess, then install all bolts finger-tight.

30 Torque the main bearing cap bolts followed by the side bolts in the correct sequence (see illustration 10.19).

31 Recheck crankshaft endplay with a feeler gauge or a dial indicator. The endplay should be correct if the crankshaft thrust faces aren't worn or damaged and if new bearings have been installed.

32 Rotate the crankshaft a number of times by hand to check for any obvious binding. It should rotate with a running torque of 50 in-lbs or less. If the running torque is too high, correct the problem at this time.

33 Install the new rear main oil seal (see Chapter 2A).

11 Engine overhaul - reassembly sequence

1 Before beginning engine reassembly, make sure you have all the necessary new parts, gaskets and seals as well as the following items on hand:

> Common hand tools
> A 1/2-inch drive torque wrench
> New engine oil
> Gasket sealant
> Thread locking compound

2 If you obtained a short block it will be necessary to install the cylinder heads, the oil pump and pick-up tube, the oil pan, the water pump, the timing belt and timing covers, and the valve covers (see Chapter 2A). In order to save time and avoid problems, the external components must be installed in the following general order:

> Thermostat and housing cover
> Water pump
> Intake and exhaust manifolds
> Fuel injection components
> Emission control components
> Spark plugs
> Ignition coils
> Oil filter
> Engine mounts and mount brackets
> Driveplate

12 Initial start-up and break-in after overhaul

✳ WARNING:

Have a fire extinguisher handy when starting the engine for the first time.

1 Once the engine has been installed in the vehicle, double-check the engine oil and coolant levels.

2 With the spark plugs out of the engine and the ignition system and fuel pump disabled (see Section 3), crank the engine until oil pressure registers on the gauge or the light goes out.

3 Install the spark plugs, hook up the plug wires and restore the ignition system and fuel pump functions.

4 Start the engine. It may take a few moments for the fuel system to build up pressure, but the engine should start without a great deal of effort.

5 After the engine starts, it should be allowed to warm up to normal operating temperature. While the engine is warming up, make a thorough check for fuel, oil and coolant leaks.

6 Shut the engine off and recheck the engine oil and coolant levels.

7 Drive the vehicle to an area with minimum traffic, accelerate from 30 to 50 mph, then allow the vehicle to slow to 30 mph with the throttle closed. Repeat the procedure 10 or 12 times. This will load the piston rings and cause them to seat properly against the cylinder walls. Check again for oil and coolant leaks.

8 Drive the vehicle gently for the first 500 miles (no sustained high speeds) and keep a constant check on the oil level. It is not unusual for an engine to use oil during the break-in period.

9 At approximately 500 to 600 miles, change the oil and filter.

10 For the next few hundred miles, drive the vehicle normally. Do not pamper it or abuse it.

11 After 2000 miles, change the oil and filter again and consider the engine broken in.

Specifications

General

Bore	3.5 inches (89.0 mm)
Stroke	Not available
Displacement	214 cubic inches (3.5 liters)
Cylinder compression pressure	135 to 163 psi (930 to 1,130 kPa)
Oil pressure at 178-degrees F (80-degrees C)	
At curb idle	10 psi (78 kPa)
At 3,000 rpm	71 psi (490 kPa)

Torque specifications	Ft-lbs (unless otherwise indicated)	Nm
Connecting rod bearing cap bolts		
Step 1	14	20
Step 2	Tighten an additional 1/4-turn (90-degrees)	
Main bearing caps (see illustration 10.19)		
Main bolts		
2004 and earlier models	56	76
2005 and later models	54	73
Side bolts	36	49
Subframe mounting bolts (see illustration 7.44c)		
Large bolts (A)*	76	103
Bracket bolts		
Bolts B	54	74
Bolts C	86	117

*Replace with New bolts

Notes

Notes

Notes

3

COOLING, HEATING AND AIR CONDITIONING SYSTEMS

1 General information

ENGINE COOLING SYSTEM

♦ **Refer to illustrations 1.1 and 1.2**

All vehicles covered by this manual employ a pressurized engine cooling system with thermostatically controlled coolant circulation (see illustration). An impeller-type water pump mounted on the engine block pumps coolant through the engine. The coolant flows around each cylinder and toward the rear of the engine. Cast-in coolant passages direct coolant around the intake and exhaust ports, near the spark plug areas and in close proximity to the exhaust valve guides.

A wax-pellet type thermostat controls engine coolant temperature. During warm up, the closed thermostat prevents coolant from circulating through the radiator. As the engine nears normal operating temperature, the thermostat opens and allows hot coolant to travel through the radiator, where it's cooled before returning to the engine (see illustration).

The cooling system is sealed by a pressure-type radiator cap, which raises the boiling point of the coolant and increases the cooling efficiency of the radiator. If the system pressure exceeds the cap pressure relief value, the excess pressure in the system forces the spring-loaded valve inside the cap off its seat and allows the coolant to escape through the overflow tube into a coolant reservoir. When the system cools the excess coolant is automatically drawn from the reservoir back into the radiator.

The coolant reservoir serves as both the point at which fresh coolant is added to the cooling system to maintain the proper fluid level and as a holding tank for overheated coolant.

This type of cooling system is known as a closed design because coolant that escapes past the pressure cap is saved and reused.

ENGINE COOLING FANS

These models are equipped with two electric cooling fans; a radiator fan and a condenser fan. The fans are controlled by relays, fans switches and the computer. There are two fan switches that detect the temperature of the coolant. Fan switch A is located in the thermostat housing and fan switch B is located in the cylinder head near the timing belt. The radiator fan main relay is located in a box directly in front of the engine compartment relay box. There is also a radiator fan relay and a condenser fan relay located in the engine compartment relay box. The computer uses the information from the fan switches, the air conditioning system and the on-board driveability computer to control the application of the two fans.

HEATING SYSTEM

The heating system consists of a blower fan and heater core located in the heater box, the hoses connecting the heater core to the engine cooling system and the heater/air conditioning control head on the dashboard. Hot engine coolant is circulated through the heater core. When the heater mode is activated, a flap door opens to expose the heater box to the passenger compartment. A fan switch on the control head activates the blower motor, which forces air through the core, heating the air.

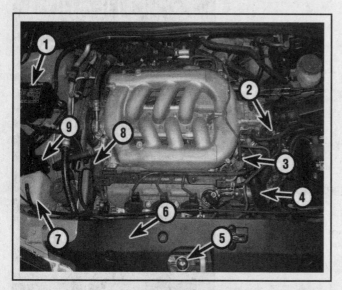

1.1 Cooling, heating and air conditioning underhood components

1. *Fuse and relay box*
2. *Radiator fan switch A (on thermostat housing)*
3. *ECT sensor*
4. *Radiator hose*
5. *Radiator cap*
6. *Radiator cover*
7. *Coolant reservoir*
8. *Radiator fan switch B (on cylinder head behind the camshaft sprocket)*
9. *Radiator fan main relay box*

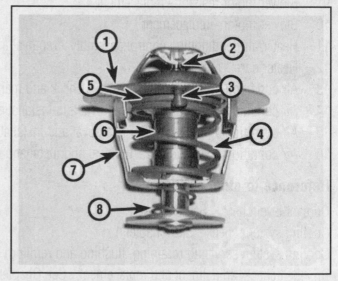

1.2 Typical thermostat

1	*Flange*	5	*Valve seat*
2	*Piston*	6	*Valve*
3	*Jiggle pin*	7	*Frame*
4	*Main coil spring*	8	*Secondary coil spring*

AIR CONDITIONING SYSTEM

The air conditioning system consists of a condenser mounted in front of the radiator, an evaporator mounted adjacent to the heater core, a compressor mounted on the engine, a receiver-drier built into the condenser and the plumbing connecting all of the above components.

A blower fan forces the warmer air of the passenger compartment through the evaporator core (sort of a radiator-in-reverse), transferring the heat from the air to the refrigerant. The liquid refrigerant boils off into low pressure vapor, taking the heat with it when it leaves the evaporator.

2 Antifreeze - general information

▶ **Refer to illustration 2.5**

❋❋ WARNING:

Do not allow antifreeze to come in contact with your skin or painted surfaces of the vehicle. Rinse off spills immediately with plenty of water. Antifreeze is highly toxic if ingested. Never leave antifreeze lying around in an open container or in puddles on the floor; children and pets are attracted by its sweet smell and may drink it. Check with local authorities about disposing of used antifreeze. Many communities have collection centers which will see that antifreeze is disposed of safely. Never dump used antifreeze on the ground or pour it into drains.

❋❋ CAUTION:

Do not mix coolants of different colors. Doing so might damage the cooling system and/or the engine. The manufacturer specifies either a green colored coolant or a yellow colored coolant to be used in these systems. Read the warning label in the engine compartment for additional information.

➡ **Note: Non-toxic antifreeze is now manufactured and available at local auto parts stores, but even this type must be disposed of properly.**

The cooling system should be filled with a water/ethylene glycol based antifreeze solution, which will prevent freezing down to at least -20-degrees F (even lower in cold climates). It also provides protection against corrosion and increases the coolant boiling point. The engines in these vehicles have aluminum heads. The manufacturer recommends that the correct type of coolant be used and strongly urges that coolant types not be mixed (see Chapter 1 Specifications).

Drain, flush and refill the cooling system at least every other year (see Chapter 1). The use of antifreeze solutions for periods of longer than two years is likely to cause damage and encourage the formation of rust and scale in the system.

Before adding antifreeze to the system, inspect all hose connections. Antifreeze can leak through very minute openings.

The exact mixture of antifreeze to water, which you should use, depends on the relative weather conditions. The mixture should contain at least 50-percent antifreeze, but should never contain more than 70-percent anti-freeze. Consult the mixture ratio chart on the container before adding coolant.

Hydrometers are available at most auto parts stores to test the coolant (see illustration). Use antifreeze that meets factory specifications for engines with aluminum heads (see Chapter 1).

2.5 Use a hydrometer (available at most auto parts stores) to test the condition of your coolant

3 Thermostat - check and replacement

❋❋ WARNING:

Do not remove the radiator cap, drain the coolant or replace the thermostat until the engine has cooled completely.

CHECK

1 Before assuming the thermostat is to blame for a cooling system problem, check the coolant level, drivebelt tension (see Chapter 1) and temperature gauge operation.

➡ **Note: These models use the coolant temperature sensor (ECT) to read coolant temperature for the temperature gauge.**

2 If the engine seems to be taking a long time to warm up, based on heater output or temperature gauge operation, the thermostat is probably stuck open. Replace the thermostat with a new one.

3 If the engine runs hot, use your hand to check the temperature of the lower radiator hose. If the hose isn't hot, but the engine is, the

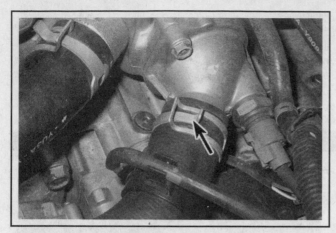

3.8 Use pliers to squeeze the coolant hose clamp and slide the clamp away from the thermostat housing

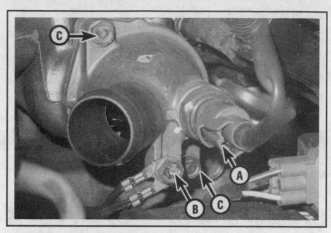

3.11 To replace the thermostat, remove the radiator fan switch connector (A), the bolt for the ground terminals (B) and the thermostat cover mounting bolts (C)

3.12 Note the location of the jiggle pin and the alignment tang on the rubber gasket

3.14a Install a new rubber seal over the thermostat

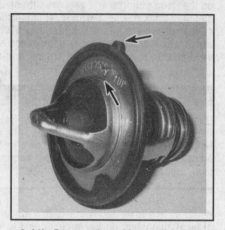

3.14b Be sure the rubber gasket is aligned properly with the rubber tang directly over the jiggle pin located at the top of the thermostat

thermostat is probably stuck closed, preventing the coolant inside the engine from escaping to the radiator. Replace the thermostat.

> ❄ **CAUTION:**
>
> **Don't drive the vehicle without a thermostat. The computer may stay in open loop and emissions and fuel economy will suffer.**

4   If the lower radiator hose is hot, it means that the coolant is flowing and the thermostat is open. Consult the *Troubleshooting* Section at the front of this manual for cooling system diagnosis.

REPLACEMENT

◆ **Refer to illustrations 3.8, 3.11, 3.12, 3.14a and 3.14b**

5   Disconnect the cable from the negative battery terminal (see Chapter 5, Section 1).
6   Drain the cooling system (see Chapter 1). If the coolant is relatively new or in good condition (see Chapter 1), save it and reuse it. Read the **Warning** in Section 2.

7   Remove the battery (see Chapter 5).
8   Follow the lower radiator hose to the engine to locate the thermostat housing cover (see illustration).
9   Loosen the hose clamp, then detach the hose from the fitting. If it's stuck, grasp it near the end with a pair of adjustable pliers and twist it to break the seal, then pull it off. If the hose is old or deteriorated, cut it off and install a new one.
10   If the outer surface of the large fitting that mates with the hose is deteriorated (corroded, pitted, etc.) it may be damaged further by hose removal. If it is, the thermostat housing cover will have to be replaced.
11   Remove the thermostat cover bolts (see illustration) and detach the housing cover. If the cover is stuck, tap it with a soft-face hammer to jar it loose. Be prepared for some coolant to spill as the gasket seal is broken.
12   Note how it's installed - with the jiggle pin up - then remove the thermostat (see illustration).
13   Remove all traces of old gasket material and/or sealant from the housing and cover.
14   Install a new rubber seal over the thermostat (see illustration). Make sure the seal is aligned correctly with the rubber tang located directly above the jiggle pin (see illustration).

15 Install the new thermostat in the housing without using sealant. Make sure the jiggle pin is at the top and the spring end is directed into the engine (see illustration 3.12).

16 Install the housing cover and bolts. Tighten the bolts to the torque listed in this Chapter's Specifications.

17 Reattach the hose and tighten the hose clamp securely. Install all components that were removed for access.

18 Refill the cooling system (see Chapter 1).

19 Reconnect the battery (see Chapter 5, Section 1).

20 Start the engine and allow it to reach normal operating temperature, then check for leaks and proper thermostat operation (as described in Steps 3 and 4).

4 Engine cooling fans - check and replacement

✳ WARNING:

To avoid possible injury or damage, DO NOT operate the engine with a damaged fan. Do not attempt to repair fan blades - replace a damaged fan with a new one.

➡ **Note: All models have two complete fan circuits - one for the condenser and one for the radiator. The following procedures apply to both.**

CHECK

▸ **Refer to illustrations 4.1a, 4.1b, 4.3 and 4.5**

1 If the engine is overheating and the cooling fan is not coming on when the engine temperature rises to an excessive level, check all the fuses first. If the fuses are okay, unplug the fan motor electrical connector (see illustrations) and then connect the motor directly to the battery with a fused jumper wire on terminal A. Use another jumper wire to ground terminal B. If the fan motor doesn't come on, replace the motor. These models are equipped with a separate fan for the condenser. If the radiator fan motor checks out okay, be sure to test the condenser fan motor.

✳ CAUTION:

Do not apply battery power to the harness side of the connector. Be sure to test the cooling fan motor only.

2 If the radiator fan motor is okay, but it isn't coming on when the engine gets hot, the fan relay(s) (radiator fan, condenser fan and main relay) might be defective.

3 Locate the fan relays in the engine compartment fuse/relay box (see illustration 1.1).

➡ **Note: The radiator and condenser fan relays are located in the engine compartment fuse/relay box. The radiator fan main relay is located in the box directly in front of the fuse/relay box (see illustration).**

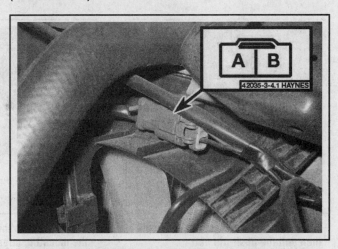

4.1a To test either fan motor, disconnect the electrical connector and use jumper wires to connect the fan directly to the battery (A) and ground (B) - if the fan still doesn't work, replace the motor (condenser fan shown)

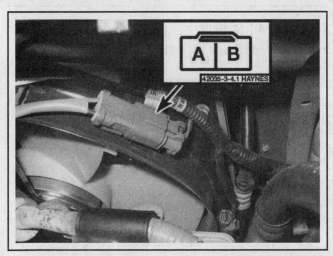

4.1b The location of the radiator fan connector

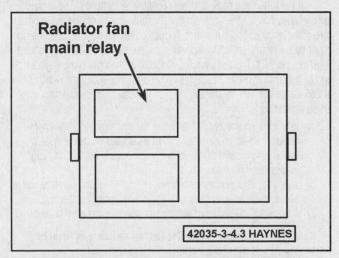

4.3 The radiator fan main relay is located in a small relay box underneath the cruise control actuator

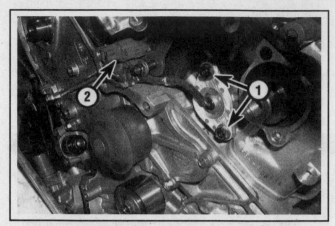

4.5 Fan switch B (the one that operates the radiator fan) is located at the front of the forward cylinder head and is retained by two bolts (1). The electrical connector (2) is located below the power steering pump (which has been removed for clarity)

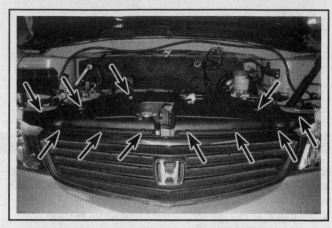

4.9a Location of the radiator cover mounting fasteners

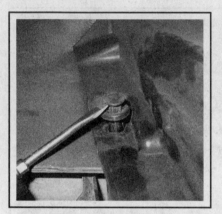

4.9b Lift up on the center release pin then pull the push-pin out

4.11a Remove the vacuum hose from the mounting clips and position the vacuum hose away from the radiator bracket

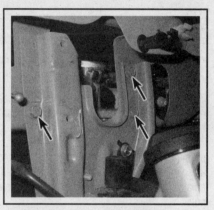

4.11b Location of the radiator bracket mounting bolts

4   Test the relay (see Chapter 12).

5   If the relays are okay, test the radiator fan switches. The radiator fan switches control the operation of the fans according to the temperature of the engine. The fan switch A (located on the thermostat housing cover [see illustration 3.11]) activates the condenser fan at 196 degrees F (91 degrees C). The fan switch B (located at the right [passenger's] end of the front cylinder head [see illustration]) operates the radiator fan at 205-degrees F (96-degrees C). These switches can be checked with an ohmmeter as follows:

a)   *When the engine is cold, or when the temperature of the engine coolant is 5 to 15-degrees F (3 to 8-degrees C) below the activation temperature stated above, there should be no continuity across the switch terminals.*

b)   *When the engine coolant reaches the activation temperature stated above, there should be continuity across the switch terminals.*

c)   *If the switch doesn't react like this, it's defective and must be replaced.*

➡ **Note:** *The electrical connector for fan switch B is located below the power steering pump.*

6   If the relay(s) and the fan switches are okay, check all wiring and connections to the fan motors.

REPLACEMENT

2004 and earlier models

▶ **Refer to illustrations 4.9a, 4.9b, 4.11a, 4.11b, 4.14a, 4.14b, 4.16a and 4.16b**

7   Disconnect the cable from the negative battery terminal (see Chapter 5, Section 1).

8   Set the parking brake and block the rear wheels to prevent the vehicle from rolling. Raise the front of the vehicle and support it securely with jackstands. Remove the lower splash pan, if equipped, from under the radiator.

9   Remove the radiator cover (see illustrations).

10   Drain the cooling system (see Chapter 1). If the coolant is relatively new or in good condition, save it and reuse it. Read the Warning in Section 2.

11   Remove the wiring harness clamp and position the harness off to the side. Remove the vacuum hose from the clamps along the bracket (see illustration). Remove the radiator bracket (see illustration).

12   Remove the battery, the battery tray and position the wiring har-

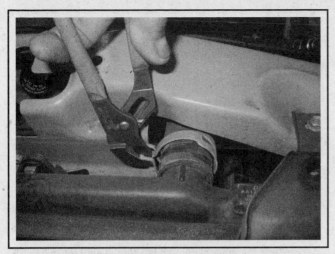

4.14a Use pliers to squeeze the hose clamp and slide the clamp off the inlet housing (neck) of the radiator

4.14b Location of the lower radiator hose clamp

4.16a Location of the radiator brackets (B) and the condenser brackets (A) (2004 and earlier models)

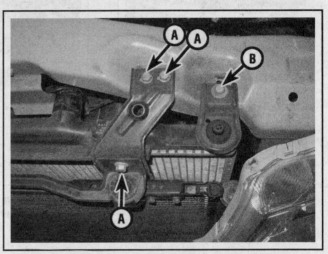

4.16b Locations for the radiator bracket bolt (B) and the condenser brackets bolts (A) (2004 and earlier models)

ness off to the side (see Chapter 5). Remove the relay box bracket and the ground cable.

13 Disconnect the fan wiring connectors (see illustrations 4.1a and 4.1b).

14 Remove the upper and lower radiator hoses. Loosen the hose clamps, then detach the radiator hoses from the fittings (see illustrations). If they're stuck, grasp each hose near the end with a pair of slip-joint pliers and twist it to break the seal, then pull it off - be careful not to damage the radiator fittings! If the hoses are old or deteriorated, cut them off and install new ones. Also disconnect the small hose to the coolant reservoir.

15 Disconnect the automatic transaxle hoses from the radiator and

plug them (see Chapter 7).

16 Remove the radiator and condenser brackets (see illustration).

2005 and later models

17 Disconnect the breather hose and the air intake duct (see Chapter 4).

18 Remove the battery and the battery tray (see Chapter 5).

19 On 2005 through 2007 models, remove the grille top cover (see Chapter 11). On 2008 and later models, remove the front bumper cover (see Chapter 11).

20 Disconnect the interfering hoses, wiring and wiring clamps.

21 Remove the coolant reservoir (see Section 5).

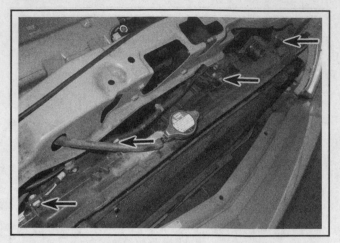

4.22 Location of the condenser fan and radiator fan mounting bolts (2004 and earlier models)

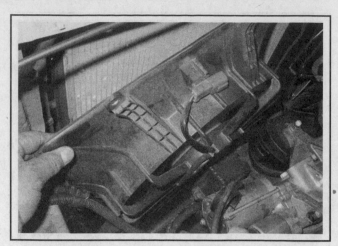

4.23a Slide the radiator cooling fan shroud until it can be removed through the cutout in the radiator support structure

4.23b Move the condenser fan down and away from the radiator support structure

4.24 To remove the fan, unscrew the nut in the center, then pull the fan blade from the motor shaft

4.25 Location of the engine cooling fan motor mounting screws

All models

▶ **Refer to illustrations 4.22, 4.23a, 4.23b, 4.24 and 4.25**

22 Remove the upper bolts and loosen the lower bolts of each fan shroud (see illustration).

23 Carefully lift the fan(s) out of the engine compartment (see illustrations).

➡ **Note: On 2004 and earlier models, the cruise control cable must first be detached from its clips.**

24 To detach the fan from the motor, remove the motor shaft nut (see illustration).

25 To detach the fan motor from the shroud, remove the mounting screws (see illustration).

26 Installation is the reverse of removal.

27 Reconnect the battery (see Chapter 5, Section 1).

5   Coolant reservoir - removal and installation

▶ **Refer to illustrations 5.1 and 5.2**

✳ WARNING:

Wait until the engine is completely cool before beginning this procedure.

1   Disconnect the reservoir hose (see illustration). Plug the hose to prevent leakage.

2   On 2004 and earlier models, lift the reservoir out of its bracket (see illustration). On 2005 and later models, remove the two mounting screws, then lift the reservoir out.

3   Clean out the tank with soapy water and a brush to remove any deposits inside. Inspect the reservoir carefully for cracks. If you find a crack, replace the reservoir.

4   Installation is the reverse of removal.

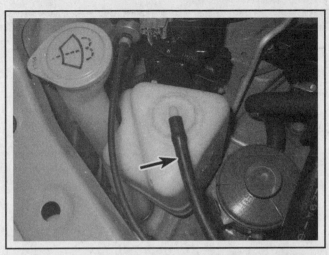

5.1 Disconnect the coolant hose from the top of the reservoir

5.2 Lift the coolant reservoir straight up out of its bracket

6 Radiator - removal and installation

✳✳ WARNING:

Wait until the engine is completely cool before beginning this procedure.

REMOVAL

2004 and earlier models

1 Disconnect the cable from the negative battery terminal (see Chapter 5, Section 1).

2 Set the parking brake and block the rear wheels. Raise the front of the vehicle and support it securely on jackstands. Remove the splash shield beneath the radiator (see Chapter 2A).

3 Drain the cooling system (see Chapter 1). If the coolant is relatively new or in good condition, save it and reuse it. Read the **Warning** in Section 2.

4 Remove the engine cooling fans (see Section 4).

2005 and later models

5 Drain the coolant (see Chapter 1). If it's in good condition, save it for reuse. See the **Warning** in Section 2.

6 Remove both fan assemblies (see Section 4).

7 Disconnect both radiator hoses and the transmission cooler lines. Plug the transmission cooler openings to prevent contamination.

8 Remove the two upper mounting brackets.

9 Remove the hood latch (see Chapter 11).

All models

▶ **Refer to illustration 6.13**

10 Carefully lift out the radiator. Don't spill coolant on the vehicle or scratch the paint.

11 Inspect the radiator for leaks and damage. If it needs repair, have a radiator shop or dealer service department perform the work as special techniques are required.

12 Bugs and dirt can be removed from the radiator by spraying with a garden hose nozzle from the back side. The radiator should be flushed out with a garden hose before reinstallation.

13 Check the radiator mounts for deterioration (see illustration) and replace if necessary.

INSTALLATION

14 Installation is the reverse of the removal procedure. Guide the radiator into the mounts until they seat properly.

15 Tighten the radiator bracket bolts to the torque listed in this Chapter's Specifications.

16 After installation, fill the cooling system with the proper mixture of antifreeze and water (see Chapter 1).

17 Reconnect the battery (see Chapter 5, Section 1).

18 Start the engine and check for leaks. Allow the engine to reach normal operating temperature, indicated by the lower radiator hose becoming hot. Recheck the coolant level and add more if required.

19 Check and add transaxle fluid as needed (see Chapter 1).

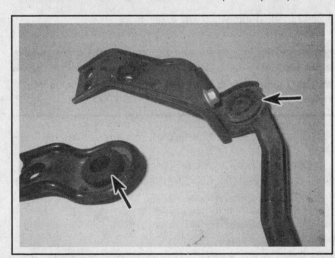

6.13 Location of the radiator bracket rubber mounts (2004 and earlier models)

7 Water pump - check

▶ **Refer to illustration 7.3**

1 A failure in the water pump can cause serious engine damage due to overheating.

2 There are two ways to check the operation of the water pump while it's installed on the engine. If the pump is defective, it should be replaced with a new or rebuilt unit.

3 Water pumps are equipped with weep (or vent) holes (see illustration). If a failure occurs in the pump seal, coolant will leak from the hole. With the timing belt cover removed, you'll need a flashlight and small mirror to find the hole on the water pump from underneath to check for leaks.

4 If the water pump shaft bearings fail, there may be a howling sound at the pump while it's running. Shaft wear can be felt with the timing belt removed if the water pump pulley is rocked up and down (with the engine off). Don't mistake drivebelt slippage, which causes a squealing sound, for water pump bearing failure.

5 Even a pump that exhibits no outward signs of a problem, such as noise or leakage, can still be due for replacement. Removal for close examination is the only sure way to tell. Sometimes the fins on the back of the impeller can corrode to the point that cooling efficiency is hampered.

7.3 The weep hole on the underside of the pump - you'll need a flashlight and small mirror to inspect it (with the timing belt removed)

8 Water pump - replacement

▶ **Refer to illustrations 8.5 and 8.10**

✳✳ WARNING:

Wait until the engine is completely cool before beginning this procedure.

1 Disconnect the cable from the negative battery terminal (see Chapter 5, Section 1).

2 Drain the cooling system (see Chapter 1). If the coolant is relatively new or in good condition, save it and reuse it. Read the **Warning** in Section 2.

3 Remove the drivebelts (see Chapter 1).

4 Remove the timing belt (see Chapter 2A), and remove the timing belt tensioner.

5 Remove the bolts (see illustration) and detach the water pump from the engine. Check the impeller for evidence of corrosion or missing fins.

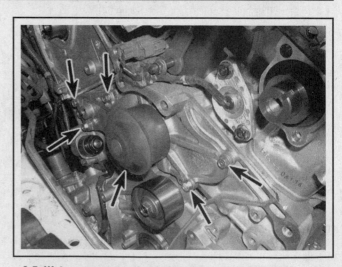

8.5 Water pump mounting bolts - one bottom bolt isn't visible in this photo

6   Clean the bolt threads and the threaded holes in the engine to remove corrosion and sealant.

7   Compare the new pump to the old one to make sure they're identical.

8   Remove all traces of old gasket sealant and O-ring from the engine.

9   Clean the engine and new water pump mating surfaces with lacquer thinner or acetone.

10 Apply a thin layer of RTV sealant to the O-ring groove of the new pump, then carefully set a new O-ring in the groove (see illustration).

11 Carefully attach the pump to the engine and thread the bolts into the holes finger tight. Use a small amount of RTV sealant on the bolt threads, and make sure that the dowel pins are in their original locations.

12 Install the remaining bolts. Tighten the bolts to the torque listed in this Chapter's Specifications in 1/4-turn increments. Don't overtighten the bolts or the pump may be distorted.

13 Reinstall all parts removed for access to the pump.

14 Refill and bleed the cooling system and check the drivebelt tension (see Chapter 1). Run the engine and check for leaks.

15 Reconnect the battery (see Chapter 5, Section 1).

8.10 Apply a thin layer of RTV sealant to the O-ring groove of the new pump, then carefully set a new O-ring in the groove

9   Blower motor resistor - replacement

✳✳ WARNING:

The models covered by this manual are equipped with Supplemental Restraint systems (SRS), more commonly known as airbags. Always disable the airbag system before working in the vicinity of any airbag system component to avoid the possibility of accidental deployment of the airbag, which could cause personal injury (see Chapter 12).

FRONT AIR CONDITIONING SYSTEMS

▶ **Refer to illustration 9.1**

1   Working in the passenger compartment under the glovebox, disconnect the electrical connector from the blower motor resistor (see illustration).

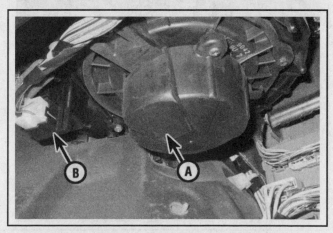

9.1 Location of the front blower motor assembly (A) and the blower motor resistor (B)

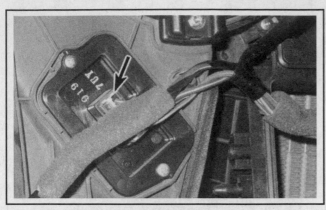

9.6 Disconnect the rear blower motor resistor electrical connector

2   Remove the blower motor resistor mounting screws and remove the resistor from the blower housing (see illustration 9.1).

3   Installation is the reverse of removal.

REAR AIR CONDITIONING SYSTEMS

▶ **Refer to illustration 9.6**

4   Remove the rear trim panels (see Chapter 11).

5   Remove the blower motor housing to access the resistor (see Section 10).

6   Disconnect the electrical connector from the blower motor resistor (see illustration).

7   Remove the blower motor resistor mounting screws (see illustration 10.8) and remove the resistor from the blower housing.

8   Installation is the reverse of removal.

---

10 Blower motor - replacement

FRONT AIR CONDITIONING SYSTEMS

▶ **Refer to illustrations 10.1 and 10.3**

1   Working in the passenger compartment under the glovebox, disconnect the electrical connector from the blower motor (see illustration).

2   Remove the blower motor mounting screws and then remove the blower motor assembly (see illustration 9.1).

3   Remove the blower motor circlip (see illustration) and remove the blower fan from the motor.

4   Installation is the reverse of removal.

REAR AIR CONDITIONING SYSTEMS

▶ **Refer to illustrations 10.6, 10.7 and 10.8**

5   Remove the rear trim panels (see Chapter 11).

6   Remove the heater blower housing mounting bolts (see illustration).

7   Disconnect the blower motor electrical connector (see illustration).

8   Remove the blower motor mounting screws (see illustration) and then remove the blower motor.

9   Remove the blower motor circlip (see illustration 10.3) and remove the blower fan from the motor.

10 Installation is the reverse of removal.

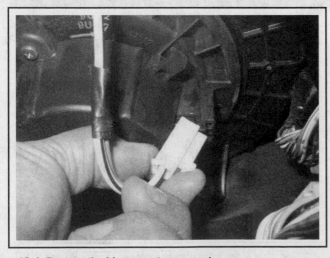

10.1 Remove the blower motor connector

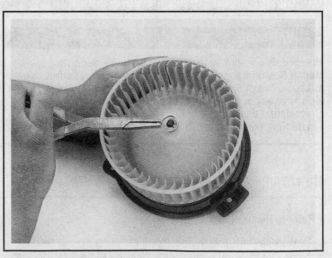

10.3 Use pliers to remove the circlip from the motor shaft and lift the blower fan from the assembly

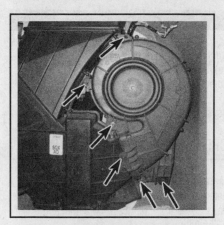

10.6 Location of the rear blower motor housing mounting bolts

10.7 Disconnect the blower motor electrical connector

10.8 Location of the rear blower motor mounting screws

11 Heater/air conditioning control assembly - removal and installation

✳✳ WARNING:

The models covered by this manual are equipped with Supplemental Restraint systems (SRS), more commonly known as airbags. Always disable the airbag system before working in the vicinity of any airbag system component to avoid the possibility of accidental deployment of the airbag, which could cause personal injury (see Chapter 12).

1 Disconnect the cable from the negative battery terminal (see Chapter 5, Section 1).

FRONT HEATER/AIR CONDITIONING CONTROL ASSEMBLY

▶ **Refer to illustrations 11.3 and 11.4**

2 Remove the dashboard center bezel (see Chapter 11).

3 Disconnect the front blower motor switch and temperature control module connectors (see illustration).

4 Pull off the knobs (2005 and later models only). Remove the heater/air conditioner control assembly retaining screws (see illustration).

5 Installation is the reverse of removal.

REAR HEATER/AIR CONDITIONING CONTROL ASSEMBLY

6 Use a panel tool to pry the control assembly from the body panel.
7 Remove the electrical connectors from the control assembly.
8 Separate the control assembly from the body panel.
9 Installation is the reverse of the removal.

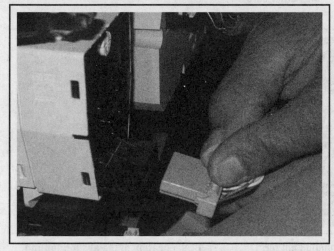

11.3 Disconnect the heater/air conditioning control electrical connectors

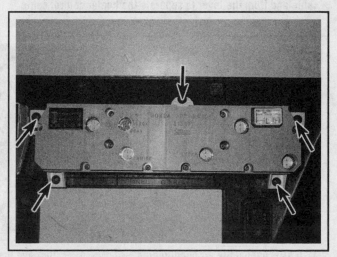

11.4 Location of the control assembly mounting screws - typical

12 Heater core - replacement

✳✳ WARNING:

The models covered by this manual are equipped with Supplemental Restraint systems (SRS), more commonly known as airbags. Always disable the airbag system before working in the vicinity of any airbag system component to avoid the possibility of accidental deployment of the airbag, which could cause personal injury (see Chapter 12).

✳✳ WARNING:

The air conditioning system is under high pressure. DO NOT loosen any fittings or remove any components until after the system has been discharged. Air conditioning refrigerant must be properly discharged into an EPA-approved container at a dealer service department or an automotive air conditioning repair facility. Always wear eye protection when disconnecting air conditioning system fittings.

1   Have the air conditioning system discharged by a dealer service department or by an automotive air conditioning shop before proceeding (see **Warning** above).

2   Disconnect the cable from the negative battery terminal (see Chapter 5, Section 1).

3   Drain the cooling system (see Chapter 1).

FRONT HEATER CORE

▶ **Refer to illustrations 12.4, 12.5, 12.6, 12.7 and 12.9**

4   Disconnect the heater control valve cable (see illustration).

5   Disconnect the heater hoses from the heater core inlet and outlet pipes at the firewall (see illustration).

6   Disconnect the evaporator inlet and outlet air conditioning lines at the engine compartment firewall (see illustration).

7   Remove the mounting nut for the heater unit located in the engine compartment (see illustration).

8   Remove the instrument panel (see Chapter 11).

9   Remove the evaporator unit mounting bolts (see illustration).

10 Remove the evaporator unit from the heater unit.

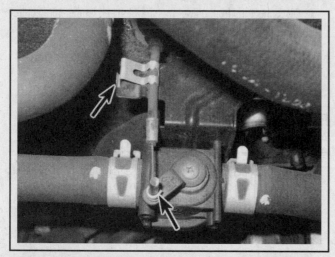

12.4 Release the clip from the cable bracket and lift the cable end from the lever to separate the heater control cable

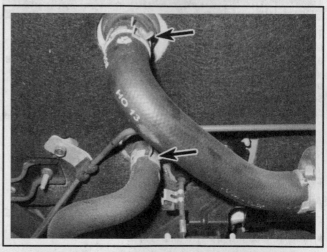

12.5 Release the clamps and separate the heater hoses from the heater core

12.6 Disconnect the air conditioning lines at the firewall

12.7 Remove the mounting nut for the heater unit inside the engine compartment

12.9 Location of the evaporator unit mounting bolts - 2004 and earlier models

11 Remove the heater roof vent cover (see illustration), the heater unit mounting bolts and remove the assembly from the passenger compartment.

12 Remove the heater core cover mounting screws from the clamps and pull the heater core from the housing by carefully gripping the edges to release it from the interior seal.

2005 and later models

13 Detach the condenser drain hose, then remove the entire heater blower assembly.

14 Remove the upper duct fitting from the heater unit.

15 Remove the passenger's air outlet and the cover from the top of the heater core.

16 Detach the heater tube clamps, then pull the heater core out of the case.

All models

17 Installation is the reverse of removal. Don't forget to reconnect the heater core inlet and outlet hoses at the firewall.

18 Reconnect the cable to the negative terminal of the battery (see Chapter 5, Section 1). Refill the cooling system (see Chapter 1). Have the air conditioning system recharged and leak tested by the shop that discharged it.

REAR HEATER CORE

▶ **Refer to illustrations 12.20, 12.21, 12.22 and 12.23**

19 Remove the rear trim panels (see Chapter 11).

20 Disconnect the air conditioning/heater housing electrical connectors (see illustration).

21 Disconnect the air duct from the housing (see illustration).

22 Disconnect the heater hoses (see illustration) and the air conditioning lines from the A/C and heater housing.

23 On 2004 and earlier models, remove the air conditioning/heater housing mounting bolts and nuts (see illustration).

24 On 2005 and later models, unbolt the wiring junction box and allow it to hang, then remove the mounting screws and pull the unit out. Disconnect the remaining wiring and remove the unit from the vehicle.

25 Remove the heater core mounting screws and clamps and lift the heater core from the housing.

26 Installation is the reverse of removal. Don't forget to reconnect the heater core inlet and outlet hoses.

27 Reconnect the cable to the negative terminal of the battery (see Chapter 5, Section 1). Refill the cooling system (see Chapter 1). Have the air conditioning system recharged and leak tested by the shop that discharged it.

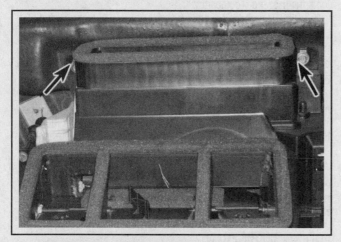

12.11 Remove the heater roof vent cover mounting bolts - 2004 and earlier models

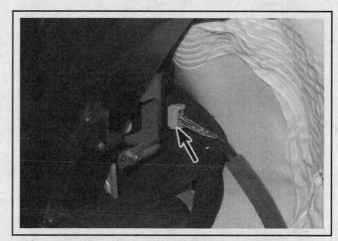

12.20 Disconnect the blend door electrical connector

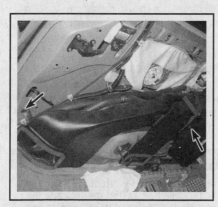

12.21 Remove the air duct housing mounting bolts

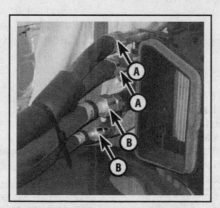

12.22 Disconnect the heater hoses (A) and the air conditioning lines (B)

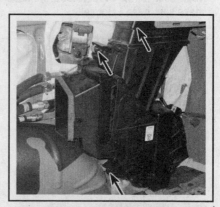

12.23 First slide the telescopic upper vent off the top portion of the housing and remove the air conditioning/ heater housing mounting bolts

13 Air conditioning and heating system - check and maintenance

▶ Refer to illustration 13.1

⁎⁎ WARNING:

The air conditioning system is under high pressure. Do not loosen any hose fittings or remove any components until after the system has been discharged by a dealer service department or service station. Always wear eye protection when disconnecting air conditioning system fittings.

1 The following maintenance checks should be performed on a regular basis to ensure the air conditioner continues to operate at peak efficiency.

  a) Check the compressor drivebelt. If it's worn or deteriorated, replace it (see Chapter 1).
  b) Check the drivebelt tension and, if necessary, adjust it (see Chapter 1).
  c) Check the system hoses. Look for cracks, bubbles, hard spots and deterioration. Inspect the hoses and all fittings for oil bubbles and seepage. If there's any evidence of wear, damage or leaks, replace the hose(s).
  d) Inspect the condenser fins for leaves, bugs and other debris. Use a "fin comb" or compressed air to clean the condenser.

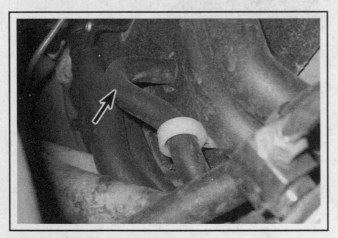

13.1 Look for the evaporator drain hose on the firewall - make sure it isn't clogged

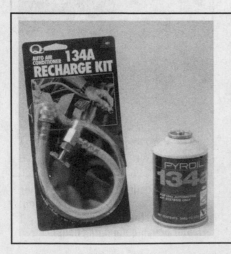

13.9 A basic charging kit for R-134a systems is available at most auto parts stores - it must say R-134a (not R-12) and so should the can of refrigerant

  e) Make sure the system has the correct refrigerant charge.
  f) Check the evaporator housing drain tube (see illustration) for blockage.

2 It's a good idea to operate the system for about 10 minutes at least once a month, particularly during the winter. Long term non-use can cause hardening, and subsequent failure, of the seals.

3 Because of the complexity of the air conditioning system and the special equipment necessary to service it, in-depth troubleshooting and repairs are not included in this manual. However, simple checks and component replacement procedures are provided in this Chapter.

4 The most common cause of poor cooling is simply a low system refrigerant charge. If a noticeable drop in cool air output occurs, the following quick check will help you determine if the refrigerant level is low.

CHECKING THE REFRIGERANT CHARGE

5 Warm the engine up to normal operating temperature.

6 Place the air conditioning temperature selector at the coldest setting and the blower at the highest setting. Open the vehicle doors (to make sure the air conditioning system doesn't cycle off as soon as it cools the passenger compartment).

7 With the compressor engaged - the clutch will make an audible click and the center of the clutch will rotate - feel the evaporator inlet and outlet lines at the firewall. The inlet (small diameter) line should feel warm and the outlet (large diameter) line should feel cold. If so, the system is properly charged.

8 Place a thermometer in the dashboard vent nearest the evaporator and operate the system until the indicated temperature is around 40 to 45-degrees F. If the ambient (outside) air temperature is very high, say 110-degrees F, the duct air temperature may be as high as 60-degrees F, but generally the air conditioning is 30 to 40-degrees F cooler than the ambient air.

➡ **Note: Humidity of the ambient air also affects the cooling capacity of the system. Higher ambient humidity lowers the effectiveness of the air conditioning system.**

ADDING REFRIGERANT

▶ **Refer to illustrations 13.9, 13.12, 13.13 and 13.15**

9 Buy an automotive charging kit at an auto parts store (see illustration). A charging kit includes a 12- or 14-ounce can of refrigerant, a tap valve and a short section of hose that can be attached between the tap valve and the system low side service valve. Because one can of refrigerant may not be sufficient to bring the system charge up to the proper level, it's a good idea to buy an additional can. Make sure that one of the cans contains red refrigerant dye. If the system is leaking, the red dye will leak out with the refrigerant and help you pinpoint the location of the leak.

⁎⁎ CAUTION:

There are two types of refrigerant used in automotive systems; R-12 - which has been widely used on earlier models and the more environmentally-friendly R-134a used in all models covered by this manual. These two refrigerants (and their appropriate refrigerant oils) are not compatible and must never be mixed or components will be damaged. Use only R-134a refrigerant in the models covered by this manual.

10 Hook up the charging kit by following the manufacturer's instructions.

11 Back off the valve handle on the charging kit and screw the kit onto the refrigerant can, making sure first that the O-ring or rubber seal inside the threaded portion of the kit is in place.

12 Remove the dust cap from the low-side charging connection and attach the quick-connect fitting on the kit hose (see illustration).

13 Warm up the engine and turn on the air conditioner. Keep the charging kit hose away from the fan and other moving parts.

➡ Note: The charging process requires the compressor to be running. Your compressor may cycle off if the pressure is low due to a low charge. If the clutch cycles off, you can detach the A/C pressure switch plug (located on the evaporator inlet (small diameter) line, right below the fuse/relay box) and attach a jumper wire to terminals 1 and 4 (see illustration). This will keep the compressor ON.

14 Turn the valve handle on the kit until the stem pierces the can, then back the handle out to release the refrigerant. You should be able to hear the rush of gas. Add refrigerant to the low side of the system until both the receiver-drier surface and the evaporator inlet pipe feel about the same temperature. Allow stabilization time between each addition.

15 If you have an accurate thermometer, place it in the center air conditioning vent (see illustration) and then note the temperature of the air coming out of the vent. A fully-charged system which is working correctly should cool down to about 40-degrees F. Generally, an air conditioning system will put out air that is 30 to 40-degrees F cooler than the ambient air. For example, if the ambient (outside) air temperature is very high (over 100-degrees F), the temperature of air coming out of the registers should be 60 to 70-degrees F.

16 When the can is empty, turn the valve handle to the closed position and release the connection from the low-side port. Replace the dust cap.

17 Remove the charging kit from the can and store the kit for future use with the piercing valve in the UP position, to prevent inadvertently piercing the can on the next use.

HEATING SYSTEMS

18 If the carpet under the heater core is damp, or if antifreeze vapor or steam is coming through the vents, the heater core is leaking. Remove it (see Section 12) and install a new unit (most radiator shops will not repair a leaking heater core).

19 If the air coming out of the heater vents isn't hot, the problem could stem from any of the following causes:

a) *The thermostat is stuck open, preventing the engine coolant from warming up enough to carry heat to the heater core. Replace the thermostat (see Section 3).*

b) *There is a blockage in the system, preventing the flow of coolant through the heater core. Feel both heater hoses at the firewall. They should be hot. If one of them is cold, there is an obstruction in one of the hoses or in the heater core, or the heater control valve is shut. Detach the hoses and back flush the heater core with a water hose. If the heater core is clear but circulation is impeded, remove the two hoses and flush them out with a water hose.*

c) *If flushing fails to remove the blockage from the heater core, the core must be replaced (see Section 12).*

13.12 Cans of R-134A refrigerant (available at auto parts stores) can be added to the low side of the air conditioning system with a simple recharging kit

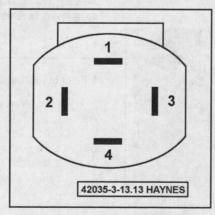

42035-3-13.13 HAYNES

13.13 Terminal identification for the A/C pressure switch electrical connector

13.15 Insert a thermometer in the center vent, turn on the air conditioning system and wait for it to cool down; depending on the humidity, the output air should be 30 to 40-degrees cooler than the ambient air temperature

ELIMINATING AIR CONDITIONING ODORS

▶ **Refer to illustration 13.23**

20 Unpleasant odors that often develop in air conditioning systems are caused by the growth of a fungus, usually on the surface of the evaporator core. The warm, humid environment there is a perfect breeding ground for mildew to develop.

21 The evaporator core on most vehicles is difficult to access, and factory dealerships have a lengthy, expensive process for eliminating the fungus by opening up the evaporator case and using a powerful disinfectant and rinse on the core until the fungus is gone. You can service your own system at home, but it takes something much stronger than basic household germ-killers or deodorizers.

22 Aerosol disinfectants for automotive air conditioning systems are available in most auto parts stores, but remember when shopping for them that the most effective treatments are also the most expensive. The basic procedure for using these sprays is to start by running the system in the RECIRC mode for ten minutes with the blower on its highest speed. Use the highest heat mode to dry out the system and keep the compressor from engaging by disconnecting the wiring connector at the compressor (see Section 14).

23 Make sure that the disinfectant can comes with a long spray hose. Point the nozzle through the air recirculation door so that it protrudes inside the evaporator housing (see illustration), and then spray according to the manufacturer's recommendations. Try to cover the whole sur-

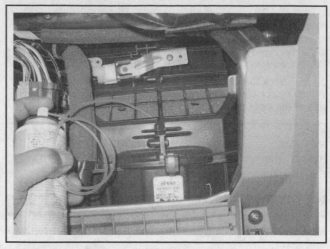

13.23 Remove the glove box (see Chapter 11) and then insert the nozzle of the disinfectant can into the evaporator housing by shoving it through the air recirculation door

face of the evaporator core, by aiming the spray up, down and sideways. Follow the manufacturer's recommendations for the length of spray and waiting time between applications.

24 Once the evaporator has been cleaned, the best way to prevent the mildew from coming back again is to make sure your evaporator housing drain tube is clear (see illustration 13.1).

14 Air conditioning compressor - removal and installation

✳ WARNING:

The air conditioning system is under high pressure. Do not loosen any hose fittings or remove any components until after the system has been discharged. Air conditioning refrigerant must be properly discharged into an EPA-approved recovery/re-cycling unit at a dealer service department or an automotive air conditioning repair facility. Always wear eye protection when disconnecting air conditioning system fittings.

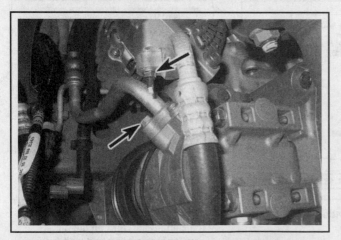

14.8 Remove the mounting bolt for the suction line (low side) and the mounting nut for the discharge line (high side) and detach the air conditioning lines from the air conditioning compressor

✳ CAUTION:

When replacing the compressor with a new one, the amount of oil inside of it must be adjusted (see Step 14). Be sure to read the can before adding any oil to the system, to make sure it is compatible with the R-134a system.

➡ **Note: The receiver-drier should be replaced whenever the compressor is replaced.**

REMOVAL

▶ **Refer to illustrations 14.8, 14.9, 14.10, 14.11 and 14.12**

1 Have the air conditioning system refrigerant discharged and recovered by an air conditioning technician.

2 Disconnect the cable from the negative battery terminal (see Chapter 5, Section 1).

3 Remove the drivebelt (see Chapter 1).

4 On 2004 and earlier models, remove the alternator (see Chapter 5).

5 Set the parking brake, block the rear wheels and raise the front of the vehicle, supporting it securely on jackstands.

6 Remove the splash shield from under the engine compartment (see Chapter 2A). On 2005 and later models detach the front of the inner fender and move it rearward.

7 Disconnect the compressor clutch wiring harness.

8 Disconnect the refrigerant lines from the compressor. Plug the open fittings to prevent entry of dirt and moisture (see illustration).

14.9 Remove the subframe bracket bolts (A) and loosen the subframe mounting bolt (B) and pivot the bracket away from the subframe

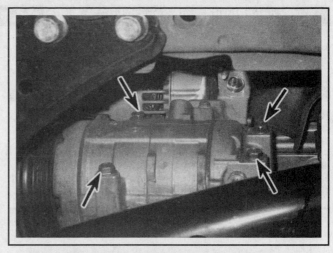

14.10 Remove the air conditioning compressor mounting bolts

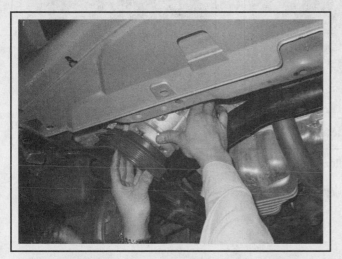

14.11 Slide the compressor through the opening between the subframe and the body of the vehicle

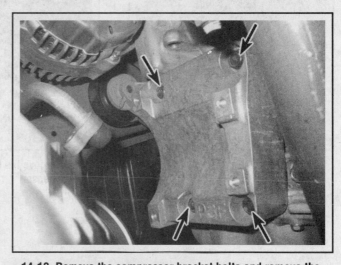

14.12 Remove the compressor bracket bolts and remove the bracket from the engine compartment

9   Remove the subframe bracket bolts, loosen the subframe mounting bolt and pivot the bracket away from the body (see illustration).

10 Remove the compressor mounting bolts (see illustration).

11 Carefully guide the compressor through the opening between the subframe and the body of the vehicle (see illustration).

12 If necessary, remove the compressor mounting bracket (see illustration). Remove the compressor bracket from the engine compartment.

INSTALLATION

13 The clutch may have to be transferred from the old compressor to the new unit.

14 Adjust the amount of refrigerant oil in the new compressor using the following calculations:

a) *Drain the refrigerant oil from the old compressor through the suction fitting and measure it in ounces.*

b) *Subtract this number from 7 ounces (210 ml).*

c) *The difference between these two figures is equal to the amount you should drain from the new compressor.*

✳✳ CAUTION:

Even if no oil came out of the old compressor, don't drain more than 1-2/3 ounces (50 ml) from the new one.

15 Installation is the reverse of removal, using new O-rings where the line fittings attach to the compressor. Tighten the subframe bracket bolts and subframe mounting bolt to the torque listed in the Chapter 2B Specifications.

16 Reconnect the battery. Refer to Chapter 5, Section 1.

17 Have the system evacuated, recharged and leak tested by the shop that discharged it.

15 Air conditioning receiver-drier - removal and installation

▶ **Refer to illustrations 15.4, 15.5 and 15.6**

⁂ WARNING:

The air conditioning system is under high pressure. Do not loosen any hose fittings or remove any components until after the system has been discharged. Air conditioning refrigerant must be properly discharged into an EPA-approved recovery/ recycling unit at a dealer service department or an automotive air conditioning repair facility. Always wear eye protection when disconnecting air conditioning system fittings.

1 Have the refrigerant discharged and recovered by an air conditioning technician.

2 Disconnect the cable from the negative battery terminal (see Chapter 5, Section 1).

3 Remove the condenser (see Section 16).

4 Remove the cap from the condenser (see illustration).

5 Remove the filter from the condenser (see illustration).

6 Remove the receiver-drier desiccant (see illustration).

7 Installation is the reverse of removal. Be sure to install new O-rings onto the receiver-drier cap. Apply a thin layer of refrigerant oil to the O-rings before installing them.

8 Reconnect the battery. Refer to Chapter 5, Section 1.

9 Have the system evacuated, charged and leak tested by the shop that discharged it.

15.4 Remove the cap from the condenser

15.5 Remove the filter from the condenser

15.6 Use pliers to remove the desiccant from the condenser

16 Air conditioning condenser - removal and installation

▶ **Refer to illustrations 16.6 and 16.7**

⁂ WARNING:

The air conditioning system is under high pressure. Do not loosen any hose fittings or remove any components until after the system has been discharged. Air conditioning refrigerant must be properly discharged into an EPA-approved recovery/ re-cycling unit at a dealer service department or an automotive air conditioning repair facility. Always wear eye protection when disconnecting air conditioning system fittings.

⁂ CAUTION:

When replacing entire components, additional refrigerant oil must be added to them. Be sure to read the can before adding any oil to the system, to make sure it is compatible with the R-134a system.

REMOVAL

1 Have the refrigerant discharged and recovered by an air conditioning technician.

2 Disconnect the cable from the negative battery terminal (see Chapter 5, Section 1).

3 On 2004 and earlier models, remove the radiator grille and the hood latch (see Chapter 11).

4 On 2005 and later models, remove the front bumper cover (see Chapter 11).

5 Remove the radiator and condenser brackets (see Section 4).

6 Disconnect the refrigerant lines from the condenser (see illustration). Cap the fittings on the condenser and lines to prevent entry of dirt or moisture.

7 Remove the condenser by lifting it from the front of the vehicle (see illustration).

INSTALLATION

8 Installation is the reverse of removal. If a new condenser was installed, add 1 1/6-ounces (35 ml) of fresh refrigerant oil. Assemble all connections with new O-rings, lightly lubricated with R-134a refrigerant oil.

9 Reconnect the battery. Refer to Chapter 5, Section 1.

10 Have the system evacuated, charged and leak tested by the shop that discharged it.

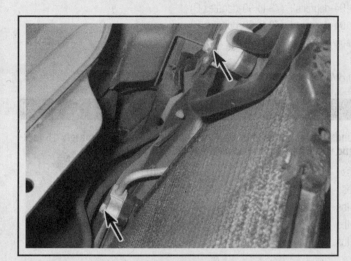

16.6 Remove the suction and discharge lines from the condenser

16.7 Lift the condenser from the engine compartment

Specifications

General

Radiator cap pressure rating	14 to 18 psi (93 to 123 kPa)
Thermostat rating (opening to fully open temperature range)	
2001 models	163 to 194-degrees F (73 to 90-degrees C)
2002 and later models	169 to 194-degrees F (78 to 90-degrees C)
Cooling system capacity	See Chapter 1
Refrigerant type	R-134a
Refrigerant capacity	Refer to HVAC specification tag

Torque specifications

➡ **Note: One foot-pound (ft-lb) of torque is equivalent to 12 inch-pounds (in-lbs) of torque. Torque values below approximately 15 foot-pounds are expressed in inch-pounds, because most foot-pound torque wrenches are not accurate at these smaller values.**

Condenser inlet and outlet nuts	86 in-lbs	10 Nm
Condenser bracket bolts	86 in-lbs	10 Nm
Radiator bracket bolts	104 in-lbs	12 Nm
Thermostat housing cover bolts	104 in-lbs	12 Nm
Water pump bolts	104 in-lbs	12 Nm

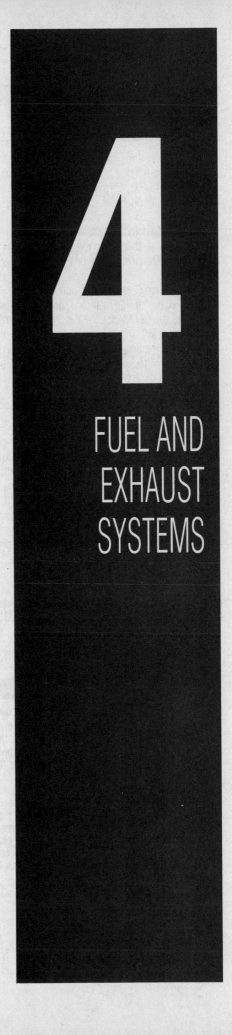

4

FUEL AND EXHAUST SYSTEMS

1 General information

AIR INDUCTION SYSTEM

The air induction system consists of the air filter assembly, the air intake duct, the throttle body and the intake manifold. The air filter assembly on the Odyssey is equipped with a small heat exchanger that warms intake air during cold weather before it gets to the intake manifold.

The throttle body contains a throttle plate. This plate is operated either by a cable attached to the accelerator pedal (2004 and earlier models), or electronically by the Powertrain Control Module (PCM) (2005 and later models). The throttle body is also the location of the Throttle Position (TP) sensor, a potentiometer that monitors the opening angle of the throttle plate and sends a variable voltage signal to the Powertrain Control Module (PCM). All of the air induction components (air filter housing, air intake duct and throttle body) are covered in this Chapter except for the intake manifold, which is covered in Chapter 2A, and the information sensors, which are covered in Chapter 6.

FUEL SYSTEM

The fuel system consists of the fuel tank, an electric fuel pump (located in the fuel tank), the fuel pulsation damper, the fuel pressure regulator, the fuel rail and the fuel injectors. Programmed Fuel Injection (PGM-FI) is a "sequential multiport" system, which means that the fuel injectors deliver fuel directly into the intake ports of the cylinders in firing order sequence (1-4-2-5-3-6). Sequential multiport systems provide much better control of the air/fuel mixture ratio than earlier fuel injection systems, and are therefore able to produce more power, better mileage and lower emissions. For more information about the PGM-FI system, see Section 11. For more information about the PCM and the information sensors, refer to Chapter 6.

FUEL PUMP AND FUEL LINES

2004 and earlier models

Fuel is circulated from the fuel tank to the fuel rail and back to the fuel tank through metal lines located on the underside of the vehicle. An electric fuel pump is located inside the fuel tank. The fuel level sending unit and the fuel filter are an integral part of the fuel pump. The fuel pump/fuel filter/fuel level sending unit module can be accessed through a cover plate in the floor of the vehicle, and any of the three components can be replaced separately from the other two. A fuel pulsation damper, which is located on the fuel supply line near the fuel rail, attenuates the hydraulic and acoustic "noise" produced by the fuel pump when it's operating. A fuel pressure regulator, which is installed on the fuel rail at the connection for the fuel return line, maintains the fuel pressure within the specified operating range.

2005 and later models

Fuel is pumped from the fuel tank to the fuel rail through a steel fuel line mounted on the underside of the vehicle. An electric fuel pump is located in the fuel tank. The fuel level sending unit, the fuel filter and the pressure regulator are part of the fuel pump module. The module can be accessed through a cover plate in the floor of the vehicle. All of the components are replaceable.

EXHAUST SYSTEM

The exhaust system consists of the exhaust manifolds, the "Y" pipe that connects both manifolds to the catalytic converter, the catalyst itself, the muffler and the tailpipe. The exhaust manifolds are covered in Chapter 2A, and the catalytic converter is covered in Chapter 6.

2 Fuel pressure relief procedure

Refer to illustration 2.2

WARNING:

Gasoline is extremely flammable, so take extra precautions when you work on any part of the fuel system. Don't smoke or allow open flames or bare light bulbs near the work area, and don't work in a garage where a gas-type appliance (such as a water heater or a clothes dryer) is present. Since gasoline is carcinogenic, wear latex gloves when there's a possibility of being exposed to fuel, and, if you spill any fuel on your skin, rinse it off immediately with soap and water. Mop up any spills immediately and do not store fuel-soaked rags where they could ignite. The fuel system is under constant pressure, so, if any fuel lines are to be disconnected, the fuel pressure in the system must be relieved first. When you perform any kind of work on the fuel system, wear safety glasses and have a Class B type fire extinguisher on hand.

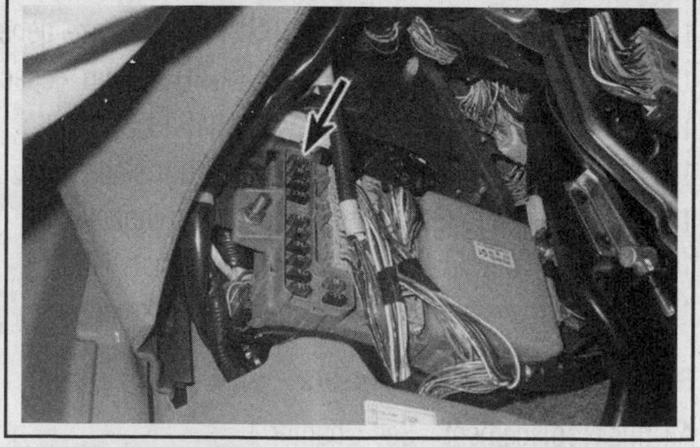

2.2 The fuel pump fuse is located in the fuse and relay box under the left end of the dash

1 Start the engine.

2 Pull out the fuel pump fuse (see illustration), which is located in the passenger compartment fuse and relay panel, under the left end of the dash. The engine will cease running immediately. The fuel pressure is now relieved, but there is still fuel in the lines, so be sure to have shop rags handy to mop up any spilled fuel when disconnecting fuel lines.

3 Before proceeding with any work on the fuel system, disconnect the cable from the negative terminal of the battery (see Chapter 5, Section 1).

3   Fuel pump/fuel pressure - check

✳ WARNING:

Gasoline is extremely flammable, so take extra precautions when you work on any part of the fuel system. See the Warning in Section 2.

GENERAL CHECKS

1   Verify that there is fuel in the fuel tank.

2   Verify that the fuel pump actually runs. Turn the ignition switch to ON - you should hear a brief whirring noise for about two seconds as the pump comes on and pressurizes the system.

➡ **Note: If you can't hear the pump from inside the vehicle, open the fuel filler neck cap, then have an assistant turn the ignition switch to ON while you listen to the pump through the fuel filler neck.**

FUEL PUMP PRESSURE TEST

▶ **Refer to illustrations 3.3, 3.5, 3.6 and 3.7**

3   To measure the fuel pressure, you'll need a fuel pressure gauge capable of reading at least 63 psi (430 kPa), some fuel hose and a suitable double flare fitting and adapter nut (see illustration).

4   Before disconnecting any fuel line fittings, relieve system fuel pressure (see Section 2), then disconnect the cable from the negative battery terminal (see Chapter 5, Section 1).

5   On 2004 and earlier models, disconnect the fuel supply line from the fuel rail hose at the connection at the firewall (see illustration). On 2005 and later models, the connection point should be at the fuel rail - you'll have to fabricate your own simple yet safe connection similar to the one shown for earlier models.

6   To tee the gauge into the fuel system on 2004 and earlier models, you'll need a double-flare fitting and nut (see illustration).

7   Connect the fuel pressure gauge to the fuel system (see illustration).

8   Reconnect the battery.

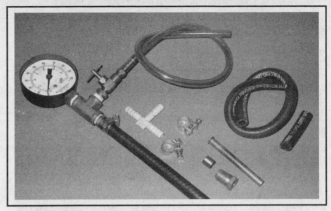

3.3 To measure the fuel pressure on the Odyssey, you'll need a fuel pressure gauge, some extra fuel hose and a suitable double-flare fitting and adapter nut - typical

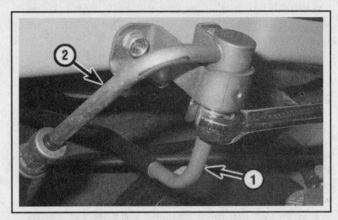

3.5 Disconnect the fuel supply line (1) from the fuel rail hose (2) at this connection on the firewall; use a flare-nut wrench, if you have one, to protect the nut - 2004 and earlier models

3.6 To tee into the fuel lines at this connection, you'll need a double-flare fitting and a suitable adapter nut

3.7 Fuel pressure gauge test rig details (2004 and earlier models)

1   *Fuel pump-to-firewall supply line*
2   *Fuel pump supply line*
3   *Fuel pressure gauge-to-tee fitting hose*
4   *Tee/fuel supply line-to-firewall hose*
5   *Firewall-to-fuel rail supply line*

9 Turn the ignition switch to ON (don't start the engine yet) with the air conditioning off. The fuel pump should run for about two seconds - pressure should register on the gauge and should hold steady.

10 Start the engine and let it warm up until it's idling at its normal operating temperature.

2001 MODELS

11 Disconnect the vacuum hose from the fuel pressure regulator (see Section 15). Note the indicated fuel pressure reading on the gauge and compare it with the operating range listed in this Chapter's Specifications. Reconnect the vacuum hose to the fuel pressure regulator, note the indicated fuel pressure and compare it with the range listed in this Chapter's Specifications. If both fuel pressure readings are within the specified range, the system is operating correctly.

12 Note that the operating fuel pressure range is slightly lower when the vacuum hose is connected to the fuel pressure regulator than when it's disconnected. This is because intake manifold vacuum is high at idle, so it raises the diaphragm inside the pressure regulator slightly, allowing fuel to return to the fuel tank, and lowering the pressure "upstream" in relation to the regulator. But when you disconnect the vacuum hose from the regulator, the spring-loaded diaphragm seals off the return line, raising the pressure upstream.

13 If the indicated fuel pressure doesn't go up when you disconnect the vacuum line from the regulator, apply vacuum to the pressure regulator with a hand-held vacuum pump and note what happens. If the fuel pressure drops, the regulator is okay, but there's probably a crack or tear in the vacuum hose. Replace the vacuum hose and retest.

14 If the indicated fuel pressure doesn't go down when you connect the vacuum hose to the regulator, inspect the vacuum hose. If it's torn or cracked, replace it and retest. If the pressure still doesn't go down with the new vacuum hose connected, replace the regulator.

15 If the indicated fuel pressure is higher than the specified range with the vacuum hose connected, verify that the fuel pressure regulator is receiving a good vacuum signal by checking it with a vacuum gauge. Vacuum should fluctuate up and down in accordance with the increase or decrease in the engine rpm (at idle the vacuum is high, but as engine speed increases the vacuum signal becomes weaker). If vacuum is present, check for a kinked, pinched or clogged fuel return hose or line. If the return line is OK, replace the regulator.

16 If the indicated fuel pressure is lower than the specified range,

start the engine and pinch off the return line. If the pressure now rises above the specified operating range, the regulator is not closing fully. Replace it (see Section 15).

17 If the indicated fuel pressure is still lower than the specified range, the fuel filter might be clogged. Replace the filter (see Sections 5 and 6). The fuel filter is an integral component of the fuel pump/fuel level sending unit assembly, so you must remove the fuel pump/fuel level sending unit module to replace the filter.

18 If the indicated fuel pressure is still lower than the specified range after replacing the filter, one or more of the fuel injectors or injector O-rings might be leaking (see Section 16), or the fuel pump might be faulty (see Sections 5 and 6). Replace the defective component(s) and retest.

19 After the test is complete, relieve the system fuel pressure (see Section 2), then disconnect the cable from the negative battery terminal.

20 Remove your fuel pressure testing rig, then reconnect the fuel supply line to the connection at the firewall. Reconnect the cable to the negative battery terminal (see Chapter 5, Section 1).

2002 AND LATER MODELS

21 Note the indicated fuel pressure reading on the gauge and compare it with the operating range listed in this Chapter's Specifications.

22 If the indicated pressure is within the specified range, the system is operating correctly.

23 If the indicated pressure is higher than the specified range, look for a kinked, pinched or clogged fuel return hose or line.

24 If the indicated pressure is lower than the specified range, the fuel filter might be clogged or the fuel pump might be defective. To rule out the possibility of a clogged fuel filter, replace the filter (see Sections 5 and 6). The fuel filter is an integral component of the fuel pump/fuel level sending unit assembly, so you must remove the fuel pump/fuel level sending unit module to replace the filter.

25 If the indicated pressure is still outside the specified range, replace the fuel pressure regulator (see Section 15).

26 After the test is complete, relieve the system fuel pressure (see Section 2), then disconnect the cable from the negative battery terminal.

27 Remove your fuel pressure testing rig, then reconnect the fuel supply line to the connection at the firewall. Reconnect the cable to the negative battery terminal (see Chapter 5, Section 1).

4   Fuel lines and fittings - general information

▸ **Refer to illustration 4.2**

✳ WARNING:

Gasoline is extremely flammable, so take extra precautions when you work on any part of the fuel system. See the Warning in Section 2.

1   Always relieve the fuel pressure before servicing fuel lines or fittings (see Section 2), then disconnect the cable from the negative battery terminal (see Chapter 5, Section 1) before proceeding.

2   The fuel supply and return lines connect the fuel pump in the fuel tank to the fuel rail on the engine. The Evaporative Emission (EVAP) system lines connect the fuel tank to the EVAP canister and connect the canister to the intake manifold. All lines are secured to the underbody

with small metal brackets that are bolted to the vehicle floorpan. The lines are attached to these metal brackets by plastic clips that are easy to detach from the brackets (see illustration).

3   Whenever you're working under the vehicle, be sure to inspect all fuel and evaporative emission lines for leaks, kinks, dents and other damage. Always replace a damaged fuel or EVAP line immediately. Leaking fuel and EVAP lines will result in loss of fuel and excessive air pollution (the leaking raw fuel emits unburned hydrocarbon vapors into the atmosphere).

4   If you find signs of dirt in the lines during disassembly, disconnect all lines and blow them out with compressed air. Inspect the fuel strainer on the fuel pump pick-up unit (see Sections 5 and 6) for damage and deterioration. And inspect the fuel filter, which is an integral component of the fuel pump/fuel level sending unit module (see Sections 5 and 6). Also inspect the fuel strainers in the fuel injectors (see Section 16).

STEEL TUBING

5   Because fuel lines used on fuel-injected vehicles are under fairly high pressure, it is critical that they be replaced with lines of equivalent specification. If you have to replace a fuel or EVAP line, use only steel tubing that meets the manufacturer's specifications. Don't use copper or aluminum tubing to replace steel tubing. These materials cannot withstand normal vehicle vibration.

6   Some steel fuel lines have threaded fittings. When loosening these fittings to service or replace components:

   a) *Always hold the stationary fitting with a wrench while turning the tube nut (this will prevent the line from twisting).*

   b) *If you're going to replace one of these fittings, use original equipment parts or parts that meet original equipment standards.*

PLASTIC TUBING

7   Some fuel lines - between the fuel supply and return pipes of the fuel pump and the front of the fuel tank, for example - are plastic. If you ever have to replace either line, use only the original equipment plastic tubing.

✳✳ CAUTION:

When removing or installing plastic fuel line tubing, be careful not to bend or twist it too much, which can damage it. And damaged fuel lines MUST be replaced! Also, be aware that the plastic fuel tubing used on the Odyssey is NOT heat resistant, so keep it away from excessive heat. Nor is it acid-proof, so don't wipe it off with a shop rag that has been used to wipe off battery electrolyte. If you accidentally spill or wipe electrolyte on plastic fuel tubing, replace the tubing.

FLEXIBLE HOSES

✳✳ WARNING:

Use only original equipment replacement hoses or their equivalent. Unapproved hoses might fail when subjected to the high operating pressures of the fuel system.

8   Don't route fuel hoses (or metal lines) within four inches of the exhaust system or within ten inches of the catalytic converter. Make sure that no rubber hoses are installed directly against the vehicle, particularly in places where there is any vibration. If allowed to touch some vibrating part of the vehicle, a hose can easily become chafed and it might start leaking. A good rule of thumb is to maintain a minimum of 1/4-inch clearance around a hose (or metal line) to prevent contact with the vehicle underbody.

DISCONNECTING AND RECONNECTING FUEL SYSTEM FITTINGS

9   Four types of fittings are used on the Odyssey fuel system. There is one threaded fitting at the connection on the firewall and one banjo-type fitting at the fuel pulsation damper. These two fittings are covered in Section 3 (threaded fitting) and Section 14 (banjo fitting). The rest of the fittings in the fuel system consist of conventional spring-type hose clamps and quick-connect fittings. Spring-type hose clamps are used

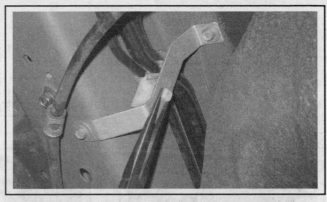

4.2 The EVAP and fuel lines are secured to the underside of the vehicle by a series of brackets and plastic clips; to release the plastic clip from the bracket, squeeze these mounting tabs together and push out the bracket, which can then be unclipped from the lines

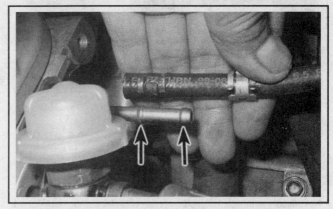

4.13 When reconnecting a fuel hose such as this return line hose to a metal line or pipe, slide the hose onto the metal line up to the second raised ridge on the line or pipe (left arrow), then center the clamp between the two ridges (the ridges create bulges in the rubber hose that indicate the location of the ridges)

to connect fuel hoses on the (low-pressure) return side of the system, i.e. between the fuel pressure regulator and the fuel tank. Quick-connect fittings are used to connect lines on the (high-pressure) supply side of the system, such as the connections at the fuel pump (supply and return line connections).

Conventional spring-type hose clamps

▸ **Refer to illustration 4.13**

10   Relieve the system fuel pressure (see Section 2), then disconnect the cable from the negative battery terminal (see Chapter 5, Section 1).

11   To disconnect a spring-type hose clamp, simply squeeze the two ends together with a pair of pliers to loosen the clamp, then slide the clamp away from the pipe to which the hose is attached.

12   If a spring-type hose clamp feels easy to squeeze open, or if it's obviously not clamping the hose tightly against the metal pipe to which the hose is connected, replace the clamp.

13   When installing spring-type hose clamps, make sure to slide the hose onto the pipe to which you're connecting it up to the second raised ridge on the pipe, then slide the hose clamp down the hose until it's centered between the two ridges (see illustration).

Manufacturer	Fuel tube color	Retainer color	Fits which end of tube?
Sanoh	Black	White	Supply line tube (both ends)
			Return line tube (both ends)
Tokai	Black	Orange	Supply line tube (pump end)
		Blue/green	Supply line tube (pipe end)
			Return line tube (pump end)
		Green	Return line tube (pipe end)

4.16 Quick-connect fitting color code

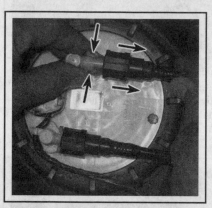

4.20 To disconnect a quick-connect fitting, squeeze the retainer tabs on the white part of the fitting and pull on the black part of the fitting until the two halves are separated

4.21 Inspect the contact surface of the line for dirt, damage and rust

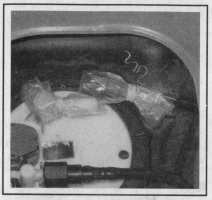

4.22 To prevent dirt and moisture from entering the system, be sure to cover the open ends of the fitting with plastic bags

14 Reconnect the cable to the negative battery cable (see Chapter 5, Section 1).

15 Start the engine and verify that no fuel is leaking out at the connection you just reconnected. If there's a leak, either the clamp is weak or it's not centered correctly between the two raised ridges on the metal line or pipe to which you connected the fuel hose. Or the hose itself is leaking because it's cracked or torn where the clamp squeezes down on it.

Quick-connect fittings

▶ **Refer to illustrations 4.16, 4.20, 4.21, 4.22, 4.23, 4.24, 4.25a, 4.25b and 4.27**

> ❊ **CAUTION:**
>
> **When disconnecting or reconnecting quick-connect fittings, be careful not to bend or twist them excessively, or they will be damaged and will have to be replaced. Also, be aware that the quick-connect fittings used on the Odyssey are NOT heat resistant, so keep them away from excessive heat. Nor are they acid-proof, so don't wipe them off with a shop rag that has been used to wipe off battery electrolyte. If you accidentally spill or wipe electrolyte on quick-connect fittings, replace them.**

16 There are quick-connect fittings at the supply and return lines at the fuel pump. Quick-connect fittings are also used at the connections in front of the tank where the lines from the pump connect to the lines leading under the vehicle to the engine compartment (these are the connections that you must disconnect when removing the fuel tank). You must also replace the quick-connect fitting retainers whenever you disconnect a quick-connect fitting. It is critical that you use the correct replacement retainer, which depends on the manufacturer of the tubing

and the end of the tube (fuel pump end or "pipe" end) on which you're installing it, because the retainers are not all the same diameter. To help you distinguish the various diameter retainers, Honda color codes them (see illustration).

➡ **Note: The "pipe" end refers to the metal fuel lines to which the plastic fuel tubing is connected in front of the fuel tank. So think of the pump end as the rear end of the fuel supply or return line tube, and the pipe end as the forward end.**

17 There are two places on the vehicle where quick-connect fittings are used: at the fuel pump, and at the front of the fuel tank. The following procedure shows how to disconnect and reconnect the quick-connect fittings at the fuel pump, but the procedure for disconnecting and reconnecting quick-connect fittings at the front of the fuel tank is identical.

18 Relieve the system fuel pressure (see Section 2), then disconnect the cable from the negative battery terminal (see Chapter 5, Section 1).

19 To disconnect the fuel line quick-connect fittings at the fuel pump, you'll have to remove the second-row seats, the carpet (see Chapter 11) and the fuel pump access cover (see Section 5). To access the quick-connect fittings at the front of the fuel tank, raise the vehicle and place it securely on jackstands.

20 Holding the black side of the fitting with one hand, squeeze the retainer tabs on the white part of the fitting with your other hand to release the tabs (see illustration), then pull the two halves of the fitting apart.

21 Inspect the contact surface of the line for dirt and damage (see illustration). If it's dirty, wipe it off with a clean shop rag. If it's rusty, remove and inspect the fuel lines, then remove and inspect the fuel pump and the fuel filter (see Section 5). If any of these components are damaged, replace them (see Section 6).

22 Cover the disconnected ends of the fitting with plastic bags to keep out dirt and moisture (see illustration).

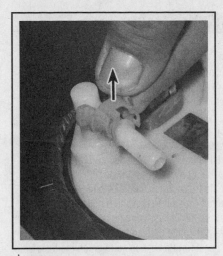

4.23 To remove the old retainer from the fitting, simply spread the two sides apart and pull it off

4.24 Inspect this O-ring inside the fitting; if it's cracked, torn or damaged, replace it

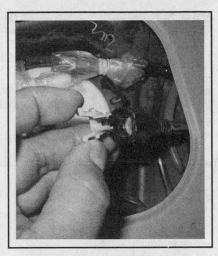

4.25a Install a new retainer in the female side of the fitting . . .

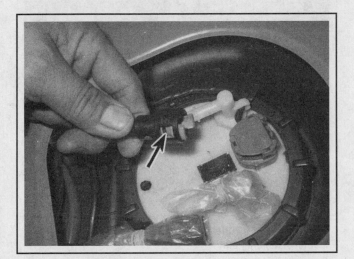

4.25b . . . and align the retainer locking pawls with the grooves in the connector

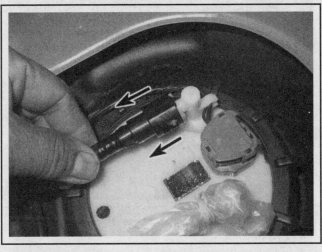

4.27 To verify that the quick-connect fitting is correctly reassembled, try to pull the two halves of the fitting apart

23 Remove the old retainer from the fitting (see illustration).

24 Inspect the old O-ring inside the bore of the fitting (see illustration). If it's cracked, torn or otherwise damaged, replace it.

25 Install a new retainer in the female side of the fitting (see illustration). Be sure to align the locking pawls of the retainer with the grooves in the side of the connector (see illustration).

26 Press the two halves of the quick-connect fitting together until both retainer tabs lock with an audible clicking sound.

27 Verify that the quick-connect fitting is correctly reconnected by trying to pull the two halves of the connector apart (see illustration).

28 Reconnect the cable to the negative battery terminal (see Chapter 5, Section 1).

29 Start the engine and check for leaks.

30 If you're servicing the quick-connect fittings at the fuel pump, replace the access cover (see Section 5), install the carpet (see Chapter 11) and install the second-row seats. If you're servicing the fittings in front of the tank, lower the vehicle.

5 Fuel pump/fuel level sending unit module - removal and installation

▶ **Refer to illustrations 5.4, 5.5, 5.7a, 5.7b, 5.8 and 5.9**

❄ WARNING:

Gasoline is extremely flammable, so take extra precautions when you work on any part of the fuel system. See the Warning in Section 2.

1 Detach the cable from the negative battery terminal (see Chapter 5, Section 1).

2 Relieve the fuel system pressure (see Section 2).

3 Remove the second-row seats, then remove the carpet from the area underneath (see Chapter 11).

4 Remove the fuel pump access cover screws (see illustration) and remove the fuel pump access cover.

5 Disconnect the fuel pump/fuel level sending unit electrical connector (see illustration).

6 Disconnect the quick-connect fittings for the fuel supply and return lines (see Section 4) and set the fuel lines aside.

7 Remove the fuel pump/fuel level sending unit locknut (see illustrations).

8 Remove the fuel pump/fuel level sending unit module from the tank (see illustration). Be sure to inspect the seal at the top of the module for cracks, tears and deterioration. If it's damaged, replace it.

9 When installing the fuel pump/fuel level sending unit module, install the seal in the hole first (see illustration). *Don't try to install it with the module*, which might cause it to become pinched or distorted.

10 Installation is otherwise the reverse of removal. Be sure to tighten the module locknut securely. If you're using a tool like the one shown in illustration 5.7a, you can use a torque wrench and tighten the locknut to the torque listed in this Chapter's Specifications.

11 Reconnect the cable to the negative terminal of the battery (see Chapter 5, Section 1).

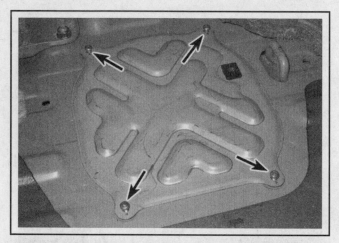

5.4 To detach the fuel pump access cover, remove these screws

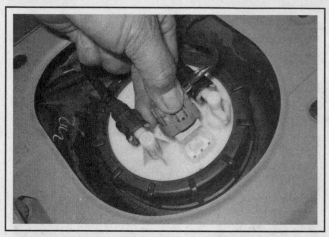

5.5 Disconnect the electrical connector from the fuel pump/ fuel level sending unit

5.7a This is the special Honda tool! (available from the manufacturer and from some automotive retailers) for loosening and tightening the fuel pump/fuel level sending unit locknut; if you can obtain one, this is the way to go because it won't damage the plastic locknut

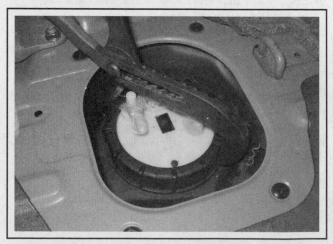

5.7b If you're unable to obtain the special Honda tool, you can use a large pair of water pump pliers as shown (we don't recommend this method because it can tear up the locknut)

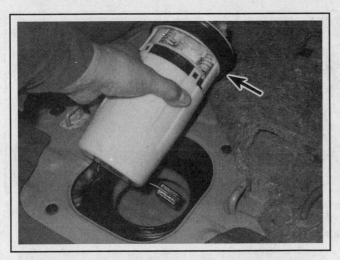

5.8 Carefully remove the fuel pump/fuel level sending unit module from the tank, then inspect the condition of the seal around the top of the module; if the seal is cracked, torn or deteriorated, replace it

5.9 Install the seal into the hole for the fuel pump/fuel level sending module *before* installing the module; if you try to install the seal by putting it on the module, it might become pinched or distorted when you try to push the module down into the hole

6 Fuel pump/fuel filter/fuel level sending unit module - replacement

DISASSEMBLY

▶ Refer to illustrations 6.4, 6.5a, 6.5b, 6.6a, 6.6b, 6.6c, 6.7, 6.8, 6.9, 6.10, 6.11a, 6.11b, 6.12 and 6.13

✳✳ WARNING:

Gasoline is extremely flammable, so take extra precautions when you work on any part of the fuel system. See the Warning in Section 2.

➡ Note: On 2005 and later models, the fuel pump module also contains the fuel pressure regulator.

1 Relieve the system fuel pressure (see Section 2), then disconnect the cable from the negative battery terminal (see Chapter 5, Section 1).

2 Remove the fuel pump/fuel level sending unit from the fuel tank (see Section 5).

3 Place the fuel pump/fuel level sending unit module on a clean workbench.

4 Disconnect the return hose from the case (see illustration).

5 Disconnect the electrical connectors for the fuel pump and for the fuel level sending unit (see illustrations).

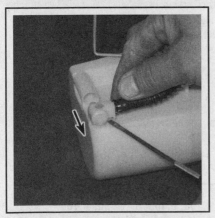

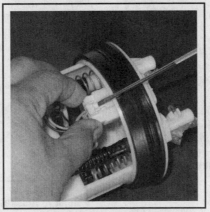

6.4 To disconnect the return hose from the case, release the locking tab with a small screwdriver and pull off the hose fitting

6.5a To disconnect the fuel pump electrical connector, release this locking tab with a small screwdriver and pull out the connector

6.5b To disconnect the fuel level sending unit connector, release this locking tab, then pull out the connector with a pair of needle-nose pliers

6.6a To separate the bracket from the case, release these two locking tabs . . .

6.6b . . . disengage the fuel pump wiring harness from the wire harness guide and release this locking tab . . .

6.6c . . . and pull the bracket and case apart

6.7 To disconnect the ground wire from its terminal on the side of the fuel filter housing, push down the locking tab on the end of the ground wire with a small screwdriver and carefully pull out the ground wire with a pair of needle-nose pliers

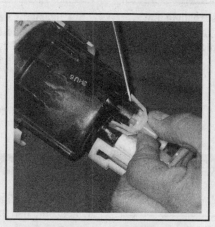

6.8 To detach the outlet tube from the fuel filter housing, pry the locking tabs loose and pull it off

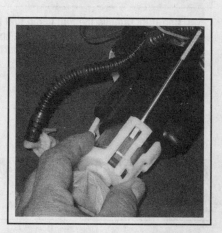

6.9 To detach the pump retainer, pry the locking tabs loose and pull it off

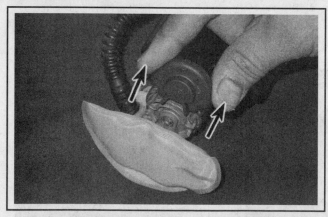

6.10 To remove the rubber isolator, simply pull it off

6   Separate the bracket and the case (see illustrations).

7   Disconnect the ground wire from its terminal on the side of the fuel filter housing (see illustration).

8   Disconnect the fuel filter outlet tube from the fuel filter housing (see illustration).

9   Remove the pump retainer (see illustration).

10   Remove the rubber isolator (see illustration).

11   Separate the fuel pump from the fuel filter housing (see illustrations). If you're simply replacing the fuel filter, no further disassembly is necessary. (The fuel filter is an integral component of the filter housing; the filter and housing are not available separately.) However, we strongly recommend cleaning the fuel inlet strainer (see Steps 14 and 15) and replacing the fuel filter inlet and outlet O-rings (see Step 16).

12   Remove the fuel inlet sock (strainer) from the fuel pump (see illustration).

13   Remove the fuel level sending unit from the case (see illustration).

14   On 2005 and later models, remove the fuel pressure regulator by pulling the retaining clip from the regulator housing. Remove the pressure regulator, its support ring and O-rings. Replace the O-rings with new ones upon assembly.

REASSEMBLY

▶ **Refer to illustrations 6.15a, 6.15b, 6.16a and 6.16b**

15   Before reassembling the fuel pump, fuel filter and fuel level sending unit, wash the fuel strainer thoroughly in clean solvent. If it's impossible to clean, replace it. When installing the strainer on the fuel pump (see illustration), use a new retainer and make sure that it's firmly seated (see illustration).

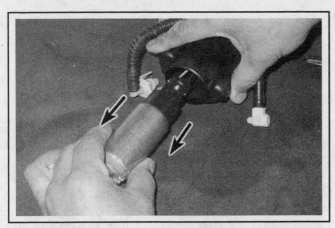

6.11a To remove the fuel pump from the fuel filter housing, pull it out . . .

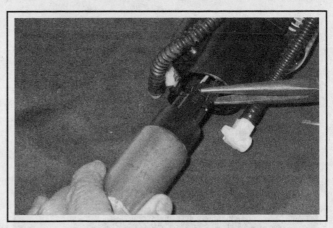

6.11b . . . and disconnect the electrical connector from the pump

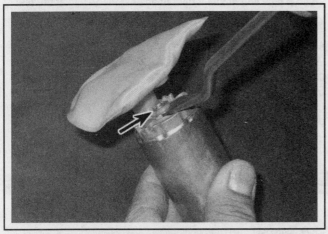

6.12 To detach the fuel inlet sock (strainer) from the fuel pump, pry it off right here, at the mounting flange for the mounting stud; prying it off will pop off - and ruin - the retainer clip, but don't bother trying to remove the retainer clip first because you'll ruin it anyway! In other words, use a new retainer clip for installation

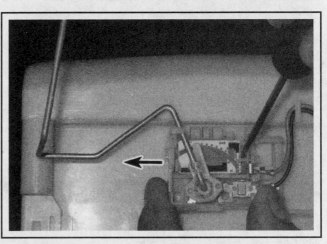

6.13 To detach the fuel level sending unit from the case, depress the locking tang with a small screwdriver and slide the sending unit to the left as indicated

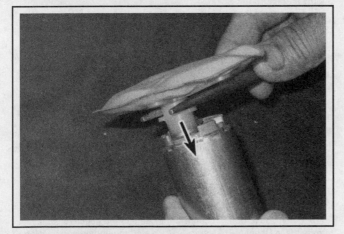

6.15a To install the strainer on the fuel pump, align the hole in the strainer mounting flange with the locator pin on the pump, then use a pair of needle-nose pliers to push against these lugs to push the strainer into the pump

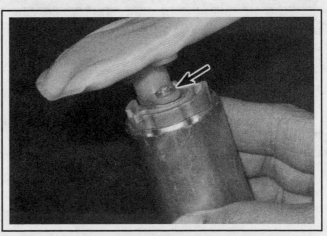

6.15b Here's how the fuel strainer should look when it's correctly installed on the pump: note the new retainer clip seated flat against the mounting flange

6.16a Inspect the O-rings for the fuel filter inlet and outlet; if either O-ring is cracked, torn or deteriorated, replace it

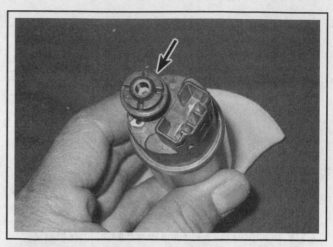

6.16b Make sure that the spacer at the top of the pump is in place and in good condition; without this spacer, the pump outlet pipe will not be a tight fit against the O-ring at the fuel filter inlet

16 Before installing the fuel pump in the fuel filter housing, inspect the condition of the fuel filter inlet and outlet O-rings (see illustration). If either O-ring is cracked, torn or deteriorated, replace it. Also make sure that the spacer at the top of the pump is in place (see illustration). This spacer insures a tight fit between the pump outlet pipe and the fuel filter inlet O-ring. If the spacer is damaged or missing, replace it.

17 Installation is otherwise the reverse of removal, but stop when you're done installing the pump. Before installing the fuel pump access cover, reconnect the cable to the negative battery terminal (see Chapter 5, Section 1), start the engine and check for fuel leaks at the pump fuel line connections. If there are no leaks, install the access cover, the carpet and the second-row seat.

7 Fuel tank - removal and installation

♦ **Refer to illustrations 7.5, 7.6a, 7.6b, 7.6c, 7.7, 7.8, 7.9a and 7.9b**

➡ **Note:** The following procedure is much easier to perform if the fuel tank is empty. The tank has no drain plug, so the fuel must be siphoned from the tank with a siphoning kit, which is available at most auto parts stores. NEVER try to start the siphoning action with your mouth!

1 Remove the fuel tank filler cap to relieve fuel tank pressure.

2 Relieve the fuel system pressure (see Section 2), then disconnect the cable from the negative battery terminal (see Chapter 5, Section 1).

3 Raise the vehicle and place it securely on jackstands.

4 If the fuel tank is empty or nearly empty, it's not necessary to siphon the remaining fuel from the tank. But if there *is* a lot of fuel in the tank, drain the fuel by removing the fuel pump/fuel level sending unit (see Section 5) and siphoning it out through the opening in the tip of the tank.

5 Disconnect the four-pin electrical connector (see illustration), which is located right in front of the tank, just below the fuel supply and return line connections. (This is the connector for the fuel pump/fuel level sending unit module.)

6 Disconnect the fuel supply and return line connections and cover the ends of the line fittings with plastic bags to prevent dirt and moisture from contaminating the fuel system (see illustrations). Also, loosen the hose clamp and disconnect the EVAP hose that's located next to the supply and return lines.

7 Disconnect the fuel filler neck hose and the three EVAP hoses (see illustration).

8 Support the fuel tank with a transmission jack (see illustration). If you don't have a transmission jack, use a floor jack. If you're going to use a floor jack, put a piece of plywood between the jack head and the fuel tank to protect the tank.

9 Unbolt the fuel tank retaining straps (see illustrations) and remove them.

10 Carefully lower the fuel tank.

11 If you need to remove the fuel pump/fuel level sending unit module, but haven't yet done so, refer to Sections 5 and 6. If you're going to have the fuel tank cleaned, refer to Section 8.

12 Installation is the reverse of removal. Be sure to tighten the fuel tank strap bolts to the torque listed in this Chapter's Specifications.

13 When you're done, reconnect the cable to the negative battery terminal (see Chapter 5, Section 1), then start the engine and check for fuel leaks.

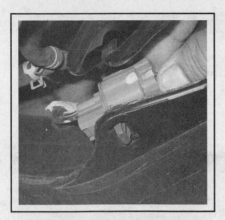

7.5 Disconnect this gray four-pin electrical connector, which is located in front of the fuel tank, near the fuel supply and return line connections (shown in the next photo)

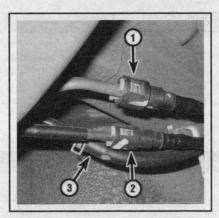

7.6a Disconnect the fuel supply line (1), the fuel return line (2) and the EVAP hose (3) at these connections, which are located in front of the fuel tank

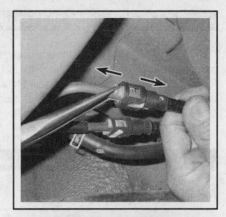

7.6b To disconnect the fuel supply and return line quick-connect fittings, squeeze the retainer with a pair of needle-nose pliers and pull the two halves of each fitting apart

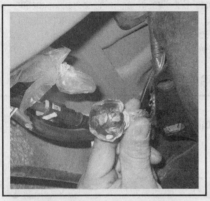

7.6c Cover the open ends of the fuel supply and return line fittings with plastic bags to prevent dirt and moisture from contaminating the fuel system

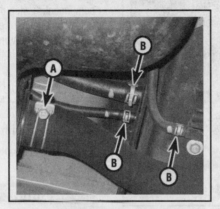

7.7 To disconnect the fuel filler neck hose, loosen this hose clamp (A) and pull off the hose; then loosen these three spring-type hose clamps (B) and disconnect the EVAP hoses (the hoses are three different diameters, so it's not necessary to label them)

7.8 Support the fuel tank with a transmission jack (shown) or with a floor jack; if you're going to use a floor jack, be sure to place a piece of plywood between the jack head and the fuel tank to protect the tank

7.9a Fuel tank strap bolts (left side)

7.9b Fuel tank strap bolts (right side)

8 Fuel tank cleaning and repair - general information

1 The fuel tanks installed in the vehicles covered by this manual are made of plastic and are not repairable. If the fuel tank has been removed for cleaning, this is a job that should be left to a professional who has experience in this critical and potentially dangerous work. Even after cleaning and flushing of the fuel tank, explosive fumes can remain.

2 If the fuel tank is removed from the vehicle, it should not be placed in an area where sparks or open flames could ignite the fumes coming out of the tank. Be especially careful inside garages where a gas-type appliance is located, because it could cause an explosion.

9 Air filter housing - removal and installation

AIR INTAKE DUCT

▶ Refer to illustrations 9.1, 9.2, 9.3, 9.4 and 9.5

1 Clearly label all cables and hoses (see illustration) that are

9.1 Note the routing of these cables and hoses, then detach or disconnect them from the air intake duct:

1 Cruise control cable
2 EVAP canister purge valve-to-throttle body hose
3 Coolant hose for air filter housing radiator
4 Coolant hose for air filter housing radiator
5 Positive Crankcase Ventilation (PCV) fresh air inlet hose

attached or connected to the air intake duct, then detach or disconnect them and set them aside.

2 Detach the left end of the air intake duct from the air filter housing (see illustration).

3 Loosen the hose clamp that secures the air intake duct to the throttle body (see illustration).

4 Remove the air intake duct (see illustration).

5 If you removed the air intake duct just to access some other component(s), skip this step. But if you're planning to replace the air intake duct itself, or either resonator, loosen the hose clamp(s) and remove the resonator(s) (see illustration).

6 Installation is the reverse of removal.

AIR FILTER HOUSING

2004 and earlier models

▶ Refer to illustrations 9.8, 9.10, 9.11a and 9.11b

✳ WARNING:

Wait until the engine is completely cool before beginning this procedure.

7 Remove the air intake duct (see Steps 1 through 4).

8 Pinch off the two coolant hoses to the radiator inside the air filter housing (see illustration). If you don't have tools suitable for safely

9.2 The left end of the air intake duct uses a spring to secure it to the air filter housing, so all you have to do is pull it off; when installing the air intake duct, be sure align the locator tab on the duct between the two ridges on the air filter housing

9.3 To detach the air intake duct from the throttle body, loosen this hose clamp screw

9.4 Before you remove the air intake duct from the engine compartment, carefully lift it up slightly and verify that there are no more cables or hoses attached or connected to it

9.5 If you're replacing the air intake duct, loosen these hose clamp screws and detach the resonators (you can also replace either of the resonators separately)

pinching off the coolant hose, drain the coolant (see Chapter 1). Then detach the coolant hose bracket from the air filter housing cover, loosen the two hose clamps and disconnect the coolant lines from the radiator hoses.

9 Remove the air filter housing cover and the air filter element (see Chapter 1).

10 Remove the two air filter housing bolts (see illustration) and remove the air filter housing.

11 If you're going to replace the radiator inside the air filter housing, remove the four radiator cover bolts (see illustration), remove the cover, remove the radiator mounting bolt (see illustration) and remove the radiator.

12 Installation is the reverse of removal.

13 Be sure to refill the cooling system (see Chapter 1) if you drained it.

9.10 To detach the air filter housing, remove these two bolts

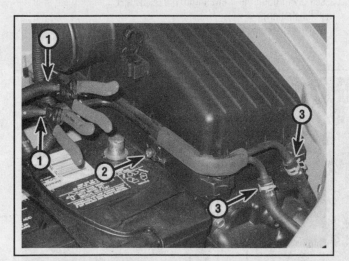

9.8 Before you can remove the air filter housing, you must:

1   *Pinch off the coolant hoses for the small radiator inside the air filter housing*
2   *Remove the screw that attaches the coolant hose bracket to the air filter housing cover*
3   *Loosen the hose clamps and disconnect the coolant lines from the radiator hoses*

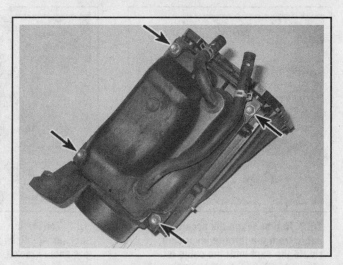

9.11a To remove the radiator cover, remove these four bolts

9.11b To detach the radiator from the cover, remove this bolt

2005 and later models

14 Disconnect the ducts from the housing.

15 Remove the two mounting bolts and lift the housing up. Installation is the reverse of removal.

---

10 Accelerator cable - removal, installation and adjustment

➡ **Note: This Section applies only to 2004 and earlier models. Later models use an electronically controlled throttle (see Chapter 6).**

REMOVAL AND INSTALLATION

▶ **Refer to illustrations 10.2, 10.3, 10.4, 10.5a, 10.5b, 10.6a and 10.6b**

1 Disconnect the cable from the negative battery terminal (see Chapter 5, Section 1).

2 Rotate the throttle lever cam until the cable is lined up with the slot in the cam, then disengage the cable from the cam (see illustration).

3 Using a pair of wrenches, loosen the accelerator cable locknut at the cable bracket (see illustration) and disengage the accelerator cable from its bracket.

4 Tracing the cable from the cable bracket back to the firewall, detach or disengage it from any clamps, clips or cable guides (see illustration).

5 Using a flashlight so that you can see underneath the dash, locate the cable connection at the top of the accelerator pedal (see illustration), push the upper end of the pedal forward and disengage the cable from the pedal arm (see illustration).

6 Remove the two nuts (see illustration) that secure the accelerator cable grommet and mounting flange to the firewall, then pull the cable assembly through the firewall from the passenger compartment side (see illustration).

7 Installation is the reverse of removal.

10.2 To disengage the accelerator cable from the throttle lever cam, rotate the cam until the cable is aligned with the slot in the cam and then pull out the cable

10.3 Loosen the accelerator cable locknut and disengage the cable from the cable bracket

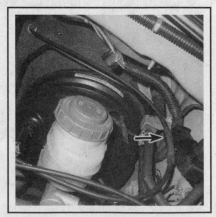

10.4 Trace the accelerator cable back from its cable bracket to the firewall and disengage it from any clamps, clips or cable guides (2000 model shown, other models might have slightly different cable routing)

10.5a The accelerator cable is connected to the top end of the accelerator pedal arm

10.5b To disengage the accelerator cable from the accelerator pedal arm, push the upper end of the arm forward, pull back on the cable end plug and pull out the cable through this slot in the pedal arm

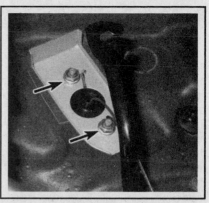

10.6a To detach the accelerator cable grommet and mounting flange from the firewall, remove these two nuts . . .

10.6b . . . then pull the cable through the firewall from the passenger compartment side

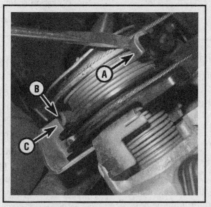

10.8a To adjust the accelerator cable, rotate the throttle cam (A) toward the cable bracket until the lever on the cam contacts the throttle stop tang (C); there should be no clearance at the point of contact (B)

10.8b Here's a better view of the lever on the throttle cam (A) contacting the throttle stop bracket (C), with zero clearance at the point of contact (B) (throttle body removed for clarity)

ADJUSTMENT

▶ **Refer to illustrations 10.8a, 10.8b and 10.8c**

8   Rotate the accelerator cable throttle cam toward the cable bracket until the small lever on the bottom of the cam contacts the throttle stop bracket (see illustrations), then measure the cable deflection (see illustration) and compare your measurement to the cable deflection listed in this Chapter's Specifications.

9   If the cable deflection is incorrect, loosen the cable locknut (see illustration 10.8c) and turn the adjustment nut until the deflection is within the specified range.

10.8c Measure the cable deflection where indicated and compare your measurement to the deflection listed in this Chapter's Specifications; if the cable deflection is out of range, adjust it by loosening the locknut (A) and turning the adjustment nut (B) until the deflection is within the specified range

11 Programmed Fuel Injection (PGM-FI) system - general information

The Programmed Fuel Injection (PGM-FI) system is a "sequential multiport" system. This means that there is a fuel injector in each intake port, and that these fuel injectors inject fuel into the intake ports in the cylinder firing order (1-4-2-5-3-6). The injectors are turned on and off by the Powertrain Control Module (PCM). When the engine is running, the PCM constantly monitors engine operating conditions with an array of information sensors, calculates the correct amount of fuel, then varies the interval of time during which the injectors are open. Sequential multiport systems provide much better control of the air/fuel mixture ratio than earlier fuel injection systems, and are therefore able to produce more power, better mileage and lower emissions.

The PGM-FI system uses the PCM and an array of information sensors to determine and deliver the correct air/fuel ratio under all operating conditions. The PGM-FI system consists of three sub-systems: air induction, electronic control and fuel delivery. The PGM-FI system is also closely interrelated with PCM-controlled emission control systems. For additional information about the PCM, the information sensors and the emission control systems, refer to Chapter 6.

AIR INDUCTION SYSTEM

The air induction system consists of the air filter assembly, the air intake duct, the throttle body and the intake manifold. The air filter assembly on 2004 and earlier models is equipped with a small heat exchanger that warms intake air during cold weather before it gets to the intake manifold. Engine coolant is routed through the heat exchanger. A hinged flap, which is controlled by a wax element, directs incoming air around the heat exchanger, or through it. When the ambient air temperature is above 32-degrees (0-degrees C), the hinged flap closes off the passage in which the heat exchanger is located. When the ambient temperature drops below 32-degrees (0-degrees C), the wax element moves the hinged flap so that incoming air is routed through the passage containing the heat exchanger.

The throttle body contains a throttle plate that regulates the amount of air entering the intake manifold. The lower part of the throttle body is heated by engine coolant to prevent icing in cold weather. The throttle body is also the location of the Throttle Position (TP) sensor, a potentiometer that monitors the opening angle of the throttle plate and sends a variable voltage signal to the Powertrain Control Module (PCM). All of the air induction components (air filter housing, air intake duct and throttle body) are covered in this Chapter, except for the intake manifold, which is covered in Chapter 2A.

When the engine is idling, the Idle Air Control (IAC) system on 2004 and earlier models maintains the correct idle speed by regulating the amount of air that bypasses the (closed) throttle plate in response to a command from the Powertrain Control Module (PCM). The IAC system consists of the IAC valve (located on the throttle body), the PCM, and several information sensors, including the Engine Coolant Tem-

perature (ECT) sensor, the Intake Air Temperature (IAT) sensor and the Manifold Absolute Pressure (MAP) sensor. The IAC valve is activated and controlled by the PCM in response to the running conditions of the engine (cold or warm running, power steering pressure high or low, air conditioning system on or off, etc.). As the PCM receives data from the information sensors (vehicle speed, coolant temperature, air conditioning and/or power steering load, etc.) it adjusts the idle according to the demands of the engine and driver.

ELECTRONIC CONTROL SYSTEM

For more information about the electronic control system, i.e. the PCM, its information sensors and output actuators, refer to Chapter 6.

FUEL DELIVERY SYSTEM

The fuel delivery system consists of the fuel pump, the fuel filter, the fuel pulsation damper, the fuel rail and fuel injectors, and the lines and fittings that carry fuel between all of these components.

The fuel pump is an in-tank design, and it can be removed from the top of the fuel tank without removing the tank. Fuel is drawn through a sock (or strainer) at the pump inlet, then pumped out the other end of the pump into an integral fuel filter (located in the same housing as the pump). After the pressurized fuel has been filtered, it's pumped through a supply line up to the fuel rail, which is located between the cylinder heads on the engine. Right before the fuel reaches the fuel rail, it's pumped through a fuel pulsation damper, which is located near the fuel rail on 2004 and earlier models. The pulsation damper attenuates the hydraulic and acoustic noise produced by the fuel pump when it's operating.

The fuel rail consists of a pair of parallel, identical tubes that are bolted to the lower intake manifold. The fuel rail houses the upper end of each fuel injector (the lower end of each injector is inserted into the intake manifold).

Each fuel injector is a solenoid-actuated, pintle-type design consisting of a solenoid, plunger, needle valve and housing. When the engine is running, there is always voltage on the hot side of each injector terminal. The PCM turns the injectors on and off by switching their ground paths on and off. When the ground path for an injector is closed by the PCM, current flows through the solenoid coil, the needle valve raises and pressurized fuel inside the injector housing squirts out the nozzle. The quantity of fuel injected each time an injector opens is determined by the pulse width, which is the interval of time during which the valve is open.

On 2004 and earlier models, the fuel pressure regulator is mounted at the fuel rail in the engine compartment. It controls the flow of fuel through the return line. On 2005 and later models, the fuel pressure regulator is part of the fuel pump module; there is no fuel return line.

12 Programmed Fuel Injection (PGM-FI) system - check

▶ **Refer to illustrations 12.7 and 12.9**

✳ WARNING:

Gasoline is extremely flammable, so take extra precautions when you work on any part of the fuel system. See the Warning in Section 2.

➡ **Note: The following procedure is based on the assumption that the fuel pump is working and the fuel pressure is adequate (see Section 3).**

1 Check all electrical connectors that are related to the system. Check the ground wire connections for tightness. Loose connectors and poor grounds can cause many problems that resemble more serious malfunctions.

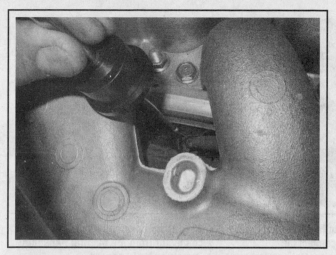

12.7 Use a stethoscope to listen to each injector; it should make a clicking sound that rises and falls with engine speed

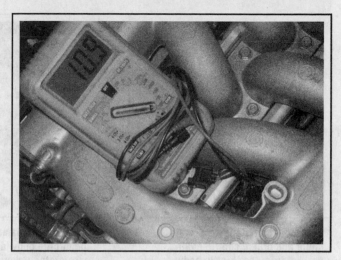

12.9 Use an ohmmeter to measure the resistance of an injector that's not working

2   Verify that the battery is fully charged. The Powertrain Control Module (PCM), information sensors and output actuators (the fuel injectors are output actuators) depend on a stable voltage supply in order to meter fuel correctly.

3   Inspect the air filter element (see Chapter 1). A dirty or partially blocked filter will severely impede performance and economy.

4   Check all fuses related to the fuel system (see Chapter 12). If you find a blown fuse, replace it and see if it blows again. If it does, look for a wire shorted to ground in the circuit(s) protected by that fuse.

5   Check the air induction system between the throttle body and the intake manifold for air leaks, which will cause a lean air/fuel mixture ratio. When the mixture ratio becomes excessively lean, the engine will begin misfiring. Also inspect the condition of all vacuum hoses connected to the intake manifold and to the throttle body. A loose or broken vacuum hose will allow "false (unmetered) air" into the intake manifold. The Manifold Absolute Pressure (MAP) sensor and the PCM can compensate for some false air, but if it's excessive, especially at idle and during other high-intake-manifold-vacuum conditions, the engine will misfire.

6   Remove the air intake duct from the throttle body and look for dirt, carbon, varnish, or other residue in the throttle body, particularly around the throttle plate. If it's dirty, clean it with carb cleaner, a toothbrush and a clean shop towel.

7   With the engine running, place an automotive stethoscope against each injector, one at a time, and listen for a clicking sound that indicates operation (see illustration). If you don't have a stethoscope, touch the tip of a long screwdriver against each injector and listen through the handle.

8   If you can hear the injectors operating, but the engine is misfiring, then the electrical circuits are functioning correctly, but the injectors might be dirty or clogged. Try a commercial injector cleaning product (available at auto parts stores). If cleaning the injectors doesn't help, the injectors probably need to be replaced.

9   If an injector is not operating, i.e. it makes no sound, disconnect the injector electrical connector and measure the resistance across the injector terminals with an ohmmeter (see illustration). Compare your measurement with the resistance value listed in this Chapter's Specifications. Replace any injector whose resistance value does not fall within the specifications.

10 If the injector is not operating, but the resistance reading is within specifications, the PCM or the circuit between the PCM and the injector might be faulty.

13   Throttle body - removal and installation

▶ **Refer to illustrations 13.4a, 13.4b, 13.5, 13.6, 13.7, 13.8, 13.9 and 13.10**

✳✳ WARNING:

Wait until the engine is completely cool before beginning this procedure.

1   Disconnect the cable from the negative battery terminal (see Chapter 5, Section 1).

2   Pinch off the two coolant hoses to the throttle body. If you don't have tools suitable for doing this, drain the engine coolant until the level in the cooling system is lower than the throttle body (see Chapter 1).

3   Remove the air intake duct (see Section 9).

13.4a To detach the accelerator cable and cruise control cable bracket from the throttle body, remove these two screws

13.4b After detaching the cable from the throttle body, disconnect the accelerator and cruise control cables from the throttle lever cam (see Section 10 if you need help)

13.5 Disconnect the electrical connector from the Manifold Absolute Pressure (MAP) sensor

13.6 Disconnect the electrical connector from the Throttle Position (TP) sensor

13.7 Pinch off the two coolant hoses connected to the throttle body, then loosen the hose clamps, slide them back and disconnect both coolant hoses from the throttle body

13.8 Loosen the hose clamp, slide it back and disconnect the Evaporative Emissions (EVAP) system purge valve hose from the throttle body

13.9 Disconnect the electrical connector from the Idle Air Control (IAC) valve, which is located underneath the throttle body - 2004 and earlier models

4   Detach the cable bracket (see illustration) from the throttle body. (By detaching the cable bracket from the throttle body, but leaving the accelerator and cruise control cables attached to the cable bracket, you won't disturb the adjustment of either cable.) Then disconnect the accelerator cable and the cruise control cable from the throttle lever cam (see illustration) the same way that you disconnected the accelerator cable in Section 10.

5   Disconnect the electrical connector from the Manifold Absolute Pressure (MAP) sensor (see illustration).

6   On 2004 and earlier models, disconnect the electrical connector from the Throttle Position (TP) sensor (see illustration).

7   Loosen and slide back the hose clamps and disconnect the coolant hoses from the throttle body (see illustration). Be prepared to mop up any coolant still in the hoses or in the throttle body. Plug the hoses to prevent coolant loss.

8   Disconnect the EVAP hose (see illustration) on 2004 and earlier models.

9   Disconnect the wiring from the IAC valve on 2004 and earlier models (see illustration). On 2005 and later models, disconnect the main wiring harness.

10 Remove the two bolts and two nuts that attach the throttle body to the intake manifold (see illustration) and remove the throttle body, the spacer and the two gaskets.

11 Remove all traces of old gasket material from the throttle body, the spacer and the intake manifold.

12 Installation is the reverse of removal. Be sure to use new gaskets and tighten the throttle body mounting bolts and nuts to the torque listed in this Chapter's Specifications.

13 When you're done, refill the cooling system if you drained it (see Chapter 1). If you didn't drain the system, be sure to check the coolant level and add some, as necessary, to bring it to the appropriate level (see Chapter 1).

14 On 2004 and earlier models, check the accelerator cable adjustment and adjust it if necessary (see Section 10).

15 Reconnect the cable to the negative battery terminal (see Chapter 5, Section 1).

16 Start the engine and check for air and coolant leaks.

13.10 To detach the throttle body from the intake manifold, remove the two upper mounting nuts and the two lower mounting bolts

14 Fuel pulsation damper - removal and installation

▶ Refer to illustrations 14.2, 14.3a, 14.3b and 14.4

➡ **Note: This procedure applies only to 2004 and earlier models. Later models do not use a pulsation damper.**

1   Relieve the system fuel pressure (see Section 2), then disconnect the cable from the negative battery terminal (see Chapter 5, Section 1).

2   Remove the small black plastic ring from the fuel pulsation damper (see illustration).

3   Remove the pulsation damper (see illustrations).

4   Use new sealing washers when installing the pulsation damper, and be sure to align the slot in the banjo fitting bracket with the locator pin on the junction block (see illustration).

5   Tighten the fuel pulsation damper to the torque listed in this Chapter's Specifications.

6   Install the black plastic ring on the fixed nut. Make sure that the ridge on the inner bore of the ring is aligned with the notches in the nut.

7   Reconnect the cable to the negative battery terminal (see Chapter 5, Section 1), then start the engine and check for leaks around the pulsation damper.

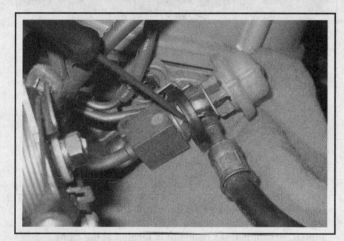

14.2 Remove this small black plastic ring from the fuel pulsation damper

14.3a Using a back-up wrench on the fixed nut to protect the metal fuel line from kinking, loosen the fuel pulsation damper with another wrench . . .

14.3b . . . remove the damper and remove and discard the old sealing washers on each side of the banjo fitting

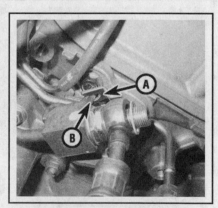

14.4 When installing the fuel pulsation damper, be sure to align the slot (A) in the banjo fitting bracket with the locator pin (B) on the junction block

15 Fuel pressure regulator - removal and installation

▶ Refer to illustrations 15.5, 15.6, 15.7a, 15.7b and 15.8

☀ WARNING:

Gasoline is extremely flammable, so take extra precautions when you work on any part of the fuel system. See the Warning in Section 2.

➡ **Note: This procedure applies only to 2004 and earlier models. The fuel pressure regulator on later models is part of the fuel pump module (see Section 6 for replacement).**

1   Relieve the system fuel pressure (see Section 2).

2   Disconnect the cable from the negative battery terminal (see Chapter 5, Section 1).

3   On 2001 models, remove the intake manifold cover (see Chapter 2A). (You can access the fuel pressure regulator without removing the cover on 2002 and later models.)

4   On 2001 models, remove the intake manifold (see Chapter 2A). (You can access the fuel pressure regulator on 2002 and later models without removing the intake manifold.)

5   Disconnect the vacuum hose from the fuel pressure regulator (see illustration). Squeeze the clamp on the fuel return hose and slide it back, then detach the fuel return hose from the pressure regulator. Be prepared for some fuel to spill out.

6   On 2001 models, remove the fuel pressure regulator from the fuel rail (see illustration). On 2002 and later models, remove the regulator from the junction block.

7   Be sure to use a new O-ring when installing the new pressure regulator. Even if you're planning to reinstall the old pressure regulator, be sure to remove and discard the old O-ring, then install a new O-ring and coat it with a little clean engine oil (see illustrations). Make sure that you don't damage the new O-ring during installation or reassembly, or it might leak when subjected to operating fuel pressure.

15.5 Disconnect the vacuum hose from the fuel pressure regulator (2001 model shown, 2002 through 2004 models similar, except that the regulator is located at the same junction block as the fuel pulsation damper)

15.6 To remove the fuel pressure regulator from the fuel rail, unscrew this big nut with a wrench (2001 model shown, 2002 through 2004 models similar except that the regulator must be unscrewed from the junction block for the fuel pulsation damper)

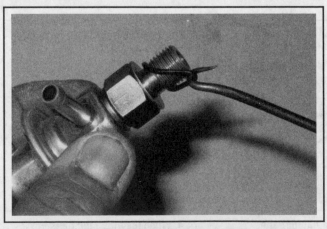

15.7a Be sure to use a new O-ring when installing the fuel pressure regulator; even if you're planning to reuse the old regulator, be sure to remove and discard the old O-ring and install a new O-ring

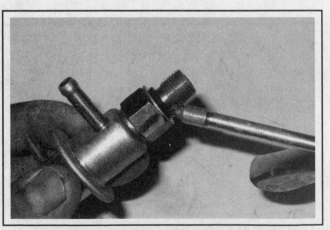

15.7b Be sure to coat the new O-ring with a little clean engine oil before installing the fuel pressure regulator to protect it from damage during installation; the O-ring will leak if it's kinked or distorted during reassembly

8   When installing the fuel pressure regulator, screw it in by hand until it stops, then turn it counterclockwise until it is properly oriented. On 2001 models, orient the regulator as shown (see illustration), with the fuel return pipe facing straight down (6 o'clock) and the vacuum pipe pointing toward the firewall at about a 45-degree angle. On 2002 and later models, orient the regulator so that the vacuum hose pipe is facing straight back (toward the firewall).

9   Installation is otherwise the reverse of removal. Be sure to tighten the fuel pressure regulator locking nut to the torque listed in this Chapter's Specifications.

10 When you're done, reconnect the cable to the negative battery terminal (see Chapter 5, Section 1), then start the engine and check for fuel leaks around the fuel pressure regulator.

15.8 This is how the fuel pressure regulator should be oriented on 2001 models before tightening the locknut: fuel return hose pipe faces straight down (6 o'clock) and the vacuum hose pipe faces toward the firewall at about a 45-degree angle

16 Fuel rail and injectors - removal and installation

REMOVAL

◆ **Refer to illustrations 16.3, 16.5a, 16.5b, 16.8, 16.9a, 16.9b, 16.9c, 16.9d and 16.10**

❈❈ WARNING:

Gasoline is extremely flammable, so take extra precautions when you work on any part of the fuel system. See the Warning in Section 2.

1   Relieve the system fuel pressure (see Section 2), then disconnect the cable from the negative battery terminal (see Chapter 5, Section 1).

2   Remove the intake manifold cover and the upper intake manifold (see Chapter 2A).

3   Disconnect the electrical connectors from the fuel injectors (see illustration).

4   On 2001 models, disconnect the vacuum hose and the fuel return hose from the fuel pressure regulator (see Section 15).

5   On 2001 models, disconnect the fuel supply hose from the front fuel rail (see illustration), then remove and discard the old O-ring (see illustration). There's another similar hose that connects the right ends of the two fuel rails. This is the crossover hose. It's not necessary to disconnect the fuel crossover hose to remove the fuel rail and injectors. However, if the engine has some miles on it, disconnect the crossover and replace both O-rings at that end.

16.3 Disconnect the electrical connectors from all six fuel injectors (2001 model shown, 2002 and later models similar)

16.5a To disconnect the fuel supply hose from the front fuel rail on 2001 models, remove this nut

6   On 2002 and later models, you have two options with respect to fuel hose disconnection. Disconnect the crossover hose from the left ends of both the front and rear fuel rails, OR disconnect the fuel hose from the junction block where the fuel pulsation damper and fuel pressure regulator are located, at the left rear corner of the engine. The crossover hose on these models is attached to the fuel rails exactly the same way as the fuel supply hose and the crossover hose on the earlier models. If you're disconnecting the crossover hose from the fuel rails, remove and discard the old O-ring at each end of the crossover hose, and replace it with a new O-ring prior to reassembly.

7   On 2001 models, remove the four fuel rail retaining bolts (see illustration 16.5b). On 2002 and later models, there are eight fuel rail mounting bolts. Four of them are similar to the fuel rail mounting bolts used on 2001 models. The other four are actually retaining bolts for the two fuel injector wiring harness covers; remove them and set the harness covers and the harnesses aside.

8   Remove the fuel rails and the fuel injectors as a single assembly (see illustration). If any of the injectors are difficult to extract from their bores, carefully pry them loose as shown.

9   Remove each injector from its bore in the fuel rail (see illustration). Remove the fuel strainer from each injector (see illustration), wash it thoroughly in clean solvent and set it aside. (If any strainer proves to be impossible to clean, replace it.) Remove and discard the upper O-ring and the cushion ring (see illustration). Remove and discard the lower O-ring (see illustration). Repeat this procedure for each injector.

➡ **Note: Even if you only removed the fuel rail assembly to replace a single injector or a leaking O-ring, it's a good idea to remove all of the injectors from the fuel rail and replace all the O-rings, cushion rings and seal rings at the same time.**

10 Remove and discard the seal ring from each injector bore in the cylinder head (see illustration).

16.5b After disconnecting the fuel supply hose from the front fuel rail, replace this O-ring (A). To detach the fuel rail, remove all four mounting bolts: two bolts on the front fuel rail (B) and two bolts on the rear fuel rail (not shown) (2001 models)

16.8 To remove the fuel rails and the fuel injectors, carefully but firmly pull up on the rails; if any of the injectors are difficult to extricate from their bores in the intake manifold, carefully pry them up with a pair of angled needle-nose pliers or some other suitable tool

16.9a To remove each injector from its bore in the fuel rail, simply wiggle it from side to side and pull on it simultaneously

16.9b Carefully remove the fuel strainer from the top of each fuel injector, wash it in clean solvent, then install it

16.9c Carefully remove the upper O-ring and the cushion ring and discard both of them

INSTALLATION

▶ **Refer to illustration 16.13**

11 Coat the new cushion rings and upper O-rings with clean engine oil and slide them into place on each of the fuel injectors. Insert the fuel strainer into the top of each injector. Coat the new lower O-rings with clean engine oil and install them on the lower ends of the injectors.

12 Coat the outside surface of each upper O-ring and cushion ring with clean engine oil, then insert each injector into its corresponding bore in the fuel rail.

13 Coat each new seal ring with clean engine oil and press it into an injector bore in the intake manifold (see illustration).

14 Install the injectors and fuel rail assembly on the intake manifold. Tighten the fuel rail mounting bolts to the torque listed in this Chapter's Specifications. On 2002 and later models, reattach the fuel injector wiring harness covers to the fuel rails.

15 The remainder of installation is the reverse of removal.

16 When you're done reassembling everything, reconnect the cable to the negative battery terminal (see Chapter 5, Section 1).

17 Turn the ignition switch to ON - this activates the fuel pump for about two seconds, which builds up fuel pressure in the fuel lines and the fuel rail - but don't operate the starter. Repeat this step two or three times, then check the fuel lines, fuel rails and injectors for fuel leaks.

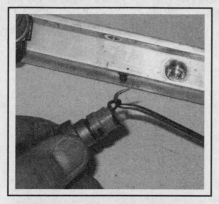

16.9d Remove and discard the lower O-ring

16.10 Carefully pry the seal ring from each of the six injector bores; be extremely careful not to damage the injector bores

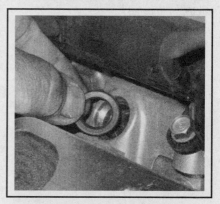

16.13 Coat each new seal ring with clean engine oil, insert it into an injector bore and push it down until it's fully seated in the bottom of the bore

17 Exhaust system servicing - general information

▶ **Refer to illustrations 17.1a and 17.1b**

✳✳ **WARNING:**

Inspect and repair exhaust system components only after enough time has elapsed after driving the vehicle to allow the system components to cool completely. Also, when working under the vehicle, make sure it is securely supported on jackstands.

1 The exhaust system consists of the exhaust manifolds, the catalytic converter, the muffler, the tailpipe and all connecting pipes, flanges and clamps. The exhaust system is isolated from the vehicle body and from chassis components by a series of rubber hangers (see illustrations). Periodically inspect these hangers for cracks or other signs of deterioration, replacing them as necessary.

2 Conduct regular inspections of the exhaust system to keep it safe and quiet. Look for any damaged or bent parts, open seams, holes,

17.1a This exhaust hanger is bolted to the underside of the vehicle; to detach it, remove these two bolts

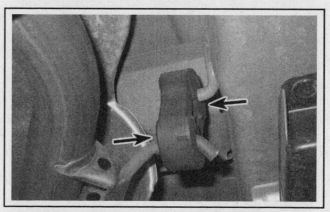

17.1b The rest of the exhaust system hangers look this one; to replace one of them, simply disengage it from the hook on the vehicle and from the hook on the exhaust bracket

loose connections, excessive corrosion or other defects which could allow exhaust fumes to enter the vehicle. Do not repair deteriorated exhaust system components; replace them with new parts.

3   If the exhaust system components are extremely corroded, or rusted together, you'll need welding equipment and a cutting torch to remove them. The convenient strategy at this point is to have a muffler repair shop remove the corroded sections with a cutting torch. If you want to save money by doing it yourself, but you don't have a welding outfit and cutting torch, simply cut off the old components with a hacksaw. If you have compressed air, there are special pneumatic cutting chisels (available from specialty tool manufacturers) that can also be used. If you decide to tackle the job at home, be sure to wear safety goggles to protect your eyes from metal chips and wear work gloves to protect your hands.

4   Here are some simple guidelines to follow when repairing the exhaust system:

a)   *Work from the back to the front when removing exhaust system components.*

b)   *Apply penetrating oil to the exhaust system component fasteners to make them easier to remove.*

c)   *Use new gaskets, hangers and clamps when installing exhaust systems components.*

d)   *Apply anti-seize compound to the threads of all exhaust system fasteners during reassembly.*

e)   *Be sure to allow sufficient clearance between newly installed parts and all points on the underbody to avoid overheating the floor pan and possibly damaging the interior carpet and insulation. Pay particularly close attention to the catalytic converter and heat shield.*

Specifications

Accelerator cable deflection	3/8 to 1/2-inch (10 to 12 mm)
Fuel system pressure	
2001	
Vacuum hose detached	43 to 49 psi (300 to 340 kPa)
Vacuum hose attached	36 to 43 psi (250 to 300 kPa)
2002 through 2004	42 to 48 psi (290 to 330 kPa)
2005 and later	55 to 63 psi (380 to 430 kPa)
Injector resistance	10 to 13 ohms

Torque specifications	Ft-lbs (unless otherwise indicated)	Nm

➡ **Note: One foot-pound (ft-lb) of torque is equivalent to 12 inch-pounds (in-lbs) of torque. Torque values below approximately 15 foot-pounds are expressed in inch-pounds, because most foot-pound torque wrenches are not accurate at these smaller values.**

Throttle body mounting bolts/nuts	16	22
Fuel rail mounting bolts	86 in-lbs	10
Fuel pressure regulator	22	29
Fuel pulsation damper	16	22
Fuel pump module locknut	69	93

Notes

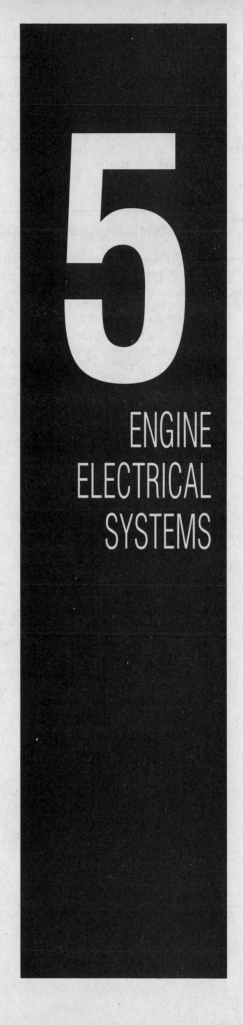

5

ENGINE ELECTRICAL SYSTEMS

1 · General information, precautions and battery disconnection

The engine electrical systems include all ignition, charging and starting components. Because of their engine-related functions, these components are covered separately from body electrical devices such as the lights, the instruments, etc. (which you'll find in Chapter 12).

PRECAUTIONS

Always observe the following precautions when working on the electrical system:

a) Be extremely careful when servicing engine electrical components. They are easily damaged if checked, connected or handled improperly.

b) Never leave the ignition switched on for long periods of time when the engine is not running.

c) Never disconnect the battery cables while the engine is running.

d) Maintain correct polarity when connecting battery cables from another vehicle during jump starting - see the "Booster battery (jump) starting" section at the front of this manual.

e) Always disconnect the cable from the negative battery terminal before working on the electrical system, but read the following battery disconnection procedure first.

It's also a good idea to review the safety-related information regarding the engine electrical systems located in the "Safety first!" section at the front of this manual, before beginning any operation included in this Chapter.

BATTERY DISCONNECTION

Some systems on the vehicle require battery power to be available at all times, either to maintain continuous operation (alarm system, power door locks, etc.), or to maintain control unit memory (radio station presets, Powertrain Control Module and other control units). When the battery is disconnected, the power that maintains these systems is cut. So, before you disconnect the battery, please note the following points to ensure that there are no unforeseen consequences of this action:

a) The radio in some models is equipped with an anti-theft system; make sure you have the correct anti-theft codes for the radio and for the navigation system, if equipped, before disconnecting the battery.

b) When the battery, or any of the components listed below, is disconnected, the engine management system's Powertrain Control Module (PCM) will lose some data from its memory regarding the engine idle characteristics. It is imperative that you perform the "PCM idle learn procedure" (see procedure below) after disconnecting any of the components listed below.

c) On a vehicle with power door locks, it's a wise precaution to remove the key from the ignition and to keep it with you, so that it does not get locked inside if the power door locks should engage accidentally when the battery is reconnected!

Devices known as "memory-savers" can be used to avoid some of these problems. Precise details vary according to the device used. The typical memory saver is plugged into the cigarette lighter and is connected to a spare battery. Then the vehicle battery can be disconnected from the electrical system. The memory saver will provide sufficient current to maintain audio unit security codes, PCM memory, etc. and will provide power to "always hot" circuits such as the clock and radio memory circuits.

✳✳ WARNING:

Some memory savers deliver a considerable amount of current in order to keep vehicle systems operational after the main battery is disconnected. If you're using a memory saver, make sure that the circuit concerned is actually open before servicing it.

✳✳ WARNING:

If you're going to work near any of the airbag system components, the battery MUST be disconnected and a memory saver must NOT be used. If a memory saver is used, power will be supplied to the airbag, which means that it could accidentally deploy and cause serious personal injury.

To disconnect the battery for service procedures requiring power to be cut from the vehicle, loosen the cable clamp nut and disconnect the cable from the negative battery post. Isolate the cable end to prevent it from coming into accidental contact with the battery post.

POWERTRAIN CONTROL MODULE (PCM) IDLE LEARN PROCEDURE

Make sure that the PCM "learns" the engine idle characteristics after you do any of the following procedures:

Disconnect the battery

Replace (or reset) the PCM

Remove (or replaced) the throttle body

Replace the Idle Air Control (IAC) valve

Remove the No. 13 (7.5 amp) CLOCK BACK-UP fuse (in the right-side fuse and relay box inside the vehicle)

Remove the 120-amp BATTERY fuse or the 40-amp BACK-UP/ACC fuse (both of which are located in the fuse and relay box in the engine compartment)

Disconnect or removed any of the wires from the engine compartment fuse and relay box

Disconnect or removed any of the wires from either the left or the right-side fuse and relay box inside the vehicle

Disconnect the electrical connector between the engine wire harness and the left engine compartment harness

Disconnect the battery ground wire from the upper radiator crossmember

Disconnect the ground wire from the engine block or from the transmission

Disconnect the ground wire from the coolant passage (near the fan switch)

Disconnect the injector ground wire from the bracket near the power steering pump

1 Make sure that all electrical components (air conditioning system, lights, rear window defogger, sound system, etc.) are turned OFF.

2 Start the engine, bring it up to 3000 rpm and hold it there, with no load, i.e. in PARK or NEUTRAL, until the radiator fan comes on or until the engine coolant temperature reaches 194-degrees F.

3 Allow the engine to idle for at least five minutes with no load on it.

➡ **Note: If the radiator fan comes on during this five-minute period, don't include the time during which the fan runs as part of the five minutes.**

RESETTING THE POWER WINDOW CONTROL UNIT (2003 AND LATER MODELS)

You must reset the power window control unit after you do any of the following procedures:

Disconnect the battery

Remove the No. 79 (20-amp) fuse from the engine compartment fuse and relay box

Disconnect the 18-pin connector from the power window control unit

Remove the window regulator, the window glass or the glass run channel

Disconnect the driver's door wiring harness

1 Turn the ignition switch to OFF, then turn it to ON.

2 Fully open the driver's window by holding the driver's switch in the AUTO DOWN position. After the window reaches its fully open position, hold the driver's switch in the AUTO DOWN position for two seconds.

3 Fully close the driver's window by holding the driver's switch in the AUTO UP position. After the window reaches its fully closed position, hold the driver's switch in the AUTO UP position for two seconds.

4 If the window doesn't operate in AUTO, reset the power window control unit by repeating this entire procedure.

2 Battery - emergency jump starting

Refer to the "Booster battery (jump) starting" procedure at the front of this manual.

3 Battery - check and replacement

❄❄ CAUTION:

Always disconnect the cable from the negative battery terminal FIRST and hook it up LAST or the battery may be shorted by the tool being used to loosen the cable clamps.

CHECK

◆ **Refer to illustrations 3.2 and 3.3**

1 Disconnect the negative battery cable, then the positive cable from the battery (see Section 1).

2 Check the battery state of charge. Visually inspect the indicator eye on the top of the battery; if the indicator eye is black in color charge the battery as described in Chapter 1. Next perform an open voltage circuit test using a digital voltmeter (see illustration).

➡ **Note: The battery's surface charge must be removed before accurate voltage measurements can be made. Turn on the high beams for ten seconds, then turn them off and let the vehicle stand for two minutes.**

With the engine and all accessories Off, touch the negative probe of the voltmeter to the negative terminal of the battery and the positive probe to the positive terminal of the battery. The battery voltage should be 12.6 volts or slightly above. If the battery is less than the specified voltage, charge the battery before proceeding to the next test. Do not proceed with the battery load test unless the battery charge is correct.

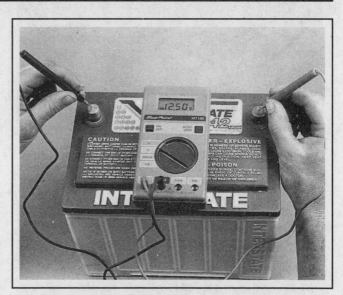

3.2 To test the open circuit voltage of the battery, touch the black probe of the voltmeter to the negative terminal and the red probe to the positive terminal of the battery; a fully charged battery should be at least 12.6 volts

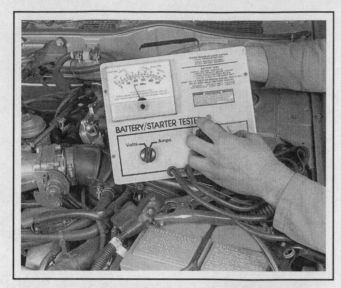

3.3 Some battery load testers (like this one) are equipped with an ammeter that allows you to vary the amount of the load on the battery (less expensive testers only have a load switch that puts the battery under a fixed load)

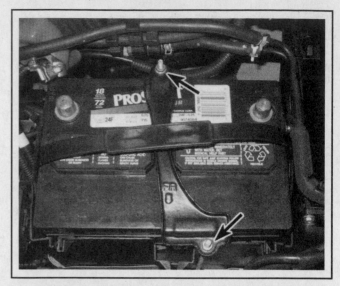

3.5 To remove the battery, unscrew these two nuts and remove the hold-down clamp; note the "FR" (front) on the clamp, indicating that this end of the clamp must face toward the front of the vehicle when you install it again

➥ **Note: Cold temperatures will cause the minimum voltage reading to drop slightly. Follow the chart given in the manufacturer's instructions to compensate for cold climates. Minimum load voltage for freezing temperatures (32 degrees F) should be approximately 9.1 volts.**

REPLACEMENT

▶ **Refer to illustrations 3.5 and 3.8**

4   Disconnect the cable from the negative battery terminal first, then (and only then!) disconnect the cable from the positive battery terminal (see Section 1).

5   Remove the battery hold-down clamp nuts (see illustration) and remove the hold-down clamp.

6   Lift out the battery. Be careful - it's heavy.

➥ **Note: Battery straps and handlers are available at most auto parts stores for a reasonable price. They make it easier to remove and carry the battery.**

7   While the battery is out, inspect the battery tray for corrosion.

8   If there's corrosion on the battery tray, remove the tray's mounting bolts (see illustration) and remove the tray from the engine compartment. Clean the deposits from the metal to prevent the battery tray from further corrosion.

9   If you are replacing the battery, make sure you get one that's identical, with the same dimensions, amperage rating, cold cranking rating, etc.

10 Installation is the reverse of removal. Be sure to connect the positive cable first and the negative cable last (see Section 1).

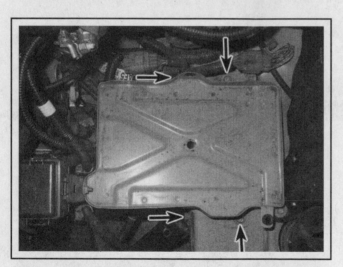

3.8 To remove the battery tray from the engine compartment, remove these four bolts (the right rear bolt, which is hidden under a wire harness, isn't visible in this photo)

3   Perform a battery load test. An accurate check of the battery condition can only be performed with a load tester (available at most auto parts stores). This test evaluates the ability of the battery to operate the starter and other accessories during periods of high current draw. Hook up a load tester to the battery terminals (see illustration). Load test the battery according to the manufacturer's instructions. Maintain the load on the battery for 15 seconds or less and observe that the battery voltage does not drop below 9.6 volts. If the battery condition is weak or defective, the tool will indicate this condition immediately.

4 Battery cables - check and replacement

▶ **Refer to illustrations 4.4a, 4.4b, and 4.4c**

1 Periodically inspect the entire length of each battery cable for damage, cracked or burned insulation and corrosion. Poor battery cable connections can cause starting problems and decreased engine performance.

2 Inspect the cable-to-terminal connections at the ends of the cables for cracks, loose wire strands and corrosion. The presence of white, fluffy deposits under the insulation at the cable terminal connection means that the cable is corroded and should be replaced. Also inspect the battery posts for distortion and corrosion. If they're corroded, clean them up

3 When removing the cables, always disconnect the cable from the negative battery terminal first and hook it up last, or you might accidentally short out the battery with the tool you're using to loosen the cable clamps. Even if you're only replacing the cable for the positive terminal, be sure to disconnect the negative cable from the battery first (see Section 1).

4 Disconnect the old cables from the battery, then trace each of

them to their opposite ends and disconnect them (see illustrations). Be sure to note the routing of each cable before disconnecting it to ensure correct installation.

5 If you are replacing any of the old cables, take them with you when buying new cables. It is vitally important that you replace the cables with identical parts. Cables have characteristics that make them easy to identify. Positive cables are usually red and larger in diameter, and negative cables are usually black and smaller in diameter.

6 Clean the threads of the solenoid or ground connection with a wire brush to remove rust and corrosion. Apply a light coat of battery terminal corrosion inhibitor or petroleum jelly to the threads to prevent future corrosion.

7 Attach the cable to the solenoid or ground connection and tighten the mounting nut/bolt securely.

8 Before connecting a new cable to the battery make sure that it reaches the battery post without having to be stretched.

9 Connect the cable to the positive battery terminal first, then connect the ground cables to the negative battery terminal (see Section 1).

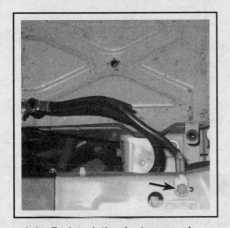

4.4a To detach the shorter ground cable from the upper radiator crossmember, remove this bolt

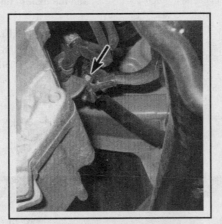

4.4b To detach the longer ground cable from the transaxle, remove this bolt

4.4c To detach the starter cable from the starter solenoid, remove this nut

5 Ignition system - general information

⁂ WARNING:

Because of the high voltage generated by the ignition system, be extremely careful when performing any procedure involving ignition components.

1 The electronic ignition system consists of the powertrain Control Module (PCM) ignition switch, the battery, the six ignition coils and the spark plugs.

2 The PCM alters ignition timing during warm-up, idle and warm

running conditions. It controls ignition timing in accordance with the engine speed, the manifold absolute pressure and the engine coolant temperature. The PCM uses data from the Camshaft Position (Top Dead Center) [CMP (TDC)] sensors to determine ignition timing during start-ups, and anytime that the crank angle is abnormal. The PCM calculates engine speed based on the data that it receives from the Crankshaft Position (CKP) sensor. It uses a Manifold Absolute Pressure (MAP) sensor to determine manifold absolute pressure. For more information about the CMP (TDC), CKP and MAP sensors, refer to Chapter 6.

6   Ignition system - check

◆ Refer to illustration 6.2

> ☀ **WARNING:**
>
> **Because of the high voltage generated by the ignition system, use extreme care when performing a procedure involving ignition components.**

1   If a malfunction occurs in the ignition system, check the following items first:

a) *Make sure that the cable clamps at the battery terminals are clean and tight.*

b) *Test the condition of the battery (see Section 3). If it doesn't pass all the tests, replace it.*

c) *Check the ignition coil connections.*

d) *Check any relevant fuses in the engine compartment fuse and relay box (see Chapter 12). If they're burned, determine the cause and repair the circuit.*

2   If the engine turns over but won't start, disconnect an ignition coil from a spark plug (see Section 7), reconnect the electrical connector to the coil, then attach a spark tester between the ignition coil high-tension terminal and the spark plug (see illustration). Spark testers are available at most auto parts stores. Crank the engine and note whether or not the tester flashes.

3   If the tester flashes during cranking, the coil is delivering sufficient voltage to the spark plug to fire it. Repeat this test for each cylinder to verify that the other coils are OK.

4   If the tester doesn't flash, remove a coil from another cylinder and swap it for the one being tested. If the tester now flashes, you know

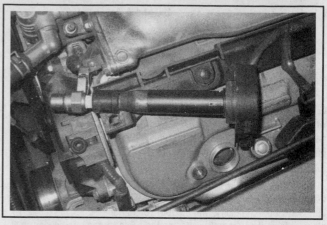

6.2 To use a calibrated spark tester, remove a coil, insert the tester into the coil, clip the tester to a good ground and crank the engine; if the coil is generating enough voltage to fire the plug, sparks will be visible between the electrode tip and the tester body

that the original coil is bad. If the tester still doesn't flash, the PCM or wiring harness is probably defective. Have the PCM checked out by a dealer service department or other qualified repair shop (testing the PCM is beyond the scope of the do-it-yourselfer because it requires expensive special tools).

5   If the tester flashes during cranking but a misfire code (related to the cylinder being tested) has been stored, the spark plug could be fouled or defective

7   Ignition coils - replacement

◆ Refer to illustrations 7.2a, 7.2b, 7.3, 7.4 and 7.5

1   Remove the ignition key from the key lock cylinder.

2   If you're removing an ignition coil from the front cylinder head, remove the ignition coil cover (see illustrations). If you're removing an ignition coil from the rear cylinder head, remove the intake manifold

cover (see "Intake manifold - removal and installation" in Chapter 2A).

3   Disconnect the electrical connector from the ignition coil (see illustration).

4   Remove the ignition coil mounting bolt (see illustration).

5   Remove the ignition coil from the spark plug (see illustration).

6   Installation is the reverse of removal.

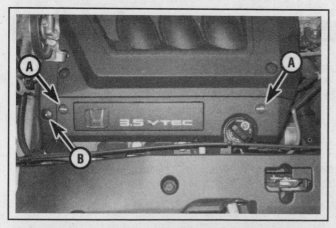

7.2a To access an ignition coil on the front cylinder head, rotate the two coil cover fasteners (A) counterclockwise a quarter-turn . . .

7.2b . . . pull up to disengage the push fastener (B in the previous illustration) and remove the coil cover

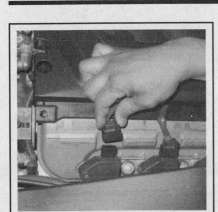

7.3 To disconnect the electrical connector from the ignition coil, depress the locking tab on the side of the connector and pull

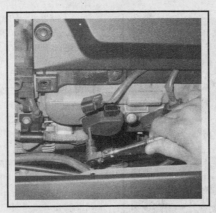

7.4 To detach an ignition coil from the valve cover, remove this bolt

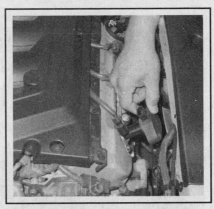

7.5 To disengage an ignition coil from the spark plug, pull firmly

8 Charging system - general information and precautions

The charging system includes the alternator (with an integral voltage regulator inside), a charge indicator light on the dash, the battery, an Electrical Load Detector (ELD), a 120-amp fuse and the wiring connecting all of these components. The charging system supplies electrical power for the ignition system, the lights, the radio, etc. The alternator is driven by a drivebelt at the one end of the engine. The alternator's voltage output is controlled by a conventional internal voltage regulator, which keeps charging output within a range of about 13.5 to 14.5 volts. The ELD, which is located in the engine compartment fuse and relay box, sends a variable voltage signal to the Powertrain Control Module (PCM) that varies in accordance with the total power demand imposed on the charging system by the electrical devices and systems in operation. The PCM uses this variable voltage signal to calculate the actual level of charging voltage needed and alters the charging voltage output accordingly.

The charging system doesn't ordinarily require periodic maintenance. However, the drivebelt, battery and wires and connections should be inspected at the intervals outlined in Chapter 1.

The dashboard warning light should come on when the ignition key is turned to ON, but it should go off immediately after the engine is started. If it remains on, there is a malfunction in the charging system (see Section 9).

Be very careful when making electrical circuit connections to a vehicle equipped with an alternator and note the following:

a) *When reconnecting wires to the alternator from the battery, be sure to note the polarity.*

b) *Before using arc-welding equipment to repair any part of the vehicle, disconnect the wires from the alternator and the battery terminals.*

c) *Never start the engine with a battery charger connected.*

d) *Always disconnect both battery leads before using a battery charger.*

e) *The alternator is turned by an engine drivebelt that could cause serious injury if your hands, hair or clothes become entangled in it with the engine running.*

f) *Because the alternator is connected directly to the battery, it could arc or cause a fire if overloaded or shorted out.*

g) *Wrap a plastic bag over the alternator and secure it with rubber bands before steam cleaning the engine.*

9 Charging system - check

▶ **Refer to illustration 9.3**

1   If a malfunction occurs in the charging circuit, do not immediately assume that the alternator is causing the problem. First, check the following items:

a) *Make sure the battery cable clamps, where they connect to the battery, are clean and tight.*

b) *Test the condition of the battery (see Section 3). If it does not pass all the tests, replace it with a new battery.*

c) *Check the external alternator wiring and connections.*

d) *Check the drivebelt condition and tension (see Chapter 1).*

e) *Check the alternator mounting bolts for tightness.*

f) *Run the engine and check the alternator for abnormal noise.*

g) *Check the 120-amp fuse in the engine compartment fuse and relay box (see Chapter 12). If it's burned, determine the cause and repair the circuit.*

h) *Check the charge light on the dash. It should illuminate when the ignition key is turned ON (engine not running). If it doesn't come on, disconnect the electrical connector and the ground wire from the alternator. The charge light should now come on (because by opening the charging circuit, you have eliminated all charging voltage. If the light still doesn't illuminate, check fuse number 6 (15 amp), which is located in the left (driver's side) passenger compartment fuse and relay box. If the fuse No. 6 is blown, troubleshoot and repair the charge light circuit and then replace the fuse. If the charge light still doesn't come on, check the bulb (see Chapter 12). If it's blown, replace it.*

i) *Make sure that the PCM hasn't stored any diagnostic trouble codes for the Electronic Load Detector (ELD) system (see Chapter 6 for more information about the ELD).*

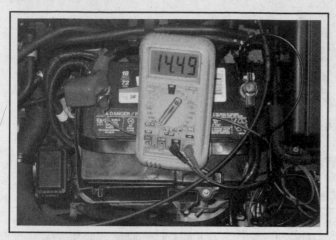

9.3 To check charging voltage, hook up a multimeter to the battery terminals and note the indicated voltage with the engine running, which should be about 13.8 to 14.8 volts

2   With the ignition key turned to the OFF position, check battery voltage with all electrical accessories (blower fan, radio, cigarette lighter, cooling fan, etc.) turned off. It should be about 12.5 volts (it might be slightly higher if the engine has been turned off for less than an hour).

3   Check the charging voltage with the engine running. Start the engine, raise the engine rpm to 1500 and check the battery voltage again. It should now be approximately 13.8 to 14.8 volts (see illustration).

4   Load the battery and observe the charging voltage. Turn on the high beam headlights, the A/C blower on HIGH, the windshield wipers and the radio. The voltage should drop and then come back up as each accessory is selected. If the charging system is working properly the voltage should stay above 13.5 volts. If the voltage drops below 13 volts, the charging system is defective.

5   Lower the engine rpm back to idle and observe the charging voltage. The charging voltage should not drop below 13 volts with the decrease in engine rpm. Apply the brakes and observe the charging voltage at idle. It should remain above 13 volts.

6   Turn off all the electrical loads (high beam headlights, the A/C blower on HIGH, the windshield wipers and the radio), run the engine at 1600 rpm and watch the charging voltage rise. It should not rise above 15 volts.

7   If the charging voltage does not exhibit distinct changes when engine rpm increases and accessory loads are added, the voltage regulator is defective. If the charging voltages are low and the drivebelts and battery are all in good condition, the alternator is defective. In this situation, replace the alternator and voltage regulator as a single unit.

10 Alternator - removal and installation

▶ **Refer to illustrations 10.4 and 10.5**

1   Disconnect the cable from the negative battery terminal (see Section 1).

2   On later models, remove the grille cover to access the alternator, if necessary.

3   Remove the drivebelt (see Chapter 1).

4   Disconnect the wiring from the alternator (see illustration).

5   Detach the interfering wiring brackets and retainers from the alternator (see illustration). On 2005 and later models, the wiring will have to be disconnected from the air conditioning compressor as well.

6   On 2005 and later models, remove the windshield washer reservoir.

7   Pull up on the power steering fluid reservoir to detach it from its mounting bracket on the right inner wheelhousing, push it aside to provide sufficient clearance, then remove the alternator.

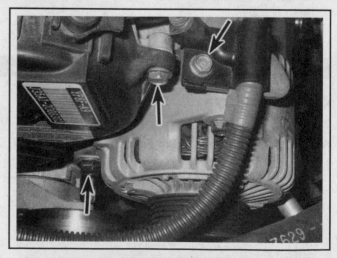

10.4 Disconnect the four-pin electrical connector from the alternator, remove this big nut from the stud type terminal and disconnect the big black output cable from the alternator

10.5 To remove the alternator, remove the wiring harness clamp bolt from the top of the alternator and remove the upper and lower alternator mounting bolts – 2004 and earlier models shown

8   If you're replacing the alternator, take the old one with you when purchasing the replacement unit. Make sure that the new/rebuilt unit looks identical to the old alternator. Look at the terminals - they should be the same In number, size and location as the terminals on the old alternator. Finally, look at the identification numbers - they will be stamped into the housing or printed on a tag attached to the housing. Make sure the numbers are the same on both alternators.

9   Many new/rebuilt alternators DO NOT have a pulley installed, so you might have to swap the pulley from the old unit to the new/rebuilt one. When buying an alternator, find out the store's policy regarding pulley swaps. Some stores perform this service free of charge. If your local auto parts store doesn't offer this service, you'll have to purchase a puller for removing the pulley and do it yourself.

10 Installation is the reverse of removal. Be sure to tighten the alternator mounting bolts to the torque listed in this Chapter's Specifications. Tighten the harness clamp bolt securely.

11 After the alternator is installed, install the accessory drivebelt (see Chapter 1).

12 Reconnect the cable to the negative terminal of the battery (see Section 1). Check the charging voltage (see Section 9) to verify that the alternator is operating correctly.

11 Starting system - general information and precautions

The starting system consists of the battery, the starter motor, the starter solenoid and the wires connecting them. The solenoid is mounted directly on the starter motor. The solenoid/starter motor assembly is installed on the front of the transaxle bellhousing.

When the ignition key is turned to the Start position, the starter solenoid is actuated through the starter control circuit. The starter solenoid then connects the battery to the starter. The battery supplies the electrical energy to the starter motor, which does the actual work of cranking the engine.

The starter can only be operated when the selector lever is in Park or Neutral.

Always observe the following precautions when working on the starting system:

a) *Excessive cranking of the starter motor can overheat it and cause serious damage. Never operate the starter motor for more than 15 seconds at a time without pausing to allow it to cool for at least two minutes.*

b) *The starter is connected directly to the battery and could arc or cause a fire if mishandled, overloaded or shorted out.*

c) *Always detach the cable from the negative terminal of the battery before working on the starting system.*

12 Starter motor and circuit - check

▶ **Refer to illustrations 12.3 and 12.4**

1   If a malfunction occurs in the starting circuit, do not immediately assume that the starter is causing the problem. First, check the following items:

a) *Make sure the battery cable clamps, where they connect to the battery, are clean and tight.*

b) *Check the condition of the battery cables (see Section 4). Replace any defective battery cables with new parts.*

c) *Test the condition of the battery (see Section 3). If it does not pass all the tests, replace it with a new battery.*

d) *Check the starter solenoid wiring and connections. Refer to the wiring diagrams at the end of Chapter 12.*

e) *Check the starter mounting bolts for tightness.*

f) *Check the fuses (fuse numbers 41 and 42) in the engine compartment fuse and relay box (see Chapter 12). If they're burned, determine the cause and repair the circuit. Also, check the ignition switch circuit for correct operation (see the wiring diagrams at the end of Chapter 12).*

g) *Check the operation of the gear position switch. Make sure the shift lever is in PARK or NEUTRAL. Refer to Chapter 7, Section 3 for the gear position switch check and adjustment procedure. This*

system must operate correctly to provide battery voltage to the starter solenoid.

h) *Check the operation of the starter cut relay. The starter cut relay is located in the fuse/relay box under the dash on the driver's side. Refer to Chapter 12 for the testing procedure.*

2   If the starter does not activate when the ignition switch is turned to the start position, check for battery voltage to the solenoid. This will determine if the solenoid is receiving the correct voltage signal from the ignition switch. Connect a voltmeter to the starter solenoid "S" terminal. Then note the indicated voltage when an assistant turns the ignition switch to the START position. It should be about the same as battery voltage. If there's no voltage at the S terminal, refer to the wiring diagrams at the end of Chapter 12 and check the starring system fuses. The two starting system fuses, which are located inside the engine compartment fuse and relay box, are No. 41 (120-amp) and No. 42 (50-amp). Also check the starter cut relay for correct operation. The starter cut relay is located inside the left (driver's side) fuse/relay panel. Refer to Chapter 12 for help with testing relays. If voltage is available but the starter motor doesn't engage and spin the driveplate ring gear, remove the starter from the engine (see Section 13) and bench test the starter (see Step 4).

12.3 To use an inductive ammeter, simply hold the ammeter over the positive or negative battery cable (whichever cable has better clearance)

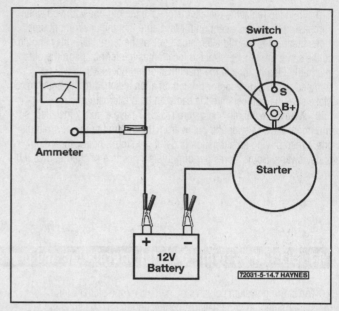

12.4 Starter motor bench testing details

3   If the starter turns over slowly, check the starter cranking voltage and the current draw from the battery. This test must be performed with the starter assembly on the engine. Crank the engine over (for 10 seconds or less) and observe the battery voltage. It should not drop below 8.5 volts. Also, observe the current draw using an ammeter (see illustration). It should not exceed 380 amps. If the starter motor exceeds these values, replace it. Several conditions might affect the starter's cranking power. The battery must be in good condition and the battery cold-cranking rating must not be under-rated for the application. Be sure to check the battery specifications carefully. The battery terminals and cables must be clean and not corroded. Also, in cases of extremely cold temperatures, make sure the battery and/or engine block is warmed before performing the tests.

4   If the starter is receiving voltage but does not activate, remove and check the starter/solenoid assembly on the bench. Most likely the solenoid is defective. In some rare cases, the engine may be seized so

be sure to try and rotate the crankshaft pulley (see Chapter 2A) before proceeding. With the starter/solenoid assembly mounted in a vise on the bench, install one jumper cable from the negative terminal (-) to the body of the starter (see illustration). Install another jumper cable from the positive terminal (+) on the battery to the B+ terminal on the starter. Install a starter switch and apply battery voltage to the solenoid S terminal (for 10 seconds or less) and observe the solenoid plunger, shift lever and overrunning clutch extend and rotate the pinion drive. If the pinion drive extends but does not rotate, the solenoid is operating but the starter motor is defective. If there is no movement but the solenoid clicks, the solenoid and/or the starter motor is defective. If the solenoid plunger extends and rotates the pinion drive, the starter/solenoid assembly is working properly.

13 Starter motor - removal and installation

▶ **Refer to illustrations 13.3 and 13.6**

1   Detach the cable from the negative terminal of the battery (see Section 1).

3   On 2004 and earlier models, unlatch the clamp for the transmission cooler hose (see illustration) and set it aside.

4   On 2005 and later models, remove the intake air duct (see Chapter 4). Also remove the wiring harness clamp from the starter.

5   On 2008 and later models with VCM, remove the bracket from the starter and the dipstick.

6   Clearly label, then disconnect the wires from the terminals on the starter motor solenoid (see illustration). Also disconnect any clips that attach the wiring to the starter assembly.

7   Remove the starter mounting bolts (see illustration 13.6) and detach the starter.

8   Installation is the reverse of removal. Tighten the starter mounting bolts to the torque listed in this Chapter's Specifications, then reconnect the cable to the negative terminal of the battery (see Section 1).

13.3 Before removing the starter, pry this clamp (A) open with a small screwdriver and pull the ATF cooler hose out of the way - (B) is the starter lower mounting bolt

13.6 Starter motor removal and installation details – 2004 and earlier models shown

Specifications

General

Battery voltage
    Engine off   12 to 12.5 volts
    Engine running   13.5 to 14.5 volts
Firing order   1-4-2-5-3-6

Torque specifications	Ft-lbs	Nm
Alternator mounting bolts		
Upper bolt	16	22
Lower bolt	33	44
Starter motor mounting bolts		
Upper bolt	33	44
Lower bolt	47	64

Section

Reference to other Chapters

6

EMISSIONS AND ENGINE CONTROL SYSTEMS

1 General information

▸ **Refer to illustration 1.4**

To prevent pollution of the atmosphere from incompletely burned and evaporating gases, and to maintain good driveability and fuel economy, a number of emission control systems are incorporated. They include the:

On-Board Diagnostic-II (OBD-II) system
Programmed Fuel Injection (PGM-FI) system (the electronic engine control system)
Electronic Load Detector (ELD)
Exhaust Gas Recirculation (EGR) system
Evaporative Emissions Control (EVAP) system
Positive Crankcase Ventilation (PCV) system
Catalytic converter

This Chapter includes general descriptions of these any other emissions-related devices and component replacement procedures (when possible) for each of the systems listed above. Before assuming that an emissions control system is malfunctioning, check the fuel and ignition systems carefully. The diagnosis of some emission control devices requires specialized tools, equipment and training. If a procedure is beyond your ability, consult a dealer service department or other repair shop. Remember, the most frequent cause of emissions problems is simply a loose or broken wire or vacuum hose, so always check all hose and wiring connections first.

➡ **Note: Because of a Federally mandated extended warranty which covers the emissions control system components, check with your dealer about warranty coverage before working on any emissions-related systems. Once the warranty has expired, you may wish to perform some of the component checks and/or replacement procedures in this Chapter to save money.**

Pay close attention to any special precautions outlined in this Chapter. It should be noted that the illustrations of the various systems might not exactly match the system installed on your vehicle because of annual changes made by the manufacturer during production and

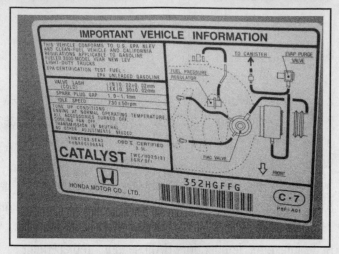

1.4 The Vehicle Emission Control Information (VECI) label is located in the engine compartment; the VECI label specifies the emission-control systems on your vehicle, and includes important tune-up specifications and a vacuum hose routing diagram

because of running changes made *during* a model year.

A Vehicle Emissions Control Information (VECI) label is attached to the underside of the hood (see illustration). This label specifies the important emissions systems on the vehicle and it provides the important specifications for tune-ups. Part of the VECI label, the Vacuum Hose Routing Diagram, provides a vacuum hose schematic with emissions components identified. If there's a discrepancy between the information in this manual and the information on the VECI label, defer to the information on the VECI label. It contains the most up-to-date information about your vehicle, and might reflect some running change made to the vehicle after the manual was published.

2 On Board Diagnosis (OBD) system and trouble codes

SCAN TOOL INFORMATION

▸ **Refer to illustrations 2.1 and 2.2**

1   Hand-held scanners are the most powerful and versatile tools for analyzing engine management systems used on later model vehicles (see illustration). Early model scanners handle codes and some diagnostics for many systems. Each brand scan tool must be examined carefully to match the year, make and model of the vehicle you are working on. Often, interchangeable cartridges are available to access the particular manufacturer (Chrysler, Ford, GM, Honda, Toyota etc.). Some manufacturers will specify by continent (Asia, Europe, USA, etc.).

➡ **Note: An aftermarket generic scanner should work with any model covered by this manual. Before purchasing a generic scan tool, contact the manufacturer of the scanner you're planning to buy and verify that it will work properly with the OBD-II system you want to scan. If necessary, of course, you can always have the codes extracted by a dealer service department or an independent repair shop with a professional scan tool.**

2.1 Scanners like these from Actron and AutoXray are powerful diagnostic aids - they can tell you just about anything you want to know about your engine management system

2   With the arrival of the Federally mandated emission control system (OBD-II), specially designed scanners were developed. Several tool manufacturers have released OBD-II scan tools for the home mechanic (see illustration).

OBD SYSTEM GENERAL DESCRIPTION

3   All models are equipped with the second generation OBD-II system. This system consists of an on-board computer known as the Powertrain Control Module (PCM), and information sensors, which monitor various functions of the engine and send data to the PCM. This system incorporates a series of diagnostic monitors that detect and identify fuel injection and emissions control systems faults and store the information in the computer memory. This updated system also tests sensors and output actuators, diagnoses drive cycles, freezes data and clears codes.

4   This powerful diagnostic computer must be accessed using an OBD-II scan tool and 16-pin Data Link Connector (DLC) located under the driver's dash area. The PCM is located below the center of the instrument panel, mounted to the firewall. The PCM is the brain of the electronically controlled fuel and emissions system. It receives data from a number of sensors and other electronic components (switches, relays, etc.). Based on the information it receives, the PCM generates output signals to control various relays, solenoids (fuel injectors) and other actuators. The PCM is specifically calibrated to optimize the emissions, fuel economy and driveability of the vehicle.

5   It isn't a good idea to attempt diagnosis or replacement of the PCM or emission control components at home while the vehicle is under warranty. Because of a Federally mandated warranty which covers the emissions system components and because any owner-induced damage to the PCM, the sensors and/or the control devices may void this warranty, take the vehicle to a dealer service department if the PCM or a system component malfunctions.

INFORMATION SENSORS

6   **Accelerator Pedal Position (APP) sensor** - All 2005 and later models have an electronic throttle control system. The throttle is not controlled by a cable on these vehicles. The PCM controls the throttle with a motor mounted on the throttle body. The APP sensor sends data to the PCM about the position of the accelerator pedal. The PCM uses this input along with other commands from cruise control and other sensors to operate the throttle.

7   **Brake Pedal Position (BPP) switch** - The BPP switch is located at the top of the brake pedal. It's a normally open switch that closes when the brake pedal is applied and sends a signal to the PCM, which interprets this signal as its cue to disengage the torque converter clutch. The BPP switch is also used to disengage the brake shift interlock. For information regarding the replacement and adjustment of the BPP switch, refer to Chapter 9.

8   **Camshaft Position (CMP) sensor** - The CMP sensor produces a signal that the PCM uses to identify the number 1 cylinder and to time the firing sequence of the fuel injectors. The CMP sensor is located on the right end of the front cylinder head.

9   **Crankshaft Position (CKP) sensor** - The CKP sensor produces a signal that the PCM uses to determine the position of the crankshaft. On models without VCM (Variable Cylinder Management), the sensor is mounted at the right end of the engine near the crankshaft pulley. On models with VCM, it's at the left lower part of the engine under a cover.

2.2 Trouble code readers like the Actron OBD-II diagnostic tester simplify the task of extracting the trouble codes

10   **Electronic Load Detector (ELD)** - The ELD monitors the electrical load on the system and keeps the PCM informed. The PCM controls the voltage output of the alternator in response to the data conveyed by this signal.

11   **Engine Coolant Temperature (ECT) sensor** - The ECT sensor is a thermistor (temperature-sensitive variable resistor) that sends a voltage signal to the PCM, which uses this data to determine the temperature of the engine coolant. The ECT sensor helps the PCM control the air/fuel mixture ratio and ignition timing. The ECT sensor is located at the left end of the engine on top of the coolant crossover housing. 2005 and later models have an additional ECT sensor located farther to the left near the thermostat housing.

12   **Fuel tank pressure sensor** - The fuel tank pressure sensor measures the fuel tank pressure when the PCM tests the EVAP system, and it's also used to control fuel tank pressure by signaling the EVAP system to purge the tank when the pressure becomes excessive. The fuel tank pressure sensor is located behind the upper rear edge of the EVAP canister, right above the EVAP bypass solenoid.

13   **Input shaft (mainshaft) speed sensor** - The input shaft (or mainshaft) speed sensor is a magnetic pick-up coil located on the front of the transaxle.

14   **Intake Air Temperature (IAT) sensor** - The IAT sensor monitors the temperature of the air entering the engine and sends a signal to the PCM. On models without VCM (Variable Cylinder Management), the sensor is mounted at the left end of the intake manifold. On models with VCM, the IAT sensor is a part of the MAF sensor, which is in the air intake duct at the air filter housing.

15   **Knock sensor** - The knock sensor is a piezoelectric crystal that oscillates in proportion to engine vibration. (The term *piezoelectric* refers to the property of certain crystals that produce a voltage when subjected to a mechanical stress.) The oscillation of the piezoelectric crystal produces a voltage output that is monitored by the PCM, which retards the ignition timing when the oscillation exceeds a certain threshold. When the engine is operating normally, the knock sensor oscillates consistently and its voltage signal is steady. When detonation occurs, engine vibration increases, and the oscillation of the knock sensor exceeds a design threshold. (Detonation is an uncontrolled explosion, after the spark occurs at the spark plug, which spontaneously combusts the remaining air/fuel mixture, resulting in a pinging or slapping sound.) If allowed to continue, the engine could be damaged. The knock sensor is located below the intake manifold,

in the valley between the cylinder heads.

16 Manifold Absolute Pressure (MAP) sensor - The MAP sensor, which is located on top of the throttle body, monitors the pressure or vacuum downstream from the throttle plate, inside the intake manifold. The MAP sensor measures intake manifold pressure and vacuum on the absolute scale, from zero instead of from sea-level atmospheric pressure (14.7 psi). The MAP sensor converts the absolute pressure into a variable voltage signal that changes with the pressure. The PCM uses this data to determine engine load so that it can alter the ignition advance and fuel enrichment.

17 Mass Air Flow (MAF) sensor - The MAF sensor is only used on 2005 and later models in addition to the MAP sensor in order to get more precise measurement of air flow. On models with VCM (Variable Cylinder Management), it's combined with the IAT sensor in one unit. The MAF sensor is mounted in the air intake duct at the air filter housing.

18 Output shaft (countershaft) speed sensor - The output shaft (or countershaft) speed sensor is a magnetic pick-up coil, which is located on top of the transaxle. The output shaft speed sensor provides the Powertrain Control Module (PCM) with information about the rotational speed of the output shaft in the transmission. The PCM uses this information to control the torque converter and to calculate speed scheduling and the correct operating pressure for the transaxle.

19 Oxygen sensors - An oxygen sensor is a galvanic battery that generates a small variable voltage signal in proportion to the difference between the oxygen content in the exhaust stream and the oxygen content in the ambient air. The PCM uses the voltage signal from the upstream oxygen sensor to maintain a stoichiometric air/fuel ratio of 14.7:1 by constantly adjusting the on-time of the fuel injectors. There are *two* oxygen sensors: one *upstream* sensor (ahead of the catalytic converter) and a *downstream* oxygen sensor (at the catalyst).

20 Power Steering Pressure (PSP) switch - The PSP switch monitors the pressure inside the power steering system. When the pressure exceeds a certain threshold at idle or during low speed maneuvers, the switch sends a voltage signal to the PCM, which raises the idle slightly to compensate for the extra load on the engine. The PSP switch is located on the power steering pressure line, at the right end of the steering rack, right above the dust boot for the right tie-rod.

21 Throttle Position (TP) sensor - The TP sensor is a potentiometer that receives a constant voltage input from the PCM and sends back a voltage signal that varies in relation to the opening angle of the throttle plate inside the throttle body. This voltage signal tells the PCM when the throttle is closed, half-open, wide open or anywhere in between. The PCM uses this data, along with information from other sensors, to calculate injector "pulse width" (the interval of time during which an injector solenoid is energized by the PCM). The TP sensor is located on the throttle body, on the end of the throttle plate shaft.

22 Transmission range switch - The transmission range switch is located at the manual lever on the left side of the transaxle. The transmission range switch functions like a conventional Park/Neutral Position (PNP) switch: it prevents the engine from starting in any gear other than Park or Neutral, and it closes the circuit for the back-up lights when the shift lever is moved to Reverse. The PCM also sends a voltage signal to the transmission range switch, which uses a series of step-down resistors that act as a voltage divider. The PCM monitors the voltage output signal from the switch, which corresponds to the position of the manual lever. Thus the PCM is able to determine the gear selected and is able to determine the correct pressure for the electronic pressure control system of the transaxle.

23 Rocker arm oil pressure sensor - This sensor is used with the VCM (Variable Cylinder Management) system on 2005 and later

models with higher trim levels. It is mounted next to the rocker arm oil control solenoid(s) on the rear cylinder head. The 2008 and later VCM system also uses two oil valves and three solenoids in addition to two oil pressure switches to operate the system. Models that only have the VTEC system use a single oil pressure switch located next to the oil control solenoid.

OUTPUT ACTUATORS

24 EVAP canister purge control solenoid valve - The EVAP canister purge control solenoid valve (or simply, "purge valve") which is located in the engine compartment, near the master cylinder, is normally closed. But when ordered to do so by the PCM, it allows the fuel vapors that are stored in the EVAP canister to be drawn into the intake manifold, where they're mixed with intake air, then burned along with the normal air/fuel mixture, under certain operating conditions. The PCM-controlled EVAP canister purge control solenoid valve also controls this vapor flow.

25 EVAP canister vent shut valve - The EVAP canister vent shut valve is located underneath the vehicle, on the left end of the EVAP canister. The canister vent shut valve is normally open, but it closes and seals off the EVAP system for inspection and maintenance tests and for OBD-II leak and pressure tests.

26 Exhaust Gas Recirculation (EGR) valve - When the engine is put under a load (hard acceleration, passing, going up a steep hill, pulling a trailer, etc.), combustion chamber temperature increases. When combustion chamber temperature exceeds 2500 degrees, excessive amounts of oxides of nitrogen (NOx) are produced. NOx is a precursor of photochemical smog. When combined with hydrocarbons (HC), other "reactive organic compounds" (ROCs) and sunlight, it forms ozone, nitrogen dioxide and nitrogen nitrate and other nasty stuff. The PCM-controlled EGR valve allows exhaust gases to be recirculated back to the intake manifold where they dilute the incoming air/fuel mixture, which lowers the combustion chamber temperature and decreases the amount of NOx produced during high-load conditions.

27 Fuel injectors - The fuel injectors, which spray a fine mist of fuel into the intake ports, where it is mixed with incoming air, are inductive coils under PCM control. For more information about the injectors, see Chapter 4.

28 Idle Air Control (IAC) valve - This valve is used only on 2004 and earlier models. On later models idle air is adjusted by electronic operation of the throttle by the PCM. The IAC valve controls the amount of air allowed to bypass the throttle plate when the throttle plate is at its (nearly closed) idle position. The IAC valve is controlled by the PCM. When the engine is placed under an additional load at idle (high power steering pressure or running the air conditioning compressor during low-speed maneuvers, for example), the engine can run roughly, stumble and even stall. To prevent this from happening, the PCM opens the IAC valve to increase the idle speed enough to overcome the extra load imposed on the engine. The IAC valve is mounted on the underside of the throttle body.

29 Ignition coils - The ignition coils are under the control of the Powertrain Control Module (PCM). There is no separate ignition control module. Instead, "coil drivers" inside the PCM turn the primary side of the coils on and off. For more information about the ignition coils, see Chapter 5.

30 Rocker arm oil control solenoid - This solenoid operates the oil control valve(s) of the VTEC and VCM systems. These solenoid valves control the operation of the rocker arms. In the VTEC system, there are high valve lift and low valve lift modes; in the VCM system, the rocker arms are actually fully disabled for some rear cylinders under certain conditions. In the VTEC system, the oil control solenoid is mounted next to the rocker arm oil pressure switch in the center of the engine at the right side. On VCM systems with one solenoid, it's located at the left side of the engine toward the rear. On later model VCM systems there is a solenoid for the front bank of cylinders at the right end of the front cylinder head. The two solenoids for the rear cylinder head are at the left end of the rear cylinder head.

31 **Electronic throttle body** - All 2005 and later models have an electronic throttle control system. The throttle is not controlled by a cable on these vehicles. The PCM controls the throttle with a motor mounted on the throttle body. There is no cruise control cable and no Idle Air Control (IAC) valve, as these functions are handled electronically by the PCM. The Throttle Position (TPS) sensor is an integral part of these throttle bodies and can't be replaced separately.

OBTAINING AND CLEARING DIAGNOSTIC TROUBLE CODES (DTCS)

32 All models covered by this manual are equipped with on-board diagnostics. When the PCM recognizes a malfunction in a monitored emission control system, component or circuit, it turns on the Malfunction Indicator Light (MIL) on the dash. The PCM will continue to display the MIL until the problem is fixed and the Diagnostic Trouble Code (DTC) is cleared from the PCM's memory. You'll need a scan tool to access any DTCs stored in the PCM.

33 Before outputting any DTCs stored in the PCM, thoroughly inspect ALL electrical connectors and hoses. Make sure that all electrical connections are tight, clean and free of corrosion. And make sure that all hoses are correctly connected, fit tightly and are in good condition (no cracks or tears). Also, make sure that the engine is tuned up. A poorly running engine is probably one of the biggest causes of emission-related malfunctions. Often, simply giving the engine a good tune-up will correct the problem.

Accessing the DTCs

▶ **Refer to illustration 2.34**

34 On these models, all of which are equipped with On-Board Diagnostic II (OBD-II) systems, the Diagnostic Trouble Codes (DTCs) can only be accessed with a scan tool. Professional scan tools are expensive, but relatively inexpensive generic scan tools (see illustrations 2.1 and 2.2) are available at most auto parts stores. Simply plug the con-

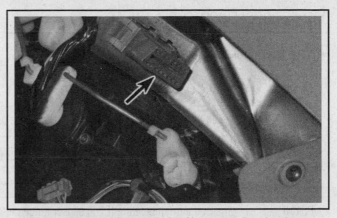

2.34 The Data Link Connector (DLC) is located under the lower edge of the dash, between the steering column and the center console

nector of the scan tool into the diagnostic connector (see illustration), which is located under the lower edge of the dash, just to the right of the steering column. Then follow the instructions included with the scan tool to extract the DTCs.

35 Once you have outputted all of the stored DTCs, look them up on the accompanying DTC chart.

36 After troubleshooting the source of each DTC make any necessary repairs or replace the defective component(s).

Clearing the DTCs

37 Clear the DTCs with the scan tool in accordance with the instructions provided by the scan tool's manufacturer.

DIAGNOSTIC TROUBLE CODES

38 The accompanying tables are a list of the Diagnostic Trouble Codes (DTCs) that can be accessed by a do-it-yourselfer working at home (there are many, many more DTCs available to professional mechanics with proprietary scan tools and software, but those codes cannot be accessed by a generic scan tool). If, after you have checked and repaired the connectors, wire harness and vacuum hoses (if applicable) for an emission-related system, component or circuit, the problem persists, have the vehicle checked by a dealer service department or other qualified repair shop.

OBD-II TROUBLE CODES

➡ **Note: Not all trouble codes apply to all models.**

Code	Probable cause
P0101	Mass air flow or volume air flow circuit, range or performance problem
P0102	Mass air flow or volume air flow circuit, low input
P0103	Mass air flow or volume air flow circuit, high input
P0107	Manifold Absolute Pressure (MAP) sensor circuit, low voltage
P0108	Manifold Absolute Pressure (MAP) sensor circuit, high voltage

OBD-II TROUBLE CODES (CONTINUED)

➡ **Note: Not all trouble codes apply to all models.**

Code	Probable cause
P0111	Intake air temperature circuit, range or performance problem
P0112	Intake Air Temperature (IAT) sensor circuit, low voltage
P0113	Intake Air Temperature (IAT) sensor circuit, high voltage
P0116	Engine Coolant Temperature (ECT) sensor range/performance problem
P0117	Engine Coolant Temperature (ECT) sensor circuit, low voltage
P0118	Engine Coolant Temperature (ECT) sensor circuit, high voltage
P0122	Throttle Position (TP) sensor circuit, low voltage
P0123	Throttle Position (TP) sensor circuit, high voltage
P0125	Insufficient coolant temperature for closed loop fuel control
P0128	Cooling system malfunction
P0131	Upstream oxygen sensor circuit, low voltage
P0132	Upstream oxygen sensor circuit, high voltage
P0133	Upstream oxygen sensor circuit, slow response
P0134	Oxygen sensor circuit - no activity detected (bank 1, sensor 1)
P0135	Upstream oxygen sensor heater circuit malfunction
P0137	Downstream oxygen sensor circuit, low voltage
P0138	Downstream oxygen sensor circuit, high voltage
P0139	Downstream oxygen sensor circuit, slow response
P0141	Downstream oxygen sensor heater circuit malfunction
P0153	Oxygen sensor circuit, slow response (bank 2, sensor 1)
P0154	Oxygen sensor circuit - no activity detected (bank 2, sensor 1)
P0155	Oxygen sensor heater circuit malfunction (bank 2, sensor 1)
P0157	Oxygen sensor circuit, low voltage (bank 2, sensor 2)
P0158	Oxygen sensor circuit, high voltage (bank 2, sensor 2)
P0159	Oxygen sensor circuit, slow response (bank 2, sensor 2)
P0161	Oxygen sensor heater circuit malfunction (bank 2, sensor 2)

Code	Probable cause
P0171	Fuel system too lean
P0172	Fuel system too rich
P0174	System too lean (bank 2)
P0175	System too rich (bank 2)
P0222	Throttle position or pedal position sensor/switch B circuit, low input
P0223	Throttle position or pedal position sensor/switch B circuit, high input
P0300	Random misfire detected
P0301	Cylinder no. 1 misfire detected
P0302	Cylinder no. 2 misfire detected
P0303	Cylinder no. 3 misfire detected
P0304	Cylinder no. 4 misfire detected
P0305	Cylinder no. 5 misfire detected
P0306	Cylinder no. 6 misfire detected
P0325	Knock sensor circuit malfunction
P0335	Crankshaft Position (CKP) sensor circuit, no signal
P0336	Crankshaft Position (CKP) sensor, intermittent interruption
P0339	Crankshaft position sensor A circuit - intermittent
P0340	Camshaft Position (CMP) sensor A, no signal
P0341	Camshaft Position (CMP) sensor A, intermittent interruption
P0344	Camshaft position sensor "A", circuit - intermittent
P0351	Ignition coil 1 primary or secondary circuit malfunction
P0352	Ignition coil 2 primary or secondary circuit malfunction
P0353	Ignition coil 3 primary or secondary circuit malfunction
P0354	Ignition coil 4 primary or secondary circuit malfunction
P0355	Ignition coil 5 primary or secondary circuit malfunction
P0356	Ignition coil 6 primary or secondary circuit malfunction
P0365	Camshaft Position (CMP) sensor B, no signal
P0366	Camshaft Position (CMP) sensor B, intermittent interruption

OBD-II TROUBLE CODES (CONTINUED)

➡ **Note: Not all trouble codes apply to all models.**

Code	Probable cause
P0369	Camshaft position sensor "B" circuit intermittent (bank 1)
P0385	Crankshaft position sensor B circuit malfunction
P0389	Crankshaft position sensor B circuit, intermittent
P0400	Exhaust gas recirculation flow malfunction
P0401	Exhaust Gas Recirculation (EGR) system, insufficient flow
P0404	Exhaust gas recirculation circuit, range or performance problem
P0406	Exhaust gas recirculation valve position sensor A circuit high
P0420	Catalyst system efficiency below threshold
P0430	Catalyst system efficiency below threshold (bank 2)
P0443	Evaporative emission control system, purge control valve circuit malfunction
P0451	Fuel tank pressure sensor range or performance problem
P0452	Fuel tank pressure sensor circuit, low voltage
P0453	Fuel tank pressure sensor circuit, high voltage
P0455	Evaporative emission (EVAP) control system leak detected (no purge flow or large leak)
P0456	Evaporative emission (EVAP) control system leak detected (very small leak)
P0457	Evaporative emission control system leak detected (fuel cap loose/off)
P0461	Fuel level sending unit range or performance problem
P0462	Fuel level sending unit, low voltage
P0463	Fuel level sending unit, high voltage
P0496	Evaporative emission system - high purge flow
P0497	Evaporative emission system - low purge flow
P0498	Evaporative emission system, vent control - circuit low
P0499	Evaporative emission system, vent control - circuit high
P0505	Idle control system malfunction
P0506	Idle control system, rpm lower than expected
P0507	Idle control system, rpm higher than expected

Code	Probable cause
P0522	Engine oil pressure sensor/switch circuit, low voltage
P0523	Engine oil pressure sensor/switch circuit, high voltage
P0560	Powertrain Control Module (PCM) back-up circuit, low voltage
P0562	System voltage low
P0563	System voltage high
P0602	Control module, programming error
P0607	Powertrain Control Module (PCM) back-up circuit malfunction
P0630	VIN not programmed or mismatch - ECM/PCM
P0685	EGM power relay, control - circuit open
P0705	Transmission range sensor, circuit malfunction (PRNDL input)
P0706	Transmission range sensor circuit, range or performance problem
P0711	Transmission fluid temperature sensor circuit, range or performance problem
P0712	Transmission fluid temperature sensor circuit, low input
P0713	Transmission fluid temperature sensor circuit, high input
P0715	Mainshaft speed sensor
P0716	Input/turbine speed sensor circuit, range or performance problem
P0717	Input/turbine speed sensor circuit, no signal
P0718	Input/turbine speed sensor circuit, intermittent signal
P0720	Countershaft speed sensor
P0721	Output speed sensor circuit, range or performance problem
P0722	Output speed sensor circuit, no signal
P0723	Output speed sensor circuit, intermittent signal
P0730	Shift control system
P0731	Incorrect gear ratio, first gear
P0732	Incorrect gear ratio, second gear
P0733	Incorrect gear ratio, third gear
P0734	Incorrect gear ratio, fourth gear
P0735	Incorrect gear ratio, fifth gear

OBD-II TROUBLE CODES (CONTINUED)

➡ **Note: Not all trouble codes apply to all models.**

Code	Probable cause
P0740	Lock-up control system
P0741	Torque converter clutch, circuit performance or stuck in off position
P0746	Pressure control solenoid, performance problem or stuck in off position
P0747	Pressure control solenoid, stuck in on position
P0751	Shift solenoid A, performance problem or stuck in off position
P0752	Shift solenoid A, stuck in on position
P0753	Shift control solenoid valve A
P0756	Shift solenoid B, performance problem or stuck in off position
P0757	Shift solenoid B, stuck in on position
P0758	Shift control solenoid valve B
P0761	Shift solenoid C, performance problem or stuck in off position
P0762	Shift solenoid C, stuck in on position
P0763	Shift control solenoid valve C
P0766	Shift solenoid D, performance problem or stuck in off position
P0767	Shift solenoid D, stuck in on position
P0776	Pressure control solenoid "B" performance or stuck off
P0777	Pressure control solenoid "B" stuck on
P0796	Transmission fluid pressure (TFP) solenoid "C" - performance or stuck off
P0797	Transmission fluid pressure (TFP) solenoid "C" - stuck on
P0812	Reverse input circuit
P0842	Transmission fluid pressure sensor/switch "A" circuit low
P0843	Transmission fluid pressure sensor/switch "A" circuit high
P0847	Transmission fluid pressure sensor/switch "B" circuit low
P0848	Transmission fluid pressure sensor/switch "B" circuit high
P0872	Transmission fluid pressure (TFP) sensor C - circuit low
P0873	Trramission fluid pressure (TFP) sensor C - circuit high

Code	Probable cause
P0962	Pressure control (PC) solenoid A - control circuit low
P0963	Pressure control (PC) solenoid A - control circuit high
P0966	Pressure control (PC) solenoid B - control circuit low
P0967	Pressure control (PC) solenoid B - control circuit high
P0970	Pressure control (PC) solenoid C - control circuit low
P0971	Pressure control (PC) solenoid C - control circuit high
P0973	Shift solenoid (SS) A - control circuit low
P0974	Shift solenoid (SS) A - control circuit high
P0976	Shift solenoid (SS) B - control circuit low
P0977	Shift solenoid (SS) B - control circuit high
P0979	Shift solenoid (SS) C - control circuit low
P0980	Shift solenoid (SS) C - control circuit high
P0982	Shift solenoid (SS) D - control circuit low
P0983	Shift solenoid (SS) D - control circuit high

3 Camshaft Position (CMP) sensor - replacement

▶ **Refer to illustrations 3.2a, 3.2b, 3.4 and 3.5**

1   Disconnect the cable from the negative battery terminal (see Chapter 5, Section 1).

2   Disconnect the CMP sensor electrical connector (see illustrations).

3   Remove the timing belt cover and the timing belt, then remove the camshaft timing belt sprocket from the front cylinder head (see Chapter 2A).

3.2a To disconnect the CMP sensor electrical connector, depress the release button (A) and pull the upper half of the connector (the harness side) straight up . . .

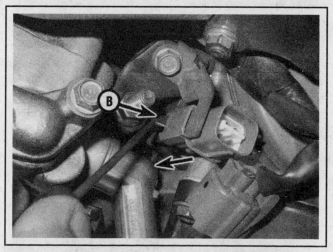

3.2b . . . and to disengage the lower half of the connector (the CMP sensor side) from its mounting bracket, depress this release button (B) and push the connector straight down

3.4 To detach the rear timing belt cover from the cylinder head, remove these two bolts – 2004 and earlier model shown

3.5 To detach the CMP sensor from the rear timing belt cover, remove these mounting bolts – 2004 and earlier model shown

4   Remove the rear timing belt cover mounting bolts (see illustration) and remove the cover.

5   Remove the CMP sensor mounting bolts (see illustration) and remove the CMP sensor.

6   Installation is the reverse of removal. Tighten the CMP sensor mounting bolts to the torque listed in this Chapter's Specifications.

7   Reconnect the cable to the negative batttery terminal (see Chapter 5, Section 1).

---

4   Crankshaft Position (CKP) sensor - replacement

ALL MODELS EXCEPT 2008 AND LATER WITH VCM

▸ **Refer to illustrations 4.5a and 4.5b**

1   Disconnect the cable from the negative battery terminal (see Chapter 5).

2   Remove the crankshaft pulley (see Chapter 2A).

3   On 2004 and earlier models, remove the dipstick and its tube.

4   Remove the upper and lower timing belt covers.

5   Disconnect the wiring from the sensor, then remove the sensor from the oil pump (see illustrations).

6   Installation is the reverse of removal.

2008 AND LATER MODELS WITH VCM

7   Raise the vehicle and support it securely on jackstands.

8   Disconnect the cable from the negative battery terminal (see Chapter 5).

9   The sensor is mounted at the left lower rear of the engine. Remove the cover from the CKP sensor.

10 Disconnect the wiring from the sensor, then remove the sensor.

11 Replace the O-ring. Installation is the reverse of removal.

4.5a The CKP sensor electrical connector is located behind the right end of the engine, above the timing belt tensioner (2007 and earlier models)

4.5b To detach the CKP sensor from the engine, remove this mounting bolt (2007 and earlier models)

5   Electronic Load Detector (ELD) - replacement

▶ **Refer to illustrations 5.3, 5.4, 5.6 and 5.7**

1   Disconnect the cable from the negative battery terminal (see Chapter 5, Section 1).

2   Remove the cover from the engine compartment fuse and relay box (see Chapter 12 if necessary).

3   Locate the ELD (see illustration) in the fuse and relay box.

4   Remove the mounting screws for the 120-amp fuse and remove the fuse (see illustration), then remove the mounting screws for the 50-amp fuse and remove it too.

5   Disconnect the electrical connector from the top of the ELD.

6   Remove the ELD (see illustration).

7   Remove the contact plate from the ELD (see illustration), inspect it for corrosion, clean it off as necessary, then install it in the new ELD. Note that the contact plate must be oriented exactly the same way it was in the old ELD. It won't fit into the fuse and relay box if it's incorrectly oriented.

8   Installation is the reverse of removal. Reconnect the cable to the negative battery terminal (see Chapter 5, Section 1).

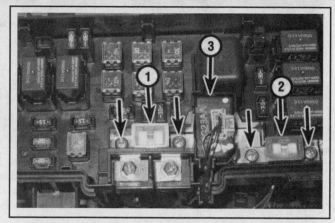

5.3 The Electronic Load Detector (ELD) is located inside the engine compartment fuse and relay box

| 1 | 120-amp fuse | 3 | ELD module |
| 2 | 50-amp fuse | | |

5.4 Remove the mounting screws for each of the big fuses and remove them from the fuse box

5.6 Carefully remove the ELD from the fuse and relay box

5.7 Before removing the contact plate from the old ELD, note how it's oriented in relation to the ELD and to the fuse and relay box; be sure to install it exactly the same way in the new unit

6   Engine Coolant Temperature (ECT) sensor - replacement

▶ **Refer to illustrations 6.3, 6.4 and 6.5**

✱✱✱ **WARNING:**

Wait until the engine has cooled completely before beginning this procedure.

➡ **Note: 2005 and later models have two ECT sensors. The secondary sensor is located at the thermostat housing.**

1   Remove the key from the ignition key lock cylinder.

2   Drain the engine coolant (see Chapter 1).

➡ **Note: If you don't drain the coolant, some coolant will run out of the coolant crossover when you remove the ECT sensor, so install the new sensor as quickly as possible.**

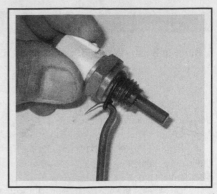

6.3 Disconnect the electrical connector from the ECT sensor

6.4 Remove the ECT sensor with a wrench (most deep sockets are too small to fit over the sensor)

6.5 Be sure to remove and discard the old O-ring from the ECT sensor; always use a new O-ring when installing the ECT sensor

3   Disconnect the electrical connector from the ECT sensor (see illustration).

4   Unscrew the ECT sensor with a wrench (see illustration). (Most deep sockets won't fit over the ECT sensor.)

✻✻ CAUTION:

If you're planning to reuse the old ECT sensor, handle it with care. Damage to the ECT sensor will adversely affect the operation of the PGM-FI system.

5   Remove and discard the old ECT sensor O-ring (see illustration). Whether you're planning to reuse the old ECT sensor or install a new unit, be sure to use a new O-ring.

6   Installation is the reverse of removal. Be sure to tighten the ECT sensor securely.

7   Input shaft (mainshaft) speed sensor - replacement

▸ **Refer to illustrations 7.4 and 7.7**

1   Remove the key from the ignition key lock cylinder.

2   Loosen the lug nuts for the left front wheel. Raise the vehicle and place it securely on jackstands. Remove the left front wheel.

3   Remove the splash shield (see Chapter 2A).

4   Locate the input shaft (mainshaft) speed sensor on the front left corner of the transaxle (see illustration).

5   Disconnect the electrical connector from the input shaft speed sensor.

6   Remove the input shaft speed sensor mounting bolt and remove the sensor.

7   Remove and discard the sensor O-ring (see illustration).

8   Installation is the reverse of removal. Be sure to use a new O-ring and to tighten the sensor mounting bolt to the torque listed in this Chapter's Specifications.

9   Install the wheel and lug nuts. Lower the vehicle and tighten the lug nuts to the torque listed in the Chapter 1 Specifications.

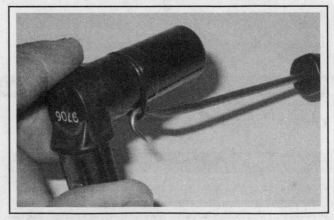

7.4 The input shaft (mainshaft) speed sensor is located at the left front corner of the transaxle; to remove the input shaft sensor from the transaxle, depress the locking tab on the electrical connector and disconnect the connector, then remove this bolt and pull the sensor out

7.7 Be sure to remove and discard the old O-ring from the input shaft sensor; even if you plan to reuse the old input shaft speed sensor, be sure to use a new O-ring

8   Intake Air Temperature (IAT) sensor - replacement

ALL MODELS EXCEPT 2008 AND LATER WITH VCM

▶ **Refer to illustrations 8.3 and 8.5**

1   Remove the key from the ignition key lock cylinder.
2   Remove the intake manifold cover (see Chapter 2A).
3   Disconnect the electrical connector from the IAT sensor (see illustration).
4   Unscrew and remove the IAT sensor.
5   Remove and discard the old IAT sensor O-ring (see illustration).

8.3 To disconnect the electrical connector from the IAT sensor, depress the locking tab on the bottom of the connector, then pull the connector straight back

Be sure to use a new O-ring, even if you're planning to reuse the old IAT sensor.

6   Installation is the reverse of removal. Be sure to use a new O-ring, and tighten the IAT sensor to the torque listed in this Chapter's Specifications.

2008 AND LATER MODELS WITH VCM

7   The IAT sensor on these models is a part of the MAF sensor. Refer to Section 16 for more information.

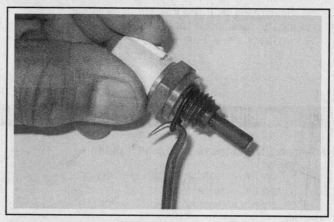

8.5 Be sure to remove and discard the old IAT sensor O-ring - use a new O-ring when installing the IAT sensor (regardless of whether you're installing the old IAT sensor or a new unit)

9   Knock sensor - replacement

▶ **Refer to illustrations 9.4, 9.5 and 9.6**

1   Disconnect the cable from the negative battery terminal (see Chapter 5, Section 1).
2   Remove the intake manifold cover and the upper intake manifold (see Chapter 2A).
3   Remove the fuel rail assembly (see Chapter 4).
4   Disconnect the electrical connector from the knock sensor (see illustration).
5   Remove the knock sensor (see illustration).

9.4 To disconnect the electrical connector from the knock sensor, depress this release button with the tip of a long slotted screwdriver and pull the connector straight up with a pair of long needle-nose pliers

9.5 You'll need to use a deep socket, a universal joint and an extension to unscrew the knock sensor

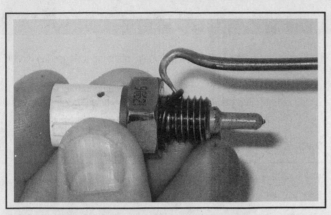

9.6 Remove the old O-ring from the knock sensor; whether you plan to reuse the old knock sensor or install a new one, be sure to use a new O-ring

6   Remove and discard the old sensor O-ring (see illustration).

7   Installation is the reverse of removal. Be sure to use a new O-ring, and tighten the knock sensor securely.

8   When you're done, reconnect the cable to the negative battery terminal (see Chapter 5, Section 1).

10 Manifold Absolute Pressure (MAP) sensor - replacement

▶ **Refer to illustrations 10.3, 10.4, 10.5 and 10.7**

1   Remove the key from the ignition key lock cylinder.

2   Remove the intake manifold cover (see Chapter 2A).

3   Disconnect the electrical connector from the MAP sensor (see illustration).

4   Remove the MAP sensor retaining screws (see illustration) and remove the MAP sensor.

5   Remove the old MAP sensor O-ring (see illustration) and discard it.

6   On 2001 models, remove the MAP sensor spacer mounting screws (see illustration 10.5) and remove the spacer.

7   On 2001 models, remove the old spacer O-ring (see illustration) and discard it.

8   Be sure to use new O-rings for the spacer (2001 models only) and for the MAP sensor. And be sure to tighten the MAP sensor retaining screws securely.

9   Installation is otherwise the reverse of removal.

10.3 Disconnect the electrical connector from the MAP sensor

10.4 To detach the MAP sensor from the throttle body, remove these two screws

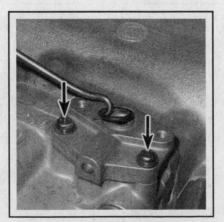

10.5 Remove and discard the old MAP sensor O-ring; to detach the MAP sensor spacer on 2001 models, remove these two screws

10.7 On 2001 models, remove and discard the old MAP sensor spacer O-ring

11 Output shaft (countershaft) speed sensor - replacement

▶ **Refer to illustration 11.3**

1   Remove the key from the ignition key lock cylinder.

2   Remove the air intake duct (see Chapter 4).

3   Locate the output shaft (countershaft) speed sensor on top of the transaxle (see illustration).

4   Disconnect the electrical connector from the output shaft (countershaft) speed sensor.

5   Remove the output shaft sensor mounting bolt and remove the sensor by pulling it straight up.

6   Remove and discard the sensor O-ring (see illustration 7.7).

7   Installation is the reverse of removal. Be sure to use a new O-ring and to tighten the sensor mounting bolt to the torque listed in this Chapter's Specifications.

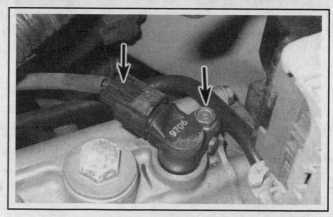

11.3 The output shaft (countershaft) speed sensor is located on top of the transaxle; to remove it, depress this tab to release the electrical connector, disconnect the connector, remove the mounting bolt and pull the sensor straight up

12 Oxygen sensors - replacement

➡ **Note: Because it is installed in the exhaust manifold or pipe, both of which contract when cool, an oxygen sensor might be very difficult to loosen when the engine is cold. Rather than risk damage to the sensor or its mounting threads, start and run the engine for a minute or two, then shut it off. Be careful not to burn yourself during the following procedure.**

1   Remove the key from the ignition key lock cylinder. Raise the vehicle and place it securely on jackstands.

2   Special care must be taken whenever a sensor is serviced.

a) Oxygen sensors have a permanently attached pigtail and an electrical connector that cannot be removed. Damaging or removing the pigtail or electrical connector will render the sensor useless.

b) Keep grease, dirt and other contaminants away from the electrical connector and the louvered end of the sensor.

c) Do not use cleaning solvents of any kind on an oxygen sensor.

d) Oxygen sensors are extremely delicate. Do not drop a sensor or throw it around or handle it roughly.

e) Make sure that the silicone boot on the sensor is installed in the correct position. Otherwise, the boot might melt and it might prevent the sensor from operating correctly.

UPSTREAM OXYGEN SENSOR

▶ **Refer to illustrations 12.3 and 12.4**

3   Detach the wire harness clip and disconnect the upstream oxygen sensor electrical connector (see illustration).

4   Remove the upstream oxygen sensor (see illustration).

5   If you're going to install the old sensor, apply anti-seize com-

12.3 To detach this wiring clip (1), squeeze the two locator pins together and pull the clip out of its bracket; then depress the locking tab and disconnect the electrical connector (2)

12.4 Use a wrench to remove the upstream oxygen sensor (there isn't room for an oxygen sensor socket)

12.8 Disconnect the downstream oxygen sensor electrical connector

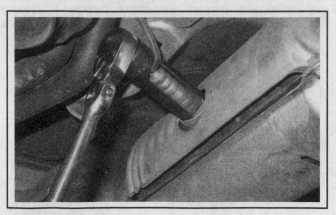

12.9 Use an oxygen sensor socket to remove the downstream oxygen sensor (use a wrench if you don't have an oxygen sensor socket)

pound to the threads of the sensor to facilitate future removal. If you're going to install a new oxygen sensor, it's not necessary to apply anti-seize compound to the threads. The threads on new sensors already have anti-seize compound on them.

6   Installation is the reverse of removal. Be sure to tighten the oxygen sensor to the torque listed in this Chapter's Specifications.

DOWNSTREAM OXYGEN SENSOR

▶ **Refer to illustrations 12.8 and 12.9**

7   Detach the wire harness clip and disconnect the upstream oxygen

sensor electrical connector (see illustration).

8   Remove the downstream oxygen sensor (see illustration).

9   If you're going to install the old sensor, apply anti-seize compound to the threads of the sensor to facilitate future removal. If you're going to install a new oxygen sensor, it's not necessary to apply anti-seize compound to the threads. The threads on new sensors already have anti-seize compound on them.

10   Installation is the reverse of removal. Be sure to tighten the oxygen sensor to the torque listed in this Chapter's Specifications.

13 Power Steering Pressure (PSP) switch - replacement

▶ **Refer to illustrations 13.3 and 13.4**

1   Remove the key from the ignition key lock cylinder.
2   Raise the vehicle and place it securely on jackstands.
3   Disconnect the electrical connector from the PSP switch (see illustration).

4   Unscrew the PSP switch (see illustration).
5   Installation is the reverse of removal. Be sure to tighten the PSP switch to the torque listed in this Chapter's Specifications.
6   When you're done, lower the vehicle and check the power steering fluid level, adding fluid of the proper type if necessary.

13.3 To release the PSP switch electrical connector, depress this locking tab, then pull off the connector

13.4 Use a wrench to remove the PSP switch; be sure to use a back-up wrench on the junction box for the power steering fluid pressure line to prevent the metal pressure line from kinking

14 Throttle Position (TP) sensor - replacement

The TP sensor is not removable. If it's defective, replace the throttle body (see Chapter 4).

15 Transmission range switch - replacement and adjustment

▶ **Refer to illustrations 15.4a, 15.4b, 15.5, 15.6, 15.7, 15.8a and 15.8b**

1 Remove the key from the ignition key lock cylinder.
2 Place the shift lever in Neutral.
3 Raise the vehicle and place it securely on jackstands.

4 Detach the transmission range switch electrical connector from its mounting bracket, then disconnect it (see illustrations).
5 Detach the wiring harness for the transmission range switch from the transaxle (see illustration).
6 Remove the transmission range switch cover bolts (see illustration) and remove the cover.

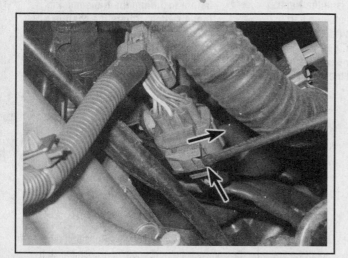

15.4a The electrical connector for the transmission range switch is secured to - and locked together by - a small metal bracket. To detach the connector from the bracket, insert a thin slotted screwdriver blade between the release lever and the connector, pry the release lever down and pull the connector off the bracket

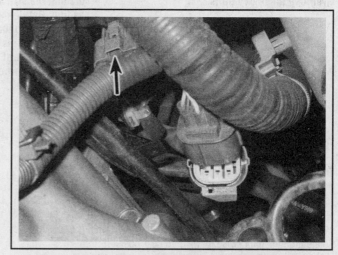

15.4b To disconnect the electrical connector, depress the release tab on top of the connector and pull the two halves of the connector apart. The release tab for the transmission range switch connector isn't visible in this photo, but the arrow indicates the release tab on a nearby connector of the same design

15.5 To detach the wiring harness from the transaxle, remove this bolt (1), then squeeze the locator pins (2) together and push this clip out of its metal bracket

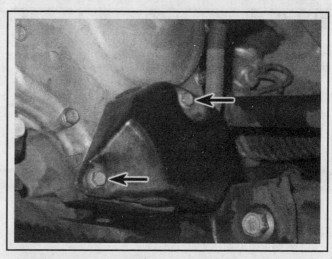

15.6 To detach the transmission range switch cover, remove these two bolts

15.7 To detach the transmission range switch from the transaxle, remove these two bolts

15.8a Before installing the transmission range switch, make sure that the switch is in the Neutral position: Rotate the moving part of the switch so that its longer inside diameter is aligned with the stationary Neutral index mark located on the upper part of the switch

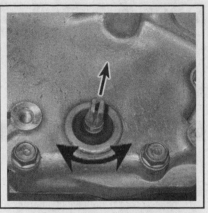

15.8b Make sure that the control shaft is also in the Neutral position before installing the transmission range switch. Rotate the shaft in a clockwise direction until it stops. As you rotate the shaft, it clicks into each gear position. Rotate it counterclockwise to the third gear position (third click), which is Neutral

7   Remove the transmission range switch mounting bolts (see illustration) and remove the switch.

8   Before installing the transmission range switch, make sure that the switch is in the Neutral position (see illustration). You'll hear/feel a click when you put the switch into Neutral. Also make sure that the control shaft is in the Neutral position before installing the transmission range switch. To do so, rotate the control shaft in a clockwise direction until it stops. As you rotate the shaft, it clicks into each gear position. Rotate it counterclockwise to the third gear position (third click), which is Neutral (see illustration).

9   The remainder of installation is the reverse of removal. Be sure

to tighten the transmission range switch mounting bolts to the torque listed in this Chapter's Specifications.

→ **Note: Be careful not to move the transmission range switch while tightening the switch mounting bolts.**

10   Turn the ignition switch to ON, move the shift lever through all the gears and verify that the transmission range switch is correctly synchronized with the gear position indicator on the instrument cluster. Then verify that the engine will NOT start in any gear position other than Park or Neutral, and that the back-up lights come on when the shift lever is in the Reverse position. If the vehicle fails to meet any of these criteria, readjust the transmission range switch.

16   Mass Air Flow (MAF) sensor - removal and installation

→ **Note: This sensor is used only on 2007 and later models. On some models, it's combined with the IAT sensor.**

1   Disconnect the electrical connector from the sensor.

2   Remove the screws, then pull the sensor from the air filter housing.

3   Installation is the reverse of removal.

17   Accelerator Pedal Position (APP) sensor (2005 and later models) - removal and installation

1   Disconnect the electrical connector from the accelerator pedal sensor.

2   Remove the mounting nuts, then remove the pedal assembly from

the firewall. Don't try to remove the sensor from the pedal; it's serviced as a complete unit and can't be disassembled.

3   Installation is the reverse of removal.

18 Rocker arm oil control sensor - removal and installation

➡ **Note: This sensor is used on vehicles with VCM (Variable Cylinder Management). This system deactivates two or three cylinders for improved economy. VCM-equipped models have one sensor located at the left rear of the engine that operates from the three rear cylinders. There is an additional sensor at the right front of the engine. All sensors are mounted adjacent to an oil control solenoid.**

1 Disconnect the electrical connector from the sensor.
2 Unscrew the sensor and discard the O-ring.
3 Installation is the reverse of removal. Replace the O-ring with a new one.

19 Rocker arm oil control solenoid - removal and installation

➡ **Note: All models have at least one rocker arm oil control solenoid. On VTEC models that don't have VCM (Variable Cylinder Management), the solenoid located at the right end of the engine next to the rocker arm oil pressure switch. On models with VCM, there are three solenoids. Two are at the left rear of the engine next to the rear rocker arm oil pressure switch and the rocker arm control valve. The other is at the right front of**

the engine next to the front rocker arm oil pressure switch and control valve.

1 Disconnect the electrical connector from the solenoid and the oil pressure sensor.
2 Remove the mounting bolts and remove the sensor.
3 Check the filter for clogging and replace it if necessary.
4 Installation is the reverse of removal.

20 Powertrain Control Module (PCM) - removal and installation

▸ **Refer to illustration 20.4, 20.5a, 20.5b and 20.5c**

2 Disable the airbag system (see Chapter 12).
3 Remove the carpet from both sides of the center console, push it aside and remove the left and right lower covers from the center console (see Chapter 11).
4 Unplug the electrical connectors from the PCM (see illustration).

✳ **WARNING:**

All models covered by this manual are equipped with a Supplemental Restraint System (SRS), more commonly known as airbags. Always disarm the airbag system before working in the vicinity of any airbag system component to avoid the possibility of accidental deployment of the airbag, which could cause personal injury (see Chapter 12).

✳ **CAUTION:**

The ignition switch must be turned OFF when pulling out or plugging in the electrical connectors to prevent damage to the PCM.

✳ **CAUTION:**

To avoid electrostatic discharge damage to the PCM, handle the PCM only by its case. Do not touch the electrical terminals during removal and installation. If available, ground yourself to the vehicle with a anti-static ground strap, available at computer supply stores.

➡ **Note: The PCM is a component of the immobilizer system (the vehicle security system). If a new PCM is installed in the vehicle, the immobilizer code must be programmed into the new PCM by a dealership service department before the engine will start. The dealer will need the vehicle, the new PCM unit and all of the vehicle keys to program the new PCM unit. So if you're planning to replace the old PCM with a new unit, a dealer service department must perform the following procedure (unless you want to have the vehicle towed to the dealer after you have installed the new PCM!).**

1 Disconnect the cable from the negative battery terminal (see Chapter 5, Section 1).

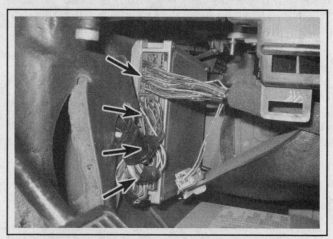

20.4 Before disconnecting the four large electrical connectors from the PCM, make SURE that the battery is disconnected and that you're grounded to the vehicle, preferably with an anti-static ground strap (available at computer supply stores)

20.5a To detach the left side of the PCM, remove this bolt

20.5b To access the right side PCM mounting nut, remove these two cover retaining nuts and remove the cover

20.5c To detach the right side of the PCM, remove this nut

5   Remove the PCM mounting bolt from the left side of the PCM, then remove the small cover and the mounting nut from the right side (see illustrations).

6   Carefully remove the PCM.

✳✳ CAUTION:

Avoid any static electricity damage to the computer by grounding yourself to the body before touching the PCM and using a special anti-static pad to store the PCM on once it is removed.

7   Installation is the reverse of removal.

8   When you're done, reconnect the cable to the negative battery terminal (see Chapter 5, Section 1).

21 Idle Air Control (IAC) valve - replacement

▶ **Refer to illustrations 21.3 and 21.4**

1   Disconnect the cable from the negative battery terminal (see Chapter 5, Section 1).

2   Remove the throttle body from the intake manifold (see Chapter 4).

3   Remove the IAC valve mounting screws (see illustration) and remove the IAC valve.

4   Remove the old IAC valve gasket (see illustration) and discard it.

5   When installing the IAC valve, be sure to use a new gasket and tighten the IAC valve mounting screws securely.

6   Installation is otherwise the reverse of removal.

7   When you're done, reconnect the cable to the negative battery terminal (see Chapter 5, Section 1).

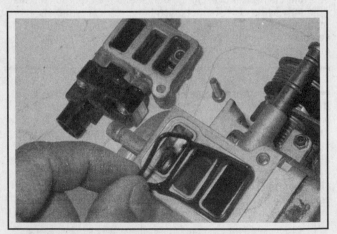

21.3 To detach the IAC valve from the throttle body, remove these two screws

21.4 Remove and discard the old IAC valve gasket, and be sure to use a new gasket when installing the IAC valve

22 Catalytic converter - general description, check and replacement

➡ **Note: Because of a Federally mandated extended warranty which covers emissions-related components like the catalytic converter, check with a dealer service department before replacing the converter at your own expense.**

GENERAL DESCRIPTION

1 A catalytic converter (or catalyst) is an emission control device in the exhaust system that reduces certain pollutants in the exhaust gas stream. There are two types of converters: oxidation converters and reduction converters.

2 Oxidation converters contain a "monolithic substrate" (a ceramic honeycomb) coated with the semi-precious metals platinum and palladium. An oxidation catalyst reduces unburned hydrocarbons (HC) and carbon monoxide (CO) by adding oxygen to the exhaust stream as it passes through the substrate, which in the presence of high temperature and the catalyst materials converts the HC and CO to water vapor (H_2O) and carbon dioxide (CO_2).

3 Reduction converters contain a monolithic substrate coated with platinum and rhodium. A reduction catalyst reduces oxides of nitrogen (NOx) by removing oxygen, which in the presence of high temperature and the catalyst material produces nitrogen (N) and carbon dioxide (CO_2).

4 Catalytic converters that combine both types of catalysts in one assembly are known as "three-way catalysts" or TWCs. A TWC can reduce *all three pollutants.* All models covered by this manual are equipped with three-way catalysts.

5 The catalytic converter is located in the exhaust pipe behind the junction of the outlet pipes of the exhaust manifolds.

CHECK

6 The test equipment for a catalytic converter (a "loaded-mode" dynamometer and a 5-gas analyzer) is expensive. If you suspect that the converter on your vehicle is malfunctioning, take it to a dealer or authorized emission inspection facility for diagnosis and repair.

7 Whenever you raise the vehicle to service underbody components, inspect the converter assembly for leaks, corrosion, dents and other damage. Carefully inspect the welds and/or flange bolts and nuts that attach the front and rear ends of the converter to the exhaust system. If you note any damage, replace the converter.

8 Although catalytic converters don't break too often, they can become clogged or even plugged up. The easiest way to check for a restricted converter is to use a vacuum gauge to diagnose the effect of a blocked exhaust on intake vacuum.

   a) *Connect a vacuum gauge to any intake manifold vacuum source (any pipe on the intake manifold with a vacuum hose connected to it will provide the necessary intake manifold vacuum).*
   b) *Warm the engine to operating temperature, place the transaxle in Park (automatic models) or Neutral (manual models) and apply the parking brake.*
   c) *Note the vacuum reading at idle and jot it down.*
   d) *Quickly open the throttle to near its wide-open position and then quickly get off the throttle and allow it to close. Note the vacuum reading and jot it down.*
   e) *Do this test three more times, recording your measurement after each test.*
   f) *If your fourth reading is more than one in-Hg lower than the reading that you noted at idle, the exhaust system might be restricted (the catalytic converter could be plugged, OR an exhaust pipe or muffler could be restricted).*

REPLACEMENT

▶ **Refer to illustrations 22.12a and 22.12b**

9 Remove the key from the ignition key lock cylinder.

10 Raise the vehicle and place it securely on jackstands.

11 Disconnect the electrical connector from the downstream oxygen sensor and remove the sensor (see Section 12).

12 Remove the retaining nuts from the front and rear catalyst mounting flanges (see illustrations).

13 Installation is the reverse of removal. Be sure to replace any rusted or damaged fasteners and to tighten all fasteners to the torque listed in this Chapter's Specifications.

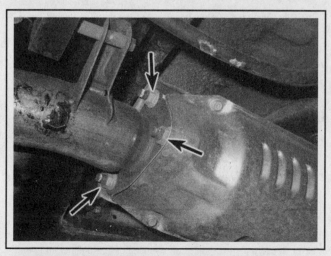

22.12a To detach the front catalyst mounting flange from the exhaust system, remove these three nuts

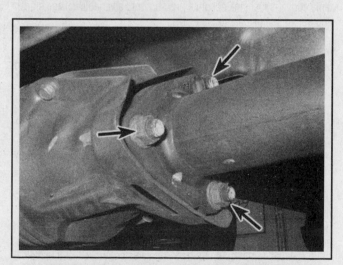

22.12b To detach the rear catalyst mounting flange from the exhaust system, remove these three nuts

23 Evaporative Emissions Control (EVAP) system - general description and component replacement

GENERAL DESCRIPTION

1 The Evaporative Emissions Control (EVAP) system prevents fuel system vapors (which contain unburned hydrocarbons) from escaping into the atmosphere. On warm days, vapors trapped inside the fuel tank expand until the pressure reaches a certain threshold. Then the fuel vapors are routed from the fuel tank through the fuel vapor vent valve and the fuel vapor control valve to the EVAP canister, where they're stored temporarily until the next time the vehicle is operated. When the conditions are right (engine warmed up, vehicle up to speed, moderate or heavy load on the engine, etc.) the PCM opens the canister purge valve, which allows fuel vapors to be drawn from the canister into the intake manifold. Once in the intake manifold, the fuel vapors mix with incoming air before drawn through the intake ports into the combustion chambers where they're burned up with the rest of the air/fuel mixture. The EVAP system is complex and virtually impossible to troubleshoot without the right tools and training. However, the following description should give you a good idea of how it works:

2 The **EVAP canister** is located under the vehicle, ahead of the fuel tank. The canister, which contains activated carbon, is a repository for storing fuel vapors. You'll have to raise the vehicle to inspect or replace the canister, or any other part of the EVAP system, except for the canister purge valve (which is located in the engine compartment). But the canister is designed to be maintenance-free and should last the life of the vehicle. There are several other important components located on or near the canister: the canister filter, the canister vent shut valve, the two-way valve, the bypass solenoid valve and the fuel tank pressure sensor.

3 The **EVAP canister filter** is located on the front side of the EVAP canister. When the canister is purged, fresh air is drawn through the filter before passing through the canister. The filter prevents dust and dirt particles from entering the EVAP canister and the EVAP system.

4 The **canister vent shut valve** is located on the left end of EVAP canister. The canister vent shut valve is normally closed, but it opens to allow fresh air from the filter to enter the EVAP canister when the canister is being purged.

5 The **fuel tank pressure sensor** is located behind the upper rear edge of the EVAP canister, above the EVAP bypass solenoid valve. The fuel tank pressure sensor monitors the pressure inside the fuel tank, converts fuel tank absolute pressure into a variable voltage signal and transmits this data to the PCM.

6 The **EVAP two-way valve** is located at the left rear corner of the EVAP canister. When the pressure of the fuel vapors inside the fuel tank exceeds the preset value of the two-way valve, the valve opens and regulates the flow of excess vapors to the canister. The two-way valve also prevents excessive vacuum in the fuel tank by drawing in fresh air through the EVAP canister.

7 The **EVAP bypass solenoid valve** is located behind the EVAP canister, below the fuel tank pressure sensor, to the right of the EVAP two-way valve. The bypass solenoid valve opens to bypass the two-way valve when the PCM does an EVAP system leak check.

8 The **EVAP canister purge control solenoid valve**, which is under the control of the Powertrain Control Module (PCM), regulates the flow of vapors being purged from the EVAP canister into the intake manifold. The canister purge valve is always closed when engine coolant temperature is below 147-degrees F (64-degrees C), which cuts off intake manifold vacuum to the EVAP canister. Above that threshold, the PCM opens or closes the purge solenoid valve in accordance with data from various information sensor inputs. The interval of time dur-

ing which the purge valve is opened by the PCM is known as its "duty cycle." The purge valve is located in the engine compartment, to the left of the power brake booster.

General system checks

9 The most common symptom of a faulty EVAP system is a strong fuel odor (particularly during hot weather). If you smell fuel while driving or (more likely) right after you park the vehicle and turn off the engine, check the fuel filler cap first. Make sure that it's screwed onto the fuel filler neck all the way. If the odor persists, inspect all EVAP hose connections, both in the engine compartment and under the vehicle. You'll have to raise the vehicle and place it securely on jackstands to inspect most of the EVAP system, since it's located under the vehicle. Be sure to inspect each hose attached to the canister for damage and leakage along its entire length. Repair or replace as necessary. Inspect the canister for damage and look for fuel leaking from the bottom. If fuel is leaking or the canister is otherwise damaged, replace it.

10 Poor idle, stalling, and poor driveability can be caused by a defective fuel vapor vent valve or canister purge valve, a damaged canister, cracked hoses, or hoses connected to the wrong tubes. Fuel loss or fuel odor can be caused by fuel leaking from fuel lines or hoses, a cracked or damaged canister, or a defective vapor valve.

11 To check for excessive fuel vapor pressure in the fuel tank, remove the gas cap and listen for the sound of pressure release If the fuel tank emits a "whooshing" sound when you open the filler cap, fuel tank vapor pressure is excessive. Inspect the canister vapor hoses and the canister inlet port for blockage or collapsed hoses. Also inspect the vapor vent valve. A complete test can only be done with a proprietary OBD-II scan tool (see Section 2), which will run a series of checks using the fuel tank pressure sensor and other output actuators to detect excessive pressure. You'll have to take the vehicle to a dealer service department or other qualified repair shop to have the EVAP system professionally diagnosed.

COMPONENT REPLACEMENT

EVAP purge control solenoid valve

▶ **Refer to illustrations 23.12, 23.13 and 23.14**

12 Disconnect the electrical connector from the purge control solenoid valve (see illustration).

13 Disconnect the vacuum hoses from the purge control solenoid valve (see illustration).

14 Remove the purge control solenoid valve (see illustration).

15 Installation is the reverse of removal.

EVAP canister air filter

▶ **Refer to illustrations 23.17, 23.18 and 23.19**

16 Raise the vehicle and place it securely on jackstands.

17 Remove the EVAP system rock guard (see illustration).

18 Clearly label the three hoses connected to the EVA canister air filter (see illustration), then disconnect them.

19 The canister air filter is secured to its mounting bracket by a pair of split-type locator pins. To detach the air filter from its mounting bracket, squeeze the two-halves of each locator pin together and pull the canister away from the bracket (see illustration).

20 Installation is the reverse of removal.

23.12 Disconnect the electrical connector from the EVAP purge control solenoid valve

23.13 Disconnect these two vacuum hoses from the EVAP purge control solenoid valve

23.14 To detach the EVAP purge control solenoid valve from its mounting bracket, simply lift it straight up

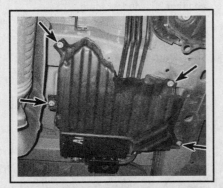

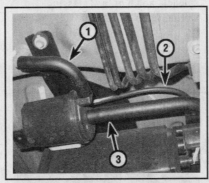

23.17 To detach the EVAP system rock guard, remove these four bolts

23.18 Clearly label the three hoses connected to the EVAP canister air filter, then disconnect them

1 Fresh air inlet hose
2 Goes to EVAP two-way valve
3 Goes to EVAP canister vent shut valve

23.19 To detach the air filter from its mounting bracket, squeeze the two halves of each locator pin together and pull the canister away from the bracket

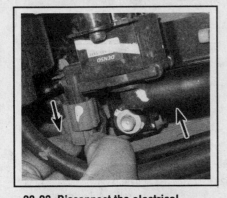

23.23 Disconnect the electrical connector from the EVAP canister vent shut valve, then disconnect the hose that connects the canister air filter to the vent shut valve

23.25 To detach the EVAP canister from its mounting bracket, remove this bolt

23.26 To detach the EVAP canister vent shut valve from the canister, remove these two screws

EVAP canister vent shut valve

▶ Refer to illustrations 23.23, 23.25, 23.26 and 23.27

21 Raise the vehicle and place it securely on jackstands.

22 Remove the EVAP system rock guard (see illustration 23.17).

23 Disconnect the electrical connector from the EVAP canister vent shut valve (see illustration).

24 Disconnect the vacuum hose that connects the EVAP canister air filter to the vent shut valve (see illustration 23.23).

25 Remove the EVAP canister retaining bolt (see illustration) and lower the canister. (It's not necessary to disconnect anything else, but the canister must be lowered before you can remove the upper vent shut valve retaining screw.)

26 Remove the vent shut valve from the EVAP canister (see illustration).

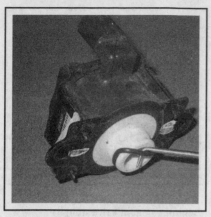

23.27 Remove the old O-ring from the EVAP canister vent shut valve and discard it; whether you're planning to reuse the old vent shut valve or install a new unit, be sure to use a new O-ring when installing the valve

23.31 To detach the mounting bracket for the two-way valve, bypass solenoid and fuel tank pressure sensor, remove this bolt

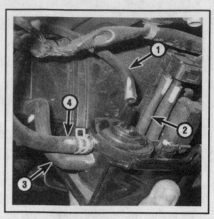

23.32 Clearly label the vacuum hoses connected to the two-way valve and then disconnect them

1 Hose to air filter
2 Hose to fuel tank pressure sensor
3 Hose to EVAP canister
4 Hose to fuel tank

23.33 Disconnect the electrical connectors from the bypass solenoid (1) and the fuel tank pressure sensor (2)

23.34 To detach the two-way valve, bypass solenoid valve and fuel tank pressure sensor assembly from the mounting bracket, remove these two screws

23.35 To detach the two-way valve from the bypass solenoid, remove these two screws

27 Remove the old O-ring from the vent shut valve (see illustration).
28 Installation is the reverse of removal.

EVAP two-way valve/bypass solenoid valve/fuel tank pressure sensor assembly

▶ **Refer to illustrations 23.31, 23.32, 23.33, 23.34, 23.35 and 23.36**

29 Raise the vehicle and place it securely on jackstands.
30 Remove the EVAP system rock guard (see illustration 23.17).
31 Detach the mounting bracket for the two-way valve/bypass solenoid valve/fuel tank pressure sensor assembly from the EVAP canister mounting bracket (see illustration).
32 Swing the mounting bracket down and disconnect the four vacuum hoses from the two-way valve (see illustration).
33 Disconnect the electrical connectors from the bypass solenoid

valve and from the fuel tank pressure sensor (see illustration).
34 Separate the two-way valve/bypass solenoid valve/fuel tank pressure sensor assembly from the mounting bracket (see illustration).
35 If you're replacing the two-way valve or the bypass solenoid valve, separate them from each other (see illustration).
36 If you're replacing the fuel tank pressure sensor, disconnect it from the two vacuum hoses (see illustration). Be sure to inspect both vacuum hoses for cracks, tears and deterioration. If either hose is damaged or deteriorated, replace it.
37 If you've separated the bypass solenoid valve from the two-way valve, be sure to remove and discard the old O-rings. Be sure to use new O-rings when reattaching the two-way valve and the bypass solenoid valve (see illustration 23.36).
38 Reassembly is the reverse of disassembly.
39 Installation is the reverse of removal.

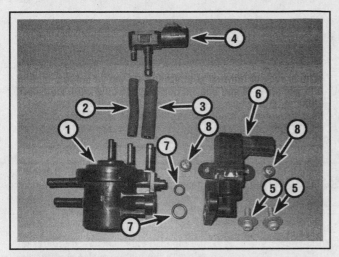

23.36 Two-way check valve/bypass solenoid valve/fuel tank pressure sensor assembly details

1. *Two-way valve*
2. *Hose connecting fuel tank pressure sensor and two-way valve*
3. *Hose connecting fuel tank pressure sensor and bypass solenoid (tees into line between two-way valve and bypass solenoid valve)*
4. *Fuel tank pressure sensor*
5. *Bypass solenoid valve-to-two-way check valve retaining screws*
6. *Bypass solenoid valve*
7. *O-rings*
8. *Two-way check valve/bypass solenoid valve/fuel tank pressure sensor assembly retaining screws*

EVAP canister

▶ **Refer to illustration 23.41 and 23.45**

40 Raise the vehicle and place it securely on jackstands.

41 Disconnect the vacuum hose that connects the air filter to the vent shut valve and disconnect the vacuum hose that connects the EVAP canister to the purge control solenoid valve (see illustration).

42 Clearly label and then disconnect any other vacuum hoses that connect any components attached to the EVAP canister with components located elsewhere (see illustration 23.32).

43 Disconnect the electrical connectors from the bypass solenoid valve and from the fuel tank pressure sensor (see illustration 23.33).

44 Disconnect the electrical connector from the canister vent shut valve (see illustration 23.41).

45 Remove the EVAP canister mounting bolt (see illustration 23.25). Then lower the rear end of the canister and disengage the slot in the front end from the mounting bracket (see illustration).

46 Installation is the reverse of removal.

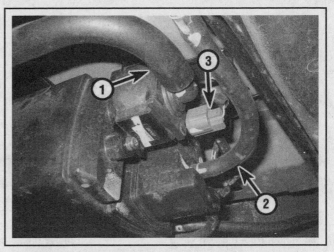

23.41 Before removing the EVAP canister, disconnect the:

1. *Hose from air filter to vent shut valve*
2. *Hose from EVAP canister to purge control solenoid valve*
3. *Vent shut valve electrical connector*

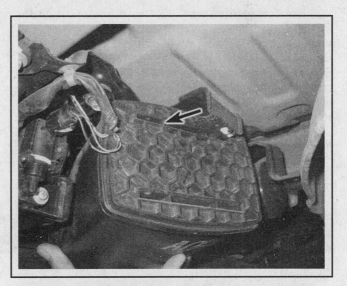

23.45 After removing the EVAP canister mounting bolt (see illustration 19.25), swing the rear end of the canister down and to the side and disengage this slot from the mounting bracket

24 Exhaust Gas Recirculation (EGR) system - general description and component replacement

GENERAL DESCRIPTION

1 Oxides of nitrogen (or simply NOx) is a compound that is formed in the combustion chambers when the oxygen and nitrogen in the incoming air mix together. NOx is a natural byproduct of high combustion chamber temperatures. When NOx is emitted from the tailpipe, it mixes with reactive organic compounds (ROCs), hydrocarbons (HC) and sunlight to form ozone and photochemical smog. The EGR system reduces oxides of nitrogen by recirculating exhaust gases from the exhaust manifold, through the EGR valve and intake manifold, then back to the combustion chambers, where it mixes with the incoming air/fuel mixture before being consumed. These recirculated exhaust gases "dilute" the incoming air/fuel mixture, which cools the combustion chambers, thereby reducing NOx emissions.

2 The EGR system consists of the Powertrain Control Module (PCM), the EGR valve, the EGR valve position sensor and various other information sensors that the PCM uses to determine when to open the

24.4 Disconnect the electrical connector from the EGR valve

24.5 To detach the EGR valve, remove these two mounting nuts

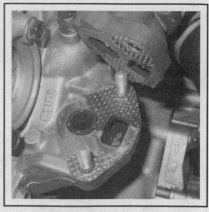

24.6 Be sure to remove and discard the old EGR valve gasket. If the gasket sticks to the mating surfaces of the EGR valve mounting flange and to the coolant crossover (as it did here) be sure to remove all traces of old gasket material with a gasket scraper, and be extremely careful not to scratch or gouge the surfaces

EGR valve. The degree to which the EGR valve is opened is referred to as "EGR valve lift." The PCM is programmed to produce the ideal EGR valve lift for varying operating conditions. The EGR valve position sensor, which is an integral part of the EGR valve, detects the amount of EGR valve lift and sends this information to the PCM. The PCM then compares it with the appropriate EGR valve lift for the operating conditions. The PCM increases current flow to the EGR valve to increase valve lift and reduces the current to reduce the amount of lift. If EGR flow is inappropriate to the operating conditions (idle, cold engine, etc.) the PCM simply cuts the current to the EGR valve and the valve closes.

EGR VALVE REPLACEMENT

▸ **Refer to illustrations 24.4, 24.5 and 24.6**

3   Remove the key from the ignition key lock cylinder.
4   Disconnect the electrical connector from the EGR valve (see illustration).
5   Remove the EGR valve mounting nuts (see illustration) and remove the EGR valve.
6   Remove and discard the old EGR valve gasket (see illustration).
7   Installation is the reverse of removal. Be sure to use a new EGR valve gasket, and tighten the EGR valve mounting nuts securely.

---

25   Positive Crankcase Ventilation (PCV) system - general description, check and component replacement

GENERAL DESCRIPTION

1   The Positive Crankcase Ventilation (PCV) system reduces hydrocarbon emissions by scavenging crankcase vapors. It does this by circulating fresh air from the air intake duct into and through the crankcase, where it mixes with blow-by gases before being drawn by intake manifold vacuum through a PCV valve to the intake manifold.

2   The main components of the PCV system are the PCV valve and a pair of vacuum hoses. The fresh air inlet hose connects the air intake duct to the left end of the front valve cover. The fresh air inlet hose draws fresh air from the air intake duct into the crankcase (via the valve cover). This fresh air combines with blow-by gases in the crankcase. This mixture of fresh air and crankcase vapors is drawn into the intake manifold by intake manifold vacuum through the PCV valve and the "crankcase ventilation hose," which connects the crankcase (via the rear valve cover) to the intake manifold.

3   To maintain idle quality, the PCV valve restricts the flow of crankcase vapors into the intake manifold when intake manifold vacuum is high, and allows full flow when intake manifold decreases.

CHECK

▸ **Refer to illustrations 25.6a and 25.6b**

➡ **Note: This procedure applies only to 2004 and earlier models. Check the PCV valve and hoses used on later models for leaks or restrictions.**

4   Remove the intake manifold cover (see Chapter 2A) and the rear ignition coil harness cover (see illustration 25.14a).
5   Inspect the two PCV system hoses/tubing for cracks, tears or deterioration. If either hose is damaged or worn, replace it.
6   Start the engine and allow it to warm up. With the engine idling, pull out the PCV valve (see illustration) and cover the open end of the valve with your finger (see illustration). You should feel intake vacuum at the PCV valve.
7   If there is no vacuum at the valve, the crankcase ventilation hose is either clogged or it has a hole in it. Remove the crankcase ventilation hose (see Steps 11 through 15), blow it out with compressed air, then inspect it for damage.

25.6a To test or to replace the PCV valve, simply pull it out of its grommet in the valve cover; before installing the PCV valve, inspect the grommet for cracks, tears and deterioration and replace it if it's worn or damaged – 2004 and earlier models

25.6b To check the PCV valve, plug it with your finger while the engine is idling and note whether you can feel the presence of intake manifold vacuum at the valve; if you can't, either the crankcase ventilation hose or the PCV valve is damaged or defective – 2004 and earlier models

25.12 On 2004 and earlier models, the PCV crankcase ventilation hose is connected to this pipe at the right rear corner of the intake manifold; to disconnect the crankcase ventilation hose, loosen the hose clamp, slide it back and pull off the hose

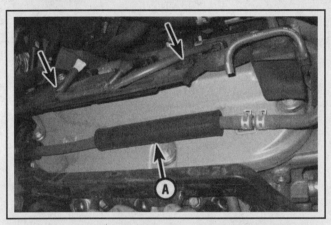

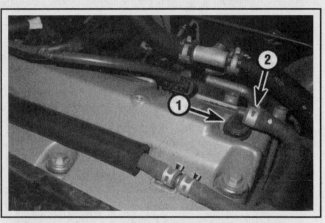

25.13a On 2004 and earlier models, remove the two bolts securing the ignition coil harness cover to the valve cover and detach the cover. The intake manifold is removed for clarity only; it's not necessary to actually remove the intake manifold to replace the crankcase ventilation hose (A)

25.13b To disconnect the crankcase ventilation hose from the PCV valve (1), loosen the hose clamp (2), slide back the clamp and pull off the hose

8   If the hose is damaged or clogged, replace it, then retest the valve. If there is still no intake vacuum at the PCV valve, replace the valve.

9   While the PCV valve is removed, inspect the PCV valve grommet for cracks, tears or deterioration. If the grommet is worn or damaged, replace it.

10 If you're not going to replace anything, install the rear ignition coil harness cover and the intake manifold cover.

COMPONENT REPLACEMENT

Crankcase ventilation hose (2004 and earlier models)

▶ Refer to illustrations 25.12, 25.13a and 25.13b

11 These models are equipped with a long crankcase ventilation

hose that begins at the PCV valve, which is located at the left end of the valve cover, and runs underneath the intake manifold to the right rear corner of the intake manifold.

12 Disconnect the hose from the intake manifold (see illustration).

13 Remove the ignition coil harness cover, then disconnect the crankcase ventilation hose from the PCV valve (see illustrations).

14 Pull the crankcase ventilation hose out from under the intake manifold.

15 Installation is the reverse of removal.

PCV valve

2004 and earlier models

16 If you're going to replace the PCV valve, disconnect the crankcase ventilation hose from the PCV valve (see illustration 25.13b).

17 Remove the PCV valve (see illustration 25.6a).

18 Inspect the PCV valve grommet for cracks, tears and other deterioration. If the grommet is worn or damaged, replace it.

19 Installation is the reverse of removal.

2005 and later models

20 Remove the engine top cover, then disconnect the electrical connector from the PCV valve.

21 Remove the mounting bolt. Pull out the PCV valve and discard the two O-rings; new ones must be used on installation.

22 Installation is the reverse of removal.

Torque specifications

➡ **Note: One foot-pound (ft-lb) of torque is equivalent to 12 inch-pounds (in-lbs) of torque. Torque values below approximately 15 foot-pounds are expressed in inch-pounds, because most foot-pound torque wrenches are not accurate at these smaller values.**

Camshaft Position (CMP) sensor mounting bolts	36 in-lbs	4 Nm
Crankshaft Position (CKP) sensor mounting bolt	104 in-lbs	12 Nm
Intake Air Temperature (IAT) sensor	156 in-lbs	18 Nm
Input shaft (mainshaft) speed sensor mounting bolt	104 in-lbs	12 Nm
Output shaft (countershaft) speed sensor mounting bolt	104 in-lbs	12 Nm
Oxygen sensors	33 ft-lbs	44 Nm
Power Steering Pressure (PSP) switch	104 in-lbs	12 Nm
Transmission range switch mounting bolts	104 in-lbs	12 Nm

7

AUTOMATIC
TRANSAXLE

Section

1 General information

All models covered by this manual are equipped with either a 4-speed or 5-speed automatic transaxle.

Because of the complexity of the automatic transaxle and the specialized equipment needed to service it, this Chapter contains only those procedures related to general diagnosis, routine maintenance, adjustment, and removal and installation.

If the transaxle requires major repair work, it should be taken to a dealer service department or an automotive or transmission repair shop. You can, however, save money by removing and installing the transaxle yourself, even if the repair work is done by a shop.

2 Diagnosis - general

1   Automatic transaxle malfunctions may be caused by five general conditions:

a) *Poor engine performance*
b) *Improper adjustments*
c) *Hydraulic malfunctions*
d) *Mechanical malfunctions*
e) *Malfunctions in the computer or its signal network*

2   Diagnosis of these problems should always begin with a check of the easily repaired items: fluid level and condition (see Chapter 1), shift cable adjustment and shift lever installation. Next, perform a road test to determine if the problem has been corrected or if more diagnosis is necessary. If the problem persists after the preliminary tests and corrections are completed, additional diagnosis should be performed by a dealer service department or other qualified transmission repair shop. Refer to the Troubleshooting section at the front of this manual for information on symptoms of transaxle problems.

PRELIMINARY CHECKS

3   Drive the vehicle to warm the transaxle to normal operating temperature.

4   Check the fluid level as described in Chapter 1:

a) *If the fluid level is unusually low, add enough fluid to bring the level within the designated area of the dipstick, then check for external leaks (see below).*
b) *If the fluid level is abnormally high, drain off the excess, then check the drained fluid for contamination by coolant. The presence of engine coolant in the automatic transmission fluid indicates that a failure has occurred in the internal radiator walls that separate the coolant from the transmission fluid (see Chapter 3).*
c) *If the fluid is foaming, drain it and refill the transaxle, then check for coolant in the fluid, or a high fluid level.*

5   Make sure the engine idle speed is correct. If the idle speed is incorrect, have it adjusted by a dealer service department or other qualified repair shop before proceeding.

6   Inspect the shift cable. Make sure that it's properly adjusted and operates smoothly (see Section 3).

FLUID LEAK DIAGNOSIS

7   Most fluid leaks are easy to locate visually. Repair usually consists of replacing a seal or gasket. If a leak is difficult to find, the following procedure may help.

8   Identify the fluid. Make sure it's transmission fluid and not engine oil or brake fluid (automatic transmission fluid is a deep red color).

9   Try to pinpoint the source of the leak. Drive the vehicle several miles, then park it over a large sheet of cardboard. After a minute or two, you should be able to locate the leak by determining the source of the fluid dripping onto the cardboard.

10 Make a careful visual inspection of the suspected component and the area immediately around it. Pay particular attention to gasket mating surfaces. A mirror is often helpful for finding leaks in areas that are hard to see.

11 If the leak still cannot be found, clean the suspected area thoroughly with a degreaser or solvent, then dry it.

12 Drive the vehicle for several miles at normal operating temperature and varying speeds. After driving the vehicle, visually inspect the suspected component again.

13 Once the leak has been located, the cause must be determined before it can be properly repaired. If a gasket is replaced but the sealing flange is bent, the new gasket will not stop the leak. The bent flange must be straightened.

14 Before attempting to repair a leak, check to make sure that the following conditions are corrected or they may cause another leak.

➡ **Note: Some of the following conditions cannot be fixed without highly specialized tools and expertise. Such problems must be referred to a transmission shop or a dealer service department.**

Seal leaks

15 If a transaxle seal is leaking, the fluid level or pressure may be too high, the vent may be plugged, the seal bore may be damaged, the seal itself may be damaged or improperly installed, the surface of the shaft protruding through the seal may be damaged or a loose bearing may be causing excessive shaft movement.

16 Make sure the dipstick tube seal is in good condition and the tube is properly seated. Periodically check the area around the speedometer gear or sensor for leakage. If transmission fluid is evident, check the O-ring for damage.

Case leaks

17 If the case itself appears to be leaking, the casting is porous and will have to be repaired or replaced.

18 Make sure the oil cooler hose fittings are tight and in good condition.

Fluid comes out vent pipe or fill tube

19 If this condition occurs, the transaxle is overfilled, there is coolant in the fluid, the case is porous, the dipstick is incorrect, the vent is plugged or the drain-back holes are plugged.

3 Shift cable - replacement and adjustment

⁕⁕ WARNING:

These models are equipped with a Supplemental Restraint System (SRS), more commonly known as airbags. Always disable the airbag system before working in the vicinity of any airbag system component to avoid the possibility of accidental deployment of the airbag(s), which could cause personal injury (see Chapter 12).

⁕⁕ WARNING:

Do not use a memory saving device to preserve the PCM or radio memory when working on or near airbag system components.

REPLACEMENT

2004 and earlier models

▶ Refer to illustrations 3.3, 3.5, 3.7 and 3.8

1 Remove the steering column covers (see Chapter 11).
2 Set the parking brake, then place the shift lever in the Neutral position.
3 Remove the locking nut from the cable adjuster, then rotate the grommet counterclockwise a quarter turn and slide the grommet along with the cable from the bracket (see illustration).
4 Raise the vehicle and support it securely on jackstands.
5 Remove the cable guide and grommet (see illustration).
6 Pull the rubber grommet and shift cable out of the vehicle.
7 Remove the fasteners securing the shift cable holder and cover (see illustration).
8 Detach the shift cable and control lever from the transaxle (see illustration).

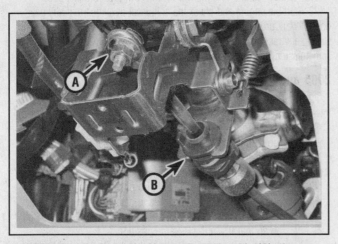

3.3 Remove the locking nut from the shift cable (A), then rotate the grommet slightly to separate the cable assembly (B)

3.5 Remove the guide bracket bolt and pry the cable body grommet from the body to separate the shift cable from the bottom

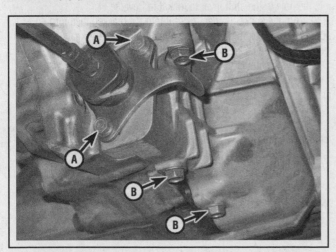

3.7 Remove the shift cable holder mounting bolts (A), then remove the control lever cover mounting bolts (B) (2004 and earlier models)

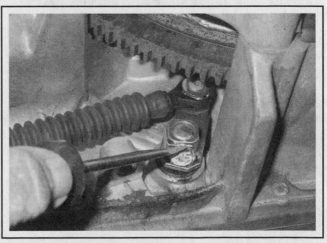

3.8 Bend the lock washer tab away from the mounting nut, then, remove the nut and slide the control lever off the transaxle (2004 and earlier models)

3.24 Insert a 15/64-inch (6.0 mm) drill bit into the positioning hole

9 Installation is the reverse of the removal procedure, noting the following points:

a) *Install a new lock washer, then bend the locking tang against the bolt head.*

b) *Adjust the cable before reattaching it to the shift lever (see Steps 22 through 28).*

2005 and later models

10 Raise the front of the vehicle and support it securely on jackstands.

11 Remove the instrument panel center trim panel and the center lower panel (see Chapter 11).

12 Turn on the ignition and shift into Reverse. Turn off the ignition.

13 Push down the lock tab of the cable end holder.

14 Use needle-nose pliers to pinch the center part of the shift cable lock and carefully pull it off of the cable end.

15 Separate the end of the shift cable from the cable end holder.

16 Twist the socket holder 90-degrees to detach it from the bracket.

17 Disconnect the shift cable retainer, then remove the firewall grommet. Pull out the cable.

18 Working at the transaxle, remove the mounting nuts near the cable end.

19 Remove the clip and separate the cable from the lever. Remove the cable from the vehicle.

20 Installation is the reverse of removal. Install a new lock in the cable end and grease all moving components.

21 After installation, turn on the ignition and make sure that the Reverse light comes on. Perform the adjustment procedure if necessary (see Steps 29 through 43).

ADJUSTMENT

2004 and earlier models

▶ Refer to illustration 3.24

22 Shift to the Neutral position, then remove the lock nut from the cable and disconnect it from the mounting bracket.

23 Push the shift cable until it stops and release your hand. Pull back two clicks until the cable stops (locks-in) in position. This is the NEUTRAL position.

24 Insert a 15/64-inch (6.0 mm) pin into the positioning hole on the shift lever bracket base (see illustration). Once the pin is slid through the positioning hole on the shift lever bracket base, align the shift lever and slide the pin into the shift lever positioning hole to lock the assembly into place.

25 Install the shift cable into the mounting bracket, then install the cable end to the shift lever mounting bolt and align the square surface with the alignment casting on the mounting bolt.

26 Install the lock nut on the cable and tighten the cable in this position.

27 Remove the alignment pin from the shift lever bracket base.

28 Start the engine and check the shift lever in all gears. If any gear doesn't work properly, refer to Section 2. If the engine won't start, or will start in any range other than Park or Neutral, check the adjustment of the Transmission Range switch (see Chapter 6).

2005 and later models

29 Remove the instrument panel center trim panel and the center lower panel (see Chapter 11).

30 Turn on the ignition and shift into Reverse. Turn off the ignition.

31 Push down the lock tab of the cable end holder.

32 Use needle-nose pliers to pinch the center part of the shift cable lock and carefully pull it off of the cable end.

33 Separate the end of the shift cable from the cable end holder.

34 Twist the socket holder 90-degrees to detach it from the bracket.

35 Push the shift cable inner rod until it stops, then release it. Pull it back one stop so that it's in the Reverse position.

36 Turn on the ignition and make sure that the Reverse light comes on. Turn off the ignition.

37 Insert a small pin through the hole in the lever bracket base and into the hole in the shift lever to lock it in Reverse.

38 Turn the socket holder, insert it into the bracket, then turn it 90-degrees to lock it in place. The holder lock will rest against the small stop pin on the bracket when it's correctly assembled.

39 Put the shift cable end into the cable end holder.

40 Install a new shift cable lock, then push it firmly up to secure it in place.

41 Remove the lock pin installed in Step 37.

42 Shift through all the gears and verify that the indicator lights correctly in all positions.

43 Replace the trim panels.

4   Shift lever - replacement

2004 AND EARLIER MODELS

▶ **Refer to illustration 4.4**

❋❋ WARNING:

These models are equipped with a Supplemental Restraint System (SRS), more commonly known as airbags. Always disable the airbag system before working in the vicinity of any airbag system component to avoid the possibility of accidental deployment of the airbag(s), which could cause personal injury (see Chapter 12).

❋❋ WARNING:

Do not use a memory saving device to preserve the PCM or radio memory when working on or near airbag system components.

1   Remove the steering column covers (see Chapter 11).
2   Set the parking brake, then place the shift lever in the Neutral position.
3   Detach the shift cable from the shift lever and bracket (see Section 3).
4   Disconnect the shift lock solenoid and the park pin switch connector (see illustration).
5   Remove the shift lever mounting bolts (see illustration 4.4), then remove the shift lever.
6   Installation is the reverse of the removal procedure, but note the following points:
  a)   *Verify the indicator for the neutral position lights with the ignition switch on.*
  b)   *Adjust the shift cable, if necessary (see Section 3).*

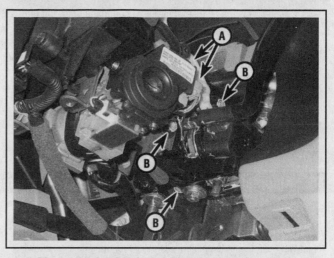

4.4 Disconnect the shift lock solenoid connector and park pin switch connector (A), then remove the shifter mounting bolts (B) (2004 and earlier models)

2005 AND LATER MODELS

7   Remove the instrument panel center trim panel and the center lower panel (see Chapter 11).
8   Disconnect the two wiring harnesses from the shift lever.
9   Turn on the ignition and shift into Reverse. Turn off the ignition.
10   Push down the lock tab of the cable end holder.
11   Use needle-nose pliers to pinch the center part of the shift cable lock and carefully pull it off of the cable end.
12   Separate the end of the shift cable from the cable end holder.
13   Twist the socket holder 90-degrees to detach it from the bracket.
14   Detach the wiring harness clamp, then remove the mounting bolts and remove the shift lever.
15   Installation is the reverse of removal. Check shift lever operation, and perform the cable adjustment procedure (see Section 3) if necessary.

5   Automatic transaxle - removal and installation

➡ **Note:** If the transaxle requires major repair work, it should be left to a dealer service department or an automotive or transmission repair shop. If you've decided that the transaxle must be removed for overhaul or major repair work, several preliminary steps should be taken. Read all removal and installation procedures carefully prior to committing this job.

➡ **Note:** Transaxle removal involves removing the engine and transaxle as an assembly, this procedure is described in Chapter 2B.

REMOVAL

1   Drain the transaxle fluid (Chapter 1).
2   Refer to Chapter 2B, Section 7 to remove the engine/transaxle assembly, then separate the transaxle from the engine as described in that Section.

INSTALLATION

3 Installation is the reverse of removal, noting the following points:

a) *Prior to installation, make sure the torque converter is fully engaged in the transaxle. To do this, rotate the converter while pushing it towards the transaxle. If it wasn't already fully in place, you'll feel it clunk into position as it engages with the input shaft and front pump. It may even clunk more than once. Lubricate the torque converter hub with multi-purpose grease.*

b) *Move the transaxle forward carefully until the dowel pins and the torque converter are engaged. Make sure the marks on the torque converter and driveplate are in alignment.*

c) *Install the transaxle-to-engine bolts. Tighten the bolts to the specified torque listed in this Chapter's Specifications.*

d) *Install the engine/transaxle assembly (see Chapter 2B).*

e) *Lower the vehicle. Install and adjust the shift cable (see Section 4).*

f) *Fill the transaxle with the recommended type and amount of fluid (Chapter 1), run the vehicle and check for fluid leaks.*

6 Automatic transaxle overhaul - general information

In the event of a problem occurring, it will be necessary to establish whether the fault is electrical, mechanical or hydraulic in nature, before repair work can be contemplated. Diagnosis requires detailed knowledge of the transaxle's operation and construction, as well as access to specialized test equipment, and so is deemed to be beyond the scope of this manual. It is therefore essential that problems with the automatic transaxle are referred to a dealer service department or other qualified repair facility for assessment.

Note that a faulty transaxle should not be removed before the vehicle has been diagnosed by a knowledgeable technician equipped with the proper tools, as troubleshooting must be performed with the transaxle installed in the vehicle.

Specifications

General

Fluid type and capacity	See Chapter 1

Torque specifications

➡ **Note: One foot-pound (ft-lb) of torque is equivalent to 12 inch-pounds (in-lbs) of torque. Torque values below approximately 15 foot-pounds are expressed in inch-pounds, because most foot-pound torque wrenches are not accurate at these smaller values.**

Torque converter-to-driveplate bolts	104 in-lbs	12 Nm
Transaxle-to-engine bolts	47 ft-lbs	64 Nm

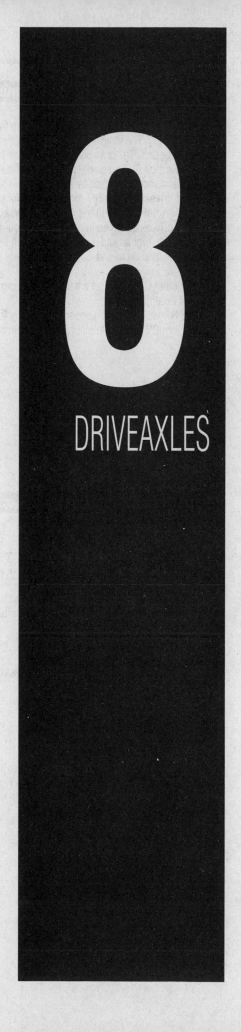

8

DRIVEAXLES

Section

1 Driveaxles - general information and inspection

1 Power is transmitted from the transaxle to the wheels through a pair of driveaxles. The inner end of each driveaxle is splined to the differential side gears. The driveaxles can be pulled out to replace the oil seals (see Section 5). The outer ends of the driveaxles are splined to the front hubs and locked in place by a large nut.

2 Each driveaxle assembly consists of an inner and outer constant velocity (CV) joint connected together by a driveaxle shaft. The inner ends of the driveaxles are equipped with a tripod joint. The design is capable of both angular and axial motion. In other words, the inner CV joints are free to slide in-and-out as the driveaxle moves up-and-down with the wheel.

3 The outer CV joints use a ball-and-cage design, capable of angular but not axial movement.

4 The boots should be inspected periodically for damage and leaking lubricant. Torn CV joint boots must be replaced immediately or the joints can be damaged. Boot replacement involves removal of the driveaxle (see Section 2).

➡ **Note: Some auto parts stores carry "split" type replacement boots, which can be installed without removing the driveaxle from the vehicle. This is a convenient alternative; however, the driveaxle should be removed and the CV joint disassembled and cleaned to ensure the joint is free from contaminants such as moisture and dirt which will accelerate CV joint wear.**

The most common symptom of worn or damaged CV joints, besides lubricant leaks, is a clicking noise in turns, a clunk when accelerating after coasting and vibration at highway speeds. To check for wear in the CV joints and driveaxle shafts, grasp each axle (one at a time) and rotate it in both directions while holding the CV joint housings, feeling for play indicating worn splines or sloppy CV joints. Also check the axleshafts for cracks, dents and distortion.

2 Driveaxles - removal and installation

REMOVAL

▶ **Refer to illustrations 2.1, 2.2, 2.8, 2.9, 2.11a and 2.11b**

1 Set the parking brake. Remove the wheel cover or hubcap. If the driveaxle/hub nut is staked, unstake it with a center punch or chisel (see illustration).

2 Loosen the driveaxle/hub nut with a large socket and breaker bar, but don't remove it yet (see illustration).

3 Loosen the front wheel lug nuts, raise the vehicle and support it securely on jackstands. Remove the wheel.

4 If you're removing the left driveaxle, drain the transaxle lubricant (see Chapter 1).

5 Remove the driveaxle/hub nut.

6 Disconnect the upper end of the stabilizer bar link (see Chapter 10).

7 Separate the control arm from the steering knuckle (see Chapter 10).

8 To loosen the driveaxle from the hub splines, tap the end of the driveaxle with a hammer and brass punch (see illustration). If the driveaxle is stuck in the hub splines and won't move, it may be necessary to push it from the hub with a puller.

9 Pull out on the steering knuckle and detach the driveaxle from

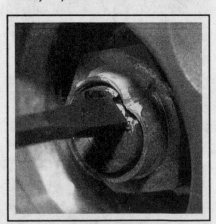

2.1 If the driveaxle is staked, use a center punch to unstake it

2.2 Loosen the driveaxle/hub nut with a long breaker bar

2.8 To loosen the driveaxle from the hub splines, tap the end of the driveaxle with a hammer and brass punch

2.9 Swing the hub/knuckle out (away from the vehicle) and pull the driveaxle from the hub

2.11a Using a long drift, carefully tap the right inboard joint off the intermediate shaft support bearing

2.11b Using a large screwdriver or prybar, pop the inner end of the left driveaxle from the transaxle

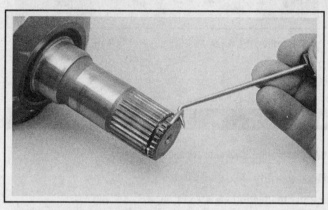

2.13a Pry the old set-ring from the inner end of the driveaxle (or the outer end of the intermediate shaft) with a small screwdriver or awl

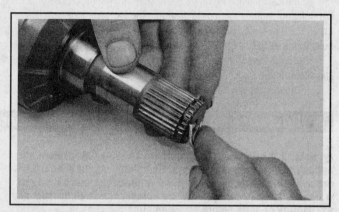

2.13b To install the new set-ring, start one end in the groove and work the ring over the shaft end, into the groove

the hub (see illustration). Suspend the outer end of the driveaxle on a bungee cord or piece of wire.

10 Before you remove the driveaxle, look for lubricant leakage in the area around the differential seal. If there's evidence of a leak, you'll want to replace the seal after removing the driveaxle (see Section 5).

11 To remove a right (passenger's side) driveaxle, tap the inboard joint off the intermediate shaft using a long drift (see illustration). To remove a left-side (driver's side) driveaxle, position the prybar against the inner joint and carefully pry the joint off the transaxle side gear (see illustration). Do not use the driveaxle to pull the on the inner joint. Doing so might damage the inner joint components. Remove the drive-axle assembly, being careful not to over-extend the inner joint or damage the axleshaft boots.

12 Should it become necessary to move the vehicle while the drive-axle is out, place a large bolt with two large washers (one on each side of the hub) through the hub and tighten the nut securely.

INSTALLATION

▶ **Refer to illustrations 2.13a and 2.13b**

13 Installation is the reverse of removal, but with the following additional points:

a) Remove the old set-ring from the inner CV joint (left driveaxle) or from the end of the intermediate shaft (right driveaxle) and install a new one (see illustration).
b) Apply a film of multi-purpose grease around the splines of the joints.
c) When installing the driveaxle, hold the driveaxle straight out, push it in sharply to seat the driveaxle set-ring into the groove in the transaxle side gear or center support bearing. To make sure the set-ring is properly seated in the gear groove, attempt to pull the driveaxle out of the transaxle by hand. If the set-ring is properly seated the inner joint will not move out.
d) Clean all foreign matter from the driveaxle outer CV joint threads. Install the new driveaxle/hub nut. Tighten the nut securely but not to the specified torque specification at this time.
e) Tighten the suspension fasteners to the torque listed in the Chapter 10 Specifications.
f) Install the wheel and lug nuts, then lower the vehicle.
g) Tighten the driveaxle/hub nut to the torque listed in this Chapter's Specifications. Using a hammer and punch, stake the nut to the groove in the driveaxle.
h) Tighten the wheel lug nuts to the torque listed in the Chapter 1 Specifications.
i) Add transaxle lubricant if it was drained or if any fluid spilled out (see Chapter 1).

3 Intermediate shaft - removal and installation

REMOVAL

▶ **Refer to illustration 3.2**

1   Remove the right driveaxle (see Section 2)

2   Remove the three bearing support-to-engine block bolts (see illustration) and slide the intermediate shaft out of the transaxle. Be careful not to damage the differential seal when pulling the shaft out.

3   Check the support bearing for smooth operation by turning the shaft while holding the bearing. If it feels rough or sticky it should be replaced. Take it to a dealer service department or other repair shop, as special tools are needed to perform this job.

INSTALLATION

4   Lubricate the lips of the transaxle seal with multi-purpose grease. Carefully guide the intermediate shaft into the transaxle side gear then install the mounting bolts through the bearing support. Tighten the bolts to the torque listed in this Chapter's Specifications.

5   Install a new spring clip on the inner CV joint (see illustrations) and seat the driveaxle into the intermediate shaft splines.

6   Reinstall the driveaxle (see Section 2).

3.2 Remove the three bearing support-to-engine block bolts

4 Driveaxle boot replacement and CV joint inspection

➡ **Note: If the CV joints or boots must be replaced, explore all options before beginning the job. Complete, rebuilt driveaxles are available on an exchange basis, eliminating much time and work. Whichever route you choose to take, check on the cost and availability of parts before disassembling the vehicle.**

INNER CV JOINT

1   Remove the driveaxle (see Section 2).

2   Mount the driveaxle in a vise with wood-lined jaws, to prevent damage to the axleshaft. Check the CV joints for excessive play in the radial direction, which indicates worn parts. Check for smooth operation throughout the full range of motion for each CV joint. If a boot is torn, the recommended procedure is to disassemble the joint, clean the components and inspect for damage due to loss of lubrication and possible contamination by foreign matter. If the CV joint is in good condition,

lubricate it with CV joint grease and install a new boot.

Disassembly

▶ **Refer to illustrations 4.4a, 4.4b, 4.5, 4.6 and 4.7**

3   Cut the boot clamps with side-cutters, then remove and discard them.

4   Using a screwdriver, carefully pry up on the edge of the CV boot, pull it off the CV joint housing and slide it down the axleshaft, exposing the tri-pod assembly. Mark the relationship of the joint housing to the tri-pod (see illustration). To separate the axleshaft and tri-pod assembly from the inner joint housing, simply pull the housing straight off (see illustration).

➡ **Note: When removing the housing, hold the rollers in place on the tri-pod to prevent the rollers and the needle bearings from falling free.**

4.4a Mark the relationship of the tri-pot to the housing

4.4b Remove the boot from the inner CV joint and slide the joint housing from the tri-pod

4.5 Remove the snap-ring with a pair of snap-ring pliers

4.6 Use a center-punch to place marks on the tri-pod and the driveaxle to ensure that they are reassembled properly

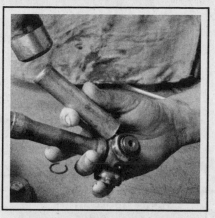

4.7 Drive the tri-pod joint from the driveaxle with a brass punch and hammer (be careful not to damage the bearing surfaces or the splines on the shaft)

4.10a Install the tri-pod with the recessed portion of the splines facing the axleshaft

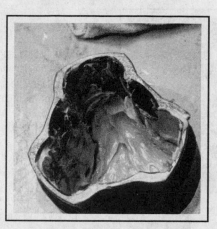

4.10b Place grease at the bottom of the CV joint housing

4.10c Install the boot and clamps onto the axleshaft, then insert the tri-pod into the housing, followed by the rest of the grease

5   Remove the tri-pod assembly snap-ring with a pair of snap-ring pliers (see illustration).

6   Mark the tri-pod to the axleshaft to ensure that they are reassembled properly (see illustration).

7   Use a hammer and a brass drift to drive the tri-pod assembly from the axleshaft (see illustration).

8   Slide the boot off the shaft.

Inspection

9   Thoroughly clean all components with solvent until the old CV joint grease is completely removed. Inspect the bearing surfaces of the tri-pod and housing for cracks, pitting, scoring and other signs of wear. If any part of the inner CV joint is worn, you must replace the entire joint. Depending on the availability of parts, you may even have to purchase a complete driveaxle assembly.

➡ **Note: If you're working on a right-side driveaxle, check the center bearing for smooth operation. If it feels rough or is noisy when rotated, take the intermediate shaft to an automotive machine shop to have the old bearing pressed out and a new one pressed in.**

Reassembly

▶ **Refer to illustrations 4.10a, 4.10b, 4.10c, 4.12, 4.13, 4.15a, 4.15b, 4.15c, 4.15d and 4.15e**

10 Wrap the splines on the inner end of the axleshaft with electrical or duct tape to protect the boots from the sharp edges of the splines and slide the clamps and boot onto the axleshaft (see illustration 4.18g). Remove the tape and place the tri-pod on the axleshaft with the recessed portion of the splines toward the shaft (see illustration). Tap the tri-pod onto the shaft with a brass drift until it's seated and install the snap-ring. Apply grease to the tri-pod assembly and inside the housing (see illustration). Insert the tri-pod into the housing and pack the remainder of the grease around the tri-pod (see illustration).

11 Slide the boot into place, making sure the raised bead on the inside of the seal boot is positioned in the groove on the interconnecting shaft. If the driveaxle has multiple locating grooves on the shaft, position the boot so only one of the grooves (the thinnest) is exposed. Position the sealing boot into the groove on the housing retaining groove.

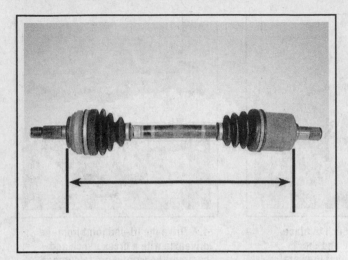

4.12 Adjust the driveaxle to the length listed in this Chapter's Specifications (this dimension is critical for maintaining the correct pressure inside sliding CV joints)

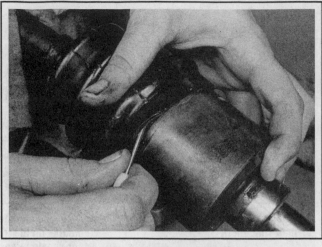

4.13 With the driveaxle set to the proper length, equalize the pressure inside the boot by inserting a small, dull screwdriver between the boot and the outer race

12 Adjust the length of the driveaxle (see illustration). Refer to the Specifications listed in this Chapter for the correct driveaxle length.

13 Equalize the pressure inside the boot by inserting a small, dull, flat screwdriver tip between the boot and the CV joint housing (see illustration).

14 Make sure each end of the boot is seated properly, and the boot is not distorted.

15 Install the boot clamps. There are three types of clamps you're likely to encounter: the band type, which requires a special tightening tool, the crimp type (which also requires a special tool), or the fold-over type (see illustrations).

16 The driveaxle is now ready for installation (see Section 2).

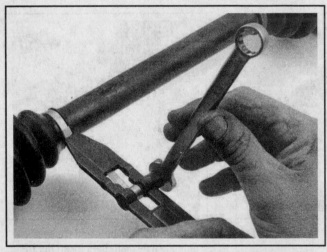

4.15a You'll need a special tightening tool to install "band" type boot clamps: Install the band with its end pointing in the direction of axle rotation and tighten it securely . . .

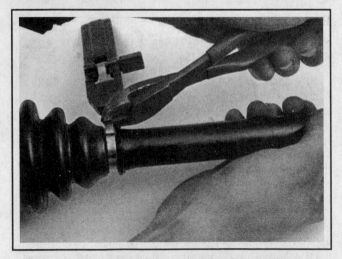

4.15b . . . then bend down the end of the clamp back and cut off the excess

4.15c If you're installing crimp-type boot clamps, you'll need a pair of special crimping pliers (available at most auto parts stores)

4.15d To install fold-over type boot clamps, bend the tang down . . .

4.15e . . . then tap the tabs over to hold it in place

OUTER CV JOINT

▶ **Refer to illustrations 4.18a through 4.18l**

17 Remove the driveaxle (see Section 2).

18 Refer to the accompanying illustrations and perform the outer CV joint boot replacement procedure (see illustrations 4.18a through 4.18l).

4.18a Cut off the band retaining the boot to the shaft, then slide the boot toward the center of the shaft

4.18b Clean all grease off the axleshaft and paint a mark on the shaft, then measure the distance from your mark to the face of the inner race and record this measurement; the inner race must be installed on the axleshaft in exactly the same position in which it was installed prior to removal

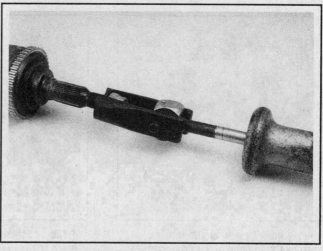

4.18c Outer CV joints can be removed with a slide hammer; you'll need an adapter and a slide hammer setup such as the one shown here

4.18d With the axleshaft firmly clamped down in a bench vise and the adapter gripping the driveaxle/hub nut, carefully extract the outer CV joint from the axleshaft

4.18e After the old grease has been rinsed away, move the inner race through its full range of motion and inspect the bearing surfaces for wear or damage

4.18f Apply CV joint grease through the splined hole, then insert a wooden dowel (slightly smaller in diameter than the hole) into the hole and push down - the dowel will force the grease into the joint. Repeat this until the joint is packed

4.18g Wrap the splined area of the axleshaft with tape to prevent damage to the boot when installing it

4.18h Install the small clamp and the boot on the driveaxle and apply grease to the inside of the axle boot until . . .

4.18i . . . the level is up to the end of axle

4.18j Install a new circlip into the groove at the end of the driveaxle. Position the CV joint assembly on the driveaxle, aligning the splines . . .

4.18k . . . then use a hammer and brass punch to carefully drive the joint onto the driveaxle to the same spot it was in before disassembly (see illustration 4.18b)

4.18l Seat the inner end of the boot in the groove and install the retaining clamp, then do the same on the other end of the boot - tighten boot clamps with the special tool

5   Driveaxle oil seals - replacement

▶ **Refer to illustrations 5.3 and 5.5**

1   The driveaxle oil seals are located on the sides of the transaxle, where the inner ends of the driveaxle and intermediate shaft are splined into the differential side gears. If you suspect that a driveaxle oil seal is leaking, raise the vehicle and support it securely on jackstands. If the seal is leaking, you'll see lubricant on the side of the transaxle, below the seal.

2   Remove the driveaxle (see Section 2) or intermediate shaft (see Section 3).

3   Using a screwdriver or prybar, carefully pry the oil seal out of the transaxle bore (see illustration).

4   If the oil seal cannot be removed with a screwdriver or prybar, a special oil seal removal tool (available at auto parts stores) will be required.

5   Using a seal installer or large socket, install the new oil seal. Drive it into the bore squarely until it bottoms (see illustration).

6   Install the driveaxle (see Section 2) or intermediate shaft (see Section 3).

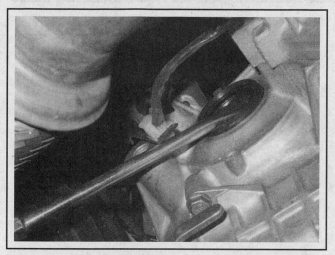

5.3 Using a large screwdriver or prybar, carefully pry the oil seal out of the transaxle (you may need to obtain a special seal removal tool - available at most auto parts stores - to do the job)

5.5 Using a seal installer, drive the new seal squarely into the bore and make sure that it's completely seated

Specifications

Driveaxle length (see illustration 4.12)

Left driveaxle
  2004 and earlier models   23.6 inches (600.7 mm)
  2005 and later models   22.2 to 22.4 inches (564 to 569 mm)
Right driveaxle
  2004 and earlier models   22.1 inches (560.8 mm)
  2005 and later models   22.6 to 22.8 inches (574 to 579 mm)

Torque specifications	Ft-lbs	Nm
Driveaxle/hub nut		
2004 and earlier models	181	245
2005 and later models	242	329
Intermediate shaft bearing support bolts	29	39
Wheel lug nuts	See Chapter 1	

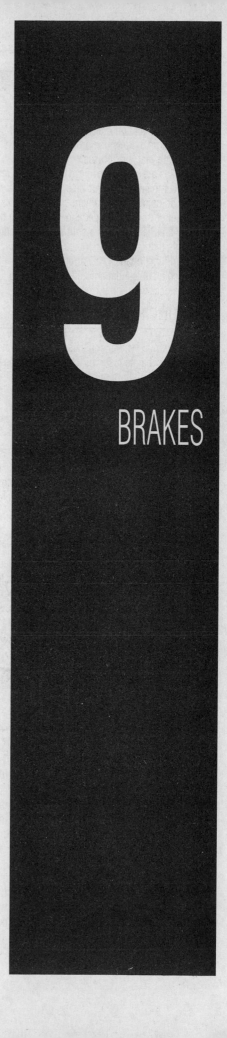

9

BRAKES

Section

1 General information

The vehicles covered by this manual are equipped with hydraulically operated front and rear brake systems. All front brake systems are disc type. Some models use drum type brakes at the rear, others are equipped with rear disc brakes.

All brakes are self-adjusting. The front and rear disc brakes automatically compensate for pad wear, while the rear drum brakes incorporate an adjustment mechanism which is activated as the brakes are applied, either through the pedal or the parking brake lever.

The hydraulic system is a split design, meaning there are two separate circuits that control the brakes. If one circuit fails, the other circuit will remain functional and a warning indicator will light up on the dashboard when a substantial amount of brake fluid is lost, showing that a failure has occurred.

HYDRAULIC SYSTEM

The hydraulic system consists of two separate circuits. The master cylinder has separate reservoir chambers for the two circuits, and, in the event of a leak or failure in one hydraulic circuit, the other circuit will remain operative. A dual proportioning valve on the firewall provides brake balance between the front and rear brakes.

POWER BRAKE BOOSTER

The power brake booster, which uses engine manifold vacuum and atmospheric pressure to provide assistance to the hydraulically operated brakes, is mounted on the firewall in the engine compartment.

PARKING BRAKE

A parking brake pedal inside the vehicle operates a cable attached to a pair of rear cables, each of which is connected to its respective rear brake. When the parking brake pedal is depressed on drum brake models, each rear cable pulls on a lever attached to the brake shoe assembly, causing the shoes to expand against the drum. When the pedal is depressed on models with rear disc brakes, the rear cables pull on levers that are attached to screw-type actuators in the caliper housings, which apply force to the caliper pistons, clamping the brake pads against the brake disc.

SERVICE

After completing any operation involving disassembly of any part of the brake system, always test drive the vehicle to check for proper braking performance before resuming normal driving. When testing the brakes, perform the tests on a clean, dry, flat surface. Conditions other than these can lead to inaccurate test results.

Test the brakes at various speeds with both light and heavy pedal pressure. The vehicle should stop evenly without pulling to one side or the other. Avoid locking the brakes, because this slides the tires and diminishes braking efficiency and control of the vehicle.

Tires, vehicle load and wheel alignment are factors which also affect braking performance.

PRECAUTIONS

There are some general cautions and warnings involving the brake system on these vehicles:

a) Use only brake fluid conforming to DOT 3 specifications.
b) The brake pads and linings contain materials which are hazardous to your health. Whenever you work on brake system components, clean all parts with brake system cleaner. Do not allow the fine dust to become airborne, and wear a filter/mask over your nose and mouth when cleaning or servicing brakes.
c) Safety should be paramount whenever any servicing of the brake components is performed. Do not use parts or fasteners which are not in perfect condition, and be sure that all clearances and torque specifications are adhered to. If you are at all unsure about a certain procedure, seek professional advice. Upon completion of any brake system work, test the brakes carefully in a controlled area before putting the vehicle into normal service.
d) If a problem is suspected in the brake system, don't drive the vehicle until it's fixed.

2 Anti-lock Brake System (ABS) - general information and speed sensor removal and installation

GENERAL INFORMATION

▶ Refer to illustrations 2.2a, 2.2b and 2.2c

1   The anti-lock brake system is designed to maintain vehicle steerability, directional stability and optimum deceleration under severe braking conditions on most road surfaces. It does so by monitoring the rotational speed of each wheel and controlling the brake line pressure to each wheel during braking. This prevents the wheels from locking up.

2   The ABS system has three main components - the wheel speed sensors, the electronic control unit (ECU) and the hydraulic unit (see illustrations). Four wheel speed sensors - one at each wheel - send a variable voltage signal to the control unit, which monitors these signals, compares them to its program and determines whether a wheel is about to lock up. When a wheel is about to lock up, the control unit signals the hydraulic unit to reduce hydraulic pressure (or not increase it further) at that wheel's brake caliper. Pressure modulation is handled by electrically-operated solenoid valves.

2.2a The ABS hydraulic unit (located below the air intake duct)

2.2b Front wheel speed sensor

2.2c Rear wheel speed sensor

3   If a problem develops within the system, an "ABS" warning light will glow on the dashboard. Sometimes, a visual inspection of the ABS system can help you locate the problem. Carefully inspect the ABS wiring harness. Pay particularly close attention to the harness and connections near each wheel. Look for signs of chafing and other damage caused by incorrectly routed wires. If a wheel sensor harness is damaged, the sensor must be replaced.

✷✷ WARNING:

Do NOT try to repair an ABS wiring harness. The ABS system is sensitive to even the smallest changes in resistance. Repairing the harness could alter resistance values and cause the system to malfunction. If the ABS wiring harness is damaged in any way, it must be replaced.

✷✷ CAUTION:

Make sure the ignition is turned off before unplugging or reattaching any electrical connections.

Diagnosis and repair

4   If a dashboard warning light comes on and stays on while the vehicle is in operation, the ABS system requires attention. Although special electronic ABS diagnostic testing tools are necessary to properly diagnose the system, you can perform a few preliminary checks before taking the vehicle to a dealer service department.

 a) *Check the brake fluid level in the reservoir.*

 b) *Verify that the computer electrical connectors are securely connected.*

 c) *Check the electrical connectors at the hydraulic control unit.*

 d) *Check the fuses.*

 e) *Follow the wiring harness to each wheel and verify that all connections are secure and that the wiring is undamaged.*

5   If the above preliminary checks do not rectify the problem, the vehicle should be diagnosed by a dealer service department or other qualified repair shop. Due to the complex nature of this system, all actual repair work (with the exception of speed sensor replacement) must be done by a qualified automotive technician.

WHEEL SPEED SENSOR - REMOVAL AND INSTALLATION

6   Loosen the wheel lug nuts, raise the vehicle and support it securely on jackstands. Remove the wheel.

7   Make sure the ignition key is turned to the Off position.

8   Trace the wiring back from the sensor, detaching all brackets and clips while noting its correct routing, then disconnect the electrical connector.

9   Remove the mounting bolt and carefully pull the sensor out from the knuckle or brake backing plate.

10   Installation is the reverse of the removal procedure. Tighten the mounting bolt securely.

11   Install the wheel and lug nuts, tightening them securely. Lower the vehicle and tighten the lug nuts to the torque listed in the Chapter 1 Specifications.

---

3   Disc brake pads - replacement

▶ **Refer to illustrations 3.5 and 3.6**

✷✷ WARNING:

Disc brake pads must be replaced on both front and rear wheels at the same time - never replace the pads on only one side. Also, the dust created by the brake system is harmful to your health. Never blow it out with compressed air and don't inhale

any of it. An approved filtering mask should be worn when working on the brakes. Do not, under any circumstances, use petroleum-based solvents to clean brake parts. Use brake system cleaner only!

➡ **Note: This procedure applies to front and rear disc brakes.**

1   Remove the cap from the brake fluid reservoir.

2   Loosen the wheel lug nuts, raise the front, or rear, of the vehicle

3.5 Spray the disc, caliper and brake pads with brake system cleaner to remove the dust produced by brake pad wear

3.6 Using a large C-clamp, push the piston(s) back into the caliper - note that one end of the clamp is on the back side of the caliper and the other end (screw end) is pressing on the outer brake pad (front caliper shown - rear caliper similar)

and support it securely on jackstands.

3   Remove the front, or rear, wheels. Work on one brake assembly at a time, using the assembled brake for reference if necessary.

4   Inspect the brake disc carefully as outlined in Section 5. If machining is necessary, follow the information in that Section to remove the disc, at which time the calipers and pads can be removed as well.

5   Before removing anything, spray the disc, caliper and brake pads with brake system cleaner to remove the dust produced by brake pad wear (see illustration). DO NOT blow the dust off with compressed air!

6   Push the piston back into the bore to provide room for the new brake pads. A C-clamp can be used to accomplish this (see illustration). As the piston is depressed to the bottom of the caliper bore, the fluid in the master cylinder will rise. Make sure it doesn't overflow. If necessary, drain off some of the fluid.

FRONT PADS

▶ **Refer to illustrations 3.7a through 3.7m**

➡ **Note: 2005 and later models have a two-piston caliper. Although the caliper appearance is different, the procedure is the same.**

7   Follow the accompanying photos, beginning with illustration 3.7a, for the actual pad replacement procedure. Be sure to stay in order and read the caption under each illustration. When you have completed the Steps described in the accompanying photos, proceed to Step 19.

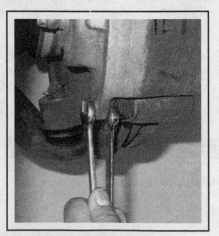

3.7a Remove the lower caliper mounting bolt while holding the caliper pin with a second wrench

3.7b Swing the caliper up and secure the caliper in this position with a piece of wire

3.7c Remove the outer brake pad and shim

3.7d Remove the inner brake pad and shim(s)

3.7e Remove and inspect the upper and lower pad retainer clips

3.7f The pad retainer clips should fit snugly in the caliper mounting bracket; if they don't, replace them. Apply a thin film of high-temperature grease to the retainer

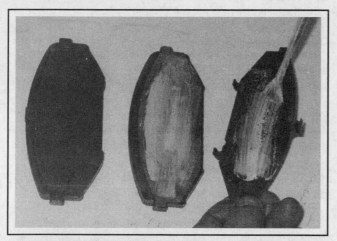

3.7g Apply a small amount of high-temperature grease to both sides of the shims

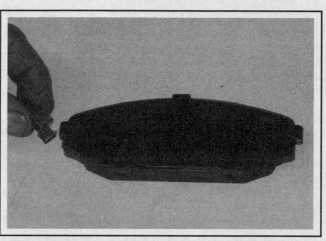

3.7h If equipped, install the brake pad wear indicator to the inner pad

3.7i Install the new inner pad and shim; make sure the "ears" on the upper and lower ends of the pad are fully engaged with their respective grooves and the pad retainer clips

3.7j Install the new outer pad and shim

3.7k Before installing the caliper, remove the caliper pin dust boots and inspect them for tears and cracks; if they're damaged, replace them. Clean off the caliper mounting bolt and coat it with high-temperature grease

3.7l Swing the caliper down over the disc and new pads (if the piston hits the inner pad, depress the piston further into the caliper bore with your C-clamp)

3.7m Install the lower bolt and tighten it to the torque listed in this Chapter's Specifications

REAR PADS

8   Remove the caliper mounting bolts while holding the caliper pins with a second wrench.

9   Remove the caliper from its mounting bracket then hang the caliper out of the way with a piece of wire. Don't let the caliper hang by the brake hose.

10 Remove the outer brake pad and shim.

11 Remove the inner brake pad and shim(s).

12 Remove and inspect the upper and lower pad retainer clips.

13 Install the pad retainer clips, they should fit snugly in the caliper mounting bracket; if they don't, replace them. Apply a thin film of high-temperature grease to the retainer.

14 Apply a small amount of high-temperature grease to both sides of the shims.

15 Install the new inner pad and shim(s). Make sure the "ears" on the upper and lower ends of the pad are fully engaged with their respec-tive grooves and the pad retainer clips

16 Install the new outer pad and shim.

17 Before installing the caliper, remove the caliper pin dust boots and inspect them for tears and cracks; if they're damaged, replace them.

18 Install the caliper mounting bolts while holding the caliper pins with a second wrench. Tighten them to the torque listed in this Chapter's Specifications.

FRONT OR REAR PADS

19 Install the wheel and lug nuts, lower the vehicle and tighten the lug nuts to the torque specified in Chapter 1.

20 Apply and release the brake pedal several times to bring the pads into contact with the brake discs. Check the brake fluid level and add fluid, if necessary (see Chapter 1).

21 Check the operation of the brakes in an isolated area before driving the vehicle in traffic.

4   Disc brake caliper - removal and installation

✳✳ WARNING:

The dust created by the brake system is harmful to your health. Never blow it out with compressed air and don't inhale any of it. An approved filtering mask should be worn when working on the brakes. Do not, under any circumstances, use petroleum-based solvents to clean brake parts. Use brake system cleaner only!

➡ Note: Always replace the calipers in pairs - never replace just one of them.

FRONT

Removal

◗ **Refer to illustrations 4.2a, 4.2b and 4.3**

1   Loosen - but don't remove - the lug nuts on the front wheels. Raise the front of the vehicle and place it securely on jackstands.

Remove the front wheels.

2   Disconnect the brake line from the caliper and plug it to keep contaminants out of the brake system and to prevent losing any more brake fluid than is necessary (see illustrations).

➡ Note: If you're simply removing the caliper for access to other components, don't disconnect the hose.

3   Remove the caliper mounting bolts while holding the caliper pins with a second wrench (see illustration).

4   Detach the caliper from its mounting bracket.

Installation

5   Install the caliper by reversing the removal procedure. Remember to replace the sealing washers on either side of the brake line fitting with new ones. Tighten the caliper mounting bolts and the banjo bolt to the torque listed in this Chapter's Specifications.

6   Bleed the brake system (see Section 10).

7   Install the wheels and lug nuts and lower the vehicle. Tighten the wheel lug nuts to the torque listed in the Chapter 1 Specifications.

4.2a Remove the brake hose banjo bolt

4.2b Using a short piece of rubber hose of the appropriate diameter, plug the brake line banjo fitting

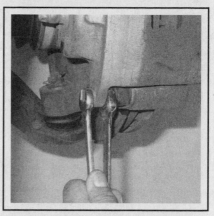

4.3 Remove the upper and lower caliper mounting bolts while holding the caliper pins with a second wrench

REAR

Removal

8 Loosen - but don't remove - the lug nuts on the rear wheels. Raise the rear of the vehicle and place it securely on jackstands. Remove the rear wheels.

9 Unscrew the banjo bolt and detach the brake line from the caliper. Plug the fitting to prevent fluid loss and contamination (see illustration 4.2b).

➡ **Note: If you're simply removing the caliper for access to other components, don't disconnect the hose.**

10 Remove the caliper mounting bolts while holding the caliper pins with a second wrench.

11 Detach the caliper from its mounting bracket.

Installation

12 Install the caliper by reversing the removal procedure. Remember to replace the sealing washers on either side of the brake line fitting with new ones. Tighten the caliper mounting bolts and the banjo bolt to the torque listed in this Chapter's Specifications.

13 Bleed the brake system (see Section 10).

14 Install the wheels and lug nuts. Lower the vehicle and tighten the lug nuts to the torque listed in the Chapter 1 Specifications.

---

5 Brake disc - inspection, removal and installation

✳ WARNING:

The dust created by the brake system is harmful to your health. Never blow it out with compressed air and don't inhale any of it. An approved filtering mask should be worn when working on the brakes. Do not, under any circumstances, use petroleum-based solvents to clean brake parts. Use brake system cleaner only!

INSPECTION

▶ **Refer to illustrations 5.2, 5.3, 5.4a, 5.4b and 5.5**

1 Loosen the wheel lug nuts, raise the vehicle and support it securely on jackstands. Remove the wheel and install the lug nuts to hold the disc in place against the hub flange.

➡ **Note: If the lug nuts don't contact the disc when screwed on all the way, install washers under them.**

If you're checking the rear disc, release the parking brake.

2 Remove the brake caliper as outlined in Section 4. It isn't necessary to disconnect the brake hose. After removing the caliper bolts, suspend the caliper out of the way with a piece of wire. Remove the two caliper mounting bracket-to-steering knuckle bolts (see illustration) or,

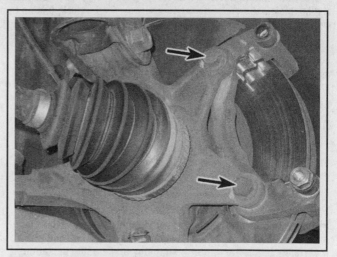

5.2 The caliper mounting bracket is retained by two bolts

on rear calipers, the bracket-to-knuckle bolts and remove the mounting bracket.

3 Visually inspect the disc surface for score marks and other dam-

5.3 The brake pads on this vehicle were obviously neglected, as they wore down completely and cut deep grooves into the disc - wear this severe means the disc must be replaced

5.4a To check disc runout, mount a dial indicator as shown and rotate the disc

5.4b Using a swirling motion, remove the glaze from the disc surface with sandpaper or emery cloth

5.5 Use a micrometer to measure disc thickness

5.6a If the disc retaining screws are stuck, use an impact screwdriver to loosen them

5.6b If the disc is stuck, thread two bolts into the disc and tighten them to force the disc off the hub

age. Light scratches and shallow grooves are normal after use and may not always be detrimental to brake operation, but deep scoring requires disc removal and refinishing by an automotive machine shop. Be sure to check both sides of the disc (see illustration). If pulsating has been noticed during application of the brakes, suspect disc runout.

4   To check disc runout, place a dial indicator at a point about 1/2-inch from the outer edge of the disc (see illustration). Set the indicator to zero and turn the disc. The indicator reading should not exceed the specified allowable runout limit. If it does, the disc should be refinished by an automotive machine shop.

➡ **Note: The discs should be resurfaced regardless of the dial indicator reading, as this will impart a smooth finish and ensure a perfectly flat surface, eliminating any brake pedal pulsation or other undesirable symptoms related to questionable discs. At the very least, if you elect not to have the discs resurfaced, remove the glaze from the surface with emery cloth or sandpaper, using a swirling motion (see illustration).**

5   It's absolutely critical that the disc not be machined to a thickness under the specified minimum thickness. The minimum (or discard)

thickness is cast or stamped into the disc. The disc thickness can be checked with a micrometer (see illustration).

REMOVAL

▶ **Refer to illustrations 5.6a and 5.6b**

6   Remove the lug nuts which were installed to hold the disc in place, or remove the two disc retaining screws (see illustration) and remove the disc from the hub. If the disc is stuck to the hub and won't come off, thread two bolts into the holes provided (see illustration) and tighten them. Alternate between the bolts, turning them a couple of turns at a time, until the disc is free. Remove the disc from the hub.

7   The rear discs may be difficult to remove because the parking brake shoes are holding them. If this is the case, remove the rubber plug and use a flat-blade screwdriver to turn the adjuster star wheel until they have loosened. Re-adjust the parking brake shoes so that there is minimal clearance, yet no drag.

INSTALLATION

8   Place the disc in position over the threaded studs. Install the disc retaining screws and tighten them securely.

9   Install the caliper mounting bracket and caliper, tightening the bolts to the torque values listed in this Chapter's Specifications.

10 Install the wheel, then lower the vehicle to the ground. Tighten the lug nuts to the torque listed in the Chapter 1 Specifications. Depress the brake pedal a few times to bring the brake pads into contact with the disc. Bleeding won't be necessary unless the brake hose was disconnected from the caliper. Check the operation of the brakes carefully before driving the vehicle.

---

6   Drum brake shoes/parking brake shoes - replacement

▶ **Refer to illustrations 6.4, 6.5, 6.6a through 6.6q and 6.7**

❋❋ WARNING:

Drum brake shoes must be replaced on both wheels at the same time - never replace the shoes on only one wheel. Also, the dust created by the brake system is harmful to your health. Never blow it out with compressed air and don't inhale any of it. An approved filtering mask should be worn when working on the brakes. Do not, under any circumstances, use petroleum-based solvents to clean brake parts. Use brake system cleaner only!

❋❋ CAUTION:

Whenever the brake shoes are replaced, the return and hold-down springs should also be replaced. Due to the continuous heating/cooling cycle the springs are subjected to, they can lose tension over a period of time and may allow the shoes to drag on the drum and wear at a much faster rate than normal.

1   Loosen the wheel lug nuts, raise the rear of the vehicle and support it securely on jackstands. Block the front wheels to keep the vehicle from rolling.

2   Release the parking brake.

3   Remove the wheel.

➡ **Note: All four rear brake shoes must be replaced at the same time, but to avoid mixing up parts, work on only one brake assembly at a time.**

4   Remove the brake drum.

➡ **Note: If the brake drum cannot be easily pulled off the axle and shoe assembly, make sure the parking brake is completely released. If the drum still cannot be pulled off, the brake shoes will have to be retracted. This is done by first removing the plug from the backing plate (see illustration). With the plug removed, push the lever off the adjuster star wheel with a screwdriver while turning the adjuster wheel with another screwdriver, moving the shoes away from the drum. The drum should now come off.**

5   Clean the brake shoe assembly with brake system cleaner before beginning work (see illustration).

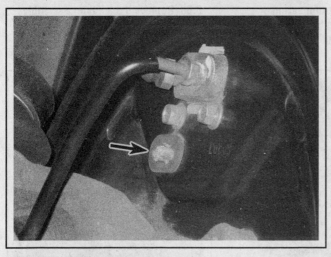

6.4 Remove this plug for access to the adjuster star wheel

6.5 Before removing anything, clean the brake assembly with brake cleaner and allow it to dry – position a drain pan under the brake assembly to catch the residue – DO NOT USE COMPRESSED AIR TO BLOW BRAKE DUST OFF THE PARTS!

6.6a Details of the rear drum brake assembly

1	Self adjuster lever	6	Self adjuster spring
2	Adjuster assembly	7	Lower return spring
3	Wheel cylinder	8	Parking brake cable
4	Upper return spring	9	Parking brake lever
5	Retainer spring		

6   Follow the accompanying illustrations for the brake shoe replacement procedure (see illustrations 6.6a through 6.6q). Be sure to stay in order and read the caption under each illustration.

7   Before reinstalling the drum, it should be checked for cracks, score marks, deep scratches and hard spots, which will appear as small discolored areas. If the hard spots cannot be removed with fine emery cloth or if any of the other conditions listed above exist, the drum must be taken to an automotive machine shop to have it resurfaced.

➡ **Note: Professionals recommend resurfacing the drums each time a brake job is done. Resurfacing will eliminate the possibility of out-of-round drums. If the drums are worn so much that they can't be resurfaced without exceeding the maximum allowable diameter (see illustration), then new ones will be required. At the very least, if you elect not to have the drums resurfaced, remove the glaze from the surface with emery cloth using a swirling motion.**

8   Install the brake drum on the hub flange. Using a screwdriver inserted through the adjusting hole in the brake backing plate (see illustration 6.4), turn the adjuster star wheel until the brake shoes drag on the drum as the drum is rotated, then back off the star wheel until the shoes don't drag. Reinstall the plug in the backing plate.

9   Mount the wheel and install the lug nuts. Lower the vehicle and tighten the lug nuts to the torque listed in the Chapter 1 Specifications.

6.6b Remove the self adjuster lever and spring

6.6c Pull the upper return spring back while supporting the brake shoe and unhook the spring from the shoe

6.6d Remove the adjuster assembly

6.6e Push down on the hold-down clip, then turn the pin to align its blade with the slot

6.6f Detach the lower return spring

6.6g Remove the parking brake lever retaining clip

6.6h Push down on the trailing shoe hold-down clip, then turn the pin to align its blade with the slot

6.6i Lubricate the brake shoe contact areas on the backing plate with high-temperature grease

6.6j Clean the adjuster bolt and clevis, then lubricate the threads and ends with high-temperature grease

6.6k Position the trailing shoe on the backing plate and secure it with the hold-down clip

6.6l Put the new trailing shoe on the parking brake lever and install the retaining clip; crimp the ends of the clip together with a pair of needle-nose pliers

6.6m Connect the lower return spring to the bottom of each shoe

6.6n Position the leading shoe on the backing plate and secure it with the hold-down clip

6.6o Install the adjuster screw, making sure it engages the slot in each shoe

6.6p Install the upper return spring

6.6q Install the adjusting lever and spring on the new leading shoe

6.7 The maximum allowable diameter is cast into the drum (typical)

10 Make a number of forward and reverse stops and operate the parking brake to adjust the brakes until satisfactory pedal action is obtained.

11 Check the operation of the brakes carefully before driving the vehicle.

PARKING BRAKE SHOES (MODELS WITH REAR DISC BRAKES)

❊❊ WARNING:

The dust created by the brake system is harmful to your health. Never blow it out with compressed air and don't inhale any of it. An approved filtering mask should be worn when working on the brakes. Do not, under any circumstances, use petroleum-based solvents to clean brake parts. Use brake system cleaner only!

Removal

12 Loosen the rear wheel lug nuts, raise the rear of the vehicle and support it securely on jackstands. Block the front wheels and remove the rear wheels. Release the parking brake.

➡ **Note: All four parking brake shoes must be replaced at the same time, but to avoid mixing up parts, work on only one brake assembly at a time.**

13 Remove the rear calipers (see Section 4). Support the caliper assemblies with a coat hanger or heavy wire and don't disconnect the brake line from the caliper.

14 Remove the rear discs (see Section 5).

15 Clean the parking brake assembly with brake system cleaner.

16 Remove the two upper return springs.

17 Squeeze the hold-down clip on the trailing shoe with pliers and turn the pin 90-degrees, then remove the clip.

18 Remove the connecting rod and rod spring.

19 Remove the lower return spring, then pull the leading shoe back

and remove the adjuster screw.

20 On the backing plate side of the trailing shoe, use diagonal cutters to pry the U-clip and washer from the top of the shoe.

21 Remove the parking brake lever from the trailing shoe and remove the shoe.

22 Squeeze the hold-down clip on the leading shoe with pliers and turn the pin 90-degrees, then remove the clip and shoe.

Installation

23 With the backing plate cleaned, apply light dabs of high-temperature grease to the shoe contact areas (see illustration 6.6i).

24 Lubricate the parking brake lever pin, then assemble the parking brake lever to the new trailing shoe.

25 Position the trailing shoe against the stationary stop at the top of the backing plate, then insert the hold-down pin through the backing plate and install the hold-down clip.

26 Clean the adjuster bolt and clevis, then lubricate the threads and ends with high-temperature grease.

27 Install the adjuster and lower return spring on each shoe, then position the leading shoe and insert the hold-down pin through the backing plate and install the hold-down clip.

28 Place the rod spring on the connecting rod, then separate the shoes and install the connecting rod.

29 Connect the two upper return springs to the top of each shoe.

30 Install the disc and caliper. Tighten the caliper mounting bolts to the torque listed in this Chapter's Specifications.

31 Using a screwdriver inserted through the adjusting hole in the backing plate, turn the adjuster star wheel until the brake shoes drag on the drum as the drum is rotated, then back off the star wheel until the shoes don't drag.

32 Mount the wheel and install the lug nuts. Lower the vehicle and tighten the lug nuts to the torque listed in the Chapter 1 Specifications.

33 Make a number of forward and reverse stops and operate the parking brake to adjust the brakes until satisfactory pedal action is obtained.

34 Check the operation of the brakes carefully before driving the vehicle.

7   Wheel cylinder - removal and installation

✳ WARNING:

The dust created by the brake system is harmful to your health. Never blow it out with compressed air and don't inhale any of it. An approved filtering mask should be worn when working on the brakes. Do not, under any circumstances, use petroleum-based solvents to clean brake parts. Use brake system cleaner only!

➡ Note: If replacement is indicated (usually because of fluid leakage or sticky operation), it is recommended that the wheel cylinders be replaced, not overhauled. Always replace the wheel cylinders in pairs - never replace just one of them.

REMOVAL

▶ **Refer to illustration 7.4**

1   Raise the rear of the vehicle and support it securely on jackstands. Block the front wheels to keep the vehicle from rolling.

2   Remove the brake shoe assembly (see Section 6).

3   Remove all dirt and foreign material from around the wheel cylinder.

4   Disconnect the brake line (see illustration). Don't pull the brake line away from the wheel cylinder.

5   Remove the wheel cylinder mounting bolts.

6   Detach the wheel cylinder from the brake backing plate and immediately plug the brake line to prevent fluid loss and contamination.

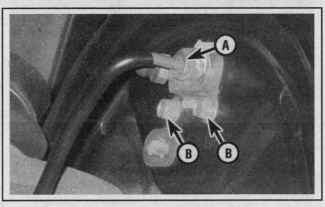

7.4 Disconnect the brake line (A) then remove the wheel cylinder mounting bolts (B)

INSTALLATION

7   Place the wheel cylinder in position and install the bolts finger tight. Connect the brake line to the cylinder, being careful not to cross thread the fitting. Tighten the wheel cylinder mounting bolts to the torque listed in this Chapter's Specifications. Now tighten the brake line fitting securely.

8   Install the brake shoe assembly (see Section 6).

9   Bleed the brakes (see Section 10).

10 Check the operation of the brakes carefully before driving the vehicle.

8   Master cylinder - removal and installation

REMOVAL

▶ **Refer to illustrations 8.4 and 8.6**

1   The master cylinder is located in the engine compartment, mounted to the power brake booster.

2   Remove as much fluid as you can from the reservoir with a syringe, such as an old turkey baster.

✳ WARNING:

If a baster is used, never again use it for the preparation of food.

3   Place rags under the fluid fittings and prepare caps or plastic bags to cover the ends of the lines once they are disconnected.

✳ CAUTION:

Brake fluid will damage paint. Cover all body parts and be careful not to spill fluid during this procedure.

4   Loosen the fittings at the ends of the brake lines where they enter the master cylinder (see illustration). To prevent rounding off the cor-

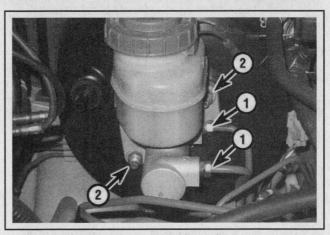

8.4 Master cylinder mounting details – 2004 and earlier models

1	Brake line fittings	2	Mounting nuts

ners on these nuts, the use of a flare-nut wrench, which wraps around the nut, is preferred. Pull the brake lines slightly away from the master cylinder and plug the ends to prevent contamination.

5   Remove the nuts attaching the master cylinder to the power booster. Pull the master cylinder off the studs and out of the engine

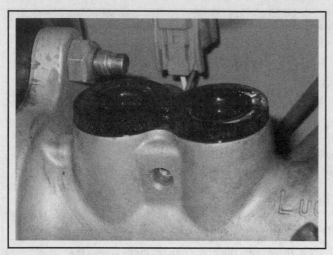

8.6 After the master cylinder reservoir has been removed, replace the seals with new ones

8.8 The best way to bleed air from the master cylinder before installing it on the vehicle is with a pair of bleeder tubes that direct brake fluid into the reservoir during bleeding

compartment. Again, be careful not to spill the fluid as this is done.

6   If a new master cylinder is being installed, remove the reservoir from the master cylinder and transfer it to the new master cylinder.

➡ **Note: Be sure to install new seals when transferring the reservoir (see illustration).**

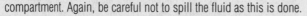

INSTALLATION

▶ **Refer to illustration 8.8**

7   Bench bleed the new master cylinder before installing it. Mount the master cylinder in a vise, with the jaws of the vise clamping on the mounting flange.

8   Attach a pair of master cylinder bleeder tubes to the outlet ports of the master cylinder (see illustration).

9   Fill the reservoir with brake fluid of the recommended type (see Chapter 1).

10   Slowly push the pistons into the master cylinder (a large Phillips screwdriver can be used for this) - air will be expelled from the pressure chambers and into the reservoir. Because the tubes are submerged in fluid, air can't be drawn back into the master cylinder when you release the pistons.

11   Repeat the procedure until no more air bubbles are present.

12   Remove the bleed tubes, one at a time, and install plugs in the open ports to prevent fluid leakage and air from entering. Install the reservoir cap.

13   Install the master cylinder over the studs on the power brake booster and tighten the attaching nuts only finger tight at this time.

➡ **Note: Be sure to install a new O-ring into the sleeve of the master cylinder.**

14   Thread the brake line fittings into the master cylinder. Since the

master cylinder is still a bit loose, it can be moved slightly in order for the fittings to thread in easily. Do not strip the threads as the fittings are tightened.

15   Fully tighten the mounting nuts, then the brake line fittings. Tighten the nuts to the torque listed in this Chapter's Specifications.

16   Fill the master cylinder reservoir with fluid, then bleed the master cylinder and the brake system as described in Section 10. To bleed the cylinder on the vehicle, have an assistant depress the brake pedal and hold the pedal to the floor. Loosen the fitting to allow air and fluid to escape. Repeat this procedure on both fittings until the fluid is clear of air bubbles.

✳ CAUTION:

Have plenty of rags on hand to catch the fluid - brake fluid will ruin painted surfaces. After the bleeding procedure is completed, rinse the area under the master cylinder with clean water.

17   Test the operation of the brake system carefully before placing the vehicle into normal service.

✳ WARNING:

Do not operate the vehicle if you are in doubt about the effectiveness of the brake system. It is possible for air to become trapped in the anti-lock brake system hydraulic control unit, so, if the pedal continues to feel spongy after repeated bleedings or the BRAKE or ANTI-LOCK light stays on, have the vehicle towed to a dealer service department or other qualified shop to be bled with the aid of a scan tool.

9 Brake hoses and lines - inspection and replacement

1 About every six months, with the vehicle raised and placed securely on jackstands, the flexible hoses which connect the steel brake lines with the front and rear brake assemblies should be inspected for cracks, chafing of the outer cover, leaks, blisters and other damage. These are important and vulnerable parts of the brake system and inspection should be complete. A light and mirror will be needed for a thorough check. If a hose exhibits any of the above defects, replace it with a new one.

FLEXIBLE HOSES

▶ **Refer to illustration 9.3**

2 Clean all dirt away from the ends of the hose.

3 To disconnect a brake hose from the brake line, unscrew the metal tube nut with a flare nut wrench, then remove the U-clip from the female fitting at the bracket and remove the hose from the bracket (see illustration).

4 Disconnect the hose from the caliper, discarding the sealing washers on either side of the fitting.

5 Using new sealing washers, attach the new brake hose to the caliper.

6 To reattach a brake hose to the metal line, insert the end of the hose through the frame bracket, make sure the hose isn't twisted, then attach the metal line by tightening the tube nut fitting securely. Install the U-clip at the frame bracket.

7 Carefully check to make sure the suspension or steering components don't make contact with the hose. Have an assistant push down on the vehicle and also turn the steering wheel lock-to-lock during inspection.

8 Bleed the brake system (see Section 10).

METAL BRAKE LINES

9 When replacing brake lines, be sure to use the correct parts. Don't use copper tubing for any brake system components. Purchase

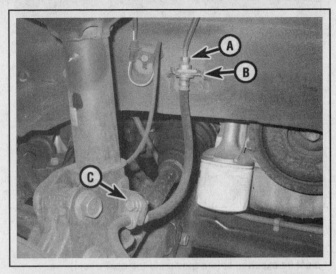

9.3 Unscrew the brake line threaded fitting with a flare-nut wrench to protect the fitting corners from being rounded off (A), then pull off the U-clip (B) with a pair of pliers and remove the brake line mounting bolt (C)

steel brake lines from a dealer parts department or auto parts store.

10 Prefabricated brake line, with the tube ends already flared and fittings installed, is available at auto parts stores and dealer parts departments. These lines can be bent to the proper shapes using a tubing bender.

11 When installing the new line make sure it's well supported in the brackets and has plenty of clearance between moving or hot components.

12 After installation, check the master cylinder fluid level and add fluid as necessary. Bleed the brake system as outlined in Section 10 and test the brakes carefully before placing the vehicle into normal operation.

10 Brake hydraulic system - bleeding

▶ **Refer to illustration 10.8**

✳ WARNING 1:

If air has found its way into the hydraulic control unit, the system must be bled with the use of a scan tool. If the brake pedal feels spongy even after bleeding the brakes, or the ABS light on the instrument panel does not go off, or if you have any doubts whatsoever about the effectiveness of the brake system, have the vehicle towed to a dealer service department or other repair shop equipped with the necessary tools for bleeding the system.

✳ WARNING 2:

Wear eye protection when bleeding the brake system. If the fluid comes in contact with your eyes, immediately rinse them with water and seek medical attention.

➡ **Note:** Bleeding the brake system is necessary to remove any air that's trapped in the system when it's opened during removal and installation of a hose, line, caliper, wheel cylinder or master cylinder.

1 It will probably be necessary to bleed the system at all four brakes if air has entered the system due to low fluid level, or if the brake lines have been disconnected at the master cylinder.

2 If a brake line was disconnected only at a wheel, then only that caliper or wheel cylinder must be bled.

3 If a brake line is disconnected at a fitting located between the master cylinder and any of the brakes, that part of the system served by the disconnected line must be bled.

4 Remove any residual vacuum (or hydraulic pressure) from the brake power booster by applying the brake several times with the engine off.

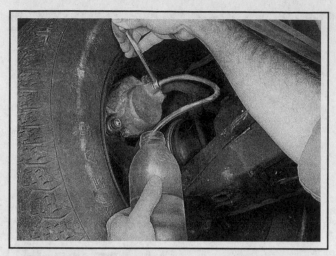

10.8 When bleeding the brakes, a hose is connected to the bleed screw at the caliper and submerged in brake fluid - air will be seen as bubbles in the tube and container (all air must be expelled before moving to the next wheel)

5   Remove the master cylinder reservoir cap and fill the reservoir with brake fluid. Reinstall the cap.

➡ **Note: Check the fluid level often during the bleeding operation and add fluid as necessary to prevent the fluid level from falling low enough to allow air bubbles into the master cylinder.**

6   Have an assistant on hand, as well as a supply of new brake fluid, an empty clear plastic container, a length of plastic, rubber or vinyl tubing to fit over the bleeder valve and a wrench to open and close the bleeder valve.

7   Beginning at the front left wheel, loosen the bleeder screw slightly, then tighten it to a point where it's snug but can still be loosened quickly and easily.

8   Place one end of the tubing over the bleeder screw fitting and submerge the other end in brake fluid in the container (see illustration).

9   Have the assistant slowly depress the brake pedal and hold it in the depressed position.

10 While the pedal is held depressed, open the bleeder screw just enough to allow a flow of fluid to leave the valve. Watch for air bubbles to exit the submerged end of the tube. When the fluid flow slows after a couple of seconds, tighten the screw and have your assistant release the pedal.

11 Repeat Steps 9 and 10 until no more air is seen leaving the tube, then tighten the bleeder screw and proceed to the right front wheel, the right rear wheel and the left rear wheel, in that order, and perform the same procedure. Be sure to check the fluid in the master cylinder reservoir frequently.

12 Never use old brake fluid. It contains moisture which can boil, rendering the brake system inoperative.

13 Refill the master cylinder with fluid at the end of the operation.

14 Check the operation of the brakes. The pedal should feel solid when depressed, with no sponginess. If necessary, repeat the entire process.

✳✳ WARNING:

Do not operate the vehicle if you are in doubt about the effectiveness of the brake system. It is possible for air to become trapped in the anti-lock brake system hydraulic control unit, so, if the pedal continues to feel spongy after repeated bleedings or the BRAKE or ANTI-LOCK light stays on, have the vehicle towed to a dealer service department or other qualified shop to be bled with the aid of a scan tool.

11 Power brake booster - removal and installation

OPERATING CHECK

1   Depress the brake pedal several times with the engine off and make sure that there is no change in the pedal reserve distance.

2   Depress the pedal and start the engine. If the pedal goes down slightly, operation is normal.

AIRTIGHTNESS CHECK

3   Start the engine and turn it off after one or two minutes. Depress the brake pedal several times slowly. If the pedal goes down farther the first time but gradually rises after the second or third depression, the booster is airtight.

4   Depress the brake pedal while the engine is running, then stop the engine with the pedal depressed. If there is no change in the pedal reserve travel after holding the pedal for 30 seconds, the booster is airtight.

REMOVAL AND INSTALLATION

▶ **Refer to illustrations 11.8 and 11.9**

5   Disassembly of the power unit requires special tools and is not ordinarily performed by the home mechanic. If a problem develops, it's recommended that a new or factory rebuilt unit be installed.

6   Remove the master cylinder (see Section 8).

7   Disconnect the vacuum hose where it attaches to the power brake booster.

8   In the passenger compartment, remove the retaining pin then disconnect the pushrod from the top of the brake pedal (see illustration).

9   Remove the nuts attaching the booster to the firewall (see illustration).

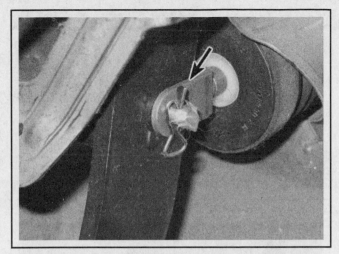

11.8 Remove the clevis pin and disconnect the pushrod from the pedal

11.9 To detach the power brake booster from the firewall, remove the four mounting nuts (one nut not visible in photo)

10 Carefully lift the booster unit away from the firewall and out of the engine compartment.

11 To install the booster, place it into position and tighten the retaining nuts. Connect the pushrod to the brake pedal.

12 Install the master cylinder. Reconnect the vacuum hose. Bleed the brakes (see Section 10).

13 Carefully test the operation of the brakes before placing the vehicle in normal service.

12 Parking brake - adjustment

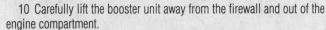 **Refer to illustration 12.3**

1 The parking brake pedal, when properly adjusted, should travel three to five clicks (rear drum brakes) or four to six clicks (rear disc brakes) when pushed with about 65 pounds of force. If it travels less than specified, there's a chance the parking brake might not be releasing completely and might be dragging on the drum. If the pedal can be depressed more than specified, the parking brake may not hold adequately on an incline, allowing the car to roll.

2 Block the front wheels, raise the rear of the vehicle and support it securely on jackstands. Depress the pedal until you hear one click.

3 Turn the adjusting nut on the pedal (see illustration) clockwise while rotating the rear wheels. Stop turning the nut when the brakes just start to drag on the rear wheels.

4 Release the parking brake and check to see the brakes don't drag when the rear wheels are turned. The travel on the parking brake pedal should be as listed in Step 1 when properly adjusted.

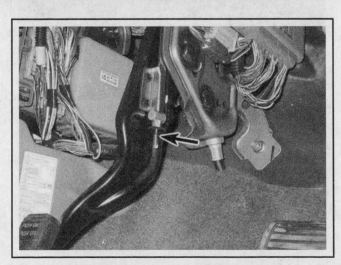

12.3 Turn this adjusting nut to adjust the parking brake

13 Brake Pedal Position (BPP) switch - replacement and clearance adjustment

▶ Refer to illustrations 13.2, 13.3a, 13.3b and 13.5

1   Using a flashlight, locate the BPP switch at the top of the brake pedal arm.

2   Disconnect the electrical connector from the BPP switch (see illustration).

3   Loosen the BPP switch locknut, then unscrew and remove the switch (see illustrations).

4   Installation is the reverse of removal, except that the BPP switch must be adjusted when installed.

5   To adjust the BPP switch, screw in the switch until its plunger is fully depressed and the threaded end of the BPP switch is contacting the pad on the brake pedal arm (see illustration). Then back off the BPP switch 3/4-turn to provide 0.010 inch (0.3 mm) clearance between the threaded barrel and the brake pedal pad.

6   Apply the brake pedal, release the pedal and verify that the brake lights go off when the pedal is released. If they don't, adjust the BPP switch again.

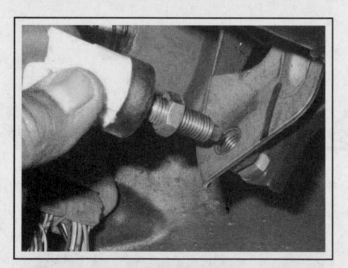

13.2 Disconnect the BPP switch electrical connector

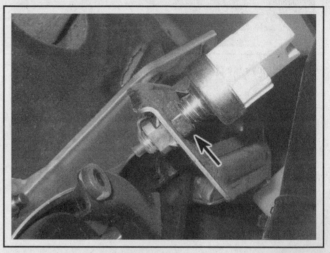

13.3a To remove the BPP switch, loosen the locknut . . .

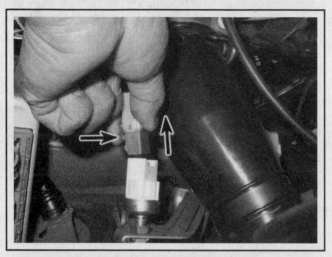

13.3b . . . then unscrew the switch from its mounting bracket

13.5 BPP switch adjustment details

1   BPP switch threaded barrel   3   Clearance point
2   Brake pedal pad

Specifications

General

Brake fluid type	See Chapter 1
Brake pedal position switch-to-stopper distance	0.010 inch (0.3 mm)

Disc brakes

Brake pad minimum thickness	See Chapter 1
Disc lateral runout limit	
2006 and earlier models	0.004 inch (0.10 mm)
2007 and later models	0.0016 inch (0.04 mm)
Disc minimum thickness	Cast into disc
Parallelism (thickness variation) limit	0.0006 inch (0.015 mm)

Drum brakes

Maximum drum diameter	Cast into drum
Shoe lining minimum thickness	See Chapter 1

Torque specifications

→ Note: One foot-pound (ft-lb) of torque is equivalent to 12 inch-pounds (in-lbs) of torque. Torque values below approximately 15 foot-pounds are expressed in inch-pounds, because most foot-pound torque wrenches are not accurate at these smaller values.

	Ft-lbs	Nm
Caliper mounting bolts		
2004 and earlier models		
Front	20	26
Rear	27	37
2005 and later models		
Front	37	50
Rear	16	22
Caliper mounting bracket bolts		
2004 and earlier models		
Front	79	108
Rear	41	55
2005 and later models		
Front	101	137
Rear	65	88
Master cylinder mounting nuts		
2004 and earlier models	18	25
2005 and later models	115 in-lbs	13
Power brake booster mounting nuts	18	25
Wheel cylinder mounting bolts	79 in-lbs	9
Wheel lug nuts	See Chapter 1	

Notes

Section

10

SUSPENSION AND STEERING SYSTEMS

1 General information

▶ **Refer to illustrations 1.1 and 1.2**

The front suspension is a strut/coil spring design. The upper end of each strut is attached to the vehicle's body strut support. The lower end of the strut is connected to the upper end of the steering knuckle. The steering knuckle is attached to a balljoint mounted on the outer end of the suspension control arm (see illustration).

The rear suspension utilizes trailing arms, shock absorber/coil spring units, one upper and two lower control arms (see illustration).

The power-assisted rack-and-pinion steering gear, which is located behind the engine/transaxle assembly, is mounted on the engine cradle. The steering gear actuates the tie-rods, which are attached to the steering knuckles. The steering column is designed to collapse in the event of an accident.

Frequently, when working on the suspension or steering system components, you may come across fasteners that seem impossible to loosen. These fasteners on the underside of the vehicle are continually subjected to water, road grime, mud, etc., and can become rusted or "frozen," making them extremely difficult to remove. In order to unscrew these stubborn fasteners without damaging them (or other components), be sure to use lots of penetrating oil and allow it to soak in for a while. Using a wire brush to clean exposed threads will also ease removal of the nut or bolt and prevent damage to the threads. Sometimes a sharp blow with a hammer and punch will break the bond between a nut and bolt threads, but care must be taken to prevent the punch from slipping

off the fastener and ruining the threads. Heating the stuck fastener and surrounding area with a torch sometimes helps too, but isn't recommended because of the obvious dangers associated with fire. Long breaker bars and extension, or cheater, pipes will increase leverage, but never use an extension pipe on a ratchet - the ratcheting mechanism could be damaged. Sometimes tightening the nut or bolt first will help to break it loose. Fasteners that require drastic measures to remove should always be replaced with new ones.

Since most of the procedures dealt with in this Chapter involve jacking up the vehicle and working underneath it, a good pair of jackstands will be needed. A hydraulic floor jack is the preferred type of jack to lift the vehicle, and it can also be used to support certain components during various operations.

⁂ WARNING:

Never, under any circumstances, rely on a jack to support the vehicle while working on it. Whenever any of the suspension or steering fasteners are loosened or removed they must be inspected and, if necessary, replaced with new ones of the same part number or of original equipment quality and design. Torque specifications must be followed for proper reassembly and component retention. Never attempt to heat or straighten any suspension or steering components. Instead, replace any bent or damaged part with a new one.

1.2 Rear suspension and related components

1	Trailing arm	3	Lower arm A	5	Rear knuckle
2	Shock absorber	4	Lower arm B	6	Drum brake assembly

1.2 Rear suspension and related components

1	Trailing arm	3	Lower arm A	5	Rear knuckle
2	Shock absorber	4	Lower arm B	6	Drum brake assembly

2 Stabilizer bar and bushings - removal and installation

BUSHINGS AND LINKS

▶ **Refer to illustrations 2.2 and 2.3**

1   Loosen the front wheel lug nuts. Raise the front of the vehicle and support it securely on jackstands. Apply the parking brake and block the rear wheels to keep the vehicle from rolling off the stands. Remove the front wheels.

2   Remove the bolts from the stabilizer bar bushing retainers (see illustration). Remove the retainers from the bushings, prying them off, if necessary.

3   Remove the nuts that attach the upper and lower ends of the stabilizer links to the strut/coil spring assembly and to the stabilizer bar (see illustration).

→ **Note: Use an Allen wrench in the end of the stud to hold it while turning the nut.**

Detach the links.

4   Inspect the retainer bushings for cracks and tears. If either bushing is broken, damaged, distorted or worn, replace both of them. If the ballstuds on the links are loose or otherwise worn, replace the links.

5   Install the links, tightening the link nuts to the torque listed in this Chapter's Specifications.

6   Install the retainer bushings. Clean the areas on the stabilizer bar where the bushings are located. Lubricate the inside and outside of the new bushings with vegetable oil (used in cooking) to simplify reassembly.

✳✳ **CAUTION:**

Don't use petroleum or mineral-based lubricants or brake fluid - they will lead to deterioration of the bushings. These bushings are split so that you can install them without having to slide them onto the ends of the stabilizer bar. Install the bushings with the slit in each bushing facing forward.

7   Install the retainers and bolts, tightening the bolts to the torque listed in this Chapter's Specifications.

8   Install the wheels and lug nuts. Lower the vehicle and tighten the lug nuts to the torque listed in the Chapter 1 Specifications.

STABILIZER BAR

9   Stabilizer bar removal involves lowering the subframe and removing the stabilizer bar with the subframe out of the vehicle. If one becomes damaged, it is most likely the result of an accident that was severe enough to damage other major components (such as the subframe itself). Damage this severe will require the services of an auto body shop. For this reason, front stabilizer bar removal and installation is not covered in this manual.

2.2 Remove the bolts attaching the stabilizer bar bracket to the subframe

2.3 Stabilizer bar link mounting nuts

3 Strut assembly - removal, inspection and installation

REMOVAL

▶ **Refer to illustrations 3.4 and 3.6**

1   Loosen the wheel lug nuts, raise the vehicle and support it securely on jackstands. Remove the wheel.

2   Disconnect the stabilizer bar link from the strut, then remove the brake hose bracket from the strut.

3   Detach the ABS speed sensor wiring harness from the strut by removing the clamp bracket bolt.

4   Mark the relationship of the strut to the knuckle (these marks will be used during installation to ensure the camber is returned to its original setting). Remove the strut-to-knuckle nuts (see illustration) and knock the bolts out with a hammer and punch.

5   Separate the strut from the steering knuckle. Be careful not to overextend the inner CV joint. Also, don't let the steering knuckle fall outward, as the brake hose could be damaged.

6   Support the strut and spring assembly with one hand and remove the three strut upper mounting nuts (see illustration). Remove the assembly from the fenderwell.

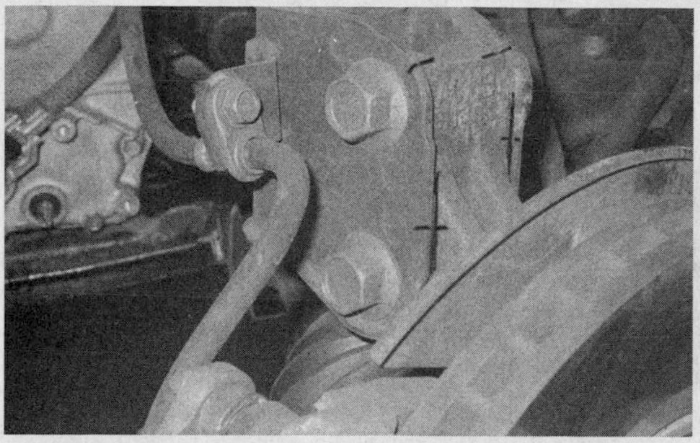

3.4 Remove the strut-to-steering knuckle nuts and bolts

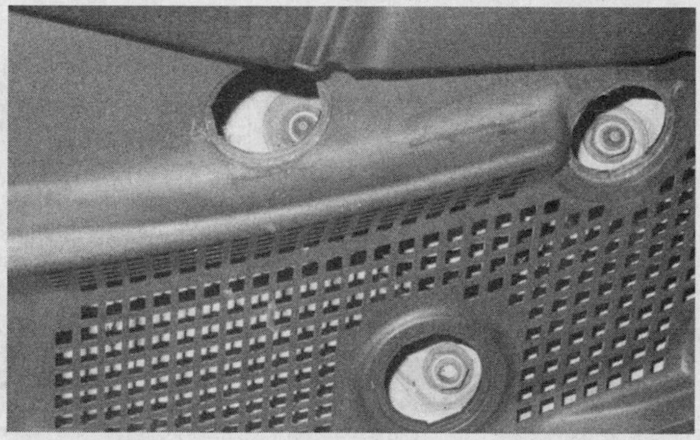

3.6 Remove the three strut upper mounting nuts

INSPECTION

7 Check the strut body for leaking fluid, dents, cracks and other obvious damage that would warrant repair or replacement.

8 Check the coil spring for chips or cracks in the spring coating (this can cause premature spring failure due to corrosion). Inspect the spring seat for cuts, hardness and general deterioration.

9 If any undesirable conditions exist, proceed to the strut disassembly procedure (see Section 4).

INSTALLATION

10 Guide the strut assembly up into the fenderwell and insert the three upper mounting studs through the holes in the shock tower. Once the three studs protrude from the shock tower, install the nuts so the strut won't fall back through. This is most easily accomplished with the help of an assistant, as the strut is quite heavy and awkward.

11 Slide the steering knuckle into the strut flange and insert the two bolts. Install the nuts, align the marks you made in Step 4, then tighten the nuts to the torque listed in this Chapter's Specifications. The manufacturer recommends that these fasteners be replaced with NEW ones upon assembly.

12 Reattach the brake hose bracket to the strut. Install the speed sensor wiring harness bracket, and reconnect the stabilizer bar link.

13 Install the wheel and lug nuts, then lower the vehicle and tighten the lug nuts to the torque listed in the Chapter 1 Specifications.

14 Tighten the three upper mounting nuts to the torque listed in this Chapter's Specifications.

15 Have the front wheel alignment checked and, if necessary, adjusted.

4 Strut/coil spring assembly - replacement

WARNING:

Struts and/or coil springs must be replaced in pairs - never replace just one of them.

1 If the struts or coil springs exhibit the telltale signs of wear (leaking fluid, loss of damping capability, chipped, sagging or cracked coil springs) explore all options before beginning any work. The strut/shock absorber assemblies are not serviceable and must be replaced if a problem develops. However, strut assemblies complete with springs may be available on an exchange basis, which eliminates much time and work. Whichever route you choose to take, check on the cost and availability of parts before disassembling your vehicle.

WARNING:

Disassembling a strut is potentially dangerous and utmost attention must be directed to the job, or serious injury may result. Use only a high-quality spring compressor and carefully follow the manufacturer's instructions furnished with the tool. After removing the coil spring from the strut assembly, set it aside in a safe, isolated area.

DISASSEMBLY

Refer to illustrations 4.3, 4.5, 4.6 and 4.7

2 Remove the strut and spring assembly (see Section 3). Mount the strut assembly in a vise. Line the vise jaws with wood or rags to prevent

4.3 Install the spring compressor following the tool manufacturer's instructions; compress the spring until all pressure is relieved from the upper spring seat (you can verify the spring is loose by wiggling it)

4.5 Lift the upper mount off the damper rod

4.6 Remove the upper spring seat and the upper pad from the damper rod

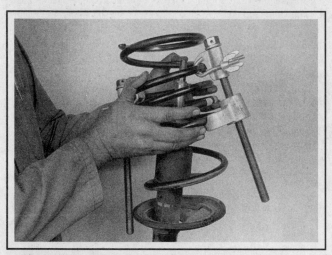

4.7 Remove the compressed spring from the strut/shock absorber assembly - keep the ends of the spring pointed away from your body

4.11 When installing the spring, make sure the end fits into the recessed portion of the lower seat

damage to the unit and don't tighten the vise excessively.

3   Following the tool manufacturer's instructions, install the spring compressor (which can be obtained at most auto parts stores or equipment yards on a daily rental basis) on the spring and compress it sufficiently to relieve all pressure from the upper spring seat (see illustration). This can be verified by wiggling the spring.

4   Hold the strut piston rod with an Allen wrench, and unscrew the thrust bearing retaining nut with a box-end wrench.

5   Remove the nut and upper mount (see illustration). Lay the parts out in the exact order in which they are removed. Inspect the bearing in the suspension support for smooth operation. If it doesn't turn smoothly, replace the upper mount. Check the rubber portion of the upper mount for cracking and general deterioration. If there is any separation of the rubber, replace it.

6   Remove the upper spring seat from the damper shaft (see illustration). Check the spring seat for cracking and hardness; replace it if necessary. Remove the upper insulator from the damper shaft.

7   Carefully lift the compressed spring from the assembly (see illustration) and set it in a safe place.

❊❊ WARNING:

When removing the compressed spring, lift it off carefully and set it in a safe place. Keep the ends of the spring away from your body.

➡ **Note: If you are disassembling both struts, mark the springs LEFT and RIGHT so you don't mix them up (they're different).**

8   Remove the dust cover plate and dust cover.

9   Slide the rubber bump stop off the damper shaft. Check the bump stop for cracking and general deterioration. If there is any deterioration of the rubber, replace it.

REASSEMBLY

▶ **Refer to illustration 4.11**

10   Extend the damper rod to its full length and install the rubber bump stop, dust cover and dust cover plate.

11   Carefully place the compressed coil spring onto the lower seat of the damper, with the end of the spring resting in the lowest part of the seat (see illustration).

12 Install the upper insulator and spring seat.
13 Install the bearing and suspension support.
14 Install the washer and nut and tighten it to the torque listed in this

Chapter's Specifications. Remove the spring compressor tool.
15 Install the strut/spring assembly (see Section 3).

5   Control arm - removal, inspection and installation

REMOVAL

♦ **Refer to illustrations 5.2, 5.3 and 5.4**

1 Loosen the wheel lug nuts on the side to be disassembled. Apply the parking brake, raise the front of the vehicle, support it securely on jackstands and remove the wheel. On 2005 and later models, disconnect the stabilizer bar links from the struts (see Section 2). Turn the stabilizer bar to access the control arm pivot bolts.
2 Remove the lock pin from the castle nut (see illustration). Loosen the nut, but don't remove it yet.
3 Use a hammer to strike the boss on the steering knuckle until it separates from the lower balljoint stud (see illustration).

✳ CAUTION:

Do not hit the lower control arm or the balljoint grease seal, be careful not to separate the inner CV joint and do not pry the lower balljoint from the steering knuckle.

Once the balljoint stud has been released from the steering knuckle, remove the castle nut. Separate the balljoint from the steering knuckle.
4 Remove the two bolts that attach the control arm to the subframe (see illustration).
5 Remove the control arm.

INSPECTION

6 Make sure the control arm is straight. If it's bent, replace it. Do not attempt to straighten a bent control arm.
7 Inspect the bushings. If they're cracked, torn or worn out, replace the control arm.

INSTALLATION

8 Installation is the reverse of removal, noting the following points:
a) *Tighten the balljoint stud castle nut to the lower torque figure listed in this Chapter's Specifications, then, if necessary, tighten it a little more to line up the slots in the nut with the hole in the stud. The manufacturer recommends that these fasteners be replaced with NEW ones upon assembly.*
b) *Install a new lock pin.*
c) *Raise the outer end of the control arm with a floor jack, then tighten the control arm-to-subframe bolts to the torque listed in this Chapter's Specifications.*

9 Install the wheel and lug nuts, lower the vehicle and tighten the lug nuts to the torque listed in the Chapter 1 Specifications.
10 It's a good idea to have the front wheel alignment checked, and if necessary, adjusted after this job has been performed.

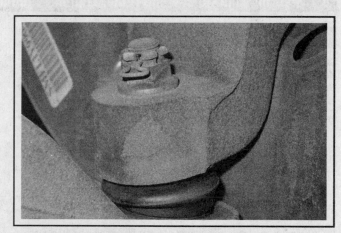

5.2 Lower control arm-to-steering knuckle nut

5.3 Strike the boss on the steering knuckle until it separates from the balljoint stud

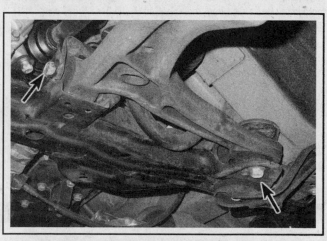

5.4 Control arm-to-subframe mounting bolts

6 Balljoints - check and replacement

CHECK

1 Raise the front of the vehicle and support it securely on jackstands. Apply the parking brake and block the rear wheels to keep the vehicle from rolling off the jackstands.

2 Place a large prybar under the balljoint and resting on the wheel, then try to pry the balljoint up while feeling for movement between the balljoint and steering knuckle. Now, pry between the control arm and the steering knuckle and try to lever the control arm down while feeling for movement between the balljoint and steering knuckle. If any movement is evident in either check, the balljoint is worn.

3 Have an assistant grasp the tire at the top and bottom and move the top of the tire in-and-out. Touch the balljoint stud nut. If any looseness is felt, suspect a worn balljoint stud or a widened hole in the steering knuckle boss. If the latter problem exists, the steering knuckle should be replaced as well as the balljoint/control arm.

4 Separate the control arm from the steering knuckle (see Section 5).

Using your fingers (don't use pliers), try to twist the stud in the socket. If the stud turns, replace the balljoint.

REPLACEMENT

5 The balljoints are not replaceable separately (the entire control arm must be replaced).

6 The balljoint dust boot can be replaced separately. This should not be done if the dust boot has cracked or been damaged while the vehicle is in use, since dirt has probably gotten into the balljoint. However, if the dust boot was damaged during removal of the control arm, the dust boot can be replaced. To do this, pry off the old dust boot. Grease the balljoint stud and the upper lip of the dust boot. Push the dust boot onto the balljoint with a special tool or a socket the same diameter as the dust boot.

7 Install the wheel and lug nuts (if removed) and lower the vehicle. Tighten the lug nuts to the torque listed in the Chapter 1 Specifications.

7 Steering knuckle and hub removal (front) - removal and installation

✳✳ WARNING:

Dust created by the brake system is harmful to your health. Never blow it out with compressed air and don't inhale any of it. Do not, under any circumstances, use petroleum-based solvents to clean brake parts. Use brake system cleaner only.

REMOVAL

1 Loosen the driveaxle/hub nut (see Chapter 8). Loosen the wheel lug nuts, raise the vehicle and support it securely on jackstands. Remove the wheel.

2 Remove the brake caliper and support it with a piece of wire as described in Chapter 9. Remove the caliper mounting bracket, then remove the brake disc from the hub. Detach the brake hose clamp and remove the wheel speed sensor from the knuckle.

3 Mark the strut to the steering knuckle, then loosen, but do not remove the strut-to-steering knuckle bolts (see illustration 3.4).

4 Separate the tie-rod from the steering knuckle arm (see Section 15).

5 Loosen the balljoint-to-control arm nut and separate the balljoint from the steering knuckle, then remove the nut (see illustrations 5.2 and 5.3). The strut-to-knuckle bolts can now be removed.

6 Push the driveaxle from the hub as described in Chapter 8. Support the end of the driveaxle with a piece of wire.

7 Separate the steering knuckle from the strut.

INSTALLATION

8 Guide the knuckle and hub assembly into position, inserting the driveaxle into the hub.

9 Push the knuckle into the strut flange and install the bolts and nuts, but don't tighten them yet.

10 Connect the balljoint to the control arm and install the nut (don't tighten them yet).

11 Attach the tie-rod to the steering knuckle arm (see Section 15). Tighten the strut bolt nuts, the balljoint-to-control arm nut and the tie-rod nut to the torque values listed in this Chapter's Specifications.

12 Place the brake disc on the hub and install the caliper mounting bracket and caliper as outlined in Chapter 9.

13 Install the driveaxle/hub nut and tighten it securely (final tightening will be carried out when the vehicle is lowered). The manufacturer recommends that these fasteners be replaced with NEW ones upon assembly.

14 Install the wheel and lug nuts.

15 Lower the vehicle and tighten the lug nuts to the torque listed in the Chapter 1 Specifications. Tighten the driveaxle/hub nut to the torque listed in the Chapter 8 Specifications.

16 Have the front wheel alignment checked and, if necessary, adjusted.

8 Hub and bearing assembly (front) - replacement

Due to the special tools and expertise required to press the hub and bearing from the steering knuckle, this job should be left to a professional mechanic. However, the steering knuckle and hub may be removed and the assembly taken to an automotive machine shop or other qualified repair facility equipped with the necessary tools. See Section 7 for the steering knuckle and hub removal procedure.

9   Shock absorber (rear) - removal, inspection and installation

▶ **Refer to illustrations 9.3 and 9.4**

⁂ WARNING:

Always replace the shock absorbers in pairs - never replace just one of them.

1   Loosen the rear wheel lug nuts. Chock the front wheels to keep the vehicle from rolling, then raise the rear of the vehicle and support it securely on jackstands placed underneath the rear jacking point. Remove the rear wheels.

2   Support lower arm B with a floor jack placed under the coil spring pocket.

⁂ WARNING:

The jack must remain in this position until the shock absorber is reinstalled.

3   Remove the shock absorber upper mounting fastener(s) (see illustration).

4   Remove the shock absorber lower mounting nut and washer and remove the shock absorber (see illustration).

5   To install the shock absorber, reverse the removal procedure. Be sure to install the washer on the lower mounting stud with the concave side facing away from the shock absorber.

6   Raise lower arm B with the jack to simulate normal ride height, then tighten the mounting bolt and nut to the torque listed in this Chapter's Specifications. The manufacturer recommends that the lower nut and washer be replaced with new ones upon assembly.

7   Repeat the procedure to replace the other rear shock absorber.

8   Install the wheels and lug nuts and lower the vehicle. Tighten the lug nuts to the torque listed in the Chapter 1 Specifications.

9.3 Rear shock absorber upper mounting bolt – 2004 and earlier models

9.4 Rear shock absorber lower mounting nut

10 Suspension arms (rear) - removal and installation

➡ **Note: All nuts and bolts used in the rear suspension arms should be replaced with new ones on assembly according to the manufacturer.**

1   Loosen the rear wheel lug nuts. Raise the rear of the vehicle and support it securely on jackstands. Block the front wheels to prevent the vehicle from rolling. Remove the wheel.

UPPER ARM

▶ **Refer to illustration 10.4**

2   Support lower arm B with a floor jack placed under the coil

spring pocket.

⁂ WARNING:

The jack must remain in this position until the new arm is installed.

3   Remove the lock pin from the castle nut. Loosen the nut, but don't remove it yet. Using a puller, separate the balljoint from the knuckle. Remove the nut.

10.4 Upper arm-to-chassis mounting bolt/nut

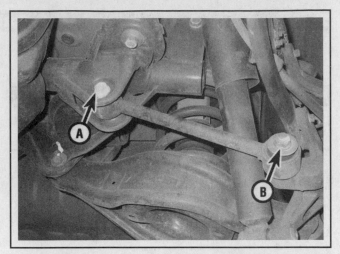

10.7 Lower arm A-to-chassis mounting bolt (A) and the arm-to-knuckle mounting nut (B)

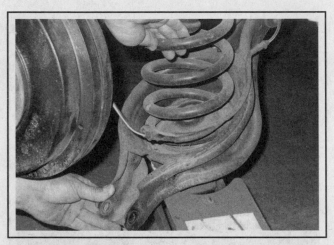

10.13 With a floor jack supporting lower arm B, slowly lower the jack until the coil spring can be removed

4   Remove the upper arm-to-chassis mounting bolt (see illustration).

5   Installation is the reverse of removal, noting the following points:

   a) *Tighten the balljoint stud castle nut to the lower torque figure listed in this Chapter's Specifications, then, if necessary, tighten it a little more to line up the slots in the nut with the hole in the stud.*

   b) *Install a new lock pin.*

   c) *Raise lower arm B with a floor jack, then tighten the control arm-to-subframe bolts to the torque listed in this Chapter's Specifications.*

   d) *Tighten the wheel lug nuts to the torque listed in the Chapter 1 Specifications.*

LOWER ARM A

▶ **Refer to illustrations 10.7**

6   Support lower arm B with a floor jack placed under the coil spring pocket.

⁂ WARNING:

The jack must remain in this position until the new arm is installed.

7   Remove the lower arm-to-chassis mounting bolt/nut and the lower arm-to-knuckle mounting bolt/nut (see illustration).

8   Remove the arm from the vehicle.

9   Installation is the reverse of the removal procedure. Be sure to install the washer on the arm-to-knuckle mounting stud with the concave side facing away from the arm. Before tightening the fasteners to the torque listed in this Chapter's Specifications, raise the rear suspension with the floor jack to simulate normal ride height. Tighten the wheel lug nuts to the torque listed in the Chapter 1 Specifications.

LOWER ARM B

▶ **Refer to illustrations 10.13 and 10.14**

10 Support lower arm B with a floor jack placed under the coil spring pocket.

11 Remove the ABS wheel speed sensor and unbolt the harness brackets from the trailing arm.

12 Remove the bolt securing the control arm to the knuckle.

13 Slowly lower the floor jack until the coil spring is extended, then remove the coil spring (see illustration).

14 Mark the relationship of the toe adjuster cam to the subframe, then remove the pivot bolt and nut from the inner end of the arm (see illustration). Remove the arm from the vehicle.

15 Installation is the reverse of removal, noting the following points:

   a) *Align the mark you made on the toe adjuster cam with the mark on the subframe.*

   b) *Raise the outer end of lower arm B with a floor jack, then tighten the fasteners to the torque listed in this Chapter's Specifications.*

   c) *Tighten the wheel lug nuts to the torque listed in the Chapter 1 Specifications.*

   d) *Have the rear wheel alignment checked and, if necessary, adjusted.*

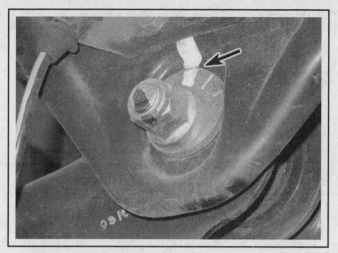

10.14 Place an alignment mark on the toe adjuster cam and the subframe, then unscrew the nut and remove the pivot bolt

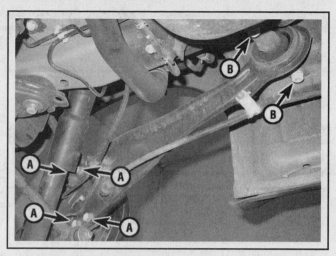

10.19 Remove the trailing arm-to-knuckle bolts (A) and the trailing arm-to-chassis mounting bolts (B)

TRAILING ARM

▶ **Refer to illustration 10.19**

16 Remove the brake shoe or disc brake assembly (see Chapter 9).

17 Unbolt the brake hose and brake line brackets from the trailing arm. Unbolt the parking brake cable brackets.

18 Support the control arm B with a floor jack placed under the coil spring pocket.

19 Remove the trailing arm-to-knuckle bolts, then remove the trailing arm-to-chassis mounting bolts (see illustration).

20 Remove the trailing arm.

21 Installation is the reverse of removal, noting the following points:

a) *Tighten all fasteners to the proper torque specifications.*

b) *It won't be necessary to bleed the brakes unless a hydraulic fitting was loosened.*

c) *Have the rear wheel alignment checked and, if necessary, adjusted.*

11 Coil spring (rear) - removal and installation

✳✳ WARNING:

Always replace the springs as a set - never replace just one of them.

1 Loosen the wheel lug nuts, raise the vehicle and support it securely on jackstands. Block the front wheels to prevent the vehicle from rolling. Remove the wheel.

2 Remove the ABS wheel speed sensor and unbolt the harness brackets from the trailing arm.

3 Support the control arm B with a floor jack placed under the coil spring pocket.

4 Remove the bolt securing the control arm to the knuckle.

5 Mark the position of the spring to the spring insulators.

6 Slowly lower the floor jack and remove the coil spring (see illustration 10.13).

7 Check the spring for cracks and chips, replacing the springs as a set if any defects are found. Also check the upper insulator for damage and deterioration, replacing it if necessary.

8 Installation is the reverse of removal, noting the following points:

a) *Be sure to position the lower end of the coil spring in the depressed area of the trailing arm.*

b) *Raise the outer end of lower arm B with a floor jack, then tighten the control arm-to-knuckle bolt to the torque listed in this Chapter's Specifications.*

c) *Tighten the wheel lug nuts to the torque listed in the Chapter 1 Specifications.*

12 Hub and bearing assembly (rear) - removal and installation

2004 AND EARLIER MODELS

▶ **Refer to illustrations 12.3, 12.4 and 12.5**

※※ WARNING:

The manufacturer recommends replacing the hub nut and the dust cover with new ones whenever they are removed.

1   Loosen the rear wheel lug nuts, raise the rear of the vehicle, support it securely on jackstands and remove the wheels.

2   Remove the brake drum or disc (see Chapter 9).

3   Remove the dust cover (see illustration).

4   Remove the hub retaining nut (see illustration).

5   Remove the hub and bearing assembly from the spindle (see illustration).

6   Before installing the hub and bearing assembly, clean the spindle and apply a coat of wheel bearing grease to the area on the spindle where the bearing rides.

7   Installation is the reverse of removal. Install a new hub nut and tighten it to the torque listed in this Chapter's Specifications.

➡ **Note: Apply a little clean engine oil to the seating surface of the nut before installing it.**

On models with rear disc brakes, tighten the caliper mounting bolts to the torque listed in the Chapter 9 Specifications.

8   Install the wheel and lug nuts. Lower the vehicle and tighten the lug nuts to the torque listed in the Chapter 1 Specifications.

2005 AND LATER MODELS

9   Loosen the rear wheel lug nuts. Raise the vehicle and support it securely on jackstands. Remove the rear wheel.

10   Remove the brake caliper, then hang it from a piece of wire so the hose isn't stretched (see Chapter 9). Remove the two washers from between the caliper and the knuckle; don't lose them.

11   Remove the four hub mounting bolts. Pull off the hub and remove the O-ring under it. Discard the O-ring.

12   Installation is the reverse of removal. Replace the O-ring and tighten all fasteners to the torque listed in this Chapter's Specifications.

12.3 Using a hammer and chisel, remove the dust cover

12.4 Remove the hub retaining nut

12.5 Remove the hub and bearing assembly from the spindle

13 Steering wheel - removal and installation

※※ WARNING 1:

These models are equipped with a Supplemental Restraint System (SRS), more commonly known as airbags. Always disable the airbag system before working in the vicinity of any airbag system component to avoid the possibility of accidental deployment of the airbag(s), which could cause personal injury (see Chapter 12).

※※ WARNING 2:

Do not use a memory saving device to preserve the PCM or radio memory when working on or near airbag system components

REMOVAL

▶ **Refer to illustrations 13.2, 13.3, 13.4 and 13.8**

1   Make sure the front wheels are pointed straight ahead, then disconnect the cable from the negative terminal of the battery (see Chapter 5, Section 1). Wait at least three minutes before proceeding.

2   Remove the airbag connector access panel from the bottom of the steering wheel (see illustration).

3   Unplug the airbag module connector and the electrical connector for the horn (see illustration).

4   Open the access panels from each side of the steering wheel. Remove the fasteners retaining the airbag module to the steering wheel (see illustration).

13.2 Remove the panel at the bottom of the steering wheel to gain access to the airbag module electrical connector

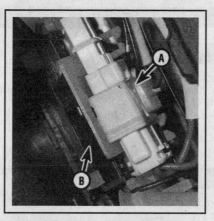

13.3 Disconnect the electrical connector for the airbag module (A), then disconnect the electrical connector for the horn (B)

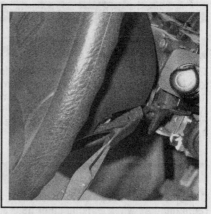

13.4 Remove the access covers for the airbag module bolts (one on each side of the steering wheel)

5   Pull off the airbag module, then carefully set it in a safe location.

❊❊ WARNING:

Carry the airbag module with the trim side facing away from you, and set the steering wheel/airbag module down with the trim side facing up. Don't place anything on top of the steering wheel/airbag module.

6   Disconnect the connectors for the radio remote switch and the cruise control switch.

7   On 2001 models, loosen the steering wheel retaining nut, or if you're working on a 2002 or later model, loosen the steering wheel retaining bolt until about 1/2-inch of threads are showing between the bolt head and the steering wheel.

8   Remove the steering wheel using a steering wheel puller (see illustration). The puller screw must be contacting the steering wheel bolt or shaft.

❊❊ CAUTION 1:

Don't thread the bolts of the puller into the steering wheel more than five turns, as they could contact the airbag clockspring and damage it.

❊❊ CAUTION 2:

While the steering wheel is removed, DO NOT turn the steering shaft. If you do so, the airbag clockspring could be damaged.

Make a mark indicating the relationship of the steering wheel hub to the steering shaft

9   If it is necessary to remove the clockspring, remove the steering column covers (see Chapter 11).

10 Unplug the clockspring electrical connector, then remove the three screws and detach it from the combination switch.

INSTALLATION

11 With the front wheels are pointed straight ahead, make sure that the airbag clockspring is centered with the arrow on the clockspring

13.8 Use a steering wheel puller to remove the steering wheel (early model shown)

pointing up. This shouldn't be a problem as long as you have not turned the steering shaft while the wheel was removed. If for some reason the shaft was turned, center the clockspring as follows:

   a) *Rotate the clockspring clockwise until it stops.*
   b) *Rotate the clockspring counterclockwise about 2-1/2 turns until the arrow on the clockspring points straight up.*

12 Be sure to align the index mark on the steering wheel hub with the mark on the shaft when you slip the wheel onto the shaft. Make sure the locating pins on the clockspring engage the holes in the backside of the steering wheel, and the notches in the steering wheel hub engage the tabs on the turn signal canceling cam. Install a NEW steering wheel bolt/nut and tighten it to the torque listed in this Chapter's Specifications.

13 Connect the radio remote switch and the cruise control switch connectors.

14 Reattach the airbag module using NEW fasteners and tighten them to the torque listed in this Chapter's Specifications.

15 Plug in the electrical connector for the horn and the airbag module.

16 Reconnect the negative battery cable (see Chapter 5, Section 1).

14 Steering column - removal and installation

✳✳ WARNING 1:

These models are equipped with a Supplemental Restraint System (SRS), more commonly known as airbags. Always disable the airbag system before working in the vicinity of any airbag system component to avoid the possibility of accidental deployment of the airbag(s), which could cause personal injury (see Chapter 12).

✳✳ WARNING 2:

Do not use a memory saving device to preserve the PCM or radio memory when working on or near airbag system components.

14.8 Remove the plastic lower push fasteners (A) and the two spring clips (B)

REMOVAL

▶ Refer to illustrations 14.8, 14.9 and 14.10

1 Park the vehicle with the wheels pointing straight ahead. Disconnect the cable from the negative terminal of the battery (see Chapter 5, Section 1).

2 Adjust the steering wheel tilt option to the Neutral position, approximately 8 mm down from the uppermost position.

3 Remove the steering wheel (see Section 13). Prevent the steering shaft from turning.

✳✳ CAUTION:

If this is not done, the airbag clockspring could be damaged.

2004 and earlier models

4 Remove the steering column covers (see Chapter 11).

5 Remove the clockspring (see Section 13).

6 Remove the multi-function switch (see Chapter 12).

7 Remove the shift cable from the shift lever and cable mounting bracket (see Chapter 7).

8 Remove the steering shaft cover (see illustration).

9 Mark the relationship of the U-joint to the intermediate shaft, then remove the pinch bolt (see illustration).

10 Remove the steering column mounting fasteners (see illustration), lower the column and pull it to the rear, making sure nothing is still connected, then remove the column.

2005 and later models

11 Remove the trim panel to the right of the accelerator pedal.

12 Remove the cover from the base of the steering column.

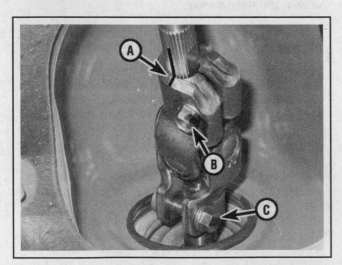

14.9 Mark the relationship of the intermediate shaft to the steering gear U-joint (A), then remove the pinch bolt (B). C is the pinch bolt securing the u-joint to the steering gear input shaft

14.10 Remove the steering column mounting fasteners (one fastener not pictured)

13 Tilt the column up as far as possible. Telescope the wheel IN as far as possible.

14 Use a long loop of wire to secure the lower part of the shaft (the upper part of the U-joint) to the uppermost part of the shaft. The shaft can't be allowed to slide out and separate.

15 Telescope the wheel out as far as possible. Lock it in place.

16 Remove the bolt from the lower U-joint. Slide the steering joint into the column.

17 Disconnect the wiring from the combination switch reel.

18 Remove the combination switch reel from the steering column shaft.

19 Disconnect the ignition switch wiring, then detach the wiring harness clips from the steering column

20 Unbolt and remove the steering column.

➡ **Note: If the inner shaft with the U-joint slides out, insert it back in, aligning the paint marks.**

INSTALLATION

21 Guide the steering column into position, then install the steering column mounting fasteners and tighten them to the torque listed in this Chapter's Specifications.

22 Connect the U-joint to the intermediate shaft. Install the intermediate shaft pinch bolt and nut, tightening it to the torque listed in this Chapter's Specifications.

23 The remainder of installation is the reverse of removal. Reconnect the negative battery cable (see Chapter 5, Section 1).

15 Tie-rod ends - removal and installation

REMOVAL

▶ **Refer to illustrations 15.2, 15.3 and 15.4**

1 Loosen the wheel lug nuts, raise the front of the vehicle and support it securely on jackstands. Apply the parking brake and block the rear wheels to keep the vehicle from rolling off the jackstands. Remove the wheel.

2 Loosen the tie-rod end jam nut (see illustration).

3 Mark the relationship of the tie-rod end to the threaded portion of the tie-rod. This will ensure the toe-in setting is restored when reassembled (see illustration).

4 Remove the cotter pin and loosen the nut from the tie-rod end ballstud a few turns. Disconnect the tie-rod end ballstud from the steering knuckle arm with a puller (see illustration).

5 Remove the nut from the ballstud, separate the tie-rod end from the steering knuckle, and then unscrew the tie-rod end from the tie-rod.

INSTALLATION

6 Thread the tie-rod end onto the tie-rod to the marked position and connect the tie-rod end to the steering arm. Install the nut on the ballstud and tighten it to the torque listed in this Chapter's Specifica-

tions. Install a new cotter pin.

➡ **Note: If necessary, tighten the nut a little more to allow insertion of the cotter pin. Never loosen the nut to align the cotter pin holes.**

7 Tighten the jam nut securely and install the wheel. Lower the vehicle and tighten the lug nuts to the torque listed in the Chapter 1 Specifications.

8 Have the front end alignment checked and, if necessary, adjusted.

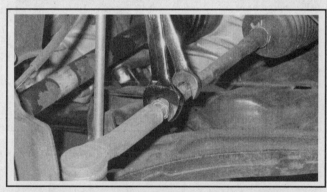

15.2 Using a back-up wrench to prevent the tie-rod from turning, loosen the jam nut

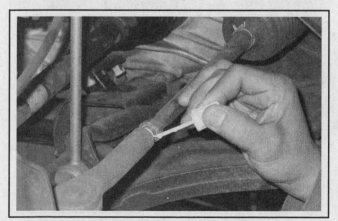

15.3 Back off the jam nut and mark the exposed threads to ensure that the new tie-rod end is threaded on the same number of turns

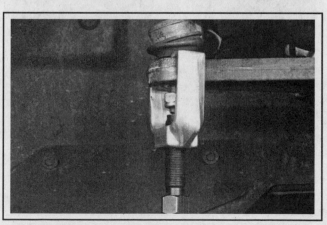

15.4 Use a two-jaw puller to push the tie-rod end stud out of the steering knuckle

16 Steering gear - removal and installation

REMOVAL

1   Disconnect the cable from the negative battery terminal (see Chapter 5, Section 1).

2   Drain the power steering fluid from the remote power steering reservoir. This can be accomplished with a suction gun or large syringe, or by disconnecting the fluid hose and draining the fluid into a container.

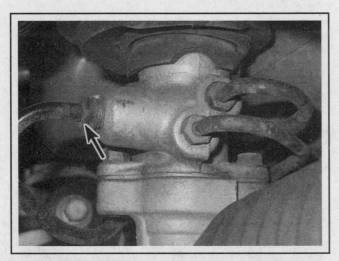

16.9 Using a flare-nut wrench, disconnect the pressure line (return hose not visible in this photo)

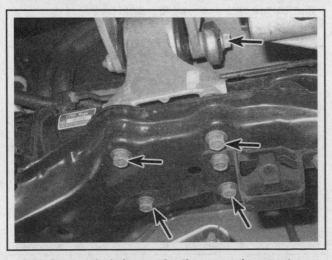

16.11 Remove the bolts securing the rear engine mount, then remove the mount

2004 and earlier models

▶ **Refer to illustrations 16.9, 16.11 and 16.13**

3   From inside the vehicle under the dashboard, remove the steering shaft cover (see illustration 14.8), then remove the pinch bolt securing the intermediate shaft to the steering gear input shaft (see illustration 14.9).

4   Loosen the front wheel lug nuts, raise the vehicle and support it securely on jackstands. Remove both front wheels.

➡ **Note: The jackstands must be behind the front suspension subframe, not supporting the vehicle by the subframe.**

5   Remove the engine splash shield.

6   Detach the tie-rod ends from the steering knuckles (see Section 15).

7   Remove the exhaust pipe-to-manifold and the catalytic converter assembly (see Chapter 4).

8   Remove the brackets securing the pressure line to the subframe.

9   Place a drain pan or tray under the vehicle, positioned beneath the steering gear. Using a flare-nut wrench, disconnect the pressure and return lines from the steering gear (see illustration). Plug the lines to prevent excessive fluid loss.

10 Secure the engine using an engine support brace that is fitted above the engine compartment. If an engine support brace is not available, install an engine hoist and a lifting chain assembly.

11 Remove the rear engine mount (see illustration).

12 Using two floor jacks, support the subframe. Position one jack on each side of the subframe, midway between the front and rear mounting points.

13 Loosen the four subframe-to-chassis mounting bolts (see illustration). Loosen the bolts approximately 1-3/16 inches (30 mm) from the mounting surface. Do not remove the bolts.

15 Remove the bolts securing the subframe stiffener plates (see illustration 16.13).

16 Lower the jacks until the subframe is sufficiently resting on the bolts that were loosened (enough to allow the steering gear to be removed).

17 Remove the steering gear mounting clamp, mounting bolts and nuts.

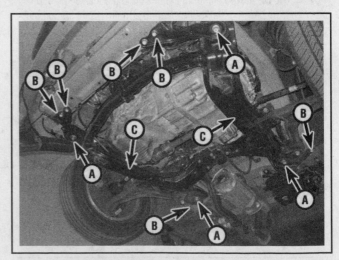

16.13 Loosen the subframe mounting bolts (A), then remove the stiffener plate mounting bolts (B). C is where the floor jacks should be placed

18 Pass the steering gear assembly through the left wheel opening and remove it from the vehicle.

2005 and later models

19 Perform Steps 11 through 16 in Section 14.

20 Disconnect any interfering wiring harnesses and brackets, then attach an engine support fixture to the top of the engine. Tighten the fixture to remove weight from the engine mounts. The engine must be securely supported from above to allow removal of the subframe.

21 Loosen the front wheel lug nuts. Raise the vehicle and support it securely on jackstands. Remove the front wheels.

22 Disconnect the tie-rod ends from the knuckles (see Section 15).

23 Remove the interfering exhaust pipe.

24 Disconnect the power steering switch wiring. Remove the front lower engine splash shield.

25 Using two floor jacks, support the subframe. Place one jack on each side of the subframe, midway between the front and rear mounting points.

26 Use paint to mark the exact location of all four corners of the subframe.

27 Remove the front subframe support bracket bolts.

28 Loosen the two front subframe main mounting bolts about 1-3/16 inches.

29 Remove the front subframe main mounting bolts and remove the rear support brackets.

30 Lower the entire subframe about 2 inches.

31 Detach the power steering line brackets from the subframe.

32 Disconnect the fluid lines from the steering gear. Seal the ends to prevent contamination.

33 Remove the power steering heat shield.

34 Remove the mount from the passenger's side of the steering gear.

35 Remove the mounting bolts from the driver's side of the gear.

36 Remove the steering gear support bracket bolt.

37 Remove the rear engine mount for clearance.

38 Disconnect the power steering return hose clip.

39 Slide the gear toward the left of the vehicle, then turn it so that the pinion shaft is facing forward. Carefully guide the steering gear out through the driver's side wheel well opening.

INSTALLATION

40 Installation is the reverse of removal, noting the following points:

a) Tighten the steering gear mounting bolts/nuts and mounting bracket bolts to the torque listed in Chapter's Specifications.

b) Tighten the subframe mounting bolts to the torque listed in Chapter 2B.

c) Tighten the engine mount bolts to the torque listed in Chapter 2A.

d) Fill the power steering pump with the recommended fluid (see Chapter 1), bleed the system (see Section 18) and recheck the fluid level. Check for leaks.

e) Run the engine and check for proper operation and leaks. Shut off the engine and recheck fluid levels.

f) Reconnect the negative battery cable (see Chapter 5, Section 1).

g) Have the front end alignment checked and, if necessary, adjusted.

17 Power steering pump - removal and installation

◆ **Refer to illustrations 17.2 and 17.4**

1 Remove the drivebelt (see Chapter 1).

2 Clamp the power steering feed hose shut so fluid loss will be minimized when the hose is disconnected, then disconnect the feed hose and pressure line at the pump (see illustration). Note the difference between the pressure and the feed hoses; the feed hose is held to the pump with a spring type clamp, and the pressure line has two bolts holding it to the pump body.

3 Cap or plug the line and hose to prevent leakage or contamination.

4 Remove the pump mounting bolts/nuts and adjuster bolt (see illustration). Remove the pump.

5 Installation is the reverse of removal. Install a new O-ring on the end of the pressure line. Be sure to adjust the drivebelt tension (see Chapter 1), check the power steering fluid level and add some, if necessary (see Chapter 1), then bleed the power steering system (see Section 18).

17.2 Power steering pump details

A Mounting bolt
B Adjusting nut
C Feed hose and clamp
D Pressure hose mounting bolts

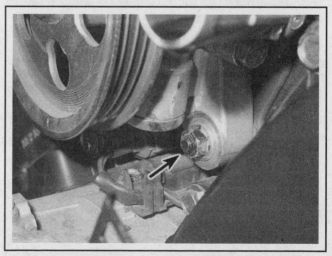

17.4 Power steering pump lower mounting bolt and nut

18 Power steering system - bleeding

1 Following any operation in which the power steering fluid lines have been disconnected, the power steering system must be bled to remove all air and obtain proper steering performance.

2 With the front wheels in the straight ahead position, check the power steering fluid level and, if low, add fluid until it reaches the MIN mark on the reservoir.

3 Start the engine and allow it to run at fast idle. Recheck the fluid level and add more if necessary to reach the MIN mark on the reservoir.

4 Bleed the system by turning the wheels from side to side, without hitting the stops. This will work the air out of the system. Keep the res-

ervoir full of fluid as this is done.

5 When the air is worked out of the system, return the wheels to the straight ahead position and leave the vehicle running for several more minutes before shutting it off.

6 Road test the vehicle to be sure the steering system is functioning normally and noise free.

7 Recheck the fluid level to be sure it is up to the MAX mark on the reservoir while the engine is at normal operating temperature. Add fluid if necessary (see Chapter 1).

19 Wheels and tires - general information

▶ **Refer to illustration 19.1**

1 All vehicles covered by this manual are equipped with metric-sized fiberglass or steel belted radial tires (see illustration). Use of other size or type of tires may affect the ride and handling of the vehicle. Don't mix different types of tires, such as radials and bias belted, on the same vehicle as handling may be seriously affected. It's recommended that tires be replaced in pairs on the same axle, but if only one tire is being replaced, be sure it's the same size, structure and tread design as the other.

2 Because tire pressure has a substantial effect on handling and wear, the pressure on all tires should be checked at least once a month or before any extended trips (see Chapter 1).

3 Wheels must be replaced if they are bent, dented, leak air, have elongated bolt holes, are heavily rusted, out of vertical symmetry or if the lug nuts won't stay tight. Wheel repairs that use welding or peening are not recommended.

4 Tire and wheel balance is important in the overall handling, braking and performance of the vehicle. Unbalanced wheels can adversely affect handling and ride characteristics as well as tire life. Whenever a tire is installed on a wheel, the tire and wheel should be balanced by a shop with the proper equipment.

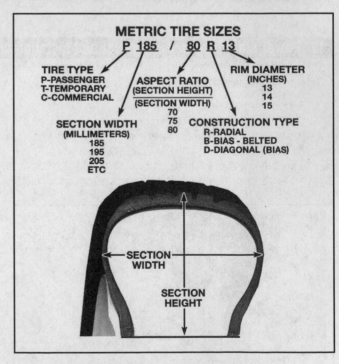

19.1 Metric tire size codes

20 Wheel alignment - general information

▶ Refer to illustration 20.1

A wheel alignment refers to the adjustments made to the wheels so they are in proper angular relationship to the suspension and the ground. Wheels that are out of proper alignment not only affect vehicle control, but also increase tire wear. The front end angles normally measured are camber, caster and toe-in (see illustration). Toe-in is the only routine adjustment made; camber on the front end is adjustable, but only after installing special strut-to-knuckle bolts. If the caster is not correct, check for bent components.

Getting the proper wheel alignment is a very exacting process, one in which complicated and expensive machines are necessary to perform the job properly. Because of this, you should have a technician with the proper equipment perform these tasks. We will, however, use this space to give you a basic idea of what is involved with a wheel alignment so you can better understand the process and deal intelligently with the shop that does the work.

Toe-in is the turning in of the wheels. The purpose of a toe specification is to ensure parallel rolling of the wheels. In a vehicle with zero toe-in, the distance between the front edges of the wheels will be the same as the distance between the rear edges of the wheels. The actual amount of toe-in is normally only a fraction of an inch. At the front end, toe-in is controlled by the tie-rod end position on the tie-rod. At the rear, it's adjusted by a cam bolt at the inner end of control arm B. Incorrect toe-in will cause the tires to wear improperly by making them scrub against the road surface.

Camber is the tilting of the wheels from vertical when viewed from one end of the vehicle. When the wheels tilt out at the top, the camber is said to be positive (+). When the wheels tilt in at the top the camber is negative (-). The amount of tilt is measured in degrees from vertical and this measurement is called the camber angle. This angle affects the amount of tire tread which contacts the road and compensates for changes in the suspension geometry when the vehicle is cornering or traveling over an undulating surface. On the front end it is adjusted using special camber adjusting bolts, which alter the relationship between the strut and the steering knuckle. At the rear end camber is not adjustable.

Caster is the tilting of the front steering axis from vertical. A tilt toward the rear is positive caster and a tilt toward the front is negative caster.

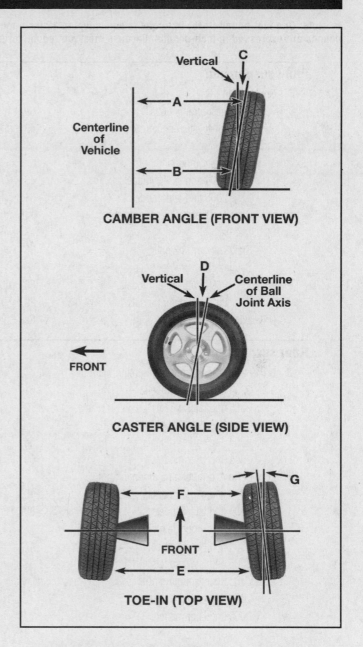

CAMBER ANGLE (FRONT VIEW)

CASTER ANGLE (SIDE VIEW)

TOE-IN (TOP VIEW)

20.1 Camber, caster and toe-in angles

A minus B = C (degrees camber)
D = degrees caster
E minus F = toe-in (measured in inches)
G = toe-in (expressed in degrees)

Torque specifications	Ft-lbs (unless otherwise indicated)	Nm

➡ Note: One foot-pound (ft-lb) of torque is equivalent to 12 inch-pounds (in-lbs) of torque. Torque values below approximately 15 foot-pounds are expressed in inch-pounds, because most foot-pound torque wrenches are not accurate at these smaller values.

Front suspension

Control arm		
Arm-to-subframe bolts	69	93
Balljoint-to-steering knuckle nut	43 to 51	59 to 69
Strut		
Strut upper mounting nuts		
2004 and earlier models	43	59
2005 and later models*	51	69
Strut-to-steering knuckle fasteners	116	157
Stabilizer bar		
Stabilizer bar link nuts	58	78
Stabilizer bar bracket bolts		
2004 and earlier models	86 in-lbs	10
2005 and later models	29	39
Driveaxle hub nut*	See Chapter 8	

Rear suspension

Lower arm B-to-subframe mounting bolt/nut		
2004 and earlier models	61	83
2005 and later models*	72	98
Lower arm B-to-knuckle bolt		
2004 and earlier models	54	74
2005 and later models*	69	93
Lower arm A-to-subframe mounting bolt		
2004 and earlier models	105	142
2005 and later models*	80	103
Lower arm A-to-knuckle mounting bolt		
2004 and earlier models	47	64
2005 and later models*	98	132
Shock absorber mounting nuts		
2004 and earlier models	47	64
2005 and later models		
Upper	33	44
Lower*	58	78
Trailing arm-to-chassis mounting bolts	75	103
Trailing arm-to-knuckle mounting bolts		
2004 and earlier models	47	64
2005 and later models*	87	118
Upper control arm-to-subframe bolt		
2004 and earlier models	47	64
2005 and later models*	61	83
Upper control arm-to-knuckle nut		
2004 and earlier models	36 to 43	49 to 59
2005 and later models*	43 to 51	59 to 69

*Replace with new fasteners upon assembly

Torque specifications (continued)	Ft-lbs (unless otherwise indicated)	Nm

➡ **Note: One foot-pound (ft-lb) of torque is equivalent to 12 inch-pounds (in-lbs) of torque. Torque values below approximately 15 foot-pounds are expressed in inch-pounds, because most foot-pound torque wrenches are not accurate at these smaller values.**

Steering

Airbag module-to-steering wheel bolts	86 in-lbs	10
Power steering pump fasteners	17	24
Steering gear mounting fasteners		
2004 and earlier models	43	58
2005 and later models	40	54
Steering gear bracket bolts		
2004 and earlier models	29	39
2005 and later models	31	42
Tie-rod end-to-steering knuckle nut*	40	54
Intermediate shaft pinch bolt		
2004 and earlier models	16	22
2005 and later models	21	28
Steering column mounting nuts	142 in-lbs	16
Steering wheel mounting nut		
2001 models	36	49
2002 through 2004 models	28	38
2005 and later models	36	49
Rear hub nut, 2004 and earlier models*	181	245
Rear hub assembly bolts, 2005 and later models	73	99

Replace with new fasteners upon assembly

Notes

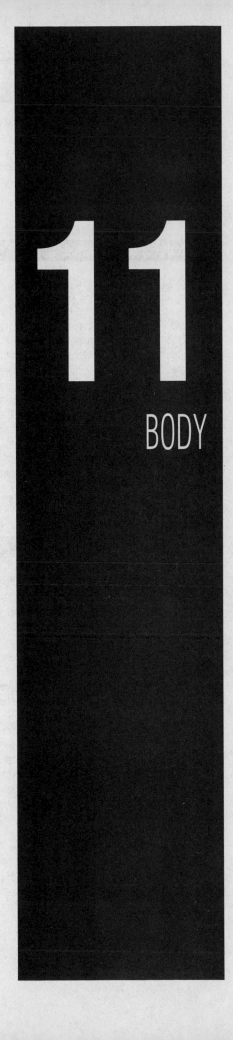

11

BODY

Section

1 General information

These models feature a "unibody" layout, using a floor pan with integral side frame rails which support the body components, front and rear suspension systems and other mechanical components.

Certain components are particularly vulnerable to accident damage and can be unbolted and repaired or replaced. Among these parts are the body moldings, bumpers, front fenders, the hood and trunk lid, doors and all glass.

Only general body maintenance practices and body panel repair procedures within the scope of the do-it-yourselfer are included in this Chapter.

2 Body - maintenance

1 The condition of your vehicle's body is very important, because the resale value depends a great deal on it. It's much more difficult to repair a neglected or damaged body than it is to repair mechanical components. The hidden areas of the body, such as the wheel wells, the frame and the engine compartment, are equally important, although they don't require as frequent attention as the rest of the body.

2 Once a year, or every 12,000 miles, it's a good idea to have the underside of the body steam-cleaned. All traces of dirt and oil will be removed and the area can then be inspected carefully for rust, damaged brake lines, frayed electrical wires, damaged cables and other problems.

3 At the same time, clean the engine and the engine compartment with a steam cleaner or water-soluble degreaser.

4 The wheel wells should be given close attention, since undercoating can peel away and stones and dirt thrown up by the tires can cause the paint to chip and flake, allowing rust to set in. If rust is found, clean down to the bare metal and apply an anti-rust paint.

5 The body should be washed about once a week. Wet the vehicle thoroughly to soften the dirt, then wash it down with a soft sponge and plenty of clean soapy water. If the surplus dirt is not washed off very carefully, it can wear down the paint.

6 Spots of tar or asphalt thrown up from the road should be removed with a cloth soaked in kerosene. Scented lamp oil is available in most hardware stores and the smell is easier to work with than straight kerosene.

7 Once every six months, wax the body and chrome trim. If a chrome cleaner is used to remove rust from any of the vehicle's plated parts, remember that the cleaner also removes part of the chrome, so use it sparingly. On any plated parts where chrome cleaner is used, use a good paste wax over the plating for extra protection.

3 Vinyl trim - maintenance

Don't clean vinyl trim with detergents, caustic soap or petroleum-based cleaners. Plain soap and water works just fine, with a soft brush to clean dirt that may be ingrained. Wash the vinyl as frequently as the rest of the vehicle.

After cleaning, application of a high quality rubber and vinyl protectant will help prevent oxidation and cracks. The protectant can also be applied to weather stripping, vacuum lines and rubber hoses, which often fail as a result of chemical degradation, and to the tires.

4 Upholstery and carpets - maintenance

1 Every three months remove the floormats and clean the interior of the vehicle (more frequently if necessary). Use a stiff whisk broom to brush the carpeting and loosen dirt and dust, then vacuum the upholstery and carpets thoroughly, especially along seams and crevices.

2 Dirt and stains can be removed from carpeting with basic household or automotive carpet shampoos available in spray cans. Follow the directions and vacuum again, then use a stiff brush to bring back the "nap" of the carpet.

3 Most interiors have cloth or vinyl upholstery, either of which can be cleaned and maintained with a number of material-specific cleaners or shampoos available in auto supply stores. Follow the directions on the product for usage, and always spot-test any upholstery cleaner on an inconspicuous area (bottom edge of a backseat cushion) to ensure that it doesn't cause a color shift in the material.

4 After cleaning, vinyl upholstery should be treated with a protectant.

➡ **Note: Make sure the protectant container indicates the product can be used on seats - some products may make a seat too slippery.**

❊❊ CAUTION:

Do not use protectant on steering wheels.

5 Leather upholstery requires special care. It should be cleaned regularly with saddlesoap or leather cleaner. Never use alcohol, gasoline, nail polish remover or thinner to clean leather upholstery.

6 After cleaning, regularly treat leather upholstery with a leather conditioner, rubbed in with a soft cotton cloth. Never use car wax on leather upholstery.

7 In areas where the interior of the vehicle is subject to bright sunlight, cover leather seating areas of the seats with a sheet if the vehicle is to be left out for any length of time.

FLEXIBLE PLASTIC BODY PANELS (FRONT AND REAR BUMPER FASCIA)

The following repair procedures are for minor scratches and gouges. Repair of more serious damage should be left to a dealer service department or qualified auto body shop. Below is a list of the equipment and materials necessary to perform the following repair procedures on plastic body panels. Although a specific brand of material may be mentioned, it should be noted that equivalent products from other manufacturers may be used instead.

Wax, grease and silicone removing solvent
Cloth-backed body tape
Sanding discs
Drill motor with three-inch disc holder
Hand sanding block
Rubber squeegees
Sandpaper
Non-porous mixing palette
Wood paddle or putty knife
Curved-tooth body file
Flexible parts repair material

1   Remove the damaged panel, if necessary or desirable. In most cases, repairs can be carried out with the panel installed.

2   Clean the area(s) to be repaired with a wax, grease and silicone removing solvent applied with a water-dampened cloth.

3   If the damage is structural, that is, if it extends through the panel, clean the backside of the panel area to be repaired as well. Wipe dry.

4   Sand the rear surface about 1-1/2 inches beyond the break.

5   Cut two pieces of fiberglass cloth large enough to overlap the break by about 1-1/2 inches. Cut only to the required length.

6   Mix the adhesive from the repair kit according to the instructions included with the kit, and apply a layer of the mixture approximately 1/8-inch thick on the backside of the panel. Overlap the break by at least 1-1/2 inches.

7   Apply one piece of fiberglass cloth to the adhesive and cover the cloth with additional adhesive. Apply a second piece of fiberglass cloth to the adhesive and immediately cover the cloth with additional adhesive in sufficient quantity to fill the weave.

8   Allow the repair to cure for 20 to 30 minutes at 60-degrees to 80-degrees F.

9   If necessary, trim the excess repair material at the edge.

10 Remove all of the paint film over and around the area(s) to be repaired. The repair material should not overlap the painted surface.

11 With a drill motor and a sanding disc (or a rotary file), cut a "V" along the break line approximately 1/2-inch wide. Remove all dust and loose particles from the repair area.

12 Mix and apply the repair material. Apply a light coat first over the damaged area; then continue applying material until it reaches a level slightly higher than the surrounding finish.

13 Cure the mixture for 20 to 30 minutes at 60-degrees to 80-degrees F.

14 Roughly establish the contour of the area being repaired with a body file. If low areas or pits remain, mix and apply additional adhesive.

15 Block sand the damaged area with sandpaper to establish the actual contour of the surrounding surface.

16 If desired, the repaired area can be temporarily protected with several light coats of primer. Because of the special paints and techniques required for flexible body panels, it is recommended that the vehicle be taken to a paint shop for completion of the body repair.

STEEL BODY PANELS

▶ **See photo sequence**

Repair of minor scratches

17 If the scratch is superficial and does not penetrate to the metal of the body, repair is very simple. Lightly rub the scratched area with a fine rubbing compound to remove loose paint and built up wax. Rinse the area with clean water.

18 Apply touch-up paint to the scratch, using a small brush. Continue to apply thin layers of paint until the surface of the paint in the scratch is level with the surrounding paint. Allow the new paint at least two weeks to harden, then blend it into the surrounding paint by rubbing with a very fine rubbing compound. Finally, apply a coat of wax to the scratch area.

19 If the scratch has penetrated the paint and exposed the metal of the body, causing the metal to rust, a different repair technique is required. Remove all loose rust from the bottom of the scratch with a pocket knife, then apply rust inhibiting paint to prevent the formation of rust in the future. Using a rubber or nylon applicator, coat the scratched area with glaze-type filler. If required, the filler can be mixed with thinner to provide a very thin paste, which is ideal for filling narrow scratches. Before the glaze filler in the scratch hardens, wrap a piece of smooth cotton cloth around the tip of a finger. Dip the cloth in thinner and then quickly wipe it along the surface of the scratch. This will ensure that the surface of the filler is slightly hollow. The scratch can now be painted over as described earlier in this Section.

REPAIR OF DENTS

20 When repairing dents, the first job is to pull the dent out until the affected area is as close as possible to its original shape. There is no point in trying to restore the original shape completely as the metal in the damaged area will have stretched on impact and cannot be restored to its original contours. It is better to bring the level of the dent up to a point which is about 1/8-inch below the level of the surrounding metal. In cases where the dent is very shallow, it is not worth trying to pull it out at all.

21 If the back side of the dent is accessible, it can be hammered out gently from behind using a soft-face hammer. While doing this, hold a block of wood firmly against the opposite side of the metal to absorb the hammer blows and prevent the metal from being stretched.

22 If the dent is in a section of the body which has double layers, or some other factor makes it inaccessible from behind, a different technique is required. Drill several small holes through the metal inside the damaged area, particularly in the deeper sections. Screw long, self tapping screws into the holes just enough for them to get a good grip in the metal. Now the dent can be pulled out by pulling on the protruding heads of the screws with locking pliers.

23 The next stage of repair is the removal of paint from the damaged area and from an inch or so of the surrounding metal. This is easily done with a wire brush or sanding disk in a drill motor, although it can be done just as effectively by hand with sandpaper. To complete the preparation for filling, score the surface of the bare metal with a screwdriver or the tang of a file or drill small holes in the affected area. This

These photos illustrate a method of repairing simple dents. They are intended to supplement Body repair - minor damage in this Chapter and should not be used as the sole instructions for body repair on these vehicles.

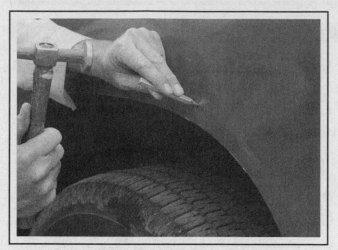

1 If you can't access the backside of the body panel to hammer out the dent, pull it out with a slide-hammer-type dent puller. In the deepest portion of the dent or along the crease line, drill or punch hole(s) at least one inch apart . . .

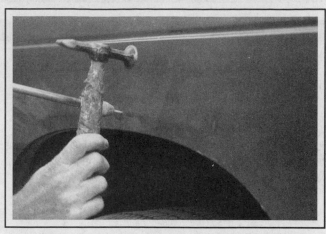

2 . . . then screw the slide-hammer into the hole and operate it. Tap with a hammer near the edge of the dent to help 'pop' the metal back to its original shape. When you're finished, the dent area should be close to its original contour and about 1/8-inch below the surface of the surrounding metal

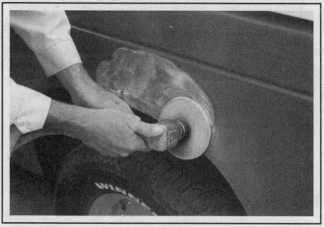

3 Using coarse-grit sandpaper, remove the paint down to the bare metal. Hand sanding works fine, but the disc sander shown here makes the job faster. Use finer (about 320-grit) sandpaper to feather-edge the paint at least one inch around the dent area

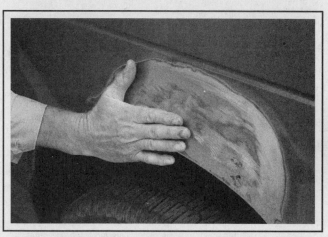

4 When the paint is removed, touch will probably be more helpful than sight for telling if the metal is straight. Hammer down the high spots or raise the low spots as necessary. Clean the repair area with wax/silicone remover

5 Following label instructions, mix up a batch of plastic filler and hardener. The ratio of filler to hardener is critical, and, if you mix it incorrectly, it will either not cure properly or cure too quickly (you won't have time to file and sand it into shape)

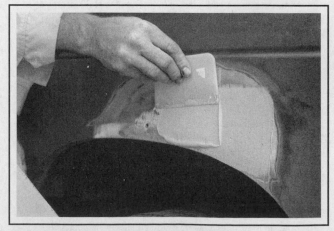

6 Working quickly so the filler doesn't harden, use a plastic applicator to press the body filler firmly into the metal, assuring it bonds completely. Work the filler until it matches the original contour and is slightly above the surrounding metal

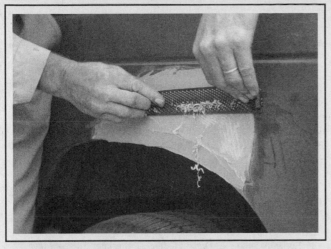

7 Let the filler harden until you can just dent it with your fingernail. Use a body file or Surform tool (shown here) to rough-shape the filler

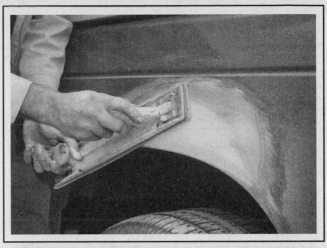

8 Use coarse-grit sandpaper and a sanding board or block to work the filler down until it's smooth and even. Work down to finer grits of sandpaper - always using a board or block - ending up with 360 or 400 grit

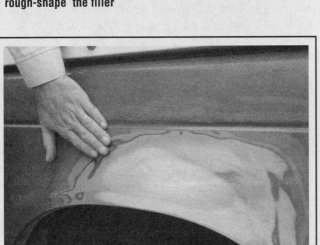

9 You shouldn't be able to feel any ridge at the transition from the filler to the bare metal or from the bare metal to the old paint. As soon as the repair is flat and uniform, remove the dust and mask off the adjacent panels or trim pieces

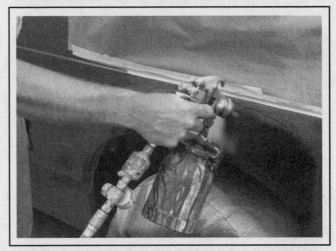

10 Apply several layers of primer to the area. Don't spray the primer on too heavy, so it sags or runs, and make sure each coat is dry before you spray on the next one. A professional-type spray gun is being used here, but aerosol spray primer is available inexpensively from auto parts stores

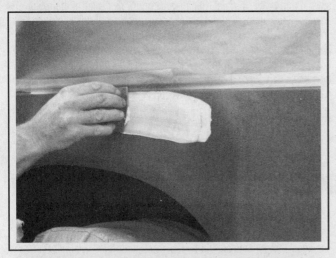

11 The primer will help reveal imperfections or scratches. Fill these with glazing compound. Follow the label instructions and sand it with 360 or 400-grit sandpaper until it's smooth. Repeat the glazing, sanding and respraying until the primer reveals a perfectly smooth surface

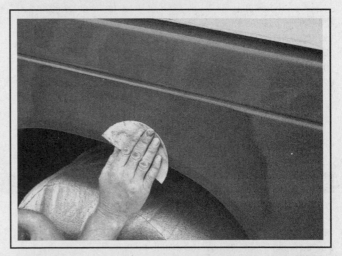

12 Finish sand the primer with very fine sandpaper (400 or 600-grit) to remove the primer overspray. Clean the area with water and allow it to dry. Use a tack rag to remove any dust, then apply the finish coat. Don't attempt to rub out or wax the repair area until the paint has dried completely (at least two weeks)

will provide a good grip for the filler material. To complete the repair, see the Section on filling and painting.

REPAIR OF RUST HOLES OR GASHES

24 Remove all paint from the affected area and from an inch or so of the surrounding metal using a sanding disk or wire brush mounted in a drill motor. If these are not available, a few sheets of sandpaper will do the job just as effectively.

25 With the paint removed, you will be able to determine the severity of the corrosion and decide whether to replace the whole panel, if possible, or repair the affected area. New body panels are not as expensive as most people think and it is often quicker to install a new panel than to repair large areas of rust.

26 Remove all trim pieces from the affected area except those which will act as a guide to the original shape of the damaged body, such as headlight shells, etc. Using metal snips or a hacksaw blade, remove all loose metal and any other metal that is badly affected by rust. Hammer the edges of the hole in to create a slight depression for the filler material.

27 Wire brush the affected area to remove the powdery rust from the surface of the metal. If the back of the rusted area is accessible, treat it with rust inhibiting paint.

28 Before filling is done, block the hole in some way. This can be done with sheet metal riveted or screwed into place, or by stuffing the hole with wire mesh.

29 Once the hole is blocked off, the affected area can be filled and painted. See the following subsection on filling and painting.

FILLING AND PAINTING

30 Many types of body fillers are available, but generally speaking, body repair kits which contain filler paste and a tube of resin hardener are best for this type of repair work. A wide, flexible plastic or nylon applicator will be necessary for imparting a smooth and contoured finish to the surface of the filler material. Mix up a small amount of filler on a clean piece of wood or cardboard (use the hardener sparingly). Follow the manufacturer's instructions on the package, otherwise the filler will set incorrectly.

31 Using the applicator, apply the filler paste to the prepared area. Draw the applicator across the surface of the filler to achieve the desired contour and to level the filler surface. As soon as a contour that approximates the original one is achieved, stop working the paste. If you continue, the paste will begin to stick to the applicator. Continue to add thin layers of paste at 20-minute intervals until the level of the filler is just above the surrounding metal.

32 Once the filler has hardened, the excess can be removed with a body file. From then on, progressively finer grades of sandpaper should be used, starting with a 180-grit paper and finishing with 600-grit wet-or-dry paper. Always wrap the sandpaper around a flat rubber or wooden block, otherwise the surface of the filler will not be completely flat. During the sanding of the filler surface, the wet-or-dry paper should be periodically rinsed in water. This will ensure that a very smooth finish is produced in the final stage.

33 At this point, the repair area should be surrounded by a ring of bare metal, which in turn should be encircled by the finely feathered edge of good paint. Rinse the repair area with clean water until all of the dust produced by the sanding operation is gone.

34 Spray the entire area with a light coat of primer. This will reveal any imperfections in the surface of the filler. Repair the imperfections with fresh filler paste or glaze filler and once more smooth the surface with sandpaper. Repeat this spray-and-repair procedure until you are satisfied that the surface of the filler and the feathered edge of the paint are perfect. Rinse the area with clean water and allow it to dry completely.

35 The repair area is now ready for painting. Spray painting must be carried out in a warm, dry, windless and dust free atmosphere. These conditions can be created if you have access to a large indoor work area, but if you are forced to work in the open, you will have to pick the day very carefully. If you are working indoors, dousing the floor in the work area with water will help settle the dust which would otherwise be in the air. If the repair area is confined to one body panel, mask off the surrounding panels. This will help minimize the effects of a slight mismatch in paint color. Trim pieces such as chrome strips, door handles, etc., will also need to be masked off or removed. Use masking tape and several thickness of newspaper for the masking operations.

36 Before spraying, shake the paint can thoroughly, then spray a test area until the spray painting technique is mastered. Cover the repair area with a thick coat of primer. The thickness should be built up using several thin layers of primer rather than one thick one. Using 600-grit wet-or-dry sandpaper, rub down the surface of the primer until it is very smooth. While doing this, the work area should be thoroughly rinsed with water and the wet-or-dry sandpaper periodically rinsed as well. Allow the primer to dry before spraying additional coats.

37 Spray on the top coat, again building up the thickness by using several thin layers of paint. Begin spraying in the center of the repair area and then, using a circular motion, work out until the whole repair area and about two inches of the surrounding original paint is covered. Remove all masking material 10 to 15 minutes after spraying on the final coat of paint. Allow the new paint at least two weeks to harden, then use a very fine rubbing compound to blend the edges of the new paint into the existing paint. Finally, apply a coat of wax.

6   Body repair - major damage

1   Major damage must be repaired by an auto body shop specifically equipped to perform unibody repairs. These shops have the specialized equipment required to do the job properly.

2   If the damage is extensive, the body must be checked for proper alignment or the vehicle's handling characteristics may be adversely affected and other components may wear at an accelerated rate.

3   Due to the fact that some of the major body components (hood, fenders, doors, etc.) are separate and replaceable units, any seriously damaged components should be replaced rather than repaired. Sometimes the components can be found in a wrecking yard that specializes in used vehicle components, often at considerable savings over the cost of new parts.

7   Hinges and locks - maintenance

Once every 3,000 miles, or every three months, the hinges and latch assemblies on the doors, hood and trunk (or liftgate) should be given a few drops of light oil or lock lubricant. The door latch strikers should also be lubricated with a thin coat of grease to reduce wear and ensure free movement. Lubricate the door and trunk (or liftgate) locks with spray-on graphite lubricant.

8   Windshield and fixed glass - replacement

Replacement of the windshield and fixed glass requires the use of special fast-setting adhesive/caulk materials and some specialized tools and techniques. These operations should be left to a dealer service department or a shop specializing in glass work.

9   Hood - removal, installation and adjustment

➡ Note: The hood is somewhat awkward to remove and install; at least two people should perform this procedure.

REMOVAL AND INSTALLATION

♦ Refer to illustration 9.3

1   Open the hood, then place blankets or pads over the fenders and cowl area of the body. This will protect the body and paint as the hood is lifted off.

2   Disconnect any cables or wires that will interfere with removal. Disconnect the windshield washer tubing from the nozzles on the hood.

3   Make marks around the hood hinge to ensure proper alignment during installation (see illustration).

4   Have an assistant support one side of the hood while you support the other. Simultaneously remove the hinge-to-hood bolts, then lift off the hood.

5   Installation is the reverse of removal. Align the hinge bolts with the marks made in Step 3.

ADJUSTMENT

♦ Refer to illustrations 9.9 and 9.10

6   Fore-and-aft and side-to-side adjustment of the hood is done by moving the hinge plate slot after loosening the bolts or nuts.

7   Mark around the entire hinge plate so you can determine the amount of movement.

8   Loosen the bolts and move the hood into correct alignment. Move it only a little at a time. Tighten the hinge bolts and carefully lower the hood to check the position.

9   If necessary after installation, the entire hood latch assembly can be adjusted up-and-down as well as from side-to-side on the radiator support so the hood closes securely and flush with the fenders. Scribe a line or mark around the hood latch mounting bolts to provide a reference point, then loosen them and reposition the latch assembly, as necessary (see illustration). Following adjustment, retighten the mounting bolts.

10   Finally, adjust the hood bumpers on the radiator support so the hood, when closed, is flush with the fenders (see illustration).

11   The hood latch assembly, as well as the hinges, should be periodically lubricated with white, lithium-base grease to prevent binding and wear.

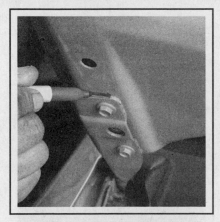

9.3 Draw alignment marks around the hood hinges to ensure proper alignment of the hood when it's reinstalled

9.9 To adjust the hood latch horizontally or vertically, mark around the perimeter of the washers, loosen the latch bolts and reposition the latch, then tighten the bolts

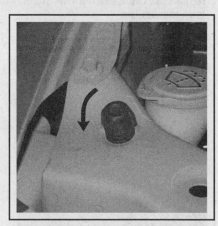

9.10 To adjust the vertical height of the leading edge of the hood so that it's flush with the fenders, turn each edge cushion clockwise (to lower the hood) or counterclockwise (to raise the hood)

10 Hood latch and release cable - removal and installation

❈ WARNING:

The models covered by this manual are equipped with Supplemental Restraint systems (SRS), more commonly known as airbags. Always disable the airbag system before working in the vicinity of any airbag system component to avoid the possibility of accidental deployment of the airbag, which could cause personal injury (see Chapter 12).

LATCH

♦ **Refer to illustration 10.2**

1   Remove the cover from the top of the grille, if equipped. Scribe a line around the latch bolts to aid alignment when installing, then remove the retaining bolts securing the hood latch to the radiator support (see illustration 9.9). Remove the latch.

2   Disconnect the hood release cable from the latch assembly (see illustration).

3   Installation is the reverse of removal.

➡ **Note: Adjust the latch so the hood engages securely when closed and the hood bumpers are slightly compressed.**

CABLE

♦ **Refer to illustrations 10.4a, 10.4b, 10.5 and 10.6**

4   Working in the passenger compartment, remove the driver's side kick panel (see illustrations).

5   Remove the hood release handle (see illustration).

6   Lift the hood release handle lever upward, then rotate the cable housing end and disengage the cable from the hood release lever handle (see illustration).

7   Attach a piece of wire or string to the end of the cable (inside the vehicle).

10.2 Detach the cable housing from the hood latch, then remove the cable end from the slotted portion of the latch mechanism

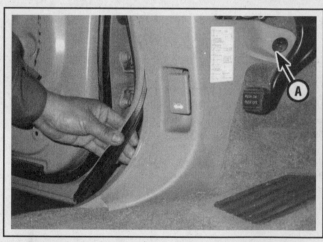

10.4a Remove the kick panel moulding from the door sill, remove the panel screw (A) . . .

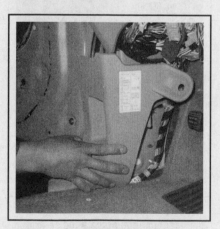

10.4b . . . then detach the panel

10.5 Remove the hood release handle mounting bolts

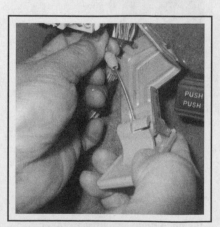

10.6 Lift upward on the handle and slide the end of the cable housing using a fine tipped screwdriver to release it from the base of the handle

8 Loosen the left-front wheel lug nuts, raise the front of the vehicle and support it securely on jackstands. Remove the left inner fender splash shield (see Section 12).

9 Working in the engine compartment, disconnect the hood release cable from the latch as described in Steps 1 and 2. Unclip all the cable retaining clips on the radiator support and the inner fenderwell.

10 Pull the cable forward into the engine compartment until it is free, then remove the wire or string from the old cable and fasten it to the new cable.

11 With the new cable attached to the wire or string, pull the wire or string back through the firewall until the new cable reaches the inside handle.

12 Seat the cable grommet where the cable passes through the body.

13 Working in the passenger compartment, connect the new cable to the hood release handle, making sure the cable housing fits snugly into the notch in the handle bracket.

14 The remainder of the installation is the reverse of removal. Tighten the wheel lug nuts to the torque listed in the Chapter 1 Specifications.

11 Bumpers - removal and installation

✳✳ WARNING:

The models covered by this manual are equipped with Supplemental Restraint systems (SRS), more commonly known as airbags. Always disable the airbag system before working in the vicinity of any airbag system component to avoid the possibility of accidental deployment of the airbag, which could cause personal injury (see Chapter 12).

1 Apply the parking brake, raise the vehicle and support it securely on jackstands.

2004 AND EARLIER MODELS

Front bumper

▶ **Refer to illustrations 11.3a, 11.3b, 11.4, 11.5, 11.6, 11.7 and 11.8**

2 Remove the radiator grille (see Section 13).

3 Remove the inner fender splash shield, disconnecting only the push-pins and screws that are attached to the splash shield and bumper cover (see illustrations). Peel back the inner fender splash shield.

4 Remove the bolts and the clips securing the front bumper cover to the chassis (see illustration).

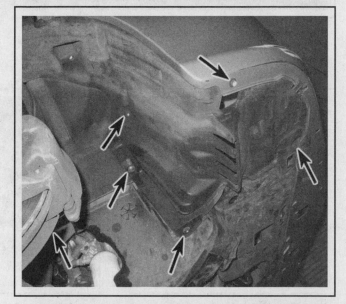

11.3a Disconnect the inner fender splash shield, removing only the push-pins and screws that are attached to the splash shield and bumper cover - right side shown, left side similar

11.3b Remove the push-pins by lifting the center release pin, then pull the push-pin out

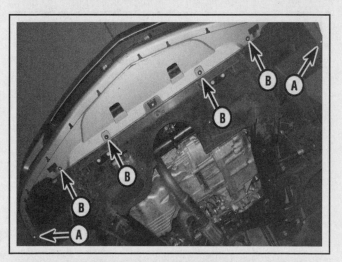

11.4 Remove the push-pins (B) and the mounting bolts (A) from the lower section of the bumper cover – 2004 and earlier models

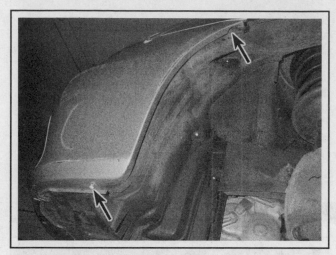

11.5 Remove the outer bolts securing the bumper cover to the inner fender

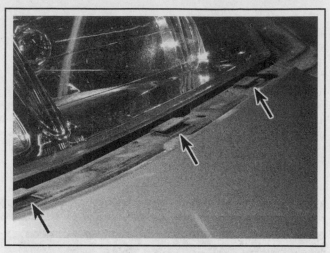

11.6 Release the bumper cover from the hooks along the upper edge and slide the cover out – 2004 and earlier models

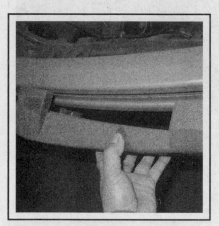

11.7 Remove the foam absorber insert from the bumper

11.8 Remove the front bumper mounting bolts (lower bolt hidden from view) - left side shown, right side similar

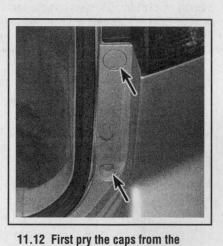

11.12 First pry the caps from the upper bumper cover and remove the bolts - right side shown, left side similar (2004 and earlier models)

11.13 Remove the upper side bolts from the bumper cover - right side shown, left side similar

5 Remove the outer bolts securing the bumper cover to the inner fender (see illustration).

6 Release the upper section of the bumper cover from the hooks (see illustration).

7 Remove the foam absorber from the front bumper (see illustration).

8 Remove the bumper mounting bolts (see illustration) and the bolts retaining the side cover beams.

9 Remove the front bumper and side cover beams from the chassis.

10 Installation is the reverse of removal.

Rear bumper

◆ **Refer to illustrations 11.12, 11.13, 11.14, 11.15, 11.16, 11.17 and 11.18**

11 Remove the rear taillights (see Chapter 12).

12 Remove the caps and the bolts from the sides of the upper bumper cover (see illustration).

13 Remove the upper side bolts from the upper bumper cover (see illustration).

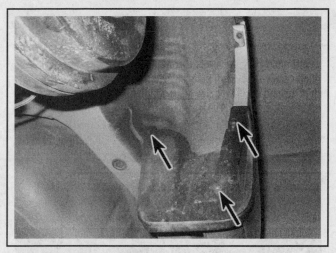

11.14 Remove the mudflap mounting screws and detach the mudflap - right side shown, left side similar (2004 and earlier models)

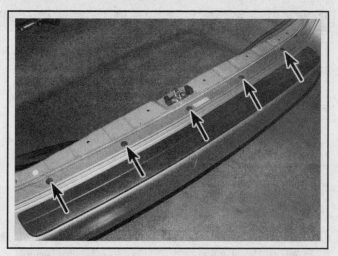

11.15 Remove the rear bumper push-pins from the upper section

11.16 Remove the push-pins from the lower section of the bumper cover

11.17 Remove the rear bumper cover, lifting the cover from the hooks and sliding the cover back

11.18 Remove the rear bumper mounting bolts (lower bolt hidden from view)

14 Remove the mudflaps to access the lower bumper cover screws (see illustration). Remove the lower bumper cover screws from the fenderwell.

15 Remove the rear bumper cover push-pins from the upper trunk area (see illustration).

16 Remove the rear bumper cover push-pins from below (see illustration).

17 Remove the rear bumper cover by lifting the cover off the hooks (see illustration).

18 Remove the rear bumper mounting bolts (see illustration).

19 Installation is the reverse of removal.

2005 AND LATER MODELS

Front bumper

20 Remove the cover from the top of the grille.

21 Raise the vehicle and support it securely on jackstands. There are push-pin retainers, bolts and screws securing the bumper cover that vary by year and model. Remove the push-pins along the bottom edge of the bumper, then remove the screws or bolts at each end.

22 Remove the upper retainers at each side of the grille.

23 With the help of an assistant, pull the rear sections of the bumper to release the hooks on the fenders.

24 Pull the bumper forward to release the hooks on the center section.

25 Carefully remove the bumper and disconnect any wiring.

26 Installation is the reverse of removal. Be sure all hooks are properly engaged.

Rear bumper

27 The procedure is the same as for 2004 and earlier models (see Steps 11 through 19).

12 Front fender - removal and installation

▶ **Refer to illustrations 12.3a, 12.3b, 12.5a, 12.5b, 12.6a, 12.6b and 12.7**

1 Loosen the front wheel lug nuts. Raise the front of the vehicle, support it securely on jackstands and remove the front wheel.

2 Remove the headlight housing (see Chapter 12).

3 Remove the inner fender splash shield (see illustrations).

4 If you're removing the passenger side fender, remove the radio antenna (see Chapter 12).

5 Remove the lower fender-to-body bolts (see illustrations).

6 Open the front door, remove the trim panel from the front pillar and remove the upper fender-to-body bolts (see illustrations).

7 Remove the remaining fender mounting bolts (see illustration).

8 Lift off the fender. It's a good idea to have an assistant support the fender while it's being moved away from the vehicle to prevent damage to the surrounding body panels.

9 Installation is the reverse of removal. Check the alignment of the fender to the hood and front edge of the door before final tightening of the fender fasteners.

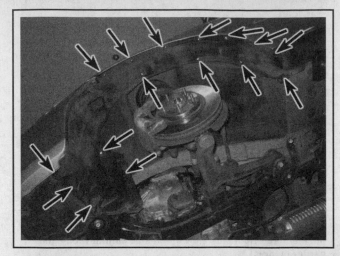

12.3a Remove the inner fender splash shield push-pin retainers, mounting screws and bolt

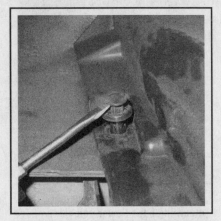

12.3b To remove a push-pin retainer, lift the center pin and pop the retainer out

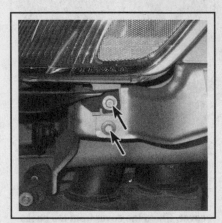

12.5a Remove the lower fender mounting bolts at the front . . .

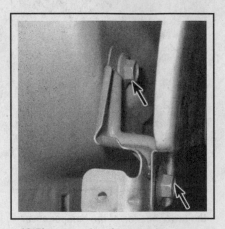

12.5b . . . and at the rear

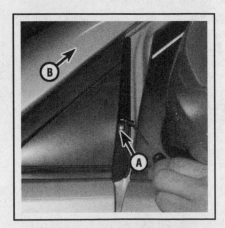

12.6a Use a screwdriver to remove the plug to access the panel screw (A). Slide the panel in the direction of arrow B to release it from the channel rails

12.6b Remove the upper fender mounting bolt

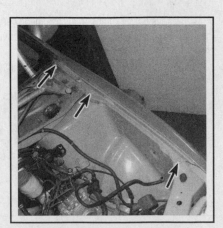

12.7 Remove the fender mounting bolts along the upper edge of the engine compartment

13 Radiator grille - removal and installation

2007 AND EARLIER MODELS

▶ **Refer to illustrations 13.1 and 13.2**

1 Remove the radiator cover (see illustration).
2 Remove the radiator grille push-pins (see illustration).
3 Lift the grille out and remove it.
4 Installation is the reverse of removal.

2008 AND LATER MODELS

5 Remove the front bumper (see Section 11).
6 Remove the six screws from the perimeter of the grille, then remove the grille molding. Remove the screws from the rear of the emblem and remove the emblem.
7 Remove the push-pin fasteners at the top corners of the grille.
8 Use a flat-blade screwdriver to release the hooks at the bottom of the grille, then pull out the grille.
9 Installation is the reverse of removal.

13.1 Location of the radiator cover push-pins (2004 and earlier models)

13.2 Location of the radiator grille retainers (2004 and earlier models)

14 Cowl cover and vent tray - removal and installation

▶ **Refer to illustrations 14.2a, 14.2b and 14.2c**

1 Remove the wiper arms (see Chapter 12).
2 Remove the push-pin fasteners and screws securing the cowl cover (see illustrations).

➡ **Note: Use a small screwdriver to pop the screw covers up to access the cowl cover mounting screws (see illustration).**

3 Installation is the reverse of removal.

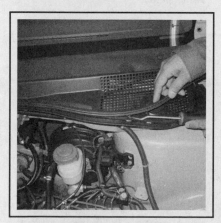

14.2a Use a panel tool to release the retainers and lift the moulding off the front edge of the cowl cover

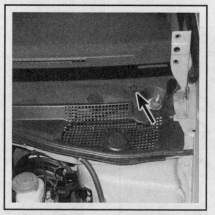

14.2b Remove the screw covers to access the cowl screws that border the upper edge - one shown; there are three total (2004 and earlier models)

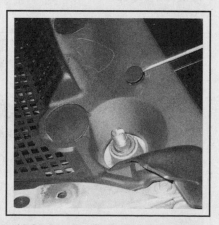

14.2c Remove the screw covers to access the cowl mounting screws

15 Door trim panels - removal and installation

⁜ WARNING:

The models covered by this manual are equipped with Supplemental Restraint systems (SRS), more commonly known as airbags. Always disable the airbag system before working in the vicinity of any airbag system component to avoid the possibility of accidental deployment of the airbag, which could cause personal injury (see Chapter 12).

1   Disconnect the cable from the negative terminal of the battery (see Chapter 5, Section 1).

2004 AND EARLIER MODELS

Front door

▶ **Refer to illustrations 15.3a, 15.3b, 15.4a, 15.4b, 15.6a, 15.6b and 15.8**

2   Remove the power mirror (see Section 20).
3   Remove the door handle screw cover (see illustration) and screw.

Carefully remove the door handle assembly, disconnect the latch rod from the bushing and disconnect the electrical connector (see illustration).

4   Remove the power window switch panel screw (see illustration). Lift the switch assembly from the door panel, disconnect the electrical connector (see illustration) and remove the switch assembly.

5   Remove the speaker mounting panel. Remove the speaker mounting screws (see Chapter 12), disconnect the speaker electrical connector and lift the speaker from the door trim panel.

6   Use a door panel tool and release the clips that retain the door trim panel (see illustrations).

7   Once all of the clips are disengaged, pull the lower edge of the trim panel away from the door, disconnect any electrical connectors and remove the trim panel from the vehicle by gently pulling it up and out.

8   For access to the inner door, peel back the watershield (see illustration), taking care not to tear it. To install the trim panel, first press the watershield back into place. If necessary, add more sealant to hold it in place.

9   The remainder of the installation is the reverse of removal. Reconnect the battery (see Chapter 5, Section 1).

15.3a Pry up the screw cover from the door handle assembly, then remove the screw

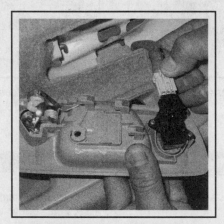

15.3b Disconnect the electrical connector from the door handle assembly

15.4a Pry up the cover and remove the screw from the power window switch panel

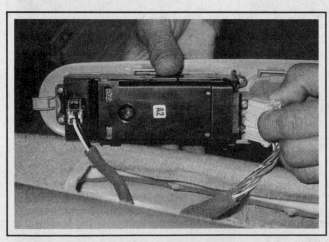

15.4b Disconnect the power window switch electrical connector

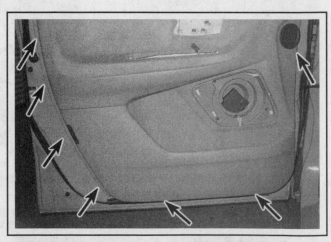

15.6a Use a door panel tool to release the clips on the door panel

Sliding door

▶ **Refer to illustrations 15.11, 15.12, 15.13 and 15.14**

10 Turn off the power sliding door main switch.

11 Release the clips that hold the rear and upper trim (see illustration) from the window directly above the power sliding door trim panel.

12 Remove the door handle by releasing the inner wire clip using a shop towel (see illustration).

13 Pry the screw cover and remove the panel mounting screw (see illustration).

14 Use a panel tool to remove the sliding door trim panel (see illustration).

➡ **Note: Door trim panel retaining clips are approximately six to ten inches apart. Pry at the clip location only. Prying in between clips will result in distorted or damaged door trim panels.**

15 Once all of the clips are disengaged, detach the trim panel and remove the trim panel from the vehicle by gently pulling it up and out.

16 For access to the inner door, peel back the watershield, taking care not to tear it. To install the trim panel, first press the watershield back into place. If necessary, add more sealant to hold it in place.

17 Installation is the reverse of removal. Reconnect the battery (see Chapter 5, Section 1).

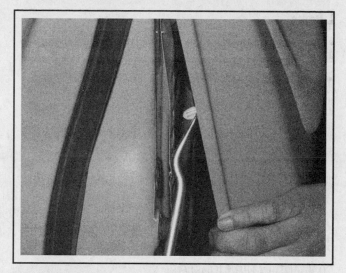

15.6b Be sure to position the door panel tool next to the clip when prying

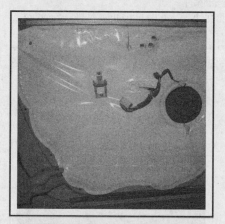

15.8 Peel back the watershield from the door

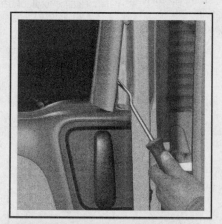

15.11 Use a panel tool to release the clips from the sliding door trim

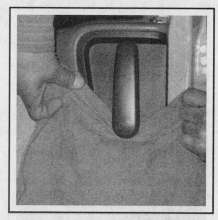

15.12 Use a shop towel to apply pressure to the release clip located at the bottom of the handle

15.13 Remove the panel mounting screw

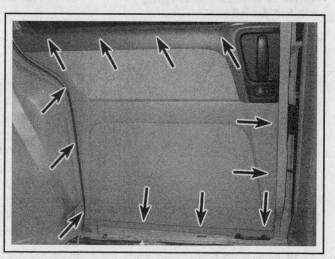

15.14 Locate the release clips on the perimeter of the sliding door trim panel

Liftgate

▶ **Refer to illustrations 15.18a, 15.18b, 15.18c, 15.19, 15.20 and 15.21**

18 Remove the liftgate upper trim (see illustrations).

19 Remove the liftgate grab handle (see illustration). On models with a power liftgate, pry out the Close switch, then disconnect the wiring.

20 Remove the liftgate trim panel screws (see illustration).

21 Using a screwdriver or trim panel removal tool, pry out the clips and remove the trim panel from the liftgate (see illustration).

22 Prior to installation of the liftgate panel, be sure to reinstall any clips in the panel which may have come out when you removed the panel.

23 Press the liftgate panel into place until the clips are seated.

24 The remainder of the installation is the reverse of removal. Reconnect the battery (see Chapter 5, Section 1).

2005 AND LATER MODELS

Front door

25 Raise the glass.

26 Carefully pry out the rear part of the door latch handle bezel to release the two hooks. Remove the screws of the handle.

27 Use a plastic trim tool or a screwdriver wrapped with tape to pry up the rear of the window switch panel. Work the tool around toward the front, releasing the hooks on the sides and front. Lift the switch assembly and disconnect the wiring.

28 Remove the door panel screws.

29 Use a door panel tool or a putty knife to release the door panel clips.

30 Lift the rear of the panel, then release the lock button. Remove the door panel.

31 Follow Steps 8 and 9 for the remainder of the procedure

Sliding door

32 Lower the glass fully.

33 Use a plastic trim tool or a screwdriver wrapped with tape to pry up the rear of the window switch panel. Work the tool around toward the front, releasing the hooks on the sides and front. Lift the switch assembly and disconnect the wiring.

34 Use a window clip tool to remove the retaining clip from the inside handle.

➡ **Note: A shop towel can also be used if necessary (see illustration 15.12).**

Pull off the handle.

35 Pry off the lower sections of the window trim molding to allow clearance for door panel removal.

36 Follow Steps 14 through 17 for the remainder of the procedure.

15.18a Remove the liftgate upper trim from the left side . . .

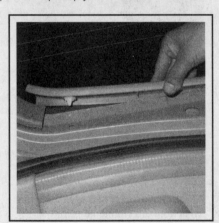

15.18b . . . the middle section . . .

15.18c . . . and the right side of the liftgate

15.19 Remove the screw covers and the mounting screws from the grab handle

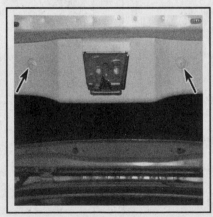

15.20 Remove the liftgate trim panel screws

15.21 Use a panel tool to release the panel clips and remove the liftgate trim panel

16 Door - removal, installation and adjustment

※※ WARNING:

The models covered by this manual are equipped with Supplemental Restraint systems (SRS), more commonly known as airbags. Always disable the airbag system before working in the vicinity of any airbag system component to avoid the possibility of accidental deployment of the airbag, which could cause personal injury (see Chapter 12).

➡ **Note: The door is heavy and somewhat awkward to remove and install - at least two people should perform this procedure.**

REMOVAL AND INSTALLATION

Front door

▶ **Refer to illustration 16.8, 16.9a and 16.9b**

1   Raise the window completely in the door, then disconnect the cable from negative terminal of the battery (see Chapter 5, Section 1).

2   Open the door all the way and support it on jacks or blocks covered with rags to prevent damaging the paint.

3   Remove the door trim panel and watershield (see Section 15).

4   Remove the door speaker (see Chapter 12).

5   Unplug all electrical connections, ground wires and harness retaining clips from the door.

➡ **Note: It is a good idea to label all connections to aid the reassembly process.**

6   Working through the door opening, detach the rubber conduit between the body and the door. Then pull the wiring harness through the conduit hole and remove it from the door.

7   Mark around the door hinges with a pen or a scribe to facilitate realignment during reassembly.

8   Remove the door stop strut (see illustration).

9   Have an assistant hold the door, remove the hinge-to-door bolts (see illustrations) from the upper and lower hinge and lift the door off.

10   Installation is the reverse of the removal. Reconnect the cable to the negative terminal of the battery (see Chapter 5, Section 1).

Sliding door

2004 and earlier models

▶ **Refer to illustrations 16.12, 16.13, 16.15, 16.16 and 16.17**

11   Open the sliding door several inches and support it on jacks or blocks covered with rags to prevent damaging the paint. Turn the power sliding door main switch off.

12   Remove the sliding door sill trim (see illustration).

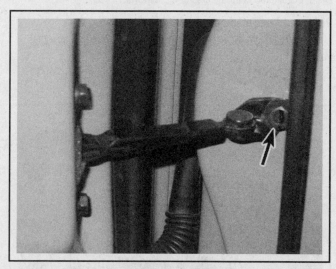

16.8 Remove the bolt from the door stop strut

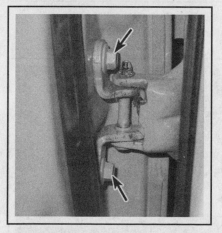

16.9a Remove the bolts from the top door hinge

16.9b Remove the bolts from the lower door hinge

16.12 Carefully remove the sill trim from the body by lifting along the inner edge to release the clips

13 On power sliding doors, remove the bolt and the stop spring (see illustration).

➡ **Note: On manual sliding doors, remove the lower roller plate.**

14 Slide the door to fully open.

15 Mark the edges of the hinge with paint and remove the bolts securing the center roller (see illustration).

16 Move the door and align the lower roller sub-base with the notch in the lower rail (see illustration). Carefully maneuver the lower roller sub-base with through the notch.

17 Hold the sliding door away from the body and slide it forward until the upper roller lines up with the notch in the upper rail (see illustration). Carefully remove the upper roller through the notch.

18 With the help of an assistant, lift the sliding door away from the body and remove it from the vehicle.

19 Installation is the reverse of the removal.

2005 and later models

20 Pull up the door sill trim panel, releasing the hooks and clips as you do so.

21 Disconnect the CESS wiring. Remove the bolt, disconnect the hooks and remove the wiring harness.

22 Remove the lower roller plate, the middle stop and the full-open stop.

23 Pull off the upper rail cover. It's attached by clips and double-sided tape; you may have to use a knife to cut the tape.

24 Have as assistant hold the door, then remove the bolts securing the roller along the middle of the door.

25 Pull the bottom of the door away from the body, then slide it so that the upper roller aligns with the notch in the top rail. Pull the top of the door out and lift it free of the vehicle.

ADJUSTMENT

Front door

▶ **Refer to illustration 16.29**

26 Having proper door-to-body alignment is a critical part of a well-functioning door assembly. First check the door hinge pins for excessive play. Fully open the door and lift up and down on the door without lifting the body. If a door has 1/16-inch or more excessive play, the hinges should be replaced.

16.13 Remove the bolt and the stop spring - power sliding door shown

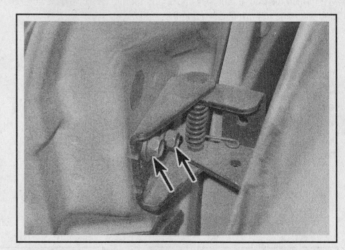

16.15 Remove the bolts from the center roller hinge

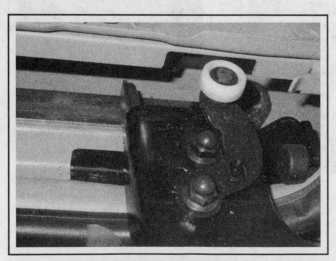

16.16 Remove the lower roller sub-base through the notch in the subrail

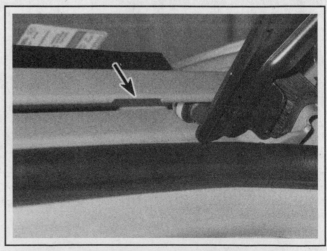

16.17 Remove the upper roller through the notch in the upper rail

27 Door-to-body alignment adjustments are made by loosening the hinge-to-body or hinge-to-door bolts and moving the door. Proper body alignment is achieved when the top of door is aligned parallel with the roof panel and the bottom of the door is aligned parallel with the lower rocker panel. If these goals can't be reached by adjusting the hinge-to-body or hinge-to-door bolts, body alignment shims may have to be purchased and inserted behind the hinges to achieve correct alignment.

28 To adjust the door closed position, first check that the door latch is contacting the center of the latch striker. If not, remove striker and add or subtract shims to achieve correct alignment.

29 Finally, adjust the latch striker as necessary (up-and-down or sideways) to provide positive engagement with the latch mechanism (see illustration) and so the door panel is flush with the center pillar.

Sliding door

30 Turn the power sliding door main switch off, if equipped.

31 Adjust the door gap(s) position by loosening the center roller bolts and moving the door as necessary (see illustration 16.15). Proper door alignment is achieved when the gap at the front of the door is smaller (approximately 0.18 inch) than the rear of the door (approximately 0.33 inch). Loosen the bolts and move the door into position by sliding the center roller hinge up or down and/or sideways.

➡ **Note: If the sliding door is significantly out of alignment, slightly loosen the bolts on the door stops and also turn the door cushion bumper clockwise, fully extended. This will allow additional sliding door movement.**

32 To adjust the door overhang (outward extension), first check that the door latch is contacting the center of the rear latch striker (up and down adjustment). Second, adjust latch striker as necessary (side-to-side adjustment) to provide positive engagement with the latch mechanism and to align the door panel with the rear quarter panel. The sliding door should not overhang the rear quarter panel by more than 0.02 inch.

33 To adjust the upper door alignment with the body, remove the upper roller bolts and install the necessary shims. Position the sliding door level with the upper body and flush with the front door.

34 To adjust the lower door with the body, loosen the three bolts on

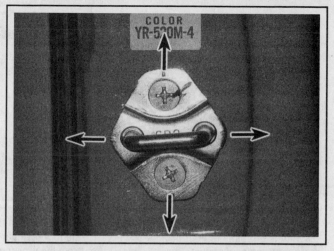

16.29 Adjust the door lock striker by loosening the mounting screws and gently tapping the striker in the desired direction

the lower roller and position the sliding door level with the lower body and flush with the front door. Loosen the lower roller bottom nut and adjust the door in or out until the door is tight against the seals.

35 Gripping the leading edge of the door, pull the door in and out and inspect the alignment with the seals. The sliding door should rest tightly against the seals. Check the top-to-bottom alignment of the sliding door. Readjust if necessary.

36 Remove the weatherstrip from the front edge of the sliding door opening. Turn on the power sliding door main switch, if equipped. Hold a piece of paper between the door and the cushion. The paper should slide out, even and tight. If the paper slides quickly or not at all, readjust the cushion.

37 Tighten the door stops if they were loosened (see Step 31). Alternate between the top and the bottom bolts until all four bolts are tight. This will prevent the stops from pivoting during the tightening sequence.

17 Door latch, lock cylinder and handles - removal and installation

1 Remove the door trim panel and watershield as described in Section 15.

➡ **Note: This step applies to both the front and sliding doors.**

FRONT DOOR

Outside handle and lock cylinder

◆ **Refer to illustrations 17.2a, 17.2b, 17.3a, 17.3b, 17.4, 17.6a, 17.6b, 17.7 and 17.8**

2 Remove the glass run channel mounting bolt (see illustration) and pull the assembly out (see illustration).

➡ **Note: The glass run channel and the center lower channel must be removed as one complete assembly.**

17.2a Remove the glass run channel bolt from the outer door

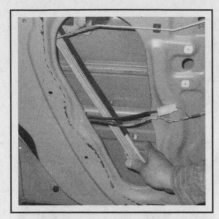

17.2b Remove the glass run channel assembly through the door access hole - early model shown

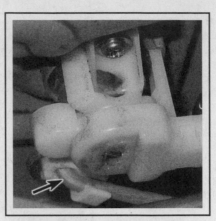

17.3a Remove the cylinder rod from the lock cylinder by releasing it first from the pressure clip and rotating it out of the bushing

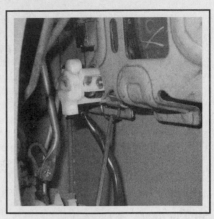

17.3b Use a pick to pull the mounting clip down

17.4 The lock cylinder mounting screw is located behind the assembly

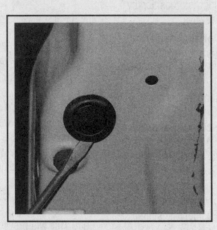

17.6a Remove the access cover . . .

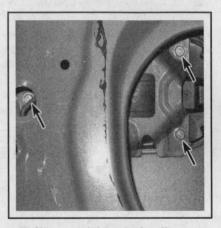

17.6b . . . and the outer handle mounting bolts

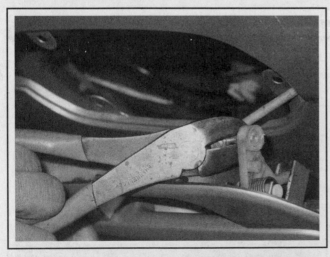

17.7 Use cutting pliers to pull the handle away from the door and pry carefully to separate the link rod from the bushing

3   Disconnect the cylinder rod (see illustration) and remove the mounting clip (see illustration).

4   Remove the mounting screw and separate the lock cylinder from the lock switch (see illustration).

5   Disconnect the lock cylinder switch connector and release the harness clip from the door.

6   Remove the access cover and the outer handle mounting bolts (see illustrations).

7   Pull the outer handle away from the door and remove the link rod from the joint (see illustration).

8   Replace the bushing on the outer handle (see illustration).

9   Installation is the reverse of removal.

Door latch

▶ **Refer to illustrations 17.13, 17.14 and 17.15**

10 Raise the window completely in the door.

11 Remove the outside handle (see Steps 2 through 9).

12 Working through the access hole in the door frame, remove the mounting screw for the lock rod protector.

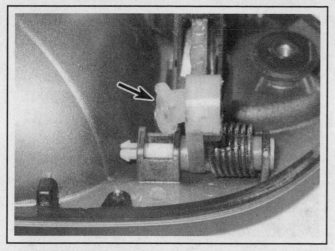

17.8 Replace the bushing

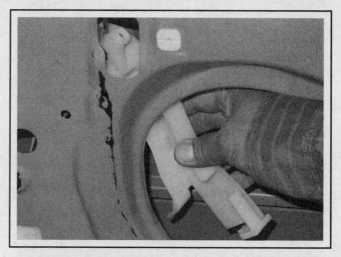

17.13 Remove the lock rod protector through the door access hole

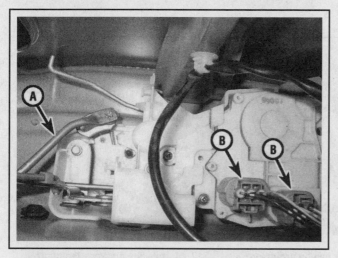

17.14 Disconnect the electrical connectors (B) and the inner handle rod (A) from the latch

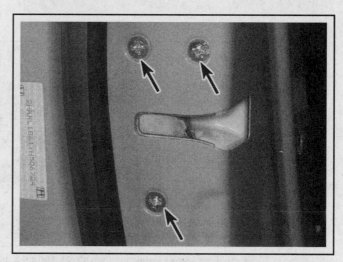

17.15 Remove the latch mounting screws

13 Unhook the lock rod protector from the door and remove it through the access hole (see illustration).

14 Disconnect the electrical connectors (see illustration) and the inner handle rod from the latch.

15 Remove the latch mounting screws (see illustration).

16 Remove the latch assembly through the access hole. Remove the latch assembly carefully to avoid bending the inner handle rod, the cylinder rod and the lock rod.

17 Installation is the reverse of removal. Make sure the lock rods are connected properly and the door opens and closes correctly.

SLIDING DOOR

Door outside handle

▶ **Refer to illustrations 17.19, 17.21, 17.22a, 17.22b, 17.23, 17.24, 17.25 and 17.26**

18 Disconnect the cable from negative terminal of the battery (see Chapter 5, Section 1).

19 Remove the lock knob mounting screws (see illustration).

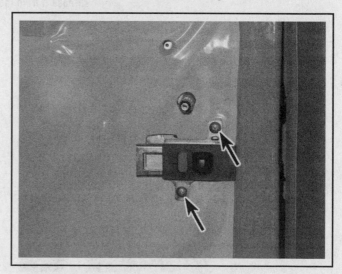

17.19 Remove the lock knob mounting screws

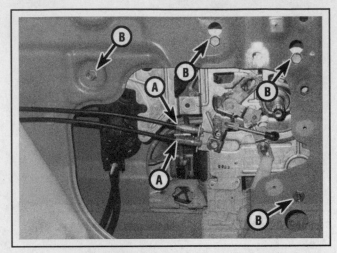

17.21 Location of the door latch cables (A) and the door latch mounting bolts (B)

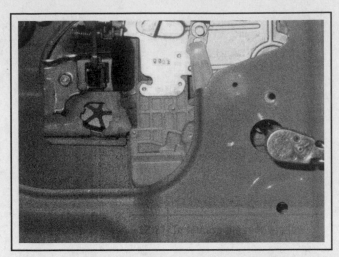

17.22a The door handle bolts can be removed through a lower access hole . . .

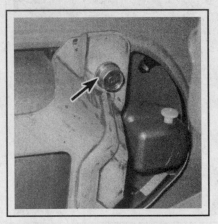

17.22b . . . and the door access hole (two bolts shown, three bolts total)

17.23 Hold the door handle protector using one hand and pull the door handle out with the other hand to release it from the clip

17.24 Note the distance the outer handle rod extends from the joint (distance between arrows)

17.25 Use cutting pliers to pry the joint from the bushing on the linkage

20 Remove the door latch cables (see illustration 17.21).

21 Remove the lower bolt and loosen the upper door lock remote control mounting bolts (see illustration). Move the remote control assembly up and to the rear but do not remove it from the door at this time.

22 Remove the outside handle mounting bolts (see illustrations).

23 Remove the outside handle from the handle protector by holding the protector and pulling out to release the clip (see illustration). Remove the handle protector.

24 Note the distance the outer handle rod extends from the joint (see illustration). Make a note for proper reassembly.

25 Position a shop rag between the outside handle and the door. Use cutting pliers to pry the joint from the linkage on the outside handle (see illustration).

26 Replace the bushing (see illustration).

27 Installation is the reverse of removal. Reconnect the cable to the negative terminal of the battery (see Chapter 5, Section 1). Make sure the outer handle rod is connected properly and the door opens and closes correctly.

17.26 Replace the bushing

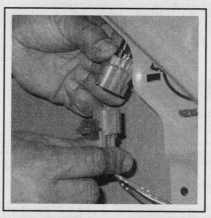

17.30 Disconnect the door lock actuator connector

17.31 Remove the door lock remote control through the access hole in the door

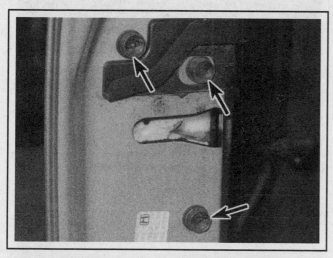

17.34a Location of the outer latch mounting bolts . . .

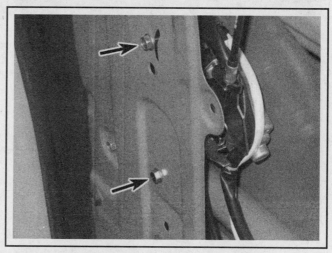

17.34b . . . and the inside latch mounting bolts

28 Re-home the power sliding door control module (see Steps 39 through 44).

Door lock remote control

▶ **Refer to illustrations 17.30 and 17.31**

29 Remove the sliding door outside handle (see Steps 18 through 28).

30 Disconnect the door lock actuator connector and the power release actuator connector from the remote control (see illustration).

31 Remove all the door lock remote control mounting bolts (see illustration 17.21) and remove the remote control through the access hole in the door (see illustration).

32 Installation is the reverse of removal.

33 Re-home the power sliding door control module (see Steps 39 through 44).

Latch

▶ **Refer to illustrations 17.34a and 17.34b**

34 Remove the bolts securing the latch to the door jamb and the inner door (see illustrations).

35 Working through the large access hole, disengage the door latch cable, the lower roller lever cable and the power door closer connector, if equipped.

36 Working through the large access hole, remove the latch from the sliding door.

37 Installation is the reverse of removal. Check the operation of the door locks. Adjust the door latch cable and the auto-close cable. Each cable has a bracket and a mounting bolt. Loosen the mounting bolt and slide the cable bracket to tension the cable or loosen the cable.

38 Re-home the power sliding door control module (see Steps 39 through 44).

Re-homing the power sliding door

39 Close the power sliding door.

40 Turn off the power sliding door main switch.

41 Manually open the power sliding door partially.

42 Turn on the power sliding door main switch.

43 Press the close button and hold it until the power sliding door is completely closed.

44 Repeat the procedure for the other power sliding door.

18 Door window glass - removal and installation

▶ Refer to illustrations 18.2 and 18.6

❋❋ **CAUTION:**

Wear gloves when working inside the door openings to protect against cuts from sharp metal edges.

1   Remove the door trim panel and the plastic watershield (see Section 15).

2   Remove the pull pocket bracket (see illustration).

3   On 2003 and later models, remove the power window control unit bracket.

4   Raise the window just enough to access the window retaining bolts through the holes in the door frame (see illustration 18.2).

5   Place a rag over the glass to help prevent scratching the glass and remove the two glass mounting bolts.

6   Remove the glass by pulling it up and out (see illustration).

7   Installation is the reverse of removal.

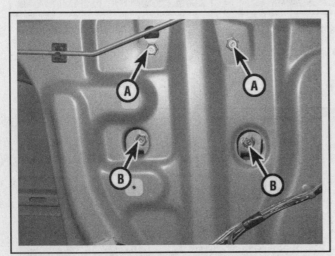

18.2 Location of the pull pocket bracket mounting bolts (A) and the window glass retaining bolts (B)

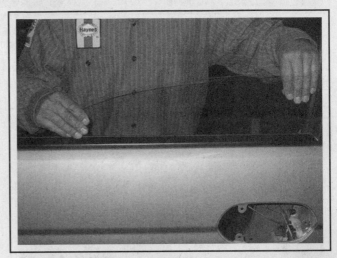

18.6 Remove the door glass by tilting it slightly and lifting up

19 Door window glass regulator - removal and installation

▶ Refer to illustrations 19.4 and 19.5

❋❋ **CAUTION:**

Wear gloves when working inside the door openings to protect against cuts from sharp metal edges.

1   Remove the door trim panel and the plastic watershield (see Section 15).

2   Remove the door window glass (see Section 18).

3   Disconnect the cable from the negative battery terminal (see Chapter 5, Section 1).

4   Disconnect the regulator connector (see illustration).

➥ **Note: On 2003 and later models, disconnect the regulator connector at the door harness bracket.**

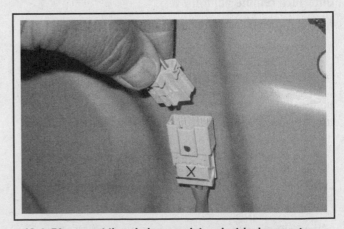

19.4 Disconnect the window regulator electrical connector

5   Remove the regulator mounting bolts and loosen the motor assembly mounting bolts (see illustration).

6   Remove the window regulator/motor assembly from the door.

7   Reconnect the battery (see Chapter 5, Section 1).

8   Installation is the reverse of removal. Lubricate the rollers and wear points on the regulator with white grease before installation.

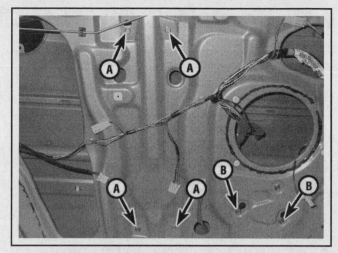

19.5   Remove the regulator mounting bolts (A) and loosen the motor assembly mounting bolts (B)

20   Mirrors - removal and installation

▶ **Refer to illustrations 20.2, 20.4 and 20.5**

1   Lower the door glass.

2   On 2004 and earlier models, pry off the mirror mount cover (see illustration). On 2005 and later models, lift the cover to release the hook, then pull off the cover.

3   If you're removing a power mirror, remove the front door trim panel (see Section 15).

4   If you're removing a power mirror, disconnect the electrical connector from the mirror (see illustration).

5   Remove the four mirror retaining bolts and push out the spring clip to detach the mirror (see illustration).

6   Installation is the reverse of removal. Be sure to position the spring clip into place correctly.

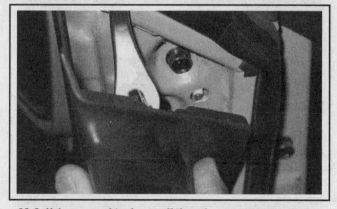

20.2   Using a panel tool, pry off the mirror mount cover

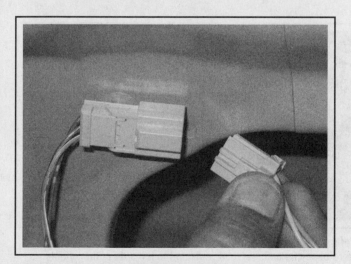

20.4   Disconnect the power mirror connector

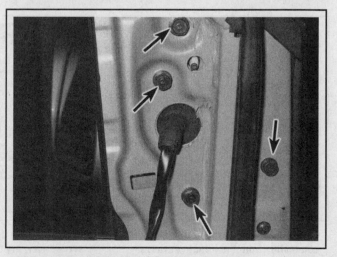

20.5   Location of the mirror retaining bolts

21 Liftgate - removal, installation and adjustment

➡ **Note: The liftgate is heavy and somewhat awkward to remove and install - at least two people should perform this procedure.**

REMOVAL AND INSTALLATION

▶ **Refer to illustrations 21.2, 21.4, 21.7, 21.9 and 21.10**

1   Remove the liftgate trim panel (see Section 15).
2   Remove the nuts from the liftgate spoiler (see illustration).
3   Disconnect the rear window washer inlet hose.
4   Remove the access cap from the liftgate (see illustration). Disengage the clip underneath.
5   Slowly lower liftgate and remove the liftgate spoiler. Partially lift the spoiler and disconnect the high mount brake light connector.
6   Have an assistant hold the door in the open position.
7   Disconnect all electrical connections, ground wires and harness retaining clips from the door (see illustration).

8   Detach the rubber conduit between the body and the liftgate. Then pull the wiring harness through the conduit hole and remove it from the liftgate.
9   Remove the liftgate support struts (see illustration).
10 With an assistant holding the door, remove the hinge-to-door bolts and lift the door off (see illustration).

➡ **Note: Draw a reference line around the hinges before removing the bolts.**

11 Installation is the reverse of removal.

ADJUSTMENT

12 Having proper liftgate-to-body alignment is a critical part of a well-functioning liftgate assembly. First check the liftgate hinge pins for excessive play. Fully open the liftgate and move it side-to-side without moving the body. If a liftgate has 1/16-inch or more excessive play, the hinges should be replaced.

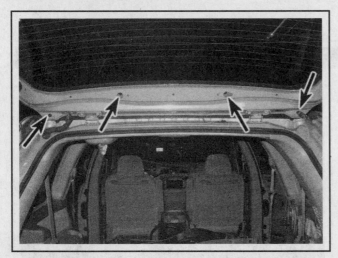

21.2 Remove the nuts that retain the liftgate spoiler to the top of the liftgate

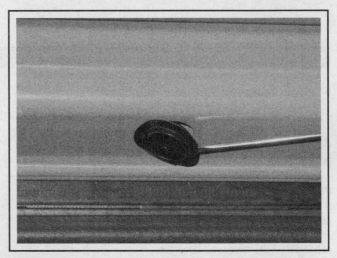

21.4 Use a small screwdriver and pry the access cap from the liftgate

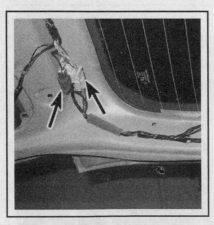

21.7 Disconnect the electrical connectors from the liftgate harness

21.9 Using the tip of a small screwdriver, pry the release clip and slide the strut off the ballstud

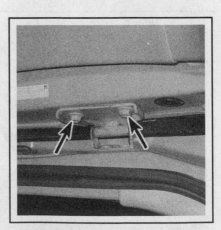

21.10 Location of the liftgate hinge nuts on the left side of the vehicle

13 Liftgate-to-body alignment adjustments are made by disconnecting the liftgate support struts while an assistant holds the liftgate in position (see illustration 21.9) and loosening the hinge-to-body bolts or hinge-to-liftgate bolts and moving the liftgate. Proper body alignment is achieved when the top of the liftgate is parallel with the roof section and the sides of the liftgate are flush with the rear quarter panels and the bottom of the liftgate is aligned with the lower liftgate sill. If these goals can't be reached by adjusting the hinge-to-body or hinge-to-liftgate bolts, body alignment shims may have to be purchased and inserted behind the hinges to achieve correct alignment.

14 To adjust the liftgate-closed position, scribe a line or mark around the striker plate to provide a reference point, then check that the liftgate latch is contacting the center of the latch striker. If not, adjust the up and down position first.

15 Finally adjust the latch striker sideways position, so that the liftgate panel is flush with the rear quarter panel and provides positive engagement with the latch mechanism.

22 Liftgate latch, lock cylinder and handle - removal and installation

LIFTGATE LATCH

▶ Refer to illustrations 22.2, 22.3 and 22.4

1 Open the liftgate and remove the door trim panel and watershield as described in Section 15.

2 Disconnect the actuating rods from the liftgate latch (see illustration).

➡ Note: All door lock rods are attached by plastic clips. The plastic clips can be removed by unsnapping the portion engaging the connecting rod and then pulling the rod out of its locating hole.

3 Remove the liftgate latch electrical connectors (see illustration).

4 Remove the screws securing the latch to the door (see illustration). Remove the latch assembly through the door opening.

5 Installation is the reverse of removal.

LIFTGATE LOCK CYLINDER

▶ Refer to illustration 22.7

6 Open the liftgate and remove the trim panel as described in Section 15.

7 Disconnect the actuating rod from the lock cylinder (see illustration).

➡ Note: The door lock rod is attached by a plastic clip. The plastic clip can be removed by unsnapping the portion engaging the connecting rod and then pulling the rod out of its locating hole.

8 Disconnect the lock cylinder connector (see illustration 22.7).

9 Remove the lock cylinder mounting bolt and rotate the assembly 45-degrees (see illustration 22.7). Remove the lock cylinder from the liftgate.

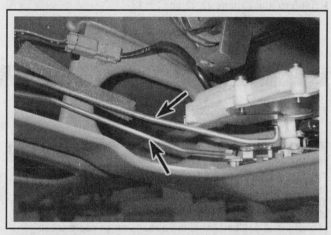

22.2 Unsnap the actuating rods at the plastic clips on the door latch

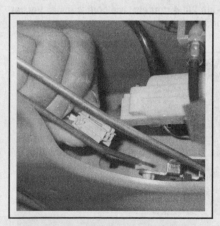

22.3 Remove the liftgate latch electrical connector

22.4 Remove the latch mounting screws

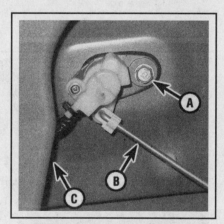

22.7 Disconnect the actuating rod (B), the electrical connector (C) and remove the mounting bolt (A) to separate the lock cylinder from the liftgate

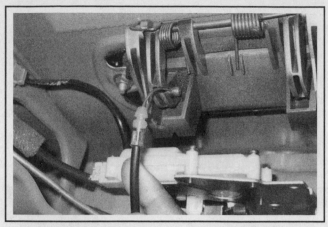

22.12 Rotate the cable and slide it through the slotted portion of the handle lever

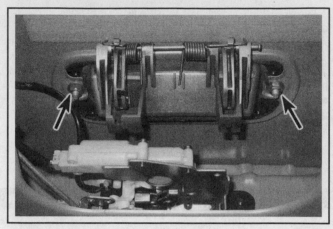

22.13 Remove the liftgate handle mounting nuts

10 The remainder of the installation is the reverse of removal.

LIFTGATE HANDLE

▶ **Refer to illustrations 22.12 and 22.13**

11 Open the liftgate and remove the door trim panel and watershield

as described in Section 15.
12 Disconnect the handle cable from the assembly (see illustration).
13 Remove the liftgate handle mounting nuts (see illustration).
14 Remove the liftgate handle from the liftgate.
15 The remainder of the installation is the reverse of removal.

23 Center console - removal and installation

▶ **Refer to illustrations 23.2, 23.3, 23.4 and 23.5**

✳ WARNING:

The models covered by this manual are equipped with Supplemental Restraint systems (SRS), more commonly known as airbags. Always disable the airbag system before working in the vicinity of any airbag system component to avoid the possibility of accidental deployment of the airbag, which could cause personal injury (see Chapter 12).

➡ **Note: This procedure applies only to 2004 and earlier models.**

1 Disconnect the cable from the negative battery terminal (see Chapter 5, Section 1).
2 Remove the push pins from the center lower console panel (see illustration).

➡ **Note: On 2002 through 2004 models with built-in navigation systems, remove the six panel clips and slide the assembly out.**

3 Remove the center lower pocket mounting screws (see illustration).

➡ **Note: On 2002 through 2004 models, the center lower pocket is designed to accommodate the navigation system unit.**

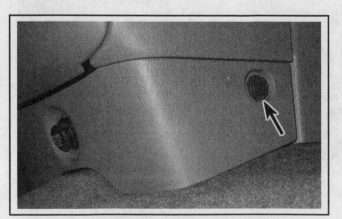

23.2 First release the interior locking tab using a screwdriver, then pull the push pin from the console panel

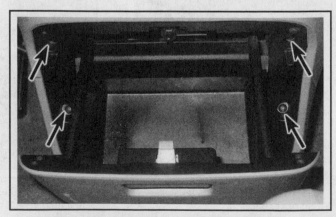

23.3 Remove the center lower pocket mounting screws

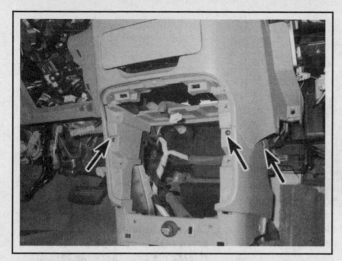

23.4 Remove the panel screws from the center lower console

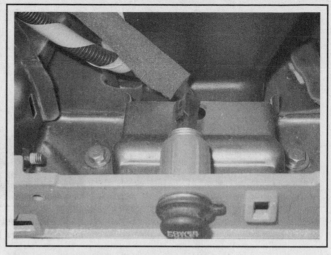

23.5 Disconnect the accessory socket connector

4 Remove the center lower console panel screws (see illustration).
5 Disconnect the accessory socket (see illustration).
6 Lift the center lower console from the vehicle.

7 Installation is the reverse of removal.
8 Reconnect the battery (see Chapter 5, Section 1).

24 Dashboard trim panels

⁂ WARNING:

The models covered by this manual are equipped with Supplemental Restraint systems (SRS), more commonly known as airbags. Always disable the airbag system before working in the vicinity of any airbag system component to avoid the possibility of accidental deployment of the airbag, which could cause personal injury (see Chapter 12).

2004 AND EARLIER MODELS

Instrument cluster bezel

▸ **Refer to illustrations 24.5, 24.6 and 24.7**

1 Disconnect the cable from the negative battery terminal (see Chapter 5, Section 1).
2 Remove the driver's switch panel (see Steps 18 through 21).
3 Remove the center trim panel (see Steps 11 through 17).
4 Tilt the steering column down.
5 Remove the screws at the top of the instrument cluster bezel (see illustration).

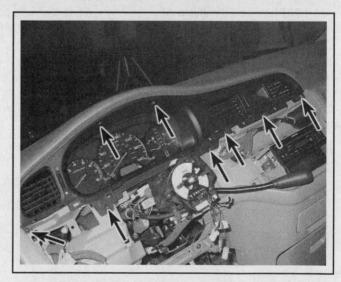

24.5 Remove the screws from the instrument cluster bezel

24.6 Grasp the bezel firmly and pull out

24.7 Disconnect the electrical connectors from the switches

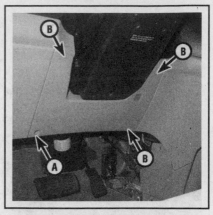

24.10a First remove the mounting screw (A) and use a panel tool to release the clips (B) on the back of the lower trim panel

24.10b Disconnect the electrical connectors from the back of the lower trim panel

24.13 Carefully pry the center trim panel using a panel tool

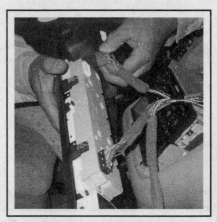

24.14a Disconnect the electrical connectors from the climate control panel . . .

6   Grasp the bezel with both hands and pull straight out to disengage the bezel from the instrument panel (see illustration).

7   Disconnect the electrical connectors from the instrument cluster bezel (see illustration).

8   Installation is the reverse of the removal procedure. Make sure the clips are engaged properly before pushing the bezel firmly into place.

9   Reconnect the battery (see Chapter 5, Section 1).

Lower trim panel

▶ **Refer to illustrations 24.10a and 24.10b**

10 Remove the mounting screws, swing the trim panel down, disconnect the electrical connectors and remove it from the instrument panel (see illustrations).

Center trim panel

▶ **Refer to illustration 24.13, 24.14a and 24.14b**

11 Disconnect the cable from the negative battery terminal (see Chapter 5, Section 1).

12 Remove the steering column covers (see Section 25).

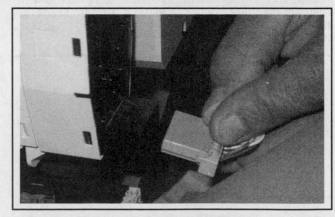

24.14b . . . and from the interior light switch

13 Using a panel tool, pry the center trim panel out (see illustration).

14 Disconnect the electrical connectors from the accessories (see illustrations).

15 Remove the center trim panel from the dash area.

24.19 Use a panel tool to pry the driver's switch panel

24.20 Disconnect all the electrical connectors from the backside of the driver's switch panel

24.22 Pull out the stop from each side of the glovebox

16 Installation is the reverse of removal. Make sure the clips are engaged properly before pushing the bezel firmly into place.

17 Reconnect the battery (see Chapter 5, Section 1).

Driver's switch panel

▶ **Refer to illustrations 24.19 and 24.20**

18 Disconnect the cable from the negative battery terminal (see Chapter 5, Section 1).

19 Carefully pry out on the driver's switch panel to release the clips from the left side (see illustration).

20 Disconnect the electrical connectors from the accessories (see illustration).

21 Installation is the reverse of removal. Reconnect the battery (see Chapter 5, Section 1).

Glove box

▶ **Refer to illustrations 24.22 and 24.23**

22 Open the glove box and pry the stops out to allow the compartment to drop (see illustration).

23 Remove the mounting bolts (see illustration).

24 Installation is the reverse of removal.

2005 AND LATER MODELS

Instrument cluster bezel

25 Tilt the steering column all the way down, then telescope it all the way out.

26 Carefully pull out at the bottom edge of the panel until the clips and hooks are released.

27 Work your way to the top of the panel, pulling out until all the retainers are free. Pull off the bezel.

28 Installation is the reverse of removal.

Center trim panel

29 Open the glove box. Use a plastic trim tool or a screwdriver wrapped with tape to carefully pry up the edge of the trim panel, releasing the clips as you go. Work your way around until all clips have been released.

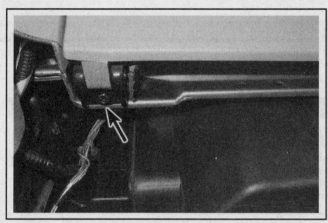

24.23 Remove the mounting bolts and detach the glovebox from the dash

30 Pull the panel off, then disconnect the wiring from the rear of the panel.

31 Installation is the reverse of removal.

End panels and driver's switch panel

32 Open the door and pry the front of the end panel out to release the hooks.

33 When you can grasp the front of the panel, pull it off carefully to release the other hooks.

34 Reach through the end panel hole and release the hook at the bottom of the driver's switch panel.

35 Push out the bottom of the panel, then continue to pry out the sides and upper part of the panel.

36 Pull out the panel and disconnect the wiring from the switches.

37 Installation is the reverse of removal.

Steering column lower trim panel

38 Remove the screw from the center bottom of the panel.

39 Pull out, starting at the bottom of the panel, to release the clips and hooks.

40 Disconnect any wiring or hoses.

41 Installation is the reverse of removal.

Center lower trim panel

42 Pry out the button-type retainers, then pull off the lower side covers (near the driver's right foot and the passenger's left foot).

43 Open the cup holder and remove the four mounting screws. Remove the cup holder assembly.

44 Use a plastic trim tool or a screwdriver wrapped with tape to carefully pry out the center lower trim panel, releasing each clip as you work your way around.

45 Pull the cover out and disconnect the wiring for the seat heater (if equipped).

46 Installation is the reverse of removal.

Passenger's lower trim panel

47 Pull down the edge nearest the rear of the vehicle to release the clips.

48 Pull the cover to the rear to detach the front pins. Remove the cover.

49 Installation is the reverse of removal.

Glove box

50 Open the glove box, then release the damper on the left side.

51 Pull out the stop from each side of the glove box.

52 Remove the two bolts from the bottom of the glove box.

53 Installation is the reverse of removal.

25 Steering column covers - removal and installation

◗ Refer to illustrations 25.2a, 25.2b and 25.2c

❊❊ WARNING:

The models covered by this manual are equipped with Supplemental Restraint systems (SRS), more commonly known as airbags. Always disable the airbag system before working in the vicinity of any airbag system component to avoid the possibility of accidental deployment of the airbag, which could cause personal injury (see Chapter 12).

1 On tilt steering columns, move the column to the lowest position.

2 Remove the screws, then separate the halves and remove the upper and lower steering column covers (see illustrations).

3 Installation is the reverse of the removal procedure.

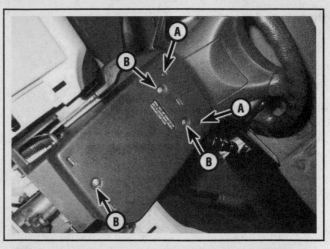

25.2a First remove the upper steering column cover screws (A) and remove the column fasteners (B)

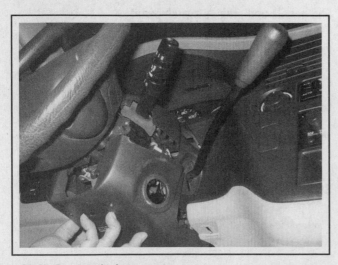

25.2b Remove the lower cover . . .

25.2c . . . and the upper cover

26 Instrument panel - removal and installation

2004 AND EARLIER MODELS

♦ Refer to illustrations 26.4a, 26.4b, 26.7a, 26.7b, 26.8a, 26.8b, 26.9, 26.11a, 26.11b, 26.12, 26.13a, 26.13b, 26.13c, 26.13d, 26.16a, 26.16b, 26.17a and 26.17b

1 Disconnect the cable from the negative battery terminal (see Chapter 5, Section 1).
2 Remove the lower trim panel (see Section 24).
3 Remove the center console (see Section 23).
4 Remove the driver's and passenger's heater covers (see illustrations).
5 Remove the glovebox (see Section 24).

6 On tilt steering columns, move the column to the lowest position. Refer to Chapter 10 and remove the steering column.
7 Remove the front door opening trim (see illustrations).
8 Remove the side kick panels (see illustrations).
9 Remove the front pillar trim (see illustration).

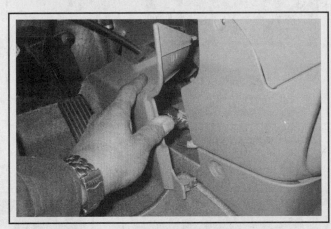

26.4a Remove the left side heater cover (by carefully releasing the clips on the back of the panel) . . .

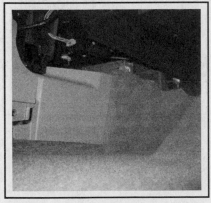

26.4b . . . and the right side heater cover

26.7a Remove the fuel door handle

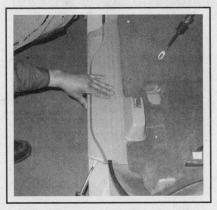

26.7b Pry the front door opening trim from the body

26.8a Pull off the rubber trim piece from the side kick panels . . .

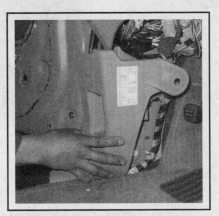

26.8b . . . then remove the screw and detach the side kick panel

26.9 Remove the front pillar trim by carefully releasing the clips

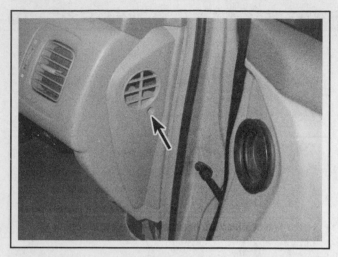

26.11a **Remove the dashboard side cover mounting screw . . .**

10 Remove the front pillar corner trim from the driver's side (see Section 12).

11 Remove the dashboard side covers (see illustrations).

12 Remove the fuse/relay box (see illustration).

13 Remove the instrument panel electrical connectors (see illustrations).

➡ **Note: A number of electrical connectors must be disconnected in order to remove the instrument panel. Most are designed so that they will only fit on the matching connector (male or female), but if there is any doubt, mark the connectors with masking tape and a marking pen before disconnecting them.**

14 Disconnect the harness for the GPS antenna, if equipped.

15 Remove the ground strap for the airbag at the airbag control unit (see Chapter 12).

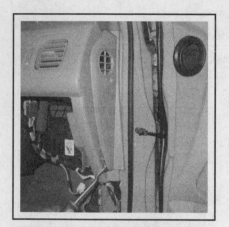

26.11b **. . . and pry the cover off using a panel tool**

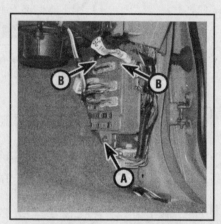

26.12 **Remove the mounting bolt (A) and release the tabs (B) to separate the fuse/relay box from the side panel**

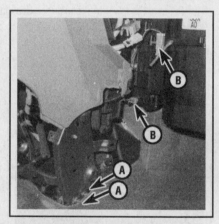

26.13a **Location of the instrument panel center mount bolts (A) and electrical connectors (B)**

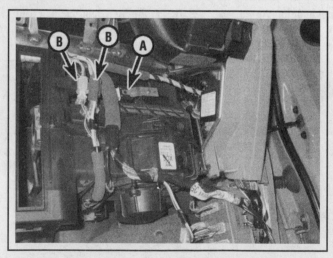

26.13b **Location of the blower relay (A) and the connectors (B)**

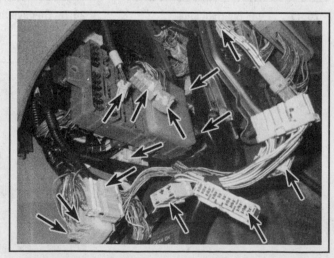

26.13c **Location of the driver's side electrical connectors for the instrument panel**

16 Remove the instrument panel mounting bolts (see illustrations).

17 Remove the crossmember mounting bolts (see illustrations).

18 Remove the instrument cluster (see Chapter 12).

19 Once all the fasteners are removed, lift the instrument panel then pull it away from the windshield and take it out through the driver's door opening.

➡ **Note: This is a two-person job.**

20 Reconnect the battery (see Chapter 5, Section 1).

21 Installation is the reverse of removal.

2005 AND LATER MODELS

22 Disconnect the cable from the negative battery terminal (see Chapter 5).

23 Remove all of the dashboard trim panels (see Section 24).

➡ **Note: It may be easier to remove the front seats prior to beginning this procedure. This allows more working room and more clearance for removing the bulky instrument panel.**

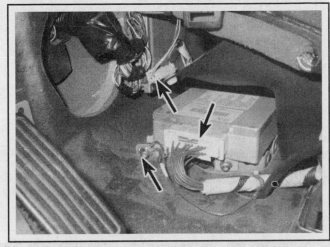

26.13d Location of the ground stud and electrical connectors for the PCM

26.16a Location of the instrument panel right side mounting bolts . . .

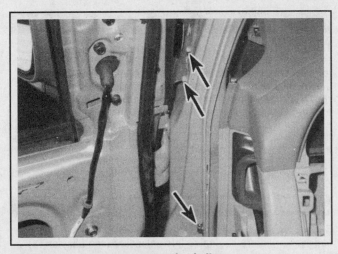

26.16b . . . and left side mounting bolts

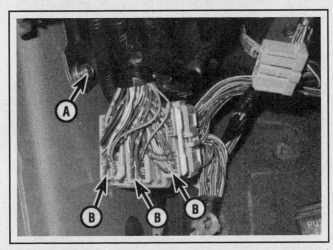

26.17a Location of the crossmember mounting bolt (A) and harness connectors (B)

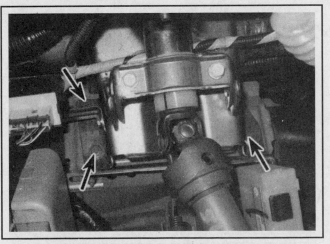

26.17b Remove the crossmember bolts from the steering column - the steering column, crossmember and instrument panel will be removed as a complete assembly

24 Remove the left and right door sills by pulling them up to release the clips.

25 Pull up the door opening trim molding around the kick panels.

26 Pull out the hood release handle, then pull off the driver's kick panel. Pull off the passenger's kick panel.

27 Use a plastic trim tool or a screwdriver wrapped with tape to pry out the windshield pillar clips. Use your hands to pull off the windshield pillar trims.

28 Using the trim tool, pry out the bottom of each door trim piece near the bottom of the windshield pillars. Slide the covers up and to the rear to release the clips.

29 Disconnect the shift cable (see Chapter 7).

30 Remove the steering column (see Chapter 10).

31 Label, then disconnect all wiring under the instrument panel including the ground connection screws.

32 Disconnect the heater lower duct.

33 Remove the instrument panel bolts from the perimeter of the instrument panel and the center frame. There are five different types of screws used, so lay them out in order as you remove them. They must all be installed in their original positions.

34 Lift the instrument panel upward to detach it from the four guide pins along the top front edge.

35 With the aid of an assistant, carefully guide the instrument panel through a front door opening.

36 Installation is the reverse of removal. Be sure the panel is installed on the guide pins securely. Tighten the center bracket and center frame bolts after tightening the other main bolts.

27 Seats - removal and installation

▶ Refer to illustrations 27.2, 27.5 and 27.6

☀ WARNING 1:

The front seat belts on some models are equipped with pre-tensioners, which are pyrotechnic (explosive) devices designed to retract the seat belts in the event of a collision. On models equipped with pre-tensioners, do not remove the front seat belt retractor assemblies, and do not disconnect the electrical connectors leading to the assemblies. Problems with the pre-tensioners will turn on the SRS (airbag) warning light on the dash. If any pre-tensioner problems are suspected, take the vehicle to a dealer service department.

☀ WARNING 2:

On models with side-impact airbags, be sure to disarm the airbag system before beginning this procedure (see Chapter 12).

2004 AND EARLIER MODELS

Front seats

▶ Refer to illustrations 27.2, 27.5 and 27.6

1 Disconnect the cable from the negative battery terminal (see Chapter 5, Section 1).

2 Slide the seat forward to access the rear riser cover (see illustration).

3 Remove the rear riser cover.

a) On 2001 and 2002 models, use a panel tool to separate the clips and remove the side and center clips on power operated seats or the side clips on manual operated seats.

b) On 2003 and 2004 models driver's side front seat, use a panel tool to separate the clips and remove the rear riser cover. On the passenger's side front seat, release the tabs on the outer edge and the clips to separate the riser cover.

4 On 2003 and 2004 models, remove the lower anchor bracket from the weight sensor on the outside seat rail.

5 Slide the seat to the rear and remove the front riser cover (see illustration).

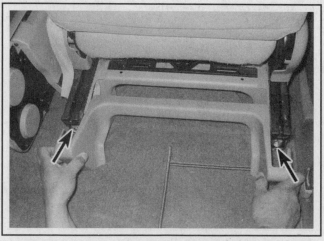

27.2 Slide the seat forward to access the rear riser cover - note the locations of the seat mounting bolts

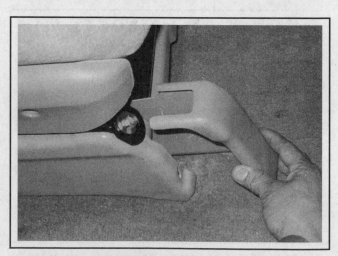

27.5 Slide the seat to the rear to access the front riser cover

a) *On 2001 and 2002 models, use a panel tool to separate the clips and remove front seat riser.*

b) *On 2003 and 2004 models driver's side front seat, use a panel tool to separate the clips and remove the front riser. On the passenger's side front seat, release the tabs on the outer edge and the clips to separate the riser from the seat.*

6 Remove the seat mounting bolts (see illustration).

7 Tilt the seat upward to access the underside, then disconnect any electrical connectors and lift the seat from the vehicle.

8 Installation is the reverse of removal.

Second row seat

▶ **Refer to illustration 27.9, 27.10a and 27.10b**

9 Fold the seat forward (see illustration).

10 Release the lock (see illustration) and tilt the seat forward to pivot the latch mechanism off the retainer (see illustration).

11 Installation is the reverse of removal.

Third row seat

12 Fold the rear seat down into the floorwell.

13 Pull back the trim cover and remove the bolts from the pivot brackets.

14 Pull the carpet back from the bottom of the seat and remove the two bolts holding the pivot bracket to the seat.

➡ **Note: It's only necessary to remove one of the pivot brackets (this will provide enough clearance to remove the seat without scratching the trim panels).**

15 With the help of an assistant, lift the seat out of the floorwell and remove it from the vehicle.

16 Installation is the reverse of the removal procedure.

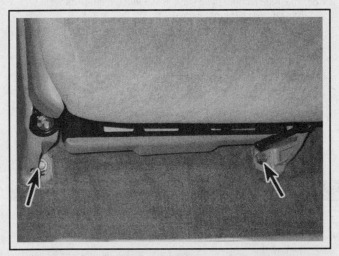

27.6 Remove the mounting bolts from the front of the seat assembly

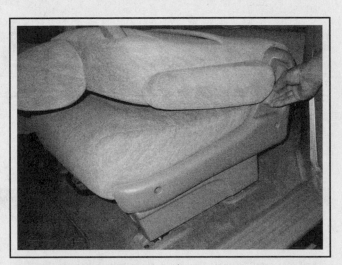

27.9 Fold the seat forward

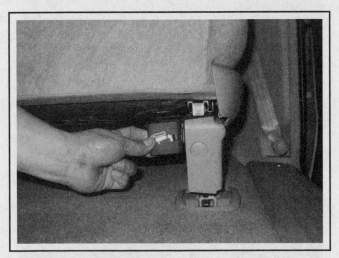

27.10a Release the lock . . .

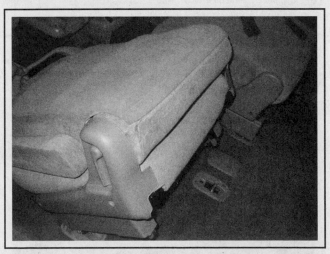

27.10b . . . and tilt the seat forward to unhook the latch mechanism from the retainers

2005 AND LATER MODELS

Front seats

17 Tilt the steering column to the highest position and telescope it in as far as possible.

18 Move the seats all the way forward.

19 Remove the covers from the rear of the passenger's seat tracks by spreading them until the clips are released.

20 Unbolt the seat belt anchor bracket from the weight sensor. Don't remove the seat belt from the bracket.

21 Remove the covers from the middle section of the seats by pulling them until the clips are released.

22 Remove the rear seat mounting bolts.

23 Adjust the seats as far forward as possible.

24 Remove the covers from the front seat tracks, then remove the front bolts.

25 Disconnect the cable from the negative battery terminal (see Chapter 5).

✳✳ WARNING:

Disarm the airbag system before continuing this procedure (see Chapter 12).

26 Lift the seats up and disconnect all wiring harnesses.

27 Remove the seats with the help of an assistant to avoid damaging trim panels or upholstery.

28 Installation is the reverse of removal.

Second row seat

29 Refer to the owner's manual for information about this procedure.

Third row seat

30 Stow both seats in the floor recess.

31 Pry off the center pivot upper cover.

32 Pull both seats up and lock them in position.

33 Pry off the center lower pivot cover.

34 Remove the covers from the center hinges.

35 Stow the right seat in the floor recess.

36 Lift the cover, then remove the hinge bolt from the center pivot bracket.

37 Remove the pivot cover.

38 Insert the stopper plate into the slot in the outer pivot shaft to keep the seat from popping open.

39 Release the hook, then lift the mat on the seat back. Remove the bolts of the left seat.

40 Remove the left seat. Remove the right seat using the same procedure.

28 Rear trim panels - removal and installation

▶ **Refer to illustrations 28.3, 28.5a, 28.5b, 28.5c, 28.6, 28.7, 28.8, 28.9a and 28.9b**

1 Disconnect the cable from the negative battery terminal (see Chapter 5, Section 1).

2 Remove the rear seat (see Section 27).

3 Remove the step panel from the side door (see illustration).

4 Unbolt the seatbelt anchor, where necessary.

5 Remove the liftgate lower trim panel (see illustrations).

6 Pry out the speaker grille (see illustration).

7 Remove the rear speaker mounting screws (see illustration).

8 Remove the passenger's side trim panel mounting screws (see illustration).

9 Use a panel tool to pry the clips (see illustration) and remove the passenger's side trim panel from the rear compartment (see illustration).

10 Installation is the reverse of removal.

11 Reconnect the battery (see Chapter 5, Section 1).

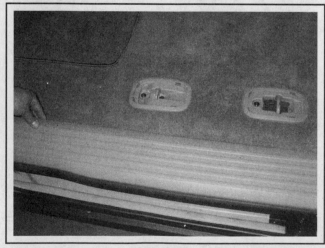

28.3 Carefully remove the sill trim from the body by lifting along the inner edge to release the clips

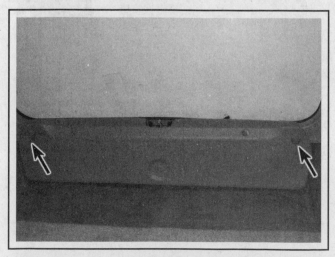

28.5a Remove the liftgate/trunk lower trim panel hole plugs

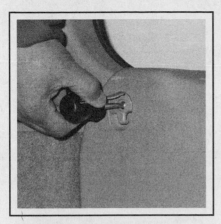

28.5b Remove the mounting screws from the panel

28.5c Lift the panel from the trunk area

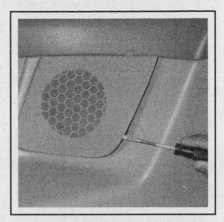

28.6 Remove the grille from the side speaker using a panel tool or flat-bladed screwdriver

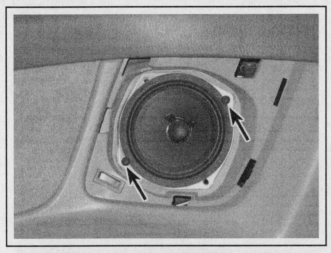

28.7 Remove the speaker mounting screws, pull the speaker out and unplug the connector

28.8 Remove the passenger's side trim panel seat belt retainers (A) and the mounting screws (B)

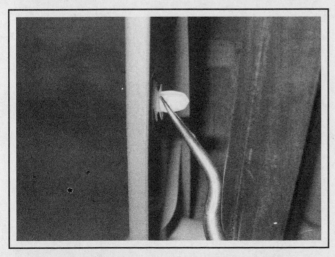

28.9a Use a panel tool to release the trim panel clips

28.9b Lift the trim panel from the rear compartment

Notes

12

**CHASSIS
ELECTRICAL
SYSTEM**

Section

1 General information

The electrical system is a 12-volt, negative ground type. Power for the lights and all electrical accessories is supplied by a lead/acid-type battery, which is charged by the alternator.

This Chapter covers repair and service procedures for the various electrical components not associated with the engine. Information on the battery, ignition system, alternator and starter motor can be found in Chapter 5.

It should be noted that when portions of the electrical system are serviced, the negative battery cable should be disconnected from the battery to prevent electrical shorts and/or fires.

2 Electrical troubleshooting - general information

▶ **Refer to illustrations 2.5a and 2.5b**

1   A typical electrical circuit consists of an electrical component, any switches, relays, motors, fuses, fusible links or circuit breakers related to that component and the wiring and connectors that link the component to both the battery and the chassis. Wiring diagrams are included at the end of this Chapter to help you pinpoint an electrical circuit problem.

2   Before tackling any troublesome electrical circuit, study the appropriate wiring diagrams to get a complete understanding of what makes up that individual circuit. Noting if other components related to the circuit are operating correctly, for instance, can often narrow trouble spots, down. If several components or circuits fail at one time, chances are the problem is in a fuse or ground connection, because several circuits are often routed through the same fuse and ground connections.

3   Electrical problems usually stem from simple causes, such as loose or corroded connections, a blown fuse, a melted fusible link or a failed relay. Visually inspect the condition of all fuses, wires and connections in a problem circuit before troubleshooting the circuit.

4   If test equipment and instruments are going to be utilized, use the diagrams to plan ahead of time where you will make the necessary connections in order to accurately pinpoint the trouble spot.

5   Basic electrical troubleshooting tools include a circuit tester, test light or voltmeter, a continuity tester, a set of test leads and a jumper wire (preferably with a circuit breaker), which can be used to bypass electrical components (see illustrations). Before attempting to locate a problem with test instruments, use the wiring diagram(s) to decide where to make the connections.

VOLTAGE CHECKS

▶ **Refer to illustration 2.6**

6   Voltage checks should be performed if a circuit is not functioning correctly. Connect one lead of a circuit tester to either the negative battery terminal or a known good ground. Connect the other lead to a connector in the circuit being tested, preferably nearest to the battery or fuse (see illustration). If the bulb of the tester lights, voltage is present, which means that the part of the circuit between the connector and the battery is problem free. Continue checking the rest of the circuit in the same fashion. When you reach a point at which no voltage is present, the problem lies between that point and the last test point with voltage. Most of the time the problem can be traced to a loose connection.

➡ **Note: Keep in mind that some circuits receive voltage only when the ignition key is in the ACC or ON position.**

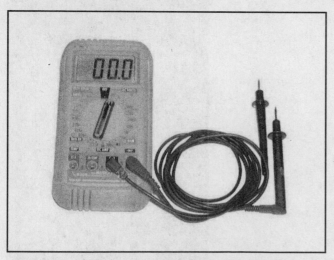

2.5a The most useful tool for electrical troubleshooting is a digital multimeter that can check volts, amps, and test continuity

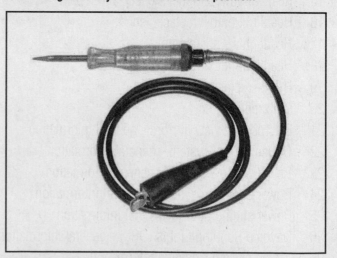

2.5b A simple test light is a very handy tool for testing voltage

FINDING A SHORT

7   One method of finding shorts in a live circuit is to remove the fuse and connect a test light in place of the fuse terminals (fabricate two jumper wires with small spade terminals, plug the jumper wires into the fuse box and connect the test light). There will be voltage present in the circuit if the circuit is shorted. Move the suspected wiring harness from side-to-side while watching the test light. If the bulb goes off, there is a short to ground somewhere in that area, probably where the insulation has rubbed through.

GROUND CHECK

8   Perform a ground test to check whether a component is correctly grounded. Disconnect the battery and connect one lead of a continuity tester or multimeter (set to the ohm scale), to a known good ground. Connect the other lead to the wire or ground connection being tested. If the resistance is low (less than 5 ohms), the ground is good. If the bulb on a self-powered test light does not go on, the ground is not good.

CONTINUITY CHECK

▶ **Refer to illustration 2.9**

9   Do a continuity check to verify that there are no opens in a circuit. With the circuit off (no power in the circuit), a self-powered continuity tester or multimeter can be used to check the circuit. Connect the test leads to both ends of the circuit (or to the "power" end and a good ground), and if the test light comes on the circuit is passing current correctly (see illustration). If the resistance is low (less than 5 ohms), there is continuity; if the reading is 10,000 ohms or higher, there is a break somewhere in the circuit. The same procedure can be used to test a switch, by connecting the continuity tester to the switch terminals. With the switch turned to ON, the test light should come on (or low resistance should be indicated on a meter).

FINDING AN OPEN CIRCUIT

10 When diagnosing for possible open circuits, it is often difficult to locate them by sight because the connectors hide oxidation or terminal misalignment. Merely wiggling a connector on a sensor or in the wiring harness may correct the open circuit condition. Remember this when an open circuit is indicated when troubleshooting a circuit. Intermittent problems may also be caused by oxidized or loose connections.

11 Electrical troubleshooting is simple if you keep in mind that all electrical circuits are basically electricity running from the battery, through the wires, switches, relays, fuses and fusible links to each electrical component (light bulb, motor, etc.) and to ground, from which it is passed back to the battery. Any electrical problem is an interruption in the flow of electricity to and from the battery.

CONNECTORS

12 Most electrical connections on these vehicles are made with multiwire plastic connectors. The mating halves of many connectors are secured with locking clips molded into the plastic connector shells. The mating halves of large connectors, such as some of those under the instrument panel, are held together by a bolt through the center of the connector.

13 To separate a connector with locking clips, use a small screwdriver to pry the clips apart carefully, then separate the connector halves. Pull only on the shell, never pull on the wiring harness as you may damage the individual wires and terminals inside the connectors. Look at the connector closely before trying to separate the halves. Often the locking clips are engaged in a way that is not immediately clear. Additionally, many connectors have more than one set of clips.

14 Each pair of connector terminals has a male half and a female half. When you look at the end view of a connector in a diagram, be sure to understand whether the view shows the harness side or the component side of the connector. Connector halves are mirror images of each other, and a terminal that is shown on the right side end-view of one half will be on the left side end view of the other half.

2.6 In use, a basic test light's lead is clipped to a known good ground, then the pointed probe can test connectors, wires or electrical sockets - if the bulb lights, the circuit being tested has battery voltage

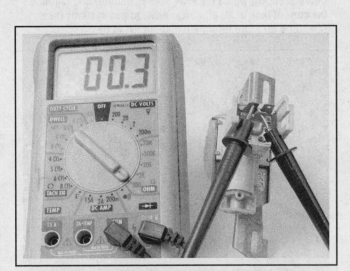

2.9 With a multimeter set to the ohm scale, resistance can be checked across two terminals - when checking for continuity, a low reading indicates continuity, a high reading or infinity indicates high resistance or lack of continuity

3   Fuses - general information

FUSES

▶ **Refer to illustrations 3.1a, 3.1b, 3.1c and 3.2**

The electrical circuits of the vehicle are protected by a combination of fuses, circuit breakers and relays (for more information about circuit breakers, refer to Section 4; for more information about relays, refer to Section 5). Fuse and relay boxes are located in the engine compartment and underneath the dashboard (see illustrations). A wide array of mini and maxi-style fuses is used to protect various circuits. These fuses, which employ a blade terminal design, can be removed and installed without special tools. Each fuse protects a specific circuit or circuits,

and the protected circuits are identified on the fuse panel cover. If the fuse panel cover is difficult to read, or missing, you can also refer to your owner's manual, which includes a complete guide to all fuses and relays in all three fuse/relay boxes.

If an electrical component fails, always check the fuse first. The best way to check a fuse is with a test light. Check for power at the exposed terminal tips of each fuse. If power is present on one side of the fuse but not the other, the fuse is blown. A blown fuse can also be confirmed by visually inspecting it (see illustration).

Be sure to replace blown fuses with the correct type. Fuses of different ratings are physically interchangeable, but only fuses of the correct rating should be used. Replacing a fuse with one of a higher or lower value than specified is not recommended. Each electrical circuit needs a specific amount of protection. The amperage value of each fuse is molded into the fuse body.

If the replacement fuse immediately fails, don't replace it again until the cause of the problem is isolated and corrected. In most cases, this will be a short circuit in the wiring caused by a broken or deteriorated wire.

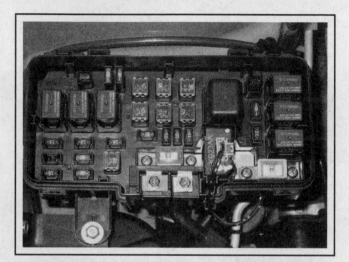

3.1a The engine compartment fuse/relay box is located at the right rear corner of the engine compartment. It contains fuses and relays related to engine compartment electrical systems, all of which are listed by location and function on the fuse/relay box cover. It also contains the Electronic Load Detector (ELD), which the PCM uses to monitor and regulate the current load of all electrical devices and systems (see Chapter 6 for more information about the ELD)

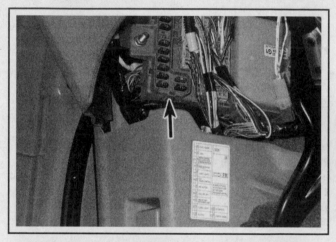

3.1b There are two fuse/relay boxes inside the passenger compartment. This one is located under the left end of the dash, above the left kick panel

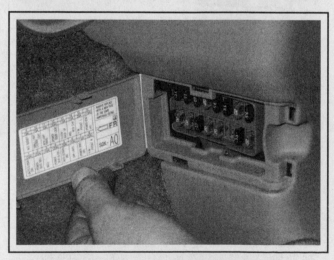

3.1c The other fuse and relay panel in the passenger compartment is located in the right kick panel; to access it, simply open this door

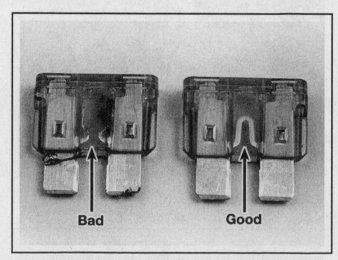

3.2 When a fuse blows, the element between the terminals melts - the fuse on the left is blown, the fuse on the right is good

4   Circuit breakers - general information

Circuit breakers protect certain circuits, such as the power windows or heated seats. The number of circuit breakers employed on your vehicle depends on its electrical accessories. Some circuit breakers are located in a fuse/relay box; others are located as stand-alone units under the dash and in other locations throughout the vehicle.

Because a circuit breaker resets automatically, a temporary or intermittent electrical overload in a circuit-breaker-protected system will cause the circuit to open momentarily, then close again. If a circuit-breaker-protected circuit does not close, or constantly opens and closes, check it immediately. There's probably an intermittent short or ground somewhere in the circuit that's causing the current overload, which causes the circuit breaker to cycle the circuit on and off.

For a basic check, pull the circuit breaker up out of its socket on the fuse panel, but just far enough to probe with a voltmeter. The breaker should still contact the sockets.

With the voltmeter negative lead on a good chassis ground, touch each end prong of the circuit breaker with the positive meter probe. There should be battery voltage at each end. If there is battery voltage only at one end, the circuit breaker must be replaced.

Some circuit breakers must be reset manually.

5   Relays - general information and testing

GENERAL INFORMATION

1   Several electrical accessories in the vehicle, such as the fuel injection system, horns, starter, and fog lamps use relays to transmit the electrical signal to the component. A relay allows a low-current circuit (the control circuit) to be used to open and close a high-current circuit (the power circuit). If a relay is defective, the component(s) powered by the high-current circuit controlled by the relay will not operate. Relays are located in the engine compartment fuse/relay box and in or near the fuse and relay boxes under the dash (see illustrations 3.1a through 3.1c). If a relay is suspect, test it using the procedure below, or have it tested by a dealer service department or a repair shop. Defective relays must be replaced, because they cannot be repaired.

TESTING

2   There are three basic types of relays used in these vehicles: normally-open Type A, normally-open Type B and the five-terminal type. Type A and Type B relays have similar internal circuitry, but their external spade terminals are arranged differently and they're numbered differently. Five-terminal relays have different internal circuitry and one more external spade terminal than Type A and Type B relays. To test a relay, remove it from the vehicle and use an ohmmeter to check for continuity.

Normally-open Type A relays

▶ **Refer to illustration 5.4**

3   Normally-open type A relays are used for:
Air-conditioning clutch relay
Air/fuel (A/F) ratio sensor relay
Condenser fan relay
Headlight relay No. 1 (2001 models)
Headlight relay No. 2 (2001 models)
Headlight relay (2002 and later models)
Horn relay
Power window relay
Radiator fan relay
Reverse relay
Starter cut relay
Taillight relay
Daytime Running Lights (DRL) relay (Canadian models)
PGM-FI main relay No. 1
PGM-FI main relay No. 2

4   Type A relays (see illustration) have four external spade terminals: two horizontal terminals, one on top of the other, with two vertical terminals, side-by-side, below them. In other words, the two horizontal terminals are perpendicular to the two vertical terminals. So an easy way to determine whether you're dealing with a Type A relay is to place the relay you want to test on a table top or workbench, with the spade terminals facing toward you. Then position it so that its two horizontal terminals are on top and its two vertical terminals are on the bottom. If that's what it looks like, it's a Type A relay. If it has four terminals, but they're all parallel to each other, it's a Type B relay. Some Type A relays have numbered terminals (1, 2, 3, 4) and some don't. If the Type A relay that you want to test doesn't have numbered terminals, how do you know which terminal is No. 1, which is No. 2, etc.? Here's a simple way to determine terminal numbering: All Type A relays are numbered from top-to-bottom and from left-to-right, so once you have your Type A relay positioned with the two horizontal terminals at the top, those are terminal Nos. 1 and 2, respectively. And the two vertical terminals below them are numbered from left to right, so those two lower terminals are Nos. 3 and 4.

5   To test a normally-open Type A relay verify that there is *no* continuity between terminal No. 1 and No. 2 when the power is disconnected. Then verify that there *is* continuity between terminal No. 1 and No. 2 when the No. 3 and No. 4 terminals are connected to power and ground, respectively.

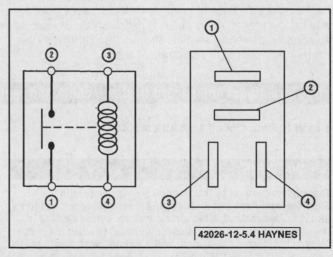

42026-12-5.4 HAYNES

5.4 Normally-open Type A relay

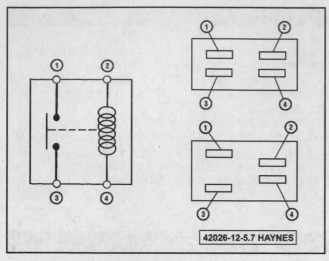

5.7 Normally-open Type B relay

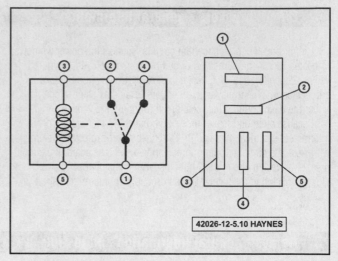

5.10 Five-terminal relay

Normally-open Type B relays

▶ **Refer to illustration 5.7**

6   Normally-open Type B relays are used for:
   Blower motor relay
   Rear window defogger relay

7   Type B relays also have four external spade terminals (see illustration), but they're arranged in two parallel rows, with two terminals per row. So to identify a Type B relay, lay it flat with the four terminals horizontal (NOT vertical!). If two of the terminals are closer together, position the relay so that those two terminals are on your right. Then the terminal in the upper left corner is No. 1, the terminal in the upper right corner is No. 2, the terminal in the lower left corner is No. 3 and the terminal in the lower right corner is No. 4. This method of identification works well on Type B relays like the type 1 and type 2 blower motor relays because they each have a set of terminals that are closer together (Nos. 2 and 4). But on Type B relays such as the rear window defogger relay, where both terminals in each row are parallel (i.e. the two on the right - Nos. 2 and 4 - are the same distance apart as terminal Nos. 1 and 3), there's no way to be sure that you have placed the relay "right side up" because it looks the same right side up or upside down. On these Type Bs, look for the number 1 next to the No. 1 terminal. If the No. 1 terminal isn't numbered, you'll have to take a guess and then see what happens when you power up the relay. If it works as it's supposed to (closes the other circuit when you power up the control circuit) then you got it right. If it doesn't, flip it over and retest it.

8   To test a normally-open Type B relay verify that there is no continuity between terminal No. 1 and No. 3 when the power is disconnected. Then verify that there is continuity between terminal No. 1 and No. 3 when the No. 2 and No. 4 terminals are connected to power and ground, respectively.

Five-terminal type relays

▶ **Refer to illustration 5.10**

9   Five-terminal relays are used for:
   Moonroof-closing relay
   Moonroof-opening relay
   Low-beam cut relay (Canadian models)

10 Five-terminal relays are easy to identify because they have five terminals (see illustration) instead of four. To determine the terminal numbering, place a five-terminal relay with its two terminals at the top and parallel to the table top, and with the other three vertical terminals underneath the two upper horizontal ones. The top terminal is No. 1, the one below it is No. 2 and the three terminals below No. 2 are, from left to right, Nos. 3, 4 and 5.

11 To test a five-terminal relay verify that there is continuity between terminal No. 1 and No. 4 when the power is disconnected. Then verify that there is continuity between terminal No. 1 and No. 2 when power and ground are connected to the No. 3 and No. 5 terminals.

---

6   Turn signal and hazard flasher - check and replacement

▶ **Refer to illustrations 6.4a, 6.4b and 6.4c**

❊❊ WARNING:

The models covered by this manual are equipped with a Supplemental Restraint System (SRS), commonly referred to as airbags. Always disable the airbag system before working in the vicinity of any airbag system component to avoid the possibility of accidental deployment of the airbag, which could cause personal injury (see Section 27).

1   The turn signal and hazard flashers are controlled from a single electronic flasher unit, which is located on the backside of the fuse/relay box under the left end of the dash.

2   If the flasher unit is functioning correctly, you can hear an audible click when it's operating. If one of the turn signal indicators on the instrument cluster flashes more rapidly than normal, the turn signal bulb for that side has a blown filament.

3   If neither turn signal indicator blinks, the problem might be a blown fuse, a faulty flasher unit, a broken switch or a loose or open connection. If the left or right turn signal fuse has blown, check the wiring for a short before installing a new fuse.

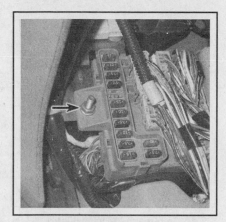

6.4a To access the turn signal and hazard flasher unit, remove this nut . . .

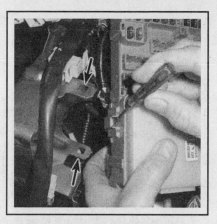

6.4b . . . release the two locking tabs from the upper and lower mounting brackets and remove the fuse and relay box

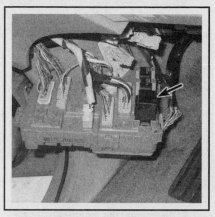

6.4c To remove the turn signal and hazard flasher unit, simply pull it out of the fuse and relay box

4   To replace the flasher unit, remove the driver's side fuse and relay box (see illustrations). Then remove the flasher (see illustration) from the backside of the fuse and relay box.

5   Make sure that the replacement unit is identical to the original. Compare the old one to the new one before installing it.

6   Installation is the reverse of removal.

7   Steering column switches - replacement

✳ WARNING:

The models covered by this manual are equipped with a Supplemental Restraint System (SRS), more commonly known as airbags. Always disable the airbag system   before working in the vicinity of any airbag system component to avoid the possibility of accidental deployment of the airbag, which could cause personal injury (see Section 27).

1   Disconnect the cable from the negative battery terminal (see Chapter 5, Section 1), then wait at least three minutes before proceeding.

2   Remove the knee bolster and the upper and lower steering column covers (see Chapter 11).

MULTI-FUNCTION SWITCH

▶ **Refer to illustrations 7.3, 7.4 and 7.5**

3   Disconnect the electrical connector from the multi-function switch (see illustration).

4   Remove the multi-function switch retaining screws (see illustration).

5   Remove the multi-function switch (see illustration).

6   Installation is the reverse of removal.

7   After you're done, reconnect the cable to the negative battery terminal (see Chapter 5, Section 1).

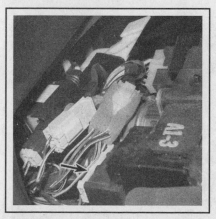

7.3 Disconnect the electrical connector from the multi-function switch

7.4 To detach the multi-function switch, remove these two screws

7.5 To remove the multi-function switch, pull it straight out to the side

7.8 Disconnect the electrical connector from the windshield wiper/ washer switch

7.9 To detach the windshield wiper/ washer switch, remove these two screws

7.10 To remove the windshield wiper/washer switch, pull it straight out to the right

WINDSHIELD WIPER/WASHER SWITCH

▶ **Refer to illustrations 7.8, 7.9 and 7.10**

8   Disconnect the electrical connector from the windshield wiper/ washer switch (see illustration).

9   Remove the windshield wiper/washer switch retaining screws (see illustration).

10 Remove the windshield wiper/washer switch (see illustration).

11 Installation is the reverse of removal.

12 After you're done, reconnect the cable to the negative battery terminal (see Chapter 5, Section 1).

8   Ignition switch and key lock cylinder - replacement

✳✳ WARNING:

All models covered by this manual are equipped with a Supplemental Restraint System (SRS), more commonly known as airbags. Always disable the airbag system   before working in the vicinity of any airbag system component to avoid the possibility of accidental deployment of the airbag, which could cause personal injury (see Section 27).

1   Disconnect the cable from the negative battery terminal (see Chapter 5, Section 1), then wait at least three minutes before proceeding.

2   Remove the knee bolster and the upper and lower steering column covers (see Chapter 11).

IGNITION SWITCH

▶ **Refer to illustration 8.4 and 8.5**

3   Detach the driver's side fuse and relay box (see Section 3).

4   Disconnect the ignition switch electrical connector from the fuse and relay box (see illustration).

5   Remove the ignition switch mounting screws (see illustration) and remove the switch.

6   Installation is the reverse of removal.

7   When you're done, reconnect the cable to the negative battery terminal (see Chapter 5, Section 1).

8   Verify that the ignition switch operates correctly in the LOCK, ACC, ON and START positions.

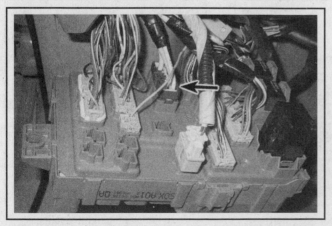

8.4 Disconnect the ignition switch electrical connector from the fuse and relay box

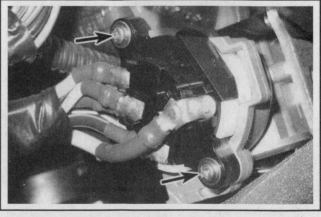

8.5 To detach the ignition switch, remove these two screws

KEY LOCK CYLINDER

▶ **Refer to illustration 8.10**

9   Remove the ignition switch (see Steps 1 through 5).

10   The lock cylinder can't be replaced by itself - the whole housing must be replaced. Remove the shear-head bolts, remove the bracket and detach the lock cylinder housing from the steering column. Shear-head bolt removal can be accomplished by drilling a hole in the center of each bolt and unscrewing them with a screw extractor (see illustration).

11   Installation is the reverse of removal. Tighten the key lock cylinder housing bolts until the hex heads break off.

12   Reconnect the cable to the negative battery terminal (see Chapter 5, Section 1).

13   Verify that the key lock cylinder works correctly.

8.10 To detach the key lock cylinder housing from the steering column, remove these two shear-head bolts

9   Dashboard switches - replacement

❊ WARNING:

The models covered by this manual are equipped with a Supplemental Restraint System (SRS), more commonly known as airbags. Always disable the airbag system before working in the vicinity of any airbag system component to avoid the possibility of accidental deployment of the airbag, which could cause personal injury (see Section 27).

SWITCHES ON DRIVER'S SWITCH PANEL

▶ **Refer to illustrations 9.2a and 9.2b**

1   Disconnect the cable from the negative battery terminal (see Chapter 5, Section 1), then wait at least three minutes before proceeding.

2   On 2004 and earlier models, carefully pry the switch trim panel loose (see illustration) and pull it out far enough to disconnect the electrical connector and remove the switch you're replacing. After disconnecting the electrical connector for the switch that you're replacing, removing the switch is simply a matter of depressing the locking springs (see illustration) and pushing the switch out through the front of the trim panel. On 2005 and later models, remove the instrument panel end cover (see Chapter 11), then reach through the opening and release the hook at the bottom of the switch panel. Pull out the switch panel. The switches can be removed after disconnecting the wires.

HAZARD FLASHER SWITCH

▶ **Refer to illustrations 9.5 and 9.6**

3   Disconnect the cable from the negative battery terminal (see Chapter 5, Section 1).

4   Remove the instrument panel trim panel (see Chapter 11).

5   Disconnect the electrical connector from the hazard flasher switch (see illustration).

9.2a Carefully pry the dashboard switch trim panel loose with a panel removal tool or with a flat-blade screwdriver; if you're going to use a screwdriver, be sure to tape the end to protect the plastic trim panel

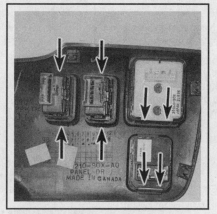

9.2b To release any of the switches located on this trim panel, simply depress the locking springs and push the switch through the front of the trim panel

9.5 To release the hazard flasher electrical connector, depress this lock tab, then unplug the connector

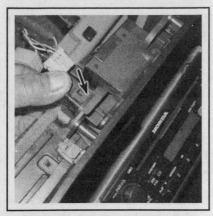

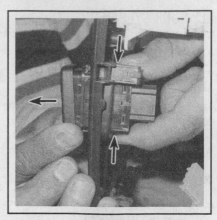

9.6 To release the hazard flasher switch from the instrument cluster trim panel, depress this lock spring on top, then push the switch through the front of the panel

9.12 To release the light control switch electrical connector, depress the lock tab with your thumb (the lock tab, not visible in this photo, is on the other side of the connector) and unplug the connector

9.13 To release the light control switch from the center trim panel, depress the locking springs at the top and bottom of the switch, then push out the switch through the front of the trim panel

6 Remove the hazard flasher switch (see illustration).

7 Installation is the reverse of removal.

8 Reconnect the cable to the negative battery cable (see Chapter 5, Section 1).

9 Verify that the hazard flasher switch works correctly (see your owner's manual, if necessary).

LIGHT CONTROL SWITCH (DASH ILLUMINATION RHEOSTAT)

▶ **Refer to illustrations 9.12 and 9.13**

10 Disconnect the cable from the negative battery terminal (see

Chapter 5, Section 1).

11 Remove the center trim panel (see Chapter 11).

12 Disconnect the electrical connector from the light control switch (see illustration).

13 Remove the light control switch (see illustration).

14 Installation is the reverse of removal.

15 When you're done, reconnect the cable to the negative battery cable (see Chapter 5, Section 1).

16 Verify that the light control switch works correctly (see your owner's manual, if necessary).

10 Clock - replacement

▶ **Refer to illustration 10.5**

✳✳ WARNING:

The models covered by this manual are equipped with a Supplemental Restraint System (SRS), more commonly known as airbags. Always disable the airbag system before working in the vicinity of any airbag system component to avoid the possibility of accidental deployment of the airbag, which could cause personal injury (see Section 27).

1 Disconnect the cable from the negative battery terminal (see Chapter 5, Section 1).

2 Remove the instrument cluster trim panel (see Chapter 11).

3 Disconnect the electrical connector from the hazard flasher switch (see illustration 9.5) and from the clock.

4 Remove the hazard flasher switch (see illustration 9.6).

5 Remove the clock from the instrument cluster trim panel (see illustration).

6 Installation is the reverse of removal.

7 When you're done, reconnect the cable to the negative battery

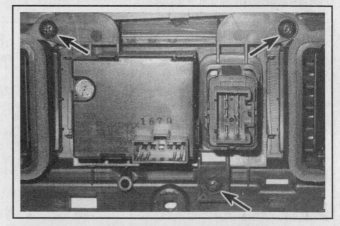

10.5 To remove the clock from the instrument cluster trim panel, remove these three screws

cable (see Chapter 5, Section 1).

8 Verify that the clock works correctly (see your owner's manual, if necessary).

11 Instrument cluster - removal and installation

▶ Refer to illustrations 11.3a and 11.3b

✳ WARNING:

The models covered by this manual are equipped with a Supplemental Restraint System (SRS), more commonly known as airbags. Always disable the airbag system before working in the vicinity of any airbag system component to avoid the possibility of accidental deployment of the airbag, which could cause personal injury (see Section 27).

1   Disconnect the cable from the negative battery terminal (see Chapter 5, Section 1).

2   Remove the instrument cluster trim panel (see Chapter 11).

3   Remove the instrument cluster retaining screws (see illustration), then pull out the cluster and disconnect the electrical connectors from the backside (see illustration).

4   Installation is the reverse of removal.

5   Reconnect the cable to the negative battery terminal (see Chapter 5, Section 1).

11.3a To detach the instrument cluster from the dashboard, remove these four screws . . .

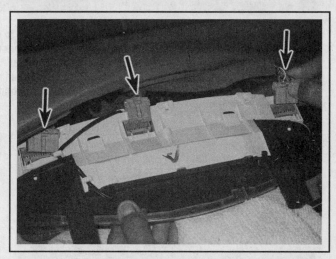

11.3b . . . then pull out the cluster and disconnect the three electrical connectors

12 Wiper motors - check and replacement

WIPER MOTOR CIRCUIT CHECK

➡ **Note: Refer to the wiring diagrams for wire colors in the following checks. When checking for voltage, probe a grounded 12-volt test light to each terminal at a connector until it lights; this verifies voltage (power) at the terminal. If the following checks fail to locate the problem, have the system diagnosed by a dealer service department or other properly equipped repair facility.**

1   If the wipers work slowly, make sure the battery is fully charged and in good condition (see Chapter 5). If the battery is in good shape, remove the wiper motor (see below) and operate the wiper arms by hand. Check for binding linkage and pivots. Lubricate or repair the linkage or pivots as necessary. Reinstall the wiper motor. If the wipers still operate slowly, check for loose or corroded connections, especially the ground connection. If all connections look OK, replace the motor.

2   If the wipers fail to operate when activated, check the fuse (see Section 3). If the fuse is OK, connect a jumper wire between the wiper motor's ground terminal and ground, then retest. If the motor works now, repair the ground connection. If the motor still doesn't work, turn the wiper switch to the HI position and check for voltage at the motor.

➡ **Note: The cowl cover will have to be removed to access the electrical connector (see Steps 7 and 8).**

3   If there's voltage at the connector, remove the motor and check it off the vehicle with fused jumper wires from the battery. If the motor now works, check for binding linkage (see Step 1). If the motor still doesn't work, replace it. If there's no voltage to the motor, check for voltage at the wiper control relays. If there's voltage at the wiper control relays and no voltage at the wiper motor, have the switch tested. If the switch is OK, the wiper control relay is probably bad. See Section 5 for relay testing.

4   If the interval (delay) function is inoperative, check the continuity of all the wiring between the switch and the wiper control module.

5   If the wipers fail to "park" (if they stop at the position that they're in when the switch is turned off instead of returning to their normal "off" position), turn the wiper switch to OFF and the ignition switch to ON, then check for voltage at the park feed wire of the wiper motor connector. If no voltage is present, check for an open circuit between the wiper motor and the fuse panel.

12.7a To remove the windshield wiper arms, remove the nut that attaches each arm to its splined shaft, then pull the arm straight off

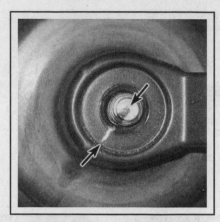

12.7b Be sure to mark each windshield wiper arm in relation to the splined shaft to ensure that the arm is installed in the same position when reassembling the windshield wiper system

12.8a Three pop fasteners secure the upper edge of the cowl cover to the vehicle body; to remove each pop fastener, carefully pry it up as shown with a small screwdriver, then pull it out

12.8b To detach the hood seal from the cowl cover, carefully pry loose each of the split-type locator pins; then remove the cowl cover

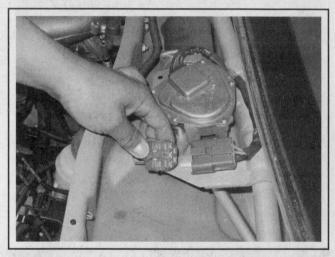

12.9 Disconnect the electrical connector from the windshield wiper motor

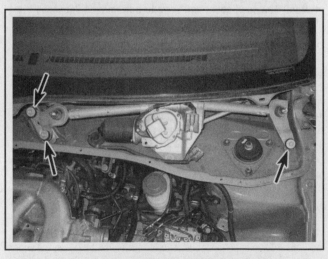

12.10a To detach the windshield wiper linkage/motor assembly, remove these three bolts . . .

WIPER MOTOR REPLACEMENT

Windshield wiper motor

▶ Refer to illustrations 12.7a, 12.7b, 12.8a, 12.8b, 12.9, 12.10a, 12.10b, 12.10c, 12.11a, 12.11b, 12.11c, 12.12, 12.13a and 12.13b

6   Disconnect the cable from the negative battery terminal (see Chapter 5, Section 1).

7   Remove the windshield wiper arm retaining nuts (see illustration). Be sure to mark the position of each wiper arm in relation to its splined shaft (see illustration), then remove the wiper arms.

8   Remove the windshield cowl cover (see illustrations). Store the pop fasteners and hood seal in a plastic bag.

9   Disconnect the electrical connector from the windshield wiper motor (see illustration).

10   Remove the windshield wiper linkage/motor assembly (see illustrations).

12.10b . . . then slide the assembly toward the passenger side of the vehicle until the rubber grommet is disengaged from the locator pin (A) . . .

12.10c . . . and remove the windshield wiper linkage/motor assembly from the cowl area

12.11a To separate the windshield wiper linkage from the wiper motor, mark the relationship of the link to the wiper motor mounting bracket . . .

12.11b . . . then holding one end of the link with a pair of locking pliers, remove the nut that attaches the link to the wiper motor shaft . . .

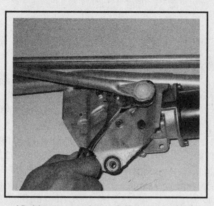

12.11c . . . and carefully pry the link off the wiper motor shaft

12.12 To detach the windshield wiper motor from its mounting bracket, remove these three bolts

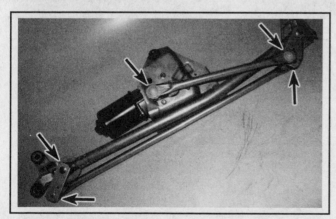

12.13a Before installing the windshield wiper linkage, it's a good idea to grease all the joints of the linkage with a grease gun

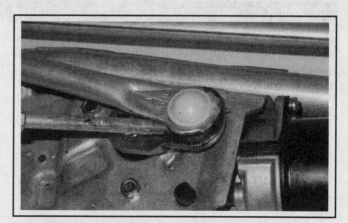

12.13b To grease each joint, carefully push the rubber bushing out of the way so that the grease is applied to the moving parts, not the bushing

11 Separate the windshield wiper linkage from the wiper motor (see illustrations).

12 Remove the windshield wiper motor mounting bolts (see illustration) and separate the motor from its mounting bracket.

13 Before installing the windshield wiper linkage (especially if you're installing the old linkage), grease the moving parts (see illustrations).

14 Installation is otherwise the reverse of removal. Be sure to align

the marks you made between the link and the motor mounting bracket and between the windshield wiper arms and the wiper arm shafts.

15 Reconnect the cable to the negative battery terminal (see Chapter 5, Section 1).

16 Turn on the windshield wipers and verify that the wiper motor operates correctly in all modes (see your owner's manual if necessary).

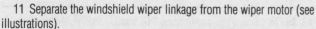

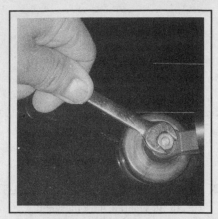

12.19 To detach the rear window wiper arm from the wiper motor shaft, flip up the hinged cover and remove the nut; before removing the arm, be sure to mark the relationship of the arm to the wiper motor shaft (see illustration 12.7b)

12.20 Remove this protective cover and then remove this big nut

12.21 To remove the rear window wiper motor, disconnect the electrical connector and remove the three motor mounting bolts

Rear window wiper motor

▶ **Refer to illustrations 12.19, 12.20 and 12.21**

17 Disconnect the cable from the negative battery terminal (see Chapter 5, Section 1).

18 Remove the tailgate trim panel (see Chapter 11).

19 Remove the rear window wiper arm (see illustration). After removing the wiper arm retaining nut, be sure to mark the relationship of the wiper arm to the wiper motor shaft (see illustration 12.7b).

20 Remove the protective cover for the rear window wiper motor

shaft nut and then remove the nut (see illustration).

21 Disconnect the electrical connector from the rear window wiper motor (see illustration).

22 Remove the rear window wiper motor mounting bolts (see illustration 12.21) and remove the motor.

23 Installation is the reverse of removal.

24 Reconnect the cable to the negative battery terminal (see Chapter 5, Section 1).

25 Turn on the rear window wiper motor and verify that it operates correctly.

13 Radio and speakers - removal and installation

❈❈ **WARNING:**

The models covered by this manual are equipped with a Supplemental Restraint System (SRS), more commonly known as airbags. Always disable the airbag system before working in the vicinity of any airbag system component to avoid the possibility of accidental deployment of the airbag, which could cause personal injury (see Section 27).

➡ **Note: Be sure that you have the anti-theft codes for the audio system and the navigation system (if so equipped) before starting this procedure.**

RADIO

▶ **Refer to illustration 13.3a, 13.3b and 13.4**

1 Disconnect the cable from the negative battery terminal (see Chapter 5, Section 1).

2 Remove the center trim panel (see Chapter 11).

3 Remove the radio mounting screws (see illustration), then pull out the radio far enough to disconnect the antenna and the electrical connector from the back of the unit (see illustration).

13.3a To detach the radio from the dash, remove these four mounting screws . . .

13.3b . . . then pull out the radio far enough to disconnect the electrical connectors and the antenna from the back of the unit

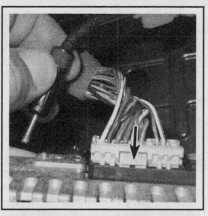

13.4 Disconnect the antenna, then depress this release tab and disconnect the electrical connector from the back of the radio unit

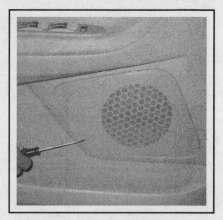

13.7 Using a small screwdriver, carefully pry off the speaker cover

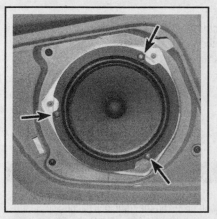

13.8 To detach the speaker from the door, remove these three screws

13.9 Disconnect the electrical connector from the speaker and remove the speaker from the door

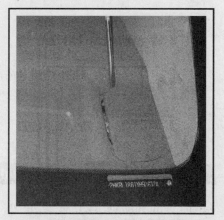

13.11 Carefully pry the tweeter out of the dash

4   Disconnect the antenna and the electrical connector from the back of the radio (see illustration) and remove the radio from the vehicle.

5   Installation is the reverse of removal.

6   Reconnect the cable to the negative battery terminal (see Chapter 5, Section 1).

SPEAKERS

Front door speakers

▶ **Refer to illustrations 13.7, 13.8 and 13.9**

7   Pry off the speaker cover (see illustration).

8   Remove the speaker mounting screws (see illustration) and pull the speaker out of its receptacle in the door.

9   Disconnect the electrical connector (see illustration) and remove the speaker from the vehicle.

10 Installation is the reverse of removal.

Tweeters

▶ **Refer to illustrations 13.11 and 13.12**

11 Pry the tweeter out of the dash (see illustration).

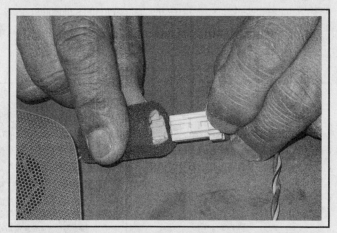

13.12 Disconnect the electrical connector from the tweeter

12 Disconnect the electrical connector from the tweeter (see illustration).

13 Installation is the reverse of removal.

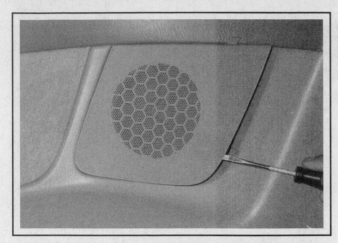

13.14 Carefully pry the rear speaker cover off the trim panel

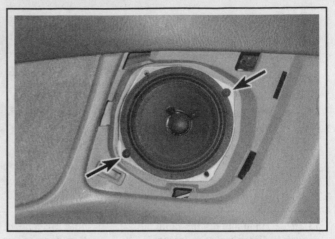

13.15 To detach a rear speaker from the trim panel, remove these two mounting screws (the rear speakers on some models have three screws)

Rear speakers

▶ Refer to illustrations 13.14 and 13.15

14 Pry off the speaker cover (see illustration).
15 Remove the speaker mounting screws (see illustration) and pull the speaker out of its receptacle.

16 Disconnect the electrical connector (see illustration 13.9) and remove the speaker from the vehicle.
17 Installation is the reverse of removal.

14 Antenna and cable - removal and installation

▶ Refer to illustrations 14.1, 14.2a, 14.2b, 14.4 and 14.5

➡ **Note: This procedure applies only to 2004 and earlier models with mast antennas. On 2005 and later models, the antenna is intgral with the right quarter glass.**

1 Remove the antenna mast (see illustration) from its mounting base.
2 Remove the antenna nut, then remove the mounting base and the rubber weather seal (see illustrations).

3 Remove the right scuff plate and the right kick panel (see "Instrument panel - removal and installation" in Chapter 11). Also remove the right inner fender splash shield (see Chapter 11).
4 Unbolt the antenna housing mounting bracket, pull out the bracket and housing and separate the housing from the bracket (see illustration).
5 Pull out the antenna cable through its grommet in the vehicle body (see illustration).
6 Installation is the reverse of removal.

14.1 Unscrew the antenna mast from its mounting base with a wrench

14.2a To remove the antenna nut, use a special antenna nut wrench (available at most auto parts stores)

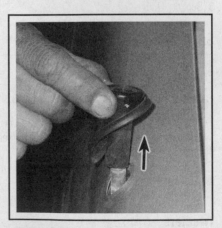

14.2b After removing the antenna nut, remove the antenna mounting base and the rubber weather seal

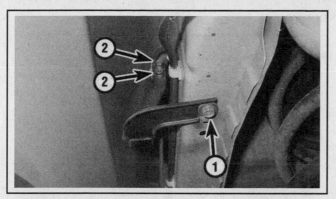

14.4 To detach the antenna housing mounting bracket from the vehicle, remove this bolt (1); to separate the antenna housing from the mounting bracket, remove these two bolts (2)

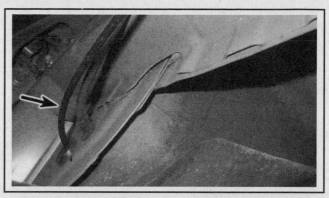

14.5 To remove the antenna cable, pull it out through its grommet in the vehicle body

15 Rear window defogger - check and repair

1   The rear window defogger consists of a number of horizontal elements baked onto the glass surface.

2   Small breaks in the element can be repaired without removing the rear window.

CHECK

▶ **Refer to illustrations 15.4, 15.5 and 15.7**

3   Turn the ignition switch and defogger system switches to the ON position. Using a voltmeter, place the positive probe against the defogger grid positive terminal and the negative probe against the ground terminal. If battery voltage is not indicated, check the fuse, defogger switch and related wiring. If voltage is indicated, but all or part of the defogger doesn't heat, proceed with the following tests.

4   When measuring voltage during the next two tests, wrap a piece

of aluminum foil around the tip of the voltmeter positive probe and press the foil against the heating element with your finger (see illustration). Place the negative probe on the defogger grid ground terminal.

5   Check the voltage at the center of each heating element (see illustration). If the voltage is 5 or 6-volts, the element is okay (there is no break). If the voltage is zero, the element is broken between the center of the element and the positive end. If the voltage is 10 to 12-volts the element is broken between the center of the element and ground. Check each heating element.

6   Connect the negative lead to a good body ground. The reading should stay the same. If it doesn't, the ground connection is bad.

7   To find the break, place the voltmeter negative probe against the defogger ground terminal. Place the voltmeter positive probe with the foil strip against the heating element at the positive terminal end and slide it toward the negative terminal end. The point at which the voltmeter deflects from several volts to zero is the point at which the heating element is broken (see illustration).

15.4 When measuring the voltage at the rear window defogger grid, wrap a piece of aluminum foil around the positive probe of the voltmeter and press the foil against the wire with your finger

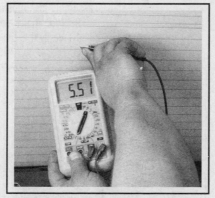

15.5 To determine whether a wire has broken, check the voltage at the center of each wire. If the voltage is five to six volts, the wire is unbroken; if the voltage is 10 to 12 volts, the wire is broken between the center of the wire and the ground side; if the voltage is zero, the wire is broken between the center of the wire and the power side

15.7 To find the break, place the voltmeter negative lead against the ground terminal, place the voltmeter positive lead with the foil strip against the heat wire at the positive terminal end and slide it toward the negative terminal end; the point at which the voltmeter deflects from several volts to zero volts is the point at which the wire is broken

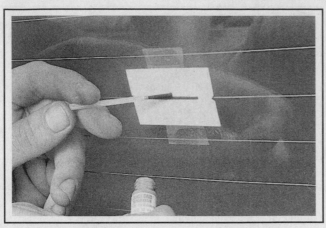

15.13 To use a defogger repair kit, apply masking to the inside of the window at the damaged area, then brush on the special conductive coating

REPAIR

▶ **Refer to illustration 15.13**

8　Repair the break in the element using a repair kit for this purpose (available at most auto parts stores). Make sure that the repair kit includes plastic conductive epoxy.

9　Prior to repairing a break, turn off the system and allow it to cool off for a few minutes.

10　Lightly buff the element area with fine steel wool, then clean it thoroughly with rubbing alcohol.

11　Use masking tape to mask off the area being repaired.

12　Thoroughly mix the epoxy, following the instructions provided with the repair kit.

13　Apply the epoxy material to the slit in the masking tape, overlapping the undamaged area about 3/4-inch on either end (see illustration).

14　Allow the repair to cure for 24 hours before removing the tape and using the system.

16　Headlight bulb - replacement

▶ **Refer to illustration 16.2, 16.3, 16.4 16.5a, 16.5b, 16.6 and 16.8**

❋❋ WARNING:

Halogen gas filled bulbs are under pressure and can shatter if the surface is scratched or the bulb is dropped. Wear eye protection and handle the bulbs carefully, grasping only the base whenever possible. Do not touch the surface of the bulb with your fingers because the oil from your skin could cause it to overheat and fail prematurely. If you do touch the bulb surface, clean it with rubbing alcohol.

1　Make sure that the headlight switch and the ignition switch are both turned off, then open the hood.

2　If you're going to replace the left headlight bulb, remove the air intake cover (see illustration).

3　Disconnect the electrical connector from the headlight assembly (see illustration).

4　Remove the rubber weather seal from the headlight assembly (see illustration).

5　Disengage the headlight bulb retainer wire, then remove the bulb from the headlight assembly (see illustrations).

6　Without touching the glass part of the new bulb with your bare fingers, insert the bulb into the headlight assembly. Make sure that the three metal tabs on the bulb are aligned with the three slots in the plastic mounting base and that the bulb mounting flange is fully seated against the base (see illustration).

7　Swing the bulb retainer wire back into place and engage the end with its slot.

8　Install the rubber weather seal on the back of the headlight assembly (see illustration).

9　Plug in the electrical connector.

10　Verify that the new headlight bulb operates correctly.

16.2 To detach the air intake cover, remove these pop fasteners (to remove a pop fastener, simply pry it loose, then pull it out)

16.3 Disconnect the electrical connector from the headlight

16.4 To remove the rubber weather seal from the headlight assembly, simply pull on one of the tabs

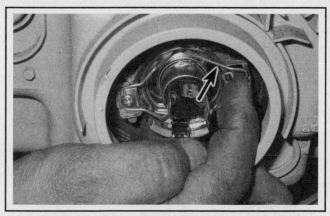

16.5a To release the headlight bulb retainer wire, push the end of the wire forward until it's disengaged from its slot, then push it up until it clears the slot and pull it back

16.5b Pull out the headlight bulb

16.6 When installing a headlight bulb, make sure that the three tabs on the headlight bulb flange are aligned with their respective slots in the plastic mounting base

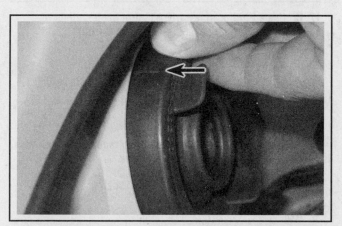

16.8 When installing the rubber weather seal on the back of the headlight assembly, make sure that the word "TOP" is at the 12 o'clock position. On other seals (like this one) there is no designated "top" but there are arrows 180-degrees apart (the arrows are aligned with the pull tabs used to remove the seal); make sure that one of the arrows is at the top

17 Headlights - adjustment

⬥ Refer to illustrations 17.1a, 17.1b and 17.3

➡ Note: The headlights must be aimed correctly. If adjusted incorrectly they could blind the driver of an oncoming vehicle and cause a serious accident or seriously reduce your ability to see the road. The headlights should be checked for correct aim every 12 months and any time a new headlight is installed or front end body work is performed. It should be emphasized that the following procedure is only an interim step that will provide temporary adjustment until the headlights can be adjusted by a properly equipped shop.

1 The adjustment mechanisms are on the rear of each headlight housing (see illustration). 2005 and later models have a single adjustment for the vertical direction only. Use a Phillips screwdriver to turn the adjusters (see illustration).

2 There are several methods for adjusting the headlights. The simplest method requires masking tape, a blank wall and a level floor.

3 Position masking tape vertically on the wall in relation to the

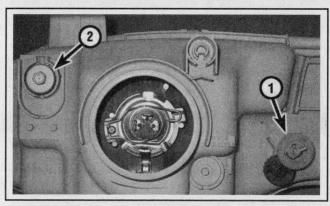

17.1a The horizontal headlight adjuster (1) and vertical headlight adjuster (2) are located on the back of each headlight housing (later models do not have a horizontal adjuster)

17.1b Use a Phillips screwdriver to turn the headlight adjusters (headlight housing removed for clarity)

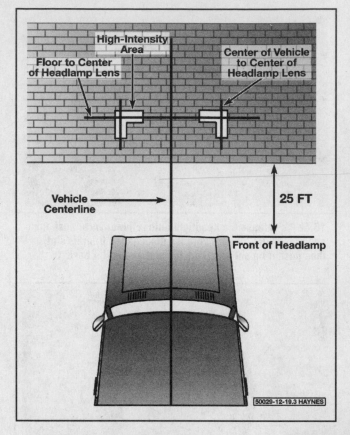

17.3 Headlight adjustment details

vehicle centerline and in relation to the centerlines of both headlights (see illustration).

4   Position a horizontal tape line in reference to the centerline of all the headlights.

➡ **Note: It might be easier to position the tape on the wall with the vehicle parked only a few inches away.**

5   Adjustment should be made with the vehicle parked 25 feet from the wall, sitting level, the gas tank half-full and no heavy load in the vehicle.

6   With the low beams turned on, position the high intensity zone so it is two inches below the horizontal line and two inches to the side of the headlight vertical line, away from oncoming traffic.

7   With the high beams on, the high intensity zone should be vertically centered with the exact center just below the horizontal line.

➡ **Note: It might not be possible to position the headlight aim exactly for both high and low beams. If a compromise must be made, keep in mind that the low beams are the most used and have the greatest effect on safety.**

8   If you had any difficulty adjusting the headlights, have them adjusted by a dealer service department as soon as possible.

18 Headlight housing - replacement

❱ **Refer to illustrations 18.4a, 18.4b and 18.5**

1   Make sure that the headlight switch and the ignition switch are turned off.

2   Remove the front bumper cover (see Chapter 11).

3   Disconnect the electrical connector from the headlight housing

(see illustrations 16.2 and 16.3).

➡ **Note: It's not necessary to remove the rubber protective boot or the bulb to remove the headlight housing. Even if you're planning to replace the headlight housing (and therefore need to remove the boot and bulb), it's easier to do so after you have removed the headlight housing.**

4   Remove the headlight housing mounting bolts (see illustrations).

5   Pull the headlight housing out and disconnect the electrical connector for the turn signal and sidemarker lights (see illustration).

6   Installation is the reverse of removal.

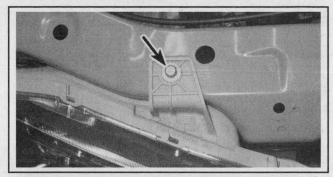

18.4a To detach the headlight housing, remove this bolt from the top . . .

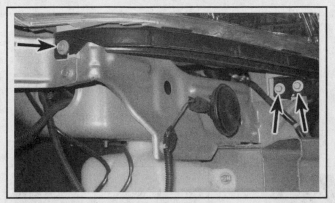

18.4b . . . and remove these three bolts from the bottom, then remove the headlight housing (2004 and earlier models shown)

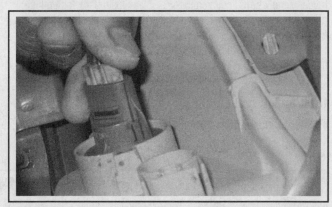

18.5 Disconnect the electrical connector for the turn signal and sidemarker lights

19 Horn - replacement

▶ **Refer to illustrations 19.3a and 19.3b**

1   Raise the vehicle and support it securely on jackstands.

2   On 2004 and earlier models, remove the front bumper cover (see Chapter 11). On 2005 and later models, remove the right front inner fender splash shield.

3   Disconnect the electrical connector from the horn (see illustrations).

4   Remove the horn mounting bracket bolt and remove the horn.

5   Installation is the reverse of removal.

19.3a Horn locations – 2004 and earlier models

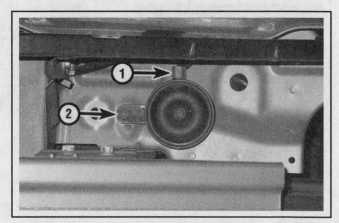

19.3b To remove a horn, disconnect the electrical connector (1) and remove the mounting bracket bolt (2)

20 Bulb replacement

EXTERIOR LIGHT BULBS

Front turn signal and sidemarker lights

▶ **Refer to illustrations 20.3 and 20.4**

1 Loosen the left or right front wheel lug nuts. Raise the front of the vehicle and place it securely on jackstands. Remove the left or right front wheel.

2 Remove the left or right inner fender splash shield (see Chapter 11).

3 Locate the front turn signal bulb holder. To remove the bulb holder, simply turn it counterclockwise (see illustration) and pull it out of the housing. It's not necessary to disconnect the electrical connector from the bulb holder.

4 Remove the turn signal bulb from the bulb holder (see illustration).

5 Installation is the reverse of removal.

High-mount brake light

▶ **Refer to illustrations 20.6a, 20.6b, 20.6c, 20.7 and 20.8**

6 Remove the small cover from the right end of the high-mount brake light, remove the screw and pull the light assembly out (see illustrations).

7 To remove the bulb holder from the high-mount brake light assembly, rotate the bulb holder counterclockwise and pull it out (see illustration).

8 To remove the old bulb from the bulb holder. simply pull it straight out of the holder (see illustration).

9 To install a new bulb, push it straight into the bulb holder.

10 Installation is the reverse of removal.

License plate light

▶ **Refer to illustrations 20.11, 20.12 and 20.13**

11 Pry the license plate light assembly from the liftgate (see illustration).

12 To remove the bulb holder from the license plate light lens, depress the release tabs on the sides of the holder and pull it out (see illustration).

13 To remove the bulb from the socket, pull it straight out (see illustration).

14 To install a new bulb in the socket, push it straight into the socket.

15 Installation is the reverse of removal.

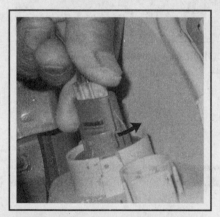

20.3 To remove the front turn signal/ sidemarker bulb holder, turn it counterclockwise and pull it out

20.4 To remove the front turn signal/ sidemarker bulb from the holder, turn it counterclockwise and pull it out

20.6a Carefully pry off this cover from the right end of the high-mount brake light lens . . .

20.6b . . . then remove this screw . . .

20.6c . . . and pull out the high- mount brake light assembly

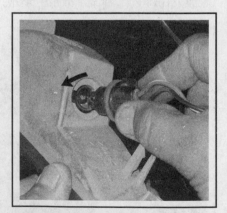

20.7 To remove the bulb holder from the high-mount brake light assembly, rotate it 1/4-turn counterclockwise and pull it out

Inner taillights (back-up lights and running lights)

▶ **Refer to illustrations 20.17 and 20.18**

16 To access the inner taillight bulbs, remove the trim panel from the liftgate (see Chapter 11).

17 After removing the liftgate trim panel, you'll see two bulb holders installed in each inner taillight assembly. The larger lower bulb holders are for the back-up light bulbs; the smaller upper bulb holders are for the running lights. To remove a bulb holder from an inner taillight, rotate the holder counterclockwise (see illustration) and pull it out.

18 To remove an inner taillight bulb from its holder, pull it straight out (see illustration).

19 To install a bulb in its socket, push it straight into the socket.

20 Installation is the reverse of removal.

Taillights (brake lights and turn signal lights)

▶ **Refer to illustrations 20.21, 20.22a, 20.22b, 20.23 and 20.24**

21 Open the liftgate and remove the two taillight mounting bolts (see illustration).

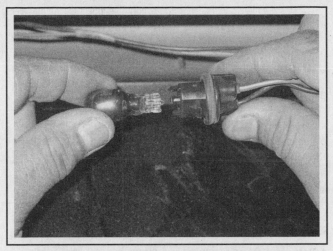

20.8 To remove the bulb from the high-mount brake light bulb holder, simply pull it straight out of the holder

20.11 Pry the license plate light assembly from the liftgate

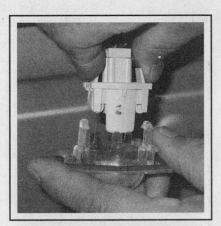

20.12 To release the bulb holder from the license plate light lens, depress the two release tabs on the sides of the holder and pull out the holder

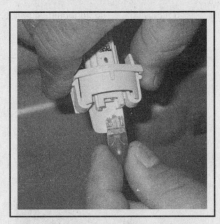

20.13 To remove the bulb from the bulb holder, pull it straight out

20.17 To remove either bulb holder from the inner taillight assembly, rotate it counterclockwise and pull it out (back-up light bulb holder shown, running light bulb holder identical)

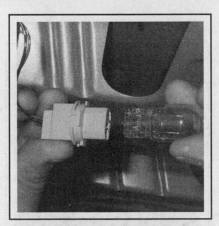

20.18 To remove a bulb from either inner taillight bulb holder, pull it straight out

20.21 To detach a taillight assembly from the vehicle body, remove these two mounting bolts

22 Pull out the weather seal grommet and disconnect the taillight electrical connector (see illustrations) then remove the taillight assembly.

23 The upper bulb holder is for the brake light and the lower holder is for the turn signal light. To remove either bulb holder, turn it counterclockwise and pull it out (see illustration).

24 To remove a bulb from its socket, simply pull it straight out (see illustration).

25 To install a bulb in its socket, push it straight into the socket.

26 While the taillight assembly is removed, be sure to inspect the condition of the weather seal grommet. If it's cracked, torn or deteriorated, replace it. Installation is otherwise the reverse of removal.

INTERIOR LIGHTS

Cargo area light

▶ **Refer to illustrations 20.27 and 20.28**

27 To remove the cargo light lens from the headliner, simply pry it loose (see illustration). Be careful not to scratch the cargo light housing assembly or the headliner.

28 To remove the cargo light bulb, simply pull it out of its holder (see illustration).

29 To install a new cargo light bulb, simply push it into its holder.

30 Installation is the reverse of removal.

Center pocket light

▶ **Refer to illustrations 20.32, 20.33 and 20.34**

31 Remove the center pocket from the center console (see Chapter 11).

32 Disconnect the electrical connector from the center pocket light assembly (see illustration).

33 Remove the center pocket light assembly (see illustration).

34 Remove the center pocket light (see illustration).

35 Installation is the reverse of removal.

Front individual map lights

▶ **Refer to illustrations 20.36 and 20.37**

36 Carefully pry off the lens from the front individual map light assembly (see illustration).

37 To replace one of the light bulbs in the interior/map reading light assembly, simply pull it out (see illustration).

38 Installation is the reverse of removal.

20.22a Pull out the weather seal grommet . . .

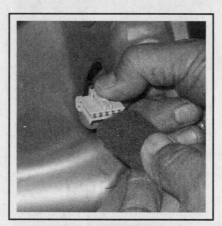

20.22b . . . and disconnect the taillight electrical connector

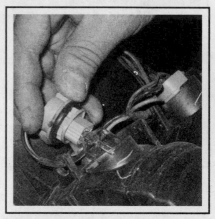

20.23 To remove a taillight bulb holder, rotate it 1/4-turn counterclockwise and pull it out

20.24 To remove a taillight bulb from its holder, simply pull it straight out

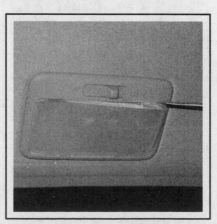

20.27 To access the cargo light, carefully pry off the lens

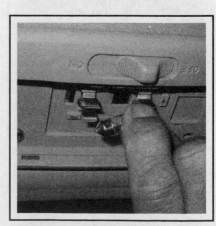

20.28 To remove a cargo light bulb, simply pull it out of its holder

Hazard flasher switch light bulb

♦ Refer to illustrations 20.40a and 20.40b

39 Remove the hazard flasher switch (see Section 9).

40 Remove the light bulb from the hazard flasher switch (see illustrations).

41 To install a new bulb in the hazard flasher switch, insert it into the mounting hole and turn it clockwise to lock it in place.

42 Installation is otherwise the reverse of removal.

Rear individual map lights

♦ Refer to illustrations 20.43 and 20.44

43 Pry off the lens from the rear individual map light assembly with a small screwdriver (see illustration).

44 Remove the old bulb from the rear individual map light assembly (see illustration).

45 Installation is the reverse of removal.

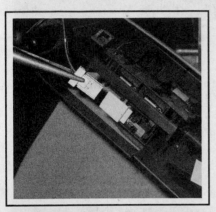

20.32 Disconnect the center pocket light electrical connector

20.33 To detach the center pocket light assembly, remove these two screws

20.34 Use a small screwdriver to pry the old center pocket light bulb out of its holders (pry only on the metal ends - NOT on the glass!)

20.36 Carefully pry off the lens from the front individual map light assembly with a small screwdriver

20.37 To remove a front individual map light bulb, simply pull it straight out

20.40a To remove the light bulb from the hazard flasher switch, turn it 1/4-turn counterclockwise . . .

20.40b . . . and pull it out with a pair of tweezers

20.43 Carefully pry off the lens from the rear individual map light assembly

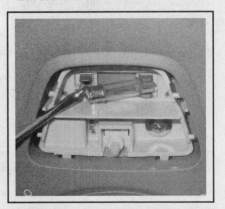

20.44 Pry out the old light bulb with a small screwdriver (pry only on the metal ends - NOT on the glass)

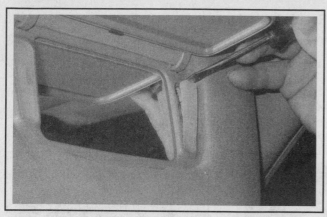

20.46 Carefully pry off the lens from the vanity mirror light

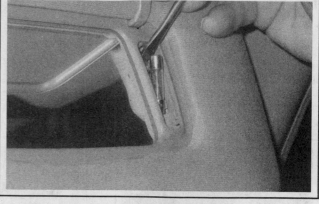

20.47 Pry out the old bulb with a small screwdriver (pry only on the metal ends - NOT on the glass)

Vanity mirror lights

▶ Refer to illustrations 20.46 and 20.47

46   Carefully pry off the lens from the vanity mirror light (see illustration).

47   Remove the old bulb from the vanity mirror light assembly (see illustration).

48   Installation is the reverse of removal.

21   Electric side view mirrors - general information

1   Most electric rear view mirrors use two motors to move the glass; one for up and down adjustments and one for left-right adjustments.

2   During mirror adjustment, the power mirror adjustment switch sends voltage to the left or right side mirror. With the ignition key turned to ON (engine not running), operate the mirror adjustment switch through all of its functions (left-right and up-down) for both the left and right side mirrors.

3   Listen carefully for the sound of the electric motors running in the mirrors.

4   If you can hear the motors but the mirror glass doesn't move, there's a problem with the drive mechanism inside the mirror.

5   If the mirrors do not operate and no sound comes from the mir-

rors, check the fuse (see Section 3).

6   If the fuse is OK, remove the power mirror adjustment switch (see Section 9). Have the switch continuity checked by a dealership service department or other qualified automobile repair facility.

7   Test the ground connections.

8   If the mirror still doesn't work, remove the mirror and check the wires at the mirror for voltage.

9   If there is no voltage in any switch position, check the circuit between the mirror and the adjustment switch for opens and shorts.

10 If there's voltage, remove the mirror and test it off the vehicle with jumper wires. Replace the mirror if it fails this test.

22   Cruise control system - general information

1   The cruise control system maintains vehicle speed with an electrically-operated motor located in the engine compartment, which is connected to the throttle body by a cable. The system consists of the Powertrain Control Module, the speed control actuator, the speed control cable, the speed control indicator light, the speed control actuator switches, the Brake Pedal Position (BPP) switch and the transmission range switch. The cruise control system requires diagnostic procedures that are beyond the scope of this manual, but there are some general procedures that will help you identify common problems.

2   Check the fuses (see Section 3).

3   Have an assistant operate the brake lights while you check their

operation (voltage from the brake light switch deactivates the cruise control).

4   If the brake lights don't come on or stay on all the time, correct the problem and retest the cruise control system.

5   Visually inspect the control cable between the cruise control motor and the throttle linkage for free movement. Replace it if necessary.

6   Test drive the vehicle to determine if the cruise control is now working. If it isn't, take it to a dealer service department or an automotive electrical specialist for further diagnosis.

23   Power window system - general information

1   The power window system operates electric motors, mounted in the doors, which lower and raise the windows. The system consists of the control switches, the motors, regulators, glass mechanisms and associated wiring.

2   The power windows can be lowered and raised from the master control switch by the driver or by remote switches located at the individual windows. Each window has a separate motor, which is reversible. The position of the control switch determines the polarity and therefore

the direction of operation.

3   The circuit is protected by a fuse and a circuit breaker. Each motor is also equipped with an internal circuit breaker, this prevents one stuck window from disabling the whole system.

4   The power window system will only operate when the ignition switch is turned to ON. There's also a main switch at the master power window control panel (in the driver's door) which, when activated, disables the switches at the rear windows and the switch at the passenger's window. So if there's a problem with the passenger window or with either of the rear windows, make sure that it's not simply a matter of flipping the main switch before proceeding.

5   The procedures listed below are general in nature, so if you can't find the problem using them, take the vehicle to a dealer service department.

6   If the power windows won't operate, always check the fuses and relays first (see Sections 3 and 5, respectively). Also verify that there's voltage to the relay and that the relay is well grounded.

7   If only the rear windows are inoperative, or if the windows only operate from the master control switch, check the main switch for continuity in the unlocked position. Replace it if it doesn't have continuity (see "Door trim panel - removal and installation" in Chapter 11).

8   Check the wiring between the switches and the fuse and relay box for continuity. Repair the wiring, if necessary.

9   If only one window is inoperative from the main switch, try the other control switch at the window.

➡ **Note: This doesn't apply to the driver's door window.**

10   If the same window works from one switch, but not the other, check the switch for continuity.

11   If the switch tests OK, check for a short or open in the circuit between the affected switch and the window motor.

12   If one window is inoperative from both switches, remove the trim panel from the affected door (see "Door trim panel - removal and installation" in Chapter 11) and check for voltage at the switch and at the

motor while the switch is operated.

13   If voltage is reaching the motor, disconnect the glass from the regulator (see Chapter 11). Move the window up and down by hand while checking for binding and damage. Also check for binding and damage to the regulator. If the regulator is not damaged and the window moves up and down smoothly, replace the motor. If there's binding or damage, lubricate, repair or replace parts, as necessary.

14   If voltage isn't reaching the motor, check the wiring in the circuit for continuity between the switches and motors. You'll need to consult the wiring diagram for the vehicle.

RESETTING THE POWER WINDOW CONTROL UNIT (2003 AND 2004 MODELS)

15   On 2003 and 2004 models, the power window control unit *might* have to be reset after any of these procedures:

The battery has been disconnected

The No. 79 (20-amp) fuse has been removed from the engine compartment fuse and relay box

The 18-pin electrical connector has been disconnected from the power window control unit

The window regulator, glass or glass run channel has been removed

The driver's door wiring harness has been disconnected

16   Turn the ignition switch to OFF, then turn it to ON.

17   Fully open the driver's window by depressing the AUTO DOWN part of the driver's door power window switch. When the window is fully open, hold the switch in the AUTO DOWN position for two seconds.

18   Fully close the driver's window without stopping by holding the switch in the UP position. When the window is fully closed, hold the switch in the UP position for two seconds.

19   If the window still doesn't work, repeat this procedure.

24   Power door lock system - general information

1   A power door lock system operates the door lock actuators mounted in each door. The system consists of the switches, actuators, a control unit and associated wiring. On some models, the power door lock system is part of the security alarm system. On these models, the power door lock system is more complex, and more difficult to diagnose. Therefore, home troubleshooting is limited to simple checks of the wiring connections and actuators for minor faults that can be easily repaired.

2   Power door lock systems are operated by bi-directional solenoids located in the doors. The lock switches have two operating positions: LOCK and UNLOCK. When activated, the switch sends a ground signal to the door lock control unit to lock or unlock the doors. Depending on which way the switch is activated, the control unit reverses polarity to the solenoids, allowing the two sides of the circuit to be used alternately as the feed (positive) and ground side.

3   The following general guidelines should help you quickly identify and repair typical problems. If you're unable to locate the trouble using these guidelines, consult a dealer service department.

4   Always check the fuses first (see Section 3 and your owners' manual).

5   Operate the door lock switches in both directions (LOCK and

UNLOCK) with the engine off. Listen for the click of the solenoids operating.

6   Test the switches for continuity. Remove the switches and have them checked by a dealer service department.

7   Check the wiring between the switches, control unit and solenoids for continuity. Repair the wiring if there's no continuity.

8   Check for a bad ground at the switches and at the control unit.

9   If only one lock solenoid doesn't operate, remove the trim panel from the door with the bad solenoid (see "Door trim panel - removal and installation" in Chapter 11) and check for voltage at the solenoid while the lock switch is operated. One of the wires should have voltage in the Lock position; the other should have voltage in the Unlock position.

10   If the inoperative solenoid is receiving voltage, replace the solenoid.

11   If the inoperative solenoid isn't receiving voltage, check for an open or short in the wire between the lock solenoid and the control unit.

➡ **Note: Wire harnesses typically break between the body and door, because repeatedly opening and closing the door fatigues and eventually breaks the wires.**

25 Power sliding doors - general information

Some models are equipped with power sliding doors. The electrical control and power circuits for these doors are quite complex. If a malfunction causes the doors to open accidentally while the vehicle is moving, it could be dangerous, so we don't recommend that you attempt to diagnose or repair these circuits. If you have any problems with the power sliding door(s), have the problem diagnosed and repaired by a dealer service department or other qualified repair shop.

26 Daytime Running Lights (DRL) - general information

The Daytime Running Lights (DRL) system illuminates the headlights whenever the engine is running. The only exception is with the engine running and the parking brake engaged. Once the parking brake is released, the lights will remain on as long as the ignition switch is on, even if the parking brake is later applied. The DRL system supplies reduced power to the headlights so they won't be too bright for daytime use, while prolonging headlight life.

If one of the headlight low beams is out, the low-beam filament is probably burned out, but check the DRL relay first (see Section 3). The DRL relay is located in the engine compartment fuse and relay box. If the relay is okay, replace the bad headlight bulb (see Section 16).

27 Airbag system - general information

GENERAL INFORMATION

1 All models are equipped with a Supplemental Restraint System (SRS), more commonly known as airbags. This system is designed to protect the driver, and the front seat passenger, from serious injury in the event of a head-on or frontal collision. It uses a single crash sensor built into the SRS control unit on 2001 models, or a pair of crash sensors mounted behind the front bumper (2002 models) or along the base of the inner fender panels (2003 and later models). The airbag assemblies are mounted on the steering wheel and inside the passenger's end of the dash. 2002 and later models are also equipped with side-impact airbags mounted in the backs of the front seats.

2 These models are also equipped with seat belt pre-tensioners. These are pyrotechnic devices that reduce the slack in the seat belts during an impact of sufficient force to trigger the airbags.

AIRBAG MODULE

Driver's side airbag

3 The airbag inflator module contains a housing incorporating the cushion (airbag) and inflator unit, mounted in the center of the steering wheel. The inflator assembly is mounted on the back of the housing over a hole through which gas is expelled, inflating the bag almost instantaneously when an electrical signal is sent from the system. A "clockspring" on the steering column under the steering wheel carries this signal to the module. This clockspring assembly can transmit an electrical signal regardless of steering wheel position. The igniter in the airbag converts the electrical signal to heat and ignites the powder, which inflates the bag. For information on how to remove and install the driver's side airbag, refer to "Steering wheel - removal and installation" in Chapter 10.

PASSENGER'S SIDE AIRBAG

4 The airbag is mounted at the top of the passenger's side of the instrument panel. It consists of an inflator containing an igniter, a reaction housing/airbag assembly and a trim cover.

5 The passenger's side airbag is considerably larger than the steering wheel-mounted unit and is mounted inside the dash, near the glove box. The airbag trim cover on top of the dash is textured and painted to match the instrument panel and has a molded seam, which splits when the bag inflates.

SRS CONTROL UNIT

6 This unit supplies the current to the airbag system (and seat belt pre-tensioners, on models so equipped) in the event of the collision, even if battery power is cut off. It checks this system every time the vehicle is started, causing the "SRS" light to go on, then off, if the system is operating correctly. If there is a fault in the system, the light will go on and stay on, or it will flash or the dash will make a beeping sound. If this happens, take the vehicle to your dealer immediately for service.

DISARMING THE SYSTEM AND OTHER PRECAUTIONS

✳✳ WARNING:

Failure to follow these precautions could result in accidental deployment of the airbag and personal injury.

7 Whenever working in the vicinity of the steering wheel, instrument panel or any of the other SRS system components, the system must be disarmed. To disarm the system:

a) *Point the wheels straight ahead and turn the key to the Lock position.*

b) *Disconnect the cable from the negative battery terminal(s). Refer to Chapter 5, Section 1 for the disconnecting procedure.*

c) *Wait at least three minutes for the back-up power supply to be depleted.*

8   Whenever handling an airbag module, always keep the airbag opening side pointed away from your body. Never place the airbag module on a bench or other surface with the airbag opening facing the surface. Always place the airbag module in a safe location with the airbag opening facing up.

9   Never measure the resistance of any SRS component or use any electrical test equipment on any of the wiring or components. An ohm-meter has a built-in battery supply that could accidentally deploy the airbag.

10 Never use electrical welding equipment on a vehicle equipped with an airbag without first disconnecting the airbag electrical connectors. The connector for the driver's side airbag is located near the bottom of the steering column (see "Steering wheel - removal and installation" in Chapter 10); the connector for the passenger's side airbag is located inside the dash, near the glove box (see below). The seat belt pre-tensioner electrical connectors are located behind the B-pillar trim panels. The electrical connectors for the side impact airbags, on models so equipped, are located under the front seats.

11 Never dispose of a live airbag module or seat belt pre-tensioner. Return it to a dealer service department or other qualified repair shop for safe deployment and disposal.

AIRBAG MODULE REMOVAL AND INSTALLATION

Driver's side airbag module and clockspring

12 Refer to Chapter 10, *Steering wheel - removal and installation*, for the driver's side airbag module and clockspring removal and installation procedures.

Passenger's side airbag module

▶ **Refer to illustrations 27.15 and 27.16 and 27.17**

13 Disarm the airbag system as described previously in this Section.
14 Remove the glovebox (see Chapter 11).
15 Disconnect the passenger side airbag electrical connector (see illustration).
16 Remove the airbag module mounting nuts (see illustration). After removing the nuts, carefully but firmly push up on the airbag module to disengage the trim cover from the top of the dash.

※ CAUTION:

The airbag module and trim cover are attached and are removed as a single assembly). Do NOT try to pry open the trim cover from up top, or you will damage the surface of the dash and/or the trim cover.

17 Working from above, pull the airbag trim cover and airbag module out of the dash (see illustration). If necessary (and only if necessary), carefully separate the airbag module from the trim cover. Be sure to heed the precautions outlined previously in this Section.
18 Installation is the reverse of removal. Tighten the airbag module mounting nuts securely.
19 Reconnect the cable to the negative battery terminal (see Chapter 5, Section 1).

Side-impact airbag

20 Under normal circumstances there would never be a reason to remove a side-impact airbag. However, if it has been determined that there is a problem with the side-impact airbag module, the work must be left to a dealer service department or other qualified repair shop.

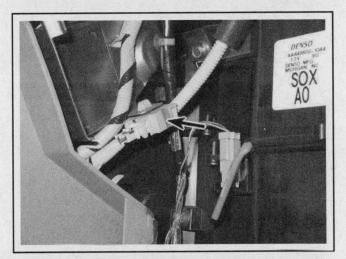

27.15 Disconnect the passenger's side airbag electrical connector

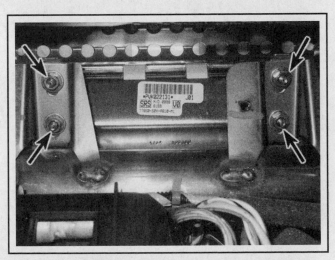

27.16 To detach the passenger's side airbag, remove these four nuts

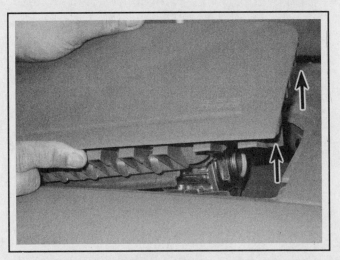

27.17 To remove the passenger airbag, push up on it from underneath and then lift it out of the dash

28 Wiring diagrams - general information

Since it isn't possible to include all wiring diagrams for every year covered by this manual, the following diagrams are those that are typical and most commonly needed.

Prior to troubleshooting any circuits, check the fuses and relays to ensure that they're in good condition. Make sure that the battery is correctly charged and check the cable connections (see Chapters 1 and 5).

When checking a circuit, make sure that all connections are clean and tight, with no broken or loose terminals. If an electrical connector is difficult to disconnect, it's probably because the two halves of the connector are locked together on one or two sides of the connector. So stop and look for the locks, which are usually small plastic tabs that must either be depressed to unlock them, or must be released with a small screwdriver. If you have a problem finding the lock(s), clean off the connector with electronic parts cleaner, then look again. If you're trying to unplug a connector that's located in a dark area, use a flashlight to find the locks. When disconnecting an electrical connector, do NOT pull on the wires; pull on the two halves of the connector itself.

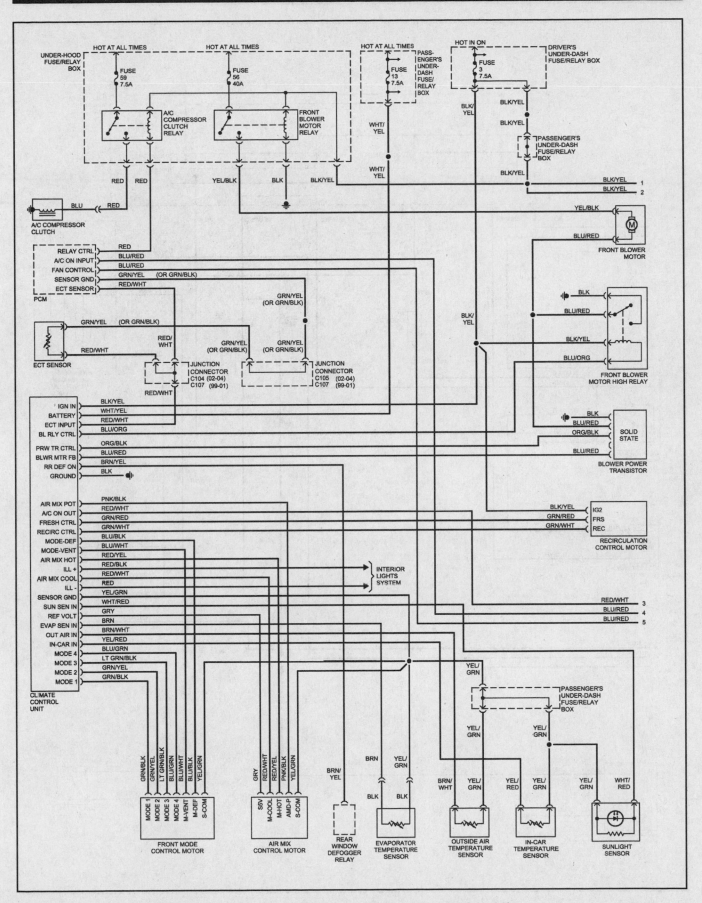

Automatic climate control system, without Navigation system (2004 and earlier EX models) (1 of 2)

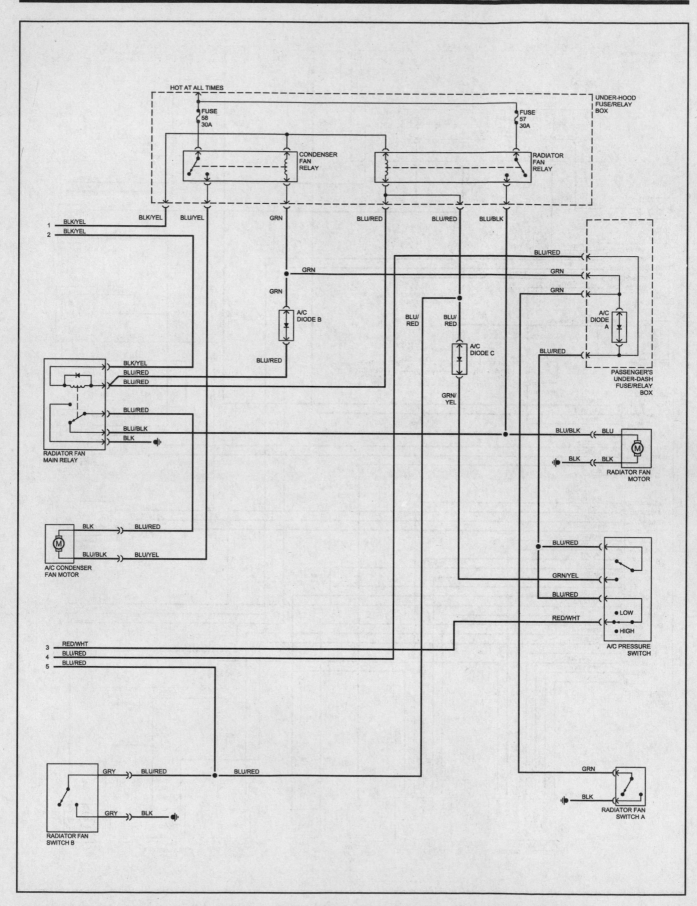

Automatic climate control air conditioning system, without Navigation system (2004 and earlier EX models) (2 of 2)

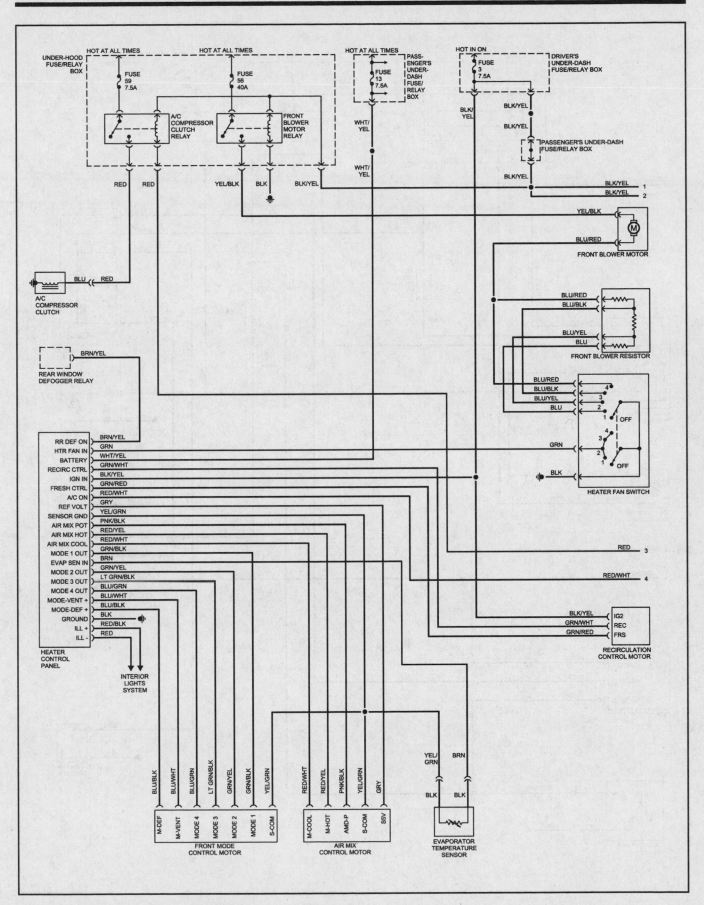

Manual air conditioning system (2004 and earlier LX models) (1 of 2)

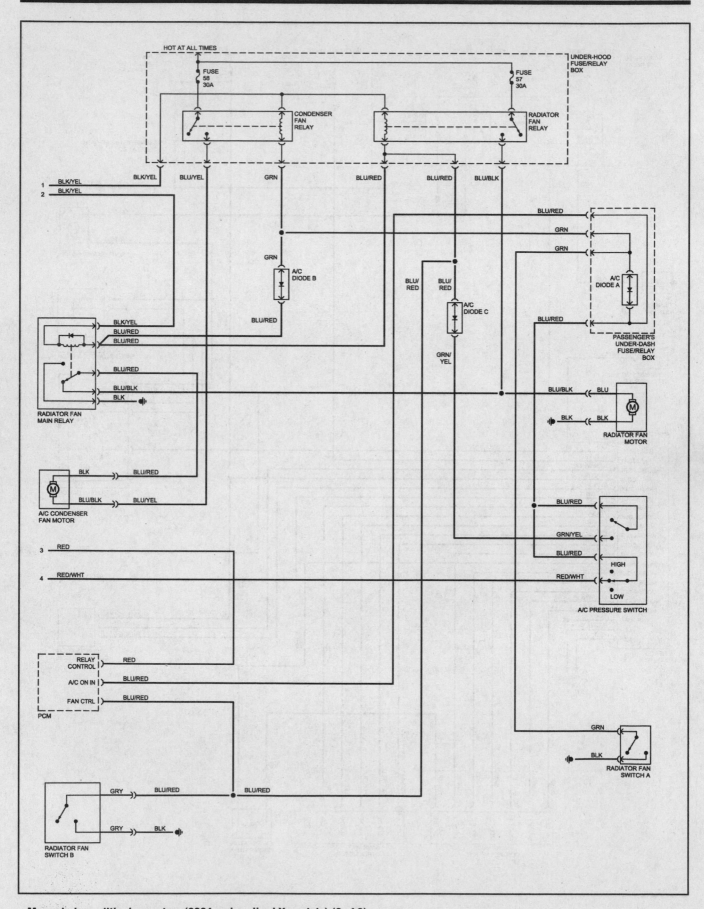

Manual air conditioning system (2004 and earlier LX models) (2 of 2)

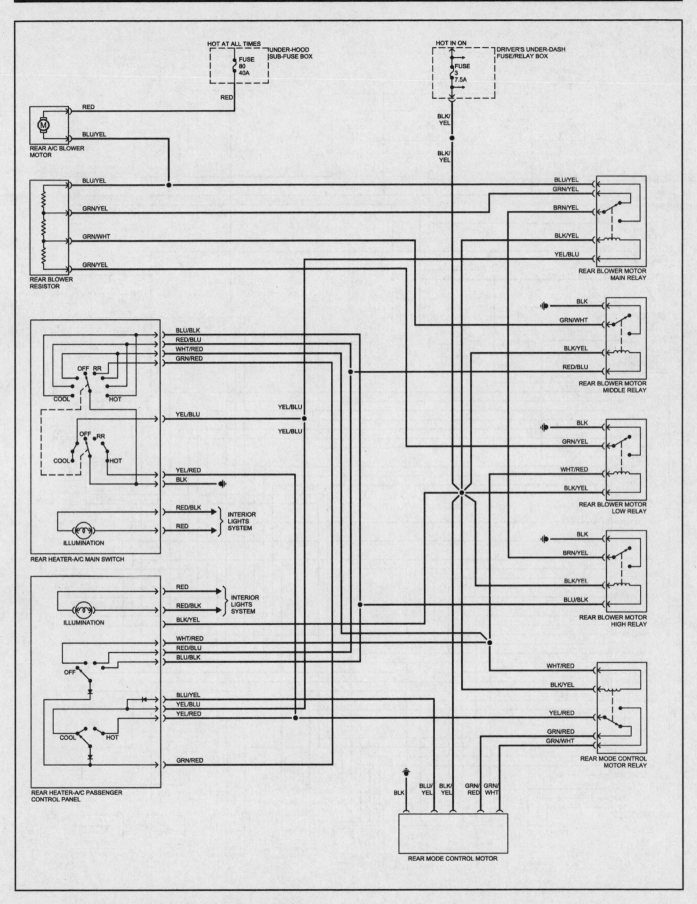

Rear air conditioning system (2004 and earlier models)

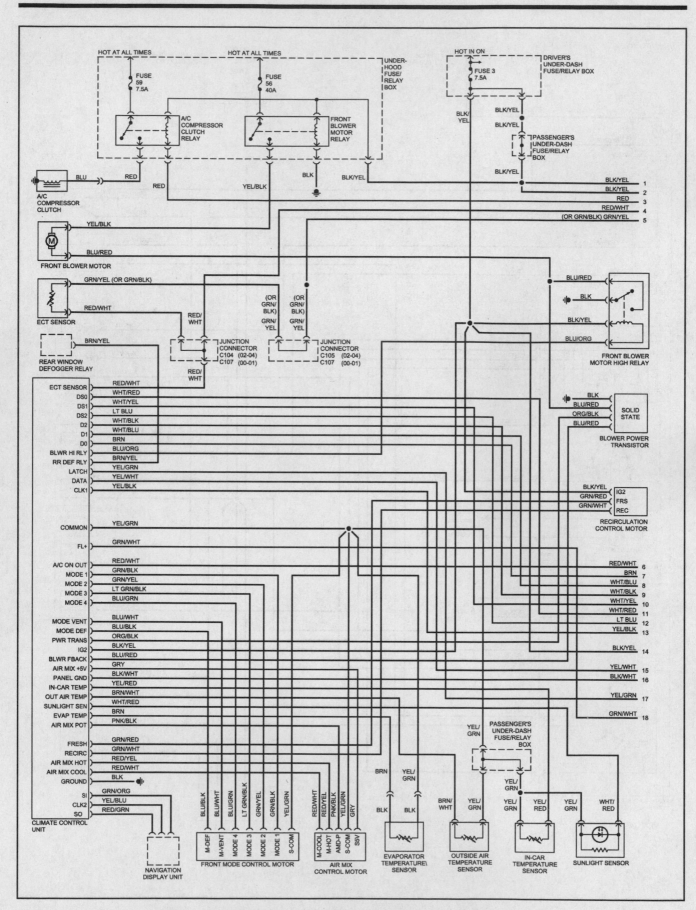

Automatic climate control system, with Navigation system (2004 and earlier EX models) (1 of 2)

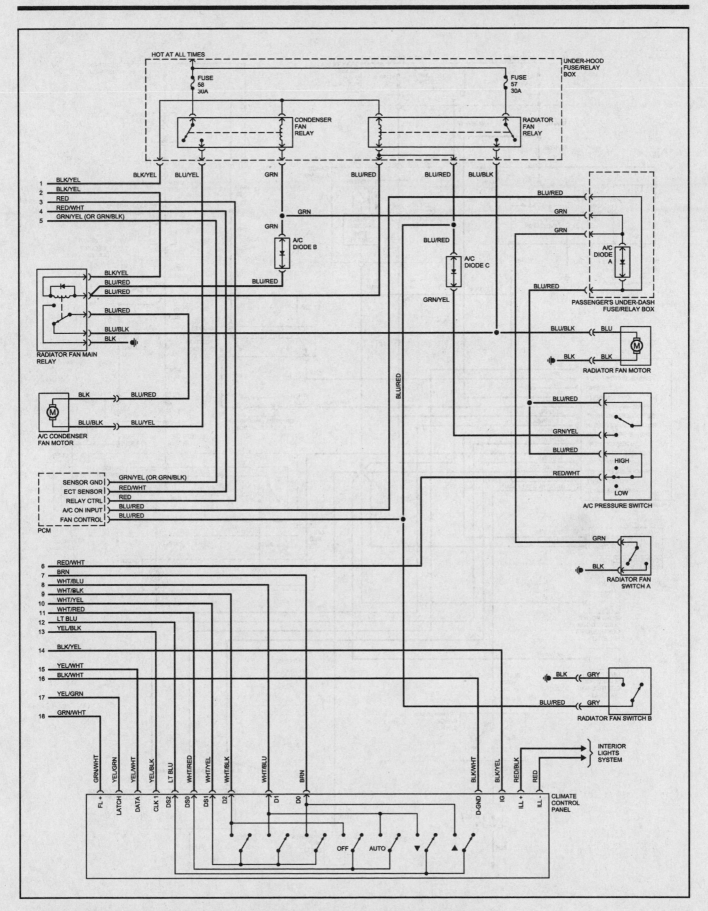

Automatic climate control system, with Navigation system (2004 and earlier EX models) (2 of 2)

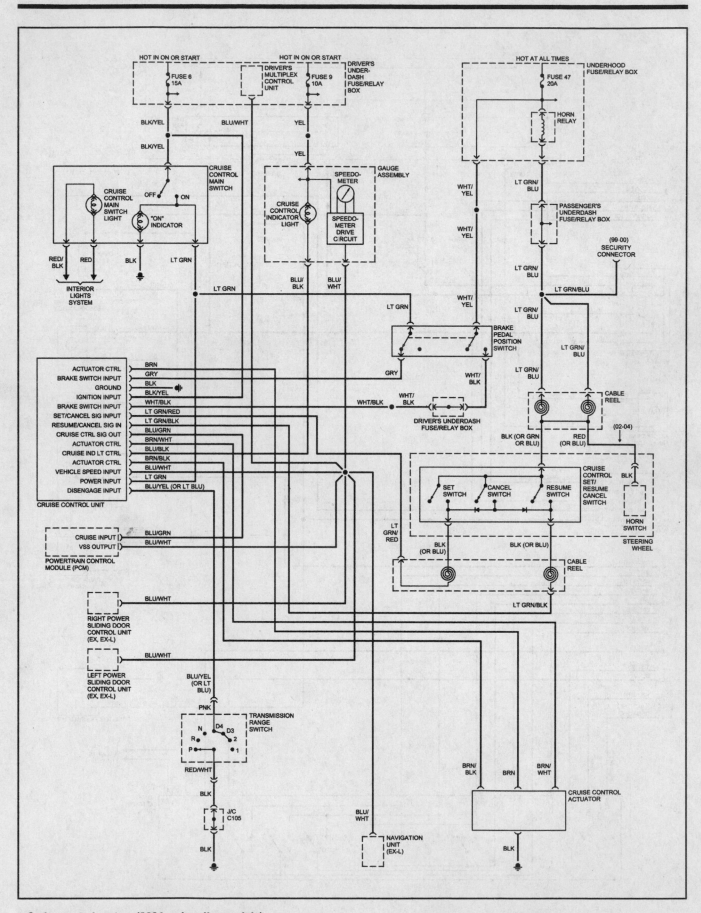

Cruise control system (2004 and earlier models)

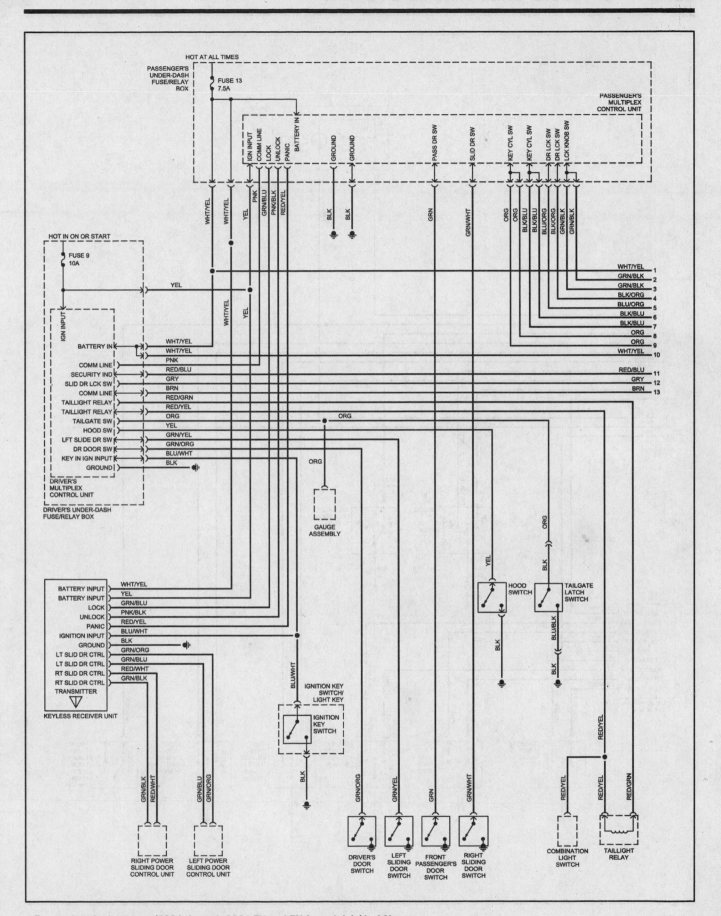

Power door lock system (2001 through 2004 EX and EX-L models) (1 of 3)

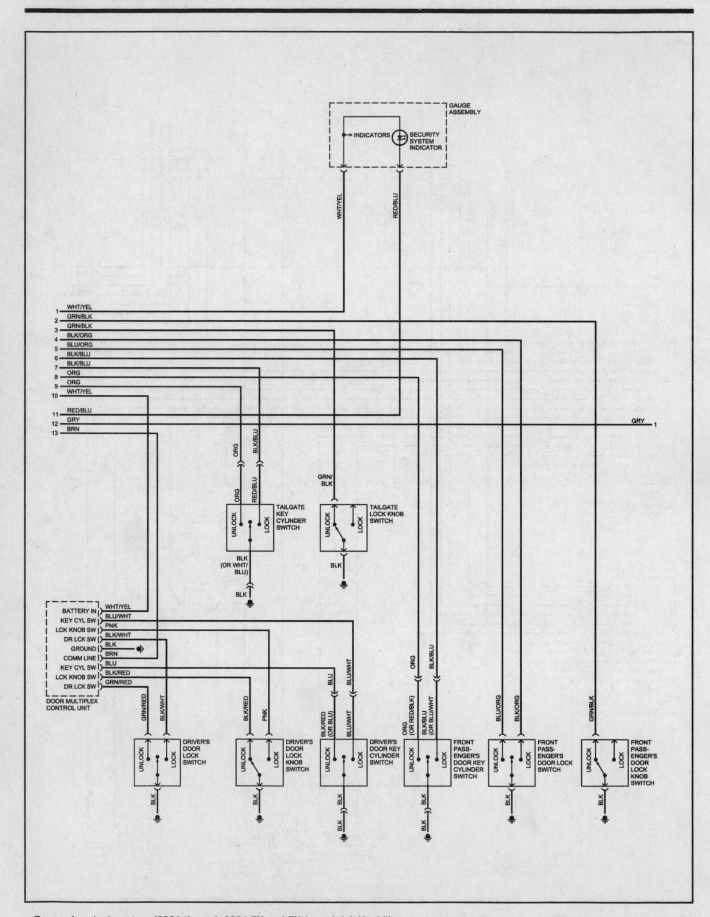

Power door lock system (2001 through 2004 EX and EX-L models) (2 of 3)

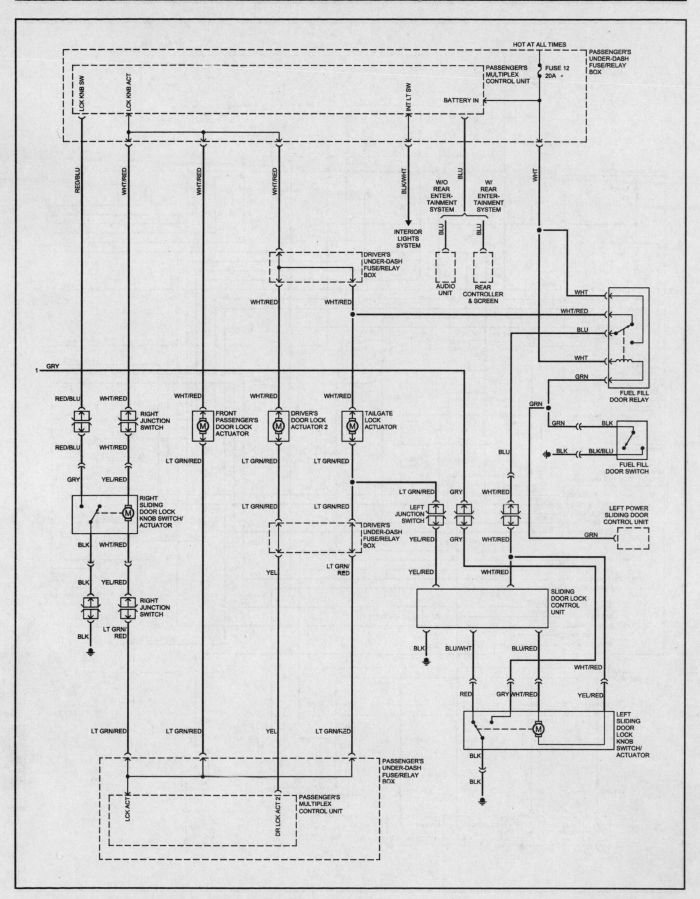

Power door lock system (2001 through 2004 EX and EX-L models) (3 of 3)

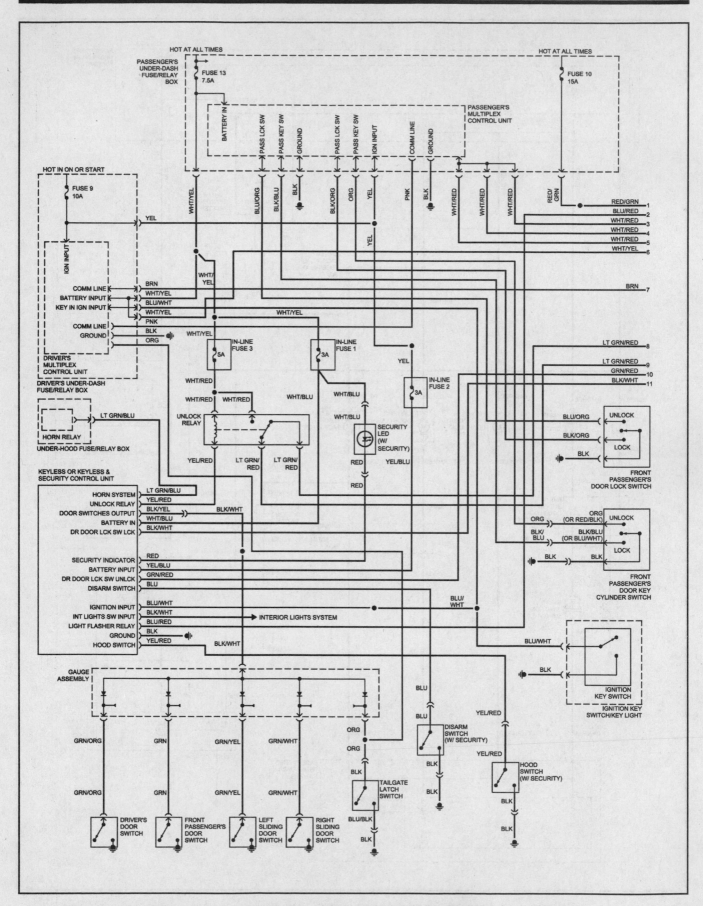

Power door lock system (2004 and earlier LX models with keyless entry system) (1 of 2)

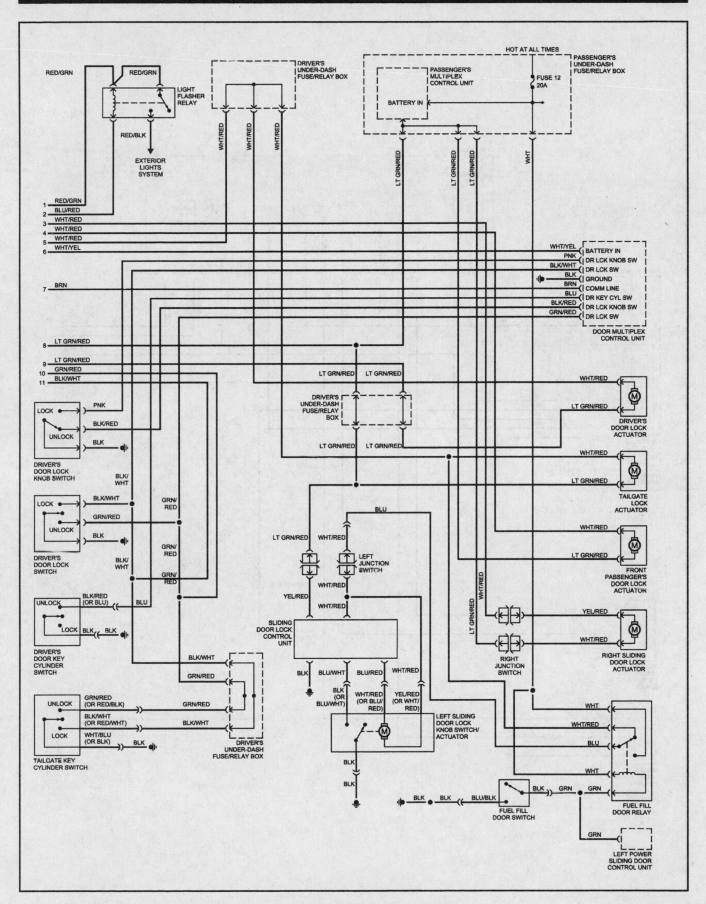

Power door lock system (2004 and earlier LX models with keyless entry system) (2 of 2)

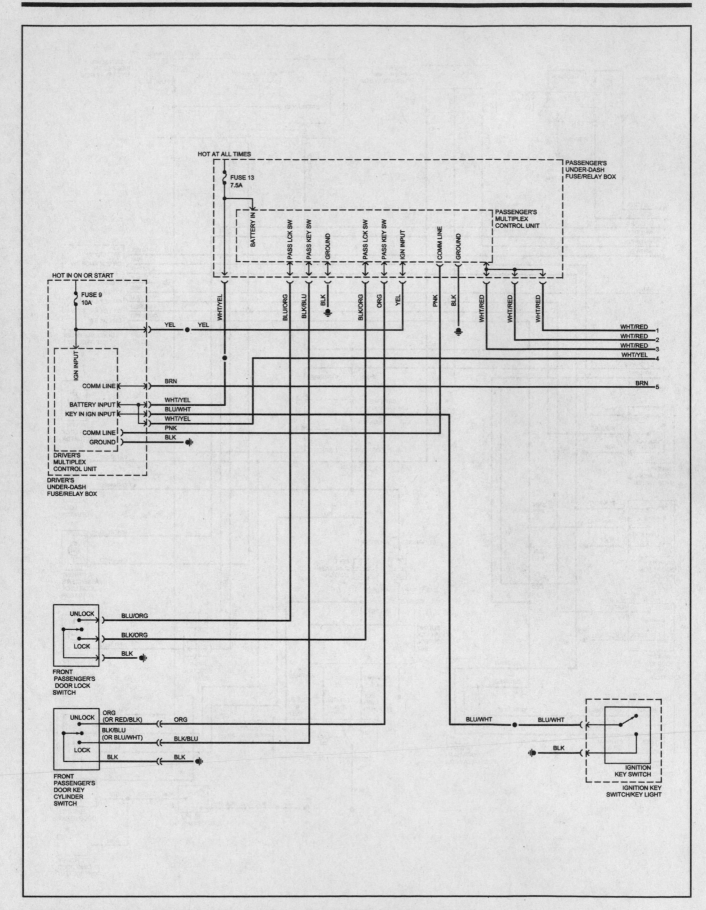

Power door lock system (2004 and earlier LX models without keyless entry system) (1 of 2)

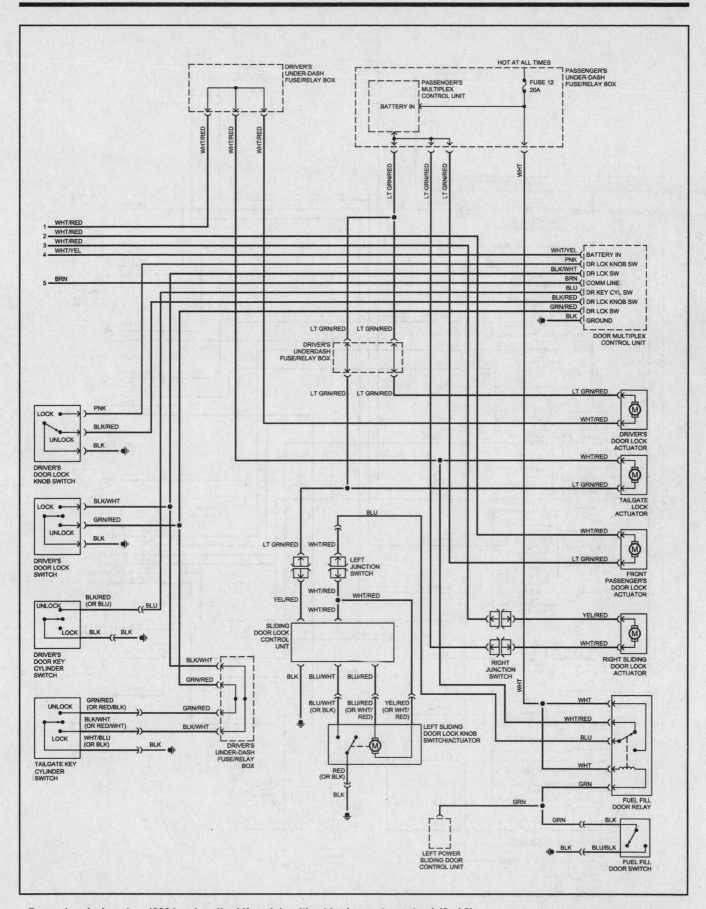

Power door lock system (2004 and earlier LX models without keyless entry system) (2 of 2)

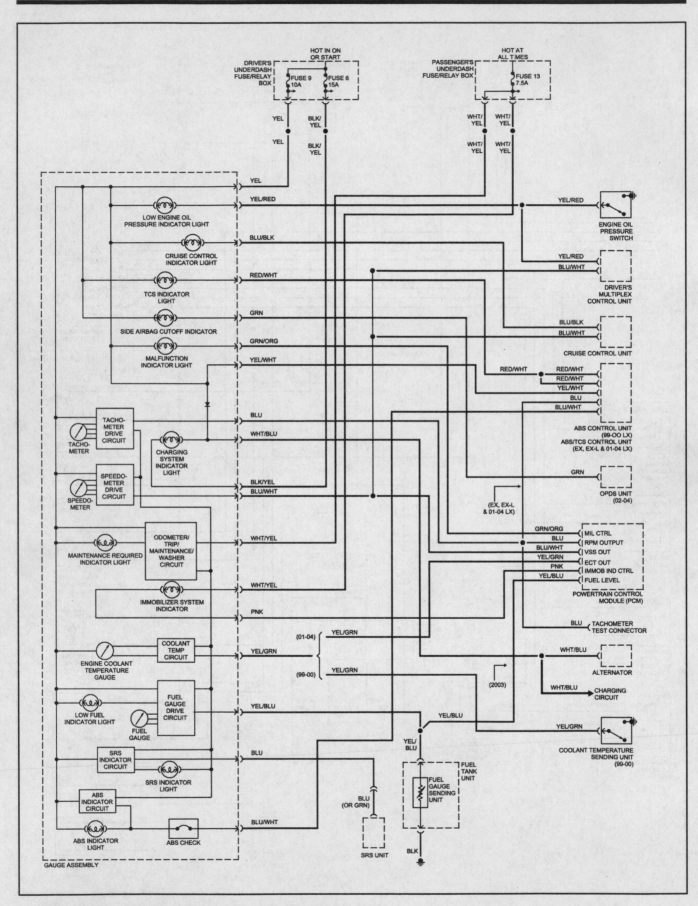

Instrument cluster and engine indicator lights (2004 and earlier models)

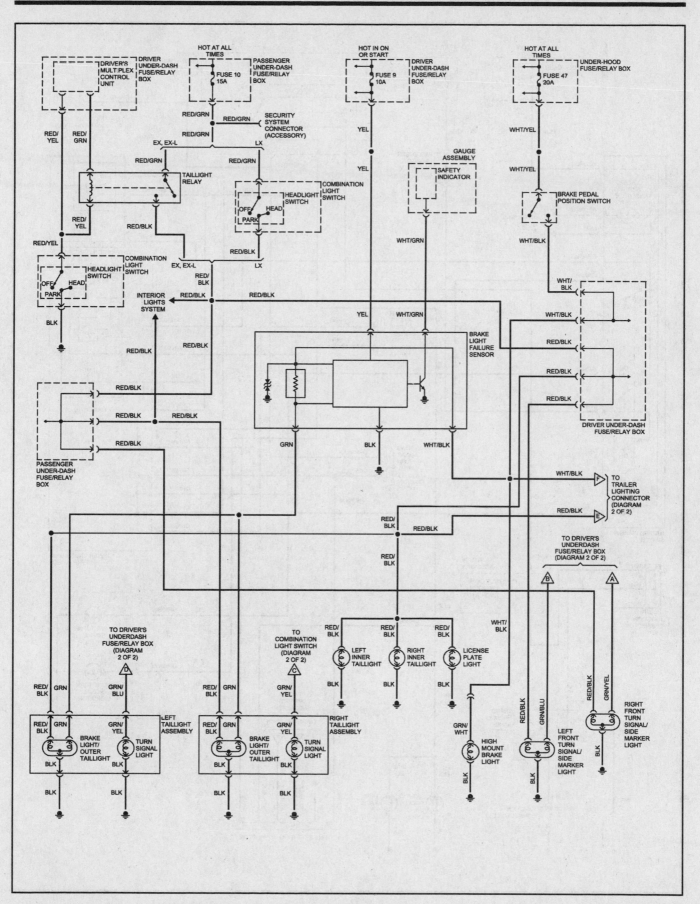

Exterior lighting systems, except headlights (2004 and earlier models) (1 of 2)

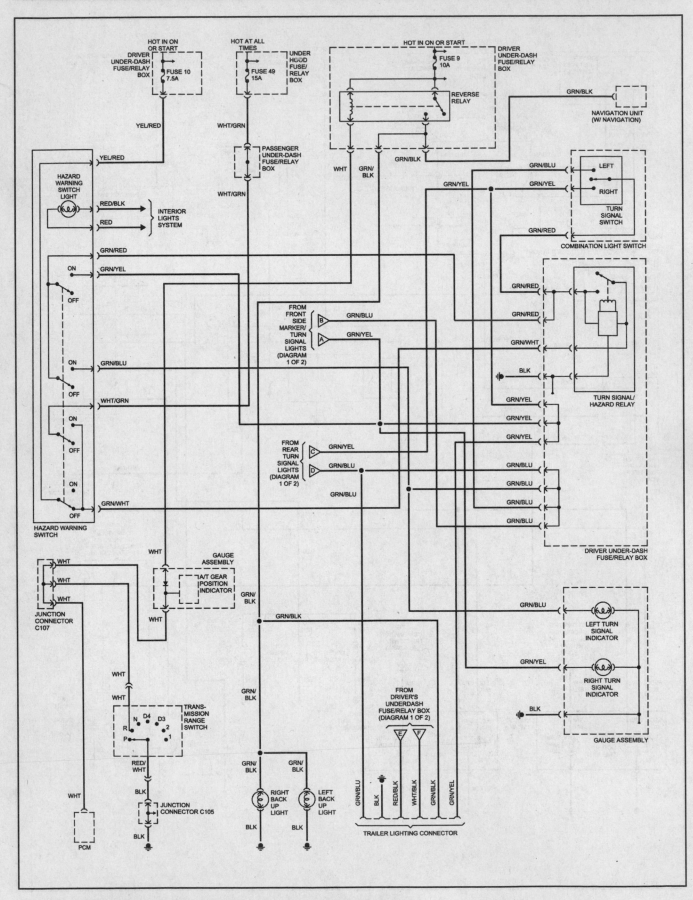

Exterior lighting systems, except headlights (2004 and earlier models) (2 of 2)

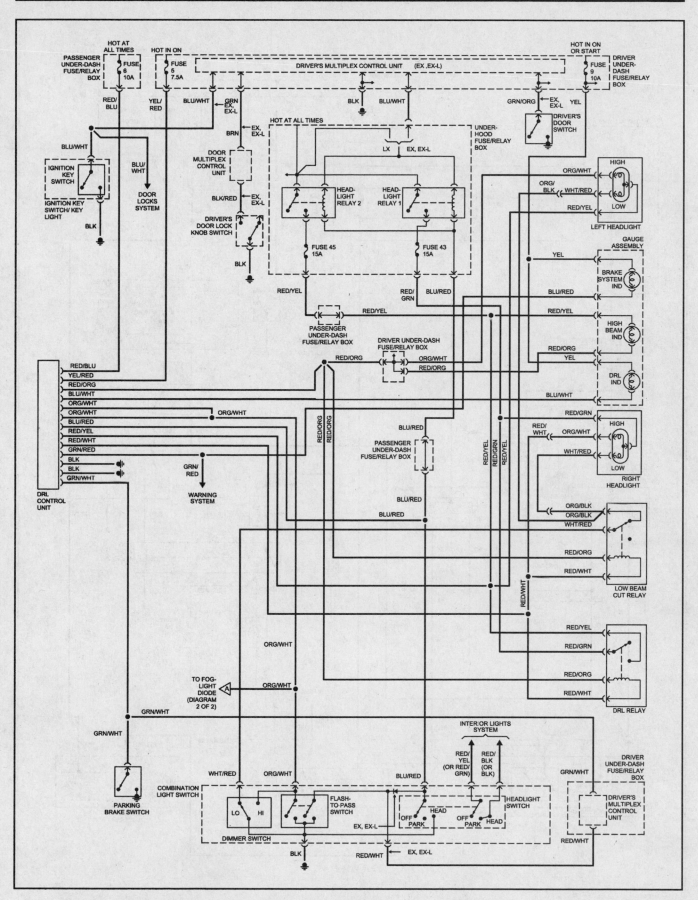

Headlight system with Daytime Running Lights (2004 and earlier models)

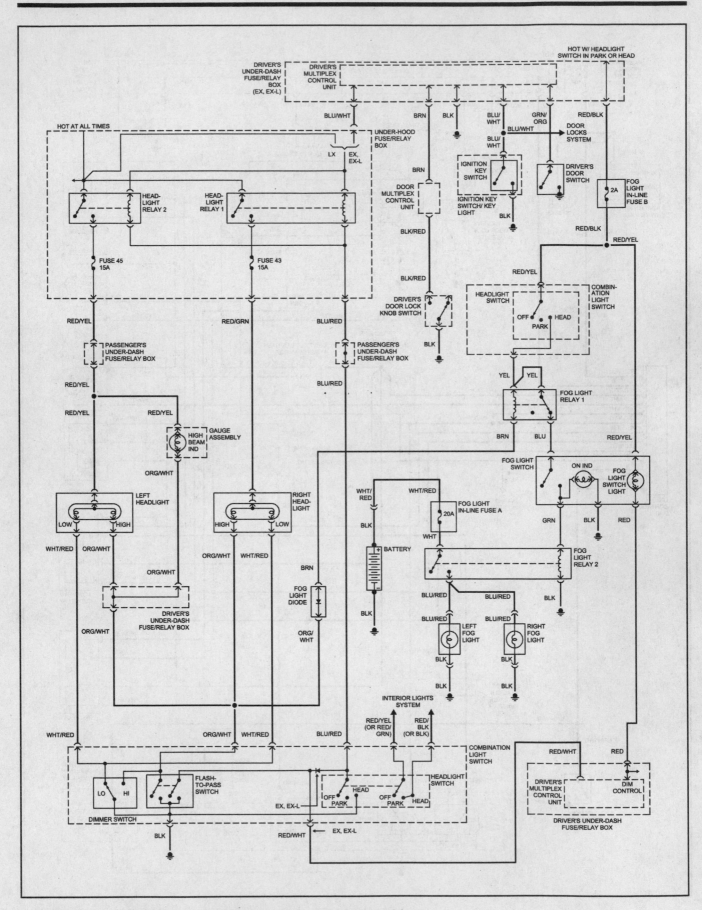

Headlight system without Daytime Running Lights (2004 and earlier models)

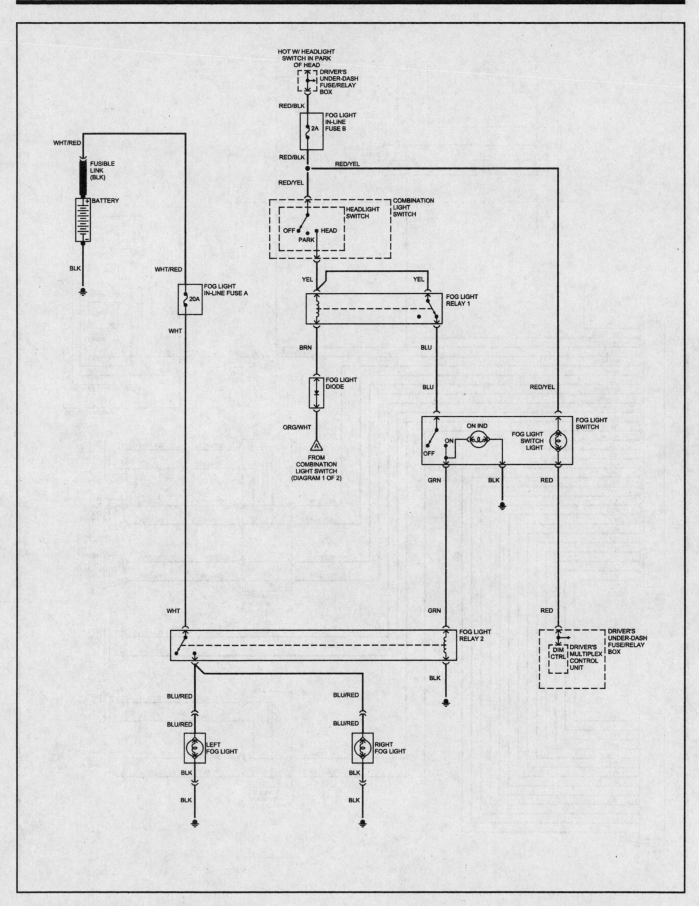

Fog light system (2004 and earlier models)

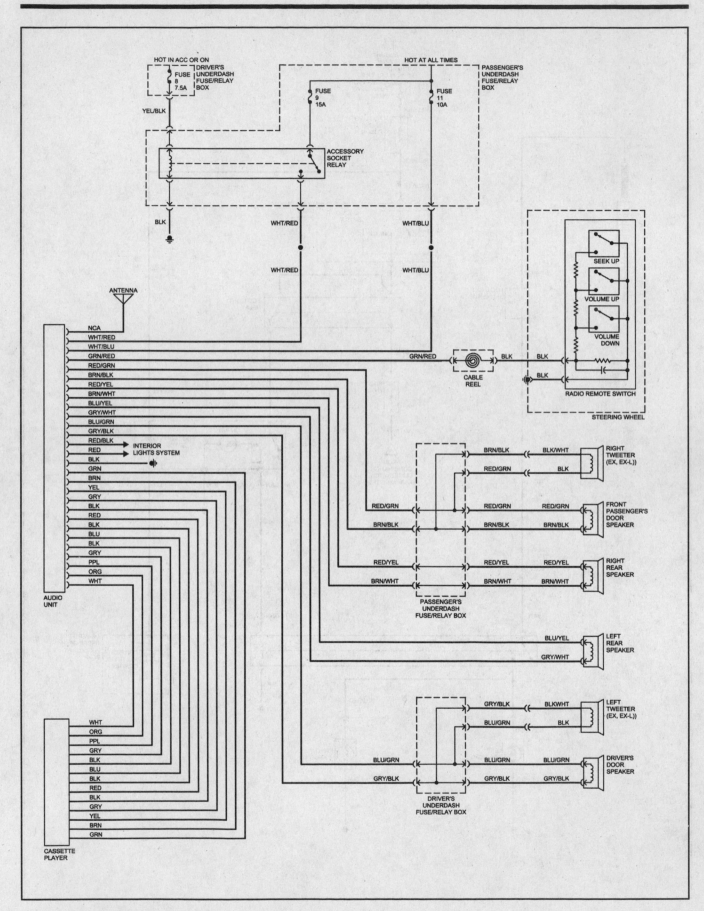

Sound system (2004 and earlier models)

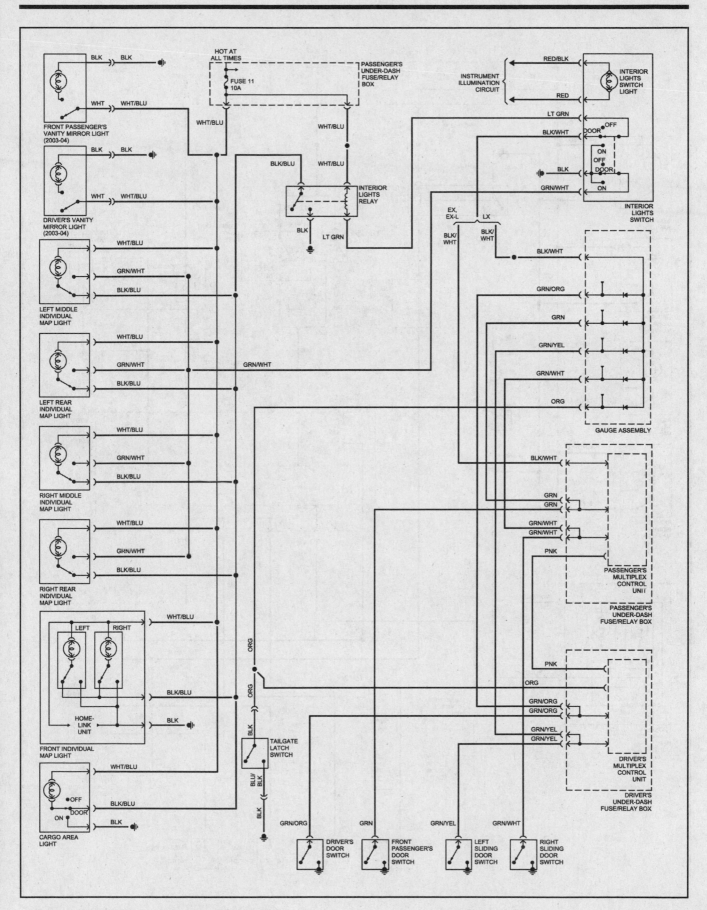

Interior lighting systems (2004 and earlier models)

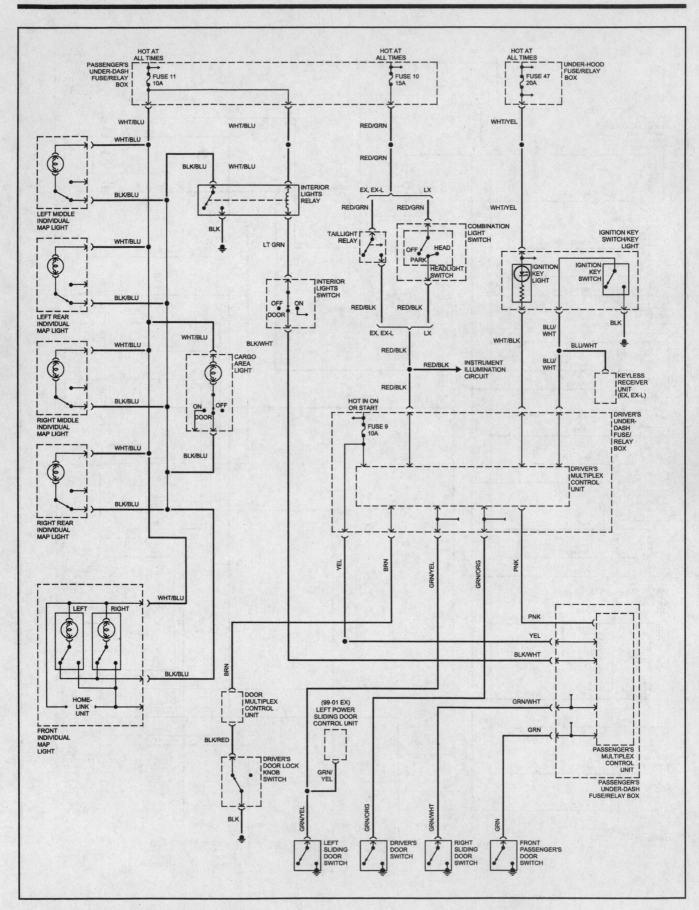

Timed entry systems (2004 and earlier models)

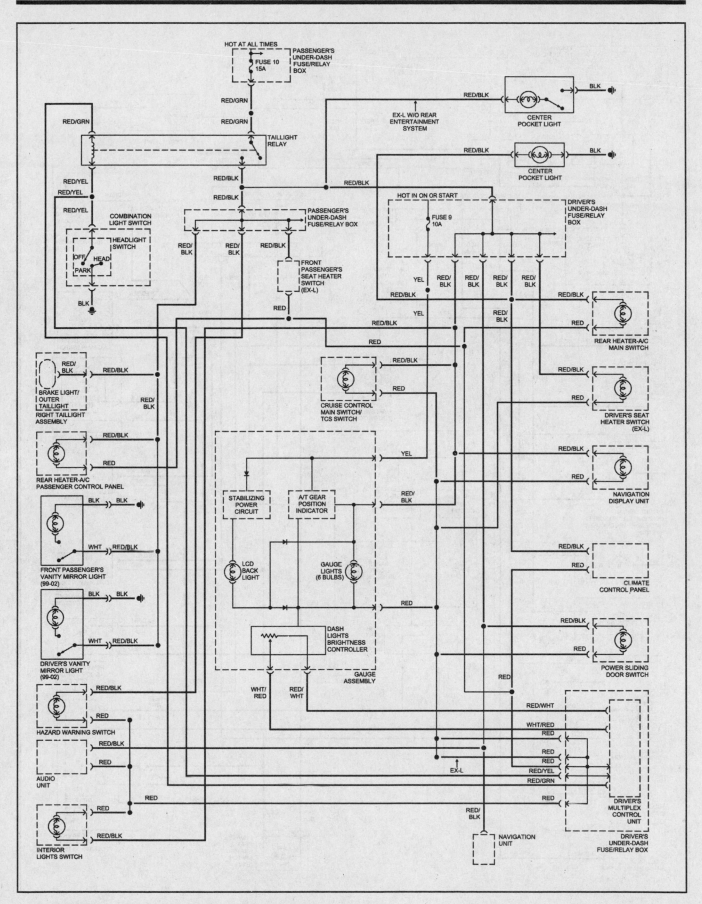

Interior lighting systems, with navigation system (2004 and earlier models)

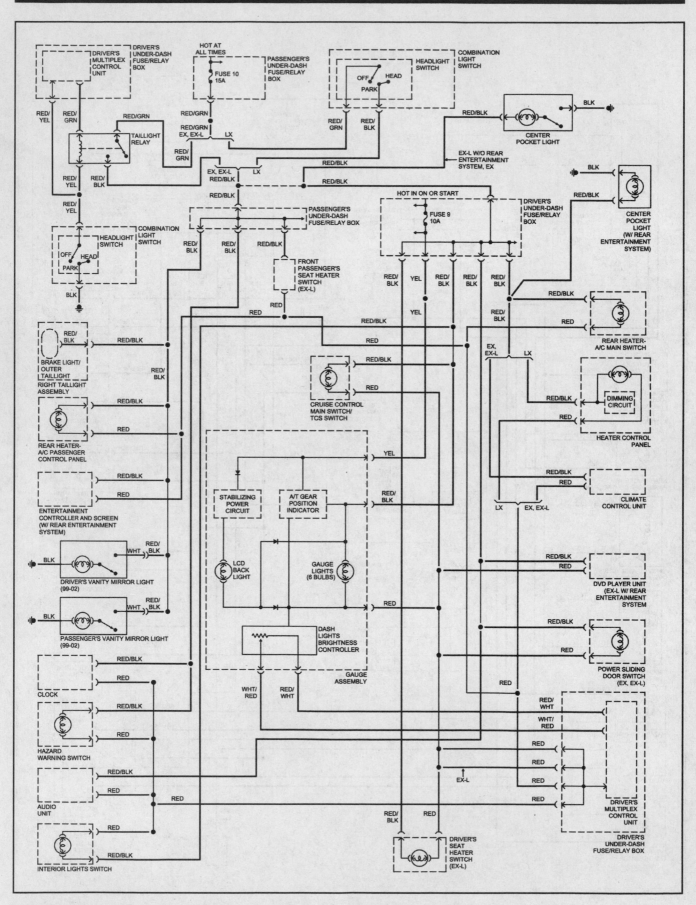

Interior lighting systems, without navigation system (2004 and earlier models)

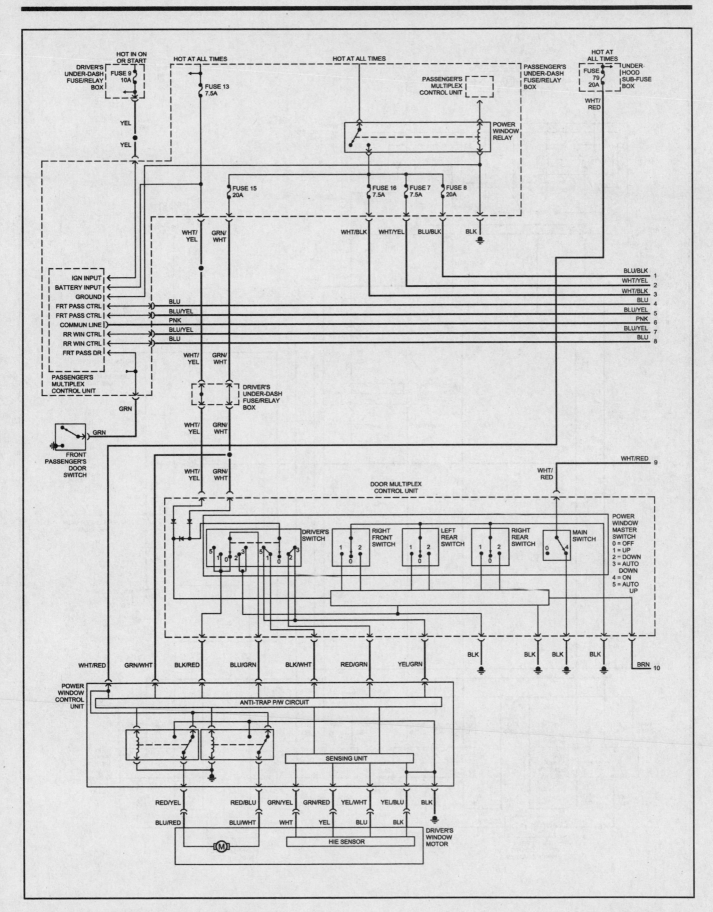

Power windows (2002 and earlier models) (1 of 2)

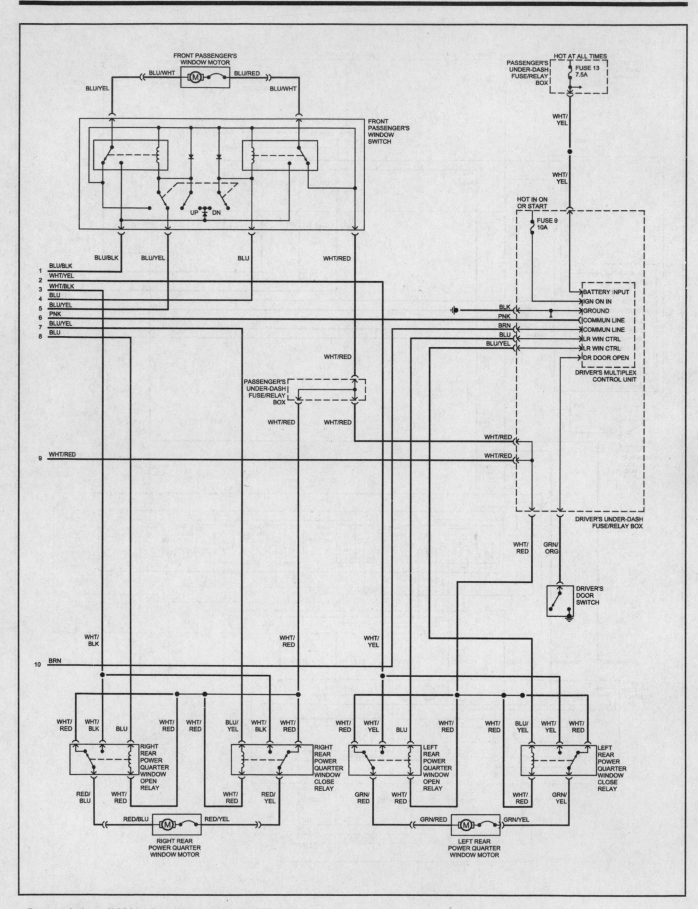

Power windows (2002 and earlier models) (2 of 2)

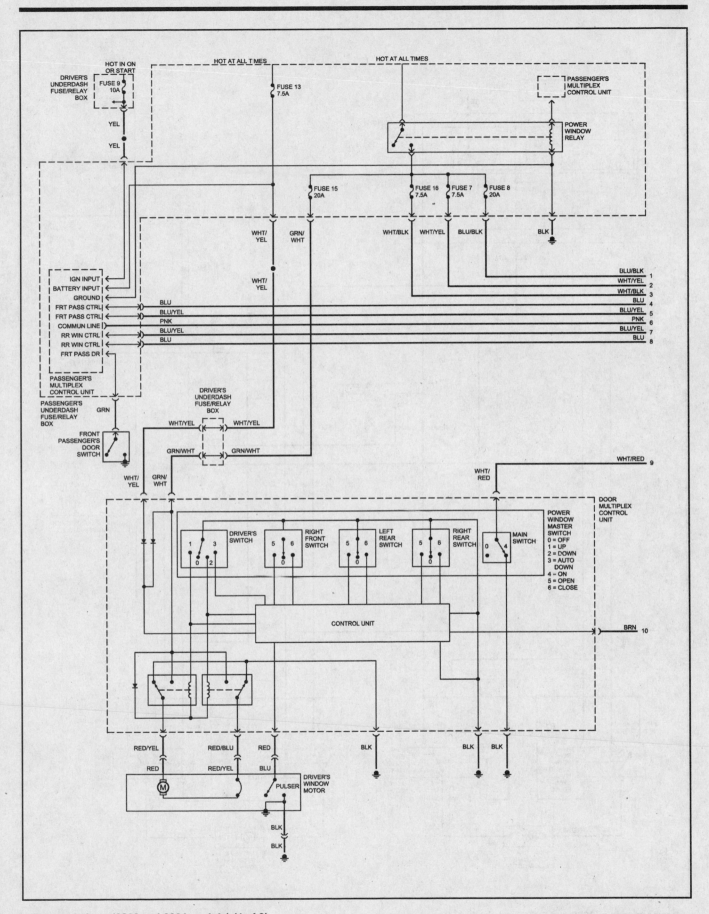

Power windows (2003 and 2004 models) (1 of 2)

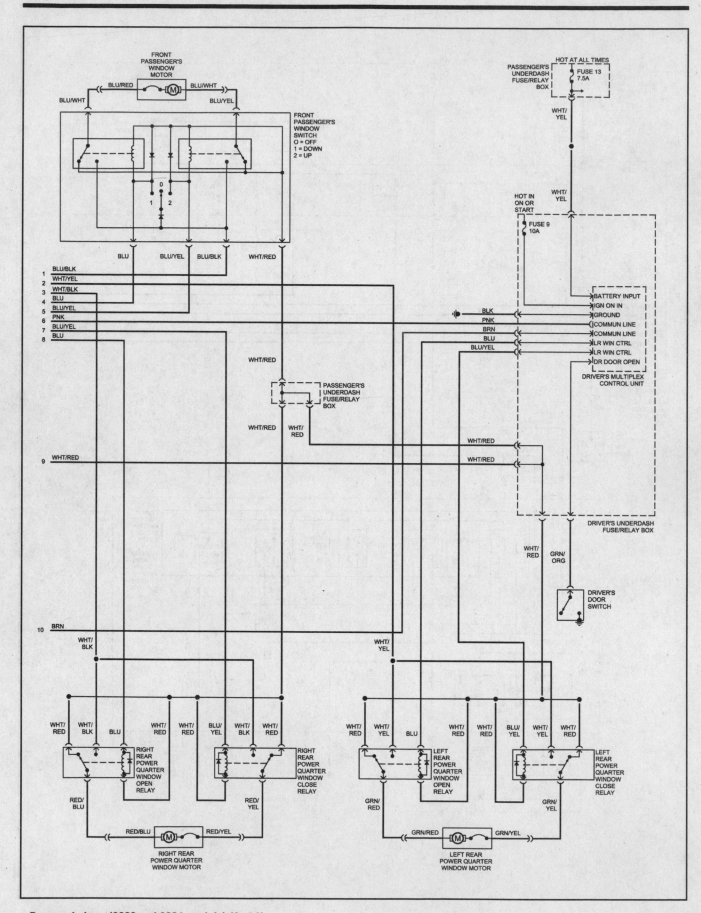

Power windows (2003 and 2004 models) (2 of 2)

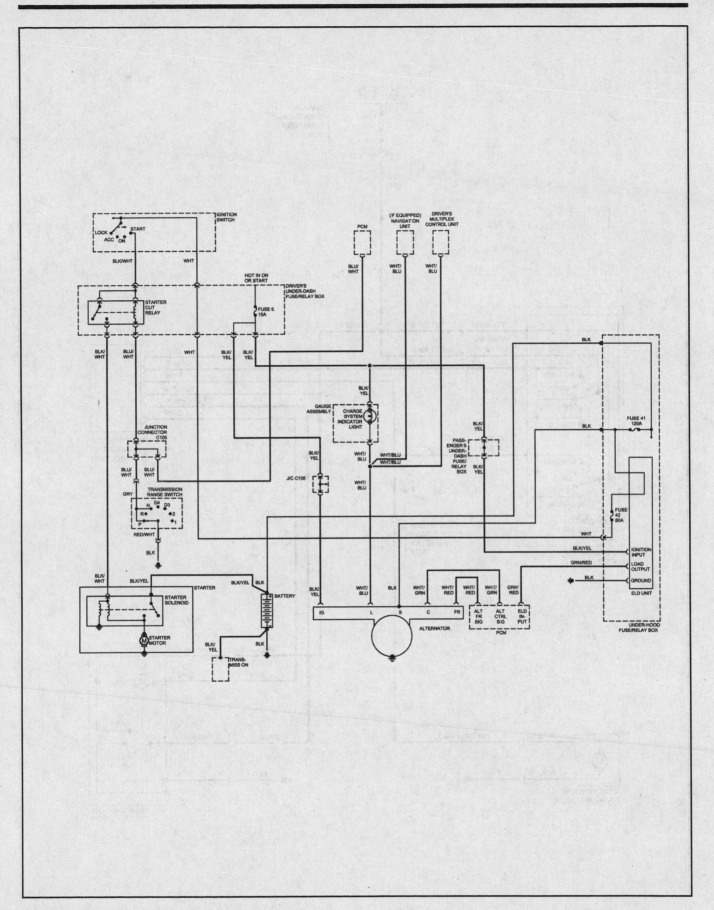

Starting and charging systems (2004 and earlier models)

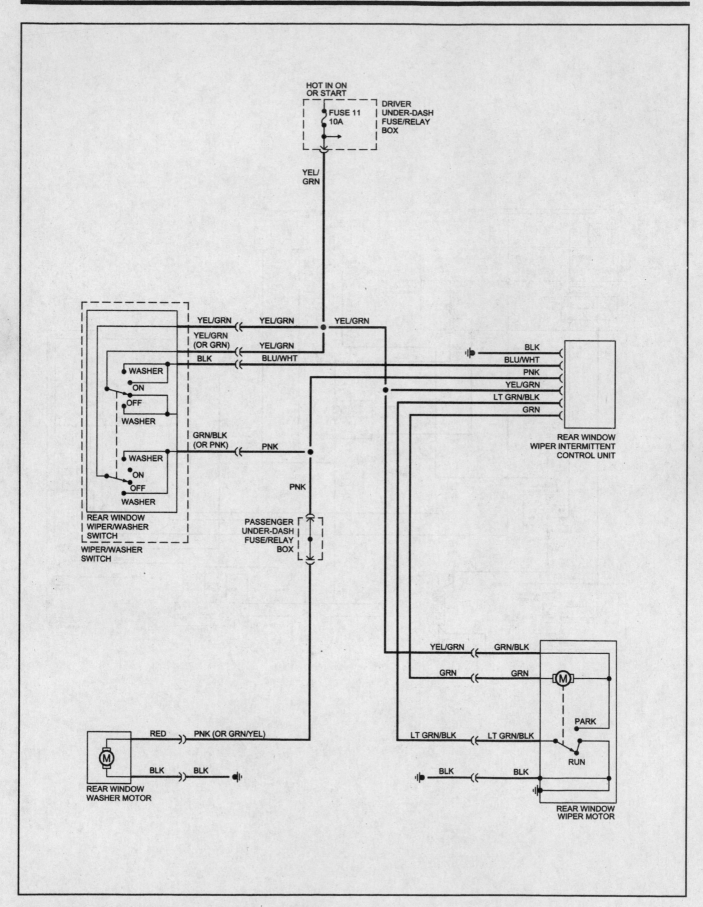

Rear window wiper/washer system (2004 and earlier models)

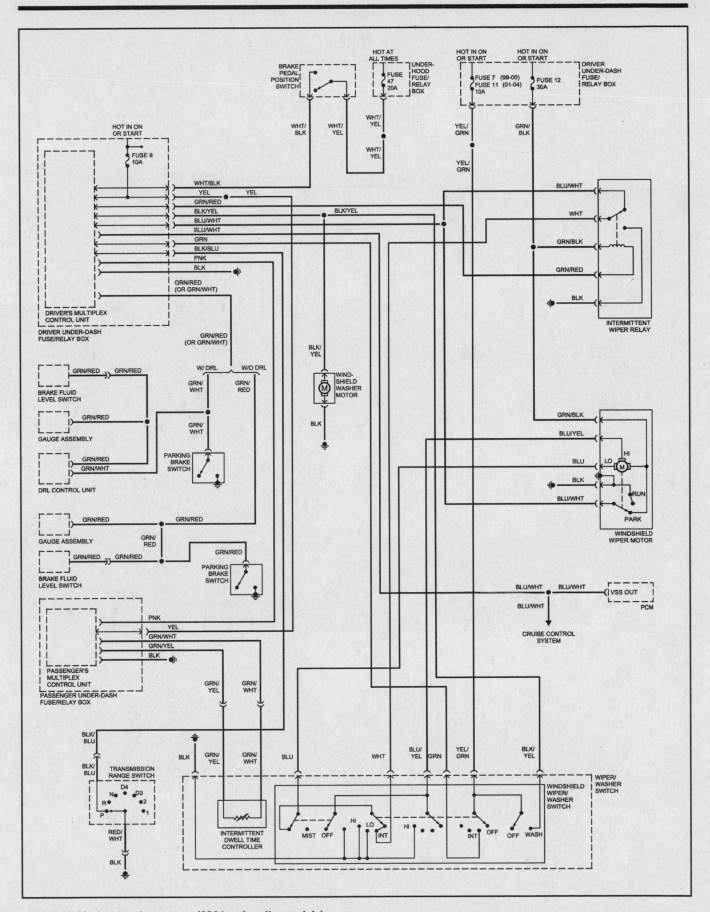

Windshield wiper/washer system (2004 and earlier models)

Notes

Notes

Notes

GLOSSARY

AIR/FUEL RATIO: The ratio of air-to-gasoline by weight in the fuel mixture drawn into the engine.

AIR INJECTION: One method of reducing harmful exhaust emissions by injecting air into each of the exhaust ports of an engine. The fresh air entering the hot exhaust manifold causes any remaining fuel to be burned before it can exit the tailpipe.

ALTERNATOR: A device used for converting mechanical energy into electrical energy.

AMMETER: An instrument, calibrated in amperes, used to measure the flow of an electrical current in a circuit. Ammeters are always connected in series with the circuit being tested.

AMPERE: The rate of flow of electrical current present when one volt of electrical pressure is applied against one ohm of electrical resistance.

ANALOG COMPUTER: Any microprocessor that uses similar (analogous) electrical signals to make its calculations.

ARMATURE: A laminated, soft iron core wrapped by a wire that converts electrical energy to mechanical energy as in a motor or relay. When rotated in a magnetic field, it changes mechanical energy into electrical energy as in a generator.

ATMOSPHERIC PRESSURE: The pressure on the Earth's surface caused by the weight of the air in the atmosphere. At sea level, this pressure is 14.7 psi at 32°F (101 kPa at 0°C).

ATOMIZATION: The breaking down of a liquid into a fine mist that can be suspended in air.

AXIAL PLAY: Movement parallel to a shaft or bearing bore.

BACKFIRE: The sudden combustion of gases in the intake or exhaust system that results in a loud explosion.

BACKLASH: The clearance or play between two parts, such as meshed gears.

BACKPRESSURE: Restrictions in the exhaust system that slow the exit of exhaust gases from the combustion chamber.

BAKELITE: A heat resistant, plastic insulator material commonly used in printed circuit boards and transistorized components.

BALL BEARING: A bearing made up of hardened inner and outer races between which hardened steel balls roll.

BALLAST RESISTOR: A resistor in the primary ignition circuit that lowers voltage after the engine is started to reduce wear on ignition components.

BEARING: A friction reducing, supportive device usually located between a stationary part and a moving part.

BIMETAL TEMPERATURE SENSOR: Any sensor or switch made of two dissimilar types of metal that bend when heated or cooled due to the different expansion rates of the alloys. These types of sensors usually function as an on/off switch.

BLOWBY: Combustion gases, composed of water vapor and unburned fuel, that leak past the piston rings into the crankcase during normal engine operation. These gases are removed by the PCV system to prevent the buildup of harmful acids in the crankcase.

BRAKE PAD: A brake shoe and lining assembly used with disc brakes.

BRAKE SHOE: The backing for the brake lining. The term is, however, usually applied to the assembly of the brake backing and lining.

BUSHING: A liner, usually removable, for a bearing; an anti-friction liner used in place of a bearing.

CALIPER: A hydraulically activated device in a disc brake system, which is mounted straddling the brake rotor (disc). The caliper contains at least one piston and two brake pads. Hydraulic pressure on the piston(s) forces the pads against the rotor.

CAMSHAFT: A shaft in the engine on which are the lobes (cams) which operate the valves. The camshaft is driven by the crankshaft, via a belt, chain or gears, at one half the crankshaft speed.

CAPACITOR: A device which stores an electrical charge.

CARBON MONOXIDE (CO): A colorless, odorless gas given off as a normal byproduct of combustion. It is poisonous and extremely dangerous in confined areas, building up slowly to toxic levels without warning if adequate ventilation is not available.

CARBURETOR: A device, usually mounted on the intake manifold of an engine, which mixes the air and fuel in the proper proportion to allow even combustion.

CATALYTIC CONVERTER: A device installed in the exhaust system, like a muffler, that converts harmful byproducts of combustion into carbon dioxide and water vapor by means of a heat-producing chemical reaction.

CENTRIFUGAL ADVANCE: A mechanical method of advancing the spark timing by using flyweights in the distributor that react to centrifugal force generated by the distributor shaft rotation.

CHECK VALVE: Any one-way valve installed to permit the flow of air, fuel or vacuum in one direction only.

CHOKE: A device, usually a moveable valve, placed in the intake path of a carburetor to restrict the flow of air.

CIRCUIT: Any unbroken path through which an electrical current can flow. Also used to describe fuel flow in some instances.

CIRCUIT BREAKER: A switch which protects an electrical circuit from overload by opening the circuit when the current flow exceeds a predetermined level. Some circuit breakers must be reset manually, while most reset automatically.

COIL (IGNITION): A transformer in the ignition circuit which steps up the voltage provided to the spark plugs.

COMBINATION MANIFOLD: An assembly which includes both the intake and exhaust manifolds in one casting.

COMBINATION VALVE: A device used in some fuel systems that routes fuel vapors to a charcoal storage canister instead of venting them into the atmosphere. The valve relieves fuel tank pressure and allows fresh air into the tank as the fuel level drops to prevent a vapor lock situation.

COMPRESSION RATIO: The comparison of the total volume of the cylinder and combustion chamber with the piston at BDC and the piston at TDC.

CONDENSER: 1. An electrical device which acts to store an electrical charge, preventing voltage surges. 2. A radiator-like device in the air conditioning system in which refrigerant gas condenses into a liquid, giving off heat.

CONDUCTOR: Any material through which an electrical current can be transmitted easily.

CONTINUITY: Continuous or complete circuit. Can be checked with an ohmmeter.

COUNTERSHAFT: An intermediate shaft which is rotated by a mainshaft and transmits, in turn, that rotation to a working part.

CRANKCASE: The lower part of an engine in which the crankshaft and related parts operate.

CRANKSHAFT: The main driving shaft of an engine which receives reciprocating motion from the pistons and converts it to rotary motion.

CYLINDER: In an engine, the round hole in the engine block in which the piston(s) ride.

CYLINDER BLOCK: The main structural member of an engine in which is found the cylinders, crankshaft and other principal parts.

CYLINDER HEAD: The detachable portion of the engine, usually fastened to the top of the cylinder block and containing all or most of the combustion chambers. On overhead valve engines, it contains the valves and their operating parts. On overhead cam engines, it contains the camshaft as well.

DEAD CENTER: The extreme top or bottom of the piston stroke.

DETONATION: An unwanted explosion of the air/fuel mixture in the combustion chamber caused by excess heat and compression, advanced timing, or an overly lean mixture. Also referred to as "ping".

DIAPHRAGM: A thin, flexible wall separating two cavities, such as in a vacuum advance unit.

DIESELING: A condition in which hot spots in the combustion chamber cause the engine to run on after the key is turned off.

DIFFERENTIAL: A geared assembly which allows the transmission of motion between drive axles, giving one axle the ability to turn faster than the other.

DIODE: An electrical device that will allow current to flow in one direction only.

DISC BRAKE: A hydraulic braking assembly consisting of a brake disc, or rotor, mounted on an axle, and a caliper assembly containing, usually two brake pads which are activated by hydraulic pressure. The pads are forced against the sides of the disc, creating friction which slows the vehicle.

DISTRIBUTOR: A mechanically driven device on an engine which is responsible for electrically firing the spark plug at a predetermined point of the piston stroke.

DOWEL PIN: A pin, inserted in mating holes in two different parts allowing those parts to maintain a fixed relationship.

DRUM BRAKE: A braking system which consists of two brake shoes and one or two wheel cylinders, mounted on a fixed backing plate, and a brake drum, mounted on an axle, which revolves around the assembly.

DWELL: The rate, measured in degrees of shaft rotation, at which an electrical circuit cycles on and off.

ELECTRONIC CONTROL UNIT (ECU): Ignition module, module, amplifier or igniter. See Module for definition.

ELECTRONIC IGNITION: A system in which the timing and firing of the spark plugs is controlled by an electronic control unit, usually called a module. These systems have no points or condenser.

END-PLAY: The measured amount of axial movement in a shaft.

ENGINE: A device that converts heat into mechanical energy.

EXHAUST MANIFOLD: A set of cast passages or pipes which conduct exhaust gases from the engine.

FEELER GAUGE: A blade, usually metal, or precisely predetermined thickness, used to measure the clearance between two parts.

FIRING ORDER: The order in which combustion occurs in the cylinders of an engine. Also the order in which spark is distributed to the plugs by the distributor.

FLOODING: The presence of too much fuel in the intake manifold and combustion chamber which prevents the air/fuel mixture from firing, thereby causing a no-start situation.

FLYWHEEL: A disc shaped part bolted to the rear end of the crankshaft. Around the outer perimeter is affixed the ring gear. The starter drive engages the ring gear, turning the flywheel, which rotates the crankshaft, imparting the initial starting motion to the engine.

FOOT POUND (ft. lbs. or sometimes, ft.lb.): The amount of energy or work needed to raise an item weighing one pound, a distance of one foot.

FUSE: A protective device in a circuit which prevents circuit overload by breaking the circuit when a specific amperage is present. The device is constructed around a strip or wire of a lower amperage rating than the circuit it is designed to protect. When an amperage higher than that stamped on the fuse is present in the circuit, the strip or wire melts, opening the circuit.

GEAR RATIO: The ratio between the number of teeth on meshing gears.

GENERATOR: A device which converts mechanical energy into electrical energy.

HEAT RANGE: The measure of a spark plug's ability to dissipate heat from its firing end. The higher the heat range, the hotter the plug fires.

HUB: The center part of a wheel or gear.

HYDROCARBON (HC): Any chemical compound made up of hydrogen and carbon. A major pollutant formed by the engine as a byproduct of combustion.

HYDROMETER: An instrument used to measure the specific gravity of a solution.

INCH POUND (inch lbs.; sometimes in.lb. or in. lbs.): One twelfth of a foot pound.

INDUCTION: A means of transferring electrical energy in the form of a magnetic field. Principle used in the ignition coil to increase voltage.

INJECTOR: A device which receives metered fuel under relatively low pressure and is activated to inject the fuel into the engine under relatively high pressure at a predetermined time.

INPUT SHAFT: The shaft to which torque is applied, usually carrying the driving gear or gears.

INTAKE MANIFOLD: A casting of passages or pipes used to conduct air or a fuel/air mixture to the cylinders.

JOURNAL: The bearing surface within which a shaft operates.

KEY: A small block usually fitted in a notch between a shaft and a hub to prevent slippage of the two parts.

MANIFOLD: A casting of passages or set of pipes which connect the cylinders to an inlet or outlet source.

MANIFOLD VACUUM: Low pressure in an engine intake manifold formed just below the throttle plates. Manifold vacuum is highest at idle and drops under acceleration.

MASTER CYLINDER: The primary fluid pressurizing device in a hydraulic system. In automotive use, it is found in brake and hydraulic clutch systems and is pedal activated, either directly or, in a power brake system, through the power booster.

MODULE: Electronic control unit, amplifier or igniter of solid state or integrated design which controls the current flow in the ignition primary circuit based on input from the pick-up coil. When the module opens the primary circuit, high secondary voltage is induced in the coil.

NEEDLE BEARING: A bearing which consists of a number (usually a large number) of long, thin rollers.

OHM: (Ω) The unit used to measure the resistance of conductor-to-electrical flow. One ohm is the amount of resistance that limits current flow to one ampere in a circuit with one volt of pressure.

OHMMETER: An instrument used for measuring the resistance, in ohms, in an electrical circuit.

OUTPUT SHAFT: The shaft which transmits torque from a device, such as a transmission.

OVERDRIVE: A gear assembly which produces more shaft revolutions than that transmitted to it.

OVERHEAD CAMSHAFT (OHC): An engine configuration in which the camshaft is mounted on top of the cylinder head and operates the valve either directly or by means of rocker arms.

OVERHEAD VALVE (OHV): An engine configuration in which all of the valves are located in the cylinder head and the camshaft is located in the cylinder block. The camshaft operates the valves via lifters and pushrods.

OXIDES OF NITROGEN (NOx): Chemical compounds of nitrogen produced as a byproduct of combustion. They combine with hydrocarbons to produce smog.

OXYGEN SENSOR: Use with the feedback system to sense the presence of oxygen in the exhaust gas and signal the computer which can reference the voltage signal to an air/fuel ratio.

PINION: The smaller of two meshing gears.

PISTON RING: An open-ended ring with fits into a groove on the outer diameter of the piston. Its chief function is to form a seal between the piston and cylinder wall. Most automotive pistons have three rings: two for compression sealing; one for oil sealing.

PRELOAD: A predetermined load placed on a bearing during assembly or by adjustment.

PRIMARY CIRCUIT: the low voltage side of the ignition system which consists of the ignition switch, ballast resistor or resistance wire, bypass, coil, electronic control unit and pick-up coil as well as the connecting wires and harnesses.

PRESS FIT: The mating of two parts under pressure, due to the inner diameter of one being smaller than the outer diameter of the other, or vice versa; an interference fit.

RACE: The surface on the inner or outer ring of a bearing on which the balls, needles or rollers move.

REGULATOR: A device which maintains the amperage and/or voltage levels of a circuit at predetermined values.

RELAY: A switch which automatically opens and/or closes a circuit.

RESISTANCE: The opposition to the flow of current through a circuit or electrical device, and is measured in ohms. Resistance is equal to the voltage divided by the amperage.

RESISTOR: A device, usually made of wire, which offers a preset amount of resistance in an electrical circuit.

RING GEAR: The name given to a ring-shaped gear attached to a differential case, or affixed to a flywheel or as part of a planetary gear set.

ROLLER BEARING: A bearing made up of hardened inner and outer races between which hardened steel rollers move.

ROTOR: 1. The disc-shaped part of a disc brake assembly, upon which the brake pads bear; also called, brake disc. 2. The device mounted atop the distributor shaft, which passes current to the distributor cap tower contacts.

SECONDARY CIRCUIT: The high voltage side of the ignition system, usually above 20,000 volts. The secondary includes the ignition coil, coil wire, distributor cap and rotor, spark plug wires and spark plugs.

SENDING UNIT: A mechanical, electrical, hydraulic or electro-magnetic device which transmits information to a gauge.

SENSOR: Any device designed to measure engine operating conditions or ambient pressures and temperatures. Usually electronic in nature and designed to send a voltage signal to an on-board computer, some sensors may operate as a simple on/off switch or they may provide a variable voltage signal (like a potentiometer) as conditions or measured parameters change.

SHIM: Spacers of precise, predetermined thickness used between parts to establish a proper working relationship.

SLAVE CYLINDER: In automotive use, a device in the hydraulic clutch system which is activated by hydraulic force, disengaging the clutch.

SOLENOID: A coil used to produce a magnetic field, the effect of which is to produce work.

SPARK PLUG: A device screwed into the combustion chamber of a spark ignition engine. The basic construction is a conductive core inside of a ceramic insulator, mounted in an outer conductive base. An electrical charge from the spark plug wire travels along the conductive core and jumps a preset air gap to a grounding point or points at the end of the conductive base. The resultant spark ignites the fuel/air mixture in the combustion chamber.

SPLINES: Ridges machined or cast onto the outer diameter of a shaft or inner diameter of a bore to enable parts to mate without rotation.

TACHOMETER: A device used to measure the rotary speed of an engine, shaft, gear, etc., usually in rotations per minute.

THERMOSTAT: A valve, located in the cooling system of an engine, which is closed when cold and opens gradually in response to engine heating, controlling the temperature of the coolant and rate of coolant flow.

TOP DEAD CENTER (TDC): The point at which the piston reaches the top of its travel on the compression stroke.

TORQUE: The twisting force applied to an object.

TORQUE CONVERTER: A turbine used to transmit power from a driving member to a driven member via hydraulic action, providing changes in drive ratio and torque. In automotive use, it links the driveplate at the rear of the engine to the automatic transmission.

TRANSDUCER: A device used to change a force into an electrical signal.

TRANSISTOR: A semi-conductor component which can be actuated by a small voltage to perform an electrical switching function.

TUNE-UP: A regular maintenance function, usually associated with the replacement and adjustment of parts and components in the electrical and fuel systems of a vehicle for the purpose of attaining optimum performance.

TURBOCHARGER: An exhaust driven pump which compresses intake air and forces it into the combustion chambers at higher than atmospheric pressures. The increased air pressure allows more fuel to be burned and results in increased horsepower being produced.

VACUUM ADVANCE: A device which advances the ignition timing in response to increased engine vacuum.

VACUUM GAUGE: An instrument used to measure the presence of vacuum in a chamber.

VALVE: A device which control the pressure, direction of flow or rate of flow of a liquid or gas.

VALVE CLEARANCE: The measured gap between the end of the valve stem and the rocker arm, cam lobe or follower that activates the valve.

VISCOSITY: The rating of a liquid's internal resistance to flow.

VOLTMETER: An instrument used for measuring electrical force in units called volts. Voltmeters are always connected parallel with the circuit being tested.

WHEEL CYLINDER: Found in the automotive drum brake assembly, it is a device, actuated by hydraulic pressure, which, through internal pistons, pushes the brake shoes outward against the drums.

Notes

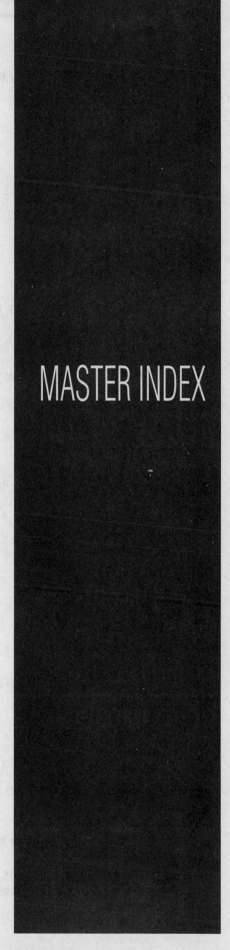

MASTER INDEX

A

B

BALLJOINTS, CHECK AND REPLACEMENT, 10-8
BATTERY
cables, check and replacement, 5-5
check and replacement, 5-3
check, maintenance and charging, 1-14
jump starting, 0-18
precautions and disconnection, 5-2
BLOWER MOTOR, REPLACEMENT, 3-12
BLOWER MOTOR RESISTOR, REPLACEMENT, 3-11
BODY REPAIR
major damage, 11-6
minor damage, 11-3
BODY, 11-1
BODY, MAINTENANCE, 11-2
BOOSTER BATTERY (JUMP) STARTING, 0-18
BRAKES, 9-1
Anti-lock Brake System (ABS), general information and speed sensor
    removal and installation, 9-2
Brake Pedal Position (BPP) switch, replacement and
    adjustment, 9-18
caliper, removal and installation, 9-6
disc, inspection, removal and installation, 9-7
fluid
    change, 1-26
    level check, 1-8
hoses and lines, inspection and replacement, 9-15
hydraulic system, bleeding, 9-15
master cylinder, removal and installation, 9-13
pads, disc brake, replacement, 9-3
parking brake
    adjustment, 9-17
    shoes, replacement, 9-9
power brake booster, removal and installation, 9-16
shoes, drum brake, replacement, 9-9
system check, 1-17
wheel cylinder, removal and installation, 9-13
BULB REPLACEMENT, 12-22
BUMPERS, REMOVAL AND INSTALLATION, 11-9
BUYING PARTS, 0-8

C

CALIPER, DISC BRAKE, REMOVAL AND INSTALLATION, 9-6
CAMSHAFT POSITION (CMP) SENSOR,
    REPLACEMENT, 6-11
CAMSHAFTS, REMOVAL, INSPECTION AND
    INSTALLATION, 2A-16
CAPACITIES, LUBRICANTS AND FLUIDS, 1-32
CATALYTIC CONVERTER, GENERAL DESCRIPTION, CHECK
    AND REPLACEMENT, 6-23

CENTER CONSOLE, REMOVAL AND INSTALLATION, 11-28
CHARGING SYSTEM
alternator, removal and installation, 5-8
check, 5-7
general information and precautions, 5-7
CHASSIS ELECTRICAL SYSTEM, 12-1
CHECK ENGINE LIGHT ON, 6-5
CHEMICALS AND LUBRICANTS, 0-19
CIRCUIT BREAKERS, GENERAL INFORMATION, 12-5
CLOCK, REPLACEMENT, 12-10
COIL SPRING (REAR), REMOVAL AND
    INSTALLATION, 10-11
COIL SPRING/STRUT ASSEMBLY (FRONT),
    REPLACEMENT, 10-6
COILS, IGNITION, REPLACEMENT, 5-6
COMPRESSOR, AIR CONDITIONING, REMOVAL AND
    INSTALLATION, 3-18
CONDENSER, AIR CONDITIONING, REMOVAL AND
    INSTALLATION, 3-20
CONTROL ARM, REMOVAL, INSPECTION AND
    INSTALLATION, 10-7
CONVERSION FACTORS, 0-20
COOLANT
level check, 1-7
reservoir, removal and installation, 3-8
temperature (ECT) sensor, replacement, 6-13
COOLING SYSTEM
check, 1-16
servicing (draining, flushing and refilling), 1-26
COOLING, HEATING AND AIR CONDITIONING
    SYSTEMS, 3-1
COWL COVER AND VENT TRAY, REMOVAL AND
    INSTALLATION, 11-13
CRANKSHAFT FRONT OIL SEAL, REPLACEMENT, 2A-12
CRANKSHAFT POSITION (CKP) SENSOR,
    REPLACEMENT, 6-12
CRANKSHAFT, REMOVAL AND INSTALLATION, 2B-16
CRUISE CONTROL SYSTEM, GENERAL
    INFORMATION, 12-26
CYLINDER COMPRESSION CHECK, 2B-4
CYLINDER HEADS, REMOVAL AND INSTALLATION, 2A-17

D

DASHBOARD
switches, replacement, 12-9
trim panels, 11-29
DAYTIME RUNNING LIGHTS (DRL), GENERAL
    INFORMATION, 12-28
DEFOGGER, REAR WINDOW, CHECK AND REPAIR, 12-17
DIAGNOSIS, 0-23

Notes